THE GREEN

G. Gsell-PHOTONONSTOP

Burgundy
Jura

MICHELIN

Travel Publications

Hannay House, 39 Clarendon Road
Watford, Herts WD17 1JA, UK
☎ 01923 205 240 - Fax 01923 205 241
www.ViaMichelin.com
TheGreenGuide-uk@uk.michelin.com

Manufacture française des pneumatiques Michelin
Société en commandite par actions au capital de 304 000 000 EUR
Place des Carmes-Déchaux – 63 Clermont-Ferrand (France)
R.C.S. Clermont-Fd B 855 200 507

No part of this publication may be reproduced in any form
without the prior permission of the publisher

© Michelin et Cie, Propriétaires-éditeurs, 2000
Dépôt légal novembre 2000 – ISBN 2-06-000067-X – ISSN 0763-1383
Printed in France 02-03/3.3

Typesetting: LE SANGLIER, Charleville-Mézières
Printing and binding: AUBIN, Ligugé

Cover design: Carré Noir, Paris 17e arr.

THE GREEN GUIDE
Spirit of Discovery

Leisure time spent with The Green Guide is also a time for refreshing your spirit, enjoying yourself, and taking advantage of our selection of fine restaurants, hotels and other places for relaxing: immerse yourself in the local culture, discover new horizons, experience the local lifestyle. The Green Guide opens the door for you.

Each year our writers go touring: visiting the sights, devising the driving tours, identifying the highlights, selecting the most attractive hotels and restaurants, checking the routes for the maps and plans.

Each title is compiled with great care, giving you the benefit of regular revisions and Michelin's first-hand knowledge. The Green Guide responds to changing circumstances and takes account of its readers' suggestions; all comments are welcome.

Share with us our enthusiasm for travel, which has led us to discover over 60 destinations in France and other countries. Like us, let yourself be guided by the desire to explore, which is the best motive for travel: the spirit of discovery.

Contents

Typical belfry in the Jura Mountains

Ready to row at Lac de Chalain

G. Magnin-MICHELIN

Ateliers M. Bevalot-

Maps
and plans

Thematic maps

Town plans

Monuments

Local maps for touring

Cabinet Ste-Cécile, Cormatin Château

Harvest time in Burgundy

Michelin maps

COMPANION PUBLICATIONS

Regional and local maps

To make the most of your journey, travel with Michelin maps at a scale of 1:200 000: **Regional maps** nos 519, 514, 515, 520 and 523 and the new **local maps**, which are illustrated on the map of France below. For each of the sites listed in this guide, map references are indicated to help you find your location on these maps.

In addition to identifying the nature of the main and secondary roads, Michelin maps show castles, churches, scenic view points, megalithic monuments, swimming beaches, golf courses, race tracks and more.

Maps of France

And remember to travel with the latest edition of the **map of France no 721**, which gives an overall view of the region of Burgundy-Jura, and the main access roads which connect it to the rest of France. The entire country is mapped at a 1:1 000 000 scale and clearly shows the main road network. Convenient Atlas formats (spiral, hard cover, "mini" and motorways) are also available.

Internet

Michelin is pleased to offer a route-planning service on the Internet:
www.ViaMichelin.com.
Choose the shortest route, a route without tolls, or the Michelin recommended route to your destination; you can also access information about hotels and restaurants from The Red Guide, and tourist sites from The Green Guide.

There are a number of useful maps and plans in the guide, listed in the table of contents.

Bon voyage!

Using this guide

● The summary maps on the following pages are designed to assist you in planning your trip: the **Map of principal sights** identifies major sights and attractions, the **Map of driving tours** proposes regional driving itineraries.

● **The Practical information** section offers useful information for planning your trip, seeking accommodation, indulging in outdoor activities, festival and carnival dates, suggestions for thematic tours on scenic railways and through nature reserves, and more. The **Map of places to stay** points out pleasant holiday spots.

● We recommend that you read the **Introduction** before setting out on your trip. The background information it contains on history, the arts and traditional culture will prove most instructive and make your visit more meaningful.

● The main towns and attractions are presented in alphabetical order in the Sights section. For addresses of **hotels and restaurants**, look for the pages or boxes bordered in blue throughout the guide. The clock symbol ⊙, placed after monuments or other sights, refers to the **Admission times and charges** section at the end of the guide, in which the names appear in the same order as in the Sights section.

● The **Index** lists attractions, famous people and events, and other subjects covered in the guide.

Let us hear from you. We are interested in your reaction to our guide, in any ideas you have to offer or good addresses you would like to share. Send your comments to Michelin Travel Publications, 39 Clarendon Road, Watford, Herts WD17 1JA, U.K. or by e-mail to TheGreenGuide-uk@uk.michelin.com.

S. Sauvignier-MICHELIN

Key

Selected monuments and sights

◉ ⇨ Tour - Departure point

⌂ ⚲ Catholic church

⌂ ⚲ Protestant church, other temple

✡ ▱ ⚱ Synagogue - Mosque

▰ Building

■ Statue, small building

⚱ Calvary, wayside cross

◎ Fountain

●━━■► Rampart - Tower - Gate

⤫ Château, castle, historic house

⫶ Ruins

⌣ Dam

✿ Factory, power plant

☆ Fort

∩ Cave

▱ Troglodyte dwelling

⋔ Prehistoric site

▼ Viewing table

Ⓦ Viewpoint

▲ Other place of interest

Sports and recreation

🐎 Racecourse

⛸ Skating rink

≋ ≋ Outdoor, indoor swimming pool

🎥 Multiplex Cinema

⚓ Marina, sailing centre

⌂ Trail refuge hut

□━■━■━□ Cable cars, gondolas

□┼┼┼┼┼□ Funicular, rack railway

🚂 Tourist train

◆ Recreation area, park

🎢 Theme, amusement park

🦌 Wildlife park, zoo

✿ Gardens, park, arboretum

🕊 Bird sanctuary, aviary

🚶 Walking tour, footpath

👶 Of special interest to children

Abbreviations

A Agricultural office (Chambre d'agriculture)

C Chamber of Commerce (Chambre de commerce)

H Town hall (Hôtel de ville)

J Law courts (Palais de justice)

M Museum (Musée)

P Local authority offices (Préfecture, sous-préfecture)

POL. Police station (Police)

⚜ Police station (Gendarmerie)

T Theatre (Théatre)

U University (Université)

	Sight	Seaside resort	Winter sports resort	Spa
Highly recommended	★★★	☆☆☆	✳✳✳	⊹⊹⊹
Recommended	★★	☆☆	✳✳	⊹⊹
Interesting	★	☆	✳	⊹

Additional symbols

🛈	Tourist information
▬▬ ▬▬	Motorway or other primary route
❶ ❶	Junction: complete, limited
▭▭▭ ▭▭▭	Pedestrian street
ɪ⁼⁼⁼⁼ɪ	Unsuitable for traffic, street subject to restrictions
▭▭▭▭ ----	Steps - Footpath
🚂 🚉	Train station - Auto-train station
🚌 🚌 S.N.C.F.	Coach (bus) station
―•―•―	Tram
Ⓜ	Metro, underground
P R	Park-and-Ride
&.	Access for the disabled
✉	Post office
☎	Telephone
⬧	Covered market
•✕•	Barracks
△	Drawbridge
∪	Quarry
✗	Mine
B **F**	Car ferry (river or lake)
🛥	Ferry service: cars and passengers
⇌	Foot passengers only
③	Access route number common to Michelin maps and town plans
Bert (R.)...	Main shopping street
AZ B	Map co-ordinates
►►	Visit if time permits

Hotels and restaurants

20 rooms:
€ 38.57/57.17   Number of rooms: price for one person/ double room

half-board or full board:
€ 42.62   Price per person, based on double occupancy

⇌ *€ 6.85*   Price of breakfast; when not given, it is included in the price of the room (i.e., for bed-and-breakfast)

120 sites:
€ 12.18   Number of camp sites and cost for 2 people with a car

€ 12.18 lunch-
€ 16.74/38.05   Restaurant: fixed-price menus served at lunch only – mini/maxi price fixed menu (lunch and dinner) or à la carte

rest.
€ 16.74/38.05   Lodging where meals are served mini/maxi price fixed menu or à la carte

meal € 15.22   "Family style" meal

reserv   Reservation recommended

⊘   No credit cards accepted

P   Reserved parking for hotel patrons

The prices correspond to the higher rates of the tourist season

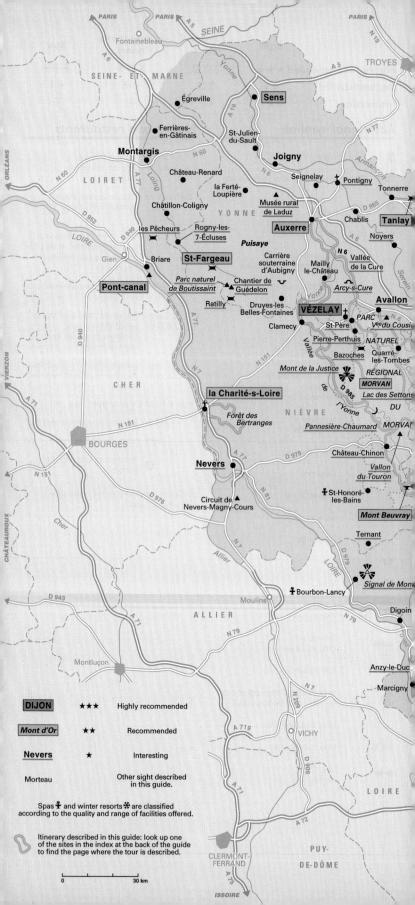

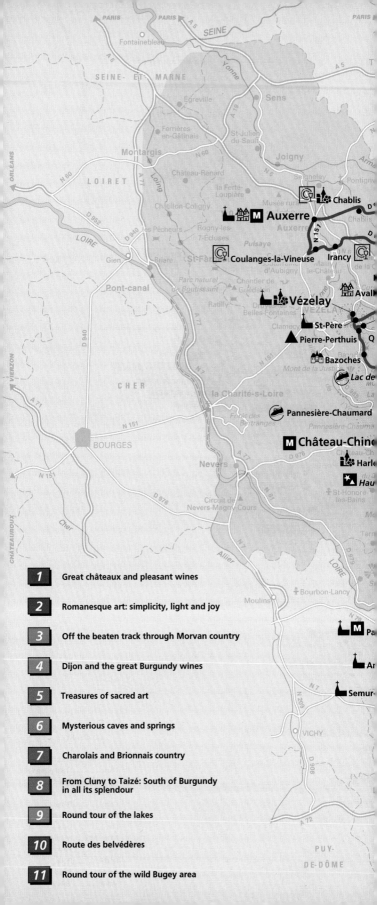

PARIS PARIS PARIS

SEINE

Fontainebleau

SEINE-ET-MARNE

Egreville

Sens

Ferrières-en-Gâtinais

Montargis

St-Julien-du-Sault

Joigny

Château-Renard

Seignelay

Pontigny

LOIRET

Chablis

Auxerre

la Ferté-Loupière

Musée ru...

Chablis

Auxerre

Rogny-les-7-Écluses

N 157

Irancy

Pulsaye

St-Fà...

Coulanges-la-Vineuse

d'Aubigny

la-Châte...

Parc naturel de Boussaint

Chantier de Guédelon

Vézelay

Aval

Ratilly

Belles-Fontaines

St-Père

Clamecy

Q

▲ **Pierre-Perthuis**

Bazoches

CHER

Mont de la Justi...

Lac de

la Charité-s-Loire

Forêt des Bertranges

Pannesière-Chaumard

Pannesière-Chaum...

BOURGES

Château-Chin

Nevers

Château-Ch...

Harle

du-b...

★ **Hau**

St-Honoré-les-Bains

Circuit de Nevers-Magny-Cours

Allier

LOIRE

CHÂTEAUROUX

Bourbon-Lancy

Moulins

Pa

1	Great châteaux and pleasant wines
2	Romanesque art: simplicity, light and joy
3	Off the beaten track through Morvan country
4	Dijon and the great Burgundy wines
5	Treasures of sacred art
6	Mysterious caves and springs
7	Charolais and Brionnais country
8	From Cluny to Taizé: South of Burgundy in all its splendour
9	Round tour of the lakes
10	Route des belvédères
11	Round tour of the wild Bugey area

Ar

Semur-

VICHY

PUY-DE-DÔME

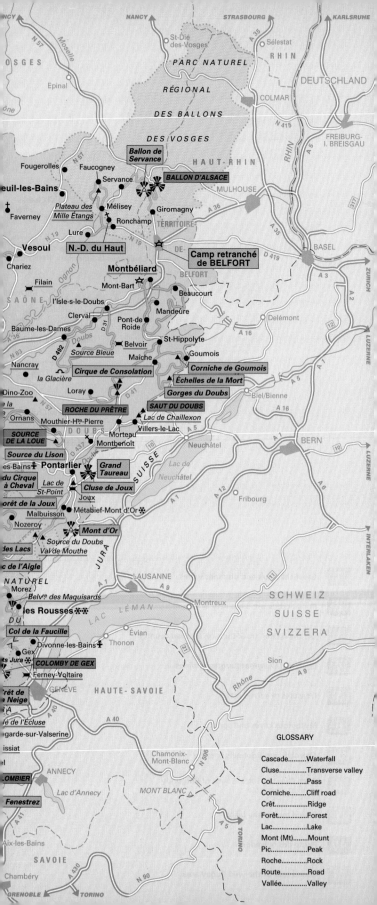

GLOSSARY

Cascade..........Waterfall	
Cluse.............Transverse valley	
Col...................Pass	
Corniche..........Cliff road	
Crêt................Ridge	
Forêt...............Forest	
Lac..................Lake	
Mont (Mt).......Mount	
Pic...................Peak	
Roche.............Rock	
Route..............Road	
Vallée.............Valley	

Principal sights

Driving tours

For descriptions of these tours, turn to the Practical Information section following.

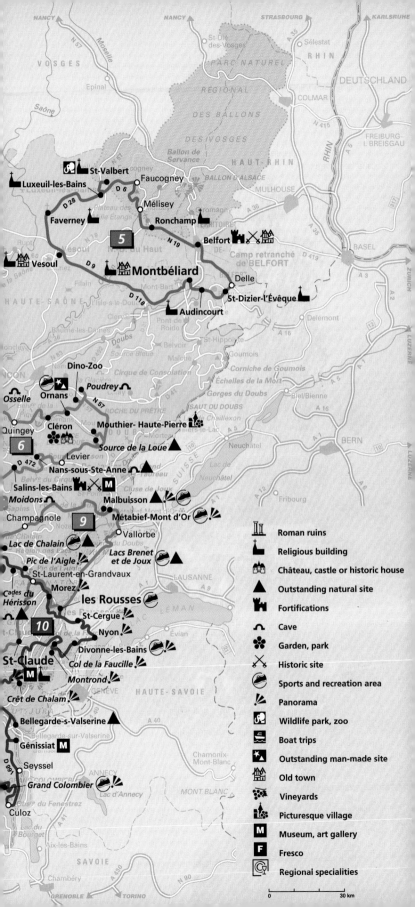

Map Legend

ⅢⅠ	Roman ruins
⛪	Religious building
🏛	Château, castle or historic house
▲	Outstanding natural site
🏰	Fortifications
⌒	Cave
✿	Garden, park
✕	Historic site
⌒	Sports and recreation area
⚐	Panorama
🐾	Wildlife park, zoo
⛴	Boat trips
★	Outstanding man-made site
🏘	Old town
🍇	Vineyards
🏙	Picturesque village
M	Museum, art gallery
F	Fresco
Ⓖ	Regional specialities

0 ─────── 30 km

Place names visible on map:

NANCY, STRASBOURG, KARLSRUHE, St-Dié-des-Vosges, Sélestat, COLMAR, DEUTSCHLAND, FREIBURG I. BREISGAU, RHIN, PARC NATUREL RÉGIONAL DES BALLONS DES VOSGES, VOSGES, Épinal, Ballon de Servance, HAUT-RHIN, BALLON D'ALSACE, MULHOUSE, St-Valbert, Luxeuil-les-Bains, Faucogney, Mélisey, Ronchamp, Faverney, Vesoul, Belfort, BASEL, Montbéliard, Delle, St-Dizier-l'Évêque, Audincourt, HAUTE-SAÔNE, Dino-Zoo, Osselle, Ornans, Poudrey, Quingey, Cléron, Mouthier-Haute-Pierre, Source de la Loue, Levier, Nans-sous-Ste-Anne, Salins-les-Bains, Moidons, Malbuisson, Métabief-Mont d'Or, Champagnole, Vallorbe, Lac de Chalain, Lacs Brenet et de Joux, Pic de l'Aigle, St-Laurent-en-Grandvaux, Morez, Cascades du Hérisson, les Rousses, St-Cergue, Nyon, St-Claude, Divonne-les-Bains, Col de la Faucille, Montrond, Crêt de Chalam, Bellegarde-s-Valserine, Génissiat, Seyssel, Grand Colombier, Culoz, HAUTE-SAVOIE, SAVOIE, Chamonix-Mont-Blanc, MONT BLANC, Lac d'Annecy, LAUSANNE, BERN, Fribourg, Lac de Neuchâtel, Neuchâtel, Biel/Bienne, ZÜRICH, LUZERN, GRENOBLE, TORINO

Canal de Bourgogne

Practical
information

Planning your trip

USEFUL ADDRESSES

Internet

www.ambafrance-us.org
The French Embassy in the USA has a Web site providing basic information (geography, demographics, history), a news digest and business-related information. It offers special pages for children, and pages devoted to culture, language study and travel, and you can reach other selected French sites (regions, cities, ministries) with a hypertext link.

www.franceguide.com
The French Government Tourist Office / Maison de la France site is packed with practical information and tips for those travelling to France. The home page has a number of links to more specific guidance, for American or Canadian travellers for example, or to the FGTO's London pages.

www.FranceKeys.com
This site has plenty of practical information for visiting France. It covers all the regions, with links to tourist offices and related sites. Very useful for planning the details of your tour in France!

www.fr-holidaystore.co.uk
The French Travel Centre in London has gone on-line with this service, providing information on all of the regions of France, including updated special travel offers and details on available accommodation.

www.visiteurope.com
The European Travel Commission provides useful information on travelling to and around 27 European countries, and includes links to some commercial booking services (such as vehicle hire), rail schedules, weather reports and more.

French tourist offices

For information, brochures, maps and assistance in planning a trip to France travellers should apply to the official French Tourist Office in their own country:

Australia – New Zealand
Sydney – BNP Building, 12 Castlereagh Street,
Sydney, New South Wales 2000
☎ (02) 9231 5244 – Fax: (02) 9221 8682.

Canada
Montreal – 1981 Avenue McGill College, Suite 490,
Montreal PQ H3A 2W9
☎ (514) 288-4264 – Fax: (514) 845 4868.
Toronto – 30 St Patrick's Street, Suite 700, Toronto, Ontario
☎ (416) 979 7587.

Eire
Dublin – 10 Suffolk Street, Dublin 2
☎ (01) 679 0813 – Fax: (01) 679 0814.

South Africa
P.O. Box 41022, Craig Hall 2024
☎ (011) 880 8062.

United Kingdom
London Maison de France – 178 Piccadilly, London WIV 0AL
☎ (09068) 244 123 – Fax: 020 793 6594.

United States
East Coast – New York – 444 Madison Avenue,
16th Floor, NY 10022-6903
☎ (212) 838-7800 – Fax: (212) 838-7855.
Mid West – Chicago – 676 North Michigan Avenue,
Suite 3360, Chicago, IL 60611-2819
☎ (312) 751-7800 – Fax: (312) 337-6339.
West Coast – Los Angeles – 9454 Wilshire Boulevard,
Suite 715, Beverly Hills, CA 90212-2967
☎ (310) 271-6665 – Fax: (310) 276-2835.
Information can also be requested from **France on Call**,
☎ (202) 659-7779.

Local tourist offices

Visitors may also contact local tourist offices for more precise information, to receive brochures and maps. The addresses and telephone numbers of tourist offices in the larger towns are listed after the symbol 🖪, in the *Admission times and charges* section at the end of the guide. Below, the addresses are given for local tourist offices of the *départements* and *régions* covered in this guide. The index lists the *département* after each town.

At regional level, address inquiries to:

Maison de la Franche-Comté, 2 boulevard de la Madeleine, 75009 Paris, ☎ 02 42 66 26 28. www.franche-comte.org

Comité Régional de Tourisme de Franche-Comté (Ain, Territoire de Belfort, Doubs, Haute-Saône, Jura), La City, 4 rue Gabriel-Plançon, 25044 Besançon Cedex ☎ 03 81 25 08 08. www.franche-comte.org

Comité Régional de Tourisme de Bourgogne (Côte-d'Or, Nièvre, Saône-et-Loire, Yonne), BP 1602, 21035 Dijon Cedex; offices: 5 avenue Garibaldi, 21000 Dijon, ☎ 03 80 28 02 80, Fax 03 80 28 03 00. www.bourgogne-tourisme.com

For each *département* within the region, address inquiries to the **Comité Départemental du Tourisme (CDT)**, unless otherwise stated:

Ain – 34 rue du Général-Delestraint, BP 78, 01002 Bourg-en-Bresse Cedex, ☎ 04 74 32 31 30.

Côte-d'Or – Côte-d'Or Tourisme, BP 1601, 21035 Dijon Cedex, ☎ 03 80 63 66 92.

Agence pour le développement économique et touristique du Doubs – Hôtel du Département, 7 avenue de la Gare-d'Eau, 25031 Besançon Cedex, ☎ 03 81 65 10 00. www.doubs.org

Jura – 8 rue Louis-Rousseau, 39000 Lons-le-Saunier, ☎ 03 84 87 08 88. www.jura-tourism.com

Nièvre – 3 rue du Sort, 58000 Nevers, ☎ 03 86 36 39 80.

Haute-Saône – Maison du Tourisme, 6 rue des Bains, BP 117, 70002 Vesoul Cedex, ☎ 03 84 97 10 70. www.haute-saone-tourism.com or www.cdt-tourism-haute-saone.fr

Saône-et-Loire – 389 avenue de Lattre-de-Tassigny, 71000 Mâcon, ☎ 03 85 21 02 20. www.cdt-saone-et-loire.fr

Yonne – 1-2 quai de la République, 89000 Auxerre, ☎ 03 86 72 92 00. www.tourisme-yonne.com

Maison du tourisme du Territoire de Belfort – 2 bis rue Clemenceau, 90000 Belfort, ☎ 03 84 55 90 90.

Tourist Information Centres (🖪) – See the *Admission times and charges* for the addresses and telephone numbers of the local tourist offices *(Syndicats d'Initiative)*; they provide information on craft courses and itineraries with special themes – wine tours, history tours, artistic tours.

Eleven towns and areas, labelled Villes et Pays d'Art et d'Histoire by the Ministry of Culture, are mentioned in this guide (Autun, Auxerre, Beaune, Besançon, Chalon, Cluny, Dijon, Dole, Joigny, Nevers and Paray-le-Monial). They are particularly active in promoting their architectural and cultural heritage and offer guided tours by highly qualified guides as well as activities for 6 to 12-year-olds. More information is available from local tourist offices and from www.vpah.culture.fr.

Embassies and consulates in France

Australia	Embassy	4 rue Jean-Rey, 75015 Paris ☎ 01 40 59 33 00 – Fax: 01 40 59 33 10.
Canada	Embassy	35 avenue Montaigne, 75008 Paris ☎ 01 44 43 29 00 – Fax: 01 44 43 29 99.
Eire	Embassy	4 rue Rude, 75016 Paris ☎ 01 44 17 67 00 – Fax: 01 44 17 67 60.
New Zealand	Embassy	7 ter rue Léonard-de-Vinci, 75016 Paris ☎ 01 45 01 43 43 – Fax: 01 45 01 43 44.
South Africa	Embassy	59 quai d'Orsay, 75007 Paris ☎ 01 53 59 23 23 – Fax: 01 53 59 23 33.
UK	Embassy	35 rue du Faubourg St-Honoré, 75008 Paris ☎ 01 44 51 31 00 – Fax: 01 44 51 31 27.
	Consulate	16 rue d'Anjou, 75008 Paris ☎ 01 44 51 31 01 (visas).
USA	Embassy	2 avenue Gabriel, 75008 Paris ☎ 01 43 12 22 22 – Fax: 01 42 66 97 83.
	Consulate	2 rue St-Florentin, 75001 Paris ☎ 01 42 96 14 88.
	Consulate	15 avenue d'Alsace, 67082 Strasbourg ☎ 03 88 35 31 04 – Fax: 03 88 24 06 95.

TRAVELLERS WITH SPECIAL NEEDS

The sights described in this guide which are easily accessible to people of reduced mobility are indicated in the *Admission times and charges* by the symbol &. On TGV and Corail trains, operated by the national railway (SNCF), there are special wheelchair slots in 1st class carriages available to holders of 2nd-class tickets. On Eurostar and Thalys, special rates are available for accompanying adults. All airports are equipped to receive physically disabled passengers.

Web-surfers can find information for slow walkers, mature travellers and others with special needs at www.access-able.com. For information on museum access for the disabled contact La Direction, *Les Musées de France, Service Accueil des Publics Spécifiques*, 6 rue des Pyramides, 75041 Paris Cedex 1, ☎ 01 40 15 35 88.

The Red Guide France and the **Michelin Camping Caravaning France** indicate hotels and camp sites with facilities suitable for physically handicapped people.

SEASONS AND WEATHER

Burgundy enjoys a semi-continental climate with marked contrasts between the seasons. The air is sharp in spite of frequent periods of bright weather except in the south of the region where the Mediterranean influence can already be felt.

Other than at the height of summer, the mountainous Jura receives a fair amount of rain which is responsible for the lush pastures and numerous cascades and waterfalls. In **winter**, it can be very cold in Burgundy even when the sun is out. The Jura summits and plateaux are covered with snow and many resorts offer very good skiing conditions. When the weather turns extremely cold, it is even possible to skate on many ponds and small lakes.

In **spring**, nights in Burgundy are fresh, even frosty, until late May. As for the Jura mountains, they are still white in late April, but when the snow starts to melt, the landscapes come to life with cascading streams and splendid foaming waterfalls.

Summer in Burgundy can be hot, although tempered by cool showers; glorious sunsets light up the façades of churches and old mansions. On the other hand, it is never too hot on the high plateaux and in the mountains of the Jura region; even down in the valleys, woods provide shade and keep the heat out.

Early **autumn** is the ideal season to enjoy Burgundian landscapes and gastronomy; the sun shines generously as the Morvan heights act as a screen against Atlantic weather. Later on fog invades river valleys and frost settles in the region's forests. In the Jura, deciduous trees put on warm golden hues which contrast with the dark green colour of fir trees; heavy rainfall turns mountain streams into gushing torrents.

Weather forecast

Météo-France offers recorded information at national, regional and local level. This information is updated three times a day and is valid for five days.

National forecast: ☎ 08 36 68 01 01.

Regional forecast: ☎ 08 36 68 00 00.

Local forecast: ☎ 08 36 68 02 followed by the number of the *département* (Ain: 01; Côte-d'Or: 21; Doubs: 25; Jura: 39; Nièvre: 58; Haute-Saône: 70; Saône et Loire: 71; Yonne: 89; Territoire de Belfort: 90).

What to pack

As little as possible! Cleaning and laundry services are available everywhere. Most personal items can be replaced at reasonable cost. Try to pack everything into one suitcase and a tote bag. Porter help may be in short supply, and new purchases will add to the original weight. Take an extra tote bag for packing new purchases, shopping at the open-air market, carrying a picnic etc. Be sure luggage is clearly labelled and old travel tags removed. Do not pack medication in checked luggage, but keep it with you.

Formalities

Documents

Passport – Nationals of countries within the European Union entering France need only a national identity card. Nationals of other countries must be in possession of a valid national **passport**. In case of loss or theft, report to your embassy or consulate and the local police.

Visa – No **entry visa** is required for Canadian, US or Australian citizens travelling as tourists and staying less than 90 days, except for students planning to study in France. If you think you may need a visa, apply to your local French consulate.
US citizens should obtain the booklet *Safe Trip Abroad* (US$1) which provides useful information on visa requirements, customs regulations, medical care etc for international travellers. Published by the Government Printing Office, it can be ordered by phone (☎ (202) 512-1800) or consulted on-line (www.access.gpo.gov). General passport information is available by phone toll-free from the Federal Information Center (item 5 on the automated menu), ☎ 800-688-9889. US passport application forms can be downloaded from http://travel.state.gov.

Customs

Apply to the Customs Office (UK) for a leaflet on customs regulations and the full range of duty-free allowances; available from HM Customs and Excise, Thomas Paine House, Angel Square, Torrens Street, London ECIV ITA, ☎ 08450 109 000. The US Customs Service offers a publication *Know before you go* for US citizens – for the office nearest you, consult the phone book, Federal Government, US Treasury (www.customs.ustreas.gov).
There are no customs formalities for holidaymakers bringing their caravans into France for a stay of less than six months. No customs document is necessary for pleasure boats and outboard motors for a stay of less than six months but the registration certificate should be kept on board.
Americans can bring home, tax-free, up to US$ 400 worth of goods (limited quantities of alcohol and tobacco products); Canadians up to CND$ 300; Australians up to AUS$ 400 and New Zealanders up to NZ$ 700.
Persons living in a member state of the European Union are not restricted with regard to purchasing goods for private use, but the recommended allowances for alcoholic beverages and tobacco are as follows:

Spirits (whisky, gin, vodka etc)	10 litres	Cigarettes	800
Fortified wines (vermouth, port etc)	20 litres	Cigarillos	400
Wine (not more than 60 sparkling)	90 litres	Cigars	200
Beer	110 litres	Smoking tobacco	1kg

Health

First aid, medical advice and chemists' night service rota are available from chemists/drugstores *(pharmacie)* identified by the green cross sign.
It is advisable to take out comprehensive insurance coverage as the recipient of medical treatment in French hospitals or clinics must pay the bill. **Nationals of non-EU countries** should check with their insurance companies about policy limitations. Reimbursement can then be negotiated with the insurance company according to the policy held.
All prescription drugs should be clearly labelled; it is recommended that you carry a copy of the prescription.
British and Irish citizens should apply to the Department of Health and Social Security for Form E 111, which entitles the holder to urgent treatment for accident or unexpected illness in EU countries. A refund of part of the costs of treatment can be obtained on application in person or by post to the local Social Security Offices *(Caisse Primaire d'Assurance Maladie)*. **Americans** concerned about travel and health can contact the International Association for Medical Assistance to Travelers, which can also provide details of English-speaking doctors in different parts of France: ☎ (716) 754-4883.

The American Hospital of Paris is open 24hr for emergencies as well as consultations, with English-speaking staff, at 63 boulevard Victor-Hugo, 92200 Neuilly-sur-Seine, ☎ 01 46 41 25 25. The hospital is accredited by major insurance companies.
The British Hospital is just outside Paris in Levallois-Perret, 3 rue Barbès.

Budget

CURRENCY

There are no restrictions on the amount of currency visitors can take into France. Visitors carrying a lot of cash are advised to complete a currency declaration form on arrival, because there are restrictions on currency export.

Notes and coins

Since 17 February 2002, the **euro** has been the only currency accepted as a means of payment in France, as in the 11 other European countries participating in the monetary union. It is divided into 100 cents or centimes. Since June 2002, it has only been possible to exchange notes and coins in French francs at the Banque de France (3 years for coins and 10 years for notes).

Banks

Although business hours vary from branch to branch, banks are generally open from 9am to noon and 2pm to 4pm and are closed either on Monday or on Saturday. Banks close early on the day before a bank holiday. A passport is necessary as identification when cashing travellers' cheques in banks. Commission charges vary and hotels usually charge more than banks for cashing cheques.

One of the most economical ways to use your money in France is by using **ATM machines** to get cash directly from your bank account (with a debit card) or to use your credit card to get a cash advance. Be sure to remember your PIN number, you will need it to use cash dispensers and to pay with your card in shops, restaurants etc. Code pads are numeric; use a telephone pad to translate a letter code into numbers. PIN numbers have 4 digits in France; inquire with the issuing company or bank if the code you usually use is longer. Visa is the most widely accepted credit card, followed by MasterCard; other cards, credit and debit (Diners Club, Plus, Cirrus etc) are also accepted in some cash machines. American Express is more often accepted in premium establishments. Most places post signs indicating which cards they accept; if you don't see such a sign, and want to pay with a card, ask before ordering or making a selection. Cards are widely accepted in shops, hypermarkets, hotels and restaurants, at tollbooths and in petrol stations.

Before you leave home, check with the bank that issued your card for emergency replacement procedures. Carry your card number and emergency phone numbers separate from your wallet and handbag; leave a copy of this information with someone you can easily reach. If your card is lost or stolen while you are in France, call one of the following 24-hour hotlines:

American Express ☎ 01 47 77 72 00   **Visa** ☎ 08 36 69 08 80
Mastercard/Eurocard ☎ 01 45 67 84 84   **Diners Club** ☎ 01 49 06 17 50

You must report any loss or theft of credit cards or travellers' cheques to the local police who will issue you with a certificate (useful proof to show the issuing company). It may be a good idea to carry some travellers' cheques in addition to your cards, and to keep them in a safe place in case of emergency.

PRICES AND TIPS

Since a service charge is automatically included in the price of meals and accommodation in France, any additional tipping is up to the visitor, generally small change, and generally not more than 5%. Taxi drivers and hairdressers are usually tipped 10-15%.

Restaurants usually charge for meals in two ways: a *menu*, that is a fixed price menu with 2 or 3 courses, sometimes with a small pitcher of wine, all for a stated price, or *à la carte*, the more expensive way, with each course ordered separately.

As a rule, the cost of staying in a hotel, eating in a restaurant or buying goods and services is significantly lower in the French regions than in Paris.

Here are a few indicative prices, based on surveys conducted by French authorities in 2001. Exchange rates change regularly, so you will have to check before you leave for an exact calculation. At press time, the exchange rate for 1€ was: USD 1; GBP 0.63; CAD 1.53; AUD 1.76.

Hotel rooms (based on double occupancy) in a city	Euros
1 star (French Tourist board standards)	27.44 – 53.36
2 star	53.36 – 76.22
3 star	76.23 – 121.97
4 star	137.21 – 228.69
4 star (luxury)	228.69 – 381.15

Notes and Coins

The euro banknotes were designed by Robert Kalinan, an Austrian artist. His designs were inspired by the theme "Ages and styles of European Architecture". Windows and gateways feature on the front of the banknotes, bridges feature on the reverse, symbolising the European spirit of openness and co-operation.

The images are stylised representations of the typical architectural style of each period, rather than specific structures.

Classical

Baroque and Rococo

Romanesque

19C iron and glass

Gothic

Renaissance

20C modern

Euro coins have one face common to all 12 countries in the European single currency area or "Eurozone" (currently Austria, Belgium, Finland, France, Germany, Greece, Ireland, Italy, Luxembourg, The Netherlands, Portugal and Spain) and a reverse side specific to each country, created by their own national artists.

Euro banknotes look the same throughout the Eurozone. All Euro banknotes and coins can be used anywhere in this area.

Food and entertainment	Euros
Movie ticket	8
River cruise	6.1 – 9.91
Dinner cruise	68.61 – 76.23
In a café: Expresso coffee	1.83
Café au lait	3.35
Soda	3.35
Beer	3.05
Mineral water	3.05
Ice cream	4.88
Ham sandwich	3.20
Baguette of bread	0.69
Soda (1 litre in a shop)	2.13
Restaurant meal (3 courses, no wine)	22.87
Big Mac menu meal	5.34
French daily newspaper	0.91
Foreign newspaper	1.52 – 2.29
Compact disc	12.00 – 21.00
Telephone card – 50 units	7.47
Telephone card – 120 units	14.86
Cigarettes (pack of 20)	2.44 – 3.25

Public transportation	Euros
Bus, street car, metro ticket	1.30
Book of ten tickets	9.60
Taxi (5km + tip)	9.91
TGV ticket Paris-Dijon 2nd class	44.90

Cafés have very different prices, depending on where they are located. The price of a drink or a coffee is cheaper if you stand at the counter *(comptoir)* than if you sit down *(salle)* and sometimes it is even more expensive if you sit outdoors *(terrace)*.

Discounts

Significant discounts are available for senior citizens, students, youth under age 25, teachers, and groups for public transportation, museums and monuments and for some leisure activities such as movies (at certain times of day). Bring student or senior cards with you, and bring along some extra passport-size photos for discount travel cards. The **International Student Travel Conference** (www.istc.org), global administrator of the International Student and Teacher Identity Cards, is an association of student travel organisations around the world. ISTC members collectively negotiate benefits with airlines, governments, and providers of other goods and services for the student and teacher community, both in their own country and around the world. The non-profit association sells international ID cards for students, youth under age 25 and teachers (who may get discounts on museum entrances, for example). The ISTC is also active in a network of international education and work exchange programmes. The corporate headquarters address is Herengracht 479, 1017 BS Amsterdam, The Netherlands, ☎ 31 20 421 28 00, Fax 31 20 421 28 10.
See the section below on travelling by rail in France for other discounts on transportation.

Tourist Pass: 100 sights for 42.69€

This pass gives unrestricted access to more than 100 historic buildings managed by the *Centre des Monuments Nationaux*. It is valid for one year throughout France as of the date of purchase and is for sale at the entrance to major historic buildings, monuments and museums. With the pass, you can save time by skipping the wait at the ticket booth. For a list of all the monuments, plus details on their history, information on travel, and other entertaining features to help you plan your trip, visit the lively web site www.monuments-france.fr.

Getting there

By air

The various international and other independent airlines operate services to **Paris** (Roissy-Charles de Gaulle and Orly airports) and **Dijon** in the heart of Burgundy. The Jura has only one regional airport, **Dole** and therefore the international airports of **Mulhouse-Basle** to the north-east and **Geneva** to the south-east are useful alternatives. Check with your travel agent, however, before booking direct flights, as it is sometimes cheaper to travel via Paris. Air France (☎ 0820 820 820), the national airline, links Paris to Dijon several times a day.

Contact airline companies and travel agents for details of package tour flights with a rail or coach link-up as well as fly-drive schemes.

By sea (from the UK or Ireland)

There are numerous **cross-Channel services** (passenger and car ferries, hovercraft) from the United Kingdom and Ireland, as well as the rail Shuttle through the Channel Tunnel (**Le Shuttle-Eurotunnel**, ☎ 0990 353-535). For details apply to travel agencies or to:

P & O Stena Line Ferries	Channel House, Channel View Road, Dover, CT17 9JT, ☎ 0990 980 980 or 01304 863 000 (Switchboard). www.p-and-o.com
Hoverspeed	International Hoverport, Marine Parade, Dover, Kent, CT17 9TG, ☎ 0990 240 241, Fax 01304 240088, www.hoverspeed.co.uk
Brittany Ferries	Millbay Docks; Plymouth, Devon, PL1 3^{E}W, ☎ 0990 360 360, www.brittany-ferries.com
Portsmouth Commercial Port (and ferry information)	George Byng Way, Portsmouth, Hampshire, PO2 8SP, ☎ 01705 297391, Fax 01705 861165
Irish Ferries	50 West Norland Street, Dublin 2, ☎ (353) 16 610 511, www.irishferries.com
Seafrance	Eastern Docks, Dover, Kent, CT16 1JA, ☎ 01304 212696, Fax 01304 240033, www.seafrance.fr

By rail

Eurostar runs via the Channel Tunnel between **London** (Waterloo) and **Paris** (Gare du Nord) in 3hr (bookings and information ☎ 0345 303 030 in the UK; ☎ 1-888-EUROSTAR in the US). In Paris it links to the high-speed rail network (TGV) which covers most of France. There is fast inter-city service on the TGV from **Paris** (Gare de Lyon) to **Montbard** *(1hr 5min)*, **Le Creusot** *(1hr 20min)*, **Dijon** *(1hr 35min)*, **Mâcon** *(1hr 35min)*, **Bourg-en-Bresse** *(2hr)*, **Beaune** *(2hr 5min)*, **Dole** *(2hr 5min)*, **Châlon-sur-Saône** *(2hr 20min)* and **Besançon** *(2hr 30min)*, with connections to other towns via the Trains Express Régionaux (TER).

Eurailpass, Flexipass, Eurailpass Youth, EurailDrive Pass and **Saverpass** are three of the travel passes which may be purchased by residents of countries outside the European Union. In the US, contact your travel agent or **Rail Europe** 2100 Central Ave. Boulder, CO, 80301 ☎ 1-800-4-EURAIL or **Europrail International** ☎ 1 888 667 9731. If you are a European resident, you can buy an individual country pass, if you are not a resident of the country where you plan to use it. In the UK, contact Europrail at 179 Piccadilly London W1V OBA ☎ 0990 848 848. Information on schedules can be obtained on Web sites for these agencies and the **SNCF**, respectively: www.raileurop.com.us, www.eurail.on.ca, www.sncf.fr. At the SNCF site, you can book ahead, pay with a credit card, and receive your ticket in the mail at home.

There are numerous **discounts** available when you purchase your tickets in France, from 25-50% below the regular rate. These include discounts for using senior cards and youth cards (the nominative cards with a photograph must be purchased – 45 and 41€, respectively), and lower rates for 2-9 people travelling together (no card required, advance purchase necessary). There are a limited number of discount seats available during peak travel times, and the best discounts are available for travel during off-peak periods.

Tickets bought in France must be validated *(composter)* by using the orange automatic date-stamping machines at the platform entrance (failure to do so may result in a fine).

The French railway company SNCF operates a telephone information, reservation and prepayment service in English from 7am to 10pm (French time). In France call ☎ 08 36 35 35 39 (when calling from outside France, drop the initial 0).

By coach

Regular coach services between **London** and **Paris** and connections to other cities:

Eurolines (UK), 4 Cardiff Road, Luton Bedfordshire, L41 IPP ☎ 0990 143219.

Eurolines (Paris), 22 rue Malmaison, 93177 Bagnolet Cedex ☎ 01 49 72 57 80.

Eurolines home page: www.eurolines.com

Motoring in France

The area covered in this guide is easily reached by main motorways and national roads. **Michelin map 726** indicates the main itineraries as well as alternate routes for avoiding heavy traffic during busy holiday periods, and gives estimated travel times. **Michelin map 727** is a detailed atlas of French motorways, indicating tolls, rest areas and services along the route; it includes a table for calculating distances and times. The latest Michelin route-planning service is available on Internet, **www.ViaMichelin.com**. Travellers can calculate a precise route using such options as shortest route, route avoiding toll roads or the Michelin-recommended route. In addition to tourist information (hotels, restaurants, attractions), you will find a magazine featuring articles with the up-to-the-minute reports on holiday destinations.

The roads are very busy during the holiday period (particularly weekends in July and August) and, to avoid traffic congestion it is advisable to follow the recommended secondary routes (signposted as *Bison Futé – itinéraires bis*). The motorway network includes rest areas *(aires)* and petrol stations, usually with restaurant and shopping complexes attached, about every 40km/25mi, so that long-distance drivers have no excuse not to stop for a rest every now and then.

Documents

Travellers from other European Union countries and North America can drive in France with a valid national or home-state **driving licence**. An **international driving licence** is useful because the information on it appears in nine languages (keep in mind that traffic officers are empowered to fine motorists). A permit is available (US$10) from the National Automobile Club, 1151 East Hillsdale Blvd., Foster City, CA 94404, ☎ 650-294-7000 or, www.nationalautoclub.com; or contact your local branch of the American Automobile Association. For the vehicle, it is necessary to have the registration papers (logbook) and a nationality plate of the approved size.

Certain motoring organisations (AAA, AA, RAC) offer accident **insurance** and breakdown service schemes for members. Check with your current insurance company in regard to coverage while abroad. If you plan to hire a car using your credit card, check with the company, which may provide liability insurance automatically (and thus save you having to pay the cost for optimum coverage).

Highway code

The minimum driving age is 18. Traffic drives on the right. All passengers must wear **seat belts**. Children under the age of 10 must ride in the back seat. Headlights must be switched on in poor visibility and at night; use sidelights only when the vehicle is stationary.

In the case of a **breakdown**, a red warning triangle or hazard warning lights are obligatory. In the absence of stop signs at intersections, cars must **yield to the right**. Traffic on main roads outside built-up areas (priority indicated by a yellow diamond sign) and on roundabouts has right of way. There are many **roundabouts** (traffic circles) located just on the edge of towns; they are designed to reduce the speed of the traffic entering the built-up area and you must slow down when you approach one and yield to the cars in the circle. Vehicles must stop when the lights turn red at road junctions and may filter to the right only when indicated by an amber arrow.

The regulations on **drinking and driving** (limited to 0.50g/l) and **speeding** are strictly enforced – usually by an on-the-spot fine and/or confiscation of the vehicle.

Speed Limits – Although liable to modification, these are as follows:
– toll motorways *(autoroutes)* 130kph/80mph (110kph/68mph when raining);
– dual carriageways and motorways without tolls 110kph/68mph (100kph/62mph when raining);
– other roads 90kph/56mph (80kph/50mph when raining) and in towns 50kph/31mph;
– outside lane on motorways during daylight, on level ground and with good visibility minimum speed limit of 80kph/50mph.

Parking Regulations – In town there are zones where parking is either restricted or subject to a fee; tickets should be obtained from the ticket machines (*horodateurs* – small change necessary) and displayed inside the windscreen on the driver's

side; failure to display may result in a fine, or towing and impoundment. Other parking areas in town may require you to take a ticket when passing through a barrier. To exit, you must pay the parking fee (usually there is a machine located by the exit – *sortie*) and insert the paid-up card in another machine which will lift the exit gate.

Tolls – In France, most motorway sections are subject to a toll *(péage)*. You can pay in cash or with a credit card (Visa, Mastercard).

Car rental

There are car rental agencies at airports, railway stations and in all large towns throughout France. European cars have manual transmission; automatic cars are available in larger cities only if an advance reservation is made. Drivers must be over 21; between ages 21-25, drivers are required to pay an extra daily fee; some companies allow drivers under 23 only if the reservation has been made through a travel agent. It is relatively expensive to hire a car in France; Americans in particular will notice the difference and should make arrangements before leaving, take advantage of fly-drive offers, or seek advice from a travel agent, specifying requirements.

Central Reservation Numbers in France:

Avis: 08 02 05 05 05

Budget France: 08 00 10 00 01

SIXT-Eurorent: 01 40 65 01 00

A Baron's Limousine: 01 45 30 21 21

Europcar: 08 03 35 23 52

Hertz France: 01 39 38 38 38

National-CITER: 01 45 22 88 40

Worldwide Motorhome Rentals offers fully equipped campervans for rent. You can view them on the company's web pages (mhrww.com) or call (US toll-free) US ☎ 888-519-8969; outside the US ☎ 530-389-8316 or Fax 530-389-8316.

Overseas Motorhome Tours Inc. organises escorted tours and individual rental of recreational vehicles: in the US ☎ 800-322-2127; outside the US ☎ 1-310-543-2590; Internet www.omtinc.com.

Petrol (US: gas) – French service stations dispense: *sans plomb 98* (super unleaded 98), *sans plomb 95* (super unleaded 95), *diesel/gazole* (diesel) and *GPL* (LPG). Petrol is considerably more expensive in France than in the USA. Prices are listed on signboards on the motorways; it is usually cheaper to fill up after leaving the motorway; check the large hypermarkets on the outskirts of town.

Where to stay, Eating out

Places to stay

This map illustrates a selection of holiday destinations which are particularly to be recommended for the accommodation and leisure facilities they offer, and for their pleasant setting. It shows **overnight stops**, fairly large towns which should be visited and which have good accommodation facilities as well as traditional destinations for a **short break**, which combine accommodation, charm and a peaceful setting. As far as Dijon and Besançon are concerned, the influence they exert in the region and the wealth of monuments, museums and other sights to which they are home make them the ideal setting for a **weekend break**.

Finding a hotel

The Green Guide is pleased to offer a new feature: lists of selected hotels and restaurants for this region. Turn to the sections bordered in blue for descriptions and prices of typical places to stay and eat with local flair. The key on pages 8-9 explains the symbols and abbreviations used in these sections. We have reported the prices and conditions as we observed them, but of course changes in management and other factors may mean that you will find some discrepancies. Please feel free to keep us informed of any major differences you encounter.

Use the **Map of places to stay** below to identify recommended places for overnight stops. For an even greater selection, use **The Red Guide France**, with its famously reliable star-rating system and hundreds of establishments all over France. Book ahead to ensure that you get the accommodation you want, not only in tourist season but year round, as many towns fill up during trade fairs, arts festivals etc. Some places require an advance deposit or a reconfirmation. Reconfirming is especially important if you plan to arrive after 6pm.

For further assistance, **Loisirs Accueil** is a booking service that has offices in some French *départements* – for further information, contact the tourist offices listed above or the Fédération nationale des services de réservation Loisirs-Accueil, 280 boulevard St-Germain, 75007 Paris, ☎ 01 44 11 10 44; www.resinfrance.com or www.fnsrla.net. A guide to good-value, family-run hotels, **Logis et Auberges de France**, is available from the French Tourist Office, as are lists of other kinds of accommodation such as hotel-châteaux, bed-and-breakfasts etc.

Relais et châteaux provides information on booking in luxury hotels with character: 15 rue Galvani, 75017 Paris, ☎ 01 45 72 90 00.

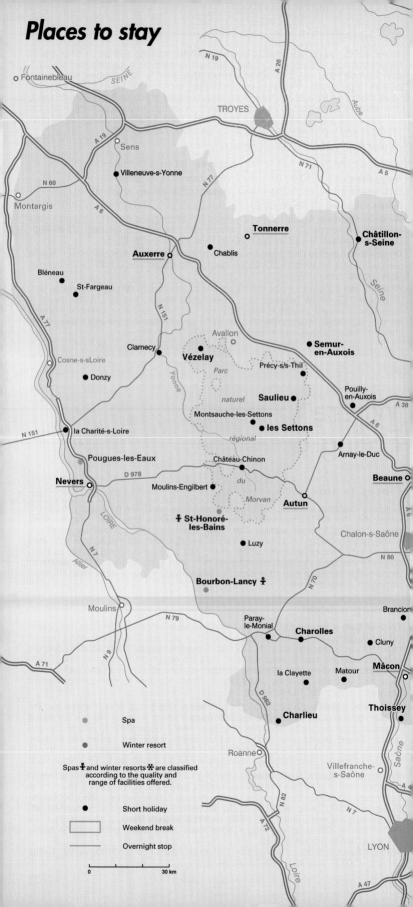

Places to stay

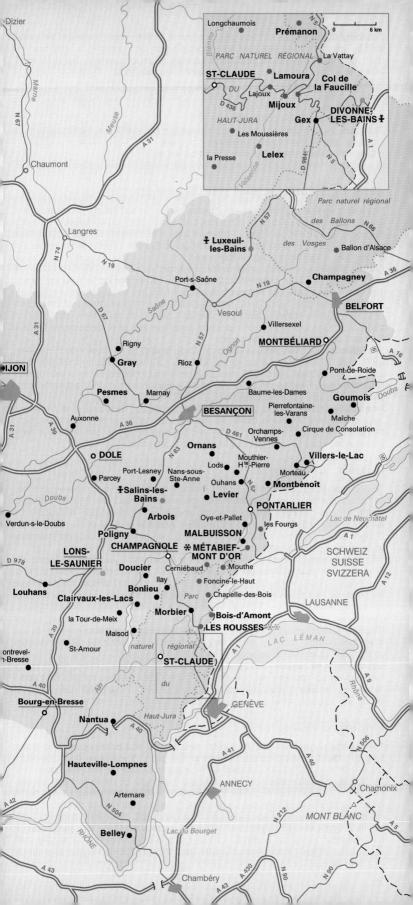

Economy Chain Hotels – If you need a place to stop en route, these can be useful, as they are inexpensive (30-45€ for a double room) and generally located near the main road. While breakfast is available, there may not be a restaurant; rooms are small, with a television and bathroom. Central reservation numbers:

– **Akena** ☎ 01 69 84 85 17
– **B&B** ☎ 0 803 00 29 29 (inside France); 33-2 98 33 75 00 (from outside France)
– **Mister Bed** ☎ 01 46 14 38 00
– **Villages Hôtel** ☎ 03 80 60 92 70

The hotels listed below are slightly more expensive (from 45€), and offer a few more amenities and services. Central reservation number:

– **Campanile, Climat de France, Kyriad** ☎ 01 64 62 46 46

Many chains have on-line reservations: www.etaphotel.com; www.ibishotel.com.

Renting a cottage, Bed and Breakfast

The **Maison des Gîtes de France** is an information service on self-catering accommodation in the Burgundy-Jura region (and the rest of France). *Gîtes* usually take the form of a cottage or apartment decorated in the local style where visitors can make themselves at home, or bed and breakfast accommodation *(chambres d'hôtes)* which consists of a room and breakfast at a reasonable price.

Contact the Gîtes de France office in Paris: 59 rue St-Lazare, 75439 Paris Cedex 09, ☎ 01 49 70 75 75, or their representative in the UK, **Brittany Ferries** *(address above)*. The Internet site, **www.gites-de-france.fr**, has a good English version. From the site, you can order catalogues for different regions illustrated with photographs of the properties, as well as specialised catalogues (bed and breakfasts, farm stays etc). You can also contact the local tourist offices which may have lists of available properties and local bed and breakfast establishments.

The **Fédération des Stations vertes de vacances et Villages de neige** (6 rue Ranfer-de-Bretenières, BP 71698, 21016 Dijon Cedex, ☎ 03 80 54 10 50; www.stationsvertes.com) is an association which promotes 581 rural localities throughout France, selected for their natural appeal as well as for the quality of their environment, of their accommodation and of the leisure activities available.

Farm holidays: three guides, *Guide des fermes-auberges*, *Bienvenue à la ferme* and *Vacances et week-ends à la ferme*, list the addresses of farms providing guest facilities which have been vetted for quality and for meeting official standards. For more information, apply to local tourist offices *(addresses above)*.

Hostels, Camping

To obtain an International Youth Hostel Federation card (there is no age requirement, and there is a senior card available too) you should contact the IYHF in your own country for information and membership applications (US ☎ 202 783 6161; UK ☎ 01727 855215; Canada ☎ 613-273 7884; Australia ☎ 61-2-9565-1669). There is a new booking service on the internet (iyhf.org), which you may use to reserve rooms as far as six months in advance.

There are two main youth hostel associations *(auberges de jeunesse)* in France, the **Ligue Française pour les Auberges de la Jeunesse** (67 rue Vergniaud, 75013 Paris, ☎ 01 44 16 78 78; www.auberges-de-jeunesse.com) and the **Fédération Unie des Auberges de Jeunesse** (4 boulevard Jules-Ferry, 75011 Paris, ☎ 01 43 57 02 60, Fax 01 43 57 53 90).

There are numerous officially graded **camp sites** with varying standards of facilities throughout the Burgundy-Jura region. The **Michelin Camping Caravaning France** guide lists a selection of camp sites. The area is very popular with campers in the summer months, so it is wise to reserve in advance.

Accommodation for ramblers: ramblers and those who enjoy ski touring, bike touring, mountaineering, canoeing etc, will find the guide *Gîtes d'étapes, refuges* by A and S Mouraret most useful. It is published by Rando-Éditions, BP 24, 65421 Ibos, ☎ 05 62 90 09 90. Internet: www.gites-refuges.com (order on-line, consult or book).

Finding a restaurant

Turn to the pages bordered in blue for descriptions and prices of selected places to eat in the different locations covered in this guide. The key on page 9 explains the symbols and abbreviations used in these sections. Use **The Red Guide France**, with its famously reliable star-rating system and hundreds of establishments all over France, for an even greater choice. If you would like to experience a meal in a highly rated restaurant from The Red Guide, be sure to book ahead! In the countryside, restaurants usually serve lunch between noon and 2pm and dinner between 7.30-10pm. It is not always easy to find something in-between those two meal times, as the non-stop restaurant is still a rarity in the provinces. However, a hungry traveller can usually get a sandwich in a café, and ordinary hot dishes may be available in a *brasserie*.

La Carte	The Menu
ENTREES	STARTERS
Crudités	Raw vegetable salad
Terrine de lapin	Rabbit terrine (pâté)
Frisée aux lardons	Curly lettuce with bacon bits
Escargots	Snails
Cuisses de grenouille	Frog's legs
Jambon de Luxeuil	Ham (speciality from the Jura)
Salade au crottin	Goat cheese on a bed of lettuce
PLATS (VIANDES)	MAIN COURSES (MEAT)
Bavette à l'échalote	Sirloin with shallots
Faux filet au poivre	Sirloin with pepper sauce
Bœuf Bourguignon	Burgundian beef casserole
Côtes d'agneau	Lamb chops
Jésus de cerf	Venison sausage from the Jura
Filet mignon de porc	Pork filet
Saucisse de Morteau, de Montbéliard	Smoked pork sausage from the Jura
Blanquette de veau	Veal in cream sauce
Nos viandes sont garnies	Our meat dishes are served with vegetables
PLATS (POISSONS, VOLAILLE)	MAIN COURSES (FISH, FOWL)
Filets de sole	Sole fillets
Dorade aux herbes	Sea bream with herbs
Saumon grillé	Grilled salmon
Pôchouse	Fish stewed in white wine
Truite au vin jaune	Trout cooked in white wine from the Jura
Coq au vin	Chicken in red wine sauce
Poulet de Bresse rôti	Free-range roast chicken from the Bresse
Poularde au vin jaune	Fat hen in *vin jaune* and mushroom sauce
Omelette aux morilles	Wild-mushroom omelette
Fondue de Franche-Comté	Hot dip made with Comté cheese melted in seasoned white wine
PLATEAU DE FROMAGES	SELECTION OF CHEESES
DESSERTS	DESSERTS
Tarte aux pommes	Apple pie
Crème caramel	Cooled baked custard with caramel sauce
Sorbet: trois parfums	Sherbet: choose 3 flavours
BOISSONS	BEVERAGES
Bière	Beer
Eau minérale (gazeuse)	(Sparkling) mineral water
Une carafe d'eau	Tap water (no charge)
Vin rouge, vin blanc, rosé	Red wine, white wine, rosé
Jus de fruit	Fruit juice
MENU ENFANT	CHILDREN'S MENU
Jambon	Ham
Steak haché	Ground beef
Frites	French fried potatoes

For information on local specialities, see the chapter on Gastronomy in the Introduction.

In French restaurants and cafés, a service charge is included. Tipping is not necessary, but French people often leave the small change from their bill on their table, or about 5% for the waiter in a nice restaurant.

Basic information

Electricity

The electric current is 220 volts. Circular two-pin plugs are the rule. Adapters and converters (for hairdryers, for example) should be bought before you leave home; they are on sale in most airports. If you have a rechargeable device (video camera, portable computer, battery charger), read the instructions carefully or contact the manufacturer or shop. Sometimes these items only require a plug adapter, in other cases you must use a voltage converter as well or risk ruining your appliance.

Metric system

France operates on the metric system. Some equivalents:

1 gram = 0.04 ounces	1 metre = 1.09 yards
1 kilogram = 2.20 pounds	1 kilometre = 0.62 miles
1 litre = 1.06 quarts	

Post and telephone

Main Post Offices open Monday to Friday 8am to 7pm, Saturday 8am to noon. Smaller branch post offices generally close at lunchtime between noon and 2pm and at 4pm.

Postage via air mail:

UK: letter (20g) 0.46€

North America: letter (20g) 0.67€

Australia and NZ: letter (20g) 0.79€

Stamps are also available from newsagents and *bureaux de tabac*. Stamp collectors should ask for *timbres de collection* in any post office.

Public Telephones – Most public phones in France use pre-paid phone cards *(télécartes)*, rather than coins. Some telephone booths accept credit cards (Visa,

Mastercard/Eurocard). *Télécartes* (50 or 120 units) can be bought in post offices, branches of France Télécom, *bureaux de tabac* (cafés that sell cigarettes) and newsagents and can be used to make calls in France and abroad. Calls can be received at phone boxes where the blue bell sign is shown; the phone will not ring, so keep your eye on the little message screen.

National Calls – French telephone numbers have 10 digits. Paris and Paris region numbers begin with 01; 02 in north-west France; 03 in north-east France; 04 in south-east France and Corsica; 05 in south-west France. Numbers beginning with 08 are special rate numbers, available only when dialling within France.

International Calls – To call France from abroad, dial the country code (33) + 9-digit number (omit the initial 0). When calling abroad from France dial 00, then dial the country code followed by the area code and number of your correspondent.

International dialling codes (00 + code):

Australia	☎ 61	New Zealand	☎ 64
Canada	☎ 1	United Kingdom	☎ 44
Eire	☎ 353	United States	☎ 1

To use your **personal calling card** dial:

AT&T	☎ 0-800 99 00 11	Sprint	☎ 0-800 99 00 87
MCI	☎ 0-800 99 00 19	Canada Direct	☎ 0-800 99 00 16

International Information, US/Canada: 00 33 12 11
International operator: 00 33 12 + country code
Local directory assistance: 12

Emergency numbers:
Police: 17   **Fire** (Pompiers):   18
SAMU (Paramedics): 15

Minitel – France Télécom operates a system offering directory enquiries (free of charge up to 3min), travel and entertainment reservations, and other services (cost per minute varies). These small computer-like terminals can be found in some post offices, hotels and France Télécom agencies and in many French homes. 3614 PAGES E is the code for **directory assistance in English** (turn on the unit, dial 3614, hit the *connexion* button when you get the tone, type in "PAGES E", and follow the instructions on the screen).

Cellular Phones in France have numbers which begin with 06. Two-watt (lighter, shorter reach) and eight-watt models are on the market, using the Orange (France Télécom) or SFR network. *Mobicartes* are pre-paid phone cards that fit into mobile units. Cell phone rentals (delivery or airport pickup provided) are available from:

Rent a Cell Express   ☎ 01 53 93 78 00, Fax 01 53 93 78 09

A.L.T. Rent A Phone   ☎ 01 48 00 06 60, E-mail altloc@jve.fr

Public holidays

Museums and other monuments may be closed or may vary their hours of admission on the following public holidays:

1 January	New Year's Day *(Jour de l'An)*
	Easter Day and Easter Monday *(Pâques)*
1 May	May Day *(Fête du travail)*
8 May	VE Day
Thur 40 days after Easter	Ascension Day *(Ascension)*
7th Sun-Mon after Easter	Whit Sunday and Monday *(Pentecôte)*
14 July	France's National Day (Bastille Day)
15 August	Assumption *(Assomption)*
1 November	All Saints' Day *(Toussaint)*
11 November	Armistice Day
25 December	Christmas Day *(Noël)*

National museums and art galleries are closed on Tuesdays; municipal museums are generally closed on Mondays. In addition to the usual school holidays at Christmas and in the spring and summer, there are long mid-term breaks (10 days to a fortnight) in February and early November.

Time

France is 1hr ahead of Greenwich Mean Time (GMT). France goes on daylight-saving time from the last Sunday in March to the last Sunday in October.

When it is **noon in France**, it is

3am	in Los Angeles
6am	in New York
11am	in Dublin
11am	in London
7pm	in Perth
9pm	in Sydney
11pm	in Auckland

R. Corbel/MICHELIN

In France "am" and "pm" are not used but the 24-hour clock is widely applied.

33

Conversion tables

Weights and measures

    ⫶

| 1 kilogram (kg) | 2.2 pounds (lb) | 2.2 pounds |
| 1 metric ton (tn) | 1.1 tons | 1.1 tons |

to convert kilograms to pounds, multiply by 2.2

| 1 litre (l) | 2.1 pints (pt) | 1.8 pints |
| 1 litre | 0.3 gallon (gal) | 0.2 gallon |

to convert litres to gallons, multiply by 0.26 (US) or 0.22 (UK)

| 1 hectare (ha) | 2.5 acres | 2.5 acres |
| 1 square kilometre (km²) | 0.4 square miles (sq mi) | 0.4 square miles |

to convert hectares to acres, multiply by 2.4

1centimetre (cm)	0.4 inches (in)	0.4 inches
1 metre (m)	3.3 feet (ft) - 39.4 inches - 1.1 yards (yd)
1 kilometre (km)	0.6 miles (mi)	0.6 miles

to convert metres to feet, multiply by 3.28, kilometres to miles, multiply by 0.6

Clothing

Women								Men
	35	4	2½		40	7½	7	
	36	5	3½		41	8½	8	
	37	6	4½		42	9½	9	
Shoes	38	7	5½		43	10½	10	Shoes
	39	8	6½		44	11½	11	
	40	9	7½		45	12½	12	
	41	10	8½		46	13½	13	
	36	4	8		46	36	36	
	38	6	10		48	38	38	
Dresses	40	8	12		50	40	40	Suits
& Suits	42	12	14		52	42	42	
	44	14	16		54	44	44	
	46	16	18		56	46	48	
	36	08	30		37	14½	14.5	
	38	10	32		38	15	15	
Blouses	40	12	14		39	15½	15½	Shirts
& sweaters	42	14	36		40	15¾	15¾	
	44	16	38		41	16	16	
	46	18	40		42	16½	16½	

Sizes often vary depending on the designer. These equivalents are given for guidance only.

Speed

kph	10	30	50	70	80	90	100	110	120	130
mph	6	19	31	43	50	56	62	68	75	81

Temperature

Celsius (°C)	0°	5°	10°	15°	20°	25°	30°	40°	60°	80°	100°
Fahrenheit (°F)	32°	41°	50°	59°	68°	77°	86°	104°	140°	176°	212°

To convert Celsius into Fahrenheit, multiply °C by 9, divide by 5, and add 32.
To convert Fahrenheit into Celsius, subtract 32 from °F, multiply by 5, and divide by 9.

Shopping

Most of the larger shops are open Mondays to Saturdays from 9am to 6.30 or 7.30pm. Smaller, individual shops may close during the lunch hour. Food shops – grocers, wine merchants and bakeries – are generally open from 7am to 6.30 or 7.30pm; some open on Sunday mornings. Many food shops close between noon and 2pm and on Mondays. Bakery and pastry shops sometimes close on Wednesdays. Hypermarkets usually stay open non-stop until 9pm or later.

People travelling to the USA cannot import plant products or fresh food, including fruit, cheeses and nuts. It is acceptable to carry tinned products or preserves.

S. Sauvignier/MICHELIN

Recovering Value Added Tax

There is a Value Added Tax in France *(TVA)* of 19.6% on almost every purchase (books and some foods are subject to a lower rate). However, non-European visitors who spend more than 183€ (amount subject to change) in any one participating store can get the VAT amount refunded. Usually, you fill out a form at the store and have to present your passport. Upon leaving the country, you submit all forms to customs for approval (they may want to see the goods, so if possible don't pack them in checked luggage). The refund is usually paid directly into your bank or credit card account, or it can be sent by mail. Big department stores that cater to tourists provide special services to help you; be sure to mention that you plan to seek a refund before you pay for goods (no refund is possible for tax on services). If you are visiting two or more countries within the European Union, you submit the forms only on departure from the last EU country. The refund is worth while for those visitors who would like to buy fashions, furniture or other fairly expensive items, but remember, the minimum amount must be spent in a single shop (though not necessarily on the same day).

Markets and local specialities

Markets – All the towns and nearly all the villages hold traditional markets on at least one day of the week. Below are some of the most important:

Monday mornings	Bresse chicken market in Louhans
	Sheep market in Moulins-Englibert
Tuesday mornings	Cattle market in Moulins-Engilbert
Wednesday mornings	Cattle market in Charolles
Thursday mornings	Cattle market in St-Christophe-en-Brionnais
Saturday mornings	Covered and open market in Beaune
Sunday mornings	Burgundy market in Chablis

Local Specialities – The name Burgundy has been synonymous with great **wine** ever since the 12C when the monks of Cîteaux Abbey developed the famous Clos Vougeot. Burgundy is fairly expensive starting at around 12€ a bottle but it is well worth it. You can find good wine in all the wine-growing cellars throughout the region and in specialised shops in large towns, such as Beaune where a famous wine sale is held during the second half of November *(see Calendar of events)*. If you wish to learn all about wine and vineyards, why not try **L'Athenaeum**, 7 rue de l'Hôtel-Dieu, 21200 Beaune, ☎ 03 80 25 08 30.

If you happen to be visiting Arbois or Château-Chalon, a bottle or two of the Jura region's unique **vin jaune** is a must; it goes well with **comté cheese**, another of the region's specialities.

Handicraft – **Nevers earthenware** is renowned worldwide and you will find a wide choice of dishes, vases and other objects in the town's specialised shops. **Pottery** is the speciality of the Puisaye and several workshops are open to visitors; the list can be obtained from the **Syndicat d'initiative intercommunal de la Puisaye nivernaise**, square de Castellamonte, 58310 St-Amand-en-Puisaye, ☎ 03 86 39 81 26.

Handicraft is so varied in the Jura region that it is difficult to list all the specialities: in St-Claude, the capital of pipe-making, local craftsmen sell a wide choice of **pipes** beautifully carved from briar root; in Moirans-en-Montagne, you will find all kinds of high-quality wooden and plastic **toys**; **lace** is the speciality of Luxeuil and **clocks** abound in the Morteau area.

Discovering the region

REGIONAL DRIVING TOURS

Here is a brief description of each of the tours shown on the map on page 13.

1 Great châteaux and pleasant wines

140km/87mi starting from Auxerre

Having visited the town, its fine Gothic cathedral, its old boatmen's district, and admired the view from the Paul-Bert bridge, you will enjoy a tour of the vineyards east of Auxerre via Irancy and Noyers. Continue east as far as Ancy-le-Franc then turn north-west down the valley of the River Armance with the Canal de Bourgogne meandering alongside it and discover a typical riverside scenery with its line of poplars, and its barges and pleasure boats queueing up at the locks. Two Renaissance jewels await you along this section of the tour: the Château d'Ancy-le-Franc, which is being restored but is well worth seeing for its superb interior decoration, and the Château de Tanlay with its bridge flanked by two obelisks. At Tonnere, turn west back towards Auxerre through the Chablis vineyards which produce a wide choice of famous wines from the modest *petits chablis* to the exclusive *grands crus*.

2 Romanesque art: simplicity, light and joy

200km/124mi starting from Vézelay

The starting point of this unusual tour is Ste-Madeleine Basilica which is the concrete expression of everything that Romanesque art stands for: the nave conveys an immediate impression of simplicity and light, whereas the carvings on the tympanum or the capitals are radiant with joy and light, rendering to perfection the serenity of Romanesque art. You can stop in several places along the twisting road to Saulieu, for instance in Bazoches and St-Léger-Vauban, where the memory of the great 17C military architect lives on; the Abbaye de la Pierre-qui-Vire a little further on offers a striking contrast. Beyond Saulieu, head north towards Fontenay Abbey, stopping at the Butte de Thil and in Semur-en-Auxois on the way. The fact that it is tucked away in a remote vale seems to emphasise the simplicity and lack of ornamentation of the Abbaye de Fontenay, making it one of the finest expressions of the very spirit of Romanesque art. Return to Vézelay via Montbard, the native town of the 18C naturalist Buffon *(see La Grande Forge)*, the Château de Montjalin and Avallon.

3 Off the beaten track through Morvan country

145km/90mi starting from Château-Chinon

The Morvan will delight sports enthusiasts, ramblers and nature lovers for it offers an abundance of lakes, forests and authentic villages such as Arleuf and Anost… Haut-Folin and Mont Beuvray (the site of the Gaulish city of Bibracte) tower above the southern part of the Morvan, offering panoramic views over vast areas.

4 Dijon and the great Burgundy wines

130km/81mi starting from Dijon

Dijon, Beaune, Clos de Vougeot, Pommard, Meursault… these names symbolise what is most prestigious in Burgundy. First of all Dijon with its two claims to fame, gastronomy and history: the order of the Golden Fleece and the tombs of the dukes of Burgundy in the Musée des Beaux-Arts for history buffs, St-Bénigne Cathedral and the Chartreuse de Champmol for those who are keen on architecture and sculpture. However, Dijon is first and foremost a fine town, with a pleasant way of life and where tourists like to stop for a day or two and stroll through the streets. South of Dijon, N 74 goes through a succession of villages which produce world-famous wines. Visits of cellars and wine-tasting sessions are a must. Take time to admire the vineyards looked after with loving care by generations of wine-growers. Beaune is still as attractive as ever with its Hôtel-Dieu containing the famous Polyptych of the Last Judgment, and its shopping district offering the thousand and one tantalising specialities of the region. The wine tour ends with Meursault and Pommard and the itinerary takes the long way back to Dijon, via three amazing castles: La Rochepot, Châteauneuf and Commarin.

5 Treasures of sacred art *215km/134mi starting from Montbéliard*

The contrast between the simplicity of the Temple St-Georges and the elaborate ornamentation of the nearby Église St-Maimboeuf is a perfect example of religious rivalry from the Reformation onwards.
Strong beliefs and traditions are expressed by a profusion of attractive religious buildings and places of pilgrimage some of which, dotted along this route, are truly amazing such as the baptistery in Audincourt or the Chapelle Notre-Dame-du-Haut in Ronchamp.

⑥ Mysterious caves and springs *270km/168mi starting from Dole*

Rain, more rain, nothing but rain... How many holidaymakers have cursed the rain that seems to fall for days on end; yet it is the rain that makes the Jura landscape what it is by swelling the streams which dig their way through deep gorges, feed vast lakes and keep pastures green year-round. In any case nature kindly provides sumptuous caves as shelter when the weather is bad!

⑦ Charolais and Brionnais country

142km/88mi starting from Charolles

Charolais is the name of a famous breed of cattle characterised by the pale colour of their coat. If you enjoy eating meat, you will want to savour a succulent piece of Charolais beef (tastings are organised by the Charolais Institute!). The surrounding area is dotted with castles... beginning with Digoine. Nearby is Paray-le-Monial and its basilica modelled, albeit on a smaller scale, on the famous Cluny Abbey. Further south, the route enters Brionnais country; churches in this area are renowned for their bell-towers and fine sculptures (Anzy-le-Duc, Semur-en-Brionnais). St-Christophe, lying in the heart of the cattle-breeding region, bustles with activity on Thursday mornings when the cattle market takes place. South to Charlieu, its fine abbey and nearby Couvent des Cordeliers (Gothic cloisters). Turn northwards back to Charolles via the Château de Drée (its interior is being beautifully restored) and Mont des Carges which offers a last glimpse of the Charolais countryside.

⑧ From Cluny to Taizé: South of Burgundy in all its splendour *120km/75mi starting from Mâcon*

South Burgundy seems to stand apart from the rest of the region, an impression which is underlined by the widening Saône Valley and the use of curved tiles on the roofs of houses. Starting from Mâcon, drive across the famous vineyards of St-Vérand and Pouilly-Fuissé on the way to the Roche de Solutré. The climb is not too hard and the view is well worth the effort. Stop by the museum of prehistory partly dug out of the rock. Continue to Milly, where Lamartine spent his childhood and visit the nearby Château de St-Point where he received all his famous friends, Victor Hugo, Franz Liszt etc. Further on lies Cluny and its abbey, once the "light of the world" but unfortunately badly damaged... However, the tradition lives on in nearby Taizé, which plays host to thousands of youths from all over the world, gathering to pray together every summer. Beyond the 17C Château de Cormatin, Burgundian Romanesque art is once more expressed in Chapaize, Brancion and above all Tournus. Take time to appreciate the city's architectural beauty and gastronomic delights before returning to Mâcon via the Bresse region and enjoying a boat trip on the River Seille as you go through La Truchère.

⑨ Round tour of the lakes *240km/149mi starting from St-Claude*

Beautiful scenery is the theme of this tour of the Jura lakes. Artificial and natural lakes are very popular in summer. Their considerable number and great diversity ensure a wide choice of leisure activities. The largest of them all is the Vouglans Lake; it offers cruises aboard an elegant paddle-boat, often including a gastronomic meal. The most beautiful is probably the Chalain Lake which attracts water sports and sailing enthusiasts. The St-Point Lake, which freezes over in winter, is famous in summer for its shimmering clear waters whereas the Abbaye lake is the paradise of anglers.

⑩ Route des belvédères *270km/168mi starting from Les Rousses*

A moderately high mountain, plateaux dotted with lakes, forests as far as the eye can see and numerous waterfalls... it takes time to discover the wealth of natural beauty the region has to offer and it is sometimes necessary to get an overall view of the Jura's varied scenery from one of the many viewpoints dotted along this route. For instance, the Pic de l'Aigle offers an unforgettable panorama of the lake region and the Col de la Faucille ovelooks the Gex area, Lake Geneva with the Alps in the distance.

⑪ Round tour of the wild Bugey area

250km/155mi starting from Nantua

The A 40 motorway wends its way across this once remote area through tunnels and over viaducts. Nantua and its lake now welcome visitors who enjoy its gastronomic speciality, the *quenelle de Nantua*. As the Bonnet silk works in Jujurieux testify, the area has traditionally been under the economic influence of the nearby Lyon region. The generally moderate altitude, the purity of the air and unspoilt nature are an inducement to relaxation even if one is reminded that this was not always so as the Maison d'Izieu testifies.

THEMATIC ITINERARIES AND VISITS

Travel itineraries on specific themes have been mapped out to help you discover the regional architectural heritage and the traditions which make up the cultural heritage of the region. You will find brochures in tourist offices, and the routes are generally well marked and easy to follow (signs posted along the roads).

History

To allow tourists to discover France's architectural heritage in a historical context, the **Fédération nationale des Routes historiques** (www.routes-historiques.com) has set the following itineraries for the region described in this guide (the list below includes a local contact):

Route historique des Ducs de Bourgogne – Information is available from Madame de Ferluc, Château de Massène, 21140 Semur-en-Auxois, ☎/ Fax 03 80 97 03 58 or from the Office de tourisme de Dijon, ☎ 03 80 44 11 44.

Route historique des Monts et Merveilles de Franche-Comté – The route includes the châteaux of Arlay, Belvoir, Filain, Gy, Joux and the Saline royale d'Arc-et-Senans. Contact the Association des Monts et Merveilles de Franche-Comté, Château de Gy, 70700 Gy, ☎ 03 84 32 92 41.

Traditions and cultural heritage

These routes cover a selection of themes of regional interest from cheese and wine to art and famous figures of the past.

Route des Châteaux de Bourgogne du Sud – The itinerary includes, among others, the châteaux of Sully, Couches, Cormatin, La Ferté Abbey... Contact Monsieur Jacques Thenard, Abbaye de la Ferté, 71240 St-Ambreuil, ☎ 03 85 44 17 96.

Route des Trésors de la Puisaye – Apply to the Office de tourisme de St-Fargeau, ☎ 03 86 74 15 72.

Route de Madame de Sévigné – Contact Madame Jacqueline Queneau, 6 impasse de l'Ancienne-Comédie, 21140 Semur-en-Auxois, ☎ 03 80 97 28 25.

Route des Mariniers de Loire – In the footsteps of the Loire bargees from Neuvy-sur-Loire to Tresnay. Apply to the Comité départemental du tourisme, 3 rue du Sort, 58000 Nevers, ☎ 03 86 36 39 80.

Route des Vins du Jura – 80km/50mi tour from Salins-les-Bains to St-Amour through the great vineyards of the Jura region; visit of the wine museum in Arbois. Contact the Comité interprofessionnel des vins du Jura, Château Pécauld, BP 41, 39602 Arbois Cedex, ☎ 03 84 66 26 14; www.jura-vins.com.

Route des Retables – This route enables visitors to discover more than 70 splendid altarpieces mostly made after the Reformation. Information is available from the Maison du tourisme de Haute-Saône, rue des Bains, BP 117, 70002 Vesoul Cedex, ☎ 03 84 97 10 70.

Routes du Comté – The famous Comté cheese represents one of the strongest traditions of the Jura region. Several itineraries have been mapped out to include visits to farms and maturing cellars as well as meetings with local people willing to share with visitors their knowledge and enthusiasm. Information from the Maison du Comté in Poligny, www.comte.com.

Route Pasteur – In the footsteps of Louis Pasteur via Dole, Arbois and Salins-les-Bains. Contact Le Triangle d'Or jurassien, Hôtel de ville, 39330 Mouchard, ☎ 03 84 73 79 53 or the Office de tourisme d'Arbois, Hôtel de ville, 39600 Arbois, ☎ 03 84 66 55 50 or the Office de tourisme de Salins, place des Salines, 39110 Salins, ☎ 03 84 73 01 34.

Nature

The routes below focus on areas of exceptional natural beauty.

Route des Mille Étangs – 61km/38mi tour of the southern part of the Vosges: Melisey, Servance, Beulotte-St-Laurent, Faucogney, Écromagny... Apply to the Comité départemental du tourisme de Haute-Saône, Maison du tourisme, rue des Bains, BP 117, 70002 Vesoul Cedex, ☎ 03 84 97 10 70.

Route des Sapins and **Route des Lacs** – See *Route des SAPINS* and *Région des LACS DU JURA* in the Sights section of the guide. Further information is available from the Office de tourisme de Champagnole, ☎ 03 84 52 43 67.

Local industry and handicraft

Burgundy and Jura have a wealth of traditional industries which perpetuate ancestral skills and contribute to technical innovation. Furthermore, the development of technical tourism has become a reality.

This has prompted the Chamber of Commerce and Industry in Dijon to publish a regularly updated guide to help visitors in their economic discovery of the Côte-d'Or *département*.

Interesting technical visits mentioned in the Sights section include:
The **Grande Forge de Buffon** near Montbard
La Mine et les Hommes in Blanzy, near Le Creusot-Montceau
The **Museum of Man and Industry** in Le Creusot
The **underground quarry** in Aubigny
The **Musée Nicéphore-Niepce** in Châlon-sur-Saône
The **Musée Jappy** in Beaucourt
The **Forge-Musée** in Étueffont, near Belfort
The **Écomusée du Pays de la Cerise et de la Distillation** in Fougerolles
The **Musée du Jouet** in Moirans-en-Montagne
The **Musée de la Lunetterie** in Morez
The **Taillanderie** in Nans-sous-Ste-Anne
The **Musée de la Mine** in Ronchamp
The **Salines** in Salins-les-Bains
The **Forges de Syam**

Wine country

The art of drinking wine – To identify and describe the qualities or defects of a particular wine, both wine buffs and wine experts use an extremely wide yet precise vocabulary. Assessing a wine involves three successive stages, each associated with a particular sense and a certain number of technical terms:

The eye – General impression: crystalline (good clarity), limpid (perfectly transparent, no particles in suspension), still (no bubbles), sparkling (effervescent wine) or *mousseux* (lots of fine, Champagne-type bubbles).
Colour and hues: a wine is said to have a nice robe when the colour is sharp and clean; the main terms used to describe the different hues are pale red, ruby, onionskin, garnet (red wine), salmon, amber, partridge-eye pink (rosé wine) and golden-green, golden-yellow and straw (white wine).
The nose – Pleasant smells: floral, fruity, balsamic, spicy, flinty. Unpleasant smells: corked, woody, hydrogen sulphide, cask.
The mouth – Once it has passed the visual and olfactory tests, the wine undergoes a final test in the mouth.

Tasting Chablis at Château Long-Depaquit

S. Sauvignier/MICHELIN

It can be described as agreeable (pleasant), aggressive (unpleasant, with a high acidity), full-flavoured (rich and well-balanced), structured (well-constructed, with a high alcohol content), heady (intoxicating), fleshy (producing a strong impact on taste buds), fruity (flavour evoking the freshness and natural taste of grapes), easy to drink, jolly (inducing merriness), round (supple, mellow), lively (light, fresh, with a lowish alcohol content) etc.

Quality control – French wines fall into various official categories indicating the area of production and therefore the probable quality of the wine. AOC *(appellation d'origine contrôlée)* denotes a wine produced in a strictly delimited area, stated on the label, made with the grape varieties specified for that wine in accordance with local traditional methodology. VDQS *(vin délimité de qualité supérieure)* is also produced in a legally controlled area, slightly less highly rated than AOC. *Vin de pays* denotes the highest ranking table wine after AOC and VDQS.

Wine cellar visits – The **Bureau interprofessionnel des vins de Bourgogne (BIVB)**, 12 boulevard Bretonnière, BP 150, 21024 Beaune Cedex, ☎ 03 80 25 04 80, Fax 03 80 25 04 81, www.bivb.com, provides information and publishes several brochures about wines including a repertory of wine cellars selling bottled wine with the names of the different estates, cooperatives and wine-producers/merchants.

Wine-tasting courses lasting from 2hr to several days are organised by the **École des vins de Bourgogne**, BIVB, ☎ 03 80 25 04 95.

In addition, 155 wine-producers/merchants, cooperatives and municipal cellars have formed an association known as the **De Vignes en Caves**. Members display a sign at the entrance of their estate and a list of all members with their location is offered to visitors in Tourist Information Centres.

Wine museums – These are described in the guide.

Beaune Musée du vin de Bourgogne
Chenôve Cuverie des ducs de Bourgogne
Vougeot Château du Clos de Vougeot
Reulle-Vergy Musée des arts et traditions des Hautes-Côtes
Cuiseaux Maison de la Vigne et du Vigneron
Romanèche-Thorins Hameau du Vin
Champvallon Pressoir

KIR

Kir is a friendly little before-dinner drink made of cool white wine and a touch of *cassis*, blackcurrant liqueur, a Dijon speciality. Its rosy colour and sweet aroma make you feel better just looking at it. Start with champagne and it becomes a *kir royal*, or innovate with other flavoured liqueurs (peach, blackberry). While the origins of the concoction itself are lost in time, the name is that of Dijon's mayor (from 1945 until his death in 1968), who tirelessly served this drink to his guests at the town hall.

Internet – Many wine-growers now have their own web site and sell their wine via the Internet. Some wine-growers, however, have chosen to be included on the portal of their merchants.

Information:

www.bourgogne.net – This portal includes numerous information web sites on the themes of economy, tourism, wine, wine-growing estates etc and is a good introduction to the region.

www.frenchwines.com – Linked to the previous portal, this web site offers a repertory of French wines with maps, a list of wine-growing villages, of events concerning wine, of wine-growers and merchants, an explanation of the *appellations* system and a vintage table with ratings (click on Hints and Tips).

www.webiwine.com/english – Repertory of a great number of wine-growing estates (including Brocard, Louis Latour, Joseph Drouhin).

www.louisjadot.com – The geographical specificity of this wine-growing estate is explained in detail. Wide list of *appellations*.

www.louislatour.com – Map of the various plots of land which make up this estate and the wines produced are described with tasting tips.

Beaune wine auction sale:

Find out all about this famous wine auction sale (the world's most important charity sale) on the web site of the Comité régional de tourisme de Bourgogne: www.crt-bourgogne.fr

Buying wine online:

www.vins-du-beaujolais.com – This elaborate web site includes a great number of wine-growers and is one of the best for buying wine.

www.vintime.com – This site offers a wide selection of great Burgundy wines; the company is also renowned for its collection of old vintages.

Address book – Below are the addresses of main wine centres and large cooperatives:

Côte de Beaune

Beaune **Maison des Vins à Beaune (BIVB)** – *See address above.*
Denis Perret – 40 place Carnot, 21200 Beaune, ☎ 03 80 22 35 47. The most important wine-merchant in Beaune; extensive choice of great vintage wines.
L'Athenaeum – 7 rue de l'Hôtel-Dieu, 21200 Beaune. ☎ 03 80 25 08 30. All you need to know about wine... books, information, video films, specialised tools, glassware, various objects.

Hautes-Côtes

Nuits-Saint-Georges **Maison des Hautes-Côtes** – Route de Villers, Marey-lès-Fussey, 21700 Nuits-Saint-Georges, ☎ 03 80 62 91 29, Fax 03 80 62 96 79.

Chablis, Auxerrois

Chablis **Maison des Vins à Chablis (BIVB)** – Le Petit-Pontigny, 1 rue de Chichée, BP 31, 89800 Chablis, ☎ 03 86 42 42 22, Fax 03 86 42 80 16. **Coopérative la Chablisienne** – 8 boulevard Pasteur, 89800 Chablis, ☎ 03 86 42 89 89, Fax 03 86 42 89 90.

Saint-Bris-le-Vineux	**Maison du Vignoble auxerrois** – 14 route de Champs, 89530 Saint-Bris-le-Vineux, ☎ 03 86 53 66 76.
Côte chalonnaise	
Chalon-sur-Saône	**Maison des Vins de la Côte chalonnaise** – Promenade Sainte-Marie, 71100 Chalon-sur-Saône, ☎ 03 85 41 64 00, Fax 03 85 41 99 83.
Mâconnais	
Mâcon	**Maison Mâconnaise des Vins** – 520 avenue De-Lattre-de-Tassigny, 71000 Mâcon, (along N 6), ☎ 03 85 22 91 30, Fax 03 85 22 91 81. Restaurant-Sale, 484 avenue De-Lattre-de-Tassigny, 71000 Mâcon, ☎ 03 85 22 91 11, Fax 03 85 22 91 12.

ANOTHER POINT OF VIEW

Tourist trains

A number of charming old steam trains, often running off the beaten track, enable visitors to discover sites otherwise inaccessible.

Petit train de la Côte-d'Or – APTCO, gare de Plombières-Canal, 21370 Plombières-lès-Dijon, ☎ 03 80 45 88 51, runs along the Ouche and the Canal de Bourgogne. Departure from Lac Kir.

Train touristique des Lavières – 6 rue des Capucins, 21120 Is-sur-Tille, ☎ 03 80 95 36 36, runs through the pine forest near Is-sur-Tille.

Chemin de fer de la vallée de l'Ouche – 4 rue Pasumot, 21200 Beaune, ☎ 03 80 20 16 65, steam or diesel train along the old track between Dijon and Épinac, leaving from Bligny-sur-Ouche Station and running to Pont-d'Ouche; July and August: daily; early May to the end of September: Sundays and holidays.

Chemin de fer des Combes – Rue des Pyrénées, 71200 Le Creusot, ☎ 03 85 55 26 23, offers a good view of Le Creusot and the Morvan heights; 10km/6mi journey through a wooded park; steam engine dating from 1917.

Chemin de fer touristique de Puisaye – Avenue de la Gare, 89130 Toucy, ☎ 03 86 44 05 58, small trucks and steam-powered tractors run along the old track; railway museum open weekends and holidays from May to the last Sunday in September.

P'tit train de l'Yonne – ATPVM, 89310 Nitry, ☎ 03 86 33 93 33 or 03 86 33 62 74, 5km/3mi through the Serein Valley between Massangis and Civry, departure from Massangis.

Coni'fer – Between Les Hôpitaux-Neufs and Fontaine Ronde *(description and information, see MÉTABIEF-MONT D'OR)*.

Saint-Claude to Morez – 1 Grande-Rue, 39170 St-Lupicin, ☎ 03 84 42 85 96. This old 25km/15mi line runs along part of the Bienne gorge, unfolding beautiful landscapes. It is dotted with tunnels and various engineering structures. The journey is often combined with thematic visits.

From above

Weather permitting, there are various ways of getting a bird's-eye view of the Burgundy-Jura region, from microlights (ULM, standing for *ultra-légers motorisés*), light aircraft or hot-air balloons *(montgolfières)*.

Microlights – École professionnelle Alizé, route de Lons, 39130 Doucier, ☎ 03 84 25 71 93.

Light aircraft – Aéroclub de promotion de l'aviation comtoise, Domergue. Aérodrome de la Vèze, 25660 La Vèze, ☎ 03 81 81 50 82.
Aéroclub de Gray, rue St-Adrien, 70100 Gray, ☎ 03 84 65 99 84.

Hot-air balloons – It is also possible to take a trip in a hot-air balloon (generally allow about half a day for 1hr-1hr 30min in the air). Balloons fly over the Côte de Beaune vineyards during the fine season; flights last from 1hr to 3hr from April to November and take place either early in the morning or towards the end of the day to take advantage of the most favourable weather conditions.

Air Adventures, rue Dessous, 21320 Chailly, ☎ 03 80 90 74 23.
Air Escargot, 71150 Remigny, ☎ 03 85 87 12 30.
France Montfolfières, 6 place de la gare, 89270 Vermenton, ☎ 03 86 81 03 70.
Montgolfières de l'Yonne, 21 rue de Valmy, 89000 Auxerre, ☎ 03 86 46 15 18.
Club aérostatique de Franche-Comté, BP 24, 90001 Belfort Cedex, ☎ 03 84 90 20 20.

Activities children will love

The region abounds in parks, zoos, museums and various attractive sites and features as well as leisure activities which will appeal to children; in the Sights section, the reader's attention is drawn to them by the symbol 🖾. Here is a short list:

Museums – The Motor Car Museum in Chauffailles, the Heads of State Limousines Museum in Montjalin, the Motorbike Collection in Savigny-lès-Beaune Castle, the Old Toys Collection in Laduz Museum.

Sites – The Briare Canal-bridge, Le Creusot mining and industrial site, the Guédelon medieval building site, the Archéodrome de Bourgogne.

Parks and zoos – Parc de l'Auxois, 21350 Arnay-sous-Vitteaux, ☎ 03 80 49 64 01; Parc naturel de Boutissaint, 89820 Treigny, ☎ 03 86 74 07 08; Parc zoologique et d'attractions Touroparc, 71570 Romanèche-Thorins, ☎ 03 85 35 51 53.

Towns designated by the Ministry of Culture as **Villes d'Art et d'Histoire** organise discovery tours and cultural-heritage workshops for children. Fun books and specially designed tools are provided and the activities on offer are supervised by various professionals such as architects, stonemasons, storytellers, actors. This scheme, called **l'été des 6-12 ans** (summer activities for 6 to 12-year-olds) operates during school holidays. The towns concerned are: Autun, Auxerre, Beaune, Besançon, Chalon, Cluny, Dijon, Dole, Joigny, Nevers, Paray-le-Monial.

Barouche rides

Ferme équestre de l'Étang Fourchu, Les Écarts de la Chapelle, 90100 Florimont, ☎ 03 84 29 61 59.

Association Picheval, 39230 Darbonnay, ☎ 03 84 85 58 27 (wagon rides from 1hr to several days).

Courses in local cookery

Burgundy is, among other things, synonymous with gastronomy and lovers of fine cuisine will not want to miss the annual themed exhibition organised by the **Maison régionale des Arts de la table**, 15 rue St-Jacques, 21230 Arnay-le-Duc, ☎/Fax 03 80 90 11 59.

If your favourite recreation takes place with pots and pans for equipment, why not spend a few days in a prestigious French kitchen for a holiday? These courses take place mainly in winter.

À la découverte de la truffe et des vins de Bourgogne, Service Loisirs Accueil Yonne, 1-2 quai de la République, 89000 Auxerre, ☎ 03 86 72 92 10; Saturday mornings from 15 September to 8 December: all about truffles with Chef Jean-Luc Barnabet and truffle-grower M. Beaucamp, ending with a tasting session.

Visit Bourgogne (Charrecey), M. Carpentier, ☎ 03 85 45 38 97; cookery lessons (1 to 5 days).

ABC de la grande cuisine (Joigny), ☎ 03 86 62 09 70; contemporary cooking presented by Jean-Michel Lorain; the course includes accommodation; cost, programme and calendar on request.

Les Toques Nivernaises (La Charité-sur-Loire), M. James Grennerat, Restaurant Le Monarque, ☎ 03 86 70 21 73; the association proposes courses on a theme which can be chosen by the participants (from 6 to 12 persons).

Le cellier du Goût (La Charité-sur-Loire), ☎ 03 86 70 36 21; this association organises meals with a commentary, attended by famous chefs, as well as tasting sessions during the summer.

ECO-TOURISM

River cruising

Three rivers – the Yonne, the Saône and its tributary the Seille – together with several canals or stretches of canal provide about 1 200km/1 931mi of navigable waterway for those who would like to visit Burgundy by boat.
The Jura region offers its fair share of rivers (the Saône and the Doubs), canals (Canal de l'Est and Canal Rhin-Rhône) and lakes (Lac de Vouglans) – all in all, over 320km/200mi of waterways – to boating enthusiasts, who can either opt for a cruise or hire their own craft.

Houseboats – No licence is required to hire a boat but the helmsman must be an adult; a practical and theoretical lesson is given at the beginning of the hire period. To pilot such a boat successfully one must observe the speed limits and heed the advice of the rental company instructor, particularly when mooring or passing through locks. Canals are usually closed to navigation from mid-November to mid-March. Before leaving it is advisable to obtain suitable maps and guides (Collection Navicarte or Éditions du Breil or Collection Vagnon). The main embarkation ports are Digoin, St-Jean-de-Losne and Tournus (Burgundy), Gray, Joigny and Montbéliard.

For information and a list of useful addresses apply to:

The **Comité régional de tourisme de Bourgogne** *(see address above)* publishes a brochure entitled *Tourisme fluvial en Bourgogne*, listing the names and addresses of all the boat-hire companies.

The **Groupement pour le tourisme fluvial**, 6 rue de Chalezeule, 25000 Besançon, ☎ 03 81 88 71 38 *(free brochure on request)*.

Boat trips – These can last for 1hr, half a day or a day; in this case a meal is often served on board.

Les Bateaux du Saut du Doubs, Compagnie Droz-Bartholet, Les Terres Rouges, 25130 Villers-le-Lac, ☎ 03 82 68 13 25; trips to Besançon and the Saut du Doubs from Easter to 1 November.

Houseboat on a canal in Burgundy

CNFS – Vedettes panoramiques, BP 30, 25130 Villers-le-Lac, ☎ 03 81 68 05 34; cruises from Besançon and Villers-le-Lac with or without meal.

Le Vagabondo, departure from quai Mavia, 70100 Gray, ☎ 06 07 42 75 54; guided trips along the Saône; also cruises with meal included.

Barge-hotels – There are about a dozen of these in Burgundy; cruises lasting from two to seven days provide full board and offer a fine chance to discover and appreciate Burgundian gastronomy. Barges can accommodate 6 to 24 passengers and prices vary from 726.25€ to 2 286.74€ per person per week, including transfer from the airport, excursions, evening entertainment and wine-cellar visits.

Nature and the environment

Nature lovers will find a wealth of information about nature trails, hiking and outdoor activities, exhibitions concerning nature and the environment and on-going projects in the brochure *La Bourgogne Loisirs nature* (available from tourist offices) and by contacting the following:

Maison de la nature des Vosges saônoises, Belmont, 70440 Le Haut-du-Them, ☎ 03 84 63 89 41.

Maison départementale de l'environnement, Étang de Malsaucy, 90350 Évette-Salbert, ☎ 03 84 29 18 12.

DPIE Atelier de l'environnement du Haut-Jura, 1 Grande-Rue, 39170 St-Lupicin, ☎ 03 84 42 85 96.

Nature parks

There are three Regional Nature Parks, one in Burgundy and two in the Jura.

Parc naturel régional du Morvan – With its forests, deep valleys, numerous waterways and lakes, the Morvan lends itself to a wide range of nature-friendly activities (rambling, themed walks, cycle tours, riding tours, sailing, swimming, white-water sports, rock-climbing...). For full information about the Regional Nature Park and the leisure activities available, apply to the **Maison du Parc**, 58230 St-Brisson, ☎ 03 86 78 79 00; www.parcdumorvan.org.

Other useful addresses include:

Guided hikes – Guides en Morvan, 71320 Charbonnat, guidesenmorvan@parcdumorvan.org.

Morvan Découverte, La Peurtantaine, école du Bourg, 71550 Anost, ☎ 03 85 82 77 74.

Cycle tours – Service Loisirs Accueil du Nivernais-Morvan, 3 rue du Sort, 58000 Nevers, ☎ 03 86 59 14 22.

France Randonnée, 9 rue des Portes-Mordelaises, 35000 Rennes, ☎ 02 99 67 42 21.

Association Morvan VTT, Maison du Parc, M. Oppin, ☎ 03 86 78 71 77.

Base de plein air, Plan d'eau du Vallon, 71400 Autun, ☎ 03 85 86 20 96.

Riding tours – Association pour la randonnée équestre en Morvan (AREM), same address as the Maison du Parc, www.morvanacheval.com; additional information available from the Maison du Parc.

Sailing, swimming, fun with water – Station voile du lac des Settons, Les Branlasses, 58230 Montsauche-les-Settons, ☎ 03 86 84 51 98.

Base Activital de loisirs, Baye, 58110 Bazolles, ☎ 03 86 38 97 39.

White-water sports – AN rafting, 58230 St-Agan, ☎ 03 86 22 65 28 (in season) or ☎ 01 42 96 63 63 (year-round); www.an-rafting.com.

Centre Sport nature de Chaumeçon, 58140 St-Martin-du-Puy, ☎/Fax 03 86 22 61 35.

Ab Loisirs, route du camping, 89450 St-Père-sous-Vézelay, ☎ 03 86 33 38 38.

Rock-climbing – Loisirs en Morvan, 105 rue des Mignottes, 89000 Auxerre, ☎ 03 86 49 55 50.

For other activities, apply to the **Maison du Parc** or send an e-mail to: morvanloisirssportsnature@parcdumorvan.org.

Parc naturel régional du Haut-Jura – Information about activities, nature trails etc is available from the Maison du Haut-Jura, 39310 Lajoux, ☎ 03 84 34 12 30.

Parc naturel régional des Ballons des Vosges – Permanent and temporary exhibitions are held in the Maison du Parc, which also provides information and welcomes visitors.

Maison du Parc, 1 cour de l'Abbaye, 68140 Munster, ☎ 03 89 77 90 34; www.parc-ballons-vosges.fr.

SPAS

The benefits of spa treatments, known to the Romans and probably the Gauls, were rediscovered in the 18C-19C. At that time, taking the waters was reserved for wealthy clients with time to spare. Today, the French national health system recognises the therapeutic value of many cures, and patients' stays are provided for, all or in part, by the social security.

J.-M. Klein/CRT Bourgogne

St-Honoré-les-Bains

Treatment occupies only part of the day, so the spas offer their guests many other activities to pass the time pleasantly: sports and recreation, various forms of entertainment. The beautiful natural settings provide the opportunity for outdoor excursions.

In addition to traditional treatment courses, which usually last three weeks, many resorts offer shorter stays for clients with a specific goal in mind: stress relief and relaxation, fitness and shaping up, giving up smoking, losing weight etc.

You can also get general information by contacting the **Fédération thermale et climatique française**, 16 rue de l'Estrapade, 75005 Paris, ☎ 01 43 25 11 85.

Via Internet, connect to www.tourisme.fr and search the category "Spas and Fitness" for precise information (in French in most cases) on accommodation, short-stay treatments, entertainment etc. If you would like to make a spa treatment part of your holiday, be sure to plan in advance. Reservations may be scarce at certain times of the year, and special conditions, including a prior medical examination, may apply.

For further general information: **Association des villes thermales de Franche-Comté**, Hôtel de Ville, place du 8-Septembre, 25000 Besançon, ☎ 03 81 81 87 50.

Bourbon-Lancy – Damona, quartier thermal (slightly radioactive waters), BP 40, 71140 Bourbon-Lancy, ☎ 03 85 89 67 37.

Divonne-les-Bains – Thermes de Divonne, ☎ 04 50 20 05 70; Espace Paul Vidart, avenue des Thermes, 01220 Divonne-les-Bains, ☎ 04 50 20 27 70 (fitness centre).

Lons-le-Saunier – Thermes Ledonia (salt waters), Parc des Bains, BP 181, 39005, Lons-le-Saunier, ☎ 03 84 24 20 34.

Luxeuil-les-Bains – Établissement thermal, avenue des Thermes, BP 51, 70302 Luxeuil-les-Bains, ☎ 03 84 40 44 22.

Saint-Honoré-les-Bains – Établissement thermal (the waters contain sulphur), BP 8, 58360 St-Honoré-les-Bains, ☎ 03 86 30 73 27.

Salins-les-Bains – Les Thermes (salt waters), place des Alliés, 39110, Salins-les-Bains, ☎ 03 84 73 04 63.

Sports and outdoor activities

Information and brochures outlining the sports and outdoor facilities available in the region can be obtained from the French Government Tourist Office or from the organisations listed below.

WATER SPORTS

Lakes and reservoirs

They are the ideal setting for windsurfing, water-skiing, fishing, rambling around the lake shore and so on.

In the Jura:

Lake / Reservoir	*Dépt*	Surface area (in hectares)	Swimming	Leisure park	Fishing
Abbaye (Lac)	39	100	–	–	yes
Allement (Barrage)	01	225	yes	yes	yes
Antre (Lac)	39	16	–	–	yes
Barterand (Lac)	01	19	yes	–	yes
Bonlieu (Lac)	39	17	–	–	yes
Chalain (Lac)	39	240	yes	yes	yes
Champagney (Bassin)	70	103	–	yes	yes
Clairvaux (Grand Lac)	39	64	yes	yes	yes
Divonne-les-Bains (Lac)	01	45	yes	yes	yes
Etival (Grand Lac)	39	17	–	–	yes
Genin (Lac)	01	8	yes	yes	yes
Ilay (Lac)	39	70	yes	–	yes
Lamoura (Lac)	39	4	yes	–	yes
Malsaucy (Lac))	90	66	yes	yes	–
Nantua (Lac)	01	141	yes	yes	yes
Narlay (Lac)	39	42	–	–	yes
Rousses (Lac)	39	100	yes	yes	yes
St-Point (Lac)	25	450	yes	yes	yes
Sylans (Lac)	01	50	–	–	yes
Val (Lac)	39	60	–	–	yes
Vouglans (Barrage)	39	1600	yes	yes	yes

To convert hectares to acres, mulitply by 2.47.

In Burgundy:

Burgundy has fewer lakes; however, the following (non-exhaustive list) are suitable for the practice of various water sports (mainly windsurfing and water-skiing): the Lac de Bourdon (near St-Fargeau), the Lac du Pont (Côte-d'Or), the Lac Kir (Dijon) and the Lac des Settons. Some sections of the Saône, the Yonne and even the Loire are also sought after by water sports enthusiasts. In addition, the water sports centre in Arc-sur-Tille, used for competitions, can seat up to 3 000 spectators.

Further information is available from the following:
Fédération française de ski nautique, 16 rue Clément-Marot, 75008 Paris, ☎ 01 47 20 05 00; www.ffsn.asso.fr
Ligue de Bourgogne de ski nautique, c/o Michel Butel, rue Skopje, 21000 Dijon, ☎/Fax 03 80 75 39 44; www.perso.wanadoo.fr/adb/arc.

Canoeing and kayaking

This method of exploring local waterways need not be exclusively reserved for seasoned canoeing experts. Sometimes this sport can be a pleasant way to discover secluded spots inaccessible by any other means. The main difference between a canoe and a kayak is that the former is propelled by a single-bladed paddle and the latter by a double-bladed paddle.

Besides the Morvan where streams and small rivers offer exciting possibilities to canoeists looking for a challenge, the Yonne, the Canal de Bourgogne, the Saône and the Loire lend themselves to canoeing trips and competitions organised by the numerous sport centres of the **Fédération française de canoë-kayak**, 87 quai de la Marne, BP 58, 94344 Joinville-le-Pont, 01 45 11 08 50; www.ffcanoe.asso.fr (map available). A guide entitled *Vacances en canoë-kayak* is published annually by the **Canoë-kayak magazine**, 25 rue Berbisey, 21000 Dijon, ☎ 03 81 91 30 28.

For additional information, contact:
Comité régional de Franche-Comté, 19 rue Roger-Martin-du-Gard, 25000 Besançon, ☎ 03 81 53 67 07; comiteregfc-canoekayak@wanadoo.fr.
Comités départementaux –
Ain: Base de Longeville, 01500 Ambronay, ☎ 04 74 39 14 17.
Doubs: M. Pierre Menissier, 8 rue des Cantons, 25400 Audincourt, ☎/Fax 03 81 30 62 14.
Jura: M. Philippe Jacques, 14 rue de Miarle, 39100 Champvans, ☎ 03 84 82 65 71.

Equipment hire:
Espace Morteau, BP 32077, 25502 Morteau Cedex, ☎ 03 81 67 48 72; www.espace-morteau.com.
Plein Air Nautisme, rue Forge, BP 67, 70110 Villersexel, ☎ 03 84 20 30 87.
Syratu Tourisme et Loisirs, route de Montgesoye, 25290 Ornans, ☎ 03 81 57 10 82.
Club de la Gauloise, 1 rue du Château, 25200 Montbéliard, ☎ 06 03 53 06 44.
Maison pour Tous, 16 rue du Gén.-Herr, Bureau du tourisme, 25150 Pont-de-Roide, ☎ 03 81 99 33 99.

Fishing

Trout, perch, tench and pike abound in the region's lakes, rivers and canals; carp and bream are less commonly found. Some of the rivers of the Jura *département* are considered to be among the best French rivers for trout fishing.

Angling
G. Magnin/MICHELIN

Regulations – They differ according to whether the water is classified as first category (contains trout) or second category (coarse fish). Generally speaking, in the case of first category rivers, the fishing season starts on the second Saturday in March and ends on the third Sunday in September. As for rivers belonging in the second category, fishing is authorised throughout the year. Stricter rules apply to fish needing special protection.

Anglers will need either to buy a special holiday fishing permit, valid for two weeks between June and September, or take out annual membership of an officially approved angling association.

National regulations state that anglers must return to the water any fish they catch below the minimum permitted length (50cm/20in for pike, 40cm/16in for pike-perch, 23cm/9in for trout, 9cm/4in for crayfish).

Brochures and folding maps *Fishing in France (Pêche en France)* are published and distributed by the **Conseil Supérieur de la Pêche**, 134 avenue Malakoff, 75116 Paris, ☎ 01 45 02 20 20; also available from local angling organisations.

Useful addresses –

Maison nationale de l'eau et de la pêche, 36 rue St-Laurent, 25290 Ornans, ☎ 03 81 57 14 49.
Étang du Châtelet (Fédération départementale de la pêche), 7 quai de Mantoue, 58000 Nevers, ☎ 03 86 61 18 98; fly-fishing from March to October, daily except Tuesday.
Domaine de Tarperon, route de St-Marc, 21510 Aignay-le-Duc, ☎ 03 80 93 83 74.

Château de Thenissey, rue Pont, 21150 Thenissey, ☎ 03 80 35 85 55.

Au fil de l'eau, 26 rue de Lyon, 89200 Avallon, ☎ 03 86 34 50 41.

Association Mâcon Pêche au Gros, 4 rue de la Liberté, 71000 Mâcon, ☎ 03 85 29 02 50; an introduction to fishing for the carnivorous sheath-fish (up to 3m/10ft long and 150kg/331lb in weight).

École française de pêche, M. Stéphane Sence, BP 16, 33450 St-Sulpice et Cameyrac, ☎ 05 56 30 24 50; www.ecoledepeche.com.

ON DRY LAND

Rambling

Short, medium and long distance footpath *Topo-Guides* are published by the **Fédération Française de la Randonnée Pédestre (FFRP)**. These give detailed maps of the paths and offer valuable information to the rambler; they are on sale at the information centre: 14 rue Riquet, 75019 Paris, ☎ 01 44 89 93 90; www.ffrp.asso.fr.

There are several long-distance footpaths *(sentiers de grande randonnée – GR – red and white markings)* covering the Jura:
– Two of them cross the region from north the south, **GR 5** which skirts the Swiss border and the **GR 59** which follows the western edge of the region.

– Another two explore the Doubs area, **GR 590** which runs through the Loue and Lison valleys starting from Ornans and **GR 595** which links GR 59 and GR 5 from Montfaucon (near Besançon) to Maison-du-Bois (near Pontarlier).

– **GR 559** crosses the Jura from Lons-le-Saunier to Les Rousses via Ilay and Bonlieu.

– **GR 9** crosses the Jura from St-Amour in the west to Les Rousses in the east then turns south.

There are also a number of regional GR *(GR de pays – red and yellow markings)*; some of them link up with the main GR.

The extensive network (6 000km/3728mi) of footpaths crisscrossing Burgundy offers ramblers the possibility of visiting lesser known areas: the Loire islands with their remarkable fauna, Cîteaux or Vauluisant forests, the Puisaye countryside, the ochre-coloured villages of the Mâconnais area or the vineyards of South Burgundy dotted with Romanesque churches.

Ready to roam

Other useful addresses:

Comité régional de la randonnée pédestre de Bourgogne, 13 rue de la Paix, 21240 Talant, ☎ 03 80 57 11 22.

Comités départementaux de randonnée pédestre –

Côte-d'Or: Hôtel du département, BP 1601, 21035 Dijon Cedex, ☎ 03 80 63 64 60.

Nièvre: 5bis rue de la Parcheminerie, 58000 Nevers, ☎/Fax 03 86 36 92 98.

Saône-et-Loire: Centre de loisirs, Vieille route d'Ozenay, 71700 Tournus, ☎ 03 85 51 06 15.

Yonne: Maison départementale des Sports, 12 boulevard de Galliéni, 89000 Auxerre, ☎/Fax 03 86 52 39 09.

Cycling and mountain biking

The **Fédération Française de Cyclotourisme** (12 rue Louis-Bertrand, 94200 Ivry-sur-Seine, ☎ 01 56 20 88 88) and its local committees recommend a number of cycling tours of various lengths.

The **Fédération Française de Cyclisme** (5 rue de Rome, 93561 Rosny-sous-Bois Cedex, ☎ 01 49 35 69 24; www.ffc.fr) publishes a guide which describes 36 000km/22 370mi of marked trails suitable for mountain biking.

Cycling holidays in Burgundy are organised by the following:

Bougogne Touring Incoming, 11 rue de la Liberté, 21000 Dijon, ☎ 03 80 30 49 49.

Bourgogne randonnée, 7 avenue du 8-Septembre, 21200 Beaune, ☎ 03 80 22 06 03.

Dili Voyages, 10 avenue de la République, 21200 Beaune, ☎ 03 80 24 24 82.

Cyclo Vert 71, 6 rue St-Nizier, 71000 Mâcon, ☎ 03 85 39 09 88.

France randonnée, 9 rue des Portes-Mordelaises, 35000 Rennes, ☎ 02 99 67 42 21.

Duvine Adventures, operating out of Somerville, Massachusetts (635 Boston Ave. Suite 2, zip code 02144), offers a six-day guided bike tour in Burgundy: charming accommodation, fine wines, 24-speed mountain bikes. Stops along the way include famous wine cellars and châteaux, monuments (Rochepot, Abbaye de Citeaux...), local markets and some excellent restaurants with star ratings in Michelin's Red Guide. US ☎ (781) 395-7440, Fax (781) 395-8472, Internet: www.duvine.com.

In addition, Burgundy has several mountain-bike (VTT) centres officially recognised by the Fédération française de Cyclisme:

Morvan: *see Parc naturel régional du Morvan, p 317.*

La Croix Messire Jean, 71190 Uchon, ☎ 03 85 54 42 06; alt 680m/2231ft – 230km/143mi of trails among rocks and ponds. Here you can learn to read maps and to find your bearings; the centre also organises night tours.

Centre VTT Les Granges, 71960 Serrières; 226km/140mi of trails running across an undulating landscape of vineyards and châteaux. The centre also has a mountain-biking school.

Centre VTT de St-Saulge, Syndicat d'initiative, 58330 St-Saulge, ☎ 03 86 58 25 74; 16 loops totalling 550km/342mi of trails through the Nièvre region.

In view of the fact that the Jura is a mountainous region, it is necessary to establish cycling itineraries according to the level of difficulty required. Information and advice can be obtained from:

Ligue de cyclotourisme de Franche-Comté (FFCT), M. Pierre Marey, 26 rue de la Banque, 70000 Vesoul, ☎ 03 84 76 84 63.

Comité régional de cyclisme de Franche-Comté, 12 rue Charles-Dornier, 25000 Besançon, ☎ 03 81 52 17 13; ffcfranchecomte@wanadoo.fr.

There are excellent possibilities for downhill or cross-country mountain biking, the most famous site being Métabief where the world, European and French championships take place. One of the possibilities is to follow the 300km/186mi trail of the **Grande Traversée du Jura** *(see cross-country skiing).*

The Indiana Saône mountain-biking trek takes place during the 3rd weekend in August across fields, forests and rivers; to take part, contact **Indiana Saône**, Espace de la Motte, 70000 Vesoul, ☎ 03 84 75 78 35; www.indiana-saone.org.

Riding

There are many riding centres in Burgundy and in the Jura. They offer courses, excursions, forest rides and riding holidays. In addition, a visit to the Cluny stud farm, one of the most renowned in France, is not to be missed (**Haras nationaux de Cluny**, 2 rue de la Porte-aux-Prés, 71250 Cluny, ☎ 03 85 59 85 00).

Cooling off

Ph. Gajic/MICHELIN

Information at national level can be obtained from:

Comité national de tourisme équestre, 9 boulevard Macdonald, 75019 Paris, ☎ 01 53 26 15 50. The Comité publishes an annual brochure entitled *Tourisme et loisirs équestres en France.*

Information on riding in Burgundy and the Jura is available from the **Comités départementaux** (list of local centres, activities, accommodation, riding tours lasting from 2 to 8 days):

Côte-d'Or: Les Randonnées de Haute Bourgogne, M. Michel Burel, 21330 Griselles, ☎ 03 80 81 46 15.
Nièvre: Mme Maligne, Mairie, 58120 Château-Chinon, ☎ 03 86 85 15 05.
Saône-et-Loire: M. Guyot de Caila, Moulin de Vaux, 71600 Nochize, ☎ 03 85 88 31 51.
Yonne: M. Bruneau, impasse de la Maladrerie, 89740 Cruzy-le-Châtel, ☎ 03 86 75 23 16; www.yonneacheval.com.
Doubs: Alain Bouchon, relais équestre de la Montnoirotte, 25340 Crosey-le-Petit, ☎ 03 81 86 83 98.
Jura: Maurice Gallet, 172 Grande-rue, 39570 Chille, ☎ 03 84 43 46 23.
Haute-Saône: Pascal Chatriot, Gaec de la Borde, 70100 Bouhans et Feurg, ☎ 03 84 32 31 98.
Territoire de Belfort: Gilles Papillard, 2 rue des Errues, 90170 Anjoutey, ☎ 03 84 54 64 21.

Other regional addresses:

Ligue bourguignonne d'équitation, de randonnée et de tourisme équestre, M. Brochant, Mairie, 58800 Corbigny, ☎/Fax 03 86 20 08 04; www.bourgogneacheval.com.
Ligue équestre de Bourgogne, 6 rue du Palais, 21000 Dijon, ☎ 03 80 30 05 08.
Association régionale de tourisme équestre de Franche-Comté, 52 rue de Dole, 25000 Besançon, ☎ 03 81 52 67 40.
Jura du Grand Huit, 8 rue Louis-Rousseau, 39000 Lons-le-Saunier, ☎ 03 84 87 08 88; www.jura-tourism.com.

Golf

The popularity of golf, which took off in the early 1980s, is steadily increasing. In 1998, more than 260 000 golf players were officially registered in France, indulging in their favourite sport on around 500 golf links.
The map *Golfs, les Parcours Français*, published by Éditions Plein Sud and based on **Michelin map no 721**, provides useful information on the location, address and type of golf course open to players throughout the country.
Fédération Française de Golf, 68 rue Anatole-France, 92309 Levallois-Perret, ☎ 01 41 49 77 00, www.ffgolf.org.

There are 18 golf courses in Burgundy's four *départements*; the web site of the **Comité régional de tourisme** (www.crt-bourgogne.fr) provides all the relevant information: list of courses with detailed address, description, prices, accommodation etc.

Mountain Safety

Choosing the right equipment for a rambling, cross-country ski or snow-shoe expedition is essential. If walking in the summer, choose flexible hiking shoes with non-slip soles, bring a rain jacket or poncho, an extra sweater, sun protection (hat, glasses and lotion), drinking water (1-2l per person), high energy snacks (chocolate, cereal bars, bananas...), and a first aid kit. Of course, you'll need a good map (and a compass if you plan to leave the main trails). Plan your itinerary well, keeping in mind that while the average walking speed for an adult is 4kph/2.5mph, you will need time to eat and rest, and children will not keep up the same pace.

For winter expeditions, plan your itinerary carefully. Even if it is beautiful and sunny when you set out, take warm, waterproof clothing in case of a sudden storm or if you are surprised by nightfall. Always have some food and water with you. Do not leave the groomed trails unless you are with an experienced guide. Read the notices at trail entrances in regard to avalanche alerts and weather reports. Protect exposed skin from the sun with an effective lotion. Always leave your itinerary and expected time of return with someone before setting out (innkeeper, fellow camper or friend).

If you are caught in an electrical storm, avoid high ground, and do not move along a ridge top; do not seek shelter under overhanging rocks, isolated trees in otherwise open areas, at the entrance to caves or other openings in the rocks, or in the proximity of metal fences or gates. Do not use a metallic survival blanket. If possible, position yourself at least 15m/16.5yd from the highest point around you (rock or tree); crouch with your knees up and without touching the rock face with your hands or any exposed part of your body.

MOUNTAIN SPORTS

Skiing

Cross-country skiing – The Jura region is ideal for **cross-country skiing**, because of the variety of relief to be found here. There are more than 2 000km/1 245mi of clearly marked, well-groomed trails.
A big event for lovers of this strenuous, yet peaceful sport is the **Transjurassienne**, a 76km/47mi race from Lamoura to Mouthe. Since 1984, the course has been included in the Nordic World Cup series, a set of races held in different countries over the season. Contact Trans'Organisation, Espace Lamartine, BP 126, 39404 Morez, ☎ 03 84 33 45 13. A visit to the web site (**www.transjurassionne.com**), with photographs and practical advice, will make you long to grab your poles and join this ski celebration.
The **Grande Traversée du Jura** (known as the GTJ to familiars) is a cross-country ski route of over 300km/186mi, with a main trail and five intermediate trails crossing through several French *départements*, along the contours of the Haut-Doubs and through evergreen forests. The national cross-country training school is at Prémanon, near Les Rousses. If you plan on skiing along this route, **Jura Randonnées**, 39370 La Pessze, ☎ 03 84 42 73 17 (www.massifdujura.com/jurarando), will help you organise your tour (accommodation, transport of luggage, guides, maps etc).

For more information about courses and ski tours, contact **Accueil Montagnard**, 25240 Chapelle-des-Bois, ☎ 03 81 69 26 19; www.accueil-montagnard.com.
To plan a ski adventure, contact the **Espace Nordique Jurassien-GTJ**, BP 132, 390304 Champagnole Cedex, ☎ 03 84 52 58 10.

Winter in Jura

M. Paygnard/MICHELIN

Alpine skiing – The Jura cannot compete with the Alps in terms of snow cover, steepness of downhill runs and equipment, yet the three ski resorts of Les Rousses, Méta-bief-Mont d'Or and Monts-Jura are expanding owing to the quality of their equipment including many snow cannon which make up for the irregularity of the snow cover. The various activities on offer are suitable for those who seek a real change of scenery and lifestyle.

Dog sledging – Races are organised at La Pesse (Jura) and Les Fourgs (Doubs). Sledge racing began in 1979 with the creation of the first dog-sledging club and this sport has grown in popularity ever since. Four different breeds of dogs are used: Siberian huskies (the fastest), Alaskan malamutes (the strongest), wolf-like Eskimo dogs from Greenland and white Arctic Samoyeds. These breeds are better suited either for touring or racing and are trained accordingly. The driver or musher either stands at the back of a sledge pulled by a team of dogs or skis beside the team harnessed to a kind of Scandinavian sledge known as a *pulka*.

The following organise sledge tours for beginners or specialists:
L'Odyssée Blanche, Le Cernois Veuillet, 25240 Chaux-Neuve, ☎ 03 81 69 20 20; www.pageszoom.com/parc-du-chien-polaire.
Visit of the husky park, sledge-driving treks (three or four dogs), possibility of sleeping in tepees.
Extrapole, 39370 La Pesse, ☎ 03 84 42 72 77. The village has several pisted or simply waymarked sledge tracks (5-15km/3-9mi).

HANG-GLIDING AND PARAGLIDING

The Jura region is ideally suited to these air-borne sports. Hang-gliding is the more complicated of the two, requiring a degree of technical understanding of aerodynamics. Beginners should only attempt under properly qualified supervision.
École de vol libre du Poupet, 9 rue du Poupet, 39110 St-Thiébaud, ☎ 03 84 73 04 56.
Club des sports des Rousses (maiden flights on a paraglider for two), 495 rue Pasteur, 39220 Les Rousses, ☎ 03 84 60 35 14.

OTHER ACTIVITIES

Rock-climbing

Burgundy offers valuable experience to would-be mountaineers at the following sites:
Saussois rocks (Yonne) and their overhangs; these overlook D 100 between Mailly-la-Ville and Châtel-Censoir;
Saffres (Côte-d'Or), 6km/3.7mi from Vitteaux, a rock-climbing school and site particularly sought after at weekends. Other sites: Bouilland, Hauteroche and Vieux-Château (for experienced climbers), Chambolle-Musigny and Talant (for learning and practising);
Clamecy area (Nièvre): Surgy and Basseville rocks.

Karting

There is a karting track (1 110m/1 214yd long, forming two loops) for the over-12s beside the Nevers-Magny-Cours Grand-Prix race track.
Other location: **Laffite Système Karting**, Complexe Automobile de Pouilly-en-Auxois, 21320 Meilly-sur-Rouvres, ☎ 03 80 90 60 77 (Wed-Sun 10am-8pm).

Four-wheel motorbikes with low-pressure tyres are fun guided forest rides along marked trails.

Suggested reading

Besançon, the capital of Franche-Comté, is the scene of Julien Sorel's theological and sentimental education in the celebrated novel by **Stendhal**, *Le Rouge et le Noir* (1830; several English translations available under the title *The Red and the Black*). It is thought that the author had Dole in mind when he described the protagonist's home town. This portrait of the foibles of French society under the Second Restoration (1815-30) is based on a contemporary newspaper account of a crime of passion. In the book, Sorel plays the ultimate opportunist, using seduction as a means to advance his career, but is undone by tender love and his final realisation of the vanity of worldly success.

Alphonse de Lamartine (1790-1869), a native of Mâcon, is celebrated on the signposted *Lamartine Heritage Trail (see p 292)*. Some of his vast lyrical output has been translated, but English readers will have to track it down in libraries or specialised shops. Charles M Lombard's *Lamartine* (1973) contains summary and commentary on his writings; William Fortescue wrote a well-researched account of the author's career in politics, *Alphonse de Lamartine: A Political Biography* (1983).

Colette is one of the best-loved writers of fiction from the region; her works are full of verve and wit, express her love of nature and her poetic childhood memories *(see p 353)*. For an introduction to her limpid style, try the *Claudine* series for starters; many of her books are available in Penguin paperbacks. Two excellent biographies are *Close to Colette*, written by her husband Maurice Goudeket, in 1957 (Farrar, Straus & Giroux), and *Colette: A Taste for Life*, by Yvonne Mitchel (Harcourt, Brace, Jovanovich, 1977).

Burgundy is of course associated with fine food and wine, and to help plan or prolong Epicurean delights, there are books both classic and new devoted to the **wines and cuisine** of the region:

Burgundy Stars: a Year in the Life of a Great French Restaurant by **W Echikson** (Little, Brown, 1996). This 12-month account of Bernard Loiseau's famous restaurant in Saulieu is fascinating in its description of the frenetic pace and flurry in the kitchen, the elegance of one of the world's finest dining rooms.

The Physiology of Taste, or Meditations on Transcendent Gastronomy by **Jean-Anthelme Brillat-Savarin**, translated by MFK Fisher, is now available in the Penguin Classics collection. Penned in the early 19C, the musings of this French judge who barely escaped death under the Reign of Terror go beyond the culinary to attain the far reaches of philosophy. This is a classic volume for lovers of fine food, good company and sensory pleasure.

MFK Fisher has also produced excellent books on the culinary arts, many of them collected in *The Art of Eating*, (Macmillan, reprinted 1990), which includes notes from her studies in Dijon. Her award-winning prose has set a standard for food writers, as she discusses cooking with war rations, the social status of vegetables, and travelling to some wonderful places. If you love food, you will love her work, which is resonant with emotion, often surprising and joyful.

Côte d'Or: A Celebration of the Great Wines of Burgundy, by **Clive Coates** (University of California Press, 1997) has been praised as the most up to date, comprehensive book on Burgundy wine. This work seems to cover even the smallest vineyards, and takes a deeper look at 60 of the best domaines, all with wit and finely tuned British understatement.

Another good, all-encompassing book on the subject is *The Great Domaines of Burgundy: A Guide to the Finest Wine Producers of the Côte d'Or*, by **Remington Norman** (Henry Holt & Co., Inc., second edition 1996). Excellent maps and many pictures accompany the text, which concentrates on about 100 growers. Serious Burgundy lovers will lap up the historical accounts and descriptions of practices in the vineyards, as well as tasting notes on many vintages.

To learn more about the **history** of the region, read the biography of *Margaret of York: Duchess of Burgundy 1446-1503*, by **Christine Weightman** (St Martins Press, 1989). By both birth and marriage, Margaret played a pivotal role in the alliance between the dukes of Burgundy and the English crown. A patron of the arts, she was also remarkably independent and influential for a woman of her time. The book includes maps, genealogies and other illustrations.

Finally, have a look at a recent volume (1998) from the popular Thames & Hudson series: *The Most Beautiful Villages of Burgundy*, photographs by **Hugh Palmer**, text by **James Bentley**.

Calendar of events

The list below is a selection of the many events which take place in this region. Visitors are advised to contact local tourist offices for fuller details of musical events, son et lumière *shows, arts and crafts fairs etc, especially during July and August.*

Festivals

Whitsun weekend

Belfort .... International university student music festival,
☎ 03 84 54 24 43.

May to July

St-Gengoux-de-Scissé .... Tour de Bassy concerts, ☎ 03 85 33 28 77.

May to September

Pontigny .... Saison musicale des amis de Pontigny (music festival),
☎ 03 86 47 54 99.

May

Auxerre .... Jazz in Auxerre, ☎ 03 86 94 08 12.

June

Divonne-les-Bains .... Chamber music festival.

St-Claude .... Haut-Jura Music Festival, ☎ 03 84 45 48 04.

Vauluisant .... Festival de Vauluisant, ☎ 03 86 86 78 40.

June-July

Belfort .... Nuits d'été au Château (theatre, concerts).
☎ 03 84 22 66 76.

Dijon .... L'Estivade, ☎ 03 80 74 51 95.

June-September

Tournus .... Tournus Passion (various events), ☎ 03 85 27 00 20.

Late June-early July

Le Creusot .... National Blues Festival, ☎ 03 85 55 68 99.

Sens .... Synodales (contemporary dance festival),
☎ 03 86 95 52 22.

Early July

Beaune, Dijon, ... International Bell-ringing Festival, ☎ 03 880 56 68 01,
Nuits-St-Georges,   03 80 51 51 83 or 03 80 71 59 86.
Selongey, Seurre

July

Beaune .... International Baroque music festival. ☎ 03 80 26 21 30.
Belfort .... Les Eurockéennes rock festival. ☎ 03 84 22 46 58.
Moirans-en-Montagne .... Idéklic (International children's festival),
☎ 03 84 42 00 28.
Tonnere and around .... Music festival, ☎ 03 86 54 45 26.

3rd week in July

Chalon-sur-Saône .... National Street Artists Festival, ☎ 03 85 48 05 22.

Autun .... Musique en Morvan festival, ☎ 03 85 82 53 81.

Semur-en-Auxois .... Musicales en Auxois Festival, ☎ 03 80 96 20 24.
and around

Château de Joux .... Festival des Nuits at the château, ☎ 03 81 39 29 36
(mid-July to mid-August).
Belfort .... Wednesdays at the château, ☎ 03 84 55 90 90.
Nantua .... Haut-Bugey international music festival,
☎ 04 74 75 24 94.

Sens .... International Organ Festival in the cathedral,
☎ 03 86 95 67 84.

Noyers-sur-Serein .... Festival des Grands Crus de Bourgogne,
Noyers-sur-Serein Music Festival,
☎ 04 86 82 83 72.

Cluny .... Jazz in Cluny, ☎ 03 85 59 15 60.

Beaune, Dijon .... Vineyard and folk festival. International popular music
and dance festival, ☎ 03 80 30 37 95.

Besançon .... International music festival and young conductors competition, ☎ 03 81 25 05 80.

Ambronay .... Festival de l'Abbaye, ☎ 04 74 38 74 00.

Beaune .... Cinema Festival, ☎ 03 80 24 50 24.

Traditional and religious feasts, fairs and pageants

Champlitte .... Feast of St Vincent, patron of wine-growers, dating back
to 1719, ☎ 03 84 67 82 00.

Arlay .... Feast of St Vincent.
Chablis, Dijon, ... Saint-Vincent Tournante, procession celebrating the
Meursault, Tonnerre patron of wine-growers, ☎ 03 86 42 80 80;
www.chablis.net, ☎ 03 80 61 07 12 (Dijon),
☎ 03 86 53 31 68 (Tonnerre).

Audincourt .... Carnival, ☎ 03 81 30 42 08.

Chalon-sur-Saône .... Carnival: musical parade and Grand Jour des Goniots; parade and costume ball for children; fun fair. Information, ☎ 03 85 48 37 97.

March

Auxonne .... Carnival, ☎ 03 80 37 34 46.
Vesoul .... Carnival, ☎ 03 84 97 10 85.
Maîche .... Carnival, ☎ 03 81 64 06 40.
Nuits-St-Georges .... Wine auction sale, ☎ 03 80 62 67 04.

May

Arlay .... Medieval feast at the château.

Dole................................. Pilgrimage to Notre-Dame-de-Mont-Roland (2nd Sunday in May and 2 August), ☎ 03 84 79 88 00.

Besançon .... Fair (week of the Ascension holiday).

Mâcon .... International Wine Fair, ☎ 03 85 38 13 48.

3rd Sunday after Whitsun

Paray-le-Monial .... Sacré-Cœur pilgrimage, ☎ 03 85 81 62 22.

June

Semur-en-Auxois .... Fête de la Bague: horse race whose origins date back to 1639, ☎ 03 80 97 05 96.
.... Medieval pageant, ☎ 03 80 97 05 96.
Poligny .... Fête du Comté (cheese festival every other year, next one in 2003).
Le Russey .... Fête des Gentianes, ☎ 03 81 43 76 91.
Levier .... Fête des Sapins, ☎ 03 81 89 53 22.
Gex................................. Fête de l'Oiseau (bird festival): parade, ☎ 04 50 41 53 85.
St-Jean-de-Losne.............. Grand Pardon des mariniers (Blessing of river boats), ☎ 03 80 29 05 48.

14 July

Clamecy .... Jousting on the Yonne (Pont de Bethléem), ☎ 03 86 27 02 51.

Mid-July

Fondremand...................... Arts and crafts day.

Pouilly-sur-Loire ....Vintage fair (auction sale of great vintage wines), ☎/Fax 03 86 39 03 75.

22 July

Vézelay .... Fête de la Sainte-Madeleine pilgrimage, ☎ 04 86 33 39 50.

Late July

Pontailler-sur-Saône .... Fête de l'Oignon, ☎/Fax 03 80 47 84 42.

22 July and 15 August

Boutissaint .... Festival of nature and wild animals, ☎ 03 86 74 07 08; www.boutissaint.com.

August

Glux-en-Glenne.................. Fête des myrtilles (Bilberry Festival), ☎ 03 86 36 39 80.

Coulanges-sur-Yonne .... Jousting tournaments, ☎ 03 86 81 70 32.

Semur-en-Auxois .... Fireworks with sound effects over the ramparts, ☎ 03 80 97 01 11.

St-Honoré-les-Bains........... Fête des Fleurs (flower festival), ☎ 03 86 30 74 87.

Different village every year Fête du Haut-Jura (local crafts and products), ☎ 03 84 34 12 30.

Anost .... Fête de la Vielle (Hurdy-gurdy Festival), ☎ 03 80 64 38 65.

Saulieu .... Fête du Charollais, ☎ 03 80 64 06 09.

Cluny................................ Harness and stallion show.

Arbois............................... Fête du Biou (wine festival), ☎ 03 84 37 47 37.

Ronchamp .... Pilgrimage to Notre-Dame-du-Haut, ☎ 03 84 20 65 13.

Alise-Ste-Reine .... Pilgrimage and Ste-Reine mystery play, ☎ 03 80 96 86 55.

Belfort............................. Wine and fine food fair, ☎ 03 84 28 30 40.

Maîche .... La vache de Semaine (horse and cow competitions).

Arc-et-Senans................... Fête des montgolfières (hot-air balloon event), ☎ 03 81 57 41 27.

Pierre-de-Bresse................ Burgundy pottery fair.

Pupillin............................ Fête du Biou (wine festival), ☎ 03 84 37 49 16.

Maîche .... Horse Festival, ☎ 03 81 64 11 88.

Vadans............................ Fête du Biou (wine festival), ☎ 03 84 66 22 01.

St-Léger-sous-Beuvray .... Chestnut fair, ☎ 03 85 82 53 00.

Chablis, Joigny, ... Yonne Wine Festival, ☎ 03 86 42 80 80 (Chablis),
St-Bris-le-Vineux .... ☎ 03 86 62 11 05 (Joigny), ☎ 03 86 53 66 76 (St-Bris).

Dijon .... International gastronomic fair, ☎ 03 80 77 39 00.

Clos Vougeot, ... The Trois Glorieuses: Brotherhood of the Chevaliers du
Beaune and Meursault Tastevin; auction of wines from the Hospices de Beaune,
☎ 03 80 61 07 12; the Meursault Paulée. ☎ 03 80 21
22 62..

Vesoul .... St Catherine's Day fair, ☎ 03 84 97 10 85.

Montbéliard .... Christmas lights, ☎ 03 81 94 45 60.

Marcigny .... Turkey and goose fair, ☎ 03 85 25 03 51.

Bourg-en-Bresse................ Plucked and drawn poultry show, ☎ 04 74 22 29 90.

Son et lumière shows

Auxerre.............................. *Son et lumière* at the cathedral, ☎ 03 86 52 23 29.

St-Fargeau .... *Son et lumière* (historical show), ☎ 03 86 74 05 67

La Clayette........................ *Son et lumière* at the château, ☎ 03 85 28 00 16.

Noyers-sur-Serein .... *Son et lumière* (historical show spanning 1 000 years),
☎ 03 86 82 81 12.

Autun .... *Son et lumière* on a historical theme: "Il était une fois
Augustodunum", ☎ 03 85 86 80 13 (town hall).

Sporting events

Lamoura-Mouthe................ Transjurassienne cross-country ski race, ☎ 03 84 33 45 13.

Les Fourgs .... Le Marabouri, cross-country ski event, ☎ 03 81 69 44 91.

Goumois .... International canoe-kayak slalom.

Nevers-Magny-Cours.......... Grand Prix de France de Formule 1, ☎ 03 86 21 80 00.

Nantua .... Mountain-bike race, ☎ 04 50 52 81 16.

Nevers-Magny-Cours.......... Bol d'Or motorcycle race, information/bookings
☎ 01 41 40 32 32 or 03 86 21 80 00.

Useful French words and phrases

SIGHTS

abbaye	abbey
beffroi	belfry
chapelle	chapel
château	castle
cimetière	cemetery
cloître	cloisters
cour	courtyard
couvent	convent
écluse	lock (canal)
église	church
fontaine	fountain
halle	covered market
jardin	garden
mairie	town hall
maison	house
marché	market
monastère	monastery
moulin	windmill
musée	museum
parc	park
place	square
pont	bridge
port	port/harbour
porte	gateway
quai	quay
remparts	ramparts
rue	street
statue	statue
tour	tower

NATURAL SITES

abîme	chasm
aven	swallow-hole
barrage	dam
belvédère	viewpoint
cascade	waterfall
col	pass
corniche	ledge
côte	coast, hillside
forêt	forest
grotte	cave
lac	lake
plage	beach
rivière	river
ruisseau	stream
signal	beacon
source	spring
vallée	valley

ON THE ROAD

car park	parking
driving licence	permis de conduire
east	Est
garage (for repairs)	garage
left	gauche
motorway/highway	autoroute
north	Nord
parking meter	horodateur
petrol/gas	essence
petrol/gas station	station essence
right	droite
south	Sud
toll	péage
traffic lights	feu tricolore
tyre	pneu
west	Ouest
wheel clamp	sabot
zebra crossing	passage clouté

TIME

today	aujourd'hui
tomorrow	demain
yesterday	hier
winter	hiver
spring	printemps
summer	été
autumn/fall	automne
week	semaine
Monday	lundi
Tuesday	mardi
Wednesday	mercredi
Thursday	jeudi
Friday	vendredi
Saturday	samedi
Sunday	dimanche

NUMBERS

0	zéro	**10**	dix	**20**	vingt
1	un	**11**	onze	**30**	trente
2	deux	**12**	douze	**40**	quarante
3	trois	**13**	treize	**50**	cinquante
4	quatre	**14**	quatorze	**60**	soixante
5	cinq	**15**	quinze	**70**	soixante-dix
6	six	**16**	seize	**80**	quatre-vingt
7	sept	**17**	dix-sept	**90**	quatre-vingt-dix
8	huit	**18**	dix-huit	**100**	cent
9	neuf	**19**	dix-neuf	**1000**	mille

SHOPPING

bank	banque	fishmonger's	poissonnerie
baker's	boulangerie	grocer's	épicerie
big	grand	newsagent,	
butcher's	boucherie	bookshop	librairie
chemist's	pharmacie	open	ouvert
closed	fermé	post office	poste
cough mixture	sirop pour la toux	push	pousser
cough sweets	cachets pour la gorge	pull	tirer
entrance	entrée	shop	magasin
exit	sortie	small	petit
		stamps	timbres

FOOD AND DRINK

beef	bœuf	lunch	déjeuner
beer	bière	lettuce salad	salade
butter	beurre	meat	viande
bread	pain	mineral water	eau minérale
breakfast	petit-déjeuner	mixed salad	salade composée
cheese	fromage	orange juice	jus d'orange
chicken	poulet	plate	assiette
dessert	dessert	pork	porc
dinner	dîner	restaurant	restaurant
fish	poisson	red wine	vin rouge
fork	fourchette	salt	sel
fruit	fruits	spoon	cuillère
glass	verre	sugar	sucre
ice cream	glace	vegetables	légumes
ice cubes	glaçons	water	de l'eau
ham	jambon	white wine	vin blanc
knife	couteau	yoghurt	yaourt
lamb	agneau		

PERSONAL DOCUMENTS AND TRAVEL

airport	aéroport	shuttle	navette
credit card	carte de crédit	suitcase	valise
customs	douane	train/plane ticket	billet de train/ d'avion
passport	passeport	wallet	portefeuille
platform	voie		
railway station	gare		

CLOTHING

coat	manteau	socks	chaussettes
jumper	pull	stockings	bas
raincoat	imperméable	suit	costume
shirt	chemise	tights	collants
shoes	chaussures	trousers	pantalon

USEFUL PHRASES

goodbye	au revoir	yes/no	oui/non
hello/good morning	bonjour	I am sorry	pardon
how	comment	why	pourquoi
excuse me	excusez-moi	when	quand
thank you	merci	please	s'il vous plaît

Do you speak English?	Parlez-vous anglais?
I don't understand	Je ne comprends pas
Talk slowly	Parlez lentement
Where's...?	Où est...?
When does the ... leave?	A quelle heure part...?
When does the ... arrive?	A quelle heure arrive...?
When does the museum open?	A quelle heure ouvre le musée?
When is the show?	A quelle heure est la représentation?
When is breakfast served?	A quelle heure sert-on le petit-déjeuner?
What does it cost?	Combien cela coûte?
Where can I buy a newspaper in English?	Où puis-je acheter un journal en anglais?
Where is the nearest petrol/gas station?	Où se trouve la station essence la plus proche?
Where can I change traveller's cheques?	Où puis-je échanger des traveller's cheques?
Where are the toilets?	Où sont les toilettes?
Do you accept credit cards?	Acceptez-vous les cartes de crédit?

In the Mille Étangs region

Introduction

The lay of the land

POLITICAL DIVISIONS

France, exclusive of its overseas territories, is divided into administrative units: 96 *départements* and 22 *régions* , including **Bourgogne** and **Franche-Comté**. The *région* of Burgundy includes the *départements* of **Côte-d'Or**, **Nièvre**, **Saône-et-Loire** and **Yonne**; Franche-Comté encompasses **Doubs**, **Jura** and **Haute-Saône**. Jura is also the name of the 250km/155mi-long mountain range running from the Rhine to the Rhone. Perhaps because the mountains cover most of the region and unify the landscape, Jura is generally used to refer to the entire region of Franche-Comté, except for expressly administrative or historical purposes.

The region of Burgundy has several distinct geographical areas which are commonly referred to as Basse Bourgogne (the Auxerre and Chablis areas), the Arrière-Côte and Côte (the limestone plateaux terminating in escarpments to the east) and the ancient granite massifs and uplands known as the Morvan, the Charollais and the Mâconnais to the south. The Jura mountains attain a maximum width of 61km/38mi; the highest summit is the Crêt de la Neige (1 717m/5 633ft). The relief, while modest in altitude, is striking, characterised by long parallel ridges and valleys running along a northeast-southwest axis and converging at either end. This pattern of folds steps down to an undulating plateau to the west, which rises again around Montbéliard to meet the Vosges.

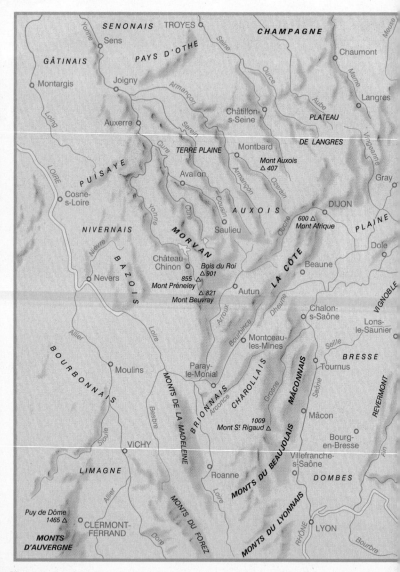

FORMATION OF THE LAND

Primary Era – This is believed to have begun about 600 million years ago. Modern France was entirely under water, until the tremendous folding movement of the earth's crust known as the **Hercynian fold** took place, which resulted in the emergence of a number of high mountain ranges. The seas that covered the Paris and Rhône basins were linked by a strait which corresponds to the "threshold of Burgundy". Erosion by the elements gradually wore the highest parts of the Morvan down to their rocky base, while the warm, humid climate gave rise to luxuriant vegetation, eventually buried under thick layers of alluvial deposits and pressurised into coal. These coal seams between the Morvan and Beaujolais massifs were to be of great benefit to modern towns such as Autun and Blanzy.

Secondary Era – This began about 200 million years ago. After the Hercynian base had subsided, the seas flooded the Paris basin and the Jura region, covering even the highest land as they advanced south. They deposited strata of sedimentary rocks – marl (calcium carbonate, or chalk, mixed with impermeable clay) and limestone (permeable rock, essentially calcium carbonate, formed from fossilised shells and fish skeletons) – on the granite seabed as they went. The formation of such sedimentary rock strata was so prolific in Jura in particular (some rock beds reach a thickness of about 1 300m/4 300ft), that geologists have named the middle period of the Secondary Era, which lasted about 45 million years, the **Jurassic** period.

Tertiary Era – This began about 60 million years ago. The parallel rock strata of the Jura region, sloping gently down to the Swiss plain, were still covered with water (the lakes of Biel, Neuchâtel and Geneva still remain). Then came the great Alpine folding movement, and the land was once again forced upwards and the seas pushed back.

The pressure during this Alpine-building period folded the Jura rock strata along a northeast-southwest axis into long parallel ridges and valleys, curving in a giant crescent between the Vosges and the Massif Central and sloping down towards the River Saône, where all the rivers drained into the great lake of Bresse (which later vanished). Nearer the Alps, the thick layers of sedimentary rock folded under pressure, giving rise to the Jura mountains. The layers of the western edge, not so thick, split along the faults formed by the movements of the earth's crust into a series of stepped plateaux. Not far from the slopes overlooking the Saône Valley, salt deposits were formed (later to become a local resource).

Quaternary Era – This began about 2 million years ago. Erosion continued to shape the region into its present appearance: ancient massifs (Morvan, Beaujolais); limestone plateaux (La Côte, l'Arrière Côte); sedimentary basins (Bazois, Terre-Plaine, Auxois); valleys (surrounding the Jura); and low-lying plains of subsidence (Saône Valley). The Quaternary Era was marked by two significant events: the appearance of man, and the coming of the Ice Age with its enormous glaciers, which invaded the valleys from the Alps. As the glaciers receded, they left in their wake a huge amount of debris, including glacial moraine, which blocked the drainage of water in many places, giving rise to the Jurassic lakes.

THE REGIONS OF BURGUNDY

From the Auxois to the Beaujolais regions, from the River Saône to the River Loire, the many and varied regions which make up Burgundy have preserved their own particular appearance, economy and way of life.

The historical links which united them during the 15C have proved strong enough, however, for several common characteristics still to be apparent to us today. Administrative divisions, modern economic demands and the attraction of Paris notwithstanding, the ties holding together the constituents of this province, of which Dijon is capital in more than name, remain unbroken.

The Alluvial Plains – The **Sénonais**, **Gâtinais** and **Puisaye** plains are situated on the northern borders of Burgundy. These are well-watered, fertile lands, rich in alluvial deposits, where the lakes and forests provide a rich catch for hunters and anglers alike. The Sénonais is furthest to the north; agriculture there is varied and productive. The Gâtinais extends from Gien (in the Loire Valley) to just north of Montargis; its resources are mostly limited to dairy farming. The Puisaye, similar in landscape, also produces fodder crops. The population is widely dispersed among the abundant woodlands; isolated houses are often half-hidden among the trees.

The Nivernais – This region of plateaux and hills, essentially a crossroads, stretches away to the west of the Morvan Massif and slopes gently down to the Loire Valley.

To the west of Château-Chinon are the verdant slopes of **Bazois**: cereal and fodder crops on the hillsides, rich pasture for stock-breeding below.

To the north, the hilly region of **Clamecy** and **Donzy** (peaks up to 450m/1 476ft high) is watered by a dense network of rivers, and used for stock-breeding and crop farming. From Nevers to Bonny the River Loire marks the boundary between the Nivernais and the Berry region. Stock-breeding pastureland alternates with wooded spurs.

Pouilly lies at the heart of a well-reputed vineyard which stretches over the hillsides overlooking the Loire Valley.

The Morvan – In the aftermath of the great Alpine thrust, the edges of the great Morvan granite massif were broken up; erosion wore away at the softer limestone strata bordering the massif, scouring out a hollow surrounding it on three sides. This depression is surrounded in turn by limestone plateaux which tower at its outer edges. The Morvan is distinguished above all by its abundant forest cover and densely woven network of rivers. Fields and meadows outlined by hedges form colourful patterns.

Long isolated in every sense of the word, like the far-flung hamlets and farmhouses found there, the Morvan has recently opened up to the outside world. It is especially popular with tourists seeking unspoiled natural landscapes.

The Auxois – To the east of the Morvan lies the Auxois region, a rich and fertile land of hard blue limestone, crisscrossed by many rivers, given over to pasture for stock-breeding.

Rocky outcrops are occupied by fortified towns, such as Semur, Flavigny-sur-Ozerain and Mont-St-Jean, or ancient *oppidums* from Roman times, such as Alésia on Mont Auxois, isolated outposts overlooking the roads and waterways.

The Charollais and the Brionnais – These regions of sweeping hillsides and plateaux, with superb rich pasturage, are the home of Charollais cattle.

The landscape of the Morvan

H. Champollion/MICHELIN

The Autun basin – During the Primary Era, this depression was a vast lake, which was gradually filled in with the coal-bearing deposits and bituminous schists later to fuel the industrial development of this region. There are still a few spoil heaps around Autun, bearing witness to past industry.

The Dijonnais – The region around Dijon reunites all the characteristics of Burgundy's various regions in a striking synthesis. It is an area of limestone plateaux, isolated outcrops, rich pastureland, wide alluvial plains and steep hillsides covered with vineyards.

The Côte – This is the edge of the last slope of the mountains (La Côte d'Or) overlooking the Saône plain. This escarpment was formed by the cracks which appeared as the Saône's alluvial plain subsided. Whereas the Arrière-Côte plateau is given over to crops, woods and pastureland, the eastern slope is covered with vines. The villages are located at the heart of the vineyards, at the mouths of the coombs which lead back into the hinterland. They soak up the abundant supply of spring water commonly found at the foot of such slopes.

The Mâconnais – This is where the mountain range formed by the Côte d'Or extends southwards. The steep faces of the escarpment are turned towards the interior, whereas along the Côte d'Or they overlook the valley of the Saône. This is a region of vine-covered hillsides and pastureland; cereal crops, beets, vegetables and poultry are also raised.

The Saône Valley – Major communications routes run through this valley which stretches along the foot of limestone cliffs. Civil engineering works have opened the river to navigation year-round. The alluvial river plains of the Saône, which are frequently flooded during winter, are covered with rich pastures and arable land. In addition to traditional wheat, beet and potato crops, there are now market gardens and fields of maize, tobacco and oilseed.

The Bresse – The Bresse plain, composed of clay and marl soil, stretches from the Saône to the foothills of the Jura, the Revermont. Numerous streams cut across the rolling countryside, which is dotted with copses. In France, the name is indissociable from the *Poulet de Bresse*, plump and delicious chickens raised here.

The Burgundy plateaux – From the northern edge of the Morvan to the Langres plateau and from Auxerre to Dijon stretches a region of limestone plateaux forming the real heartland of Burgundy. This region is known as the threshold: the point of contact between the Seine and Saône basins, and between the Vosges and the Morvan. The kingdom of Burgundy came into being at this junction of the very different regions it was to bring under its crown.

The plateaux rise to a relatively low altitude (400-500m/1 312-1 640ft), sloping gently to the north-west but dropping abruptly in the south-east. Their dry appearance contrasts with the much greener, richer one of the valleys of the rivers which intersect them; the Yonne, Serein and Armançon. The plateaux are, from west to east, the Auxerrois, the Tonnerrois and the Châtillonnais.

The Auxerrois is a rocky plateau, split across by numerous valleys, in which the limestone can often be seen dazzling white. The sunny slopes have lent themselves to the cultivation of vines, in the regions of Chablis, Auxerre and Irancy, and cherry trees.

The Tonnerrois plateau has similar characteristics to that of Langres, but it is at a lower altitude and has a climate not unlike that of the Paris basin.

The Châtillonnais is a series of monotonous plateaux, for the most part bare with the occasional rocky outcrop or dry river valley. Soil here is permeable. Water seeps down into the limestone surface, travels through a network of underground rivers, and resurfaces in the form of resurgent springs.

These plateaux used to be covered almost entirely by forests. Monks from the abbeys of Molesmes, St-Seine, Fontenay and Clairvaux cleared much of the land. In the 18C, numerous forges, foundries and nail works were active, thanks to the discovery of iron ore deposits.

Both coniferous (larch, black pine, Norwegian pine, silver pine and spruce) and deciduous (oak, beech, elm and ash) forests are being replanted; the timber industry plays an important role in the local economy.

THE REGIONS OF JURA

From the majestic outline of the mountains to the natural beauty of the forests, lakes and rivers and the more muted colours of the hillsides, the Jura region encompasses a wide variety of landscapes.

The Jura range – From the Swiss plain the Jura range appears as a high wall, a formidable unbroken fortified barrier across the horizon. From the crest, however, valleys and meadows give the countryside a less harsh appearance. Lake Geneva and the Alps of Berne and Savoy can be seen in the distance. Poets such as Goethe, Ruskin and Lamartine have sung of the splendour of this sight. Each valley constitutes a little world of its own, in which the inhabitants congregate near springs, or on the banks of rivers or lakes. The meadows, where glaciers deposited a layer of clay, contrast with the bare limestone, which looks almost like a desert in places. Among the meadows, fields of barley, rye, oats and potatoes stand out. But at this altitude, winter lasts a long time, so cereals ripen fairly late and fruit trees are few and far between.

The Jura plateaux – The best view of the Jura plateaux is from the summit called the Pic de l'Aigle. These tracts of flat land look like stair-steps descending (900-400m/2 953-1 312ft) from Pontarlier to Besançon before reaching the Bresse region and Burgundy. To the north, they extend as far as the Belfort Gap, or Trouée de Belfort, between the Jura and Vosges mountain ranges. A notable feature of these rocky plateaux is the *reculée* formation *(see diagram)*, a blind valley ending at the foot of a cliff. The region is also delightful for its gorges, river valleys, waterfalls, lakes, caves and forests.

The Vignoble – The road from Besançon to Bourg-en-Bresse, leading between the River Doubs and River Ain, runs along the continuous slope on the western rim of the Jura plateaux, part of the Revermont. The vines cultivated here for centuries have earned the region its local name, the Vignoble (vineyard).

CAVES

Caves are a common feature of the Jura plateaux, often found at the foot of the steep rocky cliffs enclosing a *reculée*. Visitors can explore an underground world of caverns, crystal-clear subterranean rivers, intricate rock formations and the vestiges of prehistoric man.

Caves in the Jura which accommodate visitors include the Grotte de Baume, with its vaulted chambers, the Grotte de la Glacière, frozen year-round, the Grottes des Moidons (concretions), the Grottes d'Osselle (multiple columns), the Grotte des Planches (good examples of features produced by limestone erosion), and the Gouffre de Poudrey. These caves can well inform the visitor about the dangers of water pollution and the difficulty of protecting these fragile environments.

Underground rivers and limestone erosion – Jurassic rivers do not only flow above ground. As in any limestone region, rainwater infiltrates the rock and dissolves the carbonate of lime, creating networks of cracks and fissures within and between the rock strata. The action of carbonic acid in rainwater enlarges existing fissures to form subterranean galleries, wells and chimneys. The water collects along these courses to emerge at ground level as a spring. In some cases, subterranean rivers are formed by an existing river dropping into a chasm and disappearing (known locally as a *perte*) to flow underground then reappear as a **resurgent spring** further on.

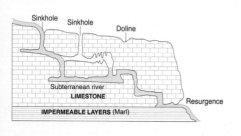

Chasms are formed either by the continued hollowing out of a depression *(doline)* at ground level until it collapses into the cave below, or by the caving in of the roof of a cave itself, as it is eroded upwards by the dissolution of limestone in the cave walls.

Caves – As it circulates underground, water deposits the lime it carries, building up concretions of fantastic shapes, which seem to defy the laws of gravity. Seeping waters deposit calcite (carbonate of lime) to form pendants, pyramids, draperies, and of course, stalactites, stalagmites and eccentrics.

Stalactites are formed on the roof by water dripping down. The concretion builds up slowly as drops deposit calcite on the surface before falling.

Stalagmites are a sort of mirror image, rising up from the floor below from dripping water, and eventually meeting the stalactite above to form a pillar.

Such concretions form very slowly; the rate of growth in temperate climates is about 1cm/0.5in every 100 years.

Eccentrics are very delicate protruberances, formed by crystallisation, which seldom exceed 20cm/8in in length. They emerge at odd angles, as slender spikes or in the shape of small translucent fans.

FOREST

In Burgundy and Jura, the forest covers an area of 1 500 000ha/3 615 000 acres, 30% and 40% of each region, respectively; well above the average for France (25%).

Vegetation – Altitude affects the distribution of the different types of trees in the forest. Deciduous trees generally give way to conifers at about 800m/2 624ft, although this can vary according to the amount of sunlight to which the slope is exposed. Beeches predominate between 500-800m/1 640-2 624ft. Higher up are the magnificent pine forests of the Joux, and above 1 000m/3 281ft, forests of spruce alternating with wooded upland pastures.

Trees – Deciduous trees lose their leaves every autumn, and grow new ones in the spring. The main trees in this group are beech and oak, and to a lesser extent ash, maple, cherry, elm and birch.

Conifers have thin, needle-like leaves which do not all die and fall from the tree at the same time, but a few at a time throughout the year. The sap of such trees is resinous, and they bear cones as fruit. Pines, firs, cypresses and spruce make up this group, and also larch, one of the few coniferous trees to lose its leaves in winter.

Spruce – This is exclusively a mountain tree, which grows best on north-facing slopes. It has a pointed top shaped like a spindle and a bushy appearance, with downward curving branches. The chocolate-brown bark becomes deeply cracked with age. The dark green needles are rounded and sharp and grow all the way round the branches and twigs. The cones hang below the branches, and when they are ripe their scales separate to release the seeds.
Timber from spruces is used mainly for roof beams and musical instruments.

Spruce   Fir   Beech

M. Janvier/MICHELIN

Fir – This has a broad top, flattened into a stork's nest in older trees. The bark remains a darkish grey colour, with blisters of resin here and there. The cones stand upright on the branches and scatter their seeds when ripe by disintegrating on the branch. The needles are soft and grow in rows along the branches, like the teeth of a comb. They are a paler green colour on their undersides, which have a double white line marking (hence the name silver fir). They are found on the deeply folded ridges of the mountain range.

Beech – This tall tree is easily recognised by its trunk, cylindrical with grey and white bark, and thin, oval leaves. A beech tree can grow at an altitude of up to 1 700m/5 577ft and live for 150 years. It grows best on well-watered slopes. In the autumn it bears oily beechnuts. The beech tree occupies a special place in the forest of Jura; its timber is used primarily for industry and handcrafts.

Other types of tree – The **larch** can be found on the sunnier slopes. It has small cones, and its delicate pale green foliage does not cast so much shade that grass is unable to grow. The **Norway pine**, with its tall, slender trunk, has bunches of 2-5 needles growing together, held by a scaly sheath, and cones with hard scales. The elegant **birch**, with its slender trunk, trembling leaves and white bark which comes off in shavings, thrives in moist soil. It provides excellent firewood. The **oak** is a beautiful tree which can grow up to 30m/98ft tall. Oak wood is valued highly by carpenters, and oak bark by tanners. Finally, the **durmast oak**, or white or truffle oak, can be found growing in dry soil above the vineyards; its typically thick trunk is protected by a deeply ridged bark which sheds itself in square-shaped chunks.

The Burgundy forest – There are forests scattered all over the province of Burgundy, but they are most extensive on the Châtillonnais, Tonnerrois and Sénonais plateaux to the north, in the Morvan and on the Nivernais plateau in central Burgundy, and around Charolles, Cluny and Mâcon to the south. The main timber areas are the forest of Othe, Châtillon, Bertranges, Planoise and St-Prix.
In the Morvan the forest is impressive for the sheer area it covers – about 137 000ha/338 540 acres – more than 50% of some communes. The most common trees are beech, oak, hornbeam and birch.
The forests of the Morvan were harvested by monks from the 10C onwards. In the 17C and 18C, the wood was floated down to Paris to be used as firewood, or converted into charcoal where it was felled. Nowadays, the Morvan has a good reputation for the quality of the wood from its conifers. Tall stands of spruce and pine are to be found particularly round Haut-Folin, and, for the last 20 or so years, the Douglas pine has been increasingly used in replanting schemes.

The alluvial land along the banks of the Saône is covered with oak forests (Auxonne, Seurre and Chalon regions) which yield high quality timber, as does the magnificent oak forest of the Nivernais plateau. Large areas of the Côte have been replanted with both broad-leaved species and pines.

Several large industries are dependant on forestry: wood distilling and charcoal making (factories in Leuglay and Prémery) for the production of charcoal, acetic acid, methylene and their by-products; sawmills; manufacturers of veneer and chipboard (at Auxerre, St-Usage, Prisse-lès-Mâcon) and so on. In addition, Burgundy produces the largest number of young trees of any region in France in the tree nurseries near St-Florentin in the Yonne and Leuglay in the Côte-d'Or, supplying French and European markets.

The Jura forest – As farming activities diminish, and in the advent of reforestation policies, the forest has gained ground, spreading out over 42% of the mountainous area.

State-owned and larger private forests are managed so that the quantity of wood cut down every year matches new growth. Healthy trees are marked by a round sign (and the letters "AF" for *administration forestière*), whereas dried out, damaged or uprooted trees are marked for removal.

In forests owned by the local authorities *(forêts communales)*, the trees destined for firewood are divided into lots which residents have the right to cut down; these lots are allocated by head count or number of fireplaces per home (very occasionally they are given out according to the size of the roof of the house, which is quite considerable in some of the villages of Jura). In some instances, the wood is sold in its entirety by the national forestry office and the profit given to the commune. In times gone by, the sale of the wood made enough money to cover the residents' taxes in some localities. Because the arrival of new residents meant a smaller share of wood for each household, newcomers were not always welcomed kindly.

Forest management is carried out under strictly observed regulations. The use of the State symbol in marking out the forests is protected by law against counterfeiting.

Historical table and notes

Prehistory

BC	The many bone fragments discovered at Solutré indicate that there was a human presence there between 18 000 and 15 000 BC.

Antiquity

6C	During the Gaulish period Burgundy is inhabited by the Aedui, the most powerful tribe in Gaul with the Arverni; their capital is Bibracte.
4C	The Sequani, originally from the Haute Seine region, settle in Franche-Comté. They build fortified camps, the most famous of which is Vesontio (Besançon).
59-51	Caesar's conquest of Gaul.
58	Under threat from the Helvetii, the Aedui ask for help from Caesar, who promptly begins his conquest of the Gauls. The Sequani also request his help, this time against the Germanic threat. Caesar drives out the Helvetii and the Germanic tribes... but stays on in Gaul himself.
52	The whole of Gaul rises up against Caesar. The Sequani and the Aedui join forces under Vercingetorix, but are forced to concede victory to Caesar at Alésia, the decisive battle for the whole of Gaul.
51	End of the Gaulish War.
AD	Roman civilization spreads throughout Gaul.
1-3C	Autun, city of Augustus, becomes capital of north-east Gaul and supplants Bibracte.
313	Edict of Milan: the Roman Emperor Constantine grants freedom of worship to Christians.
Late 4C	Christianity gradually spreads into Burgundy.
	The Roman Empire disintegrates under pressure from the Barbarians to the east.

Burgundy

5C	Burgundians, natives of the Baltic coast, settle in the Saône plain. Evidence of their civilization shows that they were more advanced than the other Barbarians. They give their name to their new homeland: Burgundia (which evolved in French into Bourgogne).
534	The Franks seize the Burgundian kingdom.
800	Charlemagne becomes Emperor of the West.
814	The death of Charlemagne plunges the Empire into a period of instability. The sons of Emperor Louis the Pious dispute his legacy.
841	Charles the Bald defeats his brother Lothar at Fontanet (Fontenoy-en-Puisaye).
843	Treaty of Verdun: Charlemagne's empire is divided between the three sons of Louis the Pious.
	Frankish Burgundy reverts to Charles the Bald. It is separated by the Saône from imperial Burgundy, Lothar's territory, the north of which becomes the County of Burgundy (or Comté).
Late 9C	Frankish Burgundy becomes a duchy and takes in Langres, Troyes, Sens, Nevers and Mâcon.

The Duchy of Burgundy

987-996	Reign of Hugues Capet.
996-1031	Reign of Robert II the Pious.
1002-1016	The King of France occupies the Duchy of Burgundy.
1032	The Germanic Emperor becomes suzerain of the Comté. But both his power and that of the count decline as the great feudal landowners gain influence, headed by the Chalons.
	Henri I, son of Robert II the Pious, to whom Burgundy returns, hands it over as a fief to his brother Robert I the Old (a Burgundian branch of the Capet family which survived until 1361).

	Under the Capetian dukes, Burgundy is one of the bastions of Christianity; Cluny, then Cîteaux and Clairvaux reach the height of their influence.
1095	First Crusade.
1270	Death of St Louis at the siege of Tunis.
1295	Philip the Fair buys the Comté as an apanage for his son Philip the Long and his descendants. This is the beginning of a period of peace and prosperity.
1337-1453	Hundred Years War.
1349	The Comté is devastated by the Black Plague; this is *l'année de la grande mort* (the year of widespread death).
1353	Switzerland frees itself from imperial domination.
1361	Duke Philippe de Rouvres dies young without issue, bringing the line of the Capet dukes to an end. The Duchy of Burgundy passes to the King of France, John the Good, who was regent during the duke's minority.
1366	The name Franche-Comté appears for the first time, on an official decree proclaiming the value the inhabitants attach to their rights, as had been done in the Franche-Montagnes of the Swiss Jura.

The Comté returns to Burgundian rule

1384-1477	Philip the Bold (son of the King of France, John the Good), who had already been given the duchy in apanage, marries the heiress to the Comté and thus takes possession of the whole of Burgundy. He is the first of the famous dynasty of the "great dukes of Burgundy", whose power came to exceed that of the kings of France. He is succeeded by John the Fearless, Philip the Good and Charles the Bold. In the Comté, these rulers keep a tight rein on the feudal lords, enforce the authority of Parliament and the State bodies and become patrons of art and literature.
1429	Orléans is saved by Joan of Arc.
1453	Constantinople falls to the Turks.
1461-1483	Reign of Louis XI.

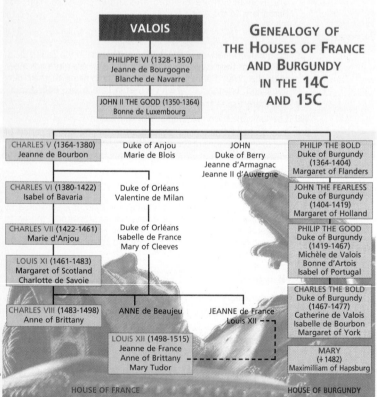

GENEALOGY OF THE HOUSES OF FRANCE AND BURGUNDY IN THE 14C AND 15C

VALOIS

PHILIPPE VI (1328-1350)
Jeanne de Bourgogne
Blanche de Navarre

JOHN II THE GOOD (1350-1364)
Bonne de Luxembourg

CHARLES V (1364-1380)
Jeanne de Bourbon

Duke of Anjou
Marie de Blois

JOHN
Duke of Berry
Jeanne d'Armagnac
Jeanne II d'Auvergne

PHILIP THE BOLD
Duke of Burgundy
(1364-1404)
Margaret of Flanders

CHARLES VI (1380-1422)
Isabel of Bavaria

Duke of Orléans
Valentine de Milan

JOHN THE FEARLESS
Duke of Burgundy
(1404-1419)
Margaret of Holland

CHARLES VII (1422-1461)
Marie d'Anjou

Duke of Orléans
Isabelle de France
Mary of Cleeves

PHILIP THE GOOD
Duke of Burgundy
(1419-1467)
Michèle de Valois
Bonne d'Artois
Isabel of Portugal

LOUIS XI (1461-1483)
Margaret of Scotland
Charlotte de Savoie

CHARLES VIII (1483-1498)
Anne of Brittany

ANNE de Beaujeu

JEANNE de France
Louis XII

CHARLES THE BOLD
Duke of Burgundy
(1467-1477)
Catherine de Valois
Isabelle de Bourbon
Margaret of York

LOUIS XII (1498-1515)
Jeanne de France
Anne of Brittany
Mary Tudor

MARY
(+ 1482)
Maximilliam of Hapsburg

HOUSE OF FRANCE

HOUSE OF BURGUNDY

THE GREAT DUKES OF BURGUNDY

It was under this dynasty, a branch of the House of Valois, that Burgundy reached the height of its power and prestige, where it remained for over a century (1364-1477).

Philip the Bold (1364-1404) – Though scarcely more than a child, Philip fought heroically at the side of his father, King John II the Good of France, at the battle of Poitiers (1356). He earned the nickname "the Bold" when, although wounded and a prisoner, he landed a well-aimed blow on an English lord who had made insulting remarks about the King of France.

By the time he became Duke of Burgundy (1364), Philip was a superb knight, who loved sport and women, and who devoted himself heart and soul to his duchy and the interests of his House. His marriage in 1369 to Margaret of Flanders, the richest heiress in Europe, made him the most powerful prince in Christendom. He lived in great splendour and kept a large and magnificent household in the palace he had built, where he employed painters and sculptors from Flanders. He was always luxuriously dressed; in his hat he wore 12 ostrich plumes, two pheasant feathers and two plumes from birds of India. A golden necklace with an eagle and a lion carrying his motto *En Loyauté*, set with a profusion of rubies, sapphires and pearls, was part of his daily apparel.

Philip founded the Chartreuse de Champmol in Dijon as a mausoleum for himself and his descendants. The finest marble from Liège and alabaster from Genoa were provided for the tomb which was designed in 1384 by the sculptor **Jean de Marville**. On his death, the decoration was entrusted to **Claus Sluter**. Philip the Bold spent so much money that, when he died in 1404, his sons had to pledge the ducal silver to pay for his funeral. In accordance with Burgundian custom, his widow came and placed her purse, her keys and her belt on his coffin as a sign that she renounced succession to any of her husband's goods.

John the Fearless (1404-19) – John succeeded his father, Philip the Bold. Although puny and unprepossessing to look at, he was brave, intelligent and ambitious. He had already shown his prowess in the crusade against the Turks. No sooner had he become Duke of Burgundy than he started a quarrel with the royal council against his cousin, Louis d'Orléans, brother of the mad king, Charles VI. As Louis had a knotted stick as his emblem, John took that of a plane to signal his intention to "plane that stick smooth". This he achieved in 1407 by having his rival assassinated. John took control of Paris, where he was staunchly opposed by the Orleanist faction which controlled the mad king. When the Orleanist leader, the poet Charles d'Orléans, was captured at Agincourt (1415) and taken off to England, where he was imprisoned for 25 years, his father-in-law, Count Bernard VII of Armagnac took over his leadership.

During the struggle between the Armagnacs and the Burgundians, in which the French were drawn into fighting each other in a civil war from which the English were able to profit considerably, John the Fearless, realising the potential harm of the struggle for French interests, sought to negotiate an agreement with the dauphin, the future king, Charles VII. He agreed to meet Charles on 11 September 1419 on the bridge at Montereau, but there he was traitorously felled by an axe and murdered.

Philip the Good (1419-67) and the Order of the Golden Fleece – Filled with desire for vengeance, Philip the Good, son of John the Fearless, allied himself with the English and in 1430 handed over to them Joan of Arc, whom he had captured at Compiègne, for the enormous sum of 10 000 livres. A few years later, however, Philip came to an understanding with Charles VII at the Treaty of Arras, which enabled him, once again, to enlarge his territory. In this way, Dijon became the capital of a powerful state which included a large part of Holland, almost all of modern Belgium, Luxembourg, Flanders, Artois, Hainaut, Picardy and all the land between the Loire and Jura.

Philip, who had an even greater taste for magnificence than his predecessors, lived like a king. Five great officers of state, the Marshal of Burgundy, the Admiral of Flanders, the Chamberlain, the Master of the Horse and the Chancellor, were part of the Duke's immediate entourage, in a court that was among the most sumptuous in Europe.

On the day of his marriage with Isabella of Portugal, 14 January 1429, Philip founded the sovereign Order of the Golden Fleece (Toison d'Or – *see DIJON*) in honour of God, the Virgin Mary and St Andrew. The Order originally had 31 members, all of whom swore allegiance to the Grand Master, Philip the Good and his successors.

Philip the Good by Rogier Van der Weyden; Musée des Beaux-Arts, Dijon

They met at least once every three years and wore the most sumptuous clothes: a long scarlet cloak, trimmed with grey squirrel fur, hung from the shoulders over a robe of the same colour, also trimmed with squirrel fur. The ducal motto, *Aultre n'auray* (not for others), stood out against a background of firestones, quartz, sparkling stones and fleeces. The neck chain of the Order was made of sparkling firestones and quartz. The headquarters of the Order was for a long time the ducal Holy Chapel at Dijon, which was destroyed during the Revolution. The Order is now one of the most prestigious and exclusive.

Charles the Bold (1467-77) – This was the last, and possibly the most famous member of the House of Valois and the dukes of Burgundy. Tall, vigorous and strongly-built, Charles loved violent exercise, and in particular hunting. He was also a cultured man, however, and spent much of his time in study. Above all he was passionately interested in history. He was a proud, intensely ambitious man, as Commynes (historian and chronicler, 1447-1511) said of him, "He was very pompous in his dress and in all other things, and altogether a little too exaggerated... He wanted great glory." As his father had borne the same name as Philip of Macedonia, Charles dreamed of becoming a second Alexander and was constantly waging war in an effort to undermine the power of Louis XI, who in turn did everything possible to break up the Burgundian state. Charles was killed during the siege of Nancy, which was defended by René of Lorraine. His body, half eaten by wolves, was found in a frozen pool.

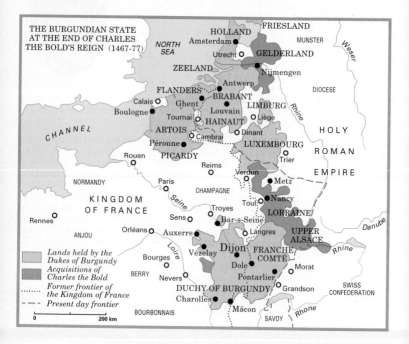

Return to the French Crown

1477	On the death of Charles the Bold, Louis XI invades the Comté. He annexes Burgundy and the Burgundian towns in Picardy to the royal territory. Mary of Burgundy, the daughter of the dead duke, deprived of a large part of her inheritance, marries Maximilian of Habsburg who thus acquires the rest of the old duchy. Their union produces Philip the Handsome whose son, the future emperor, Charles V, will continue the struggle against the Kingdom of France ruled by François I.
1519	The Comté enjoys a period of prosperity under Charles V. He includes people from the Comté, such as the Granvelles, in his immediate circle.
1556-1598	Emperor Charles V bequeaths the Comté to his son, Philip II, King of Spain, who proves to be far less sympathetic a ruler to the people of the Comté.
1589-1610	Reign of Henri IV.
1598	On the death of Philip II, the Comté passes to his daughter Isabelle, who marries the Archduke of Austria. The province of the Comté belongs to the archdukes until it is seized by the French in 1678.

The French Conquest

In order to understand the resistance to French rule of a French-speaking country with an economy closely linked with that of France, one must remember that, finding itself on the borders of the Holy Empire, Austria and Spain, the Comté had become accustomed to directing its own affairs. The independent people of the Comté regarded the rule of a Richelieu or a Louis XIV with some degree of trepidation.

1601	Henri IV acquires the territories of Bresse, Bugey, Valromey and the Gex region from the Duke of Savoy, in return for some Italian territory of his.
1609	After 50 years of struggle against the Spanish, the Netherlands wins its independence.
1610	Beginning of the reign of Louis XIII, who dies in 1643.
1618	Beginning of the Thirty Years War between the House of Austria and France allied with Sweden. The war finishes in 1648 with the Treaty of Westphalia.
1635	Richelieu gives the order to invade the Comté which gave refuge to his enemy, Gaston d'Orléans. The Ten Years War brings the country to ruin.
1643-1715	Reign of Louis XIV.
1648	Mazarin withdraws French forces from the Comté and restores it to its neutral status.
1668	Louis XIV reclaims the Comté as part of the dowry of his wife Marie-Thérèse, daughter of the deceased King of Spain. After a brief campaign, he is forced to abandon the country and return it to Spain.
1674	Louis XIV, at war with Spain, makes a fresh attempt to take control of the province, and this time is successful. His conquest is ratified by the Peace of Nimègue (1678). Besançon takes over from Dole as capital. From now on, the history of the Comté follows that of the rest of France.

From the Revolution to modern times

1715-1774	Reign of Louis XV.
1789	Fall of the Bastille.
1793	The Montbéliard region is annexed to France.
1804	Consecration of Napoleon I as Emperor of France.
1815	The battle of Waterloo. Heroic defence of Belfort by Lecourbe.
1822	Invention of photography by Nicéphore Niepce at St-Loup-de-Varenne.
1870	Colonel Denfert-Rochereau resists attack by 40 000 Germans during the siege of Belfort.
1871	General Bourbaki is defeated at Héricourt, having won victory at Villersexel, and has to fall back to Besançon.
1878	Vines devastated by the phylloxera aphid.
Late 19C-early 20C	As industrialisation gains pace, the Jura region is transformed. Great industrial dynasties such as Peugeot and Japy are born, compensating for the decline in the clockmaking industry, which is exacerbated by the war of 1914 in favour of the Swiss.
1914	Joffre gives his famous order of 6 September at Châtillon-sur-Seine.
1940	Occupation of Jura by the Germans, who use the region to block the retreat of French forces trying to reach central France along the Swiss border.
1940-1944	The Resistance movement is active is Burgundy: Army children from Autun in combat; Châtillonnais forests used as a hideout.
14 September 1944	Leclerc's division joins the army of De Lattre de Tassigny near Châtillon-sur-Seine.
November 1944	The Allied conquest of the northern part of the Doubs *département* completes the liberation of Jura.
1948	Génissiat reservoir is filled with water.
1970	The A 6-A 7 motorway from Paris to Marseille opens up the west of Burgundy (Auxerre, Beaune and Mâcon).
1981	High speed rail service (TGV) links Paris-Le Creusot-Mâcon-Lyon and Paris-Dijon-Besançon.
1986	Setting up of the Haut-Jura regional nature park.

Grandfather clocks and watchmaking in Jura

The Comtoise Clock – The first mechanical clocks, which are referred to in historical documents, stood in monastery towers. These so-called turret-clocks were weight driven, had no hands or dials and did not chime. They served to mark time for the sascritan who rang the bell to call the monks to their duties.

From the end of the 16C, weight-driven clocks in upright form came into use, and in the early 17C the mechanisms were placed inside casings. The Dutch astronomer and physicist Christiaan Huygens was the first to recognise the applications of the pendulum in keeping time, and from 1656 onward, his invention brought the clock into much wider public use. Weight-driven clocks with short pendulums were hung on the wall. An Englishmen, William Clement, introduced the long pendulum in 1670 and the grandfather clock was born.

Création J.-C. Alonet

Cabinetmakers craft the traditional long-case clocks known in France as *horloges comtoises*. The early models were usually made of oak wood, and embellished with ornaments and moulding. Beginning in 1850, pine wood became the material of choice and simple painted motifs were used to decorate the case. The pendulum, of iron or copper, is visible behind the glass window in the door of the trunk. As the pendulum swings, it regulates the descent of the weights. Enamel artists worked to create stylised clock faces.

Smaller and smaller – The first portable timepiece appeared around 1500, thanks to the inventive mind of the German locksmith Peter Henlein, who had the idea of replacing clock weights with a mainspring. As the coiled spring unwound, energy would be released and transmitted to the various parts of the movement (the balance, the wheel train, and the escapement). A friction drive to the hand on the face was provided from a wheel set to rotate at the rate of once an hour. The main defect of this early type of watch was that the spring had a much greater energy when tightly wound, and as it ran down, transmitted less and less energy to the movement, losing time. By 1540, a man known as Jacob the Czech from Prague had devised a mechanism called the fusee, which kept the torque on the spring nearly constant. A further improvement, known as a going barrel, is still the system that keeps modern wind-up watches on time.

The first French watch was made towards the end of the 15C. It was in fact a scaled-down version of a portable clock with the weights replaced by a spring. It was not long, however, before the movements were refined, and there were many models available by the second half of the 16C. At the courts of Henri II and Henri III, women would often wear watches as pendants, and men even had them set into the handles of their daggers as decoration. These timepieces only had one hand, the hour hand.

A major turning point in the clock and watch-making process was reached in 1674 when Huygens invented the spiral balance spring or hairspring. The spring acts on the balance movement much the same way that gravity acts on the pendulum. If the balance moves to one side, the spring is wound and energy stored in it; this energy is restored to the balance, causing it to move back nearly the same distance. If it were not for friction (from air, from the movement of the works against each other etc), such a watch could theoretically oscillate forever.

In 1694, the Dumont brothers, master watchmakers, brought out the first watches manufactured in Besançon, entirely handmade.

Three quarters of a century later, in 1767, Frédéric Japy of the village of Beaucourt, mechanically manufactured some rough models of watches, using machines he had invented. This was an immediate success, and his production was soon turning out 3 000 to 3 500 watches per month.

In 1793, a Swiss watchmaker, Mégevand, and 80 master watchmakers immigrated to Besançon. The *Convention* (national assembly) took them under its wing and advanced them some money to enable them to set up a factory and a national school of clock and watchmaking. They were to take in 200 apprentices per year, funded by the *Convention*. Mégevand went on to perfect assembly line production.

A matter of time – From then on, sales expanded rapidly. In 1835, 80 000 watches were produced in Besançon and in 1878, 240 000. The watchmaking industry spread to many towns in Jura. In the winter, people in the small mountain villages would work at home, producing some of the components or assembling the watches. At the end of the 19C, however, competition from Swiss watchmakers was becoming particularly tough. No longer a product of rural handicraft, modern watches were instead made in specially designed, well-equipped factories that could meet the growing demand. By the end of the 1970s, electronic watches, powered by miniature high-energy-density batteries, had almost completely replaced stem-winding watches. These timepieces use a tiny tuning fork, powered by the battery, to transmit power through minute vibrations to the movement.

19C watch and a decorative case

Today, clock and watchmaking are only of marginal importance in the economy of the region, and yet a certain reputation for quality craftsmanship has been maintained. Now only unique, very precise watches are produced for the high end of the market. Morez and Morbier still produce grandfather clocks, as they have since the 17C. Although these pieces went out of fashion in the 1960s, they hold a kind of nostalgic attraction that will never fade completely. The age-old gesture of raising the weights, the gentle sway of the pendulum, the pleasant sound of the ticking and the chiming hours in a peaceful household on a quiet afternoon... Perhaps you'd like to have one shipped to your home?

Monastic life in Burgundy

After the turmoil of the Carolingian decline, the Church used its not inconsiderable influence and long-established cultural tradition to resume a leading role in society; there was a great renewal of fervour for the monastic life throughout western Europe. France was in the vanguard of this religious revival and it was Burgundy that provided the driving force.

The first religious orders – **St Benedict and his Rule** – In 529 Benedict, who was born in Norcia in Umbria, Italy, moved from Subiaco, where he had at first led the life of a recluse, to Monte Cassino where he worked out his Constitution, soon to be adopted by many monasteries. His advice, which developed into the famous Benedictine Rule, showed great moderation: although fasting, silence and abstinence were recommended, mortification and painful penances were severely condemned. The abbots of the Benedictine monasteries, who were elected for life, had absolute authority. All relations with the outside world were to be avoided, and the community had to make itself completely self-supporting by its own labours.

Cluny and the triumph of Benedictine Rule – In 910, the founding of a monastery in the region of Mâcon by the Duke of Aquitaine, Guillaume le Pieux, marked the beginning of an important religious reform associated with the name of Cluny. A return to the spirit of the Benedictine Rule was marked by the observance of three cardinal rules – obedience, chastity and fasting – but divine service occupied the greater part of the day, reducing and almost eliminating the time for manual labour and intellectual work.

The great innovation was the complete independence of the new abbey from all political power. Under its founding charter, Cluny was directly attached to the Holy See in Rome; given the remoteness of pontifical authority, this arrangement effectively conferred complete autonomy on the order. The Cluny order expanded rapidly; by the beginning of the 12C there were 1 450 monasteries with 10 000 monks, scattered all over France, Germany, Spain, Italy and Britain, all dependant on Cluny.

This great expansion is largely explained by the personalities and the length of the reign of the great abbots of Cluny (saints Odo, Mayeul, Odilo, Hugh and Peter the Venerable), who chose their own successors and were themselves supported by extremely competent men. For two or three generations Cluny was the centre of essentially an empire. Its organisation, however, was based on extreme centralisation, with the whole weight of power vested in the abbot of Cluny.

Cîteaux and St Bernard – It was precisely to fight against the luxury and the slack discipline among the monks of Cluny that St Bernard spoke out. This young nobleman, born at the château of Fontaine near Dijon, followed a strange destiny when at the age of 21 he renounced all riches and honours and went with 32 companions to the monastery of Cîteaux in search of God's mercy. When he arrived there in 1112, the monastery was undergoing a great crisis; in a short time Bernard turned this very difficult situation around by the example and influence he exercised on all around him.

In 1115 he settled in a poor area along the borders of Burgundy and Champagne. Initially, he was completely destitute, and he had to contend with enormous difficulties: a harsh climate, sickness and physical suffering due to a life of self-denial, which he imposed as strictly on himself as on his monks.

Ph. Cajic/MICHELIN

The Benedictines of the Pierre-qui-Vire Abbey publish books in the Zodiaque collection

The monastic foundations – Bernard's fame soon attracted so many applicants for the monastic life to Clairvaux that the abbey of Trois-Fontaines was founded in the Marne in 1121. On Bernard's death in 1153, Cîteaux had 700 monks and exercised considerable influence; 350 abbeys were attached to it, including the first four "daughters": La Ferté, Morimond, Pontigny and above all Clairvaux, which, thanks to St Bernard, maintained a leading role at the heart of the Cistercian order. During Bernard's abbacy, Clairvaux was exceptionally prosperous; from 1135, a total of 1 800ha/4 448 acres of forest land and 350ha/865 acres of fields and meadows belonged to the abbey, where stone buildings had replaced the wooden structures of the earlier years.

Cistercian law – St Bernard's interpretation and application of Benedictine Rule were uncompromising. Monks wore a simple wool tunic whatever the season; their diet was frugal; seven hours a day were set aside for repose, when the monks slept fully dressed in a common dormitory on a simple straw pallet with a single blanket. The monks were roused between one and two in the morning and as the day progressed sang matins, then lauds, celebrated private Masses, recited the canonic hours (prime, tierce, sext, nones, vespers and compline), and took part in the Mass celebrated by the whole community.

The abbot, leader of the community, lived and ate with his monks, presided over their worship and also over the chapter and any other meetings. He was assisted by a prior, who took over his duties in his absence.

Like St Bernard, the Cistercians had an impact on society that went beyond issues of faith. Well organised and very efficient, the monks were able to bring prosperity to the harshest lands, often deep in valleys – sites chosen for their isolated and challenging nature. Through the hard work of clearing, draining and setting up irrigation systems, the monks became masters of hydrology, wine-growing, and even metallurgy.

The achievements of these communities were placed in peril on many occasions and for various reasons: changes in the economy, the rise of mendicant orders, the gradual isolation of the abbot from his community and finally, the French Revolution. At that time, the order was placed under interdiction and abbeys destroyed, in particular Cluny, by speculators with no thought of the future. Not until the mid-19C did a revival of interest in the communities and their monuments arise.

The contemporary order – The organisation of the Cistercian order is still based on the Charter of Charity established about 1115, a sort of link uniting the various abbeys which were all equal with each other. Today there are some 3 000 Trappist Cistercians (the name is derived from the abbey of Notre-Dame-de-la-Trappe, reformed in the 17C). Governed by an Abbot General residing in Rome, the monks are scattered throughout the world in 92 abbeys or priories, 15 of which are in France. All the abbots of the order meet at Cîteaux for the meeting of the General Chapter.

There are a further 2 000 monks belonging to 55 abbeys or priories, of which 12 are in France, ruled by the same Abbot General but with their own General Chapter.

In 1998, monks from around the world came to participate in the celebrations honouring the 900th anniversary of Cîteaux. The abbey's cows currently produce about 900 000 cheeses a year, which nicely covers their expenses.

To best appreciate the architectural qualities of Cistercian buildings in Burgundy, you should visit Pontigny and Fontenay. The latter, which is nearly entire, gives a good idea of monastic life in its heyday. To learn more about how other monks live today, you can visit the Benedictine abbey in La Pierre-qui-Vire or the Kagyu Ling Buddhist temple in La Boulaye. Taizé is a modern and flourishing ecumenical community near Cluny devoted to the Christian youth movement.

ABC of architecture

Ecclesiastical architecture

Typical ground plan of a church

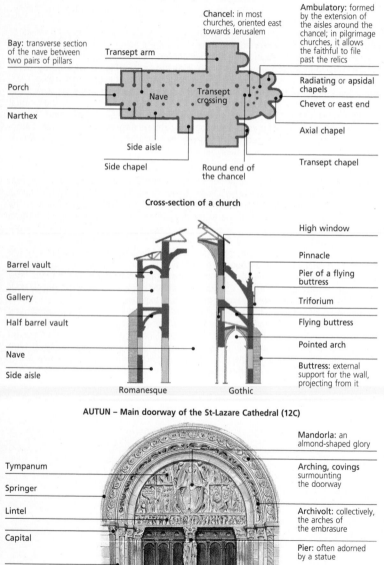

Chancel: in most churches, oriented east towards Jerusalem

Ambulatory: formed by the extension of the aisles around the chancel; in pilgrimage churches, it allows the faithful to file past the relics

Bay: transverse section of the nave between two pairs of pillars

Transept arm

Porch

Narthex

Nave

Transept crossing

Radiating or apsidal chapels

Chevet or east end

Axial chapel

Side aisle

Side chapel

Round end of the chancel

Transept chapel

Cross-section of a church

Barrel vault

Gallery

Half barrel vault

Nave

Side aisle

Romanesque

Gothic

High window

Pinnacle

Pier of a flying buttress

Triforium

Flying buttress

Pointed arch

Buttress: external support for the wall, projecting from it

AUTUN – Main doorway of the St-Lazare Cathedral (12C)

Tympanum

Springer

Lintel

Capital

Shaft

Archshaft

Mandorla: an almond-shaped glory

Arching, covings surmounting the doorway

Archivolt: collectively, the arches of the embrasure

Pier: often adorned by a statue

Jamb shaft: vertical member forming part of the jamb of a door, supporting the arches

VÉZELAY – Nave of the Ste-Madeleine Basilica

High window

Pier: a kind of pilaster supporting the column

Groined vaulting: two ribs meet at a right angle

Wall arch or stringer: lateral arch of a vault

Cornice with frieze

Abacus

Archstone (here, dark and light cut stone blocks alternate)

Historiated capital decorated with scenes or characters

Triumphant arch: a large arcade separating the central nave from the transept or the chancel

Triforium: a gallery and passageway hollowed from the thickness of the wall. At the end of the Gothic period, this feature became purely decorative

Engaged half-columns: set around the four faces of a cruciform pillar

Transverse arch: reinforces the vault

Cross-ribbed vault

Chancel

R. Corbel/MICHELIN

79

TOURNUS – St-Philibert Abbey Church (11-12C)

The fortress-like appearance of the front wall, which was a defensive feature of the abbey, is one of the first examples of Romanesque art in Burgundy, dating to around the year 1000.

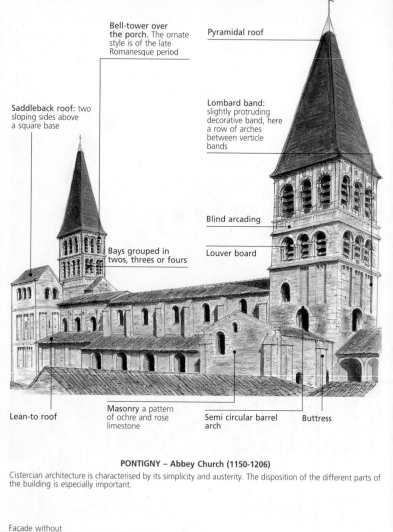

Bell-tower over the porch. The ornate style is of the late Romanesque period

Pyramidal roof

Saddleback roof: two sloping sides above a square base

Lombard band: slightly protruding decorative band, here a row of arches between verticle bands

Bays grouped in twos, threes or fours

Blind arcading

Louver board

Lean-to roof

Masonry a pattern of ochre and rose limestone

Semi circular barrel arch

Buttress

PONTIGNY – Abbey Church (1150-1206)

Cistercian architecture is characterised by its simplicity and austerity. The disposition of the different parts of the building is especially important.

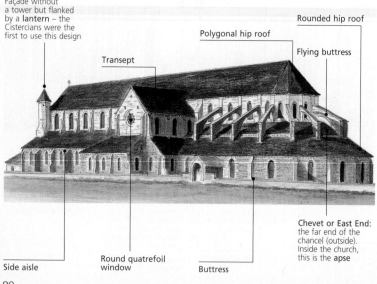

Façade without a tower but flanked by a lantern – the Cistercians were the first to use this design

Rounded hip roof

Polygonal hip roof

Flying buttress

Transept

Side aisle

Round quatrefoil window

Buttress

Chevet or East End: the far end of the chancel (outside). Inside the church, this is the apse

Military architecture

CLÉRON – Castle (14C)

This old feudal castle stands on the banks of the River Loue, which makes an excellent natural moat.

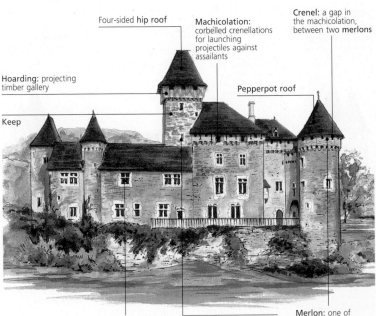

Four-sided **hip roof**

Machicolation: corbelled crenellations for launching projectiles against assailants

Crenel: a gap in the machicolation, between two **merlons**

Hoarding: projecting timber gallery

Keep

Pepperpot roof

Mullioned window

Loophole or **arrow slit**

Merlon: one of the solid intervals between two **crenels** of a battlement

BESANÇON – The citadel

An impressive sight: the fortifications hang 118m/387ft above the River Doubs. Vauban designed the citadel in the 17C.

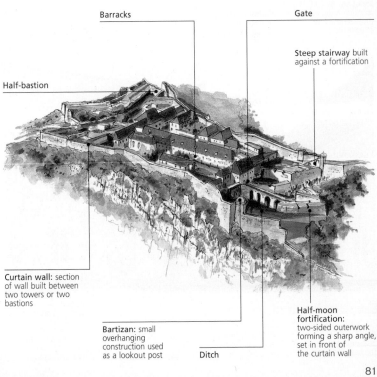

Barracks

Gate

Steep stairway built against a fortification

Half-bastion

Curtain wall: section of wall built between two towers or two bastions

Bartizan: small overhanging construction used as a lookout post

Ditch

Half-moon fortification: two-sided outerwork forming a sharp angle, set in front of the curtain wall

R. Corbel/MICHELIN

Civil architecture

NEVERS – Palais Ducal (16C)

The former home of the Dukes of Nevers was a precursor to the famous châteaux of the Loire Valley. Note the Renaissance harmony of the structure, and the great towers revealing medieval influence.

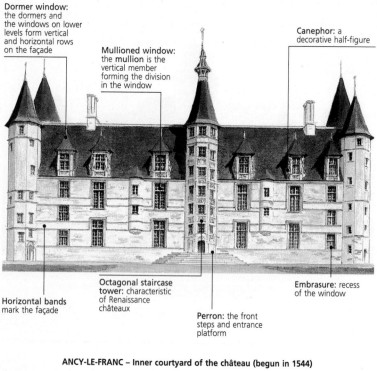

Dormer window: the dormers and the windows on lower levels form vertical and horizontal rows on the façade

Mullioned window: the **mullion** is the vertical member forming the division in the window

Canephor: a decorative half-figure

Horizontal bands mark the façade

Octagonal staircase tower: characteristic of Renaissance châteaux

Perron: the front steps and entrance platform

Embrasure: recess of the window

ANCY-LE-FRANC – Inner courtyard of the château (begun in 1544)

The square courtyard with four identical wings is an example of the architectural rhythm created by the use of alternating bays, pilasters and niches, invented by Bramante

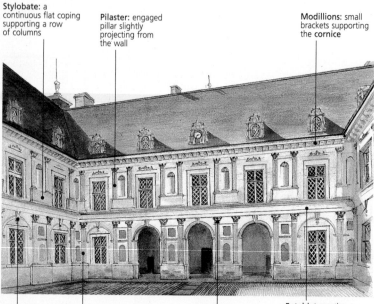

Stylobate: a continuous flat coping supporting a row of columns

Pilaster: engaged pillar slightly projecting from the wall

Modillions: small brackets supporting the **cornice**

Agrafe, clasp: an ornamental piece on the keystone of a bay

Fluting: grooves giving texture to the columns or pillars

Corinthian capital: embellished with two rows of **acanthus** leaves

Entablature: the horizontal part in classical architecture that rests on the column and consists of the architrave, frieze and cornice

SYAM – Palladian Villa

One of the forge masters, Mr. Jobez, had this villa built in 1818. He drew inspiration from the Italian villas designed by Palladio (16C)

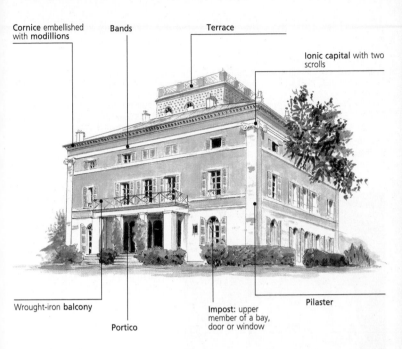

Cornice embellished with modillions

Bands

Terrace

Ionic capital with two scrolls

Wrought-iron balcony

Portico

Impost: upper member of a bay, door or window

Pilaster

VOUGLANS – Dam

Flooding part of the Ain Valley, the Vouglans Dam forms France's third largest reservoir.

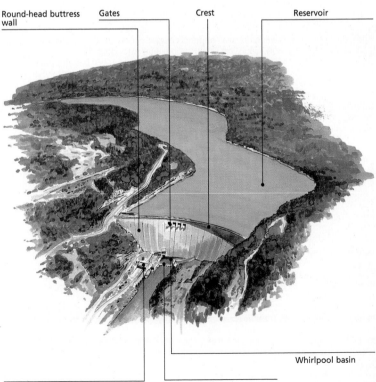

Round-head buttress wall

Gates

Crest

Reservoir

Hydro-electric plant

Coffer

Whirlpool basin

RELIGIOUS ARCHITECTURE

In Burgundy

It is not surprising that Burgundy has an incomparably rich artistic tradition, since the necessary stimulation has always existed in the area. Since Antiquity, the region has been a crossroads where a wide variety of peoples and influences have met. The treasure found near Vix shows that strong currents were active in the region of Châtillon-sur-Seine in about the 6C BC.

In the 15C, on the initiative of the Great Dukes, many groups of artists from Paris and Flanders settled in Dijon, which they made one of the most important artistic centres in Europe.

This penetration of foreign influences, and the enduring qualities of Roman civilization and ancient traditions, combined with the expression of the Burgundian temperament led to the blossoming of regional art that holds an honoured place in the artistic history of France.

Pre-Romanesque – After a period of artistic eclipse in the early Middle Ages, the Carolingian epoch (8C-9C) witnessed a period of architectural revival in Burgundy in particular. The plans of the religious buildings were simple, and stone structures basic.

A mermaid with a double tail
on this Romanesque capital

Part of the former crypt of the cathedral of St-Bénigne at Dijon and the crypts of Flavigny-sur-Ozerain and St-Germain of Auxerre are among the oldest examples of these monuments.

Romanesque – Numerous towns, wealthy abbeys and abundant building material were favourable conditions in which the Romanesque School of Burgundy flourished, showing an extraordinary vitality in the 11C and 12C, not only in architecture, but in sculpture and painting *(see below)*. Furthermore, the influence of the school spread far beyond the geographic boundaries of Burgundy.

In the year 1000, the desire to build was given fresh impetus by the end of invasions, the strengthening of royal power and the evolution of new building techniques.

Raoul Glaber, a monk of St-Bénigne at Dijon, commented that, "As the third year after the millennium was about to begin, people all over Christendom, but particularly in Italy and Gaul, set about rebuilding the churches... The Christians replaced even those which did not need to be replaced with more beautiful buildings... It seemed as if the world had shaken the dust off its old clothes to clothe everything in the white robes of its young churches...".

The first Burgundian Romanesque churches – Among the great builders of this period, Abbot Guglielmo da Volpiano, of Italian origin and related to some of the greatest families of his time, built a new basilica in Dijon on the site of the tomb of St Bénigne. The building, begun in 1001, was consecrated in 1018.

Though this abbey was completely destroyed by fire in the 12C, the church of St-Vorles in Châtillon-sur-Seine – considerably modified in the first years of the 11C by the Bishop of Langres, Brun de Roucy, a relation of Guglielmo da Volpiano – provides an example of the features of Romanesque art during this period: slipshod building methods with badly placed flat stones; massive thick pillars; crude decoration of mural niches; and cornices with Lombard arcades.

The most striking example of the architecture of this time is the church of **St-Philibert** in Tournus. The narthex and the upper storey of the narthex, built at the beginning of the 11C, are the oldest extant parts to date. The most striking aspect of this solid, powerful architecture is its sober, almost austere style.

Cluny and its school – Although, in the beginning Romanesque art owed much to foreign influences, the following period witnessed the triumphant emergence of a new style from Cluny, which was to spread throughout Burgundy, eventually reaching as far as Switzerland.

It was at Cluny that the principal characteristics of Burgundian Romanesque architecture were united for the first time.

Until St Peter's was built in Rome in the 16C, the abbey of Cluny was the largest church in all Christendom; its total internal length greatly exceeded that of the Gothic cathedrals that were built from the 13C onwards.

In 1247 an Italian churchman travelling through France remarked that "Cluny is the noblest Burgundian monastery of the Benedictine Black Monk order. The buildings are so extensive that the Pope with his cardinals and entire retinue and the king and his court may be accommodated together, without upsetting the monks' routine or putting them out of their cells".

The extent and exceptional size of the remains of the abbey, which was started by St Hugh in 1088 and completed about 1130 *(see CLUNY)*, are still impressive and allow one to recognise the general characteristics of the School of Cluny; the broken-barrel vaulting is an innovation of the period.

Burgundian architects avoided the use of semicircular vaulting as much as possible and substituted broken-barrel vaulting which was far more efficient at withstanding the strains and stresses of the building. This style of vaulting consists of each bay having a transverse arch; the use of broken arches reduces stress and thereby the weight on the walls, thus making it possible to raise the vaulting to a far greater height. The pillars are flanked by fluted pilasters in the Antique style; a false triforium of alternating bays and pilasters, surmounted by a clerestory, runs above the narrow arches. This arrangement of three storeys rising to a pointed vault is found in many churches in the region.

The completion of so large a building, in which a great many architects and artists participated, was to have a profound effect on the construction of other churches in the Mâconnais, Charollais and Brionnais regions.

The priory church of **Paray-le-Monial** is a smaller replica of the great abbey church at Cluny. It was also conceived by St Hugh and has an identical plan of construction.

At **La Charité-sur-Loire** another abbey dependant on the great abbey also shows the influence of Cluny. Other Burgundian monuments take their derivation more or less directly from the abbey of Cluny. In the church of St-Lazare at Autun, consecrated in 1130, a much simplified plan of Cluny is to be found. However Roman influence is often in evidence, for example in the fluted pilasters copied from the Antique style on the piers; the decoration of the triforium arcade is similar to that on the Arroux gateway.

At **Semur-en-Brionnais**, home of the family of St Hugh, the church is almost as high as Cluny. On the interior of the west front, the overhanging gallery recalls a similar gallery in St-Michel in Cluny.

The collegiate church of St-Andoche in Saulieu is associated with the Cluny family of churches: Notre-Dame in Beaune has more points in common with St-Lazare in Autun. Among the many village churches built under the inspiration of Cluny, particularly in the Brionnais region, those of Bois-Ste-Marie, Blanot, Montceaux-l'Étoile, Varenne-l'Arconce, Vareilles, Châteauneuf and Iguerande are particularly interesting.

Vézelay and its influence – The Cluny School was repudiated by a whole family of churches, the purest example of which is the basilica of Ste-Madeleine in Vézelay, although there are others that display characteristics even further removed from Cluny. Built at the beginning of the 12C on a hill overlooking the valley of the Cure, Vézelay constitutes the synthesis of true Burgundian Romanesque architecture.

The essential difference between this church and earlier Romanesque buildings is that the nave has groined vaulting whereas up to that time only the side aisles had this feature, their small size mitigating the risk of the vaulting subsiding as a result of lateral pressure.

This design, originally without the support of flying buttresses which were added in the Gothic period, required the incorporation of iron bars to prevent the walls of the nave from bulging outwards.

Clerestory windows placed directly above the main arches opened onto the axis of each bay, shedding light into the nave. Columns projecting slightly from the walls replace the rectangular pilasters found in the Cluny style. The vaulting is supported by semicircular transverse arches.

To break the monotony of this style of architecture, differently coloured building materials were used: vari-coloured limestone and alternating white and brown archstones.

The church in Anzy-le-Duc appears to have served as a model for the building in Vézelay; it is probable that Renaud de Semur, who came from the Brionnais region, wished to rebel against the all-powerful influence of Cluny and took as his model the church in Anzy-le-Duc, which at that time was the most perfect piece of architecture of the region. There is no shortage of points of comparison: the elevation of the storeys is the same; both have a solitary window above the main arches; both share the same style of semicircular vaulting and cruciform pillars flanked by engaged columns. This style, created in Anzy-le-Duc and perfected in Vézelay, has been copied in St-Lazare in Avallon and St-Philibert in Dijon.

Tympanum above the central doorway,
Ste-Madeleine

Ph. Gajic/MICHELIN

Fontenay and the Cistercian School – Cistercian architecture first appeared in Burgundy in the first half of the 12C (Cistercium was the Latin name for the town of Cîteaux). It is characterised by a spirit of simplicity in keeping with the teaching of St Bernard, whose influence on his times was considerable. He objected bitterly to the luxury displayed in some monastic churches, opposing the theories of some of the great builders of the 11C and 12C with extraordinary passion and vehemence. His argument against the belief of abbots such as St Hugh, Peter the Venerable and Suger, who believed that nothing could be too rich for the glory of God, was expressed for example in the letter he wrote to William, Abbot of St-Thierry, in which he asks, "Why this excessive height

Chapter house, Fontenay Abbey

B. Kaufmann/MICHELIN

in the churches, this enormous length, this unnecessary width, these sumptuous ornaments and curious paintings that draw the eye and distract attention and meditation? ...We the monks, who have forsaken ordinary life and renounced worldly wealth and ostentation for the love of Christ, ...in whom do we hope to awaken devotion with these ornaments?". There is nonetheless a certain grandeur even in the sobriety and austerity that he advocated. The uncluttered style and severe appearance truly reflected the principles of Cistercian rule, which regarded everything that was not absolutely indispensable to the development and spread of the monastic way of life as harmful.

The Cistercians almost always insisted on the identical plan of construction for all the buildings of their order and themselves directed the work on new abbeys. The abbey of Fontenay is a good example of the standard plan *(see photograph)*. This design and its architectural techniques are to be found throughout Europe from Sicily to Sweden. Every new monastery was another link with France, and craftsmen followed the monks. It was the turn of the Burgundian Cistercian monasteries to spearhead the expansion of European monasticism. In 1135, the Cistercians adopted Fountains Abbey in Yorkshire, a recent foundation (1132); there they were to build on a large scale what was to become the wealthiest abbey in England.

In **Cistercian churches**, the blind nave is covered by broken-barrel vaulting, as at Cluny; the side aisles are generally arched with transverse barrel vaulting, and their great height enables them to take the thrust of the nave. This style is to be found in many Burgundian churches of the 12C.

The transept, also of broken-barrel vaulting, juts far out and has two square chapels opening into each transept arm. The choir, of broken-barrel vaulting, is square and not very deep. It ends in a flat chevet lit through two tiers of three windows. Five windows are placed above the chancel arch, and each bay of the side aisles is also lit through a window.

The fact that most Cistercian churches have no belfry is evidence of St Bernard's desire to adhere to poverty, humility and simplicity. Living far from their fellow men, away from the frequented highways, the religious communities did not wish to attract the faithful from far and wide. Belfries, which drew attention to the existence of a church by their silhouette and shape, were thus banned.

By avoiding all decoration, be it painting or sculpture, and by eliminating every kind of superfluous ornamentation (such as stained-glass windows, or illuminated paving stones), Cistercian art achieved a remarkable purity of execution.

Gothic – About the middle of the 12C and perhaps even earlier, pointed vaulting made its appearance in Burgundy, the prelude to a new development in architecture. The Gothic style, which originated in the Parisian region (Ile-de-France), penetrated slowly into Burgundy, where it was adapted according to circumstances and trends.

Period of transition – In 1140, the gallery of the narthex at Vézelay was given pointed vaulting. The Cistercians were among the first to adopt this style of architecture and used it at Pontigny in about 1150. The choir of Ste-Madeleine at Vézelay, the work of Abbot Gérard d'Arcy, was started in the last years of the 12C; the flying buttresses were not added until the 13C. It was in the 13C that a Burgundian Gothic style emerged in religious buildings.

First half of the 13C – The church of Notre-Dame in Dijon, built without interruption between 1230 and 1251, represents the most perfect and best-known example of this style. Its characteristics are to be found in many religious buildings of the period in Burgundy; beyond the transept, the fairly deep choir is flanked by apsidal chapels (there are generally two) and ends with a high apse. The use of sexpartite vaulting permitted the replacing of the uniformly sized pillars with alternating thick and thin pillars. A triforium runs above the great arches; at the clerestory level, the nave wall is set back slightly allowing for a gallery above that of the triforium.

In the external decoration, the presence of a cornice – its form varying from one building to another – goes round the choir, the nave, the apse, or the belfry and is a typically Burgundian mode of decoration.

Among the buildings constructed in this style, the most important are: Auxerre Cathedral, the collegiate church of St-Martin in Clamecy and the church of Notre-Dame in Semur-en-Auxois. In the latter, the absence of a triforium further enhances the effect of dizzying height created by the narrow nave.

End of the 13C – Architecture now became much lighter and developed a boldness, seeming to defy the laws of gravity.

The choir of the church of St-Thibault in Auxois appears in such a style, with its keystone at a height of 27m/89ft. The five-sided apse rising to a height of four storeys is of an amazing lightness. Below the highest windows there is a clerestory composed of three tiers reaching to the ground: the top tier is a gallery, the middle tier is composed of pairs of radiant windows and the bottom tier consists of blind arcades.

The church of St-Père shares certain similarities with Notre-Dame in Dijon, but it differs in its height, being of two storeys with a gallery in front of the windows.

14C – It was at this time that the Flamboyant Gothic style, characterised by the pointed, S-shaped ogee arch, appeared; the number of ribs multiplied and the capitals were reduced to a simple decorative role or were sometimes even dispensed with completely. This period did not produce any really fine buildings in Burgundy. The church of St-Jean in Dijon has a single nave surrounded by many chapels.

Renaissance – Under the influence of Italy, Burgundian art took a new turn in the 16C, marked by a revival of the Antique styles.

In architecture the transition from Gothic to Italian art met with some resistance. The church of St-Michel in Dijon shows evidence of this: whereas the nave (started at the beginning of the 16C) is an imitation of Gothic art, the façade (built between 1537 and 1570) is a perfect example of the Renaissance style, with two towers divided into four storeys, on which Ionic and Corinthian orders are superimposed alternately, three semicircular doorways and the porch with its richly sculpted coffered vaulting all reflecting a strong Italian influence.

Jura

The religious architectural heritage of the region of Franche-Comté is indebted to the numerous monastic communities which were to be found in the region during the Middle Ages. The monks certainly played a vital role in the development of this rugged, primitive country. By the Merovingian period, two abbeys were already making waves throughout the region: Luxeuil in the north and Condat (later St-Claude) in the south. The former rapidly became an intellectual centre exerting an influence on the whole of Gaul – in particular in Lure – whereas the latter devoted its energies to spreading the Christian message and to the enormous task of clearing space in the forests of Jura. Unfortunately, the anarchy which greeted the end of Carolingian rule sounded a death knell for both these abbeys. In the 10C, the Benedictines thus faced the task of winning back territory in Burgundy. They were followed by the Cluny order, which soon dominated the province. However, in the 12C the Cluny order itself had to give way to the innumerable Cistercian communities which were springing up all over the region. At the same time, communities were being set up by the Premonstratensians, the Augustinians and the Carthusians who all threw themselves into clearing the forest and draining the soil, thus attracting their share of local residents, who set up communities round their abbeys. The churches, which are now used as parish churches, were originally monastery churches most usually built according to the rules of the religious order which was to use them: thus, the Benedictine order introduced a primitive architectural style influenced by early Italian basilicas; the Cluny order preferred Burgundian style churches; and the Cistercians built churches with a flat chevet, like that at Cîteaux, and generally paved the way for Gothic art.

Romanesque – There is in fact no Romanesque art specific to the region of Franche-Comté; the primitive churches built there during the Romanesque period drew on Burgundian and Lombard architecture for their inspiration. They generally have a basilical floor plan with a transept hardly wider than the nave itself. The chancel ends in a semicircular apse, flanked by two apsidal chapels opening into the transept, or it ends in a flat chevet (as in the church at Courtefontaine). Large arcades are supported by heavy pillars, which can be square, round or octagonal, with no capitals. The buildings and pillars are often made of small quarry stones. The nave and side aisles were originally covered by a timber roof, which was later replaced by ogival vaulting. The roofs over the side aisles are sometimes groined vaulting. The apse and apsidal chapels are closed off by half domes. The roof above the transept crossing is either a dome or a bell tower, which never features as part of the façade.

The churches of Jura are typically understated, and the absence of almost any decoration further underlines their austerity. The churches of St-Hymetière *(see photograph)* and St-Lupicin (early 12C), Boussières, the crypt of St-Denis at Lons-le-Saunier are the best preserved examples of this. The cathedral of St-Jean at Besançon is virtually the only remaining trace of Rhenish Carolingian influence in Franche-Comté; it has an apse at either end of its nave. Inside, square sturdy pillars alternate with round slender ones, creating a regular, harmonious division of space. There are also small churches by this school, which have a single nave and a bell-tower on their façade.

St-Hymetière

G. Magnin/MICHELIN

Gothic – Romanesque art continued to exert its influence in Franche-Comté for some time; one might take this as evidence of the distrust of innovation and change which is a characteristic of the region's inhabitants. Thus, at the end of the 13C, which marked the culmination of the great period of creativity in Gothic art elsewhere, there were still numerous Romanesque features evident in buildings in Franche-Comté which had adopted the new style. The most typical and best-preserved example of this period of transition is the church of St-Anatoile at Salins. This has a semicircular arched doorway, large pointed arches in the nave and a triforium with Romanesque arcades. It is in fact this long-lasting preference for semicircular arches that gives the churches of Franche-Comté their distinctive character. The Gothic style did not really become widespread in Franche-Comté until the middle of the 15C, when Flamboyant Gothic features were adopted. It did not reach its apogee there until the following century, even surviving into the middle of the 17C, when the Renaissance style was already starting to decline in other parts of France.

Flamboyant Gothic churches in Franche-Comté typically have three tall blind naves separated by elegant pointed arches supported on round pillars. The ribs from the vaulting and the moulding from the arches run down these pillars. The church is topped by an enormous bell-tower. Large windows shed light into the deep, five-sided choir (St-Claude Cathedral, Poligny Collegiate Church), which is flanked by two chapels. These open onto the transept, which is a little wider than the nave. The moderation and sobriety so dear to local people's hearts are probably responsible for the avoidance of the more excessive features of Flamboyant Gothic, which characterised the style elsewhere. In Jura, vaulting is generally uncluttered and only seigneurial chapels, such as the Chalon family chapel at Mièges, have ornate features.

Renaissance – The Italian Renaissance did not have a very marked effect on the religious architecture of Franche-Comté, which adhered to Flamboyant Gothic until quite late on. The new style was applied, once it began to make its influence felt, for the most part to church annexes, such as chapels (Pesmes) or entrance doorways (Collège de l'Arc at Dole). Sculpted decoration, in particular woodwork, adapted more successfully to the new style.

Classical to modern periods – As the Renaissance before it, so **Classical** art was slow to catch on in Franche-Comté, where the influence of the Gothic style was still strong; it only really began to make its mark from 1674 onwards, when the churches destroyed during the Ten Years War (1633-43) and the destructive campaigns of Louis XIV were being rebuilt. The small size and run-down nature of the churches which had survived from the Middle Ages, coupled with a huge rise in population figures from the middle of the 18C, may explain the great number of construction projects undertaken up until the Revolution.

The most characteristic feature from this period, which typifies the religious architecture of the region as a whole, is the way the porch is incorporated in a bell-tower, which is surmounted by an imperial style pointed dome, formed of four reversed curve sides covered with glazed tiles. There are three common layouts: a church with a single nave, with or without a transept; a church with a centralised floor plan, either octagonal or in the shape of a Greek cross; or a hall-church with three naves of equal height, generally without a transept. The naves are covered by pointed vaulting, and needed strong buttresses outside to counteract the powerful outward pressure which might otherwise have made the walls bulge at the top. The interior is often painted white, apart from the columns, pillars and ribs, which are picked out in grey. The regular façade is enlivened by frontons, pilasters and columns.

In the late 18C and early 19C, the neo-Classical style took over, with consciously simple, almost austere ornamentation. As in the Antique temples, the straight line replaced the curve, and side aisles with ceilings took the place of the side naves with pointed vaulting of the hall-churches. The central nave was covered with a barrel vault, where tall windows let in the light.

After 1850, the neo-Gothic style reintroduced pointed arches.

During the **contemporary** period, Jura is proud of the fact that it has been the setting for a revival of religious art. Since the 1950s and 1960s, some important architectural projects have been undertaken, for example, at Audincourt, Ronchamp and Dole (the church of St-Jean-l'Évangéliste). A desire to emphasize the spirituality of such places is often evident in the powerful movement of the line of the building and in the masterful way the decorative effects of light have been employed.

Many artists, such as Manessier, Gabriel Saury, Bazaine, Le Moal and Fernand Léger, have contributed in the same spirit, giving a new or renewed vitality to religious buildings with their stained-glass windows, sculptures, mosaics or tapestries.

CIVIL AND MILITARY ARCHITECTURE

In Burgundy

Gallo-Roman art – During their occupation, the Romans were responsible for the building of numerous monuments in Burgundy. To this day the town of Autun, built at the order of the Emperor Augustus to replace Bibracte, capital of the Aedui tribe, recalls Roman civilization with its two monumental gateways and its vast theatre.

Excavations undertaken at Alésia, at the presumed site of the camp where Vercingetorix made his last stand before the Roman legions of Julius Caesar in 52 BC, have led to the discovery of a complete town built a little later; paved streets, the foundations of temples and a forum, as well as many dwellings have been uncovered. Other excavations carried out at the source of the Seine have revealed the ruins of a temple and a number of bronze statuettes and unusual wooden sculptures. Numerous pieces of pottery dating from Gallo-Roman times as well as examples of gold and silver work of great value were found more than 50 years ago at Vertault, not far from Châtillon-sur-Seine.

At Dijon, the remains of an entrenched camp (Castrum Divionense), built about AD 273, have been uncovered. Excavations at Fontaines-Salées near St-Père-sous-Vézelay have revealed very extensive Gallo-Roman baths.

Gothic – Fine mansions and houses built by wealthy merchants in the 15C have survived in Dijon and some other towns, such as Flavigny-sur-Ozerain and Châteauneuf. Part of the palace of the dukes of Burgundy in Dijon (the tower on the terrace and the ducal kitchens), the synodal palace in Sens and the hospital in Beaune, a triumph in wooden architecture, all date from this period. Among the fortified castles of the 13C, those of Châteauneuf, built by Philippe Pot the Seneschal of Burgundy, Posanges and the ducal palace at Nevers are particularly interesting.

Renaissance – There was no blossoming of great Renaissance châteaux in Burgundy, as there was in the valley of the Loire, however, towns such as Ancy-le-Franc, Tanlay and Sully boast some magnificent mansions.

Classical – The reunion of Burgundy with the crown of France marked the end of the duchy's political independence, but its artistic expression survived. Classical art, initially imitated from Paris and later Versailles, is to be seen in Dijon in the layout of the Place Royale, the alterations to the old Palais des Ducs and in the building of the new Palais des Ducs. Many fine mansions were built by the families of parliamentarians who were in favour at

Ancy-le-Franc

Court at the time and who held high positions. Although retaining the characteristics of the Renaissance period, the Hôtel de Vogüé (built 1607-14) features the new design where the living quarters are set back behind a courtyard having access to the street only through the coach gateway, with the opposite façade of the house opening onto the gardens.

Among the numerous châteaux built in the 17C and 18C, those of Bussy-Rabutin, Commarin, Grancey, Beaumont-sur-Vingeanne, Menou and Talmay deserve a special mention. The sculptors – Dubois in the 17C and Bouchardon and Attiret in the 18C – were very influential, as were painters and draughtsmen such as Greuze and François Devosge and above all Mignard, master painter at the court of Louis XIV.

Burgundy prides itself on its contribution to the musical world, **Jean-Philippe Rameau**, born in Dijon at the end of the 17C. He was a contemporary of Bach and Handel and ranks as one of the great French classical composers. Besides many pieces for the harpsichord, he composed some operas, of which one, *Les Indes Galantes*, is still included in the contemporary repertoire.

19C and 20C – In architecture, **Gustave Eiffel** (1832-1923), an engineer from Dijon, specialised in metal construction: bridges, viaducts etc. The mention of his name conjures up the tower he erected in Paris for the universal exhibition in 1889; its structure is based on a web of girders.

In Jura

The architectural heritage of the region of Franche-Comté reflects its turbulent history even now, after centuries as a point of meeting and exchange of ideas and people passing through, not to mention the strategic value its position was perceived to give it, regardless of which particular power claimed to have authority over it at the time. The region was regularly subjected to the ravages of war and invasion, and it spent most of its infrequent periods of peace rebuilding its ruins. For this reason, there are relatively few real architectural masterpieces. However, the restrained style of the buildings has its own particular charm, with occasional hints of foreign influences. During the **Gallo-Roman** period, Sequania was wealthy, but little trace of this glorious past remains after the invasions of the 9C and 10C, which cost the Sequani dear as they struggled to defend themselves. The Roman triumphal arch which the inhabitants of Besançon call Porte Noir (the black gate), the Roman road at Boujailles, the remains of a theatre at Mandeure near Montbéliard are about all that is left from this period.

The Middle Ages – After the Carolingian invasions and the subsequent disintegration of Carolingian rule, power devolved into the hands of local lords. These immediately felt the need to protect themselves and their property, and turned to the Scandinavians for a design of fairly crude castle: the **keep** or **castle mound** (11C). This construction consisted of a mound (of earth) surrounded by a moat, and surmounted by a square wooden tower, which was later replaced by a stone tower.

At the same time, **stone fortresses** (Pesmes, Champlitte) made their appearance, generally built on existing hills. The surrounding fortified wall – a stone embankment with a moat around its outer edge – enclosed the living quarters and outbuildings, whereas the keep remained the stronghold. This kind of fortress reached its apogee in the late 12C and the 13C.

At this point, a new kind of seigneurial dwelling evolved with the rise of the middle-ranking class of knights: the **fortified house** (especially after 1250). This would be located just outside the village near a stream or river, and would be constructed on a man-made platform surrounded by a water-filled moat. The buildings – residential wings and outbuildings – are arranged around a central courtyard.

Fortresses did not fare at all well during the 14C and 15C, as first the Hundred Years War, then the guns of Louis XI's troops wreaked devastation. However, the Château du Pin (15C), which is very well preserved, is an interesting example of medieval military architecture.

At the end of the Gothic period, town houses began to feature more prominently, and were decorated in particular with mullioned windows surmounted by ogee arches.

Renaissance – The return of peace and prosperity to Franche-Comté during the 16C was marked by numerous castles being modified to reflect the new style, while at the same time having their defences reinforced to withstand the new metal cannon balls, which were much more destructive than the old stone ones (reinforcement of the ramparts, piercing of loopholes for guns, construction of gun towers to protect the entrance etc). But the aristocracy tended to prefer their mansions in town where Renaissance art really came into its own.

Unlike religious architecture, civil architecture drew very little inspiration from Gothic art, while it was wide open to the graceful, attractive lines and forms which arrived from Italy. Emperor Charles V's Chancellor, Perrenot de Granvelle, set the example by building himself a mansion in Besançon in 1534. On the façades of Franch-Comté, different styles were superimposed on columns (Hôtel de Ville at Gray), moulded bands were added between storeys, ogee arches above windows gave way to simpler geometric forms. On the ground floor, the basket-handle arch was used for doorways or open arcades, introducing a regular movement clearly Spanish in inspiration (the interior courtyard of the Palais Granvelle at Besançon). Architectural renewal was apparent in floral decoration, as on the façade of the château of Champlitte *(see photograph)*. The decorative artist and architect Hugues Sambin (1518-1601), born near Gray and well known for the projects he completed in Burgundy, left a magnificent example of his energetic artistic creativity on the polychrome façade of the Palais de Justice at Besançon (1581), which is his finest piece of work in Jura.

Classical – In the 17C, Franche-Comté was crushed by the Ten Years War. It was not until after 1674, when the province was incorporated into France, that a new architectural impetus came to life. The strategic position of the region, between the Vosges and the Jura mountain ranges, compelled the French kingdom to consider implementing a comprehensive project of fortification without further ado. The task was entrusted to Vauban, who paid particular attention to the defence of the points along the routes leading to Switzerland which were the only possible way to get through. Although part of it has been destroyed, Vauban's monumental work has left an indelible impression on parts of the Jura countryside. The royal architect's greatest achievement is to have developed the concept of bastion layout (adopted during the 16C) to its maximum potential, the underlying principle being to run a curtain wall between two bastions in such a way that the two protect

Château de Champlitte

each other. This idea had undergone significant development before Vauban, but he not only refined it to its definitive form, but was able to adapt it to suit the terrain of any site, whether it be a fortified town wall (Belfort, Besançon – which also has an impressive citadel) or an isolated fortress (Fort St-André near Salins-les-Bains).

Civil architecture flourished in its turn in the 18C, which was a richly productive period for art in Franche-Comté. The most original work of this period is the royal salt works at Arc-et-Senans, designed as an ideal town by visionary architect Ledoux *(see Arc-et-Senans)*. Châteaux (typically on a horseshoe layout, as at Moncley), private houses and civil buildings display perfectly symmetrical façades, pierced with large windows surmounted by triangular or rounded pediments. Another characteristic of these monuments, which some consider to be on a level of perfection with the Louis XVI style, is their traditional high roof.

19C and 20C – In the region of Franche-Comté, military architecture continued to evolve throughout the 19C and 20C. In the 19C, a number of fortresses were built (including the large fort at Les Rousses) to improve sites vulnerable to gun warfare. Most of these constructions have survived, although they are not easily seen nowadays. The invention of the torpedo shell in 1885, then of the double-action fuse meant that forts were abandoned in favour of semi-underground concrete bunkers. During the Second World War, the French High Command even went so far as to build 30 or so blockhouses to protect Swiss neutrality. Modern architecture has produced some great works of civil engineering in the region; in the 19C, impressive viaducts (Morez) were built to span some of the Jura gorges. Since the war, engineers have been concerned mainly with constructing dams; the Génissiat dam (1948) on the Rhône and the Vouglans dam (1968) in the Ain Valley are two impressive examples.

RURAL ARCHITECTURE

The wine-growers of Burgundy have large, comfortable houses, vertical in construction; the wine vats and storerooms are on the ground floor, whereas the living quarters are on the first floor. An outside staircase protected by a roof leads from the ground floor up. Often the houses are built into the hillside. The storage rooms may be partly underground, but are protected from fluctuations in temperature in any event by thick stone walls.

The farmhouses of the riche **Bresse plain**, often standing in solitary splendour in the middle of the fields, look pretty much the same as they always did, although the cob walls and thatched roofs have

Farmhouse in Saint-Trivier-de-Courtes

gradually given way to bricks and tiles. The houses are low, with a wide overhanging roof for drying maize. Inside, there is the traditional stove room. An unusual feature of a few 17C and 18C houses is the **Saracen chimney**, sitting high atop the roof like a belfry *(see page 187)*.

The rooftops of Burgundy

While Burgundy naturally brings to mind good wine and food, and is steeped in European history, the pictoral image it first inspires is certainly the colourful rooftops of the Hôtel-Dieu in Beaune, the Hôtel de Vogüe in Dijon or the château at Rochepot.

Tiled roof,
les Hospices de Beaune

These **glazed ploychrome tiles**, laid out in various geometrical designs, may have arrived in Burgundy from Central Europe via Flanders, it is not certain. The intricate patterns carry symbolic messages, relating to politics or religion; they may signify the social status of a noteworthy resident, or the reputation of a religious or lay community.

Finials in glazed earthenware, ornate weathervanes and crockets are all decorative features of the pinnacles and crests of the distinctive roofs of Burgundy, especially in the Côte d'Or region.

Upland, the broad, slanted roofs are covered in flat tiles known as **tuiles de Bourgogne**; long and narrow, they are dark brown in colour. Cistercian monks (at Pontigny in particular, where they dug out the clay) used these tiles to cover their abbeys. Manufactured tiles came to replace this traditional material, yet its use has been widespread in Ile-de-France and Normandy and even as far away as Perigord.

Some tiles, known as **laves** are by-products from quarrying operations. An upper layer was removed from the surface of building stones below. Roofers used these leftover pieces, interspersed with small rocks (as in the church at Ozenay in the Mâconnais region), to provide a well-aerated covering, protected from freezing temperatures. The considerable weight (600-800kg/1 320-1 760lb per m^2) of the tiles required heavy-duty (and expensive) framework. In the Morvan, thatch has slowly replaced tile and slate as roofing material.

The area around Tournus is a transitional zone where flat tiles are used on the main house, and rounded tiles, **tuile canal** on the outbuildings or porch roof. Rounded tiles are more prevalent in the southern reaches of Burgundy; the pitch of the roofs decreases (less than 35°), framing is different. In Beaujolais, the style already shows Mediterranean influence.

In **Jura**, besides the traditional **chalets** (wooden buildings on a stone foundation) scattered across the alpine meadows, there are **mountain houses** which consist of living quarters, stable and barn all under the same roof. These houses are squat and compact; they are built as close to the ground so as to shut out the wind. The low, thick stone walls have tiny windows; those on the sides exposed to wind and snow are protected by wooden slats known as *tavaillons*. Roofing materials are the tiles typical of Jura or, more commonly, steel sheeting. The living quarters occupy the

House in Haute-Saône

ground floor: the *houteau*, or kitchen, in which there is almost always a huge fireplace, and the *poêle*, a big heated room used as a bedroom or, on special occasions, a dining room. The stable next door is joined to the house so that it can be entered without having to go outside. The barn is on the first floor and has a special opening through which fodder can be thrown down into the stable below. The barn can also be accessed from outside up a short steep slope.

The typical dwelling of the plateaux shares similarities with that of the mountains, not least the accommodation of man and beast under the same roof. However, these houses are usually taller and have a rectangular roof with edges that slope steeply downwards, covered in the tiles typical of Jura or else ordinary red tiles.

Two partition walls divide the ground floor interior lengthwise to separate the living quarters from the stable by the barn in between. The barn can be entered through a side door with a semicircular arch. The main rooms are as above, but the first floor is often also given over to bedrooms.

PAINTING AND SCULPTURE

In Burgundy

Pre-Romanesque – During this period, sculpture was clumsily executed: the crypt of Flavigny-sur-Ozerain, all that remains of an 8C basilica, contains four shafts of columns, of which three appear to be Roman and the fourth Carolingian. The capitals are of great interest: they carry a decoration of fairly crudely executed flat foliage. Two of the capitals in the crypt of the cathedral of St-Bénigne at Dijon are decorated on each face by a man with his arms raised in prayer.

The capitals, which were sculpted in situ, reflect the experimental nature of the work; some sides are no more than rough outlines.

During the same period, frescoes and glazed surfaces were used in the decoration of the walls of religious buildings. In 1927, fine frescoes representing the stoning of St Stephen (among other secenes) were discovered in the crypt of St-Germain in Auxerre.

Romanesque sculpture – The Cluny School of sculpture is the most significant development in the Romanesque period. The great Benedictine abbey of Cluny attracted large numbers of sculptors and image-carvers, thus becoming almost the only creative centre from 1095 to 1115.

An art form was born that payed great attention to form and detail. Artists revealed a new interest in nature in the variety of vegetation and keenly observed poses of the human figures they carved on the capitals in the choir (only rare examples survive). The figures are draped in flowing tunics, creating an outline which is in keeping with the serenity they were desired to express. The influence of Cluny's sculpture was at first apparent in the church of Ste-Madeleine at Vézelay – both in the carved capitals and in the tympanum of the doorway in the narthex, which shows Christ sending out his Apostles before his ascension into heaven. The composition contains a sweeping movement which represents the Holy Spirit; the bodies and draperies seem to be caught up in a wind. This sculpture (1120) has much in common with the doorway of the church of St-Lazare in Autun, where the Last Judgment (1130-1135) contains elongated figures draped in pleated robes more closely moulded on the bodies than at Vézelay.

Gislebertus, the sculptor at Autun, here and elsewhere in his work

Capital illustrating the flight from Egypt, Autun

B. Kaufmann/MICHELIN

expresses the full range of human attitudes and sentiments. The capitals in the nave and choir depict scenes from the Bible and the lives of the saints; they provided inspiration for the vigorous talent of the artists who created St-Andoche in Saulieu.

The two doorways of the church of St-Lazare in **Avallon**, which date from the mid 12C, reveal a desire for a new style: luxuriant decoration including wreathed columns, an expression of the Baroque tendency of Burgundian Romanesque art, is depicted side by side with a column statue which recalls Chartres. The gravity and troubling presence of the round bosses on the tomb of St Lazarus in Autun (1170-1184) already point forward to the Gothic style.

The Brionnais, where there is an unusual profusion of sculpted doorways, seems to have been the oldest centre for Romanesque sculpture in Burgundy. From the mid-11C to the great projects of Cluny this region produced a slightly crude and gauche style: the figures are bunched and their movements lack elegance. After working in Cluny, where they were summoned by Abbot Hugh of Semur, the Brionnais artists introduced a new grace into their work, elongating the figures and creating less rigid compositions. These sophisticated trends appeared beside traditional elements, such as a taste for short compact figures, and evolved towards a certain mannerist decorative style (tympanum of St-Julien-de-Jonzy).

Romanesque painting – The crypt of the cathedral in Auxerre contains some 11C frescoes depicting Christ on horseback, holding a rod of iron in his right hand. At Anzy-le-Duc, restoration work carried out in the choir in the middle of the 19C uncovered a large collection of mural paintings which had different characteristics from those at Auxerre: very subdued, dull tints with dark outlines covering a background composed of parallel bands.

Another style (blue backgrounds) appears at Cluny and at Berzé-la-Ville, in the chapel of the Château des Moines, where one can see a fine collection of Romanesque mural paintings. These frescoes, uncovered at the end of the 19C, were painted in the early years of the 12C. The use of glossy, bright paints is the distinctive feature of this innovative technique. As Berzé-la-Ville was one of the residences of the abbots of Cluny where St Hugh came to stay on several occasions, it appears certain that these frescoes were painted by the same artists employed in the building of the great abbey. The imposing Christ in Majesty, surrounded by six Apostles and numerous other figures, is of Byzantine inspiration and seems to have been copied from the mosaics of the Empress Theodora in the church of San Vitale in Ravenna.

This similarity between Cluniac and Byzantine art is explained by the leading role played by St Hugh, who used examples furnished by the Roman and Carolingian basilicas, which were strongly influenced by Byzantine art. Thus, in architecture, sculpture and painting, the influence of Cluny was the determining factor in the art of the 12C, and the destruction of the majority of the great abbey at the end of the 18C can be viewed as an irreparable loss. The remains that have survived give a very incomplete idea of what was without doubt the synthesis of Romanesque art.

S. Sauvignier/MICHELIN

Fresco in the crypt of the
Auxerre Cathedral museum

Gothic sculpture – This concedes nothing in vitality and quality to Romanesque sculpture.

13C – The influence of the Paris and Champagne regions is evident in the composition and presentation of subjects, but the Burgundian temperament appears in the interpretation of some scenes, where local artists have given free rein to their fantasy and earthy realism.

A great part of the statuary of this period was destroyed or damaged during the Revolution; some examples of this 13C art survive in Vézelay, St-Père, Semur-en-Auxois, St-Thibault, Notre-Dame in Dijon and Auxerre.

In Notre-Dame in Dijon, some masks and faces are treated with an extremely elaborate realism, whereas others have an authenticity and an expression of such good nature that one is forced to think that they are portraits of Burgundians taken from real life. The doorway of St-Thibault-en-Auxois presents a number of scenes depicting the Virgin Mary but, more noticeably, five large statues portraying Duke Robert II and his family, among others. This rare example of lay personalities represented on the doorway of a church of this period is explained by the important part played by the Duke in the building of this church.

At St-Père the sculpted decoration of the gable on the west front is repeated in an interesting floral decoration on the capitals. It is probable that the gable of the Vézelay basilica was inspired by St-Père, but the statutes in St-Père are of a much finer workmanship than those in Vézelay.

The tympanum of the Porte des Bleds in Semur-en-Auxois depicts the legend of St Thomas: the figures are heavy and the draperies lack grace – characteristics of the Burgundian style. This style was modified at the end of the 13C and became more plastic: the bas-relief sculptures on the base of the doorways on the western side of Auxerre Cathedral are of a delicacy and grace never achieved before. These masterpieces were unfortunately badly damaged during the Revolution.

14C – The advent of the Great Dukes of Burgundy in 1364 coincided with a period of political expansion and the spread of artistic influence in the Duchy of Burgundy.

In 1377, Philip the Bold began the construction of the Chartreuse de Champmol at the gates of Dijon, destined to be the burial place of the new dynasty. The Duke spared no expense in the decoration of this monastery, bringing to Burgundy from his northern territories a large number of artists, many of whom were of Flemish origin.

Of the artists who in turn worked on the magnificent tomb now to be seen in the guard-room in the Dijon museum, Claus Sluter (c 1345-1405) is incontestably the greatest. He knew how to give the personalities he depicted an outstanding poise, movement and vitality. His work was continued by his nephew, Claus de Werve, who abandoned the brutal realism of his uncle's style in favour of a more gentle approach. The draperies and clothes on the statues of Philip the Bold and Margaret of Flanders in the doorway of the Chartreuse de Champmol, which are regarded as authentic portraits, are treated with consummate artistry, and the faces have a striking realism. The tableau includes the Virgin and Child against the central pillar and the donors' patron saints: St John the Baptist and St Catherine.

A new trend in sculpture emerged: statues ceased to be part of pillars and doorways; facial expressions were treated with realism, and the artist, searching for authentic representation first and foremost, did not hesitate to portray ugliness or suffering.

Claus Sluter was also the artist of the great cross that was to have surmounted the well in the charter house cloisters (Puits de Moïse). The fine head of Christ, which luckily escaped destruction, is kept at the archaeological museum in Dijon. The faces of Moses and the five Prophets represented on the base of the calvary are striking in their realism, and the costumes are long flowing draperies in broken folds. In both cases the subjects have been carefully studied and then portrayed in extraordinary detail, giving the composition an outstanding vitality and great intensity of expression, which have won the work acclaim as one of the great masterpieces of 14C sculpture.

Detail of the Puits de Moïse

15C – The tomb of Philip the Bold has given rise to many imitations: the mausoleum of John the Fearless and Margaret of Bavaria is a faithful replica; the tomb of Philippe Pot, Seneschal of Burgundy, shows more originality, since it is the mourners who support the flagstone bearing the recumbent figure.

Sculpture now turned to a different style from that of the 13C; proportions were more harmonious and the draperies simpler. The Virgin Mary in the Musée Rolin at Autun is a good example of this particular Burgundian style.

Representations of the Entombment or the Holy Sepulchre became more popular. The most remarkable of these compositions, grouping seven figures around the dead Christ, are to be found in the hospital at Tonnerre, in the church of Notre-Dame in Semur-en-Auxois and in the hospital at Dijon.

Some carved and gilded wooden retables were executed at this time by Jacques de Baërze: the retable of the Crucifixion and the retable of the Saints and Martyrs are on display in the Salle des Gardes of the Dijon museum.

Two other 15C Flemish retables, one depicting the Passion and the other the Virgin Mary, are preserved in the little church at Ternant.

Gothic painting – The great Valois dukes surrounded themselves with painters and illuminators whom they brought from Paris or from their possessions in Flanders. In Dijon, Jean Malouel, Jean de Beaumetz and André Bellechose, natives of the north, created an artistic style remarkable for its richness of colour and detail of design, a synthesis of Flemish and Burgundian styles.

Among the best-known works, the polyptych in the Hôtel-Dieu at Beaune by Roger van der Weyden and the paintings in the Dijon museum are of great interest. During the Gothic period, frescoes came into favour again. Apart from the frescoes in the church of Notre-Dame in Beaune by Pierre Spicre, a painter of Dijon, the curious Dance of Death in the little church at La Ferté-Loupière is also noteworthy. Pierre Spicre created the designs for the remarkably bright tapestries in the church of Notre-Dame at Beaune.

The tapestries in the Hôtel-Dieu at Beaune, commissioned by Chancellor Nicolas Rolin in the 15C, are among the most beautiful of this period.

The Last Judgment, polyptych in Beaune's Hôtel-Dieu

Renaissance sculpture – While Burgundian Renaissance architecture was characterised by the triumph of horizontal lines and semicircular arches, sculpture of this style used the antique form of medallions and busts in high relief, and gradually replaced sacred subjects with the profane.

In the second half of the 16C, ornamental decoration such as that conceived by Hugues Sambin, artist of the gateway of the Palais de Justice in Dijon and probably also of a large number of mansions, was much in vogue in the city.

In the 16C, decorative woodwork – door panels, coffered ceilings, church stalls – was prevalent. The 26 stalls in the church of Montréal, carved in 1522, are a work of local inspiration in which the Burgundian spirit is plain for all to see.

Classical to modern – The transition from the 18C to the 19C is marked by Girodet, the famous citizen of Montargis. Proud'hon and Rude, both pupils of Devosges and attached to the academic tradition, were producing paintings and sculpture at the beginning of the 19C; the work of the former is characterised by muted tones and dreamy, sensual figures; that of the latter recalls his Neoclassical debut, and the force of his subsequent expression of his romantic temperament in the Marseillaise on the Arc de Triomphe in Paris.

They were followed by Cabet, Jouffroy, and the contemporary sculptor François Pompon, all of whom contributed to the artistic reputation of Burgundy.

In Jura

Jura cannot pride itself on having been home to a regional school of painting or sculpture. However, despite having been under the influence mainly of Burgundian and Flemish artists, local artists produced numerous works of art which reflect their talent. Unlike painting, sculpture was overlooked by local artists as a way of expressing their ideas during the Romanesque period, and only appeared in very rare cases on capitals (Besançon Cathedral) or church doorways.

Romanesque painting – The art of painting underwent significant development during the 12C and 13C, while sculpture was making little progress. During the Romanesque and Gothic periods, artists turned to frescoes in particular to decorate the interiors of churches.

Gothic sculpture – During the 13C, craftsmen produced emotive wooden statues in a naïve style, mainly Virgins. It was not until the 14C that a real surge of creativity burst onto the scene, inspired by Burgundian art and in particular the work of Claus Sluter *(see above)*. The influence of the master's realism and expressive power can be clearly seen in the art of Franche-Comté of the 15C and even 16C (several examples at the collegiate church of Poligny, splendid statue of St Paul at Baume-les-Messieurs). The production and decoration of religious furniture also developed during this period: the magnificent choir stalls at St-Claude (15C) and the even more elaborate ones at Montbenoît (16C) are some interesting examples.

Carvings on a stall in Monbenoît Abbey

G. Magnin/MICHELIN

Gothic painting – In the 14C and 15C, the art of painting altarpieces spread at the same time as the fresco technique. Painters of altarpieces were primarily inspired by Flemish artists *(see the Passion altarpiece in the museum at Besançon)*. Unfortunately, in the 16C, the initial impetus of the primitive artists of Franche-Comté petered out. Jacques Prévost, trained in Italy, was the only artist to produce works of any quality (triptych at Pesmes). The aristocracy and merchant classes took advantage of their travels abroad to buy Flemish and Italian paintings, some of which are still part of the artistic heritage of Jura (church at Baumes-les-Messieurs, cathedral and Musée des Beaux-Arts at Besançon).

Renaissance sculpture – In the 16C, sculptural forms became less tortured, and Italian sculptors were brought in to participate in projects in Franche-Comté. The Gothic tradition was gradually dropped as local artists such as Claude Arnoux, known as Lullier (altarpiece of the Chapelle d'Andelot in the church at Pesmes), and Denis le Rupt (pulpit and organ loft in Notre-Dame at Dole) adopted the new style.

Classical to modern sculpture – During the Classical period, religious statuary became bogged down in academism. Only furniture still showed signs of the originality and good taste of the local artists (Fauconnet woodwork at Goux-les-Usiers). Later, some sculptors achieved a certain degree of fame, such as Clésinger, Luc Bretonand and above all Perraud (1819-76), who were inspired by the Romantic movement to produce sensitive, emotive works *(see LONS-LE-SAUNIER: Musée des Beaux-Arts)*.

At the end of the century, Bartholdi immortalised the resistance of the city of Belfort in 1870, by sculpting an enormous lion out of rock.

Classical to modern painting – From the 17C, French art became less regionalised. Famous artists from Jura include Jacques Courtois (1621-76), who specialised in painting battle scenes, Donat Nonotte (1708-85), a portrait painter from Besançon, and above all Courbet (1819-77), an ardent defender of realism.

Wine

Burgundy

Burgundy wines are so well known that the name itself is synonymous with the deep red colour of some of the great vintages; yet the fine white wines are certainly not to be neglected!

S. Sauvignier/MICHELIN

Irancy village and vineyards

The history of Burgundy wine – The cultivation of vines was introduced to the region by the Romans and spread rapidly. Wine from Burgundy was quick to win accolades, a historical fact confirmed by the names of certain vineyards (Vosne-Romanée) which recall the popularity of the wines with the Roman prefects of the province of Maxima Sequanorum.

In the 12C, Cistercian monks built up the vineyards, in particular the famous Clos-Vougeot. The local historian, Claude Courtépée, records that in 1359 Jean de Bussières, the Cistercian abbot, made a gift of 30 barrels of wine from the Clos de Vougeot vineyards to Pope Gregory XI. The grateful Pope did not forget this handsome gift and made the abbot a cardinal four years later. In the 15C the dukes of Burgundy took to styling themselves "lords of the best wines in Christendom" and supplying their wine to royalty. Louis XIV is known to have contributed to the fame of Côte de Nuits, whereas Madame de Pompadour favoured Romanée Conti, and Napoleon enjoyed his glass of Chambertin.

In the 18C, the wine trade began to evolve: the first commercial warehouses opened at Beaune, Nuits-St-Georges and Dijon, sending representatives all over France and Europe (Britain, Belgium, Scandinavia, Switzerland, Germany) to find new markets for Burgundy wines.

One of the enemies of the vine is a small aphid from America, phylloxera, which made its appearance in the Gard *département* in 1863. In 1878, it was found at Meursault and within a short time it had completely ravaged all the Burgundy vineyards, ruining local production. Luckily, disaster was checked by grafting French vines onto American root stock, which are resistant to phylloxera, enabling the gradual restoration of the Burgundy vineyards while preserving the quality of the wines.

Distribution of vineyards – 37 500ha/15 172 acres of vineyards producing officially registered vintages are to be found in the Yonne, Nièvre, Côte-d'Or, Saône-et-Loire and Rhône *départements*. Average annual production of high quality wines is about 1 800 000hl/40 000 000 gal.

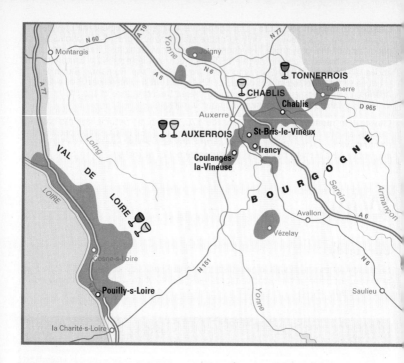

In the Yonne, the region of **Chablis** produces some excellent crisp, dry white wines, and the hillsides of the Auxerrois some pleasant rosés and reds (**Irancy, Coulanges-la-Vineuse**). Well-known wines such as **Pouilly-Fumé** come from Pouilly-sur-Loire in Nièvre. These wines have a flinty taste not unlike that of the neighbouring Sancerre wines. In the **Côte-d'Or** highly reputed vineyards stretch from Dijon to Santenay. The **Côte de Nuits** produces almost exclusively top vintage red wines, some of the most famous of which are **Gevrey-Chambertin, Morey-St-Denis, Chambolle-Musigny, Vougeot, Vosne-Romanée** and **Nuits-St-Georges**. The **Côte de Beaune** wines include both magnificent reds, such as **Aloxe-Corton, Savigny-lès-Beaune, Pommard** and **Volnay**, and very fine whites, such as **Corton-Charlemagne, Meursault, Puligny-Montrachet** and **Chassagne-Montrachet**.

In Saône-et-Loire, the Mercurey region (Côte Chalonnaise) produces high quality red (**Givry, Rully**) and white wines (**Rully-Montagny**), whereas the Mâconnais is justly proud of its **Pouilly-Fuissé**, which many consider to be one of the greatest white wines of France.

The many ingredients of a fine wine – The quality of a wine depends on grape variety *(cépage)*, and the type of soil and climate in which the vines grow. The work put in by the wine-grower also affects the final result.

Pinot Noir grapes

Grape varieties – All the great red Burgundy wines are made from the **Pinot Noir**, the aristocrat of grapes. It was already highly prized at the time of the Great Dukes, as illustrated by an edict issued by Philip the Bold in 1395 defending it against the more common Gamay. The Pinot Noir is native to Burgundy but has been successfully cultivated in Switzerland, and even in South Africa, in Cape Province. The juice of the Pinot Noir grape is colourless, and a special vinification process produces Champagne.

The **Chardonnay** grape is to white wines what the Pinot Noir is to red. It makes all the great white wines of the Côte d'Or (Montrachet-Meursault), the famous vintages of the Côte Chalonnaise (Rully), of the Mâconnais where it grows best (Pouilly-Fuissé) and the wines of Chablis (where it is known as the Beaunois grape).

Other grape varieties include the **Aligoté**, which has been cultivated for centuries in Burgundy, as it grows in

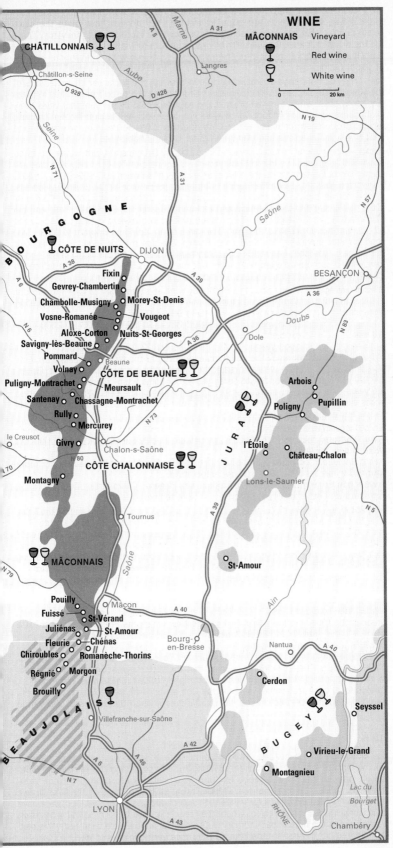

WINE

MÂCONNAIS Vineyard

Red wine

White wine

0   20 km

CHÂTILLONNAIS

Châtillon-s-Seine

Langres

B O U R G O G N E

CÔTE DE NUITS   DIJON

BESANÇON

Fixin

Gevrey-Chambertin

Chambolle-Musigny   Morey-St-Denis

Vosne-Romanée   Vougeot

Aloxe-Corton   Nuits-St-Georges

Savigny-lès-Beaune

Pommard   Beaune

Volnay   CÔTE DE BEAUNE

Puligny-Montrachet   Meursault

Santenay   Chassagne-Montrachet

Rully

Mercurey

le Creusot

Givry   Chalon-s-Saône

CÔTE CHALONNAISE

Montagny

Tournus

Dole

Doubs

Arbois

Pupillin

Poligny

l'Étoile

Château-Chalon

Lons-le-Saunier

J U R A

MÂCONNAIS

Pouilly

Fuissé   St-Vérand

Juliénas   St-Amour

Fleurie   Chénas

Chiroubles   Romanèche-Thorins

Régnié   Morgon

Brouilly

B E A U J O L A I S

Villefranche-sur-Saône

St-Amour

Mâcon

Bourg-en-Bresse

Nantua

Cerdon

B U G E Y

Seyssel

Virieu-le-Grand

Montagnieu

LYON

Chambéry

Lac du Bourget

RHÔNE

the areas where the Pinot Noir and Chardonnay grapes do not thrive, and which produces white wines which are popular, even if they do not have quite the same reputation for character and quality as those from the more famous vineyards. These are the wines that are combined with blackcurrant liqueur *(cassis))* to make the popular French apéritif known as Kir after the man who is credited with its invention, a mayor of Dijon, Canon Kir.

Soil – The soil type plays an important role in allowing the particular characteristics of the vines to develop, establish themselves and finally to come to fruition. It is in these dry, stony soils, which are well-drained and easily warmed by the sun, that vines grow best. Limestone soils produce wines with rich bouquets and a high alcohol content, which can be aged for many years (Côte de Nuits, Côte de Beaune), whereas mixed soils of silicas, limestone and clay yield lighter wines (Chablis).

Climate – The general climate prevailing in Burgundy is temperate, but winter frosts do occur and must be taken into consideration by the wine-grower. Burgundy vineyards are usually laid out in terraces on the hillsides at altitudes of between 200-500m/656-1 640ft. They seem to thrive best when facing south-east, in the case of the Chablis vineyards, south-west, in the case of those at Pouilly-sur-Loire, east-south-east for the Côte d'Or (Côte de Nuits and Côte de Beaune) and east and south for the Côte Chalonnaise and the Mâconnais. In each village, the vineyards are divided into *climats*, as determined by the soil content and exposure of the plot. The name of an individual vineyard with excellent conditions for producing fine wine, often known as a *clos*, may be added to the name of the village on the label; Beaune-Clos des Mouches is just one example. Some of the *climats* have earned such an excellent reputation over the years that their name alone suffices to identify them: Chambertin, Musigny, Clos de Vougeot and Richebourg.

Millésime and aging – When selecting a Burgundy wine, it is important to take into account the year in which it was bottled, as the weather conditions have a big impact on quality.

White wine:	excellent years:	1989-95-96-97
	good years:	1986-88-90-91-92-93-94-98-99-2000
Red wine:	excellent years:	1985-90-95-96-99
	good years:	1988-89-91-92-93-9497-98-2000

Although they do not enjoy the exceptional longevity of the famous *vin jaune du Jura*, Burgundy wines mature well and reach their peak after a few years of aging. Generally, they are best kept for five to seven years, but some white wines can age eight to ten years, and exceptional reds can be stored for up to 15 years. Wines mature best under carefully controlled conditions: a dark, well-ventilated area at a constantly cool temperature and about 70% humidity.

Serving Burgundy wines – Certain dishes enhance the pleasure of drinking Burgundy wines:
– with oysters, shellfish, fish: Chablis, Meursault, Pouilly-Fuissé, Mâcon, or other dry white wines, chilled;
– with fowl, veal, pork and light dishes: Côte de Beaune, Mercurey, Beaujolais or other light red wines served at the storage temperature;
– with game, red meat, wild mushrooms and cheese: Chambertin, Côte de Nuits, Pommard and other hearty reds served at room temperature.

Beaujolais wine – The Beaujolais vineyards cover an area 60km/37mi long and 12km/7.5mi wide from the Mâcon escarpment to the north to the Azergues Valley to the south. This area occupies about 22 500ha/55 595 acres and yields an average of 1 250 000hl/27 375 000 gallons of wine a year. The majority of these (99%) are red, exclusively from the Gamay grape. There are three categories of Beaujolais wine, starting with the *crus*, the best vintages, followed by **Beaujolais Villages** and **Beaujolais supérieurs**.

The 10 leading *crus* are **Moulin-à-Vent**, an elegant wine with lots of substance, which can be kept for 5-10 years, closely followed by **Morgon** with its fine bouquet, which has often been described as the "Beaujolais most like a Burgundy". Firm and fruity **Juliénas**, well-rounded **Chénas**, classy **Fleurie** and **Côte de Brouilly** all have a keen following, whereas the fresh and lively **Saint-Amour**, **Chiroubles** (which the French consider to be a feminine wine), **Brouilly** and **Régnié-Durette** (the baby of the *crus*, having been promoted in 1988) are best enjoyed young.

Fruity Beaujolais-Villages is at its best after about a year in the bottle. Beaujolais or Beaujolais *supérieurs* (the only difference being that the latter have a slightly higher alcohol content) do not age well and are best served slightly chilled (unlike most red wines).

Various local wine fraternities, such as the Compagnons de Beaujolais or the Gosiers secs (dry throats) de Clochemerle, voluntarily take it upon themselves to spread the good reputation of these wines abroad.

Jura

The vineyards of the historic Franche-Comté extend south-west of Salins, along a narrow strip of land 5km/3mi wide, covering the limestone and mixed clay and limestone slopes of the western edge of Jura. Four vintages are produced from these vineyards: **Arbois**, the most famous, **Château-Chalon**, **Étoile** and those of the **Côtes du Jura** appellation, which includes local wines such as Poligny and Arlay. Wine-growers have their work cut out in this region, where they regularly have to carry soil that has been washed down the hillside back to their vineyards. An annual Jura wine festival is held each September in Arbois – the Fête du Biou *(see Calendar of events)*.

Jura wines – Despite their knee-buckling effects, local followers of Bacchus sing their praises thus: *Du vin d'Arbois, Plus on en boit, Plus on va droit* (Wine of Arbois, the more you drink, the straighter you walk). Presumably one becomes hardened to their effect with regular consumption...

Grape varieties – The grape varieties cultivated in Jura include Trousseau for red wines, Poulsard for rosé, Chardonnay for white wines, and Savagnin, used to create the celebrated *Vin Jaune du Jura*.

Red wines are produced in small quantities and are fresh and fruity when young, developing a subtle, characteristic bouquet with age. The most famous **rosé wines** come from Arbois and Pupillin. With age,

Château-Chalon vineyards

M. Rock-Cephas Picture Library/TOP

the wines take on a pretty colour, like that of an onion skin. These lively but not over-powering wines have a pleasant fruity flavour. Local **white wines** are dry, yet supple, and fairly heady. They are produced essentially in the Arbois and Étoile regions. Not only do these wines accompany local dishes, they are excellent *apéritif* wines as well. The region also produces some **sparkling wines**, both white (Étoile, Arbois and Côtes du Jura) and rosé (Arbois and Côtes du Jura).

Vin jaune is a speciality of the Jura region (Château-Chalon and Arbois), made from the Savagnin grape only. The wine is left to age in barrels for 6-10 years, where it begins to oxidise and acquires its characteristic deep yellow colour and distinctive bouquet and flavour beneath a film of yeasts which forms over its surface (similar to the production of sherry). A good vintage can be kept for over a century. *Vin jaune* is relatively rare and expensive, and a degree of circumspection is required when choosing what to eat with it, because of its strong flavour. It is best savoured at room temperature, and a good companion to another local speciality, Comté cheese.

Vin de paille, straw wine, also particular to the Jura region, earns its name from the fact that the almost over-ripe grapes are dried on a bed of straw for a couple of months before being pressed. This produces a strong, sweet dessert wine, which is however quite rare (it takes about 100kg/220lb of grapes to produce 18l/4 gal of *vin de paille*!) and therefore expensive.

Macvin is another Jura dessert wine, made from grape must blended with Franche-Comté eau-de-vie, and it can reach up to 16-20% alcohol content. It is usually drunk chilled as an apéritif.

Red and rosé **Bugey wines** are light and fruity, but it is the white Bugey wines which are the best. Particularly good examples of these are Roussette and Seyssel, followed by more rare wines such as Virieu or Montagnieu. This region also produces some sparkling wines, **Seyssel** and **Cerdon**.

Gastronomy

In Burgundy

Burgundy's reputation as a gastronomic paradise has been established for a very long time. Dijon has been a city of fine food ever since Gallo-Roman times, judging from the culinary inscriptions and signs engraved on the stone tablets in the archaeological museum. In the 6C, Gregory of Tours praised the quality of Burgundian wines, and King Charles VI, still sane at the time, lauded the gastronomic delights available from Dijon, both good wines and local dishes. Under the Great Dukes, the Dijon palace was redolent with the odours of culinary artistry. The historic États Généraux de Bourgogne and the gastronomic fair at Dijon perpetuate this tradition of good food and wine in the region.

The raw materials – Land of many blessings, Burgundy is home to first-class beef cattle in the regions of Auxois, Bazois and Charollais, as well as some of the tastiest game in France. It produces incomparable vegetables, many varieties of fish (white fish from the Saône and Loire and trout and crayfish from the rivers and springs of the Morvan), the most delicious mushrooms (*cèpes*, *girolles*, *morilles* and *mousserons*), snails which are famous the world over and mouth-watering fruit (cherries from the Auxerre region, for example). And of course, Dijon is forever associated with the **mustards** produced there.

Burgundian cuisine is both rich and substantial, reflecting the Burgundian temperament and robust appetite; people here expect both quality and quantity at the table. Wine, the glory of the province, naturally plays an all important part: the *meurette* wine sauces are the pride of Burgundian cuisine; made from wine thickened with butter and flour with flavourings and spices added. These sauces blend well with fish – carp, tench and eel – brains, poached eggs and the famous **bœuf bourguignon** (Burgundian beef casserole).

The simple things in life

Cream is used in the preparation of many dishes: **jambon à la crème** (cooked ham in a cream sauce) and **champignons à la crème** (mushrooms in a cream sauce). **Saupiquet** is a spicy, wine and cream sauce that dates back to the 15C; its name is derived from the old French verb *saupiquer* – to season with salt.

Burgundian specialities – Beyond the long-simmering *boeuf bourguignon*, the cuisine of this region is renown for **escargots** (snails cooked in their shells with garlic, butter and parsley), **jambon persillé** (ham seasoned with parsley), **andouillette** (small sausages made from chitterlings), **coq au vin** (chicken in a wine sauce), **pauchouse** (stew of various types of fish cooked in white wine) and **poulet en sauce** (chicken cooked in a cream and white wine sauce).

In the Nivernais and Morvan regions, home-cured ham and sausage, ham and eggs, calf's head *(sansiot)*, eggs cooked in wine *(en meurette)*, roast veal and pullet fried with bacon and pearl onions *(jau au sang)* figure among the traditional dishes.

Perhaps the greatest moment in the meal comes with the **cheese** course. A good vintage wine enhances the experience of eating **Soumaintrain**, **Saint-Florentin**, **Époisses**, **Bouton-de-culotte**, or **Citeaux**, all produced locally. A traditional preparation that honours a great vintage is **gougère**, cheese pastry.

In Jura

Poultry and freshwater fish go particularly well with Jura wines, and **coq au vin jaune** or **truite au vin jaune** are classic local specialities.

Game is in abundant supply throughout Jura, and there are many traditional local recipes for hare, young wild boar, venison, woodcock etc. Wild hare in a white wine sauce with diced bacon, venison casserole with cream, and roast thrush (yes, really!) flambéed in Marc d'Arbois are just a few popular local dishes.

Potée is made with a variety of vegetables cooked slowly in a casserole, with a strong smoky flavour added by the inclusion of delicious Morteau sausage, a speciality of this region, as is sausage from Montbéliard. Local *charcuterie*, such as Jésus from Morteau and the numerous smoked hams (Luxeuil-les-Bains), is also widely appreciated.

Fondue de Franche-Comté

For 4-5 people. Put 1/4 pint - 2/3 cup of dry white wine into a saucepan with a chopped clove of garlic and cook it until the wine is reduced by half. Strain it and leave it to cool.

In a bowl beat 6 eggs with 1/2 lb of grated Gruyère cheese, 4 tablespoons of butter, some ground black pepper and a little salt. Add the wine, pour the mixture into an ovenproof dish and stir constantly over a low flame until smooth and creamy.

Serve at once in the pan in which it has cooked, bubbling hot. Squares of bread or toast are dipped in the fondue (it gets even better towards the bottom of the pot) using a long-handled fork. This fondue is different from the Swiss variety, which does not include eggs, and uses a dash of kirsch.

Pork and bacon were for centuries the only meat eaten in the mountain regions. The pig was therefore the object of great care and attention on the farms, and careful calculation went into the diet on which it was fattened. On pig-killing day, an occasion for great celebration in the family, a pig feast was prepared consisting simply of black pudding (boudin), sausages made from tripe (andouilles), head-cheese (fromage de tête), chops and various other bits and pieces from the pig.

In Jura, there are as many types of fish as there are rivers and lakes for them to thrive in: char and trout from the Loue; carp and pike from the Doubs; tench and perch from the Ain. In the lakes there are fish from the salmon family (Coregonidae), white fish and small fry. Meurette sauces and pauchouse stew are as popular here as in Burgundy in the preparation of fish dishes.

Mushrooms from the forests – morilles, chanterelles and cèpes – add their delicate flavour to aromatic sauces or blend with unctuous creamy sauces and a good local wine.

It would be a crime to leave Jura without appreciating some of the local cheeses: **Comté**, with its hazelnut flavour, can be melted in a saucepan with white wine to make a **fondue**, for dipping chunks of crusty bread. Try a mild and delicate **Emmenthal**, rich and creamy **Morbier**, or **Mont d'Or**, a subtly flavoured cheese made from milk from cows that have been kept on mountain pastures. **Gex Septmoncel** is a blue cheese with a delicate parsley flavour; the famous **Cancoillotte**, a soft fermented cheese, is one of the region's oldest and most typical specialities.

To top off your meal in style, all the local vineyards produce good quality **marc** spirits, but the **kirsch** from the Loue Valley (Mouthier-Haute-Pierre, Ornans) is particularly well regarded. Pontarlier, generally acknowledged as the capital of absinthe, produces an apéritif based on green aniseed, **Pontarlier Anis**. Liqueurs made from gentian and pine in the Haut-Jura plateaux are also popular.

How Comté cheese is made

Comté is a registered product subject to quality control. The cheese is made from the milk of Montbéliard stock or red and white cows from the east of France, which have been fed exclusively on grass and hay. The milk is skimmed of 5-15% of its cream content to produce a cheese which has a fat content of about 48-50g/1.7-1.8oz per 100g/3.5oz of dry mass. The milk is then poured into huge copper cauldrons, with a capacity of 800, 1 400 or even 2 500l (177, 311 or 555gal), where it is heated to about 32°C/90°F and curdled with rennet. It is then drained, and the curds are beaten and heated to between 54-56°C/129-133°F, put into a linen cloth, placed into a mould and then pressed. The resulting round of cheese can weigh up to 40-50kg/88-110lb. The cheese is put into a cold cellar for a few days, where it is salted and rubbed to speed up the formation of the rind. After this, the maturing process begins. The cheese is kept for a maximum of three to nine months in a cellar, initially at a temperature of 16-18°C/60-65°F for two months, and thereafter at between 10-12°C/50-54°F. The rind is rubbed with a cloth soaked in salt solution to encourage the growth of the moulds which give the Comté cheese its characteristic hazelnut flavour.

The uninitiated believe that the more holes there are in a Gruyère cheese, the better it is. However, this is certainly not the case with Comté. The finest, richest Comté cheese is that with no (or at least, very few) holes.

Glazed tiles on the roof of the Hôtel-Dieu in Beaune

ALISE-STE-REINE

Population 674
Michelin map 320: G-4
16km/10mi north-east of Semur-en-Auxois

Alise-Ste-Reine is situated on the steep slopes of Mont Auxois (407m/1 335ft) between the Oze and Ozerain valleys overlooking the plain of Les Laumes. The first part of the village's name is derived from Alésia, a Gaulish, then Gallo-Roman settlement on the plateau. The second part recalls a young Christian woman, Reina, who was martyred locally *(see Additional Sights below)* in the 3C; her feast day in September attracts many pilgrims.

Siege of Alésia – After his defeat at Gergovie (near Clermont-Ferrand in the Auvergne) in the spring of 52 BC, **Caesar** retreated towards the north to join forces with the legions of his lieutenant, Labienus, near Sens. Once the legions were united they began marching towards the Roman base camps, but on the way they were intercepted and atttacked near Alésia by the army of the Gauls, under **Vercingétorix**. Despite the surprise of their attack and their superior numbers, the Gauls suffered a crushing defeat, and Vercingetorix, fleeing from Caesar, decided to retreat with his remaining troops to the camp at Alésia.

Vercingétorix
B. Kaufmann/MICHELIN

A memorable siege began. Caesar's legions worked with pick and shovel to surround the camp with a double line of fortified earthworks, such as trenches, walls, palisades of stakes and towers; the inner ring of earthworks faced Alésia and was designed to prevent any attempts on the part of the besieged to escape, and the outer ring faced outwards to fight off any attacks from Gaulish armies trying to relieve the besieged camp. For six weeks Vercingetorix tried in vain to break through the rings that Caesar had set up. A rescue army of Gauls, 250 000 strong, was also powerless to reach the besieged and finally withdrew, abandoning them to their fate. With all hope of escape gone, Vercingetorix was forced to surrender and, to save his army, gave himself up to Caesar, who paraded him in triumph and eventually had him strangled after imprisoning him for six years in the Tullianum in Rome.

A battle of experts – During the 19C, some historians hotly disputed the site of Alésia as the scene of the siege, placing the combat between Caesar and Vercingetorix at Alaise, a little village in the *département* of Doubs, near the road from Ornans to Salins. To put an end to the controversy, Napoleon III had excavations carried out at Alise-Ste-Reine from 1861 to 1865. These revealed the presence of extensive military works built by Caesar's legions in the whole region of Mont Auxois, as well as the bones of men and horses and a mass of objects left behind during the siege: silver coins, millstones for cereals, weapons and weaponry. However, the erection of a huge statue to Vercingetorix on the site in 1865 by no means put an end to the polemics. The opposing theory had a keen advocate in the erudite **Georges Colomb** (1856- 1945) who, under the pseudonym of Christophe, was also the author of two well-known books for young people, *La Famille Fenouillard* and *L'Idée fixe du savant Cosinus*. More recently, excavations at Chaux-des-Crotenay to the south-east of Champagnole in the Jura have revealed another site which also claims to be Alésia.

Modern technology – aerial photographs and sample bores – has been pressed into service in support of the Burgundian claim. Information panels and markers at the side of the roads around Mont Auxois show where these roads intersect the ditches recognised by archaeologists as Roman trenches, or more precisely, the circumvallation and contravallation Caesar had built around Alésia.

The latest excavation work (1991-98) undertaken in the area could not reconcile Caesar's account of the battle with what was found on location and, in November 1998, it was officially stated that Alise was no longer considered as the site of the battle of Alesia. The mystery remains intact.

★ MONT AUXOIS

★ Panorama – There is a good viewpoint from beside the bronze statue of Vercingetorix by Millet. The panorama *(viewing table)* extends over the plain of Les Laumes and the site of the Roman outworks as far as the outskirts of Saulieu.

Les Fouilles ⊙ **(Excavations)** – The summit of the fortified settlement *(oppidum)* was occupied by a Gallo-Roman town which derived its prosperity from its metallurgical activity. The tour *(signs and numbered sites)* indicates the different districts grouped round the forum.

The western district contained the theatre (which in its final form dates from the 1C AD), the religious buildings and a civilian basilica. The northern district was prosperous and has shops, the bronze-workers' guild house and a large mansion, heated by a hypocaust (an ancient form of central heating beneath the floor), where a statue of the mother goddess was found in the cellar, hence the name

Cave à la Mater. The craftsmen's district to the south-east is composed of small houses, some with a yard where the craftsman plied his trade. To the south-west, the ruins surrounded by a cemetery belong to a Merovingian basilica dedicated to St Reina; this was the last building to be constructed on the plateau before the population moved down to the site of the present village.

The finds uncovered during the excavations are on display in the Musée Alésia.

Musée Alésia ⊘ – The museum is owned by the Société des Sciences of Semur-en-Auxois and contains all the objects found during the excavation of the Gallo-Roman town: statues and statuettes, fragments of buildings, reconstructed façade of a Gallo-Roman chapel, coins, pottery and other objects made of bronze, iron or bone. The 4C set of sacred vessels is dedicated to St Reina. In addition, various exhibits evoke the siege of Alésia.

ADDITIONAL SIGHTS

Fontaine Ste-Reine – Legend has it that a miraculous fountain gushed up from the spot where St Reina, a young Christian woman condemned to death for refusing to marry the Roman governor Olibrius, was beheaded. Up to the 18C, the curative powers of its waters were much esteemed; the fountain still attracts many pilgrims even now. The nearby chapel contains a much venerated 15C statue of the saint.

Église St-Léger – This 7C-10C church, now restored to its original appearance, was built on the usual basilical layout with a timber roof over the nave and an over-vaulted apse. The south wall is of Mervingian construction; the one facing it dates from the later Carolingian period.

Théâtre des Roches – The theatre was built in 1945, modelled on ancient theatres, for performances of the mystery play performed as part of the annual pilgrimage in honour of St Reina *(see Calendar of events)*.

AMBRONAY

Population 2 146
Michelin map 328: F-4 – 6km/3.7mi N of Ambérieu

Ambronay developed around a Benedictine abbey founded in the 9C by St Bernard, one of Charlemagne's knights (ruins of the old Carolingian church have been found under the choir and chancel).

The abbey has, for over 20 years, been the main venue of a renowned Baroque music festival.

Ancienne abbaye ⊘ – The church, cloister and chapter-house, as well as most of the conventual buildings, remain of the **abbey**, which has been re-built several times.

Cloisters

★ **Church** – This dates mainly from the 13C and 15C, with one or two even older remains. Many of the figures on the façade were destroyed during the Rev-olution. The lintel of the door-way on the left represents scenes from the Life of the Vir-gin. The Resurrection of the Dead can be seen on the lintel of the central doorway (13C, extensively restored); at the centre, Abraham is gathering souls into the fold of his cloak. There is a beautiful line of smooth round columns (15C) along the south side of the nave, topped with sim-ple ring capitals, which support the arches of the vaulting. A 15C polychrome stone Pietà can be seen in a wall niche in the north side aisle.

The **Chapelle Ste-Catherine**, north of the chancel, contains the 15C **tomb**★ of Abbot Jacques de Mauvoisin, who had the church restored.

Cloître – *Access through a door in the south side aisle*. The cloisters, a beautiful 15C construction, consist of arcades with graceful tracery, surmounted by a gallery which one can reach by taking the substantially restored, Louis XIV corner staircase.

Château d'ANCY-LE-FRANC★★

Michelin map 319: H-5 – 18km/11mi SE of Tonnerre

This **château** ⊘ on the banks of the River Armançon is one of the most beautiful Renaissance mansions in Burgundy. Antoine III de Clermont, Governor of the Dauphiné and Grand Master of Waters and Forests, husband of Anne-Françoise de Poitiers (sister of François I's beautiful mistress Diane), had it built in 1546, using plans drawn by Sebastiano Serlio. This talented architect, who helped implant the principles of the Italian Renaissance in France, was an influential figure in the court of François I.

In 1684, the château was sold to Louvois, Minister of War under Louis XIV. The Louvois family held on to it until the mid-19C, when the Clermont-Tonnerre family recovered it; upon the death of the last duke, the property reverted to his nephews, the princes of Mérode. In 1980, the estate and its contents were sold and between 1985 and 1999 the castle was more or less abandoned.

Exterior – Louvois filled in the moats and Le Nôtre created the French gardens for him. The château, with four identical wings linked by corner pavilions, forms a perfectly symmetrical square.

Interior – Regional artists contributed to the sumptuous interior decoration, along with students of Primaticcio and Nicolo dell'Abbate. Over the years, the ambient humidity took its toll on these fragile works, which were restored in the 19C; while some works are more intact than others, they are remarkable on the whole. Most of the 16C furnishings were in place when the château was built. The overall effect is true to the original spirit.

Ground floor – *Closed for restoration*. Of particular interest are the **Salle de Diane**, where the Italian-style vaulted ceiling dates from 1578, and the vast kitchens.

First floor – Beginning in the south wing, admire the **Chapelle Ste-Cécile★**, on two levels, which, restored in 1860, is covered with barrel vaulting. The *trompe-l'œil* paintings (1596) depict the Fathers of the Desert; they are the work of André Meynassier, a Burgundian artist.

The impressive **Salle des Gardes**, was decorated especially for Henri III, although he never did live here. Facing the monumental fireplace is a full-length portrait of Marshall Gaspard de Clermont-Tonnerre (1759) by Aved. Note the varying attitude of the horses featured along the walls of the **Galerie Pharsale**. Beyond this gallery and the Chambre des Fleurs, the **Chambre des Arts★** contains a rare 16C Italian cabinet with inlaid decorative work. The walls of the **Chambre de Judith** are hung with nine high-quality paintings from the late 16C, depicting the story of Judith.

Judith and Holopherne are seen here as likenesses of Diane de Poitiers and François I.

The **Cabinet du Pasteur Fido★**, with its sculpted oak panelling, boasts a magnificent Renaissance coffered ceiling. The scenes decorating the upper part of the walls are based on an Arcadian oracle mentioning a faithful shepherd, hence the name of the room.

The library, which houses 3 000 volumes and the **Galerie des Sacrifices** lead to the **Salon Louvois★** (the former king's chamber where Louis XIV slept on 21 June 1674).

Chambre des Arts

P. Lefevre

ARBOIS ★

Population 3 698
Michelin map 321: E-5

Arbois is at the entrance of one of the beautiful blind rift valleys known as *reculées* in the Jura, on either bank of the Cuisance. It is a picturesque little town surrounded by vineyards, and is a very popular holiday centre. It is possible to taste some of the famous local wine in several wine-growers' cellars which are open to the public. From the path winding along the west bank of the Cuisance there is a beautiful view of the church of St-Just, the Château Bontemps (once the residence of the dukes of Burgundy), several old mills and the town.

In town, the **Pont des Capucins** offers a lovely view of the Cuisance, the hills, the old houses and the remains of the fortifications with two old towers, the Tour Gloriette and the Tour Chaffin.

Atelier M. Bevalot

Arbois

Hot tempers – The people of Arbois are renowned throughout Jura for their particularly irreverent and independent spirit. The Arbois wine-growers have always been acknowledged to have a relatively short fuse. People have lost count of the number of times they have staged some sort of uprising. So it was that they were quick to proclaim the Republic in 1834, when Lyon rose in revolt. But they were disconcerted to realise that the new regime did not extend beyond the walls of their own little town. They were forced, albeit reluctantly, to finally accept Louis-Philippe. This particular uprising gave birth to the famous remark "We are all the leader" (*No sin tous t'sefs*), when the Arbois citizens who had come to collect some gunpowder from Poligny were asked to name those who had led them in their revolt.

The Fête du Biou – This is the great Jura wine festival. On the first Sunday in September, the wine-growers of Arbois parade with an enormous bunch of grapes weighing 80-100kg/176-220lb, which is made of many smaller bunches of grapes bound together. It is carried by four men, who march along behind fiddle players, and behind these march the local dignitaries and wine-growers, escorted by soldiers of the *garde-fruits* carrying halberds festooned with vine shoots. After the procession, the *Biou* is hung in the nave of the church as an offering to St Just, the patron saint of Arbois.

PASTEUR IN ARBOIS

Pasteur's youth – Although Louis Pasteur was born in Dole, his true home in Jura was the town of Arbois. After his parents moved there in 1827, he spent his youth there, his parents died there, and to the end of his days Pasteur never failed to spend his holidays in Arbois. When the Pasteur family moved to Arbois, they settled in a tannery which the scientist later turned into a large comfortable residence. The father did all types of leather work; the mother ran the household, raised the children, and kept the accounts. The close family life in which a high moral code was adhered to marked the young Louis for life.

He attended primary school, then secondary school (the sundial he made is still in the school yard). He was a conscientious, serious worker, who devoted so much careful thought to things that he gave the impression of being rather slow, and he was never considered more than a

G. Magnin/MICHELIN

Louis Pasteur

Eating out

BUDGET

La Finette - Taverne d'Arbois – *22 av. Pasteur -* ☎ *03 84 66 06 78 - 14.94/45.43€*. This friendly tavern with its rustic decor and wooden tables extends a warm welcome to travellers. Sample regional cuisine, washed down by a fine selection of country wines.

MODERATE

Caveau d'Arbois – *3 rte de Besançon -* ☎ *03 84 66 10 70 - contact@sylver-tours.com - closed 4-26 Nov, Sun evenings and Mon Oct-Apr - 14/29€*. This country house stands near Arbois, which is famed for its vineyards. The traditional cuisine featuring a few regional dishes accompanied by local wines is served in a bright, sparsely furnished dining room.

La Balance Mets et Vins – *R. de Courcelles -* ☎ *03 84 37 45 00 - closed 9 Dec-30 Jan, Sun evenings and Mon (except 14 Jul-25 Aug and public holidays) - 17/34€*. If you come here in winter, you will have an opportunity to taste the generous cuisine, prepared by the owner on an old stove before your very eyes. Whatever the season, you will be treated to fresh ingredients, imaginative recipes and an interesting wine list.

Where to stay

BUDGET

Hôtel des Messageries – *R. de Courcelles -* ☎ *03 84 66 15 45 - hotel.lesmes-sageries@wanadoo.fr - closed Dec-Jan - 26 rooms: 27/51€ -* ☐ *5.80€*. This former coaching inn situated in the town centre is an old house overgrown with ivy. Cheap prices for somewhat basic comfort: some rooms have no bathrooms.

MODERATE

Le Prieuré (annexe of the Hôtel Jean-Paul Jeunet) - ☎ *03 84 66 05 67 -* 🅿 *- 6 rooms: 69/79€ -* ☐ *12.50€*. This hotel is set up in a family house fronted by a flowered courtyard. Quiet, carefully kept rooms furnished in the old-fashioned style.

---

slightly above average student. His greatest interest was drawing. He drew portraits in pastels and pencil of his parents and friends, in which a certain talent is apparent. To be able to study for his baccalaureate, the young man entered the grammar school of Besançon as a teaching assistant.

A scientific genius – With his admission to the École Normale in 1843, Pasteur embarked on the career which was to distinguish him as one of the greatest minds in the history of mankind. He began with the study of pure science, where his studies of the geometry of crystals soon attracted attention. He then turned to practical problems. His study of various types of fermentation led him to discover the pasteurisation process by which wine, beer and vinegar could be prevented from going off; his work on the illnesses of silkworms were invaluable to the silk industry. He produced vaccines to cure rabies in man and anthrax in animals. He put forward theories in the field of microbiology which were to revolutionise surgery and medicine in general, leading to the use of antiseptic, sterilisation, and isolation of those with contagious diseases. Pasteur also paved the way for immunisation therapy (using antiserums).

Holidays – Every year the great scientist returned to Arbois with his family for the holidays, where he nonetheless continued his work, as vital to him as the air he breathed. While his Paris office and laboratory were strictly out of bounds to visitors, in Arbois visitors flocked to ask for his support or advice; local wine-growers considered him a kind of viticultural magician and came knocking on his door as soon as a bottle developed some kind of problem. Pasteur's patience and goodwill were inexhaustible. He was also believed to be a great doctor, and the hope of a free consultation brought many a thrifty Arbois citizen to his office. He would participate enthusiastically in the parade for the *Fête du Biou* and the harvest celebrations.

In 1895, illness prevented the great scientist from going to Arbois as usual. On 28 September of that year, he died.

SIGHTS

★**Maison de Pasteur** ⊘ – 📷 A visit to the house where Pasteur spent his youth is a moving experience. On the banks of the Cuisance, his father operated a small tannery, which the scientist progressively expanded and modernised, both to accommodate his own workshop and for the sake of his children.

Restored on the occasion of the centennial of Pasteur's death, the house looks much the same as it did when the family lived there.

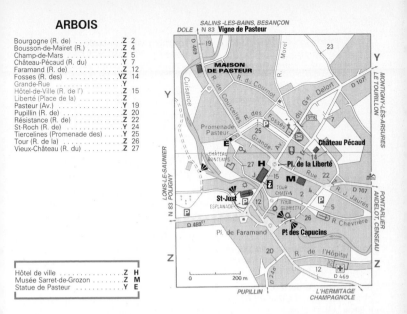

ARBOIS

The slightly ostentatious vestibule gives way to the comfortable billiard room, where numerous personal mementoes are on display. These include family portraits and a painting showing J-Baptiste Jupille, a brave shepherd from the Jura mountains, saved from death thanks to Pasteur's discovery of a treatment for rabies. On the first floor, two drawings from his youth show his hidden talent as an artist. It seems as though Pasteur himself has just left the room where his plume and inkwell stand ready.

In the laboratory are Pasteur's instruments and tools as well as the cultures he used in experiments on spontaneous generation. Some of the amenities were quite exceptional for their time: running water and a gas line, cork insulation around the warming cupboard. Finish the visit in the pleasant riverside garden.

Not far from the house, under the lime trees bordering the Promenade Pasteur, stands a statue of the scientist.

★**Église St-Just** – The church, which dates from the 12C and 13C, stands on a large open square from where there is a view of the Cuisance. The most striking feature of this former priory church is its **bell-tower**, which overlooks the town from the height of 60m/197ft.

It was built in the 16C, using a yellow ochre-coloured stone and has a bell-shaped top, fairly common in Jura. A lantern campanile contains the chimes.

Inside, great semicircular arches and massive pillars separate the side aisles from the narrow, Gothic vaulted nave. The sculpted wooden pulpit dates from 1717; the flat east end of the chancel is pierced by a large Flamboyant window, on which the twelve Apostles are depicted. At the south door there is an epitaph to Capitaine Morel. The sculpted confessionals and the organ case date from the 18C. There is a particularly beautiful late-14C Virgin with Child in the north side aisle.

Musée Sarret-de-Grozon ⊙ – This old 18C mansion still has original furniture and woodwork, which evoke the atmosphere of a relatively well-to-do home of the period. Beautiful collections of paintings (works by the Jura artist A Pointelin), china and silverware (from Dole and Besançon) are also on display.

Musée de la Vigne et du Vin ⊙ – The restored Château Pécaud, which formed part of the old fortifications of Arbois, houses the museum and the institute of Jura wine. An outdoor display illustrates the various activities of the wine-grower, whereas inside there is a collection of exhibits evoking the history of local viticultural activity.

EXCURSIONS

L'Ermitage – 2.5km/1.5mi by D 469 S on the town plan; 1.5km/0.9mi out of town, leave D 469 and turn right onto a road climbing in a series of hairpin bends to an esplanade. From the edge of the plateau, near the chapel, there is a fine view of Arbois and the Cuisance Valley.

Pupillin – 3km/1.9mi S along D 246. One of the most famous local vineyards, specialising in one type of vine, ploussard. Because of the quality of its wines, Pupillin has been allowed to use the appellation **Arbois-Pupillin**, which includes several renowned wine-growing estates such as that of Désirée Petit et Fils. On the way out of the village, there is an interesting view of part of the vineyards.

Tourillon viewing-table – *3km/1.9mi E along D 107.* View of Arbois lying at the foot of the Ermitage plateau bound by the sheer drop of the Fer à Cheval.

Grottes des Moidons ⏱ – *10km/6.2mi S.* 📷 Situated deep in the forest, these caves contain a wealth of **concretions★**. The visit ends with a *son et lumière* show which highlights the water pools in their setting.

★★ Reculée des Planches

21km/13mi – allow one day

Leave Arbois on D 107, then take D 247 to the right near the church in Mesnay. This picturesque road soon enters the Reculée des Planches, in which the village of Planches nestles. Go past the church on coming to Planches-près-Arbois, head past the stone bridge and take the narrow surfaced road sharply to the left, along the foot of the cliffs. Leave the car 600m/660yd further on, near a little refreshment stand.

Grande source de la Cuisance – This is the more interesting of the two sources of the Cuisance, a tributary of the Loue. In rainy seasons the water cascades from a cave, which is also the entrance to the cave of Les Planches.

★**Grotte des Planches** ⏱ – 📷 This cave was formed by the erosive action of water running between rock strata. Two of the galleries have been set aside for tourists, who can trace the underground path of the water as it flows through the rock.

In rainy seasons the course of the River Cuisance flows through the lower gallery in a series of spectacular thundering cascades. During dry periods, the floor of the gallery is occupied by a string of lakes, the innermost of which is over 800m/880yd from the entrance to the cave. The crystal clear waters of these lakes are strikingly blue. The effects of erosion can also be seen during dry periods: long galleries almost completely bare of concretions, their ceilings polished by the underground river; vents enlarged by the pressure of whirlpools; underground pools and, more commonly, **giants' cauldrons★** in various stages of development *(mainly in the upper gallery)*.

The exploration, formation and modification for visitors of the cave, and also the formation of the *reculée*, are described in an adjoining cave. Excavations beneath the exit, brought to light layers of evidence of habitation dating from the bronze, Neolithic and Paleolithic ages.

Petite source de la Cuisance – *500m/550yd from leaving Les Planches, then 1hr there and back on foot. On reaching Arbois head for Auberge du Moulin; leave the car in the park next to the river.*

🚶 Follow the path uphill. This waterfall in its pretty setting is formed by the young river and the spring itself during periods of heavy rainfall.

Retrace your steps. Straight after the bridge over the Cuisance, before the church in Les Planches, turn left on D 339, a narrow surfaced road leading uphill. Then take D 469, cut into the rock face, on the left. The road goes through a tunnel in the rock face. Leave the car in the car park, which is 30m/33yd further on.

Retrace your steps to enjoy a view of the Fer-à-Cheval (horse-shoe) amphitheatre, which closes off the Planches *reculée*.

Return to the car and take D 469.

★★**Belvédère du cirque du Fer-à-Cheval** – *Leave the car near an inn and take the signposted path (10min there and back on foot) on the left.*

🚶 The path goes through a little wood, at the edge of which the amphitheatre opens out *(protective barrier)*. There is a superb **view** of the *reculée* from the viewpoint overlooking the valley floor from nearly 200m/656ft up.

Return to Arbois on D 469.

★ The vineyards

90km/56mi round tour – allow one day

The region is divided into four different AOC areas (Appellation d'Origine Contrôlée, a label guaranteeing the origin of the wine): Arbois, Château-Chalon, l'Étoile and the most extensive, Côtes-du-Jura, which stretches from Port-Lesney in the north to St-Amour in the south. For more information, refer to the chapter on Wine in the Introduction.

Leave Arbois on N 83 W.

The road continues with views of the Jura plateau.

Poligny – *See POLIGNY.*

Take N 5 towards Champagnole.

★ **Culée de Vaux** – There is a difference in height of 240m/787ft between Poligny and the top of the plateau. N 5 runs along the steep valley side of the Culée de Vaux. The Glantine, which flows through Poligny, rises in this valley.

Vaux-sur-Poligny – There is an old Cluniac church here with an unusual roof of multicoloured varnished tiles.

★ **Belvédère de Monts-de-Vaux** – This well-appointed viewpoint *(car park)* offers a beautiful **view** along the length of the *reculée*. The slopes are a pretty patchwork of meadows and woodland.

Rejoin N 5 towards Poligny: after about 3.5km/2mi D 257 towards Chamole leads off to the right.

As the road climbs there are **views**★ over the Culée de Vaux, Poligny and the Bresse region.

Return to Poligny. Leave the town on D 68 S.

Plasne – A stroll around this hilltop village offers pretty **views**★ of the Bresse region. The **Fruitière de Plasne** ⊙ offers guided tours of the premises where Comté cheese, a renowned speciality of the region, is made and of the cellars where it is left to mature.

Now take D 96, a narrow, bumpy road.

★★ **Belvédère du Cirque de Ladoye** – *There is a car park for this viewpoint located above the* reculée, *to the right of the road about 40m/44yd beyond the intersection of D 96 and D 5.*
The **view** is impressive. A tributary of the Seille flows out from the bottom of the amphitheatre.

Take D 204 at Granges-de-Ladoye. This narrow, winding road first heads down to Ladoye-sur-Seille, before following the beautiful Seille Valley. Turn left at the junction with D 70, towards Baume-les-Messieurs.

★★★ **Baume-les-Messieurs** – *See BAUME-LES-MESSIEURS.*

Drive S to D 471 and turn right towards Lons-le-Saunier. Shortly beyond a deep bend which affords a vast panorama of the vineyards, turn right onto a minor road towards Panessières. Follow the signposts to the Château du Pin.

★ **Château du Pin** ⊙ – The castle stands among pastures and vineyards. Built in the 13C by Jean de Chalon, Count of Burgundy and Lord of Arlay, it was destroyed by Louis XI, rebuilt in the 15C and restored in the 20C. From the 15C keep, there is a fine view of the surrounding area.

Continue to N 83 and turn left towards Lons-le-Saunier; 1km/0.6mi further on, turn right onto D 38 towards St-Didier and L'Étoile.

L'Étoile – L'Étoile is indeed a star among wine-producing villages in the area, since it boasts one of the most renowned vintages. In spite of its small size, it has no fewer than five châteaux and several wine-growing estates where tourists can take part in a convivial wine-tasting and appreciate the distinctive bouquet of the famous local white wine, a mixture of flint and hazelnuts.

★ **Château d'Arlay** ⊙ – The château stands on the south bank of the River Seille, among famous vineyards. The medieval fortress gave way to an imposing 18C château, which contains fine regional furniture, is surrounded by a superb park and has its own wine-producing estate. The apartments of the Prince of Arenberg, who lived in the château around 1830, are open to visitors. Note the library and the doll's bedroom.

▣ The Park extends uphill to the medieval ruins of the original fortress. It offers a pleasant walk along fine alleyways lined with lime trees and a wealth of decorative features (grotto, open-air theatre...). The ruins of the old castle form an appropriate setting for demonstration flights of birds of prey (**Jurafaune**).

The **Jardin des Jeux**, close to the château, is laid out so as to suggest a set of dominoes, a draughtboard, a croquet course....

Follow D 120 towards Voiteur then turn onto the winding D 5 to Château-Chalon.

JURAFAUNE

Observe birds of prey in flight

Eating out

MODERATE

Les 16 Quartiers – *Pl. de l'Église* - ☎ *03 84 44 68 23* - *closed end of Oct to end of Mar, Sun evenings and Wed* - *16.01/20.58€.* Time seems to stand still in this charming 16C village house with its pretty dining room and shaded terrace. Treat yourself to tasty regional cooking or to a few medieval specialities! Jura wines served by the glass.

Where to stay

BUDGET

Chambre d'Hôte Le Château de la Muyre – *39210 Domblans - 8km/5mi W of Château-Chalon by D 5 until you reach Voiteur then D 120 to Domblans then D 57ᴱ on the left* - ☎ *03 84 44 66 49* - *closed Jan-Feb* - ☞ - *5 rooms: 27.44/53.36€* - ☑ *5.34€.* This fine 12C and 14C residence extends a simple and unpretentious welcome to travellers. Apart from the huge, stylish wedding room, the accommodation is somewhat basic and looks out onto fields and wooded parkland. Shared bathroom facilities. Wine tastings. Wine for sale.

Chambre d'Hôte Le Jardin de Misette – *R. Honoré-Chapuis - 39140 Arlay - 12km/7.5mi W of Château-Chalon by D 5 until you reach Voiteur then D 120* - ☎ *06 11 63 86 58* - ☞ - *4 rooms: 42€* - *meals 14.50€.* Misette and her husband, who used to run a restaurant, left the business to settle here near the river. Needless to say, the meals served here are of the highest standard. Comfortable rooms. You might want to choose Chabotte, set up in a small cottage as it is by far the prettiest.

★**Château-Chalon** – This former stronghold built on top of a rocky outcrop is surrounded by vineyards producing the famous **Vin Jaune** which takes on a characteristic golden colour after being allowed to mature for six years.

The village has retained a fortified gate and the ruins of its castle. The flower-decked streets are lined with high wine-growers' houses; some of these have a wide rounded doorway and outside access to the cellars.

The 10C Église St-Pierre, built in transitional style, features some of the first pointed vaulting characteristic of Gothic architecture.

Saline royale d'ARC-ET-SENANS★★

Population 1 381
Michelin map 321: E-4

Not far from the River Loue stands the old royal saltworks of Arc-et-Senans, one of the most unusual architectural essays in the Classical style and a rare example of 18C industrial architecture, now on UNESCO's World Heritage List.

An ideal town in the 18C – In 1773, the King's Counsel decreed that a royal saltworks should be founded at Arc-et-Senans, drawing on the salt waters of Salins which could be directed there in wooden conduits. The decision to built a saltworks at Arc-et-Senans was based on the fact that the nearby forest of Chaux would provide the fuel necessary for the processing of the salt. **Claude-Nicolas Ledoux** (1736-1806), inspector general of the saltworks in the Lorraine and Franche-Comté regions and already a famous architect, was commissioned to design the new saltworks. He had not yet designed the toll-houses in the so-called Farmers General fortified wall around Paris – most notably the rotundas in the Parc de la Villette and the Parc Monceau – but the private houses he had designed had won him a reputation for bold and ambitious ideas. He built the royal saltworks at Arc-et-Senans, his masterpiece, between 1774 and 1779. Only the cross-axis and half the first ring of buildings (workshops and workers' accommodation) envisaged by Ledoux were actually completed. What we see today is however enough to evoke the idea of an ideal 18C city. His plan was ambitious; a whole town laid out in concentric circles with the director's residence at the centre, flanked by storehouses, offices and workshops, and extending out to include a church, a market, public baths, recreational facilities etc. Ledoux's vision makes him one of the forerunners of modern architecture and modern design.

Unfortunately, the saltworks never produced as much salt as had been forecast – 40 000 hundredweight per annum instead of 60 000. Partially due to improved technology elsewhere, but mainly due to defective pipelines which led to the pollution of the drinking water with leaking salt water, the saltworks were closed down in 1895.

Part of the buildings now houses a cultural centre, the **Fondation Claude-Nicolas Ledoux**, which organises a number of events.

★★ SALINE ROYALE ⌚ (ROYAL SALTWORKS)

Gatehouse – The road to Salins leads straight to the entrance of the gatehouse, which features a peristyle of eight Doric columns. Artificial grottoes recall the origins of salt. The building once housed the guards, and also the communal oven (which could be used for a fee), the wash-house, the law court and the prison for the saltworks community. The building now houses the reception, a bookshop and another shop selling miscellaneous items.

Director's residence – The director's residence has been the object of much needed restoration work, having been badly damaged by fire in 1918 and, as if that were not enough, the victim of a dynamite attack which wrecked the façade just as the building was about to be listed as a historical monument. The columns of the peristyle consist of alternating cylindrical and square drums. The salt warehouse was in the basement, whereas management occupied the ground and first floors. The landing of the main staircase was fitted out as a chapel, and above that was the administration department.

The rooms of the director's residence are now used for conferences and presentations. In the basement, the **lieu du sel** contains a display explaining why this place was chosen as the site of the royal saltworks and how the saltworks operated, with a slide show and a film on the saltworkers of the early 20C.

J.-H. Lelièvre/EXPLORER

Director's residence, Saline royale

Courtyard – The semicircular courtyard, now a lawn, gives a good impression of the beauty and originality of the design of this complex. All the buildings around its perimeter face the director's residence, which is symbolically placed at the centre of the enterprise. They are decorated with carved motifs: petrified water flowing out of the necks of urns, evoking the source of the saltworking industry. This stylistically unified

Eating out

BUDGET

Le Relais – *Pl. de l'Église - 25610 Arc-et-Senans - ☎ 03 81 57 40 60 - closed 15 Dec-15 Jan and Sun evenings - 10/25€.* This restaurant opposite the church on the main square is accessible to all budgets. Enter by the small terrace where meals are served in summer. The dining room has stone walls, exposed beams and old-fashioned tiled floors. A few simple, tidy rooms.

Chaumière du Val d'Amour – *39380 Chissey-sur-Loue - 5km/3.1mi W of Arc-et-Senans by D 17 - ☎ 03 84 37 61 40 - closed Mon, Tue, Wed and Thu - ⊠ - reservations recommended - 20.73/22.87€.* Large cottage in a small village nestled in the Val d'Amour. Settle in the country-style dining room with exposed beams and a fine fireplace and tuck into tasty regional dishes.

Where to stay

BUDGET

Chambre d'Hôte Le Val d'Amour – *29 rte de Salins - 39380 Ounans - 13km/8.1mi SW of Arc-et-Senans by D 17 E then D 32 and D 472 - ☎ 03 84 37 62 28 - ⊠ - 4 rooms: 34/41€.* The owners extend a warm welcome at this private residence not far from Arc-et-Senans. In summertime, breakfast is served on the terrace, which looks out onto the meadows. Simple yet comfortable rooms.

Hôtel De Hoop – *36 Grande-Rue - 25610 Arc-et-Senans - ☎ 03 81 57 44 80 - closed 2 Nov-1 May - P - 6 rooms: 39/54€ - ☕ 7€ - restaurant 15/22€.* This former 18C post house owned by a friendly and talented Dutch organist is located next to the Saline Royale. Comfortable rooms giving onto the pretty garden or the Saline. The specialities here are *saucisse de Morteau* (smoked pork sausage), *bœuf batave* (beef stew) and exotic cuisine.

complex is all the more striking for the beauty and solidity of its masonry. The influence of Palladio, the 16C Italian architect, makes itself felt in the Antique style columns and pediments, whereas the roofs are constructed in the manner typical of the region.

Firewood was once unloaded for storage in this courtyard, now used by hot-air balloons as their taking-off point.

Coopers' building – The cooper's building houses the **musée Ledoux**, a collection of about 60 architectural models at a scale of 1:200 and 1:100 which reveal Claude-Nicolas Ledoux's ideas about life in the ideal society. The right wing contains buildings by Ledoux which are only partially extant, or even not at all: the theatre at Besançon, of which only the façade remains; the saltworks at Arc-et-Senans; and the Château de Maupertuis. In the left wing, the ideal city of Chaux, the gun forge and the guardians' house at the source of the Loue are all projects that Ledoux was never able to realise. Prints and photographs complete the exhibition of the architect's work. On the first floor, there is a display of toll-houses.

Salt storehouses – *On either side of the director's residence.* The old salt store-houses have been converted and during the summer now host concerts, temporary exhibits and other events.

EXCURSION

Val d'Amour

This is the delightful name of part of the Loue Valley, best-known for its legends and attractive river. A variety of crafts, mostly linked to timber, livened up the valley until the early 20C.

Chissey-sur-Loue – The interesting 13C church has a majestic-looking doorway, on which the tympanum features a sculpture of Christ Bound. The upper part of the walls is decorated with a frieze of small trefoil arches. Inside, note the stone baboons supporting the cornice of the main nave, the pulpit (18C), the gilded altarpiece of St Christopher (17C), and the giant polychrome stone statue of St Christopher (15C).

Chamblay – Downriver from Chissey, this small village had a long-standing tradition of timber-floating. This activity developed during the 18C in order to supply timber to the navy; later on timber was used by factories and for heating purposes. Chaux Forest is nearby and for a long time the fast-flowing River Loue provided the best means of transport, although it was rather dangerous for the men guiding the large rafts when the river was in spate. The **Confrérie St-Nicolas des radeliers de la Loue** has been reviving this traditional craft every year since 1994 through a series of interesting events.

La Vouivre

Once upon a time in Jura, there lived a beautiful, but cold-hearted princess. Haughty, cruel and merciless, she was the terror of the valley.

One day, a noblewoman came to visit and spoke to her at length about the virtues of compassion and generosity.

The princess turned a deaf ear, and her visitor, who was really a fairy, turned her into a *vouivre*, (in local parlance, a nasty snake). To top it off, the wicked one was given the wings of a bat, and crowned with a ruby tiara which, legend tells us, would bring a fortune to any person who could make away with it. The only time the monster removed the jewel was when she bathed in the River Loue.

Many have tried, and all have drowned. The moral of the story: never swim with snakes.

---

* **Port-Lesney** – This pretty village on the River Loue is a popular place in summer for a country holiday. On Sundays, fishermen, boating enthusiasts and lovers of trout and fried fish flock to the village.

There is a footpath *(1hr round trip)* from the Chapelle de Lorette which leads through the undergrowth to the Belvédère Edgar-Faure overlooking the village and the entire valley.

HIKE

Chemin des Gabelous

As you leave the saltworks, turn left then right at the roundabout along rue des Graduations. The signposted trail begins from the camp site; 5hr 30min on foot, 2hr 30min by bike.

The 24km/15mi waymarked path follows the historic salt trail which led from the salt-extraction site in Salins to Arc-et-Senans.

AUTUN★★

Population 16 419
Michelin map 320: F-8 – Local map see MORVAN

The city of Autun is flanked by wooded hills overlooking the valley of the Arroux and the vast plain that extends westwards. The cathedral, the museums and the Roman remains bear witness to the city's past greatness.

The remaining forests (Forêt des Battées and Forêt de Planoise, which is principally an oak forest) have enabled Autun to develop a high-quality furniture industry.

HISTORICAL NOTES

The Rome of the Gauls – Autun, derived from Augustodunum, was founded by Emperor Augustus as a prestige Roman town, with the purpose both of honouring the Aedui, the local tribe, and of making them beholden to Rome. The splendour of the new town, which was known as the sister and rival of Rome, soon eclipsed the contemporary Gaulish settlement at Bibracte *(see Mont BEUVRAY)*. The city's location on the great commercial and military road between Lyon and Boulogne brought it wealth and prosperity. By the 3C, however, this extraordinary focus of Roman civilization suffered several disastrous invasions. All that remains today of the fortified enclosure and the numerous public monuments are two gates and traces of the largest Roman theatre in Gaul.

AUTUN

Arbalète (R. de l')	**BZ** 2	Dijon (R. de)	**BY** 13
Arquebuse (R. de l')	**BZ** 3	Dr-Renaud (R.)	**AZ** 15
Cascade (R. de la)	**BZ** 4	Eumène (R.)	**AY** 16
Chauchien (Gde-Rue)	**BZ** 6	Gaillon (R. de)	**BY** 18
Cocand (R.)	**AZ** 7	Gaulle (Av. Ch.-de)	**AYZ** 19
Cordeliers (R. des)	**BZ** 9	Grange-Vertu (R.)	**AY** 21
Cordiers (R. aux)	**BZ** 12	Guérin (R.)	**BY** 23
		Jeannin (R.)	**BZ** 26
		Lattre-de-Tassigny (R. de)	**BZ** 27

Laureau (Bd.)	**BY** 28
Marbres (R. des)	**BZ** 29
Notre-Dame (R.)	**AZ** 31
Paris (R. de)	**ABY** 32
Passage couvert	**BZ** 33
Pernette (R.)	**AZ** 35
Raquette (R.)	**BZ** 37
St-Saulge (R.)	**AZ** 40
Vieux-Colombier (R. du)	**BZ** 42

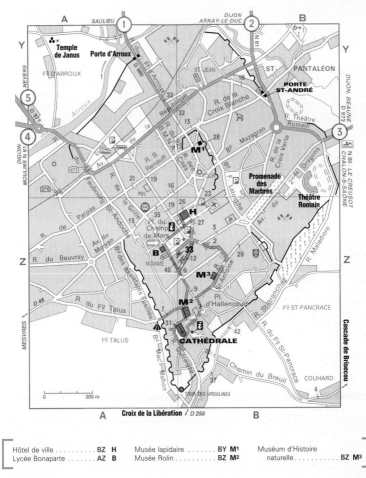

Hôtel de ville	**BZ** **H**	Musée lapidaire	**BY** **M¹**	Muséum d'Histoire
Lycée Bonaparte	**AZ** **B**	Musée Rolin	**BZ** **M²**	naturelle . . . **BZ** **M³**

Eating out

BUDGET

Le Chalet Bleu – *3 r. Jeannin -* ☎ *03 85 86 27 30 - closed 12 Feb-5 Mar, Sun evenings and 15 Nov-31 Mar, Mon evenings and Tue - 14/43€.* A warm welcome awaits you in this friendly establishment in the town centre, tucked away behind the town hall. The dining room is light, with pretty potted plants and wall paintings. The thoughtful cuisine successfully combines tradition with fresh regional produce. Highly affordable prices.

Le Relais des Ursulines – *2 r. Dufraigne -* ☎ *03 85 52 26 22 - welcome@hotelursuline.fr - 16.33/25.49€.* A stone's throw from the cathedral, this old house half way between a restaurant and a bistrot possesses an unusual decor: a wooden counter adorned with copperware, antique pieces picked up from flea markets, tables covered with red and white checked fabric, a player piano... The bill of fare includes pizzas and grilled meats cooked over an open fire.

MODERATE

Hostellerie du Vieux Moulin – *Rte de Saulieu -* ☎ *03 85 52 10 90 - closed Jan-Feb, Sun evening and Mon out of season. - 22.87/38.11€.* The Porte d'Arroux leads to this former 1878 mill nestling on the river banks. Fronted by a delightful garden, this restaurant exudes the country charm of bygone days. Traditional cooking made with home-grown vegetables. Enjoy the terrace and the few old-fashioned bedrooms.

Where to stay

MODERATE

Hôtel St-Louis et Poste – *6 r. de l'Arbalète -* ☎ *03 85 52 01 01 - louis-poste@aol.com -* 🄿 *- 33 rooms: 75/115€ -* ⛛ *10€ - restaurant 26/45€.* The tidy rooms of this 18C *hôtel particulier* have been tastefully renovated in the old-fashioned style and appointed with wrought-iron or cane furniture. Meals are served on the terrace or in the cosy yet light dining room. Conveniently close to place du Champ-de-Mars.

Sit back and relax

Irish Pub – *5 r. Mazagran -* ☎ *03 85 52 73 90 - open Tue-Sun 11am-2am, Fri-Sat until 3am.* The charming couple who run this pub will make sure you spend a highly enjoyable evening. Mix in with the trendy and appreciative crowd who throng here to listen to live music played by French, Celtic and Irish bands.

Le Lutrin – *1 pl. du Terreau -* ☎ *03 85 52 48 44 - open Mon-Fri 10am-2am, Sat-Sun 10am-3am.* A staircase plastered with old advertising posters will take you down to a vaulted cellar embellished with a host of curious items and furnished with tables mounted on old mining carts. Settle comfortably in one of the beige leather armchairs and enjoy the concerts of blues or Irish music in this convivial pub.

The century of the Rolin family – In the Middle Ages Autun became prosperous once again, largely because of two men: Nicolas Rolin and one of his sons. Born in Autun in 1376, **Nicolas Rolin**, whose name is linked with the foundation of the Hôtel-Dieu at Beaune, became one of the most celebrated lawyers of his time. He attracted the attention of the Duke of Burgundy, Philip the Good, who made him Chancellor. Despite rising to such heights, he never forgot his native town, helping to restore its economic activity to a level it had not attained since Roman times. One of his sons, **Cardinal Rolin**, who became Bishop of Autun, made the town a great religious centre. The completion of the cathedral of St-Lazare, the building of the ramparts to the south of the town and the construction of many private mansions date from this period.

THE UPPER TOWN

Start from place du Champ-de-Mars (parking area, tourist office).

Lycée Bonaparte – This was once a Jesuit college, built in 1709, and provides a noble focal point for place du Champ-de-Mars. The splendid wrought-iron **grille★**, dating from 1772, is adorned with gilded motifs of medallions, globe, astrolabes and lyres. On the left, the 17C **church of Notre-Dame** was originally the college chapel. Notable pupils included the whimsical Bussy-Rabutin and the three Bonaparte brothers, Napoleon, Joseph and Lucien. Napoleon spent only a few months here in 1779 before going on to the military school at Brienne.

Walk along rue St-Saulge, admiring the 17C Hôtel de Morey at no 24; continue along rue Chauchien and note the façades decorated with wrought-iron balconies.

Rue Cocand leads to the ramparts.

Les Remparts – The walk round the ramparts begins at boulevard des Résistants Fusillés to the west of town. Follow the ramparts south as far as the Tour des Ursulines, a 12C keep.

Walk towards the cathedral along rue Notre-Dame (Hôtel de Millery at no 12), then stroll along rue Dufraigne (timber-framed houses) and impasse du jeu de Paume (Hôtel Mac-Mahon). From place d'Hallencourt, it is possible to enter the courtyard of the bishop's residence. Continue towards rue St-Antoine.

A little further on, turn left onto rue de l'Arbalète which leads to the pedestrianised area of rue des Cordiers.

Passage de la Halle – This covered passageway dating from the mid-19C, opens onto place du Champ-de-Mars through an imposing Classical doorway.

Follow rue De-Lattre-de-Tassigny, lined with 18C private mansions.

Hôtel de Ville – The town hall houses a large **library** ⊘ including a rich collection of **manuscripts★** and incunabula, displayed in rotation during summer exhibitions.

Finally, walk along rue Jeannin, situated behind the town hall, and enter one of the gardens through a *porte-cochère*.

★★CATHÉDRALE ST-LAZARE *30min*

In the 12C the Bishop of Autun decided to supplement the existing cathedral (destroyed in the 18C) with a new church, to house the relics of St Lazarus, which had been brought back from Marseille by Gérard de Roussillon in about 970, hoping to create thereby a place of pilgrimage to rival the Basilique Ste-Madeleine in Vézelay. Construction took place from 1120 to 1146, and the cathedral was consecrated in 1130 by Pope Innocent II.

The exterior of the cathedral no longer looks particularly Romanesque because of later modifications. The belfry was destroyed by fire in 1469, and when it was rebuilt later that century, a Gothic spire was added to it. The upper part of the choir and the chapels in the right aisle date from the same period. Those in the left aisle are 16C. The two towers flanking the main front, which resemble those at Paray-le-Monial, were added in the 19C during large-scale restoration work by Viollet-le-Duc. The building was seriously damaged in the 18C, during the French Revolution; the cathedral canons demolished the rood screen, the tympanum of the north doorway and the tomb of St Lazarus which stood behind the high altar *(what remains can be seen in the Musée Rolin)*.

★★★**Tympanum of the central doorway** – The tympanum (1130-35), one of the masterpieces of Romanesque sculpture, bears the signature of its creator, **Gislebertus**, beneath the feet of Christ. Nothing is known about him, except that his work suggests he was trained in Vézelay, and perhaps also in Cluny. Unlike his contemporaries, he did not conform to the Cluniac tradition, but produced his own distinctive style. His creative genius, his sense of form and his individual power of expression are evident in all the cathedral sculpture. The composition of the central tympanum is a masterly solution of the problems posed by the decoration of such a large area. The theme is the Last Judgment. Despite its apparent complexity, the design is highly structured. At the centre, dominating the composition, is the tall figure of Christ in Majesty (**1**) surrounded by a mandorla supported by four angels. Below are the dead rising from their graves, summoned by four angels blowing trumpets (**4**, **7**, **8**, **9**); in the centre of the lintel, an angel is separating the blessed (**2**) from the damned (**3**). At the left hand of Christ, the Archangel Michael confronts Satan, who is trying to upset the weighing of souls by pressing on the beams of the scales (**6**). Behind him yawns the mouth of Hell, which is squeezed to the extreme right of the tympanum (**7**), whereas Heaven occupies the whole of the upper register with *(right)* two

Apostles or Enoch, the patriarch, and Eli, the prophet, transported straight to Heaven (**9**) and *(left)* Mary (**8**) in the heavenly Jerusalem (**4**) and the Apostles (**5**) attending the weighing of souls. St Peter, distinguished by the key on his shoulder, lends a hand to one of the blessed, while a soul tries to escape by clinging to the robe of an angel.

The human figure, which is the dominant subject of the tympanum, is treated in very diverse ways. The figures of God, His heavenly host, and the biblical characters are all

Ph. Gajic/MICHELIN

dressed in light finely pleated garments. The diaphanous material, fluted at the hem, emphasises the insubstantial essence of the owners and the spiritual harmony of the heavenly kingdom. The smaller figures of the dead, sculpted in high relief, present a very different picture; the state of their souls is revealed through the simple but varied attitudes of their naked bodies; the more numerous blessed progress in a peaceful and orderly file, their faces turned towards Christ. By contrast, the fear and agony of the damned are expressed in the chaotic poses and irregular composition of the figures. Out of the parade of human beings, a few prelates and lords among the blessed *(left)* are draped with a cloak, which still leaves them largely naked like their fellows; the cloak is a distinguishing attribute and not a symbol of grace like the clothing of the divine figures in the upper register of the tympanum. Two pilgrims can be identified by their bags; one is decorated with a scallop shell, and the other with the cross of Jerusalem. Among the damned, on the right of the person in the clutches of the devil, is an adulterous woman with serpents (the symbol of lust) at her breast, whereas on the left is a miser with his money bag round his neck. The angular lines of the procession of the damned are repeated more forcefully in Hell, where the monstrous faces of the devils and the straining muscles of their misshapen limbs express their cruelty.

The whole composition is crowned by three orders of rounded arches. The outer order (**A**) represents the passing of time, the labours of the months alternating with the signs of the zodiac in the medallions; in the centre, between Cancer and Gemini, is a small crouching figure representing the year. The middle order (**B**) bears a serpentine garland of leaves and flowers. The inner order, destroyed in 1766 when the tympanum was plastered over, showed the elders of the Apocalypse.

Interior – The pillars and vaulting date from the first half of the 12C. The Cluniac Romanesque style survives in spite of much alteration: three rows of elevation (large pointed arches, false triforium and high windows), massive cruciform pillars divided by fluted pilasters, broken-barrel vaulting with transverse ribs in the nave and rib vaulting in the aisles.

The chancel conforms to the early Christian design of an apse flanked by two apsidal chapels. The over-vaulting disappeared in the 15C when the tall windows were inserted by Cardinal Rolin (the stained glass in the pointed windows dates from the 19C, that in the Romanesque windows from 1939). In 1766 the canons demolished the tomb of St Lazarus and used the marble to cover the chancel and the apse; the marble was removed in 1939.

The use of fluted pilasters surmounted by foliated capitals, which are to be found throughout the upper gallery, gives a sense of unity to the interior of the cathedral; these elements would have been familiar to the local masons from the many ancient buildings in Autun.

The majestic effect is enlivened by the carved capitals *(binoculars are useful here)*. The most admirable features are:

1) and 2) Simon the Sorcerer tries to ascend to Heaven watched by St Paul and St Peter with his key. Simon falls head first under Peter's approving eye. The devil (visible from the main nave) is beautifully portrayed.

3) The stoning of St Stephen.

4) Symbolic representation of Samson pulling down the temple.

5) The loading of the Ark, with Noah supervising from an upper window.

6) 16C sacristy door.

7) Statues of Pierre Jeannin, who died in 1623, President of the Burgundian Parliament and a minister of Henri IV, with his wife.

8) The relics of St Lazarus are placed under the high altar.

9) Jesus appearing to Mary Magdalene against a background of curled foliage.

10) The second temptation of Christ. Oddly enough the devil is the only figure placed high up on the roof.

11) A 16C stained-glass window representing the Tree of Jesse in the burial chapel of the bishops of Autun.

12) Painting by Ingres (1834) representing the martyrdom of St Symphorian, by the Porte St-André.

13) The Nativity. St Joseph meditating in a strange, arched chair.

Chapter-house – *Access by the stairs*. The chapter-house was built in the early 16C, using some fine **capitals**★★ made of heavily grained stone containing mica, which originally capped the pillars in the chancel. The most remarkable are on the right of the doorway:

– The hanging of Judas between two devils who are pulling the ropes.

– The Flight into Egypt, which should be compared with the representation of the same scene at Saulieu.

– The Magi asleep, all in the same bed with their crowns on. An angel is waking them to show them the star in the shape of a daisy. The scene is depicted with delightful simplicity.

– The Adoration of the Magi. St Joseph has been relegated to the right and seems to be waiting for the end of all the ceremony.

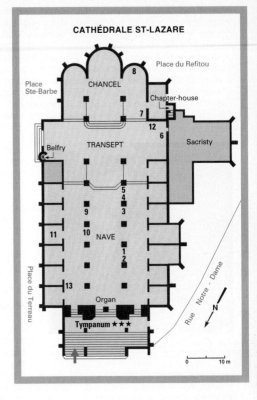

CATHÉDRALE ST-LAZARE

Belfry – The belfry (80m/262ft high) was built by Bishop Jean Rolin in 1462, when an earlier structure was struck by lightning. From the top *(230 steps)* there is a good **view**★ of the old roofs of the town, the bishops' palace, the unusual conical silhouette of the two old spoil heaps at Les Télots (relics of bituminous schist mines which once made an important contribution to the local economy) and *(east)* the blue hills of the Morvan.

Fontaine St-Lazare – This charming fountain stands to the north of the cathedral. It was built in 1543 by the cathedral chapter and has a dome and small lantern. The first dome of the Ionic order supports a second smaller one of the Corinthian order, and the whole is crowned by a pelican, a copy of the original of which is in the Musée Rolin.

ADDITIONAL SIGHTS

★ **Musée Rolin** ⊘ – The museum, located on the site of the former Rolin mansion, displays its collections in some 20 rooms.

The medieval collection is housed in a wing built in the 15C for Chancellor Nicolas Rolin. Gallo-Roman archaeology, post-16C European painting and regional historical collections are exhibited in the adjacent Hôtel Lacomme dating from the 19C. Seven rooms on the ground floor of the Hôtel Lacomme house the Gaulish and Gallo-Roman collections. Relics of the oppidum at Bibracte are on display (large collection of tombstones). Gallo-Roman culture is illustrated through dress, jewellery and toilet articles (Roman helmet with a human face), through religious cults of Roman, Eastern or traditional local deities such as Epona, and through art (handsome statues and a mosaic known as Neptune's Victory).

The last room is devoted to late Antiquity and the Middle Ages; note in particular fragments from the tomb of Brunehaut (543-613), who founded St-Martin Abbey and was buried there.

Paintings, sculptures and furniture from the Renaissance to the present are displayed on the first floor (rooms 13 to 20).

Cross the courtyard to the ground floor of the Rolin mansion.

Two rooms (8 and 9) are devoted to masterpieces of Roman **statuary**★★; most of it is the work of the two great sculptors of the Burgundian School, Gislebertus and Martin, a monk. Gislebertus' **Temptation of Eve**★★ expresses sensuality through the curves of the body and the plants; the carving adorned the lintel of the north door of the cathedral before 1766. Martin created part of the **tomb of St Lazarus**, which took the form of a miniature church and stood behind the altarpiece in the chancel of the cathedral until it was destroyed during the changes made by the canons in 1766. The surviving figures from the main group, which depicted the resurrection of Lazarus, are the slim and poignant figures of St Andrew and Lazarus' sisters, Martha (who is holding her nose) and Mary. The rest of the work is represented by a few fragments supplemented by a sketch.

The first floor houses 14C and 15C sculptures from the Autun workshops (15C Resurrection of Lazarus in polychrome stone) and works by French and Flemish Primitive painters. The room devoted to the Rolin family contains the famous

H. Champollion/MICHELIN

Detail of the Nativity

15C painting of the **Nativity**★★ by the Master of Moulins; the attention to detail and the muted colours betray the Flemish origin of the painter but the serene and solemn beauty and plasticity are characteristic of French Gothic painting. 15C Burgundian statuary is represented by the **Virgin**★★ of Autun in polychrome stone and a St Catherine attributed to the Spanish sculptor Juan de la Huerta who worked in the region during the reign of Philip the Good.

Muséum d'Histoire Naturelle ⊘ – This Natural History Museum concentrates on the geological evolution of the Autun basin, the Morvan and Burgundy. Included in the mineralogical collection are specimens of quartz (gemstones) and coal with the imprints of plants and animals (actinodon) from the Primary Era. There are also fossils from the Secondary Era and the bones of a now extinct species of wild ox (auroch) and mammoths from the Quaternary Era.

Children will no doubt appreciate the display of stuffed birds from Burgundy.

THE GALLO-ROMAN TOWN

Théâtre romain – The remains reveal the size of the largest theatre in Gaul (capacity: 12 000). Gallo-Roman stone fragments are incorporated into the wall of the porter's house.

Promenade des Marbres – Near the broad tree-lined promenade, in a French-style garden, stands a fine 17C building. It was designed by Daniel Gitard, architect to Anne of Austria, as a seminary, but was later converted into a military training school.

★ **Porte St-André** – This gate is where the roads from Langres and Besançon meet. It is the one survivor of four original gates in the Gallo-Roman fortifications, which were reinforced with 54 semicircular towers. It has two large arches for vehicles, flanked by two smaller ones for pedestrians, surmounted by an upper arcade of 10 even smaller arches. One of the guard-houses has survived by being converted into a church in the Middle Ages. Tradition has it that St Symphorian was martyred near this gateway.

Porte d'Arroux – This gateway was the Roman Porta Senonica, leading towards Sens and the Via Agrippa which ran from Lyon to Boulogne. Less massive and not so well preserved as the Porte St-André, it has similar arches. The upper arcading, decorated with fluted pilasters topped by Corinthian capitals, dates from the time of Emperor Constantine.

Musée Lapidaire ⊘ – The lapidary museum is housed in the Chapelle St-Nicolas, a 12C Romanesque chapel with a Christ in Majesty painted in the apse. Some exhibits are also in the galleries around the adjoining garden. The stone fragments on display include architectural features, mosaics and tombstones from the Gallo-Roman period as well as sarcophagi and capitals from the Middle Ages, all of them too large to be housed in the Musée Rolin. There are also pieces of statuary.

Temple de Janus – *Follow rue du Morvan then faubourg St-Andoche*. The two walls of a square tower (24m/80ft high) which stand alone in the plain on the far bank of the Arroux, are probably the remains of the sanctuary *(cella)* of a temple dedicated to a god who has not been identified (despite the name).

EXCURSIONS

★ **Croix de la Libération** – *6km/4mi S.* The road climbing in a series of hairpin bends offers a fine view of the cathedral, the old town and Morvan in the distance; 50m/55yd beyond the entrance to Montjeu Castle, a steep path on the right leads up to the granite cross, put up in 1945 to commemorate the liberation of Autun; from the cross, there is a good **view**★ of Autun and the surrounding area.

Cascade de Brisecou – *2km/1.2mi S then 45min on foot there and back; park the car in Couhard, near the church.*

🚶 A pleasant walk along a stream to this waterfall, tumbling over rocks in a pretty wooded **setting**★. On the way back, make a detour (along a path starting from the parking area) to the **Pierre de Couhard**, a strange-looking pyramid believed to be a funeral monument built at the same time as the Roman theatre.

★ **Château de Sully** ⊘ – *15km/9.3mi NE along the road to Nolay.* This château is a Renaissance mansion flanked by outbuildings and set in a vast park; in its layout and decoration it is similar to the château of Ancy-le-Franc.

The building was begun early in the 16C by Jean de Saulx, who had already acquired the land at Sully, and continued by his son, the Maréchal de Tavannes.

The château was the birthplace of Maréchal Mac-Mahon, Duke of Magenta and President of the French Republic from 1873 to 1879.

The surrounding moat is fed by the River Drée. Four wings, flanked by four square corner towers set at an angle, enclose an inner courtyard.

The west façade, containing the entrance, consists of wide bays separated by pilasters at first-floor level. Two turrets flank the chapel in the south façade.

From the north façade, which was rebuilt in the 18C, a monumental stair gives access to a terrace, bordered by a handsome balustrade, overlooking a stretch of water.

Couches – *25km/16mi SE via D 978.* In town, note the handsome early-17C Maison des Templiers, and on the outskirts of town visit the much-restored 15C **château** ⊘ of Margaret of Burgundy, with many of its early defensive features (drawbridge, traces of curtain wall and towers), 15C chapel and 12C keep (containing weapons and Aubusson tapestries). After the visit, you are invited to taste the wines produced on the estate.

AUXERRE★★

Population 37 790
Michelin map 319: E-5

Auxerre (pronounced Oh-ssair), the capital of Lower Burgundy (Basse Bourgogne), is built on a sloping site on a hillside beside the River Yonne, at the beginning of the Nivernais canal. The site has also lent itself to the building of a pleasure boat harbour. The town's fine monuments, testifying to its great past, are highlighted in summer by a *son et lumière* show near the cathedral; its shady boulevards, its steep and busy streets and its old houses contribute to its overall interest. From the bridges, most particularly from Pont Paul-Bert *(statue)* and the right bank of the river, there are some very fine **views**★ of the town, made all the more striking as the chevets of the churches rise straight up along the river bank. The town is at the centre of a vineyard area, of which the most famous wines are Chablis and Irancy.

Auxerre on the banks of the River Yonne

S. Sauvignier/MICHELIN

HISTORICAL NOTES

Near a simple Gaulish village (Autricum), the Romans built the town of Autessiodurum, which, like Autun, lay on the impressive road from Lyon to Boulogne. From the 1C it was a large town, as objects found during excavation in the area demonstrate.

The importance of Auxerre as an intellectual and spiritual centre in the Middle Ages rested largely on the influence of the bishops who ruled it, in particular St Germanus in the 5C. The saint's tomb became the object of pilgrimages, and Auxerre was declared a Holy City by the Pope in the 12C.

Two great figures in French history have visited Auxerre. In 1429 **Joan of Arc** passed through the town twice, first with the handful of brave followers who accompanied her from Vaucouleurs to Chinon, and then a few months later at the head of an army of 12 000 men with Charles VII, whom she was taking to Reims for his coronation. On 17 March 1815, **Napoleon** arrived in Auxerre on his return from Elba: Maréchal Ney, who had been sent to oppose him, embraced him and the Maréchal's troops swelled the ranks of the Emperor's small army.

Auxerre was the birthplace of the physiologist **Paul Bert** (1833-86), who was later to enter politics and become minister during the Third Republic, and of the poet **Marie Noël** (1883-1967) whose works were full of hope and serenity.

TOWN WALK

Start from quai de la Marine (parking areas).

Quartier de la Marine – This part of town with its narrow winding streets was once home to the boatmen. Take rue de la Marine *(no 37 on the town plan)* to see the remains of the north-east tower of the Gallo-Roman fortified wall. Walk across the pretty little place St-Nicolas *(no 45 on the town plan)*, overlooking quai de la Marine. The square is named after the patron saint of boatmen. Rue du Mont-Brenn leads to the place du Coche-d'Eau *(no 8 on the town plan)*. At no 3, a 16C house is host to temporary exhibitions as part of the local **Musée du Coche-d'Eau**. Go up rue du Docteur-Labosse *(no 10 on the town plan)* to reach rue Cochois.

Walk towards the town centre via place St-Étienne in front of the cathedral then rue Maison-fort on the left prolonged by rue Joubert.

Town centre – There are still many interesting old houses here, most of which are 16C with half-timbering.

Rue Fécauderie intersecting with rue Joubert has two half-timbered houses with a sculpted corner post; it leads to **place de l'Hôtel-de-Ville** where a polychrome figure recalls the poet Marie Noël; note also nos 4, 6, 16, 17 and 18.

Tour de l'Horloge – This Flamboyant clock tower was built in the 15C on Gallo-Roman foundations (old fortified wall). It was also called the Tour Gaillarde, after the gateway it defended, and was part of the fortifications. The belfry and the clock were symbols of the communal liberties granted by the Count of Auxerre. The clock (17C) has two faces showing the apparent movements of the sun and moon. The astronomical dial was mentioned by Restif de la Bretonne, a prolific 18C novelist (Nicolas-Edme Restif 1734-1806), who spent several years of his youth working as a printer's apprentice in the workshop at the base of the tower. A vaulted passageway beside the clock tower leads to place du Maréchal-Leclerc.

Beneath the vault a plaque commemorates **Cadet Roussel** (1743-1807), a court official whose blighted ambitions are immortalised in a famous French song.

Continue along **rue de l'Horloge**: no 6 (sculpted corner post) and the four houses opposite; then along **rue de la Draperie**: note the houses occupied by a bank and a jeweller's. It leads to **place Charles-Surugue** which has a fountain in honour of Cadet Roussel and interesting houses at nos 3, 4, 5 and 18.

Strolling through the area, you will come across:

The **Église St-Eusèbe**, all that remains of an old priory. The church has a lovely 12C tower decorated with multifoil

Astronomical clock

S. Sauvignier/MICHELIN

Eating out

MODERATE

Auberge Les Tilleuls – *89290 Vincelottes - 16km/10mi S of Auxerre by N 6 and D 38 -* ☎ *03 86 42 22 13 - closed 19 Dec-21 Feb, Thu Oct-Easter and Wed - 22.11/49.55€.* Why not make a small detour and stray from the beaten track? This small village inn will delight you thanks to its pretty setting, its summer terrace running along the banks of the Yonne and its succulent cuisine.

Chamaille – *89240 Chevannes - 8km/5mi SW of Auxerre by N 151 and D 1 -* ☎ *03 86 41 24 80 - lachamaille@wanadoo.fr - closed 1-17 Jan, Sun evenings 14 Nov-14 Feb, Mon and Tue - reservations required - 23/56€.* You could not hope for a more charming setting! Chamaille is surrounded by a delightful garden cut across by a small stream meandering through fields stretching as far as the eye can see... The tastefully restored farmhouse has a pretty verandah.

Auberge du Château – *89580 Val-de-Mercy - 18km/11.2mi S of Auxerre by N 6, D 85 and D 38 -* ☎ *03 86 41 60 00 - delfontaine.j@wanadoo.fr - closed 31 Jan-5 Mar, Sun evenings, Tue lunch and Mon out of season - reservations required - 22.11€ lunch - 27.14/35.85€.* A charming country inn offering a warm welcome. Spacious, carefully appointed rooms. The decoration features works by local artists. In summer the simple but tasty meals are served on the terrace, against a colourful backdrop of flowers.

EXPENSIVE

Barnabet – *14 quai de la République -* ☎ *03 86 51 68 88 - contact@restaurant-barnabet.com - closed 23 Dec-15 Jan, Sun evenings and Mon - 34/51€.* This imposing residence tucked away from the quays flanking the Yonne is the perfect address for gourmets. Delicious, lovingly prepared meals are served in the elegant dining hall decorated in pastel hues or on the terrace inside the courtyard.

Where to stay

BUDGET

Chambre d'Hôte Domaine Borgnat Le Colombier – *1 r. de l'Église - 89290 Escolives-Ste-Camille - 9.5km/5.8mi S of Auxerre by D 239 -* ☎ *03 86 53 35 28 - domaineborgnat@wanadoo.fr - closed mid-Nov to Feb - 5 rooms: 37/46€ - meals 19.82/33.53€.* This magnificent fortified 17C farmhouse is a haven for wine buffs! As far as accommodation is concerned, you can choose between the *chambres d'hôtes* or the self-catering formula in the dovecot. Whatever your decision, you will enjoy relaxing by the pool on the terrace, while sipping one of the delicious wines produced on the estate.

MODERATE

Hôtel Le Cygne – *14 r. du 24-Aug -* ☎ *03 86 52 26 51 - hcygne@3and1hotels.com -* 🅿 *- 30 rooms: 42/68€ -* ⛲ *6.40€.* A modern hotel near the town centre offering simple, comfortable rooms. Some of the attic rooms exude considerable charm and feature sloping ceilings.

Chambre d'Hôte Château de Ribourdin – *89240 Chevannes - 9km/5.6mi SW of Auxerre by N 151 and D 1 then a minor road -* ☎ *03 86 41 23 16 -* ✉ *- 5 rooms: 50/65€.* A sumptuous 16C château surrounded by meadows, located below the village. The cosy bedrooms and spacious breakfast room are housed in the 18C outbuildings, which give out onto the countryside.

Sit back and relax

Le 5 Germain Pub – *5 r. St-Germain -* ☎ *03 86 46 90 09 - open Tue-Thu 5pm-1am, Fri-Sat 5pm-2am, Sun 5pm-1am; Jun-Sep: Mon-Sat 5pm-2am, Sun 7pm-2am.* This lively pub patronised by a cosmopolitan clientele, decorated with posters and beer mats, is presided over by a huge portrait of Che Guevara. The wooden benches, white curtains and pretty courtyard add to its quaint charm.

Le Fin Palais – *3 pl. St-Nicolas -* ☎ *03 86 51 14 03 - open daily 9.30am-7.30pm - closed Nov-late Mar: Sun afternoons and Mon.* This shop offers a mouthwatering selection of the best regional produce, including liquors, wine brandies, beer from Sens, Burgundy wines and the famous *nonnette* sweet-meats (iced gingerbread filled with jam). Also on sale is the pretty sapphire blue stoneware pottery from Puisaye. Charming welcome.

Le Galion – *2 r. Étienne-Dolet* - ☎ *03 86 46 96 58 - summer: open daily 10am-2am; the rest of the year 10am-1am - closed Tue and 25 Dec-1 Jan.* This small galleon lulled by the Yonne waters offers splendid views of Auxerre and the surrounding countryside. A lively ambience and the odd improvised concert make for a highly attractive café frequented by many regular customers.

Pullman Bar – *20 r. d'Egleny* - ☎ *03 86 52 09 32 - open Mon-Fri 4pm-1am, Sat 4pm-2am - closed 3 weeks in Aug.* This unassuming bar has much to offer: more than 110 special beers from 18 different countries and over 40 cocktails, with or without alcohol... Add to that a cosy atmosphere, a warm welcome and blues music... and you have the perfect combination! Ask to see the cigar box.

Domaine Jean-Pierre-Colinot – *1 r. des Chariats - 89290 Irancy* - ☎ *03 86 42 33 25 - open Mon-Sat 8.30am-6.30pm, Sun 9.30am-noon.* The wines made on the Colinot estate are distilled and matured in accordance with long-standing Burgundy tradition. Wine tastings are organised in the storehouse. Beautiful vaulted cellars dating back to the 17C.

arches. The stone spire dates from the 15C. Inside, note the rib vaulting in the high hexagonal drum above the Renaissance chancel, the beautiful axial chapel and the 16C stained-glass windows *(closed for restoration work)*.

The oldest house in Auxerre, dating from the 14C and 15C, is at no 5 **place Robillard**. Note the lovely Renaissance mansion, known as Hôtel de Crole, with dormer windows and a sculpted cornice at no 67 **rue de Paris**.

Head towards the footbridge over the River Yonne via rue des Boucheries and **rue Sous-Murs**; this street owes its name to the walls of the Gallo-Roman city which ran alongside it; note the houses at nos 14 and 19.

PRINCIPAL SIGHTS

★★ **Cathédrale St-Étienne** ⊘ – The fine Gothic cathedral was built between the 13C and 16C. An earlier building, dating from the foundation of a sanctuary by St Amâtre c 400, succumbed to fire. In 1023, Hugues de Chalon began to construct a Romanesque cathedral. In 1215 Guillaume de Seignelay started all over again with a Gothic one. By 1400 the nave, the aisles, the chapels and the south transept were complete. The building was practically finished by 1525.

West front – The Flamboyant style façade is framed by two towers with sculpted buttresses. The south tower is incomplete. The façade is composed of four storeys of arcades surmounted by gables. Above the centre doorway is a rose window (7m/23ft across) slightly recessed between the buttresses.

The sculptures on the entrance doorways (13C-14C) were mutilated in the 16C during the Wars of Religion, and the soft limestone has weathered badly. The tympanum over the centre door shows Christ enthroned between the Virgin Mary and St John. The lintel depicts the Last Judgment. Christ presides with the Wise Virgins on his right and the Foolish Virgins (lamps upside down) on his left. These 12 statues are placed on the pilasters. Beneath the niches of the base (containing seated figures), there are bas-relief sculptures in two sections: on the left, the Life of Joseph *(read from right to left)*; on the right, the parable of the Prodigal Son *(read from left to right)*.

The sculptures framing the north door trace the lives of the Virgin Mary, St Joachim and St Anne. The Coronation of the Virgin is on the tympanum. The medallions along the base are masterly representations of scenes from Genesis.

The sculptures round the south door are 13C. The **tympanum**, divided into three, and the recessed arches are dedicated to the childhood of Christ and the life of John the Baptist. Six scenes of the love of David and Bathsheba are on the upper section of the base – eight statuettes placed between the gables of the trefoiled arches symbolise Philosophy *(on the right with a crown)* and the seven

Frescoes in the Crypt of St-Étienne

S. Sauvignier/MICHELIN

Liberal Arts.

On the right of the doorway, a high relief represents the Judgement of Solomon. The more interesting of the side entrances is the 14C south door, which is dedicated to St Stephen; the north door is dedicated to St Germanus.

Interior – The nave, built in the 14C, was vaulted in the 15C. On the end wall of the south transept are four consoles supporting amazingly realistic figures. The glass of the rose windows, dating from 1550, shows God the Father surrounded by celestial powers.

The rose window of the north transept (1530) represents the Virgin Mary surrounded by angels and her own emblems.

The **choir and the ambulatory** date from the beginning of the 13C. In 1215, Guillaume de Seignelay, Bishop of Auxerre, who was a great admirer of the new architecture then known as the French style (the term Gothic was not used until the 16C), decided to pull down the cathedral's Romanesque choir; rising above the 11C crypt is the beautiful piece of architecture which he had built to replace it, which was completed in 1234.

The ambulatory is lit by a magnificent array of **stained-glass windows**★★ composed of 13C medallions in which blue and red are the dominant colours. They represent scenes from Genesis, the stories of David, of Joseph and of the Prodigal Son and many saintly legends. The base is emphasised by a blind arcade decorated with sculpted heads, mostly representing the prophets and sibyls.

On the left side of the ambulatory, there is a 16C painting on wood representing the Stoning of St Stephen.

The beautiful **stained glass** of the rose window dates from the 16C. Note also the exquisite craftsmanship of the stained-glass window situated above the statue of the Virgin Mary in the Chapelle Notre-Dame-des-Vertus.

★ **Romanesque crypt** – The crypt, a fine architectural unit and the only remaining element of the 11C Romanesque cathedral is decorated with fine 11C-13C frescoes. The scene on the vault, showing Christ on a white horse surrounded by four mounted angels, is the only example of such a representation in France. The fresco in the apse shows Christ in Majesty surrounded by the symbols of the four Evangelists and two seven-branched candlesticks.

★ **Treasury** – The many interesting exhibits include a collection of 12C-13C chased enamels, manuscripts, 15C-16C books of hours and miniatures.

To reach the old abbey of St-Germain, go along the north side of the cathedral and down rue Cochois which is part of the Quartier de la Marine (see above).

Pass the Préfecture, once the residence of the bishops of Auxerre *(explanatory plaque)*, then the entrance doorway of the old bishops' palace.

★★ **Ancienne abbaye St-Germain** ⊙ – This celebrated Benedictine abbey was built in the 6C by Queen Clotilda, the wife of Clovis, on the site of an oratory where St Germanus, the 5C Bishop of Auxerre, was buried. In the times of Charles the Bald the abbey had a famous school which attracted such teachers as Héric and Rémi of Auxerre; the latter was tutor to St Odo of Cluny. St Patrick, who converted the Irish people to Christianity, was one of the school's famous students.

Abbey church – The upper part of the church was built from the 13C-15C and is Gothic in style; it replaced a Carolingian Romanesque church. The 10-sided Lady Chapel, dating from 1277, is linked to the ambulatory by a short passageway and overlies two semi-underground chapels *(see below)* from the same period. In 1811, a number of bays were demolished at the western end of the church isolating the beautiful 12C Romanesque **bell-tower** (51m/167ft high), known as the tower of St-Jean. The square base, surmounted by the belfry, makes a strong contrast with the soaring stone spire.

The interior of the church is of fine proportions.

★★ **Crypt** – The crypt forms a semi-underground church consisting of a nave and two aisles; the barrel vaulting dates from the Carolingian period. The confessio, raised on three steps in the centre of the crypt, provides a fine view of the Carolingian, Romanesque and Gothic vaulting; four Gallo-Roman columns, capped by composite capitals (acanthus leaves and crockets), support two millennial beams made of oak. The ambulatory is decorated with **frescoes**★ which date from 850 and are some of the oldest in France; they depict the life and martyrdom of St Stephen, and four bishops, in shades of red and ochre.

The vault (5m/16ft deep), where St Germanus' body was enshrined, is covered by a ceiling spangled with painted suns (symbol of eternity), reminiscent of the mosaics in Ravenna where St Germanus died.

The axial chapel, dedicated to St Maxime, was rebuilt in the 13C on the site of the rotunda of the Carolingian crypt. The vaulted roof is divided by ribs into 10 panels. Below is the Chapelle St-Clément, which can be reached via a narrow staircase *(to the right on leaving the Chapelle Ste-Maxime)*. The steeply sloping ground means that only part of the chapels are underground, so there are good views of the valley from some windows.

Musée St-Germain – This museum is in the old conventual buildings of the abbey, including the abbot's residence rebuilt at the beginning of the 18C *(entrance to abbey and museum)*, the 14C cellars, the monks' dormitory, the 12C chapter-house (the latter's beautiful façade was discovered behind the cloisters – *restoration work in progress*) and the sacristy.

The main staircase leads to the monks' dormitory, which houses an **archaeological collection**. In the Gallo-Roman room, note in particular a small Gaulish horse from Guerchy, a cauldron from Cravant, an Etruscan tripod and various imported Etruscan receptacles discovered at the site at Gurgy. On the second floor, the room on pre- and proto-history contains displays on the four major periods (Paleolithic, Neolithic, Bronze and Iron) with explanatory panels. In the centre, a large display case exhibits reconstructions for each of these periods.

AUXERRE

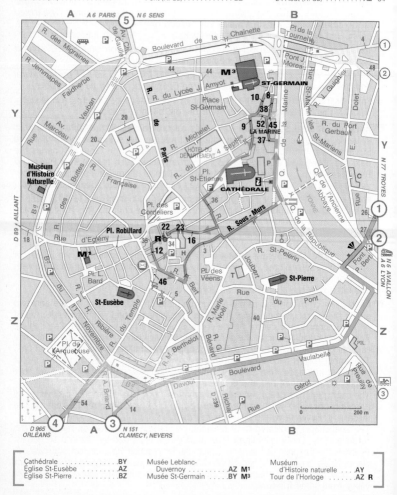

ADDITIONAL SIGHTS

Église St-Pierre – A Renaissance doorway from an old abbey, flanked by two modern buildings, leads off rue Joubert into the courtyard in which this church stands. It is a Classical building which still bears traces of Renaissance decoration. The Flamboyant tower, which has had a lot of work done on it, draws its inspiration from the north tower of the cathedral.

Musée Leblanc-Duvernoy ⊘ – This museum in an 18C residence is mainly devoted to faience ware, with many exhibits from French or local ceramists (there is a particularly large collection of earthenware from the time of the Revolution). The museum also houses a series of magnificent 18C Beauvais tapestries depicting scenes from the life of the Emperor of China, a collection of Italic and Greek (black figure and red figure) pottery as well as earthenware from Puisaye.

Musée d'Histoire Naturelle ⊘ – The Natural History Museum is housed in a pavilion surrounded by a small botanical garden and contains exhibitions on subjects related to the natural sciences of the world at large. One room contains a display on the life and work of Paul Bert.

EXCURSIONS

Seignelay – *10km/6mi N.* Charming town in a hillside setting. Note in particular the 17C covered market on place Colbert and the church of St-Martial. All that remains of the castle destroyed during the Revolution is a section of the curtain wall, a tower restored during the 19C, a 17C gatehouse and the former park.

Prehistoric paintings
in the Grande Grotte

▶▶ **Vallée de l'Yonne from Auxerre to Clamecy** – *59km/38mi along D 163 and D 100; allow 3hr.* Between Auxerre and Cravant, at the confluence of the River Yonne and River Cure, the road runs through a wide valley overlooked by low hills planted with vines and cherry trees. Upriver from Cravant, the valley becomes narrower and the river flows faster, hemmed in by steeper hills.

▶▶ **Vallée de la Cure from Auxerre to Vézelay★** – *60km/38mi.* The River Cure flows into the Yonne at Cravant *(see above).* Beyond Cravant, the road runs close to the river through a hilly landscape of woodlands and vineyards. Upriver from Arcy-sur-Cure, the limestone cliffs towering above the west bank are riddled with caves; the ◎ **Grande Grotte★** is the only one open to visitors. From there, there is a pleasant walk 🚶 along the Cure, beneath limestone escarpments and other caves which are being excavated.

AUXONNE

Michelin map 320: M-6

From its past as a fortified border town, Auxonne has retained its barracks, arsenal, ramparts, shooting range and fortress. Tree-lined alleyways run alongside the River Saône flowing peacefully by.

Lieutenant Bonaparte – In 1788, at the age of 18, second lieutenant Napoleon Bonaparte joined an artillery regiment stationed at Auxonne while he was still a student of the Royal Artillery School. He returned to his native Corsica a year later and came back in 1791 accompanied by his younger brother Louis. In April of that year, he left Auxonne to join his regiment in Grenoble. Five years later he became commander-in-chief of the French Army in Italy.

SIGHTS

Park the car near the town hall gardens.

Located behind the tourist office, the **Porte de Comté**, dating from 1503, is all that remains of the town's fortifications.

COUNTRY-STYLE

Virion – *21130 Les Maillys - 8km/5mi S of Auxonne on D 20 - ☎ 03 80 39 13 40 - michel.virion@wanadoo.fr - closed Sun evening and Mon, Dec-Feb - 13/33.50€.* A friendly village tavern next to the church. There are two dining rooms: one with exposed beams and a fireplace, the other (non-smoking) with a contemporary decor. Simple; well prepared regional dishes at reasonable prices.

Chambre d'hôte Les Laurentides – *27 r. du Centre - 21130 Athée - ☎ 03 80 31 00 25 - ⊡ - 4 rooms: 31/42€ - meals 17€.* This charming and comfortable farmhouse dates from 1870. The rooms, in the old attic, are decorated with paintings created by the proprietress. The nicest ones have a view over the lovely garden.

Église Notre-Dame – The 12C church is decorated with a profusion of gargoyles and statues. On the south side of the transept stands the original Romanesque tower. The 16C porch shelters statues of the prophets carved by Buffet in 1853. Works of art decorating the interior include a late-15C statue of the Virgin with grapes from the School of Claus Sluter (apsidal chapel on the right-hand side).

Nearby, in the centre of place d'Armes stands the **statue of Lieutenant Napoleon Bonaparte** by Jouffroy (1857). Opposite is the 15C brick-built **town hall**.

Rue du Bourg then rue de l'Hôpital (old houses) lead to the castle.

Musée Bonaparte ⊙ – The museum, housed in the largest of the castle's towers, displays mementos of the young lieutenant as well as weapons used by soldiers during the 1st- and 2nd-Empire periods.

EXCURSIONS

Château de Talmay ⊙ – The great 13C square keep (46m/151ft high), topped by a Louis XIV roof and surmounted by a lantern tower, is all that remains of the feudal castle destroyed in 1760 and replaced by the present charming **château** in the Classical style.

There is a curious decoration on the fronton of the 18C main building: the Phrygean goddess, Cybele, mother of the gods, stands in the centre with the sun and the moon on either side. The gardens, through which the Vingeanne flows, are laid out in the French style.

The different floors of the keep are furnished with taste; first there are fine Renaissance rooms with sculpted ceilings and 17C woodwork; on the upper floors are a library, a room decorated with a Louis XIV wainscot, and the guard-room, which has a handsome fireplace.

From the top of the tower there is a wide panorama: La Côte to the west prolonged to the north by the Langres plateau with the Jura mountains rising to the south-east.

▶▶ **Vallée de la Saône downriver from Talmay** – Interesting itinerary through the fertile alluvial valley of the River Saône, with picturesque sites such as the confluence of the River Saône and River Doubs at Verdun-sur-le-Doubs, the old lock and lock-keeper's house at Gigny or the charming lock with restaurants and boat hire at La Truchère, south of Tournus, where the Saône is joined by the Seille. On the way south to Mâcon, there are Romanesque churches at Farges-lès-Mâcon, Uchizy and St-Albain.

AVALLON★

Population 8 217
Michelin map 319: G-7

This pretty town, located on a rocky outcrop high above the Cousin Valley, still has its old **fortified town centre★**. Avallon is also the ideal starting point of excursions into the surrounding area and the Morvan region.

A powerful stronghold – Avallon was during the Middle Ages one of the key cities of Burgundy; anyone wanting to conquer the duchy had to take Avallon. In 1432, Jacques d'Espailly, known as Forte-Épice, and his band of adventurers from the nearby Nivernais region seized several castles of lower Burgundy. Protected by their fortifications, the people of Avallon did not feel threatened; however, Forte-Épice took the guard by surprise, climbed the walls and seized the town. Called to the rescue, the Duke of Burgundy hurried back, made a breach in the city walls with a bombard and launched an attack, but his troops were forced to withdraw. Infuriated by this delay, he immediately called on knights and cross-bowmen whereupon Forte-Épice disappeared through one of the posterns opening onto the riverside, abandoning his men there and then.

Eating out

BUDGET

Le Grill des Madériens – *22 r. de Paris - ☎ 03 86 34 13 16 - relais-des-gourmets@wanadoo.fr - closed Feb, Sun evenings and Mon - reservations required Sat-Sun - 11/23€*. The owners of this restaurant, who are very fond of Madeira, have used this island as a source of inspiration for their decor. The vaulted dining rooms feature white and blue azulejo tiling on the walls, lace fabrics and traditional costumes for the waitresses. Try the delicious grilled meats on skewers served with salads, spicy fish fritters and vegetable dishes with Caribbean seasoning. Lively atmosphere.

Ferme-Auberge des Châtelaines – *3km/1.9mi S of Avallon by D 127 then a minor road - ☎ 03 86 34 16 37 - closed 15 Nov-15 Mar, Mon-Fri out of season and Mon-Wed 1 Jul-1 Sep - ⊠ - reservations recommended - 11/19€*. Pigs, rabbits and lambs are raised on this farm lying in the vicinity of the Cousin Valley... which may explain why the home-grown vegetables and produce are so delicious! Tasty cheese pies and cakes are served in the rustic-style dining room decorated with oilcloth, farming tools and waffle irons. Pretty views of Avallon.

MODERATE

Relais des Gourmets – *47 r. de Paris - ☎ 03 86 34 18 90 - relais-des-gourmets@wanadoo.fr - 14.50/56€*. Local diners come from afar to enjoy the generous helpings of hearty cuisine served on the verandah, on the lovely flowered terrace or in the dining room embellished with exposed beams. Reasonable prices.

Where to stay

MODERATE

Dak'Hôtel – *Rte de Saulieu - ☎ 03 86 31 63 20 - dakhotel@voila.fr - 🅿 26 rooms: 44.21/48.79€ - ⊡ 6.10€*. A modern hotel away from the bustling town centre. The sound-proofed bedrooms, functional and sparsely appointed, are all identical. The breakfast room opens out onto the garden and its swimming pool.

BUDGET

Chambre d'Hôte Haras de Kenmare – *19 rte du Morvan, Le Meix - 89630 St-Germain-des-Champs - 10km/6.5mi S of Avallon by D 944, D 10 then D 75 - ☎ 03 86 34 27 63 - kenmare89@aol.com - ⊠ - 5 rooms: 40/50€ - meals 18/25€*. This welcoming family manor house built in the 19C presents a fine collection of curios and furniture pieces. The bedrooms carry the names of local writers such as Vauban, Lamartine, Vincenot, Colette and story-teller Marie Christmas; their works can be found as bedside books.

EXPENSIVE

Chambre d'Hôte Château d'Island – *89200 Island - 7km/4.3mi SW of Avallon by D 957 then D 53 - ☎ 03 86 34 22 03 - closed 10 Jan-1 Feb and 15 Nov-15 Dec - ⊠ - 11 rooms: 77/153€ - meals 38/61€*. Guests may choose between a bedroom and a suite in this 15C and 18C château nestling in a lovely park. Imposing beams, antique furniture and stately fireplaces await you in this prestigious hotel which affords lovely views of the leafy grounds. Franco-Vietnamese cuisine.

★THE WALLED TOWN

Start from the bastion of the Porte auxerroise to the north.

Tour of the ramparts – From the hospital, an early-18C building, follow rue Fontaine-Neuve overlooked by the Tour des Vaudois; next comes the Bastion de la Côte Gally towering over a ravine. Continue along rue du Fort Mac-Mahon (**9**) to the Bastion de la Petite-Porte, past the Tour du Chapitre (1454) and the Tour Gaujard.

From the **Promenade de la Petite Porte**, a terrace shaded by lime trees, there is a lovely view of the Cousin Valley 100m/109yd below, of several manor houses and of the Morvan heights in the distance.

Continue eastwards round the ramparts.

This section of the town walls overlooks another ravine and runs past the well-preserved Tour de l'Escharguet and the Tour Beurdelaine, the oldest tower built in 1404 and reinforced in 1590 by a bastion flanked by a corbelled bartizan.

AVALLON

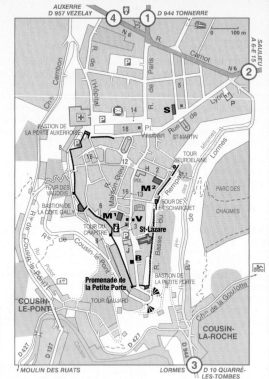

Grenier à sel	**B**
Musée de l'Avallonnais	**M¹**
Musée du Costume et de la Mode	**M²**
Salle de cinéma	**S**
Tour de l'Horloge	**V**

Église St-Lazare – Built of the site of several previous sanctuaries, the church has two interesting **doorways**★ on the façade. Note in particular the richly carved archivolt of the main doorway.

The carvings on the tympanum and lintel of the small doorway have been badly damaged but it is possible to see the Adoration, the Three Kings riding and visiting Herod then the Resurrection and the Descent in limbo. The archivolt is decorated with flower motifs.

To the right is the old Église St-Pierre which now houses temporary exhibitions.

The interior is on different levels, the chancel being 3m/10ft lower than the west doorway. In the south aisle there are 17C statues in polychrome wood, a 15C Virgin with St Ann and a 14C stone statue of St Michael slaying the dragon.

The chapel to the right of the chancel is profusely decorated with *trompe-l'œil* paintings dating from the 18C.

Do not miss the splendid 15C organ loft.

Nearby, in rue Bocquillot, there is a salt storehouse, a former 15C winepress with its recess and mullioned windows.

Tour de l'Horloge – This elegant 15C tower surmounting the Porte de la Boucherie is flanked by a slate-roofed turret topped by a campanile intended for a watchman.

ADDITIONAL SIGHTS

Musée de l'Avallonnais ⊘ – The local museum, founded in 1862, contains an eclectic collection of exhibits, including a number of Gallo-Roman artefacts (a mosaic thought to be of Venus) and an exceptionally fine collection of Roman and medieval coins.

In the Fine Arts section, local artists are well represented; note also the famous 58-plate expressionist series of the **Miserere**★ by Georges Rouault (1949).

Musée du Costume et de la Mode ⊘ – Housed in the old Hôtel de Condé (17C-18C) the fashion museum contains exhibitions of period costume which are rotated annually.

EXCURSIONS

Château de Montjalin ⊘ – *7km/4.3mi E along D 957.*

The outbuildings of this elegant 18C castle house the **Musée des Voitures de chefs d'État**★. Some 30 official cars, mostly black and very long, either convertible or armoured, imposing or dashing, give an insight into the personality of heads of State. Note De Gaulle's Citroën DS 19 with its bullet holes, President Kennedy's

Lincoln Continental, identical to the car in which he was assassinated, Pope Paul VI's Papamobile or the extravagant Cadillac of the Emir of Abou Dhabi...

Ste-Magnance –

19km/9.3mi SE towards Saulieu (N 6). The Gothic **church** of this small village was erected in 1514. The chancel and the apse are covered with Flamboyant vaulting. Inside, note the unusual tomb of St Mag-

A Lincoln Continental
model built for John F. Kennedy

Musée des Voitures de chefs d'État

nance, dating from the 12C. Damaged during the Revolution, it was subsequently restored. The low-relief carvings depict the legend of St Magnance and the miracles she performed.

▶▶ **Vallée du Cousin★** – D 427 follows the River Cousin which wends its way through verdant countryside; the itinerary is dotted with castles and picturesque watermills.

Massif du BALLON D'ALSACE★★★

Michelin map 315: E-9/10 and 314: I to J-6

The Ballon d'Alsace is the southern peak of the rounded granite summits *(ballons)* of the Vosges range. The massif has beautiful forests of pines and larches, delightful woodland, spectacular gorges and, on the uplands, huge mountain pastures covered in colourful alpine flowers. From the highest peak (1 250m/4 101ft) there is a magnificent panorama; in fine weather, you can see as far as the Alps. Unfortunately, the view is often obscured by fog.

★★★BALLON D'ALSACE

From Giromagny to the Ballon d'Alsace

Giromagny – This small town, an important crossroads in the upper valley of the Savoureuse, was for many years a major centre for the textile industry. **Fort Dorsner** at Giromagny, built between 1875 and 1879, has a sizeable weaponry and constituted the link in the line of defensive fortifications between the upper Moselle Valley and the fortress at Belfort. The fort here is now open to the public, having been the object of several restoration projects after years of disuse.

Musée de la Mine et des Techniques minières ⊘ – This small museum of mining and mining technology is to be found in the cultural centre *(Place des Commandos d'Afrique)*. It retraces the history (15C-19C) of mining for copper and lead glance.
Having passed **Lepuix**, a small industrial town, the road follows a narrow gorge.

Roches du Cerf – These rocks line the end of an old glacial valley. They have deep horizontal stripes scoured out by the lateral moraine of the glacier. A rock-climbing school exploits the challenging natural features of this site.

Maison forestière de Malvaux – The forester's lodge is in a pretty setting at the end of the rocky gorge.

Saut de la Truite – The Savoureuse tumbles over a rocky fissure as a waterfall known as the Trout's Leap.

Cascade du Rummel – *15min there and back on foot.*
🏃 A signposted footpath leads to a bridge and then the waterfall, not far from D 465.
Continue along D 465 (leaving the Masevaux road to your right).

The road leads upwards through pretty countryside. The rocky slopes to either side are covered with magnificent pine and beech trees. In the distance, you should be able to see the lakes of Sewen and Alfeld, then across the Alsace plain and the valley of the Doller.

★★★**Ballon d'Alsace** – *30min there and back on foot.*
🏃 The footpath to the summit leads off D 465, from in front of the Ferme-Restaurant du Ballon d'Alsace. It leads across the meadows to a statue of the Virgin Mary. Before Alsace was returned to France, this statue marked the frontier. The Ballon d'Alsace (1 250m/4 101ft high) is the most southerly peak of the Vosges range. Its grassy crest towers above the last foothills of the Vosges. From the viewing terrace, there is a **panorama★★** as far as Donon, to the north, the Alsace plain and the Black Forest, to the east, and Mont Blanc, to the south.

Ski area ⊘ – The Ballon d'Alsace ski area provides 19 downhill runs and 8 cross-country skiing tracks totalling 40km/25mi. Information is available from the **École de ski**.

Eating out

BUDGET

Le Saut de la Truite – *90200 Giromagny - 7 km/4.3mi N of Giromagny by D 465 and rte du Ballon d'Alsace -* ☎ *03 84 29 32 64 - closed 15 Dec-1 Feb and Fri - 15/28€.* In a quiet, peaceful valley, this restaurant's charming garden is enhanced by a quaint wooden bridge spanning a stream. Choose a table by the window, looking out over pine trees. A few simple but carefully kept rooms.

Where to stay

BUDGET

Grand Hôtel du Sommet – *At the summit of the Ballon d'Alsace - 90200 Lepuix-Gy -* ☎ *03 84 29 30 60 - closed Mon except school holidays. -* 🅿 *- 25 rooms: 37€ -* ⌨ *5€ - restaurant 13/23€.* Waking up in the mountains, breathing in the bracing country air, surrounded by cows in their peaceful meadows... is what awaits you in this comfortable hotel, which commands pretty views of Belfort Valley or, on a fine day, the Swiss Alps.

MODERATE

Chambre d'Hôte Le Lodge de Monthury – *70440 Servance - 4.5 km/2.8mi N of Servance by D 263 -* ☎ *03 84 20 48 55 - closed Christmas and New Year - 6 rooms: 50.31/56.41€ - meals 16.77/25.92€.* Facing the Ballon de Servance, this 18C farmhouse dominating Ognon Valley is lost in the Jura countryside. Simple, comfortable rooms. Regional cuisine. Fishing facilities in private ponds for keen anglers.

★★BALLON DE SERVANCE

A few miles west of the Ballon d'Alsace, the Ballon de Servance reaches 1 216m/3 990ft; the River Ognon begins a tumultuous descent here.

Saut de l'Ognon

M. Paygnard/MICHELIN

The pass route

Leave Servance by D 486 towards the Col des Croix.

Servance – 🚶 On the way out of the village to the right, a path (15min there and back) leads to the **Saut de l'Ognon**, a picturesque waterfall gushing out of a narrow gorge.

Col des Croix – Alt 678m/2 225ft. The Château-Lambert fort overlooks the border between the regions of Lorraine and Franche-Comté. This watershed is the dividing line between waters which flow to the North Sea and those which flow to the Mediterranean.

Château-Lambert – Located 1km/0.6mi beyond the Col des Croix, this charming mountain village is home to the **Musée de la Montagne** ⊙. Among the displays, you will find a rural miner's dwelling, a mill, a forge, a 17C winepress, a sawmill, exhibits on foresters' trades and local geology. Nearby, visit the 17C chapel and the St-Antoine Oratory.

Back at the Col des Croix, take D 16 to the right; this old strategic roadway runs along a ridge top. Views of the Ognon Valley open up below, before the path winds into the trees.

★★**Panorama: Ballon de Servance** – *Leave your car at the entrance to the Fort de Servance army road (off-limits).*
🚶 *Follow the blazed trail leading to the top (15min there and back on foot).*
A fabulous prospect stretches out all around; to the west, the Ognon Valley, the Esmoulières glacier plateau studded with ponds and the Langres plateau, to the north-west, the Faucilles mountains and farther on, the Moselle Valley. North-east, you will see from Hohneck to Gresson, passing by the distant Grand Ballon, the outline of the Vosges mountain range. Eastward looms the rounded contour of the Ballon d'Alsace; to the south and south-east lie the foothills of the Vosges.

BAUME-LES-DAMES

Population 5 284
Michelin map 321: I-2

Baume-les-Dames is prettily located against a backdrop of greenery at a point where the valley of the River Doubs widens. The town earns its livelihood in part from small businesses (printing, machine building, furniture, food industry); the famous Ropp pipes are made here. The relatively small historic town centre fortunately escaped destruction during the Second World War and is being gradually restored.

As is the case with Baume-les-Messieurs, Baume-les-Dames, once Baume-les-Nonnes, owes its name partly to an old Celtic word meaning cave, and partly to an old abbey run by Benedictine nuns. The abbey was founded in the 7C on the site of a castle, where St Odilia, blind from birth and driven from Alsace on that account by her father, is said to have lived and recovered her sight through baptism.

In the 18C the canonesses of Baume-les-Dames represented the cream of the aristocracy; in order to be admitted, they had to prove that they had 16 noble ancestors (reflected in the quarterings on their coats of arms).

The physicist Jouffroy d'Abbans (1751-1832) first tested a steamboat at Baume-les-Dames in 1778; a monument near the Doubs bridge commemorates the event.

Église abbatiale ⊙ – *Access under the archway on place de la République.*
The former abbey did not fully live up to its hopes; twice rebuilt, the second project proved too great an undertaking and the church was never finished. Some of the interior furnishings were dispersed under the First Empire. Today, the building is used for temporary exhibits.

St-Martin – This church was rebuilt at the beginning of the 17C. The two chapels on either side of the chancel are adorned with Louis XIII altarpieces with 17C cabled columns. The chapel to the south contains a 1549 Pietà, whereas the north chapel has two statues: a 16C polychrome wooden statue of St Barbara, and a late 18C statue of St Vincent, patron saint of wine-growers. There is a beautiful marble, bronze and wrought-iron lectern in the chancel by Nicole (1751).
There are some beautiful 18C houses around place de la République, to the south of the church. A little further on, a Renaissance house with a beautiful door and a corbelled turret graces the corner of place du Général-de-Gaulle and Place de la Loi.

Usines de pipes Ropp ⊙ – Located on the banks of the Cusancin, this factory has been producing high-quality pipes, sought after by connoisseurs, since the 19C.

EXCURSIONS

The Cusancin Valley

25km/15.5mi round tour – allow 3hr 30min

Drive south out of Baume-les-Dames along D 50 to Pont-les-Moulins then turn left onto D 21.

The picturesque road runs through the green Cusancin Valley to the source of the river at Val de Cusance.

★**Source Bleue** – This is the place where the Cusancin springs up; to the left, the Source Bleue (the Blue Spring), a pool of still waters hemmed in by woods; to the right, the Source Noire (the Black Spring), which flows out of a cave at the foot of a limestone cliff.

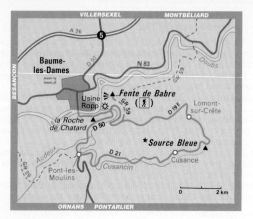

Follow the narrow road up to Lomont-sur-Crête and turn left onto D 19ᴱ. Continue past the 2nd fork to Villers-St-Martin, turn right onto the forest road of Bois de Babre then onto the path leading to Fente de Babre and the top of the cliff.

Fente de Babre – *15min on foot there and back.*

A pleasant path running through a wooded area leads to the Fente de Babre, a joint in the rock which overlooks the south bank of the Doubs and offers a pleasant **view**★ of Pont-les-Moulins and the Audeux Valley, Baume-les-Dames and the surrounding area.

Return to D 19E and turn right towards Baume-les-Dames.

Valley and mountain

Drive east out of Baume-les-Dames towards Montbéliard.

The road winds along the Doubs Valley through a pleasant rolling country landscape. Small villages make a very pretty picture, their red roofs reflected in the river.

Clerval – Clerval is a small community between the forest of Côte d'Armont and Montfort mountain, in which a few small businesses have set themselves up. There are some particularly interesting works in the **church** ⊙: two 16C statues on each side of the crucifix and a 16C wooden Pietà in a side aisle.

The road runs between wooded cliffs and gentle foothills, straying from the river's edge when the valley is wide enough for it to do so, only to return and stick close to the river's winding course a moment later.

L'Isle-sur-le-Doubs – Interestingly, the Doubs divides this town into three districts: the "Ile" (island) in the middle of the river; the "Rue" (street) on the north bank; and "Le Magny" on the south bank. The banks of the Canal du Moulin are very picturesque.

Return to the entrance to the town, driving towards the A 36 interchange and continue along D 31 which runs south under the motorway to Belvoir.

★**Château de Belvoir** – *See Château de BELVOIR.*

Continue to Sancey-le-Grand and turn right onto D 464 to Vellevans, Servin and Vaudrivillers. At the intersection with D 50, turn left to Orsans then right onto D 120 to the Grotte de la Glacière.

Grotte de la Glacière ⊙ – This 66m/217ft deep glacial cave lets in daylight through a large opening.

The **Maison des cristaux**, at the entrance to the cave, displays a rich collection of minerals from various countries.

Continue along D 120 towards Aissey, then turn right onto D 492 which runs into D 50 on the way back to Baume-les-Dames.

BAUME-LES-MESSIEURS★★★

Population 194
Michelin map 321: D-6

Baume-les-Messieurs stands in a grandiose **setting** at the convergence of three valleys, one of which is the magnificent blind valley *(reculée)* of the Baume amphitheatre. The village, framed by rocky cliffs, is famous for the ruins of its old abbey, which make a very interesting visit. There is a beautiful view of the site from the viewpoint at the foot of the church of Granges-sur-Baume *(4km/2.5mi north)*.

Cirque and village of Baume-les-Messieurs

Monks and Gentlemen – The abbey at Baume was founded c 870 and adopted the Benedictine Rule. One of its claims to glory is that in 909 six of its monks were among the founders of the illustrious abbey at Cluny. Monastic life, however, grew increasingly lax, as it did at St-Claude *(see ST-CLAUDE)*; from the 16C onwards, the humble monks of the abbey's beginnings were replaced by canons of noble birth, who had a much more worldly view of life. These high and mighty Messieurs lost no time in modifying the name of their home, thus Baume-les-Moines became Baume-les-Messieurs. This state of affairs lasted until the Revolution; in 1793 all the possessions of the abbey were seized and sold off at public auction.

The adventurous life of Jean de Watteville – Jean de Watteville was one of the abbots of Baume in the 17C, as well as one of the most extraordinary characters of his age, if one is to believe the Memoirs of St Simon. His numerous adventures have almost certainly been embellished by hearsay.

Soldier, Franciscan friar, Carthusian monk, Turkish Pasha... – Watteville initially followed a military career. While a minor officer in the Burgundy regiment during the Milan campaign he fought a duel with a Spanish nobleman in the service of the Queen of Spain and killed him. He was obliged to flee and went underground in Paris. While there, he overheard a sermon on the dangers of hell in a church one day and, overcome with remorse, converted to Christianity. The ex-soldier became a Franciscan friar, then entered the abbey of Bonlieu as a Carthusian monk.

It was not long before Watteville tired of monastic life. However, he was caught climbing the wall in his bid for freedom by the prior himself. Without a second's hesitation, Watteville shot the man with his pistol and made good his escape. After many an adventure, he crossed the Pyrenees into Spain.

Leaving behind a second noble Spanish corpse, the victim of our hero's prowess in another duel, Watteville fled to Constantinople. The ex-monk converted to Islam and put his military talents to the service of the Sultan, who was so impressed with him that he promoted him first to Pasha, then to Governor of the province of Morea.

Abbot of Baume... – After several years of living the high life surrounded by a sizeable harem, Watteville made an offer to the Venetians, whom he had been engaged by the Sultan to fight: if they could promise him papal absolution for his past crimes as well as the abbey of Baume as a reward, he would surrender his troops. This outrageous deal was struck, and our opportunist ex-Pasha shaved his head for the second time and took charge of the abbey of Baume and its resident monks, directing them very much as if they were soldiers in a military campaign.

137

The abbot remained as impetuous as ever, as several anecdotes from this stage of his life illustrate. For example, Watteville had the series of ladders, which had previously been the only way of getting to the bottom of the valley from Crançot, replaced by steps cut into the rock (the Échelles de Crançot). Seeing his monks taking infinite pains not to break their necks on the steep, slippery steps, the abbot flew into a rage, had his mule brought to him, leapt onto the long-suffering animal's back and drove it down the steps, berating the anxious monks as he went for their cowardice.

Parliamentary Intermediary – When Louis XIV invaded Franche-Comté, Watteville, after cunningly weighing up the French chances of winning, offered his services to the French king. Thanks to his skilful use of language and his clever scheming, he won over the last centres of resistance (Gray, Ornans, Nozeroy) to the French king's cause without a single shot being fired, greatly simplifying Louis XIV's 1668 campaign.

After the Nijmegen peace treaty of 1678, Watteville returned to his abbey, where he led a life of luxury and splendour more befitting a great lord. His eventful life finally came to an end in 1702, when he was 84.

Detail of altarpiece,
abbey church of
Baume-les-Messieurs

A. Le Toquin/EXPLORER

ABBAYE ⊙

A vaulted passageway leads into the first courtyard of the abbey, around which are the old guesthouse, the abbot's residence, the keep, the tower used as a court *(tour de justice)* and the church.

Church – The 15C façade has an interesting doorway: God the Father giving Blessing is depicted on the central pillar and angels enthusiastically playing musical instruments in the side niches. The nave was once paved with tombstones, of which about 40 remain; the most interesting are leaning against the wall of the north side aisle. Close by it the tomb of Abbot Jean de Watteville. The Chapelle de Chalon, the mausoleum of the aristocratic Chalon *(see NOZEROY)* family, is to the north of the chancel. It contains a 16C statue of St Catherine and a 15C stone **statue of St Paul**, as well as various tombs of the Chalon family. There is a beautiful painted and sculpted early 16C Flemish **altarpiece★★** depicting Christ's Passion.

Cour du cloître – A door in the middle of the nave on the south side leads to what used to be the cloisters. The monks' dormitory and refectory overlooked this courtyard, which still has its **fountain**.

Abbey buildings – Go through an arch on the left. This leads into another courtyard surrounded by buildings which once contained the apartments of the aristocratic canons.

Return to the old cloisters and the first courtyard through a vaulted passageway via the 13C cellars.

EXCURSION

★★★ Cirque de Baume

21km/13mi round tour

Information on walks and rambles is available in the café-restaurant Le Grand Jardin, near the abbey (open all year).

Leave Baume-les-Messieurs on D 70E3 over the Seille; then take D 70E1 to the left, which goes down to the bottom of the amphitheatre along the banks of the Dard.

The tall rocky cliffs which form this amphitheatre are an awe-inspiring sight. Leave the car near the Chalet des Grottes de Baume.

★Grottes de Baume ⊙ – The source of the Dard, a tributary of the Seille, was once to be found in these caves. Following heavy rainfall, the overspill from the Dard does still flow from here in a great cascade. The resurgent spring is below and to the left of the entrance to the caves which feature impressive cracks in the rock.

Having gone along the entrance gallery, visitors are taken through tall, narrow chambers to the **great hall**, which has superb acoustics. Then the visit goes around a little lake containing small white blind shrimp of the *niphargus* genus. The ceiling of the **Catafalque gallery** is 80m/262ft high.

Return to D 70 and then turn right to Crançot.

There is a view after the second hairpin bend of Baume and its abbey, which can be seen nestling at the bottom of the valley, at the foot of white limestone cliffs.

La Croix viewpoint – *Stop at the crossroads of D 70 and D 210.* ⓚ *Take the path on the right which leads to the forest, following the blue trail markers (20min there and back on foot). At the end of the path, near the cross, there is a great* **view★** *over Baume-les-Messieurs, the abbey and the reculée below.*

Turn back, and if you like, head for the village of Granges-sur-Baume.

DINING AL FRESCO ...

Les Grottes – *Near the caves - 3 km/1.9mi S of Baume -* ☎ *03 84 44 61 59 - closed 1 Oct-Easter and Wed except Jul-Aug – reservations required - 13/24€. This restaurant is truly astounding! The pretty 1900 pavilion enjoys a shaded terrace that offers breathtaking views of the surrounding waterfalls. In winter you can take refuge in the dining room with its old-fashioned decor.*

... A BED IN THE ABBEY

Chambre d'Hôte Gothique Café – ☎ *03 84 44 64 47 - 3 rooms: 60€ - meals 14.50/18.50€.* Housed in one of the abbey buildings, this hotel has nicely decorated, spacious, cosy rooms that look out onto the pretty town down below and its remarkable natural site. The Gothique Café restaurant offers tasty regional cuisine in a medieval setting.

A belvedere at the town limits *(follow the signs)* offers another remarkable **view★**. In the distance, you can see the *reculée* and the waterfall.

Go back to the crossroads. Further ahead turn right on D 4, then right again at Crançot on D 471, then right once more towards the Belvédère des Roches-de-Baume, also known as the Belvédère de Crançot.

★★★ Belvédère des Roches-de-Baume – ⓚ Walk along the edge of the cliff which forms the famous viewpoint. At the last minute an astounding view of the entire amphitheatre unfolds though a gap in the rocks. The rocky outcrops crowning the cliff are surprisingly thick. *Near the viewpoint furthest to the right there is a path down in the shape of steps cut into the rock.* These steps, known as the **Échelles de Crançot**, lead to the floor of the amphitheatre and to the caves.

Return to D 471 and follow it to Crancot then take D 4 back to Baume-les-Messieurs.

BEAUNE★★

Population 21 923
Michelin map 320: I-7 – Local map see La CÔTE

At the heart of the Burgundian vineyards lies Beaune, a name synonymous with good wine; that is why a visit to this ancient city, which boasts a splendid architectural heritage and some fine museums, is not complete without a tour of the vineyards of La Côte.

HISTORICAL NOTES

The capital of Burgundy wine

Birth of a town – First a Gaulish centre and then an outpost of Rome, Beaune was the residence of the dukes of Burgundy up to the 14C, before they moved permanently to Dijon. The original charter of communal liberties granted by Duke Eudes in 1203 is still in the town's archives.

The fortifications and towers that exist today were built from the 15C onwards. After the death of the last Duke of Burgundy, Charles the Bold, in 1477, the town stubbornly refused all efforts to annex it by Louis XI and surrendered only after a siege lasting five weeks.

There has always been a degree of rivalry, if not outright animosity, between the citizens of Dijon and Beaune. This was particularly pronounced during the 18C and was an ample source of inspiration to the Dijon poet **Alexis Piron** (1689-1773), who did not restrict himself merely to penning offensive odes about the residents of Beaune, but

S. Sauvignier/MICHELIN

Wine auction in Beaune

actually went there to insult them in person. His audacity almost cost him dear, however; he was cornered by an angry crowd baying for his blood and would certainly have been set upon, had a kindly citizen not rescued him and smuggled him out of the town at night.

Wine auction at the Hospices de Beaune – This is certainly the main local event of the year and draws a large crowd to the town. The Hospices de Beaune (this name includes the Hôtel-Dieu, the Hospice de la Charité and the hospital) acquired a very fine vineyard (58ha/143 acres) between Aloxe-Corton and Meursault through Chancellor Rolin. The wines from this vineyard have won international acclaim, and the honour of being a wine-producer for the Hospices is highly sought after. The proceeds of the auction sales, **"Les Trois Glorieuses"**, which are known as the "greatest charity sale in the world", go to the modernisation of the surgical and medical facilities and the maintenance of the Hôtel-Dieu.

TOWN WALK

The town centre

Parking is available near boulevard Foch and boulevard Joffre. Enter the town centre through Porte St-Nicolas, a triumphal arch erected during the reign of Louis XV.

Among the many picturesque old houses, note those at nos 18, 20, 22 and 24 **Rue de Lorraine**, which form a fine 16C ensemble.

★ **Hôtel de la Rochepot** – *Not open to the public.* This 16C building has an admirable Gothic façade.

In Place Monge stand a 14C belfry and a statue by Rude of **Gaspard Monge** (1746-1818), a local shopkeeper's son who became a famous mathematician. He is considered to be the founder of descriptive geometry (application of geometry to construction problems).

No 4 **Place Carnot** is a 16C house with attractive sculptures.

Place de la Halle – This is the very heart of the city. The Hôtel-Dieu with its fine slate roof overlooks the square.

All around the square and along the adjacent streets, attractive shop fronts display regional specialities: wine, spirits and confectionery.

Avenue de la République and rue d'Enfer lead to the former mansion of the dukes of Burgundy, dating from the 15C and 16C, now the museum of Burgundy wine.

Continue to Notre-Dame.

★ **Collégiale Notre-Dame** – The daughter house of Cluny, begun about 1120, was considerably influenced by the church of St-Lazare in Autun; it is a fine example of Burgundian Romanesque art despite successive additions.

Exterior – The façade is concealed by a wide 14C porch with three naves. The sculpted decoration was destroyed during the Revolution, but the 15C carved door panels have survived.

Walk clockwise round the church to get the best view of the chevet. Three different phases of construction – the pure Romanesque of the ambulatory and apsidal chapels, the 13C refurbishment of the chancel and the 14C flying buttresses – can be detected in the handsome proportions of the whole. The crossing tower, which is formed of Romanesque arcades surmounted by pointed bays, is capped by a dome and a 16C lantern.

Interior – The lofty nave of broken-barrel vaulting is flanked by narrow aisles with groined vaulting. A triforium, composed of open and blind bays, goes round the building, which is strongly reminiscent of Autun with its decoration of arcades and small fluted columns.

The transept crossing is covered by an octagonal dome on squinches. Behind this, the ambulatory, with three semi-domed apsidal chapels opening into it, leads off around the harmoniously proportioned choir. Note the 12C black Virgin.

Eating out

BUDGET

Le Bouchon – *Pl. de l'Hôtel-de-Ville - 21900 Meursault - 8 km/5mi SW of Beaune by N 74 -* ☎ *03 80 21 29 56 - closed 20 Nov-28 Dec Sun evenings and Mon - 10.06/25€*. Le Bouchon is a small, popular restaurant in the town centre with a thriving local clientele. Regional dishes are served in a simply decorated dining room with small but pretty square tables. Good choice of menus.

MODERATE

Bénaton – *25 r. du Fg-Bretonnière -* ☎ *03 80 22 00 26 - lebenaton@libertysurf.fr - closed Thu except evenings in high season and Wed - 20/41.50€*. Small restaurant far from the madding crowd with a pretty covered terrace for the summer days. Pleasant dining room with stone walls and bright decorative hues. Attractive quality/price ratio for light yet delicious meals made with fresh seasonal produce.

Le Caveau des Arches – *10 bd Perpreuil -* ☎ *03 80 22 10 37 - restaurant.caveau.des.arches@wanadoo.fr - closed 5-26 Aug, 23 Dec-5 Jan Sun and Mon - 20/26€*. In summer remember to bring a cardigan with you as the vaulted dining rooms of this restaurant set up on the ramparts can be somewhat chilly... Admire the ruins of an old bridge which once gave access to the city. Traditional Burgundy cooking.

Where to stay

BUDGET

Chambre d'Hôte Le Meix des Hospices – *R. Basse (near the church) - 71150 Demigny - 10 km/6.2mi S of Beaune by D 18 -* ☎ *03 85 49 98 49 -* ✍ *- 3 rooms: 34/49€*. This former hospice annexe consists of several outbuildings arranged around a square courtyard. The quiet, simple rooms, one of which is set up beneath the eaves, are sparsely appointed with modern furniture. The dining room features exposed beams, stone flooring and a fireplace.

MODERATE

Hôtel du Parc – *21200 Levernois - 5 km/3.1mi SW of Beaune by rte de Verdun-sur-le-Doubs, D 970 then D 111L -* ☎ *03 80 24 63 00 - hotel.le.parc@wanadoo.fr - closed 24 Nov-23 Jan -* 🅿 *- 25 rooms: 45/83€ -* ⌑ *6€*. Covered with Virginia creeper and bursting with flowers in summertime, this hotel is quite simply charming. The two buildings are separated by a small patio. Bright, sober accommodation. The park at the back looks out over peaceful meadows.

EXPENSIVE

Hôtel Le Cep – *27 r. Maufoux -* ☎ *03 80 22 35 48 - resa@hotel-cep-beaune.com -* 🅿 *- 57 rooms: 153/320€ -* ⌑ *15€*. Ravishing 16C house in the old quarter. The bedrooms, decorated in old-fashioned style, carry the names of famous vintages from the Côte-d'Or. Breakfast is served in the vaulted cellar or, weather permitting, in the courtyard with its pretty Renaissance arcades and medallions.

Hostellerie du Château de Bellecroix – *Rte de Chalon - 71150 Chagny - 18 km/11.2mi SW of Beaune by N 74 then N 6 -* ☎ *03 85 87 13 86 - chateau.de.bellecroix@wanadoo.fr - closed 18 Dec-13 Feb Thu lunchtime and Wed -* ⌑ *- 20 rooms: 84/182€ -* ⌑ *13€ - restaurant 43/56.50€*. The two towers of this 18C château stand amid wooded parkland. Nearby lie the turrets of a former 12C Knights Templars commanderie belonging to the Order of Malta. The bedrooms are appointed with antique furniture. There are some fine replicas of medieval wainscoting in the dining hall.

On the town

Le Bistrot Bourguignon – *8 r. Monge -* ☎ *03 80 22 23 24 - bistrobourgogne@aol.com - open Tue-Sat 11am-3pm, 6-11pm - closed mid-Feb to mid-Mar*. Relax on the charming terrace or sink into one of the comfortable armchairs inside this old house, sipping a glass of excellent wine to the strains of a few popular songs... A café with irresistible charm.

Place Carnot – *Pl. Carnot*. This large, recently restored square has many outdoor cafés where you can sit in the sun all day. The perfect place to have breakfast, lunch... or dinner!

Winelovers' paradise

L'Athenaeum de la Vigne et du Vin – *7 r. de l'Hôtel-Dieu -* ☎ *03 80 25 08 30 - athenaeum@mail.com - open daily 10am-7pm - Closed 25 Dec-1 Jan*. This bookshop has earned quite a reputation as the ultimate authority on the art of oenology, Burgundy and fine gastronomy. It also presents a collection of miscellaneous items related to wine: corkscrews, glasses, cellarman's knives...

Cordeliers wine cellar

Cave Patriarche Père & Fils – *7 r. du Collège -* ☎ *03 80 24 53 78 -
www.patriarche.com - open Oct-Mar: daily 10-11.30am, 2-5.30pm; Apr-Sep:
daily 9.30-11.30am, 2-5.30pm - closed 25 Dec-1 Jan.* Burgundy's largest
cellars (15 000m²/18 000sq yd) are housed in a former convent dating from
the 14C and 16C. Guided tours and tasting sessions of 13 different wines.

Caves de La Reine Pédauque – *Porte St-Nicolas -* ☎ *03 80 22 23 11 -
www.reine-pedauque.com - open end of Nov to Mar: daily 10am-noon, 2-5pm;
Apr-Nov: daily 9.30am-12.30pm, 2-7pm - closed Christmas and Jan.* After
exploring the 18C vaulted cellars, visitors may take part in a wine tasting session
around an imposing round marble table! An opportunity not to be missed!

L'Hallebarde – *24 bis r. d'Alsace -* ☎ *03 80 22 07 68 – open Tue-Sat and
bank holiday weekends: 9-2am - closed Feb school holidays.* The owners of this
bar have painstakingly recreated the setting of a medieval inn, which evokes
vivid images of opulent banquets and chivalrous knights in armour... Have a
beer or a glass of wine while enjoying the decor.

La Cave des Cordeliers – *6 r. de l'Hôtel-Dieu -* ☎ *03 80 24 53 79 – open
Oct-Mar: daily 10.30am-noon, 2-6pm; Apr-Sep: daily 9.30am-7pm - closed 25
Dec-1Jan.* The Couvent des Cordeliers, built in 1242, provides a splendid backdrop to these wine cellars, which you can visit before tasting six fine Burgundy
wines. In the courtyard, note the 1580 low relief depicting the Adoration of
the Magi.

Le Comptoir Viticole – *1 r. Samuel-Legay -* ☎ *03 80 22 15 73 – open Mon-
Sat 9am-noon, 2-7pm - closed public holidays.* Wine buffs and amateur
vignerons will adore this shop, which sells all manner of devices related to wine-
making: bottling machines, corkscrews, bottle racks, jeroboams, balthasars...

Le Pickwick's – *2 r. Notre-Dame -* ☎ *03 80 22 55 52 – open daily 11am-
3pm, 5pm-2am.* The work of an Englishman, this pub offers a refined setting
and a cosy, comfortable atmosphere typical of the best British establishments:
fireplace, leather armchairs, wood panelling and a tribute to famous author
Charles Dickens. In addition to the traditional beers and whiskies, the wine list
features bottles from all over the world.

Marché aux Vins – *2 r. Nicolas-Rolin -* ☎ *03 80 25 08 20 -
www.marcheauxvins.com - open mid-Jun to mid-Sep: daily 9.30am-5.45pm;
mid-Sep to mid-Jun: 9.30am-noon, 2-5.30pm - closed 25 Dec-1 Jan.* Housed
in Beaune's oldest church (13C and 14C) opposite the famous hospice, this
wine market offers 18 wines of between 3 and 15 years of age, to be sipped
and relished slowly. If requested, a cellar containing some extremely rare vintages, which have been maturing since 1911, can also be opened to visitors.

Palais des Gourmets – *14 pl. Carnot -* ☎ *03 80 22 13 39 – open May-Sep:
daily 7am-7.30pm; Oct-Apr: Tue-Sun 7am-7.30pm.* This delightful pâtisserie-
tea room serves many a local delicacy, including *cassissines* (blackcurrant fruit
jelly flavoured with blackcurrant liquor), *roulés au cointreau* (pancakes with a
Cointreau filling) and chocolate medallions depicting the Hôtel-Dieu.

Vins de Bourgogne Denis-Perret – *40 r. Carnot -* ☎ *03 80 22 35 47 - denis.perret@denisperret.fr - open May-Oct: Mon-Sat 9am-7pm, Sun 9am-noon; the rest of the year Mon-Sat 9am-noon, 2-7pm, Sun 9am-noon.* Five wine-growers and a bunch of landowners have teamed up to offer you some of the most prestigious names from the Burgundy region: Romanée-Conti, Clos-Vougeot, Montrachet, Chambertin... Such a rich selection could easily leave you speechless but, not to worry, for several young oenologists are there to help you make your choice and to suggest the best dishes to go with each wine.

Besides the decoration of the small columns in the transept, it is worth noting the band of rosettes under the false triforium in the choir, and the sculptures on certain capitals in the nave representing Noah's Ark, the Stoning of St Stephen and a Tree of Jesse. The second chapel in the north aisle contains 15C frescoes depicting the Resurrection of Lazarus, which are attributed to Burgundian artist Pierre Spicre, and a 16C Pietà. There are two altarpieces in the third chapel.
Note the Renaissance chapel with the fine coffered ceiling off the south aisle.

BEAUNE

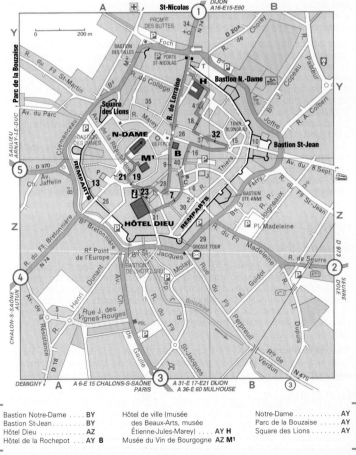

★★ Tapestries – In the choir behind the high altar there are some magnificent tapestries which mark the transition from medieval to Renaissance art. Five richly coloured panels, worked in wool and silk, trace the whole life of the Virgin Mary in a series of charming scenes. They were commissioned in 1474, woven from cartoons by Spicre based on outlines supplied by Chancellor Rolin and offered to the church in 1500 by Canon Hugues le Coq.

Cloisters – A Romanesque doorway in the south transept leads to what remains of the 13C cloisters and the chapter-house, which have both been restored.

Go back to the Hôtel-Dieu.

At no 2 **Rue E.-Fraysse**, the Maison du Colombier is a pretty Renaissance house which can be seen from the square in front of the church of Notre-Dame; no 13 **Place Fleury** is the Hôtel Saulx, a mansion with a quaint tower and an interior courtyard. The Maison des Vins (wine-tasting) is located along rue Rolin, just beyond the Hôtel-Dieu.

Continue along this street to the small place Carnot and on to place Ziem, opposite the Chapelle St-Étienne; rue de l'Enfant and rue des Tonneliers lead to place du Dr-Jorrot.

At no 10 **Rue Rousseau-Deslandes** there is a house with its first floor decorated with trefoiled arcades.

Rue Favart and rue Belin lead to the town hall.

Hôtel de ville – The town hall occupies the buildings of a 17C Ursuline convent. The right wing houses two **museums** (see Additional Sights).

The ramparts

The relatively well-preserved ramparts form an almost continuous wall walk (2km/1mi) – parts of which are now private property. The wall was built between the end of the 15C and the middle of the 16C, of roughly rectangular blocks. It is adorned with a few surviving towers and eight rustic bastions of various shapes – the double one, originally a castle, is known as the **Bastion St-Jean**. In places the ramparts are hidden by bushes or private houses; the encircling moat is now occupied by gardens, tennis courts etc.

A tour of the ramparts is possible on foot or by car.

Tour of the ramparts – *From the Bastion St-Jean follow the outer boulevards, beginning with Boulevard Joffre, counter-clockwise.* The north tower of the Bastion St-Jean has several gargoyles and a niche occupied by a Virgin and Child. It overlooks a cherry orchard in the moat. Pass the Blondeau tower, which protrudes from the ramparts, to get to the **Bastion Notre-Dame**, with its trees and a charming turret covering the spur. The line of the ramparts is broken by the 18C Porte St-Nicolas at the end of Rue Lorraine. Next come the Bastion des Filles, spoilt by the addition of an ugly new roof, and the now filled-in Bastion St-Martin forming a triangular terrace **(Square des Lions)** overlooking a shaded garden.

The route now takes you past the Bastion des Dames (pretty house and trees), the **Rempart des Dames** (walkway bordered by fine plane trees) and the now-abandoned Bastion de l'Hôtel-Dieu, with a stream at its foot which served the wash-houses in days gone by. The 15C Grosse Tour (great tower) on the Rempart Madeleine is followed by the overgrown Bastion Ste-Anne sporting a turret overlooking the moat. The tour ends in front of the castle's **south tower** overlooking the hedges and bamboo in the moat. Stand back a little to obtain a better view of this outwork crowned by a small house against a background of varnished tile roofs.

Beyond the walls

Église St-Nicolas – *Leave by ① on the town plan, N 74.* This 13C church in the midst of the wine-growers' area has a Romanesque tower with a fine stone spire. A 15C timber porch, covered with tiles and supported by pillars of dressed stone, shelters a 12C doorway. The monolithic tympanum depicts the Golden Legend of St Nicholas, in which he saves three young girls, whose father was too poor to provide them with a dowry, from a life of prostitution by giving them each a golden ball.

Parc de la Bouzaise – *Take Avenue du Parc (Faubourg St-Martin).* The fine shady trees and artificial lake fed by the river make this an agreeable spot for a walk (boating).

★★★ HÔTEL-DIEU ⊘

The Hôtel-Dieu in Beaune, a marvel of Burgundian-Flemish art, was founded as a hospital by Chancellor Nicolas Rolin in 1443. The medieval building with its perfectly preserved medieval decor has survived intact and was used as a general hospital until 1971. Today it is a very successful tourist attraction.

The Grand'Salle, Hôtel-Dieu

Street façade – The principal decorative elements of this sober façade with its tall and steeply-pitched slate roof are the dormer windows, the weather vanes, the delicate pinnacles and lacework cresting of lead. The roof line is broken by the bell turret surmounted by a slim Gothic spire 30m/98ft high.

The lovely, delicate roof above the entrance porch is composed of three slate gables terminating in worked pinnacles. Each weather vane bears a different coat of arms. On the beautifully panelled door, note the ironwork grille with sharp points and the door knocker, a magnificent piece of sculpted wrought-iron work.

Courtyard – The courtyard is surrounded by buildings which give it a charming overall effect in which cheerfulness, wealth and homeliness combine to make this seem more like a dwelling fit for royalty than a hospital for the poor. The wings to the left and the rear have magnificent roofs of coloured glazed tiles (recently restored) arranged in striking geometric patterns. These roofs are punctuated by turrets and a double row of dormer windows, surmounted by weather vanes adorned with heraldic bearings and small spires of worked lead.

A timbered gallery at first floor level rests on light stone columns forming cloisters on the ground floor. The building on the right, erected in the 17C, on the site of outbuildings, does not mar the beauty of the overall effect. On the reverse side of the façade, the pavilions that frame the entrance doorway were built during the 19C. The old well, with its wrought-iron well-head and its stone curb, is graceful.

★★★ **Grand'Salle or Chambre des Pauvres** – ⊙ This immense hall (72m long by 14m wide by 16m high/ - 236ft x 46ft x 52ft), used as the poor ward, has a magnificent timber roof in the shape of an upturned keel which is painted throughout; the ends of the tie-beams disappear into the gaping mouths of monsters' heads. The paving is a reproduction of the original flag stones. All the furniture is original or else copied from the original models.

In earlier times on feast days the 28 four-poster beds *(see photograph)* were covered with fine tapestry bedspreads, now displayed in the Salle du Polyptyque. Even without the tapestries, the double row of beds with their red and white bedclothes, hangings and testers makes a striking impression. At the end of the room stands an arresting, larger than life-size polychrome wooden statue (15C) of **Christ seated and bound**★ carved from a single piece of oak.

The Flamboyant style screen separating the Grand'Salle from the chapel was reconstructed in the 19C together with the large stained-glass window. The famous altarpiece by Roger van der Weyden, now in the Salle du Polyptyque, used to be above the altar. The chapel exhibits a copper funerary plaque in memory of Guigone de Salins, wife of Nicolas Rolin and co-founder of the Hôtel-Dieu. The Clermont-Tonnerre collection of sacred art (priestly vestments and objects) is displayed in showcases.

Salle Ste-Anne – The linen room, visible through the windows, was originally a small bedroom reserved for the nobility. The work of the nursing nuns is illustrated by life-size models dressed in the habits worn by the staff until 1961.

Salle St-Hugues – This ward, which was taken out of use in 1982, has been partially refurbished with its 17C decor; the beds are those which were in use from the end of the 19C. The frescoes, by Isaac Moillon, depict St Hugues, as bishop and Carthusian monk, and the nine miracles of Christ.

Salle St-Nicolas – This ward, where those in danger of death were nursed, now houses a permanent exhibition on the history of the Hôtel-Dieu and the healing of the body and mind which it offered to the poor and sick. A glass slab in the centre reveals the Bouzaise stream which flows beneath the hospital and which carried away the waste.

Cuisine – *Son et lumière presentation every 15min.* In the kitchen, an old-fashioned scene has been set up round the huge Gothic fireplace with its double hearth and automatic spit, which dates from 1698.

Pharmacie – The first room of the pharmacy contains pewter vessels displayed on a handsome 18C dresser; the second, which is panelled, contains a collection of 18C Nevers porcelain and a huge bronze mortar.

Salle St-Louis – The walls are hung with early-16C tapestries from Tournai depicting the parable of the Prodigal Son and a series woven in Brussels (late 16C) illustrating the story of Jacob.

Salle du Polyptyque – This room was designed to exhibit the famous **polyptych of the Last Judgment★★★** by Roger van der Weyden. This masterpiece of Flemish art, commissioned by Nicolas Rolin to grace the altar in the Grand'Salle and completed between 1445 and 1448, was extensively restored in the 19C and sawn in two so that both faces could be displayed simultaneously. A mobile magnifying glass enables viewers to study the smallest detail on the highly expressive faces of the subjects.

In the central panel Christ presides at the Last Judgment; he is enthroned on a rainbow surrounded by golden clouds suggestive of Paradise; four angels carrying the instruments of the Passion stand at his sides in the flanking panels. St Michael is weighing the souls, with angels sounding their trumpets on either side of him. In attendance on the central figures are the Virgin Mary and St John the Baptist appealing to the Saviour for mercy. Behind them are the Apostles and a few important people (including the donors) who are interceding on behalf of humankind.

The reverse side of the polyptych is on the wall to the right. In the past, only this face was usually visible, as the polyptych was opened only on Sundays and feast days. The fine portraits of Nicolas Rolin and his wife are accompanied by monochromes of St Sebastian and St Anthony, the first patrons of the Hôtel-Dieu, and the Annunciation. On the wall to the left hangs a beautiful early-16C *mille-fleurs* tapestry depicting the legend of St Eligius.

The tapestries hanging opposite the Last Judgment belonged to Guigone de Salins; against the deep rose-coloured background, scattered with turtle doves, are the arms of the founder of the hospital, an interlaced G and N and the motto *Seulle* (you alone) expressing Nicolas Rolin's faithful attachment to his wife. In the centre is St Anthony the hermit, patron saint of Guigone de Salins.

ADDITIONAL SIGHTS

★ **Musée du Vin de Bourgogne** ⓥ **(Burgundy Wine Museum)** – The museum is laid out in the former mansion of the dukes of Burgundy, a building of the 15C and 16C in which stone and woodwork complement each other harmoniously. The inner courtyard recalls the decor of a theatre and displays a reduced scale model (1:200) of the town's ramparts. The porter's lodge, to the right of the entrance doorway, dates from the 15C. The wine cellar (14C), reached through a large door, contains an impressive collection of winepresses and vats.

The entire history of Burgundian vineyards and the cultivation of the vine is explained in a comprehensive exhibit on the ground floor. The 16C polychrome statue is known as the Virgin Mary with a Bunch of Grapes or Notre-Dame de Beaune. On the first floor, a large room decorated with two immense Aubusson tapestries, one by Lurçat and one by Michel Tourlière, is the headquarters of the Ambassade des Vins de France (Embassy of the Wines of France).

Musée des Beaux-Arts ⓥ – This fine arts collection includes numerous works by local artist **Félix Ziem** (1821-1911), 16C and 17C Flemish and Dutch paintings, medieval (14C bagpipes player) and Renaissance (16C St Anne) sculpture and a small Gallo-Roman section (statue of a river goddess discovered in Gissey-le-Vieil).

Musée Étienne-Jules-Marey ⓥ – The doctor and physiologist Étienne-Jules Marey was passionately interested in the phenomenon of movement. He invented a number of medical instruments (exhibited here), including the sphygmograph – a machine for recording the pulse graphically. From 1867 he held the chair of natural history in the Collège de France. He also contributed to the development of the motion picture, inventing a drum in which there was a series of photographs which, when the drum was turned, seemed to represent motion (he studied birds in flight with this). The Lumière brothers went on to develop his makeshift motion picture camera further. Several other inventions of his are on display, including the photographic rifle camera.

EXCURSIONS

The vineyards of "La Côte" – Beaune can be the starting point of the itineraries suggested in the chapter "La Côte".

Montagne de Beaune – *4km/2.5mi NW*. From the viewing-table located near the cenotaph (about 600m/656yd south of the statue of Notre-Dame-de-la-Libération), there is an extensive view of the town and its lovely brown-tiled roofs, of the vineyards and of the Mâconnais hills to the south.

★**Château de Savigny-lès-Beaune** ⊙ – *5km/2mi NW*. In this village known for its quality wines, stands a 14C castle with some interesting collections on display. The smaller 17C château, remarkable for the masonry course in heavy limestone, is now home to a wine-tasting and sales room and an exhibit of **Arbath endurance cars**. Visitors to the park will see 60 **jet fighter planes** from the world's most powerful armies, including: Mirages (I to V), a Jaguar (1971) which took part in the Gulf War, MIG 21 US (1962), Lightening, FAIT, Sikorsky helicopters and more. Built by Jean de Frolois, Maréchal de Bourgogne, the château was restored by the Bouhier family in the 17C. At that time, the wing which closed off the courtyard was demolished and more windows were put in. The interior was restored more recently, with a view to accommodating receptions and conferences. An upper floor has been set aside for the **collection of motorcycles★**. With more than 500 models from around the world, including some very rare ones, these machines give a good overview of changes in mechanics and design over the 20C.

Archéodrome de Bourgogne ⊙ – *7km/4.3mi S along D 18 and D 23*. Located along the A 6 motorway, the Archéodrome de Bourgogne gives a panoramic view of the region's history, from Paleolithic times to the year 1000.

Audio-visual presentations are designed to plunge the visitor deep into the past: the Chronoscope gives a delineation of the major periods of human history, whereas the Espace Bourgogne develops regional themes of cultural heritage.

The outdoor areas invite the visitor to stroll among spectacular vestiges of the past, whether prehistoric, protohistoric or from Antiquity, gathered together on a single site. Carefully executed reconstructions of archaeological digs include the Arcy-sur-Cure Paleolithic dwelling; the "Dame de Passy" Neolithic burial site (from the Yonne region); the tombs of an early Iron Age dignitary and a woman from Vix, among others. The site's lay-

Ph. Gajic/MICHELIN

Gaulish farm
replica at the Archéodrome

out creates an authentic atmosphere, with its archaeologist's marks, digging tools, and objects only semi-unearthed. A scale model of the Alésia fortifications provides a good perspective on that impressive feat of defensive strategy, based on the most recent discoveries concerning it, and there is a life-size reconstruction of one section outdoors, based on 19C archaeology as well as descriptions by Julius Caesar. Even the restaurant serves meals in the ancient Roman style!

BELFORT★

Population 50 417
Michelin map 314: J-7

Belfort is divided by the River Savoureuse into two distinct parts. On the river's west bank are extensive industrial and commercial areas and housing estates; on the east bank, at the foot of the rock on which the castle is sited, is the impregnable citadel built by Vauban.

The Belfort Gap – Lying at an altitude of 350m/1 148ft between the Jura mountain plateaux (ranging from 800-1 000m/2 625-3 281ft) to the south and the Vosges range (Ballon d'Alsace summit: 1 247m/4 091ft) to the north, the 30km/19mi wide Belfort Gap (or Trouée de Belfort, sometimes known as the Burgundian Gate) provides a natural passage between the two great valleys of the Rhine and the Rhône.

The gap has attracted all sorts of communications routes – roads, railways, the Rhône-Rhine canal – and, in the past, many invading armies.

HISTORICAL NOTES

An invasion route – The Belfort Gap has drawn successive waves of invaders; Celts, Germanic tribes, soldiers of the Holy Roman Empire... in short, Belfort's history is a battered one. The town was subject to Austrian rule (the Habsburgs) from the mid 14C until the French conquest, but the citizens of Belfort took all this philosophically, knowing that their civil rights were protected by a charter dating from 1307.
During the Thirty Years War, in 1638, the town was taken by the French, under the leadership of the Comte de La Suze for Montbéliard, who managed to break through the fortifications in a bold nocturnal attack. Suze was made Governor of Belfort by Richelieu and went down in the local annals for his succinct instructions to the commander of the garrison – *Ne capitulez jamais* (Never surrender). The French conquest was ratified by the Westphalia treaties in 1648, and Louis XIV ordered Vauban to make Belfort impregnable. The resulting fortified town is the great military engineer's masterpiece. Subsequently, the town was able to withstand the three sieges commemorated by Bartholdi's monument (in 1814, 1815 and 1870).

The Verdun of 1870 – In the course of the Franco-Prussian War of 1870, 40 000 German troops were held up for a month before Belfort by the Mobile Guards commanded by Colonel Denfert-Rochereau. Rather than shutting himself and his troops up in the fortress, as expected, he and his 16 000 courageous but inexperienced men retired in good order to the citadel, defending all approaches tenaciously as they went. This leisurely retreat took a month, and once in the fortress, they withstood a 103-day siege. During this time the enemy employed 200 huge cannon, unleashing a hail of shells onto the beleaguered town; they fired over 400 000 rounds in 83 days – that is about 5 000 per day, enormous for that day and age. Denfert-Rochereau and his men only consented to march out (with full battle honours) on the direct orders of the French government, 21 days after the armistice signed at Versailles. In the struggle between President Thiers and Bismarck, the German Chancellor, over the cession of French territory, this exemplary resistance made it possible for Belfort to escape the fate of Alsace-Lorraine; it became instead the capital of its own tiny territory, which was to acquire considerable economic importance.

Rapid Expansion – After 1870, Belfort underwent a radical transformation. Until then it had been essentially a military town (it produced more generals to serve France than any other town: 20 in a single century), with only 8 000 inhabitants. Within 30 years, Belfort had become a thriving conurbation with 40 000 inhabitants. One reason for this dramatic growth was the establishment of a number of subsidiaries of businesses belonging to residents of Alsace-Lorraine, anxious to keep up their connections with France in the wake of the German annexation. As pressure built up on the town to expand, Vauban's ramparts were demolished. The new districts, with their wide streets and huge squares, give Belfort the appearance of a small capital city.

The capture of the Fort du Salbert – On 14 November 1944 the First French Army, having been blocked for two months in its advance towards the Rhine by the bristling defences of the retreating Wehrmacht at Belfort, began the offensive which would break through to upper Alsace and the Rhine. Fort du Salbert, north-west of the town, was in the way, so they attacked it on the night of 19 November. Fifteen hundred commandos of the Army of Africa slipped into Salbert forest and put the German

---

Records

1926 and 1990 are dates which reflect the main thrust of Belfort's industrial activity this century. In 1926, the first electric train was produced in the Belfort workshops of the Société Alsacienne de Constructions Mécaniques; on 18 May 1990, the high-speed train TGV-Atlantique, built in Belfort (GEC-Alsthom), broke the world rail speed record by reaching 515.3kph/320mph.

Eating out

BUDGET

Le Molière – *6 r. de l'Étuve -* ☎ *03 84 21 86 38 - closed Feb school holidays, 22 Aug-12 Sep, Tue and Wed - 15.24/38.11€.* Located in a renovated area of the old town, this restaurant offers an extremely wide choice of menus. Meals are served in the cosy dining room or on the terrace, depending on the weather.

Auberge du Lac – *27 r. du Lac - 90350 Evette-Salbert - 3 km/1.9mi N of Belfort by D 24 -* ☎ *03 84 29 14 10 - closed 2 Jan-15 Feb, 15-30 Oct, Tue lunchtime and Mon - 13/24.40€.* This former ice house stands on the shores of Malsaucy Lake, opposite the venue chosen for the Eurockéennes Festival. Settle in the panoramic dining room and sample their speciality, fried fish.

Le Choix de Sophie – *90600 Grandvillars - 19 km/11.8mi SE of Belfort by N 19 -* ☎ *03 84 27 76 03 - closed 3-19 Aug, 22 Dec-2 Jan, Sat and Sun except public holidays - 13.57/27.44€.* You will like this simple country inn with its half-timbered structure and its beams painted in blue. Warm welcome. Regional cuisine with seasonal produce.

MODERATE

Le Pot au Feu – *27 bis Grande-Rue -* ☎ *03 84 28 57 84 - closed 1-12 Jan, 1-18 Aug, Sat lunchtime, Mon lunchtime and Sun - 19€ lunch - 27/41€.* You are certainly not expected to dress for dinner in this small restaurant in the old town. Relax in the cosy dining room with its stone vaulting and neat checked tablecloths. Sample tasty regional cuisine in an easy-going, laid-back atmosphere.

Where to stay

MODERATE

Hôtel Vauban – *4 r. du Magasin -* ☎ *03 84 21 59 37 - hotel.vauban@wanadoo.fr - closed Feb school holidays, 25 Dec-2 Jan and Sun - 14 rooms : 46/56€ -* ⌒ *7€.* This small hotel is a paragon of discretion. The carefully kept rooms are decorated by pictures that were painted by the owner. Relax in the pretty garden near the River La Savoureuse.

Hôtel Les Capucins – *20 fg de Montbéliard -* ☎ *03 84 28 04 60 - closed 2-18 Aug and 20 Dec-6 Jan - 35 rooms: 48/55€ -* ⌒ *6.10€ - restaurant 15/30€.* This handsome building near the banks of La Savoureuse and the pedestrian district exudes considerable charm. The comfortable rooms are appointed with modern furniture; you would do better to choose the renovated ones at the back. For meals, two formulas are available: a restaurant and a brasserie.

Grand Hôtel du Tonneau d'Or – *1 r. Reiset -* ☎ *03 84 58 57 56 - tonneaudor@tonneaudor.fr - 52 rooms: 60.67/97.72€ -* ⌒ *9.45€ - restaurant 21.34/35.06€.* In the heart of the old quarter, this imposing turn-of-the-century house has been extensively restored and now boasts lofty ceilings, columns and fine stuccowork. Spacious rooms furnished in the 1900 style. The ambience in the restaurant is reminiscent of a Parisian brasserie. Piano-bar.

Sit back and relax

Finnegans Irish Pub – *6 bd Carnot -* ☎ *03 84 28 20 28 – open daily 2pm-1am.* This Irish pub is situated near the town centre. The perfect place to meet up with friends and have a drink. Good selection of beers and whiskies.

Hemingway Bar – *Av. de l'Éspérance -* ☎ *03 84 58 85 58 - www.atria-novotel.com - open daily 6am-midnight.* This bar set up in the Novotel Hotel tends to attract a cosmopolitan clientele. However, the jazz evenings that are organised every third Wednesday of the month are also popular with local residents. Try one of the many reasonably priced cocktails.

Le Bistrot des Moines – *22 r. Dreyfus-Schmitt -* ☎ *03 84 21 86 40 – open Mon-Fri 10.30-1am, Sat 10.30-2am.* This bar is paradise for beer drinkers. Only draught beer is sold here, a fact evidenced by the numerous copper and china pumps and the huge still dominating the room. Beer cocktails are the speciality of the house.

Le Piano-Bar – *23 fg de France -* ☎ *03 84 28 93 35 – open Mon-Sat 8.30pm-1am.* This is undoubtedly the trendiest bar in town. Customers of all ages flock to this vaulted cellar in the town centre. The thematic evenings are especially popular; they include karaoke on Thurday and jazz-blues on Friday and Saturday.

Épicerie Perello – *4 r. Porte de France -* ☎ *03 84 28 04 33 – open Mon-Sat 8am-12.30pm, 2.30-7.30pm.* A Spaniard native of the Balearic Islands settled here in 1938 and bought one of the oldest stores in France, dating from 1825… It has remained in the same family ever since, offering fine produce from Spain, Italy and Algeria: rice, semolina, beans, one hundred brands of tea and coffee, and an outstanding list of wines and liquors.

BELFORT

sentries out of action. They used ropes to drop into the deep moats surrounding
the fort, without raising the enemy's alarm, and then managed to take the garrison
by surprise and subdue it. Belfort was finally liberated on 22 November, after tank
battles and street fighting. The French Army's thrust in the direction of Mulhouse
could continue.

★ OLD TOWN

It was not until the end of the last century that Belfort was able to get rid of its
fortifications and link its old town with the new districts springing up on the west
bank of the Savoureuse.

The old town has been undergoing restoration since 1986, and the colourful
façades of the houses, in blue-green, green, pink or ochre coloured washes, with
pale stone decoration around the windows lend a much friendlier atmosphere to
the streets and squares of the once austere garrison town. Particularly charming
examples are to be found in place de l'Arsenal, place de la Grande-Fontaine,
Grande-Rue and place de la Petite-Fontaine.

*Park the car in place de la République and walk along rue de la Porte-de-France
to place d'Armes. Across the square stands the austere-looking cathedral.*

Statue "Quand même" – This statue, erected on place d'Armes in memory of the
siege of 1870-71, is the work of Mercié (1884).

Cathédrale St-Christophe – The church, built of red sandstone, has an 18C Classical façade. The exterior architecture and the interior decoration are highly unified
in style. The frieze of angels' heads in relief runs all around the nave. The beautiful **gilded wrought-iron grille** enclosing the choir is similar to the railings by Jean
Lamour in Place Stanislas in Nancy. Note in the transept paintings by the Belfort
painter G Dauphin: an *Entombment of Christ (on the right)* and *The Ecstacy of
St François-Xavier (on the left)*. The 18C **organ★**, by Valtrin, has a beautifully carved
and gilded wooden case.

*Walk round the north side of the cathedral along rue de l'Église. Turn left onto
rue du Général-Roussel which leads to the foot of the ramparts and turn right onto
rue des Bons-Enfants to the Porte de Brisach.*

★ **Porte de Brisach** – This gateway, constructed by Vauban in 1687, has been preserved in the original. It features a pilastered façade decorated with the Bourbon
coat of arms with *fleurs de lys* and, on the pediment, the coat of arms of Louis XIV:
the sun surmounted by the famous motto *Nec pluribus impar.*

Rue de la Grande-Fontaine, opposite the gate, leads to place de la Grande-Fontaine.

Place de la Grande-Fontaine – The square owes its name to the successive fountains which have decorated it; the latest dates from 1860.

Turn right towards place de l'Arsenal and place d'Armes.

Hôtel de Ville ○ – The town hall was built in the Classical style. The beautiful
Salle Kléber on the ground floor is a good example of late 18C French art (Rococo
style). There are paintings depicting Belfort's history in the main hall *(Salle
d'honneur)* on the first floor.

BELFORT

There is a beautiful view of the Belfort Lion from avenue du Général-Sarrail, south of the Hôtel de Ville.

Rue des Nouvelles leads to place de la République with its large central monument.

Monument des Trois Sièges – This work by Bartholdi depicts France and the city of Belfort with their three defenders (Legrand in 1814, Lecourbe in 1815 and Denfert-Rochereau in 1870). It stands in the middle of place de la République, which houses the Préfecture, the Palais de Justice (law courts) and the Salle des Fêtes (festival hall), not far from the covered market or **Marché couvert Fréry.**

On the west bank of the Savoureuse – Since the 1970s, a modern town has sprung up on the west bank of the Savoureuse between Les 4-As and the Faubourg de France. It has a lively pedestrian shopping zone.

Royal gateway

Walk along boulevard Carnot, admiring on the way the fine early-20C buildings; cross the river and continue on the other side along faubourg de France. Further on to the right, a passageway leads to rue de l'As-de-Carreau; turn right.

In a car park on the rue de l'As-de-Carreau there is an unusual **fresco★** by Ernest Pignon-Ernest, painted onto the walls of a U-shaped building: 47 life-size figures of men and women represent the art and science of Latin and Teutonic countries, with Beethoven and Picasso rubbing shoulders with Rimbaud and Goethe.

★★ THE BELFORT LION

The great beast (22m/72ft long and 11m/36ft high), carved from red Vosges sandstone, just below the fort symbolises the spirit and strength of Belfort's defenders in 1870 and marks the response of the French people to their heroism. It is the work of **Frédéric Bartholdi** (carved from 1876 to 1880 and put together bit by bit on site), who here gave free rein to his patriotic fervour and ardent creativity. A path leads from the **viewing platform** ⊙ at the base of the Lion to the memorial *(take the stairs from the car park and turn right into the tunnel, from which a doorway opens almost immediately on the left to the memorial).* The Lion is even more awe-inspiring when it is floodlit at night. The sight from the viewing platform is similar to that from the terrace of the fortress.

Frédéric Auguste Bartholdi (1834-1904)

This sculptor was born in Colmar and showed his artistic prowess from an early age. He won a competition held by his home town in 1856 to find someone to execute a memorial statue of General Rapp. His travels in Egypt and the Far East affected his later work. After the Franco-Prussian war in 1870, he sculpted a large number of patriotic monuments, the most famous of which are the Belfort Lion and the statue of Liberty Lighting the World at the entrance to New York harbour.

★★ THE CITADEL

A key strategic position – As early as 1625 Richelieu, anxious to secure an access route into Alsace and the German Empire, had tried to annex Belfort. However, Tilly defended the fortress successfully with the help of Croatian troops.
From 1687 Vauban began his master work; he surrounded the existing fortress and town with several pentagonal fortified walls anchored to the rocky cliff on which the buildings stood. Construction lasted about 20 years. Belfort played the role assigned to it by Vauban – of major military garrison between Alsace and Franche-Comté – until the end of the Napoleonic Empire. Commandant Legrand was another heroic defender of this fortified site in 1814.

G. Magnin/MICHELIN

The Belfort Lion

As military strategy developed away from the idea of entrenched warfare towards that of mobile warfare, first Général Lecourbe (from 1815) and then Général Haxo (from 1825) undertook not only to build at Belfort a means of protecting the town, but also a fortified military site that would enable resident troops to guard the Belfort Gap. In this way, they increased Belfort's military role considerably.

This plan was still in force at the time of the siege in 1870. It was further endorsed by the plans of Général Séré de la Rivière, who sought to fortify Verdun, Toul, Épinal and Belfort and link them together in a line of fortifications.

After 1885, in the wake of progress made in the development of efficient weaponry, many forts were modernised. Concrete replaced stone walls, and smaller batteries less easy to spot than fortresses were built for the artillery.

Shortly before the outbreak of the First World War, Belfort had reached the capacity to accommodate 7 500 men in peacetime and 10 times that number in the event of war. The line of fortifications between Épinal and Belfort was ready to play its role in the defence of the nation.

FORTIFICATIONS ⊙

The terrace of the fort – This public terrace is at the top of the barracks which houses the museum of art and history. It is an excellent viewing point, from which you will be able to place the fortress in its geographical context and gain a better understanding of its comprehensive system of defence.

The **panorama**★★ reveals to the south the Jura mountain chain on the horizon; to the west the old town, the industrial zones and the Fort du Salbert; to the north the southern Vosges with the peaks of the Ballon de Servance, the Ballon d'Alsace, the Baerenkopf and the Rossberg; to the east the curtain walls of the fortress and the Belfort Gap.

You can make out the outline of the **Grand Sousterrain**, a covered moat dating from the reign of Louis XV, which was used to provide troops and horses with shelter during attacks, and further to the east the moat known as the **Grand Couronné**, with its bastions, and the moat round the intermediate curtain wall (3rd moat) and that round the outer curtain wall (4th moat).

At the foot of the barracks to the east, the **cour d'honneur** (main courtyard) is surrounded by the Haxo casemates, which have been converted into art galleries. One of them houses the thousand-year-old **well** which reaches a depth of 67m/220ft.

The curtain walls (enceintes) – *1hr.* ⬛ *Follow the path at the foot of the fortress through the tunnel beneath the Lion and carry on along it until you get to the 4th moat.*

Note the impressive proportions of the moats and, towards the motorway, the **glacis**, a vast area of bare land which slopes gently away. Walking along the 4th or 3rd moats, between the mighty scarp and counterscarp walls, is a good way to see the defence system in detail: numerous embrasures allowed soldiers to fire down into the moats, fortifications with horn-shaped projections *(ouvrages à cornes)*, bastions. The tour ends at the **Tour des Bourgeois**, the old tower from the medieval curtain wall demolished by Vauban.

Promenade des Courtines – Walkway reached through the semicircular room in the Tour des Bourgeois *(if closed, go via Place des Bourgeois)*.

The terrace above the Porte de Brisach gives a good view of the *demi-lune* fortification in front of the gateway. The double line of fortifications from Vauban's time are also visible.

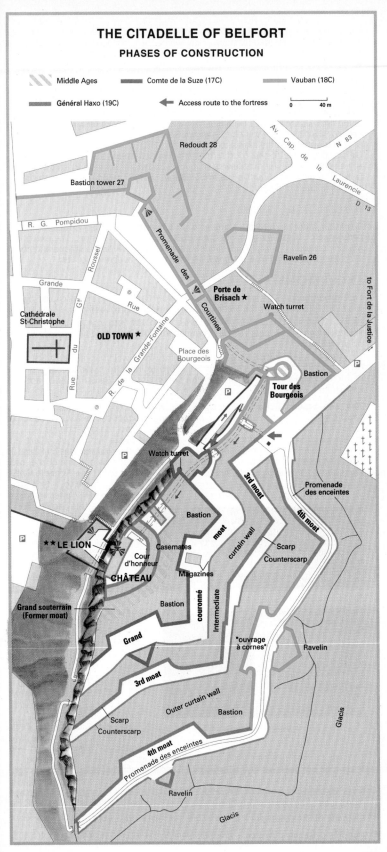

THE CITADELLE OF BELFORT

PHASES OF CONSTRUCTION

Middle Ages
Comte de la Suze (17C)
Vauban (18C)
Général Haxo (19C)
Access route to the fortress

0   40 m

Redoudt 28

Bastion tower 27

Av. Cap. de la Laurencie   N 83

D 13

R. G. Pompidou

Roussel

Grande

Rue

Rue du G.

Cathédrale St-Christophe

OLD TOWN ★

R. de la Grande Fontaine

Place des Bourgeois

Promenade des Courtines

Ravelin 26

Porte de Brisach ★

Watch turret

to Fort de la Justice

Bastion

Tour des Bourgeois

P

Watch turret

P

3rd moat

Promenade des enceintes

4th moat

★★ LE LION

P

Bastion

moat

curtain wall

Scarp

Counterscarp

Casemates

Cour d'honneur

Magazines

intermediate

couronné

CHÂTEAU

Grand souterrain (Former moat)

Bastion

Grand

"ouvrage à cornes"

Ravelin

3rd moat

Scarp
Counterscarp

Outer curtain wall

Bastion

Glacis

4th moat

Promenade des enceintes

Ravelin

Glacis

Carry on to the **Tour bastionnée 27** (the different parts of the old fortress have been numbered for easier identification), from where there is a view back to the fortress and its grass-covered walls, dating from Haxo's modifications.

Musée d'Art et d'Histoire ⊙ – The basement contains artefacts from the Neolithic, Gallo-Roman and Merovingian periods (earthenware, weapons, tools from the Cravanche cave, a mosaic from a villa in Bavilliers, belt buckles and a reconstruction of a tomb from a Burgundian cemetery). More recent history is also evoked. Exhibits include a reproduction of Vauban's relief model of his fortifications in 1687, and numerous military artefacts (weapons, helmets, trophies, documents, swords, medals). Articles which belonged to Colonel Denfert-Rochereau or to French and Prussian officers bear witness to the resistance against the 1870-71 siege.

On the other side of the courtyard, in the Haxo battery, collections of paintings (by Gustave Doré, Heim, Maximilien Luce, Guillaumin, as well as engravings by Dürer), sculptures (Camille Lefèvre, Dalou, Barye, Rodin) and photographs (A Villers) are on display.

ADDITIONAL SIGHT

★ **Donation Maurice Jardot – Cabinet d'un amateur** ⊙ – In 1997, Maurice Jardot bequeathed 110 paintings by modern artists to the city of Belfort. The exceptionally fine collection, which icludes little-known works by Picasso, Braque and above all Léger, is exhibited in a restored villa overlooking square E-Lechten.

EXCURSIONS

Fort du Salbert – The best view of the Belfort Gap and the site occupied by the town of Belfort is from the **Fort du Salbert** *(8km/5mi north-west)*.

Leave the town on avenue Jean-Jaurès. Turn left into rue de la 1re-Armée-Française, which runs into rue des Commandos-d'Afrique, then take rue du Salbert off to the right.

A winding forest road *(D 4)*, leads to the fort, which is at an altitude of 647m/2 123ft. The vast terrace *(200m/220yd to the left – viewing table)* gives a marvellous **panorama**★★ over Belfort, the Swiss Alps, the Ballon d'Alsace and the surrounding mountains.

The Hills around Belfort – *You should allow about 2hr for this walk. Leave the town through the Porte de Brisach and turn right alongside the fortress as far as a car park. Take the foot bridge on the left over avenue de la Laurencie.*

⚑ The path brings you first of all to the **Fort de la Justice**. On the left, there are look-out points which give a good overall view of the Vosges. One of these is directly opposite a dovecot for carrier pigeons with examples of some of the messages carried by the pigeons fixed to its façade. Beyond this is the **Fort de la Miotte**, distinguishable by its tower, rebuilt in 1947 after a succession of disasters had befallen it in 1724, 1835, 1870, 1875 and 1940.

A venerable forge

Étang des Forges – *Park near the sailing base.*

⚑ A nature trail leads round this lake, at times right by the water's edge, at others cutting through the reed beds. Information boards describe the flora and fauna to be found in this area (the little bittern, the smallest heron in Europe, the crested grebe and the coot).

Etueffont: Forge-Musée ⊙ – *15km/9.3mi NE. Leave Belfort on N 83; after 10km/6.2mi, turn left on D 12.*

Four generations of the Petit-jean family, plying the two trades of blacksmithing and farm labour, lived between 1844 and 1975 in a house at the heart of the village. Many tools are displayed in the forge, which is still in working order. Numerous agricultural tools, generations old, are to be seen in the attics, the barn and the stable. Other trades such as that of the sabot-maker, the ironmonger or the joiner are also represented. The house is furnished as it would have been at the turn of the 20C.

★★ **Chapelle de Ronchamp** – *22km/13.7mi NW. See RONCHAMP.*

★★★ **Massif du Ballon d'Alsace** – *28km/17.4mi N. See Massif du BALLON D'ALSACE.*

Population 10 846
Michelin map 328: H-4

This small industrial town, on the confluence of a gushing mountain stream with the Rhône, lies at the heart of a region which offers visitors a wealth of fine excursions. Bellegarde owes its recent development to its position on the main route from Lyon to the Mont-Blanc tunnel and on the Paris-Geneva TGV railway line.

THE VALSERINE VALLEY

It is preferable to explore the Valserine Valley during the afternoon, in a south-north direction.

Where to stay and Eating out

BUDGET

Auberge de la Fontaine – *01200 Châtillon-en-Michaille - 5 km/3.1mi NW of Bellegarde by D 101 - ☎ 04 50 56 57 23 - aubergefontaine@minitel.net - closed 7-29 Jan, 4-11 June, 1-8 Oct, Tue evenings except Jul-Aug, Sun evenings and Mon - 19.06/45.73€.* A pretty fountain decked with flowers greets you at the entrance to this inn. Meals are served on the shaded terrace in fair weather. A few unpretentious rooms. Tasty, generous cuisine at reasonable prices.

Auberge Le Catray – *01200 Bellegarde-sur-Valserine - 12 km/7.5mi W of Bellegarde by D 101 - ☎04 50 56 56 25 - closed 11-15 Mar, 3-7 Jun, 9-20 Sep, 12-22 Nov, Mon evenings and Tue - 🄿 - 7 rooms: 28/43€ - ☕ 5€ - restaurant 15/22€.* This mountain chalet lost in the country commands lovely vistas of Mont Blanc and the Alpine range. Unpretentious rooms with wooden panelling on the walls. Family cooking.

Hôtel Le Sorgia – *01200 Lancrans - 2 km/1.2mi N of Bellegarde by D 16 - ☎04 50 48 15 81 - closed 23 Aug-17 Sep, 21 Dec-7 Jan, Sat lunchtime, Sun evenings and Mon - 🄿 - 17 rooms: 38/41€ - ☕ 6.10€ - restaurant 12/27.50€.* This house has belonged to the same family for five generations, a fact of which the present owner is rightfully proud. Spacious, carefully kept rooms. Prim, tidy dining room. Simple bill of fare.

The River Valserine is 50km/31mi long and drops 1 000m/3 280ft from its source to its confluence with the Rhône at Bellegarde-sur-Valserine. This mountain stream runs through a charming valley known as "Valmijoux" bounded on both sides by parallel mountain ranges with two high peaks almost facing each other. The **Crêt de la Neige** (1 717m/5 633ft), the highest summit of the Jura mountains, is so called because it retains year-round a few patches of snow on its north face. The equivalent climb on the other side of the valley is that to the **Crêt de Chalam** (1 545m/4 069ft).

Whereas the valley and lower slopes are covered with meadows, there are forests and heathland higher up. The valley narrows into a gorge in several places.

★ **Berges de la Valserine** – *From the town centre (Tourist office), follow N 84 towards Lyon. Park the car just behind the railway viaduct (rue Louis-Dumont).*
🚶 The Valserine skirts the town but, because it is hemmed in by steep banks, it was difficult to reach it in the past. A path starting from the viaduct now enables visitors to walk all the way to the Pertes de la Valserine *(allow 2hr there and back)*. There are many steps along the way and in rainy weather the stones can be slippery.

★ **Pertes de la Valserine** – To get there quickly, drive north out of Bellegarde along N 84. Pass beneath the railway line and continue for 2km/1.2mi. There is a parking area on the right-hand side of the road.
🚶 Follow the steep path *(45min there and back)* running down through the woods *(many steps)*. It leads to the place, where the Valserine disappears from view amid a setting of rocky crevices and great cauldrons *(oulles)* scoured out in the rocks by the river. The waterfall is a little further upstream.

★DÉFILÉ DE L'ÉCLUSE

32km/20mi round tour. Leave Bellegarde east along N 206.

This picturesque transverse valley separates the Grand Crêt d'Eau and Montagne de Vuache ranges. The river, the N 206 Franco-Swiss highway and the scenic D 908A all run through the valley.

Beyond Longeray, just before the entrance to the tunnel, turn right towards Fort de l'Écluse.

Fort de l'Écluse

★**Fort de l'Écluse** ⊘ – This remarkable mountain fort is being restored. The fortifications were erected high above the River Rhône between 1820 and 1840. Owing to its strategic position, the fort was bitterly fought over in 1944. It is a hard climb *(800 steps, 45min to 1hr there and back)* to the top, but the view is well worth it.

Go through the tunnel and continue along N 206 to the right; in Chevrier, turn right onto D 908ᴬ and return to Bellegarde via N 508.

HAUT-BUGEY

136km/85mi round tour - allow 6hr

Drive south out of Bellegarde along N 508; turn right onto D 168 towards St-Germain-sur-Rhône. The road soon runs into D 214 which leads to the Génissiat dam.

★**Barrage de Génissiat** – See Barrage de GÉNISSIAT.

D 72 leads to D 991; turn left.

Seyssel – See GRAND COLOMBIER.

Beyond Seyssel, follow D 991 towards Ruffieux.

South of Seyssel, the Rhône, joined by the Fier, spreads out and wanders through a stony marsh dotted with islets, known as the Marais de Chautagne.

As you reach Ruffieux, turn right onto D 904 which runs through marshland, crosses the Rhône and heads for Culoz.

The River used to cut its way across the Jura mountains from east to west via a series of transverse valleys, a route now used by the Culoz-Ambérieu road, but today it continues south to Yenne.

From Culoz, climb up to the Grand Colombier.

★★★**Grand Colombier** – See GRAND COLOMBIER.

A steep narrow road leads to Virieu-le-Petit on the west side of the Montagne du Grand Colombier. From Assin, just south of Virieu, D 69 leads to Don. From there take D 31 then a surfaced track on the left above the Cerveyrieu waterfall.

★**Cascade de Cerveyrieu** – Impressive drop by the River Séran forming a picturesque waterfall

Return to D 31 and turn right onto D 30ᴮ.

Vieu – The village stands on the site of the Roman capital of the Valromey region. Here, Brillat-Savarin *(see BELLEY)* had a country residence where he could put his principles into practice and regale his friends.

Champagne-en-Valromey – This is now the main town of the area; it has retained a few old houses and organises a festival of traditional crafts in summer.

Drive towards Lochieu (D 69ᶠ).

Lochieu, Musée Rural du Valromey ⊘ – Housed in a Renaissance building (1501), this local museum preserves the living memory of the valley: objects of daily life, clothes, crafts, religious objects. A spiral staircase leads up to the dovecot which only the nobility could own.

Return to D 31 and drive north towards Ruffieu then follow D 9 and D 30 to the Col de Richemont.

★**Col de Richemont** – There is a **view** from the pass (alt 1 036m/3 399ft) of the Michaille region, an undulating landscape stretching at the foot of the mountain as far as the Rhône, whose course is blocked by the dams at Seyssel and Génissiat; of the Grand Crêt d'Eau mountain range (1 534m/5 062ft); the Défilé de l'Écluse, through which the Rhône flows into the Jura; and, in clear weather, the Mont Blanc mountain range.

Go back to Ruffieux, turn right and drive north via the Petit and Grand Abergement, along D 39 then D 55 and D 101 to the Retord plateau.

Plateau de Retord – The gently undulating verdant countryside conveys an impression of peace and remoteness. In late May and early June it turns into a vast field of daffodils. There are views of the Valromey region, of the Rhône Valley and of the Jura mountains.

From the viewing-table at Le Catray, the view extends across the Alps with Mont Blanc to the south-east, the Valserine Valley, the Défilé de l'Écluse and the Lac du Bourget.

Return to Bellegarde via D 101.

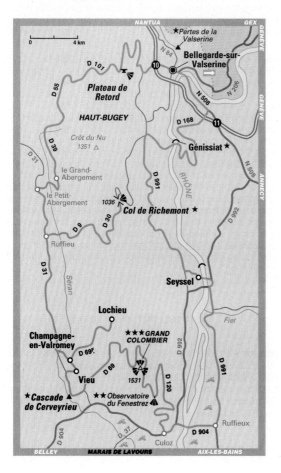

Leave Bellegarde via N 84 leading to the Pertes de la Valserine (see above); 4km/2.5mi beyond Châtillon-de-Michaille, turn right onto D 14 to Montanges then right again onto D 14ᴬ.

Pont des Pierres – This one-arch bridge spans the Valserine between Montanges and La Mulaz, towering 60m/197ft above the water. In rainy weather, the sight is impressive: mountain streams carrying stones and soil can be seen cascading down to the foaming river squeezed between sheer cliffs.

In La Mulaz, turn left onto D 991.

The road runs up the valley along wooded cliffs. From Chézery-Forens to Lélex, the river flows through the 5km/3mi long Défilé de Sous-Balme over which tower the summits of Crêt de Chalam and Le Reculet.

Continue upstream to the Monts Jura winter resort.

✱ **Monts Jura** – See MONTS JURA.

From Lélex, the resort extends along the valley to the Col de la Faucille famous for its panorama.

BELLEY

Population 8 004
Michelin map 328: H-6

This peaceful town lies in a charming little valley watered by the Furan, in the heart of the green and pleasant Bugey region. Destroyed by a fire in 1385, Belley was rebuilt and surrounded by fortifications by Amadeus VII of Savoy (the Bugey region and its capital Belley had belonged to the House of Savoy since 1077; they were not to become part of France until the Treaty of Lyon in 1601). The gateway (Vieille Porte) at the end of Boulevard du Mail is a remnant of these ramparts.

The poet Lamartine went to secondary school in Belley (a statue of him stands in front of the Collège Lamartine in honour of this). The town also won fame in the world of gastronomy for being the birthplace of the great toast of taste-buds everywhere, Brillat-Savarin.

The Physiology of Taste – When **Jean-Anthelme Brillat-Savarin** was born in Belley in 1755 his career was already mapped out for him; he would be a lawyer like his father. He settled into the quiet way of life typical of Belley, visiting family or entertaining friends in town or at his country home in Vieu, all of which left him plenty of time to indulge his interest in the sciences as well as the arts. In 1789, the year of Revolution, he was elected deputy of the Third Estate and executed this role with kindness and tolerance. Nonetheless, even he was not above suspicion during the years of the Terror and in 1794, having been elected mayor back in Belley, he was forced to flee, first to Switzerland, then to the United States. He returned to France under the Consulate and became councillor to the Supreme Court of Appeals in Paris. In his free time he wrote, initially legal or political works, then the little masterpiece which earned him his fame: *The Physiology of Taste*. In 30 essays he examines the various aspects of and issues associated with good living and good food; philosophical principles appear side by side with reflections on gluttony, sleep and dreams; he passes from scientific theories to culinary precepts, adopting the light-hearted, entertaining tone characteristic of all his scholarly writings. He died in 1826, and Belley, in recognition of his achievements, put up a statue on the "Promenoir" bearing the inscription of one of his maxims: "Inviting guests into your home means looking after their well-being as long as they are under your roof."

Eating out

BUDGET

Auberge de Contrevoz – *01300 Contrevoz - 9 km/5.6mi NW of Belley by D 69 then D 32 -* ☎ *04 79 81 82 54 - auberge.de.contrevoz@wanadoo.fr - closed 25 Dec-31 Jan, Sun evenings except Jul-Aug and Mon - 14/34€.* The flowered garden planted with fruit trees is a pretty sight indeed. This old inn has retained all its country charm, with its fine fireplace and its farming tools adorning the dining room walls. Regional cuisine.

MODERATE

Auberge La Fine Fourchette – *01300 Belley - 3 km/1.9mi SE of Belley on the road to Chambéry -* ☎ *04 79 81 59 33 - closed 21 Dec-10 Jan, Sun evenings and Mon - 22/54€.* The open countryside and an ornamental lake can be glimpsed through the large bay windows of the dining room, which has wainscoting along its ceiling. In fair weather, settle on the terrace to enjoy the view. Traditional cooking.

Where to stay

BUDGET

Chambre d'Hôte Les Charmettes – *La Vellaz, St-Martin-de-Bavel - 01510 Virieu-le-Grand - 11 km/6.8mi N of Belley by N 504 until you reach Chazey-Bons then D 31^C -* ☎ *04 79 87 32 18 -* ⊅ *- 3 rooms: 30/37€.* This charming Bugey farmhouse in the midst of the countryside has converted its stables into pretty, comfortable bedrooms, one of which has been specially equipped for the handicapped. Cooking facilities are available for guests.

Chambre d'Hôte Ferme des Grands Hautains – *Le Petit Brens - 01300 Brens - 3 km/1.9mi S of Belley by D 31^A -* ☎ *04 79 81 90 95 - closed 15 Nov-20 Dec and Sun -* ⊅ *- 4 rooms: 31/37€ - meals 10/13€.* Settle under the oak tree and sip a drink at the large stone table while admiring the pretty arbour... Or take a stroll through the vegetable garden, where the owners pick their homegrown produce to prepare succulent meals. Cosy rooms beneath the eaves appointed with family heirlooms. For non-smokers.

BELLEY

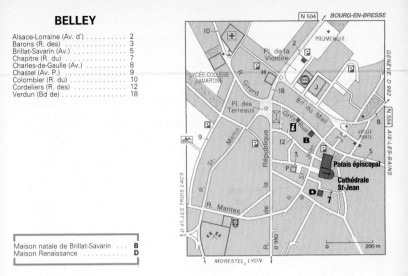

SIGHTS

Cathédrale St-Jean – Although the cathedral was almost entirely rebuilt in the 19C, it still features its original north portal, dating probably from the 14C: a door beneath a pointed arch, between two blind arcades.

Inside, the spacious six-bayed **chancel★** (1473) and the triforium with its pretty openwork balustrades are also original. Five richly decorated chapels open onto the ambulatory. The Lady Chapel, behind the high altar, contains an imposing marble statue of the Virgin Mary by Chinard (1756-1813).

There is a shrine reliquary to St Anthelme, bishop of Belley from 1163 to 1178 and patron of the town, to the left of the altar. It is made of gilt bronze decorated with enamel work and depicts 12 scenes from the saint's life. The blue globe, the cross and the stars above the shrine evoke the Carthusian Order to which he belonged.

Maison natale de Brillat-Savarin – *No 62 Grande-Rue.* Brillat-Savarin's birthplace is a beautiful, two-storied house decorated with round arches on the façade. An inner courtyard leads into a garden graced by a loggia, and in which an old well is also to be seen. The façade of the garden wing features three floors of galleries and balustrades. The bust of Brillat-Savarin is at the northern end of the Promenoir, opposite the Grand Colombier mountainside he loved, where he had his country château at Vieu.

Rue du Chapitre – There is a beautiful 15C Renaissance house with a turret at no 8; a Gothic inscription can be seen above the door.

Palais épiscopal – A bishop was in residence in Belley from 555. The 18C bishop's palace is thought to have been constructed following designs by Soufflot. It now houses the municipal library, the music school and a concert and exhibition hall.

EXCURSIONS

Les Trois lacs – *13km/8mi. Drive west out of Belley along D 41. Turn right as you leave Appregnin.* **Arborias** and **Armaille** lakes, reached via picturesque narrow roads, are a favourite haunt of anglers and picnic fans. **Ambléon** Lake, on the other hand, offers swimming facilities…and there are others in the area.

Bas-Bugey

170km/106mi round tour – allow one day

Leave Belley on N 504, north of the map, then turn right onto D 69, and after Billieu turn right again as far as D 37.

Shortly after Pollieu, the road brings you to **Lac de Barterand** *(see Practical information: Sports and outdoor activities)*, or Lac de St-Champ as it is sometimes called after the neighbouring village, a lake set in peaceful, green surroundings.

Take D 992 on the left which runs alongside the canal, then take D 37 on the right. Before reaching N 504, turn right towards Chemillieu.

The view opens up to the Yenne basin, the Dent du Chat, Mont Revard (glimpsed through the gap of the Col du Chat), and the Chartreuse mountain range (the Grand-Som and Grande Sure summits).

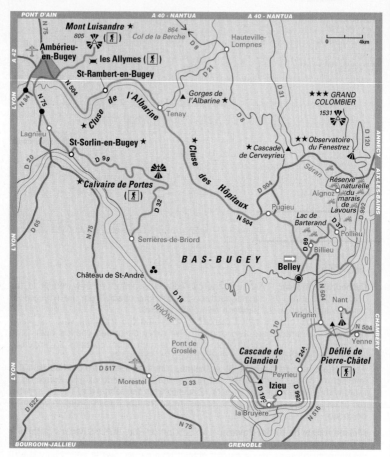

Leave the car near the wash-house in the hamlet of Nant. Take the tarmac path on the immediate left, which soon becomes a stone track (closed to vehicles) leading along the rock face to the top of the gorge.

Défilé de Pierre-Châtel – *1hr 30min there and back on foot.*

There is a **view**★ of the ravine from the top of a rocky outcrop left of the path. The Rhône has found a crack in the Jura mountains' armour; it cuts into the mountain range at the Col de Pierre-Châtel, forming a gorge, then flows on into a valley which it follows as far as its confluence with the Guiers. The buildings of an old Carthusian monastery tower above the ravine. The **Chartreuse de Pierre-Châtel**, founded in 1383, soon had fortifications added to it, before being fully converted into a fortress in the 17C, when it found itself situated on the frontier, as the Bresse and Bugey regions were handed over to France.

The elegant arch of the bridge spanning the Rhône at La Balme is eye-catching.

Return to D 37 and take N 504 which runs along the bottom of the ravine. Cross the Rhône on this road. At Virignin take D 31^A on the left, then D 24 on the left, as far as Peyrieu, where you rejoin D 992.

The road follows the course of the river as it once more changes its course, this time to bypass the Izieu mountain mass. At its confluence with the Guiers, it flows off northwest along a channel in the plateau.

Take D 19^C on the right to the outskirts of La Bruyère then turn right to Izieu.

Izieu – The country road winds upwards through brush, woodlands and orchards, leading to this peaceful village, forever linked in the memory of the French nation with one of the more tragic events of the Second World War. Forty-four Jewish children who had found refuge there, as well as the adults accompanying them, were betrayed and then deported to Auschwitz. None returned.

Musée-Mémorial ⊙ – Mme Sabine Zlatin, principal of the school at the time the tragedy occurred, has worked tirelessly for 50 years to establish this memorial. The daily routine in the short-lived safe haven is evoked in the classroom, dormitory and dining hall. An exhibit relates the trials endured by families under Nazi occupation.

Return to La Bruyère and turn right onto the old D 19 running through the villages of Brégnier-Cordon and Glandieu.

Cascade de Glandieu – During the week the waterfall is harnessed by two small hydroelectric plants at its foot.

Carry on north along D 19.

Notice the suspension bridge at Groslée, a rare example of a lightweight metal alloy construction for unlimited tonnages. Shortly after Flévieu the road runs past the ruins of the **château de St-André**.

At Serrières-de-Briord take D 32 to the right, then D 99 to the left which leads to the Calvaire de Portes.

★ **Calvaire de Portes** – The mountain summit on which this calvary stands (alt 1 025m/3 363ft) at the tip of a rocky spur can be seen from a long way off.

🏃 *Park your car in the car park at the side of the road and take the path towards the calvary (15min there and back on foot).*

From the viewing table, the view encompasses the small, pointed mountain called Dent du Chat (cat's tooth; alt 1 390m/4 203ft), to the left the towering form of the Grand Colombier (alt 1 531m/5 023ft) and to the right the broad expanse of the plain through which the Ain flows on its way to the Rhône.

D 99 leads down towards Lagnieu, providing a view of the Rhône Valley as it goes.

St Christopher

G. Magnin/MICHELIN

★ **St-Sorlin-en-Bugey** – In season, there are flowers, particularly roses, wherever you go in this village. It occupies a picturesque site at the foot of a cliff which overlooks a curve in the Rhône Valley. Visitors should allow themselves time to wander through the narrow streets and admire the carefully restored houses on the way up to the church; at the intersection with the montée des Sœurs, note the fine 16C **fresco depicting St Christopher**.

The village church has undergone several extension and restoration projects, the most ambitious of which completely rebuilt the interior, raising the roof vault and adding tall Gothic pillars supporting a network of ribs in the vault. There is a beautiful view of the whole village from the second hairpin bend in the road climbing beyond the church, from where the old château stands.

The Rhône at this point has returned to the same latitude as Culoz, although the broad meander it has made in the south, has in the meantime taken it across the whole of the Bas-Bugey. It now flows into the Dombes plain, where it picks up the tributary of the Ain and flows on towards Lyon.

Ambérieu-en-Bugey – Ambérieu, an important junction for major railway lines and roads, is expanding in the Ain plain at the mouth of the Albarine gorge.

On reaching the church in Ambérieu, take a road on the left that climbs toward the Château des Allymes. Leave the car at the edge of the hamlet of Brédevent. From here you can take a walk to either Mont Luisandre or the Château des Allymes.

★ **Mont Luisandre** – *1hr 15min there and back on foot.*

🏃 Take the steep, stone track between two houses in the village, to the left of the wash-house. A 15min walk brings you to a steep bank, where you take the path to the right which leads up through meadows and fallow land to the summit.

There is a cross at the summit (alt 805m/2 641ft). Walk round the grove to obtain a sweeping **view**★ of the Château des Allymes on one of the spurs of the Bugey, the Dombes plateau sparkling with reflected light from its lakes, the confluence of the Ain and the Rhône and the wooded summits of the Bugey region, slashed by the deep gorges of the Albarine.

Château des Allymes ⊙ – *30min there and back on foot from Brédevent.*

🏃 This fortified château was laid out as a square. The courtyard in its centre is protected by a solid, square keep in one corner, and a round tower with a lovely **timber roof**★ in the other. Walk round the second storey of the curtain wall to obtain glimpses through the openings of the Dombes plain and the Bresse region.

The tour continues through the Albarine and Hôpitaux *cluses*, which separate the Bugey region into two parts.

★ **Cluse de l'Albarine** – This valley cuts across from Ambérieu to Tenay. The Albarine, the railway line and the road wind along together between the steep slopes on either side. The lower part of these slopes is carpeted with vines here and there. The upper slopes, which are wooded, culminate in limestone ridges in which the rock strata run diagonally and at times almost vertically, in between crumbling boulders. The valley twists and turns, and then suddenly narrows off, giving you the impression that you are in fact in a cirque, and about to bump into its far side; it is not until the last moment that you find the way out.

St-Rambert-en-Bugey – This little industrial town in a green valley on the banks of the Albarine houses a **Maison de Pays** ⊙, in which traditional industries are on display along with a reconstruction of the inside of a house from days gone by. The road between Argis and Tenay, at the bottom of the *cluse*, passes one factory after another, surrounded by workers' homes. These factories used to specialise in handling silk by-products, but now produce nylon and its derivatives.

★ **Cluse des Hôpitaux** – This valley opens up between Tenay and Pugieu. It is not as green as the Cluse de l'Albarine, as there is only a tiny stream trickling through it. Its steep rocky sides, taller and craggier than those of the Cluse de l'Albarine, and its plunging gorge give the landscape a bleak and rugged air, accentuated by the almost complete absence of houses.

Return to Belley on N 504.

Château de BELVOIR★

Michelin map 321: J-3 – 24km/15mi to the west of Maîche

The fortress of Belvoir, built in the 12C by the barons of Belvoir, is perched on a promontory overlooking the Sancey Valley south of the Lomont mountains. It remained the property of the Belvoirs and their descendants (the House of Lorraine and the princes of Rohan) until the 19C. Vincent de Belvoir, to whom St Louis entrusted the writing of the first encyclopaedia, was born here.

Inside the château

Tour of the castle ⊙ – Restoration began in 1955, and the many rooms of the Château de Belvoir now house costly furnishings.

The visit includes the kitchen with its gleaming copper utensils, the guard-room, the former arsenal, and the weaponry in which arms and armour from the Middle Ages to the 19C are on display.

A living room and study have been attractively furnished in the Madge-Fà tower, which owes its curious name to the strange bearded character crouching on a monster's head beneath the *cul-de-lampe* which supports the turret overlooking the road.

From the keep, there is a beautiful panorama of the surrounding countryside: the Lomont mountains to the north; the Maîche plateau to the south; and a landscape of hills and plateaux to the east and west.

Musée de la Radio et du Phonographe ⊙ – This museum illustrates the history of sound recording and reproducing techniques, which already spans 100 years. Exhibits include an Edison phonograph dating from 1905, which used a rotating wax cylinder to record and reproduce sound waves.

EXCURSION

Sancey-le-Long – *2km/1.2mi S.* This village was the birthplace of St Jeanne-Antide Thouret, founder of the Besançon Sisters of Charity; there is a pilgrimage church in her memory.

BESANÇON ★★

Population 117 733
Michelin map 321: G-3

The capital of the Franche-Comté lies in an almost perfect ox-bow meander of the Doubs, overlooked by a rocky outcrop on which Vauban built a fortress.

The strategic advantages of the site were appreciated early on by Caesar, who described it in his account of the Gallic Wars.

Over the centuries Besançon's role expanded from the purely military to include that of an ecclesiastical and then industrial centre. During the Revolution, the town became the hub of the French clockmaking industry, and local manufacturers of modern high-precision instruments draw on this early expertise. Fine private mansions, including the famous Palais Granvelle, line the narrow pedestrianised streets, testifying to the city's rich history.

There has been an annual international music festival here since 1948, which takes place in September, during which a prize is awarded to the best young conductor (prize-winners include Seiji Ozawa in 1959 and Michel Plasson in 1962).

Famous people born here include: the portraitist Donat Nonotte (1708-85); the philosopher and economist Charles Fourier (1772-1837), who envisaged an ideal society composed of cooperative working communities known as phalanxes; the novelist Charles Nodier (1780-1844); the great poet and writer Victor Hugo (1802-85); the sociologist Pierre-Joseph Proudhon (1809-65); and the Lumière brothers, Auguste (1862-1954) and Louis (1864-1948).

HISTORICAL NOTES

A centre for Christianity – Vesontio, as Besançon was called by the Romans during their occupation of Gaul, was converted to Christianity by two missionaries of Greek origin: **St Ferréol** and **St Ferjeux**, who set up home c 180 in a cave in the middle of the woods, now the site of a basilica which was been built there in their memory. For 30 years they preached the Gospel throughout the region. They were finally beheaded in the amphitheatre, because they refused to make sacrifices to the old pagan gods.

However, religious persecution did not prevent the new religion from gaining ground, and finally being adopted by the Emperor Constantine himself. The town subsequently became an important archbishopric.

Archbishop Hugh – When **Hugh of Salins** was made archbishop of Besançon in 1031, virtually the whole of France was in the grip of a terrible famine. Hugh came from one of the most illustrious families in the Franche-Comté and had been chaplain to Rudolph III, King of Burgundy. Later, when Heinrich III became the German Emperor, Hugh proved to be an astute politician and was quick to begin forging connections with the new sovereign. In 1042, the Emperor presided over an assembly at Besançon. He granted a degree of autonomy to Burgundy and appointed Hugh, who had won his confidence, as chancellor. Now that Hugh was second only to the Emperor, Besançon gained the status of an imperial city, no longer answerable to the Comté, with the power to administer its own justice and mint its own money.

The archbishop's power was increased still further when a friend of his, Brunon de Toul, acceded to the Papal Seat as **Pope Leo IX**. Hugh entered the services of the Pope and sat in on all the Church Councils of the day, where he initiated many reforms. He also carried out a number of construction projects in Besançon, until his death in 1066. The city owes the church of St-Étienne (1050) and the cathedral of St-Jean (1061) to him.

Quai Vauban on the Doubs

The rise of the Granvelle family – In the 16C, the fame of the Granvelle family cast a reflected glow on Besançon also. This family's success was touched with genius. The Granvelle forebears were the Perrenots, humble peasants from the Loue Valley, who saved up enough to buy their liberty and set themselves up as craftsmen in Ornans. One of them managed to become a notary and sent his son to the university of Dole. This gifted young man, having qualified as a doctor of law and become a lawyer, married the daughter of a wealthy Besançon merchant, who brought a substantial dowry with her. In 1518, at the age of 32, he was appointed Parliamentary adviser. This might have been enough to fulfil most people's ambitions, but young Perrenot, now Lord of Granvelle, did not allow himself to be content with this honour. He carried on working, and his career continued its meteoric climb, until finally, at the age of 46, he was appointed Chancellor to Charles V, who placed such trust in him that he referred to his chancellor as "my bed of rest".

As was the custom of his age, Granvelle had made a fortune from his various offices. He had a vast palace built in Besançon and collected sumptuous works of art to put in it. Having ensured that his five sons and six sons-in-law held the most coveted positions in the Franche-Comté and at Court, this humble village boy from Ornans had indeed reached the pinnacle of his potential.

With infinite care, the chancellor groomed his son Antoine to succeed him. He desired his son not only to inherit material wealth and power, but also to win spiritual prestige by becoming a leading figure in the Church. Antoine de Granvelle went on to become Cardinal, Prime Minister of the Netherlands, where he advised the ruler Margaret of Parma, Viceroy of Naples, and as Minister for Foreign Affairs he was the only nobleman from the Franche-Comté whom Philip II of Spain would allow into his presence. Despite all these honours, Granvelle never forgot the town of his birth. He liked nothing better than to return to Besançon and his magnificent family seat, which he continued to embellish with works of art and other treasures.

Besançon falls under Spanish rule – In 1656, unbeknown to its inhabitants, the imperial city of Besançon was traded for Frankenthal and became Spanish territory. A turbulent period in the city's history ensued.

In 1668, 10 years after the death of Charles V, Condé took over the city after Louis XIV had laid claim to the Franche-Comté and Flanders as his inheritance. He had hardly done this, when the Treaty of Aix-la-Chapelle, signed the same year, returned the Franche-Comté to Spanish rule.

Nonetheless, in 1674 Louis XIV's troops, 20 000 men strong, assembled once more at the gates of Besançon. The siege was commanded by Vauban. In the meander of the Doubs, 5 000 men put up a heroic defence, withstanding the hail of French cannon balls which rained down of them from Chaudanne and Bregille for 27 days. Finally they had to admit defeat, although their leader, the **Prince de Vaudemont**, did not give himself up for another week.

In 1677, Louis XIV made Besançon the capital of the new French province, and the Treaty of Nijmegen (1678) annexed the Franche-Comté to France once and for all.

Capital of the Franche-Comté – Parliament, treasury, university and Mint all now moved from Dole to Besançon. At first the city's residents were delighted, but their pride soon changed to dismay when they were presented with a bill of 15 000 to 30 000 livres for each transfer by royal officials, who on top of that, more than trebled their taxes. Nevertheless, local trade, industry and the arts all made greater strides than ever before thanks to the city's new status. Besançon owes much to one of the royal commissioners in particular, the **Intendant de Lacoré**, who endowed the city with beautiful monuments and parks during the 18C.

★★ OLD TOWN 2hr

1 The lower town

Bound by the meander of the River Doubs, this part of town was once enclosed within walls.

The old town should be visited on foot (much of it is pedestrian zones). Park your car either in the car park on the Promenade Chamars, or on the north-west bank of the Doubs. Cross the Battant bridge.

View of the old town and cathedral of Besançon with the citadel in the background

Eating out

BUDGET

Au Petit Polonais – *81 r. Granges -* ☎ *03 81 81 23 67 - jean-michel.viennot@wanadoo.fr - closed 14 Jul-15 Aug, Sat evenings and Sun - 9.91/23.93€*. In 1870 this restaurant was founded by a Pole, whose story is recounted on the menu. Simple, unpretentious setting. Traditional and regional cuisine. Warm, congenial atmosphere.

MODERATE

Le Chaland – *Prom. Micaud, near Pont Brégille -* ☎ *03 81 80 61 61 - chaland@chaland.com - closed 29 Jul-20 Aug and Sat lunchtime - 15/58€*. Settle in the restaurant on this charming old barge moored along the Doubs, offering views of the old town and the Promenade Micaud. In fair weather, meals are served on the upper deck, from where you can see the cormorants circling above the water.

Vauban – *In the citadel -* ☎ *03 81 83 02 77 - closed 1 Nov-28 Feb, Sun evenings and Mon - 16.50/30.50€*. This restaurant, nestled in the fortifications of Vauban's citadel, commands breathtaking views of the city of Besançon. Meals are served on the terrace or in one of the two pretty dining rooms with stone vaulting. Classical bill of fare.

Barthod – *22 r. Bersot -* ☎ *03 81 82 27 14 - closed Feb school holidays, Sun and Mon - 23.08/45.38€*. Sit down on the charming terrace bursting with bushes and potted plants and admire the view of the nearby waterfall... The owner is a wine buff who proposes lovingly prepared menus (prices include wine) washed down by an interesting selection of vintages. Don't forget to drop by the shop on your way out.

Where to stay

BUDGET

Régina – *91 Grande-Rue -* ☎ *03 81 81 50 22 – closed 3-10 Aug and 24 Dec-2 Jan - 20 rooms: 28.97/38.11€ -* ☲ *4.88€*. This hotel is ideally located to stroll through the streets of the old town. The rooms are both quiet and comfortable; some have a balcony while others look out onto the citadel.

Hôtel du Nord – *8 r. Moncey -* ☎ *03 81 81 34 56 - hoteldunord3@wanadoo.fr - *🅿* - 44 rooms: 33.60/51.90€ -* ☲ *5.35€*. Situated in the historic quarter, this hotel is a perfect base for venturing out into the old town. The spacious, traditional rooms are equipped with all modern conveniences.

On the town

Brasserie Granvelle – *Pl. Granvelle -* ☎ *03 81 81 05 60 - brasserie-dreyfus@nge.fr - open daily 7-1am*. Get away from the bustle of the town centre and settle on the terrace of this quiet brasserie, patronised by a trendy clientele and regular visitors to the nearby law courts.

Brasserie du Commerce – *31 r. des Granges -* ☎ *03 81 81 33 11 - open daily 8-1am - closed 25 Dec-1 Jan*. This brasserie founded back in 1873 has retained its original decor and has become something of an institution. Its old-fashioned atmosphere is indeed charming but its popularity is such that, on some evenings, it is almost impossible to find a table... or a seat!

L'Auberge Comtoise – *195 r. de Belfort -* ☎ *03 81 50 83 83 – open Fri-Sat at 9pm*. Lovers of accordion music will adore this dance hall where all types of music are performed: waltz, paso doble, java and tango. Dancers of all ages are welcome at this friendly establishment, which exudes old-fashioned charm.

Le Brystol – *4 av. Édouard-Droz -* ☎ *03 81 53 04 00 - open daily 10pm-4am – appropriate clothing is required*. This little house with its cosy decor has become a temple of karaoke to which people come from all over the Besançon area. Lively ambience guaranteed. Interesting choice of cocktails.

Le Vin et l'Assiette – *97 r. Battant -* ☎ *03 81 81 48 18 - Tue-Sat 9am-9.30pm - closed 2 weeks in Aug*. This former wine-grower's cellar in the old quarter is housed in a 14C building which is an officially listed site. Wine buffs will be able to taste wine by the glass, accompanied by a plate of *rosette* (dry pork sausage) or Comté cheese.

Sit back and relax

Barthod – *22 r. Bersot* - ☏ *03 81 82 27 14 - Mon 2-7.15pm, Tue-Sat 9am-12.15pm, 2-7.15pm - closed public holidays*. This shop offers a wide selection of regional wines, all of an extremely high standard. The owner is a dedicated wine buff who will be delighted to give you advice and help you choose.

Baud – *4 Grande-Rue* - ☏ *03 81 81 20 12 - ste-baud@baud-traiteur.fr - Tue-Sat 7.30am-7.30pm, Sun 7.30am-12.30pm; public holidays 7.30am-1pm*. This family business has literally become an institution in Besançon on account of the delicious food it provides: cakes and pastries, ice cream, take-away dishes. If the terrace is crowded, just grin and bear it: it's definitely worth the wait.

Before going down the Grande-Rue, take a few steps back along the bridge to get a better view of the 17C residences with beautiful grey-blue stone **façades★** which line the banks of the Doubs.

Head north along quai (or promenade) Vauban to passage Vauban leading to place de la Révolution; when the river is in spate, follow the road running parallel to the quai Vauban.

Place de la Révolution – This lively square, better known as place du Marché, is at a junction with the **Musée des Beaux-Arts et d'Archéologie★★** (see description below) on one side and old buildings along Rue des Boucheries.

On the north-east corner of the square stands the church of the ancien hôpital du Saint-Esprit, which has been a Protestant place of worship since 1842. The courtyard has a carved timber gallery dating probably from the early 16C.

Follow rue des Granges (behind the covered market) and turn immediately right onto rue R-L Breton leading to place Pasteur and Grande-Rue.

Grande-Rue – This street is an old Roman highway which crossed Vesontio from one side to the other and which, 2 000 years later, is still the main road through the city. Part of it, between the Pont Battant and Place du 8-Septembre, has been sectioned off as a pedestrian zone. Note at no 44 the **Hôtel d'Emskerque**, a late 16C mansion and residence of Gaston d'Orléans for a time, with elegant grilles on the ground floor.

Opposite, at no 53, the interior courtyard has a remarkable stone and wrought-iron staircase. At no 67, the **Hôtel Pourcheresse de Fraisans** also has a lovely staircase in the courtyard. No 68, once the Hôtel Terrier de Santans, was built in 1770 and has a pretty interior courtyard. No 86 used to be a **convent for Carmelite nuns**; it dates from the 17C and has an arcaded courtyard. At no 88 stands the old entrance doorway to the **convent of the Great Carmelites** with a 16C fountain to the left of it. The sculptor Claude Lullier depicted the Duke of Alva, Philip II of Spain's military chief, as Neptune. No 103 has a lovely timber staircase in the courtyard.

Hôtel de Ville – The town hall dates from the 16C. Its façade is decorated with alternately blue and ochre-coloured rustic work.

Opposite, the unusual façade of the **church of St-Pierre** is the work of Besançon architect Bertrand (late 18C).

Palais de Justice – The central park of the building which houses the law courts has a pretty Renaissance façade by Hugues Sambin. The wrought-iron gates in the entrance doorway are really beautiful. The Parliament of the Franche-Comté sat in session inside, on the first floor.

★ **Palais Granvelle** – The mansion was built from 1534 to 1542 for Chancellor Nicolas Perrenot de Granvelle. It has an imposing Renaissance façade overlooking the street, which is divided into three storeys and five bays. The high roof has crow-stepped gables at each side and three dormer windows with richly sculpted frontons. There is a pretty rectangular interior **courtyard★** surrounded by porticoes with depressed basket-handle arches.

The **Musée du Temps** (clock museum) was installed in the palace in 2002 *(see additional sights).*

The Promenade Granvelle is a pleasant shady walk through the old palace gardens, which is particularly popular during the summer. It leads past the Kursaal, a concert and meeting hall.

Carry on along the Grande-Rue.

Victor Hugo was born at no 140, and the **Lumière brothers**, inventors of the first motion picture camera, were born at no 1 place Victor-Hugo.

Roman ruins – Rue de la Convention, the extension of Grande-Rue, offers a good view of the Square archéologique A-Castan, a pretty little park with a row of columns which once formed part of the peristyle of a nymphaeum. The channels of the aqueduct which supplied the basin can still be seen.

Opposite the square is the old archbishops' palace, dating from the early 18C, which now houses the local education authority.

Go through the **Porte Noire**, a Roman triumphal arch built in the 2C, which no doubt earned the name "black gate" from its very dark patina. It would have stood once upon a time in solitary splendour. The sculpture work on it, although partially restored in the 19C, has been very badly eroded by the weather.

★ **Cathédrale St-Jean** ⊙ – The cathedral, most of which was built in the 12C, is dedicated to St John the Baptist. Interestingly, it has two apses, one at either end of the central nave. The bell-tower collapsed in 1729 and was rebuilt in the 18C, along with one of the apses (Saint-Suaire, *left of entrance*) which was damaged when the tower fell in. The Saint-Suaire apse is Baroque in style and contains paintings from the 18C (Van Loo, Natoire, de Troy). In the south aisle, left of the great organ loft, is the famous painting by Fra Bartolomeo, the **Virgin Mary with Saints**★, executed in 1512 in Rome for the cathedral's canon Ferry Carondelet, abbot of Montbenoît and councillor to Charles V. The prelate is depicted on his knees on the right. Electric lighting *(switch located to the right below the painting)* enables viewers to appreciate fully the detail and colours of this work. The left apsidal chapel houses the marble tomb of Abbot Ferry Carondelet.

On the north side of the nave is the beautiful Gothic pulpit, made of stone, from which St François de Sales is believed to have preached. The second chapel off the north aisle contains a round paleochristian altar in white marble, known as the **Rose de St Jean**, which is decorated with a chrismon (Greek letters symbolising Christ) with, rather surprisingly, an eagle above it (the symbol of St John the Evangelist). Another chapel in the north aisle, near the Rose de St Jean, is dedicated to a Virgin and Child painted by Dominico Cresti in 1630, which was twice miraculously saved: in the first instance, it was rescued after a shipwreck near Toulon and then it was not damaged during the Revolution. In the chancel is a replica of the throne used in the consecration of Napoleon I.

At no 5 Rue de la Convention is an old 18C town mansion, or *hôtel*, which now houses the Palais de l'Archevêché (archbishops' palace).

★ **Horloge astronomique** ⊙ – *On the ground floor of the bell-tower.*

⊡ The astronomical clock, a marvel of mechanics comprising 30 000 parts, was designed and made between 1857 and 1860 by A-L Vérité from Beauvais, and reset in 1900 by F Goudey from Besançon. It serves as a timepiece for the public, since it is connected to the clock faces on the bell-tower. The 62 dials indicate among other things the days and seasons, the time in 16 different places all over the world, the tides in 8 ports, the length of daylight and darkness, the times at which the sun and the moon rise and set and, below the clock, the movement of the planets around the sun. Several automata are activated on the hour.

Take the pretty rue du Chambrier down to the Porte Rivotte.

Porte Rivotte – This gate is the remains of 16C fortifications. After the French conquest, Louis XIV had the fronton decorated with a symbolic sun. The cliffs of the citadel rise with their horizontal strata tower above the gate. These cliffs once plunged straight into the river. The narrow strip of land along which the road passes was dug and blasted out of the rock face. A 375m/1 230ft long canal cuts through the cliffs in a tunnel, providing a short cut past the Doubs meander.

Walk round the cathedral along rue du Chapitre and turn right onto rue du Palais. On the left is the fine Hôtel Bonvalot.

Porte Rivotte

C. Gauthier

Hôtel Bonvalot – Built between 1538 and 1544, this rather austere mansion is brightened up by its ogee-arched stained-glass windows. *Rue du Cingle leads to rue de la Vieille-Monnaie; turn right.*

Maison espagnole – 10-12 rue de la Vieille-Monnaie. Although built after the region was united to the kingdom of France, this house displays unmistakable Spanish features.

Rue de la Vieille-Monnaie is prolonged by rue Mégevand.

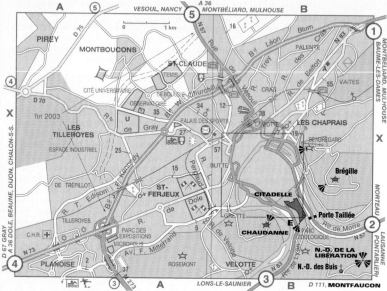

Index of street names and sights in Besançon, see page 169

Rue Mégevand – At the beginning of this street, at the junction with rue Ronchaux, there is a lovely 18C fountain representing the River Doubs. A little further on to the right, place du Théâtre offers a very appropriate setting to the Classical-style theatre, the work of C.N. Ledoux. On the left side of the street, the University is flanked by the former St Vincent Abbey (now the Église Notre-Dame) which has retained the old bell-tower and 16C doorway.

On reaching place de Granvelle, turn left onto rue de la Préfecture.

★**Préfecture** – The erstwhile Palais des Intendants was built in the 18C after designs by the architect Louis.

Outside, on the corner of Rue Ch-Nodier, stands the pretty Fontaine des Dames (18C), or Ladies' Fountain, decorated with a mermaid (copy of a 16C bronze).

Return to the junction with rue de la Préfecture and follow rue Ch.-Nodier to place Saint-Jacques then turn right towards rue de l'Orme-de-Chamars.

Hôpital St-Jacques – This hospital dates from the 17C. It has a splendid **wrought-iron gate**★ and a pretty 18C **pharmacy** ⊙.

Chapelle Notre-Dame-du-Refuge – This chapel owes its name to an establishment founded in 1690 by the Marquis de Broissia to shelter young girls in danger of falling into vice. It was built by the architect Nicolas Nicole in 1739, and became part of the hospital in 1802. Even the building's architecture takes on a religious significance: the shape of the interior gradually changes from an oval to a circle, the symbol of perfection. Note the beautiful Louis XV woodwork.

Rue de l'Orme-de-Chamars is prolonged by rue Pasteur which leads back to the beginning of Grande-Rue.

② Quartier Battant

Situated on the north-west bank of the Doubs, this lively district, one of the oldest in Besançon, used to be the wine-growers' area, and the surrounding slopes covered with modern houses were once covered with vines. On the banks of the river, near the Pont Battant, stands a statue of Jouffroy d'Abbans, who sailed one of the first ever steamboats down the Doubs.

Église Ste-Madeleine – This church was built in the 18C; the towers were built later on in 1830. The interior is vast, with elegant vaulting supported on fluted columns. The great organ (restored) is the work of Callinet.

Walk along rue de la Madeleine.

On the corner of Rue du Petit-Charmont and Rue du Grand-Charmont stands the **Hôtel Jouffroy** which dates from the late 15C and early 16C.

Retrace your steps to the Église Ste-Madeleine and walk along the famous rue Battant.

BESANÇON

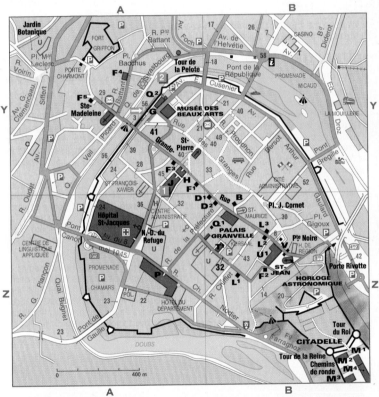

Besançon – Hôtel de Champagney

J.-P. Tupin/Mairie de Besançon

Hôtel de Champagney – This mansion was built for Nicolas de Granvelle's widow in the 16C. The heads of its four gargoyles jut out over the pavement.

Pass through the archway to admire the inner courtyard with its arcades. The passage leads through the **Clos Barbusier**, a garden of old roses, to Fort Griffon from where there is a good view of the rooftops of Besançon.

From the square containing the Bacchus fountain go down rue du Petit-Battant on the right.

Tour de la Pelote – The rather curious late-15C tower was integrated into Vauban's defence system, thus saving it from destruction. It now houses a restaurant.

Walk across the Pont Denfert-Rochereau then turn right onto avenue E.-Cusenier to return to place de la Révolution.

★★CITADELLE ⊘ AND MUSEUMS

Take the steep, winding rue des Fusillés-de-la-Résistance up behind the cathedral.

During Roman occupation this high ground was crowned with a temple, the columns of which now feature on the town's coat of arms. Later, a church dedicated to St Stephen stood on this spot. After the French conquest in 1674, **Vauban** had most of the earlier buildings demolished to make way for the fortress which now overlooks the River Doubs from a height of 118m/387ft. The citadel of Besançon has played a variety of roles – barracks, military cadet academy under Louis XIV, state prison and fortress besieged in 1814 – and both its natural setting and historical interest have much to offer the visitor.

The fortress was built on a gentle ridge and has a more or less rectangular ground plan. Three bastions (or *enceintes* or *fronts*) with large esplanades in between them stretch across its width one after the other on one side: Front St-Étienne towards the town, Front Royal in the centre and Front de Secours nearest the fortress. The whole site is surrounded by fortified ramparts, along which a watch-path runs. Several watchtowers (**Tour du Roi** to the east and **Tour de la Reine** to the west) and bartizans remain.

Chemins de Ronde (Watch-paths) – The watch-path to the west, which begins at the Tour de la Reine *(on the right in the first esplanade)*, reveals a wonderful **view★★** of Besançon, the valley of the Doubs and the Chaudanne and Les Buis hills. The watch-path which leads off towards the Bregille gives a good view of Besançon and the Doubs meander. On the side of the fortress away from the town the **Échauguette sur Tarragnoz**, reached via the **Parc Zoologique**, overlooks the valley of the Doubs.

B. Kaufmann/MICHELIN

Citadelle Front Royal

★ **Musée Comtois** – This museum, in 15 or so rooms in two buildings, houses a considerable collection of exhibits of traditional local arts, crafts and folklore from all over the Franche-Comté.

The left wing is devoted to the ironmonger's craft and contains some of the most original exhibits in the museum, including cast iron wall plates, andirons, kitchen ranges and cauldrons.

Several rooms house a large collection of puppets from a so-called mechanical theatre dating from 1850. Regional landscapes are also illustrated by a relief map, photographs, old maps and documents which can be accessed by computer.

Espace Vauban – The Cadet's building now houses an exhibit and film which trace the history of the citadel, reviewing the civil and military context of Louis XIV's reign, in particular the brilliant engineering accomplishments of Vauban.

★ **Musée d'Histoire naturelle** – ☑ The Natural History Museum is in two wings of the old arsenal and contains clear, up-to-date exhibitions on exotic fauna, with stuffed animals and birds, skulls and skeletons, and displays on insects, including a large butterfly collection. The art of Black Africa is represented by everyday objects and dance masks from the Ivory Coast.

Also of interest are:

– The **Insectarium**, an unusual attraction, is located on the first floor of the Petit Arsenal. If roaches, spiders and scorpions give you the shivers, take inspiration from the hard-working ants on their farm.

On the floor above, there is a section on **Astronomy** and **Meteorology**.

– The **Aquarium Georges-Besse** is located in a large room on the ground floor of the Petit Arsenal. A succession of tanks (50 000l/11 000 gallons) imitates the course of the River Doubs, complete with trout, perch, carp, pike and catfish. Outside, in the ponds thrive lake fish and flora; a small crayfish farm is in operation in a courtyard building.

– The **Parc Zoologique** (2.5ha/5 acres) at the far end on the fortress on the slope known as the Glacis du Front St-Étienne and the Front de Secours moat. About 350 animals live there, including a growing number of felines and primates.

– In the shadows of the **Noctarium**, former powder magazine, can be seen creatures of the night such as mice and rats.

★ **Musée de la Résistance et de la Déportation** – This museum on the French Resistance and deportation occupies 22 rooms and comprises an extensive collection of photographs, objects, posters and documents on the birth and rise of Nazism, the Second World War, the invasion of France in 1940, the Vichy régime, the French Resistance, deportation and the liberation of France. Pictures, paintings and sculptures done by inmates of German prison camps are also on display, along with contemporary works on this theme. An audio-visual room completes the visit. The statue near the entrance is by Georges Oudot.

Poteaux des Fusillés – These posts were put up in memory of the members of the French Resistance shot during the war.

ADDITIONAL SIGHTS

★★ **Musée des Beaux-Arts et d'Archéologie** ⊙ – The Museum of Fine Arts and Archaeology is in the old grain hall, which dates from 1835. It has been extended since the 1970s, by a follower of Le Corbusier, Louis Miquel, who built an original construction of concrete in the courtyard consisting of a succession of gently sloping ramps with landings in between them.

The museum contains some rich collections of works of art, some of which come from the Granvelle family, or more particularly from Nicolas de Granvelle.

At the heart of the building, the ground floor houses a collection of **Egyptian antiquities** (**Seramon's sarcophagus★** still containing his mummy) and statues and objects from the Middle Ages and the Renaissance. In the side galleries, there is a chronological display of local archaeological finds (**Gallo-Roman mosaic** depicting a quadriga, a bronze bull with three horns, god with a hammer).

The section of **paintings★** includes a wide variety of works by non-French schools, signed by some of the greatest names of the 14C to the 17C. Some of the most remarkable works include: *The Drunkenness of Noah* by Giovanni Bellini (1430-1516) in Venice; *Deposition from the Cross* by Bronzino (1503-1572) in Florence; the central panel of the *Triptych of Our Lady of Seven Sorrows* by Bernard Van Orley (1488-1541) in Brussels; *Ill-Assorted Pair* and *Nymph at the Fountain* by Lucas Cranach the Elder (1472-1553) in Germany. Flemish paintings is also represented by fine portraits of animals and humans (*Portrait of a Woman* by Dirck Jacobs). In the gallery of 18C works, note the two panels illustrating *Scenes of Cannibalism* by Goya.

The French collection includes some 18C and 19C French masterpieces: tapestry cartoons on a Chinese theme by Boucher; works by Fragonard and Hubert Robert; sketches by David; and, best of all, landscapes by Courbet, *The Conche Hill* and the monumental painting *Death of a Stag*. Make a point of looking at some works by artists from the Franche-Comté (J Gigoux, T Chartran, JA Meunier).

A fine relief model of Besançon shows the triumphal arch, no longer extant, which once stood on the Quai Vauban, and the old bell-tower of the cathedral.

The 20C has not been neglected: the Besson collection of paintings, watercolours and drawings includes some of Bonnard's best paintings, such as *Place Clichy* and *Café du Petit Poucet*, as well as the portrait of Madame Besson by Renoir, *The Seine at Grenelle* and *Two Friends* by Albert Marquet and *Yellow Sail* by Paul Signac. The Cabinet des Dessins *(open by appointment only)* houses a comprehensive collection of over 5 000 drawings, including the famous red chalk sketches of the Villa d'Este by Fragonard. The drawings are exhibited in rotation, with only a selected few at a time on display.

Musée du Temps ⊘ – *Palais Granvelle*. The clock-making industry, established in Besançon in 1793, remained the town's main activity until the 1920s. This museum, housed in the restored Palais Granvelle, exhibits all kinds of objects connected with time: a rich collection of clocks, watches, tools and engravings from the 16C to the 19C.

★ **Bibliothèque Municipale** ⊘ – Marvellous illuminated manuscripts, incunabula, old books, drawings and bookbindings.

EXCURSIONS

Chaudanne – *2km/1mi S, and then 15min there and back (see the town plan). Leave Besançon on the Charles-de-Gaulle bridge towards Planoise, go under a bridge and, 100m further, turn right onto rue G.-Plançon then take the first right, rue de Chaudanne. Follow rue du Fort-de-Chaudanne until you get to the lookout point in front of the entrance to the fort.*

There is a lovely **view** of Besançon and the Doubs meander; at 419m/1 375ft, this is one of the most interesting lookout points in the area.

From right to left, the view takes in the cathedral and the old town of Besançon, at the foot of the citadel, then the church of St-Pierre and the business district. On the far bank of the Doubs, the old wine-producing district of Battant can be seen. Directly below Chaudanne lies the administrative centre around the prefecture. Note the formidable Ruty barracks, general staff headquarters, by the Bregille bridge.

★ **Notre-Dame-de-la-Libération** – *3.5km/2mi SE*. On a vast platform, located 400m/437yd from the chapel, stands a statue of the Virgin Mary erected as a gesture of gratitude for the liberation of Besançon. A large Romanesque crypt houses marble slabs bearing the names of the region's inhabitants who died during the war. From the viewing table, the **view**★ extends over Besançon and the surrounding area and as far as the Vosges (weather permitting).

★ **Nancray, Musée de Plein Air des Maisons Comtoises** ⊘ – *16km/10mi E*.
◎ This open-air museum of typical Franche-Comté houses (Territoire de Belfort, Doubs, Haute-Saône and Jura) stages demonstrations of ancient crafts on Sundays as well as festivals, fairs and markets throughout the year.

Boussières – *17km/11mi SW along N 83 and D 104*. This village of the Doubs Valley downriver from Besançon boasts one of the few Romanesque churches in the region.

★ **Église St-Pierre** – The massive porch built in 1574 opens onto the splendid four-storey Romanesque **bell-tower**★ (11C), decorated with lombard bands with pilasters stopping at the third storey. A few openings break the overall uniformity. Inside, on the north side of the nave, there is an odd-looking 16C statue of St James.

Mont BEUVRAY★★

Michelin map 320: E-8 – 8km/4.8mi west of St-Léger-sous-Beuvray – Local map see MORVAN

A powerful Gaulish tribe known as the Aedui established their capital in a fortified settlement *(oppidum)* on one of the highest points of the Haut-Morvan, and baptised it Bibracte. Dating from the first half of the 2C BC, it was protected by a double line of fortifications – Bibracte was probably a term designating twice fortified – of wood, earth and stone.

Extensive excavations have focused attention on the site and led to the opening of a large museum offering a fascinating insight into Celtic history.

A historic site – Of the 200ha/494 acres thus enclosed, about 40 were built up. The dwellings, earth walls shored up by wooden beams, may have sheltered as many as 10 000 people. In times of danger, farmers from the surrounding area could seek refuge behind the walls of the encampment.

Strategically located at the crossroads of trade routes linking the Mediterranean regions to Celtic Europe, the capital was also a political, religious and crafts centre. Bibracte has its place in history: in the year 52 BC, the Gaulish hero **Vercingétorix** lead the local resistance against Roman occupants; the following winter, **Julius Caesar** began writing his "Commentaries" of the Gaulish Wars there.

In the early Christian era, under Augustus, Bibracte diminished in importance as Augustodunum (presently Autun) grew. Yet even after the site was largely abandoned by its inhabitants, it remained an important centre for trade up to the 16C.

Access: *via D 274, a one-way loop from D 3.*

A few nice perspectives appear through the trees.

★ **Centre Archéologique Européen** – The complex includes a **Research Centre** *(located at Glux-en-Gienne, 5km/3mi north on D 300)*, with a documentation service open to the public, and a **Musée de la Civilisation celtique** ⊘, at the foot of the hill, below the fortified camp.

Open to the public as of 1995, the museum displays artefacts from ancient Bibracte, from early and recent digs, amphorae, ceramic vases, bronze dishes, tools, weapons, jewellery and sculpture. On the first floor, a survey of Celtic culture is developed through objects from other famous sites such as Alésia, Argentomagus, La Tène (Switzerland), Manching (Germany) and Titelberg (Luxembourg). Video films, computer terminals, maps, photos taken during excavations, models, dioramas etc. provide a wealth of information about the daily life of the Celts arranged thematically (economy, religion, funeral traditions, Gaulish wars...), which illustrates the cultural unity of the Celtic civilisation.

A. de Vlaroger/MICHELIN

Dumnorix, Celtic chieftan

The Gaulish Wars

It was in Bibracte, in 52 BC, that the king of the Arverni, Vercingetorix, was chosen to lead the combined Gaulish forces in their fight against the Romans. The Aedui, who, at first, were allies of the Romans, changed sides after Caesar's defeat at Gergovia in the Auvergne. This only delayed for a while Caesar's final victory at Alesia where Vercingetorix waited in vain for reinforcements *(see ALISE-STE-REINE)* and gave himself up to save his army.

The following winter, Caesar began writing his *Commentaries on the Gaulish Wars* in which he reveals his talent as a historian as well as his huge personal ambition.

Oppidum de Bibracte ⊘ – While the first archaeological excavations took place in the late 19C, it was not until 1984 that an international effort got underway to explore these vestiges of Celtic civilisation. Today, the site (135ha/333 acres) offers a look at the organisation of the ancient city: the craftsmen's quarter, the network of streets, a section of the ramparts and one of the monumental gateways (Porte de Rebout) have been partially restored.

★★ **Panorama** – From the platform with its orientation table, set amid gnarled beech trees, there is a magnificent view over Autun, the Uchon beacon *(See Le CREUSOT-MONTCEAU)* and Mont St-Vincent. On a clear day, you can see as far as the Jura range and even Mont Blanc.

BOURBON-LANCY ★

Population 5 634
Michelin map 320: C-10

Built on a hill overlooking the Loire Valley, Bourbon-Lancy is both an ancient town and a renowned spa.

OLD TOWN

★**Maison de bois et tour de l'Horloge** – At no 3 rue de l'Horloge stands a 16C timber-framed house featuring ogee-shaped windows, a corner pillar, glazed medallions and an ancient statue.

Nearby, the former belfry which surmounts a fortified gate (the present clock tower), houses the "village idiot" who strikes the hours and sticks out his tongue.

From the belfry, follow the 4km/2.5mi long rampart trail through pleasant scenery.

Musée de l'Uniforme militaire ◷ – The museum contains a collection of dummies dressed in French army uniforms dating from the Second Empire to the Third Republic. There are also paintings by the military specialist Merlette and suitable background music played on the barrel-organ.

> **BEDS BY THE BELFRY**
>
> **Tourelle du Beffroi** – *17 pl. de la Mairie -* ☎ *03 85 89 39 20 - 8 rooms: 45/69€ -* ☲ *6.50€*. A patio overgrown with Virginia creeper and wisteria welcomes you to this modest hotel a stone's throw from the church tower. Small, comfortable rooms with wooden flooring, each decorated in its own style.

Bourbon-Expo ◷ – This museum, housed in a large hall, illustrates the history of agricultural machinery produced by the Puzenat factory (1902-56) which drastically changed agricultural techniques at the beginning of the 20C: harrows, harvesters, tedders...

Église St-Nazaire and museum ◷ – This 11C church (note the panelled ceiling) was under the authority of the Cluniac priory founded by Ancel de Bourbon. Since 1901, it has housed a museum displaying local antiquities including Gallo-Roman statues of Venus discovered in 1984, stone fragments from nearby churches as well as early-19C paintings and sculptures (Barrias's *The Abolition of Slavery by Victor Schoelcher*).

THE SPA DISTRICT

Royal spring – In 1544, after 11 years of marriage, Catherine de' Medici had yet to give her royal husband an heir to the throne of France. Afraid of being repudiated, she decided to try the waters in Bourbon-Lancy, which were reputed to cure sterility... and she subsequently bore ten children!

Hospice d'Aligre – The chapel contains a fine pulpit, carved in 1687 and offered to the abbess of St-Cyr by King Louis XIV. To the left of the chapel, on the landing of the main staircase, stands the silver statue of her descendant, the marquise d'Aligre (1776-1843), the benefactress of the hospice.

The thermal establishment – At the foot of the fortified hill, in the courtyard of the thermal baths, water springs up at a temperature varying from 46° to 58° C and at the rate of 400 000l/88 000gal per day. The waters are used for the treatment of rheumatism and circulatory complaints.

EXCURSIONS

Signal de Mont – *7km/4.3mi NE along D 60 then 15min on foot there and back*. From the viewpoint (alt 469m/1 539ft), there is a fine panorama of the Val de Loire, the Morvan hills, the Signal d'Uchon, the Charolais region and even the Auvergne mountains in clear weather.

Ternant – *20km/12.5mi N along D 973 then D 198 left*. Art lovers should not miss going to Ternant to see the two magnificent 15C Flemish triptychs in the little village church.

★★**The triptychs in the church** – The triptychs were given to the church between 1432 and 1435 by Baron Philippe de Ternant, Chamberlain to Philip the Good, Duke of Burgundy, and his son Charles de Ternant. They are made of wood – carved, painted and gilded.

The **large triptych** is devoted to the Passion of Christ. The centre panel portrays Christ's death. Below, a fainting Virgin Mary is supported by St John and the holy women; the donor Charles de Ternant and his wife Jeanne are shown kneeling in the foreground.

The left-hand panel is a Pietà including the figures of St John, Mary Magdalene and the holy women. To the right is the Entombment. The folding panels show scenes from the Passion: the Agony in the Garden, Christ carrying the Cross, the Resurrection and the Descent into Hell.

The **small triptych**, which is older, is devoted to the Virgin Mary. In the centre of the carved panel is a scene from the Assumption: a little angel, his head covered by a hood, draws the Virgin's soul, depicted as a little girl at prayer, out from her head. Above this is shown the later scene of the Assumption of the Virgin, when she is carried to heaven on a crescent moon held by an angel, symbolising her chastity. The last meeting of the Virgin with the Apostles is shown on the left of the central motif; on the right is her funeral procession.

The panel paintings are remarkable. Besides the scenes from the life of the Virgin Mary – the Annunciation, the Crowning of the Virgin, Christ holding the world, the Virgin's funeral – one can see the donor, Philippe de Ternant, dressed in chequered material – the arms of his house – the Order of the Golden Fleece about his neck, and his wife Isabella, in full state dress, accompanied by the crowned Virgin Mary, her patron saint.

BOURG-EN-BRESSE★★

Population 57 198
Michelin map 320: L-12

Bourg (pronounced Bourk) is and has always been the centre of the rich Bresse region, noted for its poultry which make the local markets famous. On market days or when there is a livestock fair, Bourg is picturesque and animated as crowds of farmers come into town. The annual exhibition *(see Calendar of events)* of Bresse capons and roasting chickens is held in the Parc des Expositions. The chickens' flesh is soaked in milk, making it a pearly colour. The town has also got a good reputation for the manufacture of Bresse country-style furniture *(meubles "rustique bressan")* using fruit trees (cherry, wild cherry, pear and walnut) and ash trees.

The combination of traditional and modern industries contributes to Bourg's dynamic image, whereas its reputation as an artistic centre rests on the many marvellous works of art to which the town is home, not least of which are the outstanding art treasures at the old monastery of Brou.

HISTORICAL NOTES

In the 10C, Bourg was still a little village of thatched cottages clustered round a castle. When the family of the lords of the manor died out in the 13C, the dukes of Savoy, powerful neighbours, took over the inheritance. They established the province of Bresse and made Bourg, now a busy township, its capital.

In 1536 the Duke of Savoy refused François I permission to cross his lands to invade the Milanese. The king forced his way through and, to secure his lines of communication, took possession of Bresse, Savoy and Piedmont. These territories were handed back by Henri II with the Treaty of Cateau-Cambrésis (1559). In 1600 Henri IV invaded the region. The Treaty of Lyon (1601) forced the Duke to exchange Bresse, Bugey, Valromey and the Pays de Gex for the marquisate of Saluces, last of France's possessions in Italy. Bourg thus became part of France.

The Vow of Margaret of Bourbon – In 1480 Philip, Count of Bresse, later Duke of Savoy, had a hunting accident. His wife, Margaret of Bourbon (grandmother of François I), made a vow that, if her husband recovered, she would transform the humble priory of Brou into a monastery. The Count recovered but Margaret died, leaving the task to her husband and her son Philibert the Handsome. Her vow however remained unfulfilled.

Twenty years went by. Philibert, who had married Margaret of Austria, died suddenly. His wife saw a heavenly punishment in this. So that her husband's soul should rest in peace, she hurried to fulfil the vow of Margaret of Bourbon. She lost no time for two reasons; firstly to affirm her sovereignty, and secondly to outshine her sister-in-law Louise of Savoy, who was soon to become Regent of France. These motivations aside, Brou has been a testament to the love of the two Margarets for their husbands for over 400 years now.

III-fated Margaret of Austria – **Margaret of Austria**, the daughter of Emperor Maximilian of Austria and Mary of Burgundy (and granddaughter of Charles the Bold), was two years old when her mother died. The following year she was taken to the court of Louis XI and, in a religious ceremony, married to the Dauphin Charles, heir to the French throne, also a child. The little girl's dowry was the Franche-Comté.

Five years later, quarrels over the succession to the duchy of Brittany began. Maximilian succeeded in winning the favour of the heiress, Duchess Anne, who had many suitors, and they were married by proxy. Unfortunately, once it became known that

Margaret of Austria

Ph. Gajic/MICHELIN

the bridegroom, who had had to borrow money to pay for his first wedding, would not be able to pay the 2 000 livres costs of his journey to Nantes for his latest wedding, Duchess Anne was quick to hand back her ring. Charles VIII took advantage of the predicament and proposed that Anne of Brittany become Queen of France instead of Empress of Austria. The two unconsummated marriages were annulled: Charles repudiated Margaret of Austria and Anne repudiated Maximilian, who thus suffered a double insult as father of the rejected Margaret and rejected husband himself.

At the age of 17 the unfortunate Margaret was married to the heir to the Spanish throne, who died after only a few months, leaving her to bear a still-born child shortly afterwards. Four years later, her father gave her in marriage for the third time to Philibert of Savoy, a frivolous and fickle young man, who was however astute enough to acknowledge his wife as "intelligent enough for two" and remained content to let her practically govern in his stead. Margaret was to have three years of happiness at her handsome duke's side, before fate struck her another cruel blow: her young husband died after catching cold out hunting. Widowed

BOURG-EN-BRESSE

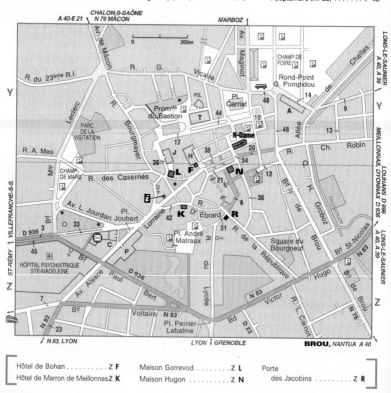

for the second time, 24 year old Margaret was to remain faithful for the rest of her days to the memory of Philibert, whom she had loved dearly despite his weaknesses. This high-ranking woman, well-read and artistic, knew how to take care of herself, selecting trustworthy advisers and commanding absolute obedience. She now devoted herself to affairs of State. In 1506 she became Regent of the Low Countries and the Franche-Comté. Her wise and liberal policies won her the loyalty, respect and affection of all who lived in the Franche-Comté.

Fulfilment of the Vow – In 1506 work began on the construction of the monastery buildings in Brou. These were arranged around three cloisters, one of which was part of the original Benedictine priory.

The priory church was then pulled down to make way for the magnificent building which was to serve as the shrine for the three tombs of Philibert, his wife and his mother. Margaret, who was living in Flanders, entrusted the construction to a Flemish master mason, Loys Van Boghem, who was both architect and general contractor. This remarkable man brought life and strength to the faltering undertaking and succeeded in erecting the fabulous building in the record time of 19 years (1513-1532). Sadly, Margaret died two years before the church was consecrated.

Brou was lucky enough to survive the Wars of Religion and the Revolution relatively unscathed. The monastery became successively a pig farm, a prison, a barracks, a home for beggars, a lunatic asylum, a seminary in 1823, and it now houses the museum of Brou (since 1921).

TOWN WALK

Old houses – There are two late-15C timber-framed houses: **Maison Hugon** (*on the corner of rue Gambetta and rue V.-Basch*) and **Maison Gorrevod** (*rue du Palais*). Equally attractive are the fine 17C stone façade of the **Hôtel de Bohan** (*on the corner by the town hall*) and the 18C **Hôtel de Marron de Meillonnas**, which houses the Trésorerie Générale (*rue Teynière*). A row of medieval half-timbered corbelled houses adjoins the Porte des Jacobins, built in 1437 (*rue J.-Migonney*).

Église Notre-Dame – Although the church was begun in 1505, building was not completed until the 17C. The apse and nave are in the Flamboyant Gothic style, whereas a triple Renaissance doorway is the centrepiece of the façade. The central door is surmounted by a Virgin and Child, copied from a work by Coysevox (17C). The tall belfry was erected under Louis XIV, but the dome and the small lantern on top are modern. A carillon plays at 7.50am, 11.50am and 6.50pm.

Interior – The church contains interesting works of art and furnishings, in particular the finely carved 16C stalls★ in the apse. The high altar, eagle-shaped lectern, the pulpit and organ loft are all fine examples of 18C woodcarving. The altar in the chapel north of the chancel is 19C. The chapel of St-Crépin (*third off the north aisle*) has polychrome statues, and a stained-glass window depicting the Crucifixion, a diptych showing the Last Supper, all dating from the 16C. The mid-20C stained glass in the aisles is by Le Chevallier (*north aisle*) and Auclair (*south aisle*). Note the series of twelve 17C and 18C canvases depicting scenes from the life of the Virgin Mary.

The 13C black Madonna, in whose honour the church was built, stands in the Chapelle de l'Annonciation to the south of the choir.

★★★ BROU *SE on the town plan*

Brou was once a small village clustered round a Benedictine priory, attached to Bourg. It is now part of the south-eastern suburbs of the town. The church and the monastery were built in the 16C in fulfilment of the vow made by Margaret of Bourbon.

A short history and the family tree of the founders are to be found in the south aisle of the church.

★★ Church ⊘

The church has now been deconsecrated. The building, in which the Flamboyant Gothic style is influenced by the Renaissance, was built at the same time as the Château of Chenonceau in the Loire Valley. On the flat ground in front of the façade there is a huge sundial which was reset in 1757 by the astronomer Lalande, a citizen of Bourg.

Exterior – The central park of the triangular façade is richly sculpted. The tympanum above the fine Renaissance **doorway★** shows Philibert the Handsome and Margaret of Austria and their patron saints at the feet of Christ Bound. On the pier is St Nicolas of Tolentino, to whom the church is dedicated (his feast falls on the day of Philibert's death). Surmounting the ornamental doorway arch is a statue of St Andrew; St Peter and St Paul flank the doorway on the arch shafts.

Eating out

BUDGET

Le Chalet de Brou – *168 bd de Brou -* ☎ *04 74 22 26 28 - closed 1-15 Jun, 23 Dec-23 Jan, Mon evenings, Thu evenings and Fri - 14/35€*. This small family restaurant opposite Brou Church offers regional cooking at moderate prices. Traditional dining room with tapestries and wood panelling. Warm welcome.

MODERATE

Le Français – *7 av. Alsace-Lorraine -* ☎ *04 74 22 55 14 - info@le-francais.fr - closed 8-12 May, 5-27 Aug, 24 Dec-2 Jan, Sat evenings and Sun - 21.30/48.50€*. This turn-of-the-century brasserie located in the town centre has a truly authentic decor, complete with huge mirrors and stucco ceilings. Traditional French cuisine with special emphasis on fish and sea food. Warm, congenial hospitality.

Where to stay

BUDGET

Chambre d'Hôte Les Vignes – *01310 Montcet - 12 km/7.5mi W of Bourg-en-Bresse by D 936 then D 45 -* ☎ *04 74 24 23 13 - jean-louis.gayet2@libertysurf.fr - ⊠ - 4 rooms: 40/50€ - meals 18€*. Lost in the countryside, this typical Bresse house made of brick and wood is surrounded by a charming garden bursting with vegetation. The cosy bedrooms feature wood panelling on the walls. Have breakfast on the terrace or the verandah or take a relaxing nap down by the pool.

MODERATE

Logis de Brou – *132 bd de Brou -* ☎ *04 74 22 11 55 - closed 22 Dec-5 Jan - ▣ - 30 rooms: 47/61€ -* ☕ *7€*. This pleasant hotel situated in the vicinity of Brou Church offers comfortable, well-kept rooms appointed with modern, rustic or bamboo furniture. Nice garden.

Shopping

Émaux Bressans Jeanvoine – *1 r. Thomas-Riboud -* ☎ *04 74 22 05 25 – open Tue-Sat 9am-noon, 2-7pm - closed public holidays*. Designed by a Parisian craftsman who settled in Bourg-en-Bresse, Bresse enamels are currently manufactured by the Jeanvoine establishment. The enamel pieces are made by hand and embellished with gold motifs according to a tradition dating from 1850.

Sit back and relax

Bière en Brousse – *1 bis r. Teynière -* ☎ *04 74 45 20 70 – open Mon-Wed 11am-1pm, Thu-Fri 11am-3pm, Sat 5pm-3am; Jul-Aug: Mon-Wed 5pm-1am, Thu-Sat 5pm-3am - closed 2 weeks in Aug*. Beer drinkers will love this unassuming bar, whose selection of rare and unusual beers is quite astounding. Every month you can discover a new beer (Maredsous, Estrella, Kriek). Another good point is the high quality of the music, be it Afro-Cuban, rock, reggae or blues.

The Albion Public House – *37 r. Bourgmayer -* ☎ *04 74 22 19 10 – open daily 5pm-1am*. With its long counter, its parquet floors and its wooden decor, this pub is a popular meeting-place for the younger generation. Light meals are provided by the barbecue set up in the leafy courtyard adjoining the back of the building.

The decorative sculpture includes a variety of Flamboyant Gothic floral motifs (leaves and fruit), some showing a decidedly Renaissance influence (laurel, vine and acanthus), intermingled with symbolic motifs, such as palms interlaced with marguerites. The decoration at Brou comprises other motifs: the initials of Philibert and Marguerite linked by love-knots (twisted fillet moulding festooned between the two letters) and intermingled with crossed batons, the arms of Burgundy.

The simpler façade of the north transept has a pinnacled gable. The five-storey square belfry stands on the south side of the apse.

From 1996 to 1998, the church roof benefited from an ambitious restoration project. Its appearance had already been modified significantly during works undertaken in 1759. The recent works provided an opportunity to return the roof to its original design; Mansard frameworks were replaced by more steeply sloping forms. Flat roof tiles laid in a diamond pattern have been glazed in colours typical of the region: dark brown, gingerbread, yellow and green.

Nave – On entering the church one is struck by the light which bathes the nave and its double aisles. The light entering through the clerestory windows falls on the false stonework marked on the surface of the walls. The pillars, formed by numerous little columns, thrust upwards in an unbroken line to the vaulting and open out into a network of ribs meeting at the carved keystones. A finely sculpted balustrade runs below the windows of the nave. The overall impression is one of elegance, magnificence and good taste.

In the second bay of the nave *(right)* is a 16C black marble font (**1**) bearing Margaret's motto *(Fortune infortune fort une – see below)*.

The south transept is lit through a beautiful stained-glass window (**2**) depicting Susanna being accused by the Elders *(above)* and being exonerated by Daniel *(below)*.

To the right of the rood screen is the Montécuto chapel (**3**) which contains models explaining the construction of the church.

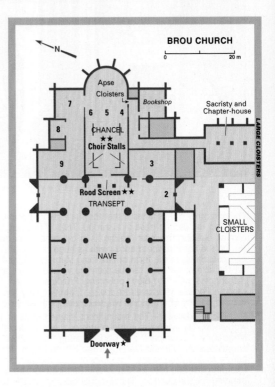

BROU CHURCH

0   20 m

N

Apse
Cloisters

Bookshop

Sacristy and
Chapter-house

LARGE CLOISTERS

7

6 5 4

8   CHANCEL
     ★★
     Choir Stalls

9   3

Rood Screen ★★

TRANSEPT   2

SMALL
CLOISTERS

NAVE

1

Doorway ★

★★ **Rood screen** – The richly decorated screen, which separates the nave and transepts (accessible to the faithful) from the chancel (reserve of the clergy and for burials), is composed of three basket-handled arches supporting seven religious statues.

Chancel – Margaret spared no expense to make this, the most important part of the church, as perfectly resplendent as possible. Taken as a whole, the sculpted decoration might seem to border on the excessive, but the longer and closer one examines the ornamentation, the greater its charm, since the smallest detail is treated with quite extraordinary craftsmanship.

★★ **Choir stalls** – The 74 stalls, which line the first two bays of the choir, were carved from oak in the astonishingly short time of two years (1530-32). The master carpenter, Pierre Berchod, known as Terrasson, had to mobilise all the wood craftsmen of this locality, where woodcarving was, and still is, extremely popular.

The stalls are carved in the same manner as the sculptures on the tombs, and the designs appear to be those of the same artist, **Jean de Bruxelles**. The seats, the backs and the canopies have an extraordinary wealth of decorative detail and statuettes, which are considered to be masterpieces of their kind.

The stalls on the north side feature scenes from the New Testament and satirical characters. Those on the south side feature characters and scenes from the Old Testament.

★★★ **The tombs** – Many artists collaborated in the decoration of these three monuments, the high point of Flemish sculpture in Burgundy. The designs were sketched by Jean de Bruxelles, who furnished the sculptors with life-size drawings. The ornamentation and the statuary, much admired by visitors, are attributed for the most part to a Flemish workshop which was set up in Brou, in collaboration with French, German and Italian sculptors. The statues of the three princely personages are the work of Conrad Meyt, born in Germany but trained in Flanders. The effigies of the prince and princess are carved in Carrara marble. The great blocks were brought from Italy by sea and then transported up the River Rhône. The final part of their journey was in huge carts drawn by nine horses travelling at three to four miles per day. Philibert and the two Margarets are represented, each lying on the tomb on a slab of black marble, their heads on finely embroidered cushions. Following tradition, a dog, emblem of fidelity, lies at the feet of the two princesses, and a lion, symbol of strength, lies at the feet of the prince. Cherubim, symbolising the entry of the three in heaven, surround the statues. The tomb of Margaret of Bourbon (**4**) occupies a recessed niche hewn in the south wall of the choir.

The Seven Joys of the Virgin Mary

The two other tombs differ in that they have two recumbent effigies: the first depicted alive and the second dead in a shroud. That of Philibert (**5**), the most sober in conception but also the most moving, is in the centre. The tomb of Margaret of Austria (**6**), on the north of the chancel, with its huge canopy of chiselled stone, prolongs the parclose. Sibyls in the form of charming statuettes mount guard around the effigies. On the sole of her foot can be seen the wound which, according to legend, caused the princess' death by blood poisoning. Princess Margaret's motto is inscribed on the canopy: *Fortune infortune fort une,* or "Fate was very hard on one woman", recalling the sad destiny of a princess whose constancy in adversity never wavered.

★★**Stained-glass windows** – The magnificent stained glass at Brou was made in a local workshop. The windows in the centre of the apse depict Christ appearing to Mary Magdalene *(upper part)* and Christ visiting Mary *(lower part)*, scenes taken from engravings by Albrecht Dürer. On the left and right, Philibert and Margaret kneel before their patron saints. The coats of arms of their families are reproduced above them in glittering colours: Savoy and Bourbon for the duke, and Imperial and Burgundian for the duchess. The armorial bearings of the towns of the State of Savoy are also represented.

★★★**Chapels and Oratories** – The chapel of Margaret (**7**) opens to the north of the choir. An altar screen and a stained-glass window, both fine works of art, deserve to be admired.

The **altar screen** depicts the Seven Joys of the Virgin Mary. It is executed in white marble and is exceptionally well preserved. It is a masterpiece of delicate workmanship, a fantastic work of art which leaves the viewer quite stunned. A scene of the Seven Joys is set in each of the niches, designed for the purpose: on the left, below, is the Annunciation; on the right, the Visitation; above, the Nativity and the Adoration of the Magi; higher still are the Assumption, framed by Christ appearing to his mother, and Pentecost. The retable is crowned by three statues: the Virgin and Child flanked by St Mary Magdalene and St Margaret. On either side of the retable note St Philip and St Andrew. The **stained-glass window**, in magnificent colours, is inspired by an engraving by Albrecht Dürer representing the Assumption. The glass workers have added Philibert and Margaret kneeling near their patron saints. The frieze of the window, in monochrome, depicts the Triumph of Faith based on a design by Titian. Christ, in a chariot, is drawn by the Evangelists and characters from the Old Testament; behind them is a throng of scholars of the church and New Testament saints.

The oratories of Margaret were arranged for her personal use. They are next to the Chapelle de Madame (**8**) and are placed one above the other, linked by a staircase. The lower oratory is on the same level as the choir, the upper one is on a level with the gallery of the rood screen. These two chambers, decorated with tapestries and warmed by fireplaces, were effectively little drawing rooms. An oblique window, or squint, below a highly original arch, allowed the princess to follow the religious services.

The nearby chapel (**9**), which has the name of Laurent de Gorrevod, one of Margaret's councillors, has a remarkable stained-glass window representing the incredulity of St Thomas and a triptych commissioned by Cardinal de Granvelle.

Leave through the doorway to the right of the choir to see the monastery.

★Museum ⊘

The museum is housed in the monastic buildings which are ranged around three two-storey cloisters, unique in France. By 1506 the old Benedictine priory had become so damp and dilapidated that the monks obtained permission from Margaret of Austria to rebuild, beginning with the living quarters rather than the church.

Small cloisters – The first of the three cloisters at Brou to be built were the small cloisters which allowed monks to pass from the monastery to the church under cover. One of the galleries on the first floor gave access to the private apartment of Margaret of Austria, but she died before it was completed. The other gallery was to allow the princess to reach the chapel directly by way of the rood screen. On the ground floor the sacristy and the chapter-house, now one room, are used for temporary exhibitions. From the galleries, now a stone depository with fragments of cornice and pinnacles, enjoy the view of the south transept gable and the spire.

Great cloisters – This is where the monks used to walk and meditate. It leads to the second chapter-house, now converted into the museum reception.

First floor – A staircase leads up to the dormer where the old monks' cells now house collections of paintings and decorative art. On the landing and in the recess in the middle of the great corridor are some fine pieces of Bresse furniture and a showcase of 18C Meillonnas earthenware.

The cells on the south side are devoted to 16C-18C art. Among the Flemish and Dutch works is a fine **portrait of Margaret of Austria**★ painted by B Van Orley c 1518 and a triptych of the life of St Jerome (1518). The following rooms are hung with 17C and 18C examples of the Italian School (Magnasco: *Monks Practising Self-Flagellation*) and 18C examples of the French School (Largillière and Gresly), as well as Burgundian and Lyonnais furniture (Nogaret) and French religious *objets d'art*. In the north gallery the rooms on the right are devoted to 19C French painting (Gustave Doré, Gustave Moreau, the Lyonnais School); those on the left exhibit the troubadour style and early-20C work. Margaret of Austria's great hall of State contains a collection of contemporary art.

In the south-east corner of the Great cloisters is the entrance to the refectory which displays 13C-17C religious sculpture, in particular a Romanesque Madonna (12C), a Holy Sepulchre (1443) and Philibert and St Philibert from the tympanum of Brou Church (early 16C). The refectory leads into the third cloisters.

Kitchen cloisters – Unlike the other two, these cloisters exhibit features typical of the region, such as the rounded arches and the gently sloping roof of hollow tiles.

BRANCION★

Michelin map 320: I-10 – 15km/9mi south-west of Tournus
Local map see Le MÂCONNAIS

The old feudal market town of Brancion is perched on a spur overlooking two deep ravines, forming a picturesque and most unusual sight.

TOUR

Since vehicles are not allowed into the town, visitors must park their cars in the car park provided outside the town walls.

Once through the gateway in the 14C ramparts, visitors will be pleasantly surprised to find the imposing ruins of a fortress, narrow streets lined with medieval-style houses covered with vines, the 15C covered market *(halles)* and the church standing proudly at the end of the spur. Some of the houses have been well restored.

Château ⊙ – This feudal castle dates back to the beginning of the 10C. It was enlarged in the 14C by Duke Philip the Bold, who added a wing to lodge the dukes of Burgundy. In the 16C it was assaulted by Catholic League militants, and finally

Château and St-Pierre church

ruined by d'Ornano's troops. The keep has been restored. From the viewing platform *(87 steps)* there is a good **view★** of the town and its church, the Grosne Valley and, to the west and north-west, the mountains of Charollais and Morvan.

St-Pierre – The church is a squat 12C building built in the Romanesque style, surmounted by a square belfry. The simplicity and purity of line, the harmonious colours of the stone and the roofing of stone tiles are all striking features. Inside, there are 14C frescoes commissioned by Eudes IV, Duke of Burgundy, a recumbent effigy of Jocerand IV of Brancion (13C), a cousin and companion of St Louis,

who died on the Seventh Crusade, and numerous funerary stones. The 14C and 15C mural paintings on the south wall of the apse have sadly deteriorated. They represent the Resurrection of the Dead.

There is an attractive view of the valley from the church terrace, built at the end of the spur.

La BRESSE★★

Michelin map 328: D-2 to E-3

A land of culture, traditions and fine cuisine, the Bresse region is the southernmost part of Burgundy; a lovely and often overlooked destination. The sedimentary plain is bordered on the west by the Saône and on the east by the Revermont plateau. The

Famous Fowl

landscape is enlivened by pretty brooks and streams darting around the traditional hedgerows of the French countryside, by old windmills and fine timber-framed farmhouses. The Bresse is beloved by gourmets for the authentic *Poulet de Bresse*, fat white chickens which feast on the corn seen drying in the region's distinctively shaped barns.

BRESSE, NORTH AND SOUTH

The influence of Burgundy and of the Mediterranean regions draws a line between the north and the south of this region, which also delinieates two different destinies. The northern part is known as *Bresse bouguignonne* and the southern part as *Bresse savoyarde*.

La Bresse louhannaise or bourguignonne – The proximity of the powerful Duchy of Burgundy long overshadowed the modest Bresse. These lands along the Saône were often the subject of dispute and acted as a border until the southern part of the Bresse and Franche-Comté were united to France in the 17C. Not popular with the nobility and left without effective local administration, the region slowly built its own identity through the excellence of its agricultural output and the eventual emergence of a bourgeois class which took the management of business and government in hand. Playing the role of a cultural centre, the **Écomusée de la Bresse bourguignonne** highlights the specific character of the region.

La Bresse bressane or savoyarde – In what is now the Ain *département*, the southern area of the Bresse is better known than its northern neighbour, largely due to the dynamic little city of Bourg-en-Bresse. Political unity was established much earlier here, under the auspices of the Bâgé family. In 1272, the marriage of Sibylle de Bâgé and Amédée V Le Grand, Count of Savoy, brought the province under the dominion of the House of Savoy. There it remained until the Treaty of Lyon (1601), by which Henri IV obtained its return to the kingdom of France. The region owes a great deal to the unfortunate Margaret of Austria *(see page 175)*, whose works in Brou contributed to the prestige and influence of the Bresse.

Despite these historical differences, visitors will discover that the Bresse has a shared regional culture, evidenced in its fine agricultural products and cuisine, its unique rural architecture, and a cultural identity well worth discovering.

CULTURE AND TRADITIONS

Rich rural heritage – The farmers of the Bresse, are lucky indeed, compared with their neighbours, for their lands are fertile and fruitful. One of their traditional country dishes is a porridge made of cornmeal, which gave them the nickname of "yellow bellies" – but the French idiom has nothing to do with courage!

Bresse is well-forested, with few stone deposits, so the houses are quite naturally made of wood. Generally half-timbered and filled in with cob or other materials, a few exceptional houses still boast their Saracen chimneys.

Bresse chicken – As for the famous local fowl, their glorious reputation dates back to the 17C. Besides making some poultry farmers quite wealthy, *poulet de Bresse* has made a considerable contribution to the local economy. As consumer awareness has grown and claims of quality come under greater scrutiny, regional production has passed all the tests for standards of excellence, and has worn a special label guaranteeing its origins since 1957. The snow white birds are raised free-range, for four to five months, feeding on grains. Their last days are spent in a pen where they are fattened up. Pullet hens and capons are fattened over a longer period and are especially appreciated for their firm and succulent flesh.

Eating out

BUDGET

Vuillot – *71480 Cuiseaux* - ☎ *03 85 72 71 79* - *closed Jan, Sun evenings and Mon* - *13/33€*. This restaurant fronted by a stone façade has two dining rooms extended by two terraces, one glassed-in, one out in the open, facing the pool. Simple fare. Light snacks available at the bar.

MODERATE

Ferme-Auberge du Poirier – *At Bourg de Cuet* - *01340 Montrevel-en-Bresse* - *1 km/0.6mi SW of Montrevel by D 67* - ☎ *04 74 30 82 97* - *closed 30 Oct-20 Mar and Sun evenings to Fri lunchtime* – *reservations required* - *16/20€*. Charolais cows, pigs, chickens and capons are bred on the grounds surrounding this large farmhouse, whose architecture is typical of the region. The dining room has a fireplace, exposed beams and a collection of clogs adorning the walls. Needless to say, all the ingredients are farm-fresh!

L'Ancienne Auberge – *01540 Vonnas* - ☎ *04 74 50 90 50* - *auberge1900@georgesblanc.com* - *closed Jan* - *17/40€*. Conveniently located on the main square, this restaurant has chosen a decor reminiscent of the early 20C, when the former owners ran it as a café. The setting is charmingly simple with checked tablecloths. Tasty, unpretentious cuisine.

Where to stay

BUDGET

Au Puits Enchanté – *71620 St-Martin-en-Bresse* - ☎ *03 85 47 71 96* - *chateau.jacky@wanadoo.fr* - *closed 6-29 Jan, 24 Feb-2 Mar, 24-30 Jun, Mon (except evenings 11 Mar-15 Oct), Sun evenings (except Jul-Aug) and Tue* - ☐ - *13 rooms: 39/50€* - ☐ *6.50€* - *restaurant 16/38€*. In a leafy setting in the town centre, this family establishment offers small, tidy rooms. Breakfast is served on the small verandah or in the dining room with flowered curtains. The cuisine is well prepared and the prices reasonable.

MODERATE

Pillebois – *Rte de Bourg-en-Bresse* - *01340 Montrevel-en-Bresse* - *2 km/1.2mi S of Montrevel by D 975* - ☎ *04 74 25 48 44* - *closed Sun Oct-Apr* - ☐ - *30 rooms: 52/58€* - ☐ *7.50€*. This modern Bresse house at the entrance to the village has a sheltered terrace facing the swimming pool. The rooms are decorated in pastel colours and appointed with painted white furniture. The dining hall decor focuses on the sea, a theme echoed by the pirogue proudly erected in the centre of the room.

EXPENSIVE

Georges Blanc – *01540 Vonnas* - ☎ *04 74 50 90 90* - *blanc@relaischateaux.fr* - *closed Jan* - *32 rooms: 165/335€* - ☐ *23€* - *restaurant 95/215€*. Be extravagant and treat yourself to a regal stay at the Georges Blanc! This elegant half-timbered mansion along the banks of the Veyle has sumptuously appointed rooms, each decorated in its own style. As for the restaurant, it serves delicious regional cuisine of the highest standard.

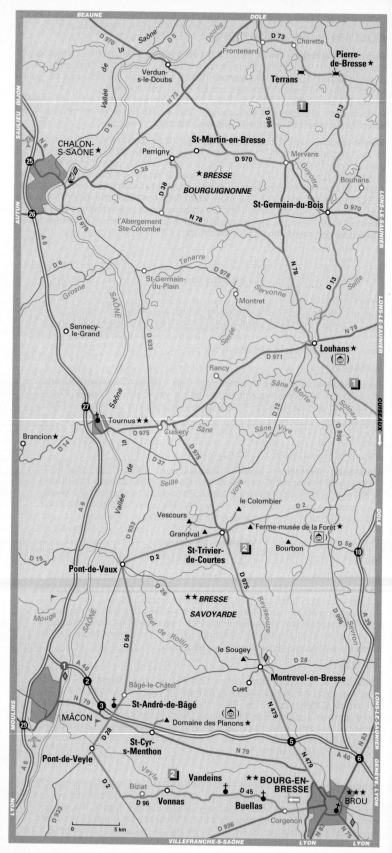

★LA BRESSE BOURGUIGNONNE

138km/86mi round tour

Cuiseaux – This former fortified town lies on the border between Burgundy and Franche-Comté. It is set in a peaceful, green agricultural landscape and is well-known for its cooked meats and sausages *(charcuterie)*. There are a few vestiges left of the 12C fortifications, which originally included 36 towers. The area around Cuiseaux lends itself to pleasant walks in the forest or the countryside.

Church – The chancel is interesting; in addition to the 16C polychrome wood statues, there are two Italian primitive paintings to be seen. The lovely 15C carved wooden stalls further enhance the beauty of the interior. There is a highly venerated 13C black statue of the Virgin Mary in the north aisle.

Maison de la Vigne et du Vigneron ⊘ – This wine museum, part of the Écomusée de la Bresse bourguignonne at Pierre-de-Bresse, is inside the fortifications of the château which once belonged to the princes of Orange. It recalls that Cuiseaux was an important wine-growing region until the end of the 19C. The museum has a display on Jura vineyards, along with wine-growers' tools and equipment and the reconstruction of a wine-grower's room (*chambre à feu*).

Drive to Louhans 19km/12mi away along D 972.

★ **Louhans** – *see LOUHANS.*

Leave Louhans travelling northward on D 13 towards St-Germain-du-Bois.

St-Germain-du-Bois: Agriculture bressane ⊘ – *15km/9mi north.* This farm centre is associated with the Écomusée de la Bresse bourguignonne, and devoted to rural life. Among other items on display, are a collection of farm implements from the 19C to today, and exhibits on local products, in particular corn and chicken (audio-visual presentation).

There is also a section on horses, complete with a harness and saddle shop.

Continue on D 13 towards Pierre-de-Bresse.

★ **Pierre-de-Bresse, Écomusée de la Bresse bourguignonne** – The Château de Pierre-de-Bresse is set in a park (30ha/74 acres); it is a handsome 17C building constructed of limestone bricks with a slate roof. The moat and U-shaped plan, guarded by four round corner towers capped by domes, reveal that it stands on the foundations of a fortified building. The central block is ornamented by an arcade of round-headed arches opening into a gallery. The pediment above the delicate central section is detached from the high mansard roof. In the 18C the axis of the courtyard was extended by the addition of an outer court bordered by extensive outbuildings encircled by a second moat.

The left wing of the château houses the **Écomusée de la Bresse bourguignonne** ⊘. The stairs in the entrance lobby with their beautiful wrought-iron bannister and two rooms (18C and 19C) restored in period style show how the interior of the château used to be. The exhibitions on three floors cover the natural environment, history, the traditional way of life and the present economic situation in Burgundian Bresse (*several audio-visual presentations including one 18min long at the end of the tour*). The museum, which illustrates the activities and traditions of Bresse, has established several branches throughout its territory at Louhans, Rancy, St-Germain-du-Bois, St-Martin-en-Bresse, Verdun-sur-le-Doubs and Cuiseaux (vineyards and viticulture).

Continue on D 73 towards Charette.

Château de Pierre-de-Bresse

J. Cartier/Château de Pierre-de-Bresse

Château de Terrans – The design of the château, begun in 1765, is sobre. An attractive wrought-iron gate closes off the courtyard, beyond which the elegant façade rises, guarded by two stone lions at the bottom of the stairway leading to the front door.

Continue along D 73 as far as Frontenard and take D 996 to the left towards Louhans. At Mervans, take D 970 to the right, continue for 7km/4mi and turn left towards St-Martin-en-Bresse.

St-Martin-en-Bresse – *In St-Martin, follow along D 35 until you reach the town of Perrigny.*

Maison de la Forêt et du Bois de Perrigny ⊘ – Amid the Bresse woodlands, the Écomusée de la Bresse bourgignonne has set up this exhibit on the different kinds of trees found in the region, and on trades and crafts related to them. The sculptures are by Alan Mantle.

Take D 38 towards l'Abergement-Ste-Colombe, drive back to Louhans on N 78 and return to Cuiseaux along D 972.

★★ LA BRESSE SAVOYARDE

104km/65mi round tour

★★ Bourg-en-Bresse *(see BOURG-EN-BRESSE)*

Leave Bourg-en-Bresse travelling west towards Villefranche-sur-Saône. At Corgenon, turn right on D 45 as far as Buellas.

Buellas – The **church** ⊘, with a rustic canopy in front, has a pretty chancel with Romanesque arcading and some interesting statues.

Follow D 45 to Vandeins.

Vandeins – The **church** has a sculpted doorway dating from the 12C. The tympanum shows Christ giving his blessing; a fine piece of Romanesque sculpture, with angels supporting the central figure. The Last Supper is a plainer piece, carved on the doorway and positioned between two groups of the damned embellishing the vertical sides.

Continue along D 96 to Vonnas.

Vonnas – This peaceful little town, bright with flowers in the fine season, is a favourite stopping place for gourmets, at the crossroads of the Bresse and the Dombes. There is an interesting **harness and coach museum** ⊘ set up in a former mill.

Take D 96 towards Bizat and catch up with D 2, which leads to Pont-de-Veyle.

Pont-de-Veyle – On the banks of the Veyle, surrounded by former moats, this village developed in the 13C and was a secretive gathering place for Protestants until the revocation of the Edict of Nantes (1685). Some fine vestiges remain, including **Porte de l'Horloge**, the Maison du Guetteur (16C), the Maison de Savoie (66 Grande Rue – 15C) and the church (1752).

Leave Pont-de-Veyle travelling north on D 28. 3km further on, take N 79 towards Bourg-en-Bresse.

St-Cyr-sur-Menthon – There are several distinguished traditional-style homes in this small town. North of N 79, stands one of the region's largest feudal mounds: 46m/151ft in diameter and 9.6m/30ft high. A bit farther north, around the hamlet of La Mulatière, several farms have Saracen chimneys, including a large one at the **Domaine des Planons★**.

Domaine de Planons in St-Cyr-sur-Menthon

A magnificent example of local architecture, the Domaine is home to the **Musée de la Bresse** ⊙. 🔲 Built with an enclosed farmyard, unusual in the region, the farm buildings are accessible by means of a wide *passou* or entranceway. The living quarters, beneath the Saracen chimney, were first built in 1490 and have since been renovated, using traditional methods. An inventory dated 1784, found on the premises, made it possible to re-establish the organisation and disposition of the farmhouse and of its furnishings in the 18C. Behind the house, the vegetable garden has been recreated. The other farm buildings (some complete with sound effects!) demonstrate poultry farming and certain aspects of rural life. The vast park has much to entertain visitors: a duck pond, a bowling game, a woodworking exhibit, information on raising Bresse poultry today. The musuem is still growing, and more exhibits on life in the region should be opening soon.

Return to St-Cyr-sur-Menthon and take N 79 as far as the crossroads with D 28. Turn right towards Bâgé-le-Châtel. The church is off to the left, visible just before you enter the village.

St-André-de-Bâgé – The church, built at the end of the 11C with the help of monks from Tournus, sits in the middle of a cemetery. An elegant, octagonal **bell-tower★** rises above the apse with its radiating chapels, topped by a graceful stone spire. In the chancel, note the slim columns with historiated capitals.

Continue on past Bâgé-le-Châtel and north on D 58 to Pont-de-Vaux.

Pont-de-Vaux – The town grew up around a meander of the River Reyssouze, a tributary of the Saône well-known to fishing enthusiasts. Part of the river, downstream from town, is navigable. The historic hamlet has a quaint setting (half-timbered houses, buildings and façades from the 16C and 17C), and reveres the memory of General Joubert, commander-in-chief of the Italian Army (d 1799). The **musée Chintreuil** ⊙ contains some interesting paintings by Jules Migonney and A Chintreuil (a student of Corot).

Leave Pont-de-Vaux travelling north-east on D2 towards St-Trivier-de-Courtes.

St-Trivier-de-Courtes – Formerly a strategic possession of the lords of Bâgé, the town became a county in 1575. It is a good place to start a tour of Saracen chimneys, as many have been preserved in the surrounding villages.

Saracen chimneys

The 30 or so which have survived date from the 17C and 18C. Within the house there is an enormous hearth, set away from the wall and covered by a hood, under which a man can stand upright; the flue is lined with wood panels. The chimney pots resemble small belfries or, more rarely, reliquaries built in the Romanesque, Gothic and sometimes Byzantine style; their shapes are round, square (modelled on the belfry of St-Philibert in Tournus) or octagonal (the belfry of St-André-de-Bâgé); they have one or two bands of vents and are capped by a cone, a pyramid or a Baroque belfry.

They are unusually high (3-5m/10-16ft) and surmounted by a wrought-iron cross. In the past some may have housed a bell, a useful feature in the daily life of these traditionally isolated farms. Saracen, the adjective, does not describe the chimneys' geographical provenance but is a survival of the medieval use of the word Saracen to mean "belonging to a foreign, old or unknown culture"; the term was therefore quite naturally applied to these unusual chimneys.

Saracen chimneys are to be found at:

St-Trivier – *1.5km/1mi west via D 2.* **Grandval** farm.

Vescours – *5km/3mi west of St-Trivier; on the left at the entrance to the village.*

Vernoux – *3km/2mi north-east of St-Trivier.* **Colombier** farm.

Ferme-Musée de la Forêt ⊙ – *3km/2mi east of St-Trivier.*
🔲 This attractive 16C-17C farm has been restored and converted into a Bresse farm museum. The small building with the wooden balcony contains a traditional interior; the chimney over the open hearth (4m2/43sq ft) is supported by a beam weighing 4 tonnes. The second building displays a collection of old agricultural implements.

St-Nizier-le-Bouchoux – *6km/4mi east of St-Trivier.* **Bourbon** farm *(beware of the dogs).*

Return to St-Trivier, and take D 975 south towards Bourg-en-Bresse.

Montrevel-en-Bresse – Former fief of the Montrevel family, the town is also the country of St Pierre Chanel (1803-1841), a missionary martyred on Futuna Island, and since named patron saint of Oceania. The old village of **Cuet**, now part of the municipality, pays hommage to the saint.

The **farm at Sougey** has preserved its square cowl (17C).

In the Reyssouze Valley, the **Montrevel recreation area** is a popular place to relax and play.

Continue along N 479 to Bourg-en-Bresse.

BRIARE

Population 5 994
Michelin map 318: N-6

This quiet town on the banks of the Loire is the meeting point of two canals which connect the basins of the Seine and Loire rivers. Today, commercial navigation has given way to leisure, and the town marina has been newly equipped to accommodate recreational boating. Steps lead down to the banks of the Loire which offer pleasant walks and a picturesque view of the magnificent canal bridge built by Eiffel.

In the early 20C, the town's prosperity came from the manufacture of enamels used in architectural decoration, jewellery and button-making.

The canal bridge at Briare

The Briare Canal – The canal was completed in 1642, 38 years after its conception. Along its 57km/36mi path, six locks move the waters from the Loire Lateral Canal (which runs alongside that river) to the Loing Canal. It was the first canal in Europe designed to link up two different canal networks in this way. At Rogny-les-Sept-Écluses, about 15km/9mi north on the towpath, the seven original locks, no mean feat of engineering at the time, are no longer in use; they form a sort of giant's stairway, in an admirable natural setting.

SIGHTS

★★ **Pont-Canal** – 🖾 The canal bridge (662m/2 172ft long, 11m/37ft wide), completed in 1890 and inaugurated in 1896, may no longer fulfil an important economic role in the transportation of merchandise, but it does transport the visitor who takes the time to stroll across it. The waters of the Loire ripple below while ducks glide on the calm surface of the brimming canal, suspended high above. The ironwork, which can be seen from stairs down to the river, was created by the Société Eiffel.

> **WATERSIDE INN**
>
> **Auberge du Pont Canal** – 19 r. du Pont-Canal - ☎ 02 38 31 24 24 - auberge-du-pont-canal@wanadoo.fr - closed Sun evenings and Mon 12.96€ lunch - 17.53/28.97€. In a sleepy setting along the Briare Canal, this small restaurant with its 1960s façade is a haven of tranquillity. The accommodation is housed in a modern building. Traditional dishes made with fresh seasonal produce.

Musée de la Mosaïque et des Émaux ⓥ – The museum devoted to the local enamel crafts is located in the manufactory, which is still in operation. One main theme is the history of Jean-Félix Bapterosses, a skilled mechanic and technician and inventor of the first machine able to produce buttons in industrial quantity, a step ahead of the British, who were still stamping them out one at a time. The collection on display is impressive in its variety. The museum also presents late-19C mosaic work typical to the town, and in particular the work of Art Nouveau precursor Eugène Grasset. The mosaic technique has been used to decorate the floor of the town's church, where a winding pattern recalling the waters of the Loire swirls around images representing the ages of man and the five senses.

▶▶ **La Bussière** – 13km/8mi N. Louis XIII-style **Château des Pêcheurs** ⓥ★ with interesting patterned brickwork and exhibition on fresh-water fishing.

Le BRIONNAIS★★

Michelin map 320: E-12 to F-12

This region south of Paray-le-Monial, enclosed by the River Loire and the River Sornin, is known as the Brionnais. Semur-en-Brionnais is the regional capital. The rolling countryside is given over mainly to cattle rearing. There are about a dozen **Romanesque churches★**, inspired by the great abbey of Cluny, in the area *(see map)*, which are well worth a visit.

The yellowish, fine-grain limestone of the region is relatively easy to work but at the same time very durable, making it the ideal medium for decorative sculpture on façades and doorways. It gives the churches a lovely warm ochre or yellow colour, which looks particularly beautiful in the rays of the setting sun. Harder stone like granite or sandstone, which cannot be worked in detail, is better suited to emphasise line or mass, as in the churches at Varenne-l'Arconce, Bois-Ste-Marie, Châteauneuf and St-Laurent-en-Brionnais. Certain themes predominate, although the attitudes and expressions of the figures do vary. The tympanum usually depicts Christ in Majesty, in a mandorla and surrounded by the four Evangelists or their symbols, or Christ ascending into Heaven. The decoration on the lintels is very elaborate (Last Supper scene at St-Julien-de-Jonzy); multitudes of tiny figures throng round the central figure of the triumphant Christ.

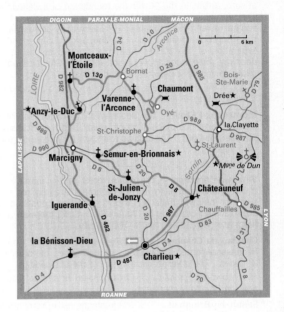

CHURCHES AND CASTLES OF THE BRIONNAIS REGION

This itinerary runs through the very heart of the Brionnais region.

Drive west out of Charlieu along D 487 then D 4.

La Bénisson-Dieu – The village **church** ⊙ and the imposing 15C square bell-tower standing in front of it are all that remains of the abbey founded in the 12C by disciples of St Bernard, which became a nuns' convent in the 17C. The early-Gothic nave is roofed with superb glazed tiles forming diamond motifs. The south aisle contains interesting 15C works of art: an abbey stall and several stone statues from the school of Michel Colombe. The Lady Chapel, on the right-hand side as you go in, was added in the 17C; note the murals and the fine white-marble statue of the Virgin.

Drive back towards the Loire, cross the river and turn left onto D 482.

Iguerande – The 12C massive church features a remarkable purity of line. It stands at the top of a steep hill overlooking the Loire and offering an interesting view of the Loire Valley, the Forez to the left and the Madeleine hills to the right. The nave and the chancel contain some unusual capitals; note, in particular, the "musician-cyclop" at the top of the first pillar on the left.

Marcigny – This picturesque town lying close to the Loire, on the edge of the Brionnais region, has retained some 16C timber-framed houses *(round the church)* and a mansion dating from 1735 *(between place du Cours and place Reverchon)*. The town hall occupies another mansion, the Hôtel Jacquet du Chailloux.

Tour du Moulin ⊙ – The 15C tall tower, once part of ramparts protecting a Benedictine priory, has unusual walls decorated with stone cannon balls. It houses a museum of local history: collection of earthenware including Italian Majolica, sculpture from the 12C to the 17C, 113 chemist's jars in Nevers faience and two 16C sweet jars by Bernard Palissy. The last floor reveals the impressive timber work of the roof.

Follow D 10 towards Charolles.

★ Anzy-le-Duc – This hillside village in the Arconce Valley possesses one of the most beautiful Romanesque churches in the area.

The harmonious **church** in golden stone was probably built in the early 11C. Its fine doorway is now on display in the Musée du Hiéron in Paray-le-Monial. The building is surmounted by a magnificent Romanesque belfry, a polygonal tower with three storeys of bays. The nave, remarkable for its purity of style and harmony of line, is roofed with groined vaulting and lit through the clerestory windows. The capitals have been well preserved; those in the nave represent biblical and allegorical scenes. The frescoes of the apse, now in poor condition, portray the lives of St John the Baptist and Hugues d'Anzy. Those in the choir show the Ascension of Christ. One fresco alludes to Letbaldus, the provost of Semur, who donated his property at Anzy-le-Duc in the 9C for the foundation of a Benedictine community.

The outbuildings of the old priory, now occupied by a farm, are overlooked by a square tower. The tympanum of a very early **doorway** in the precinct wall shows the Adoration of the Magi *(left)* and Original Sin *(right)*. The lintel portrays the separation of the blessed from the damned at the Last Judgement. The main doorway *(mentioned above)* is still very beautiful, although its decoration has been badly damaged; it depicts Christ in Majesty.

If you have time, make a short detour north along D 174 then drive directly to Varenne along D 130.

Montceaux-l'Étoile – The doorway of the **church** features a tympanum and lintel carved out of one block of stone, illustrating the Ascension as at Anzy-le-Duc and St-Julien-de-Jonzy. The arching framing the tympanum rests on columns decorated with capitals.

In Bornat, turn right onto D 34.

Varenne-l'Arconce – The **church** looks rather massive owing to its projecting transept and square tower. Its decoration was limited by the use of hard sandstone as building material. Note the elegant tympanum surmounting the south doorway and depicting the Agnus Dei. Inside, there are wooden statues (some of them are polychome), and a 16C crucifix.

Château de Chaumont – *5km/3mi to the south-east along D 158 (near Oyé).* The Renaissance façade is flanked by a round tower, the other façade in the Gothic style is modern. The sheer extent and size of the outbuildings are quite remarkable.

Head towards Semur via St-Christophe-en-Brionnais, famous for its cattle markets held on Thursday mornings.

★ Semur-en-Brionnais – The village stands on a promontory which is covered with vines and fruit trees. The château, the Romanesque church, the former priory and 18C court room (now the *mairie*, or town hall) make an attractive ensemble in pinkish stone.

★ Église St-Hilaire ⊘ – The church, which was built in the Cluniac style, has a very fine chevet; its squat appearance is relieved by the height of the gable walls at the end of the chancel and the transept arms, and its austerity is offset by the carved cornice below the roof. The elegant octagonal belfry is decorated with a double band of twin Romanesque arcades; the upper band is framed by a series of recessed arches.

The west doorway is richly decorated although the sculptures show a certain lack of skill in the modelling. As at Charlieu, a haloed lamb is carved on the external keystone. The lintel depicts a scene from the life of St Hilary of Poitiers: condemned by a council of Arian bishops, he sets off into exile, a begging bag on his shoulder; on the road he meets an angel who gives him hope and returns him to his place among the bishops; meanwhile the devil makes off with the soul of the Council President.

The nave is very attractive; at the west end the triforium, which consists of an arcade with twin arch stones, forms a bowed gallery which is supported by an impressive corbel springing from the keystone of the west door.

The belfry of St-Hilaire

B. Kaufmann/MICHELIN

The gallery may be an imitation of the chapel of St-Michel above the west door of Cluny abbey church. The dome on squinches above the transept crossing is decorated with arcades similar to those of the triforium.

Château St-Hugues ⊘ – The 9C rectangular keep was the birthplace of the famous abbot, St Hugh of Cluny. The two round towers served as a prison in the 18C. There is a view of the vineyard-covered slopes and in the distance the summits of Le Forez and La Madeleine.

Follow D 9.

St-Julien-de-Jonzy – From its location on top of one of the highest hills in the area, the village offers a fine panorama of the Brionnais and Beaujolais rolling countryside.

The present church has retained the square bell-tower and lovely carved doorway of its 12C Romanesque predecessor.

Doorway★ – The tympanum and lintel are carved out of a single block of sandstone by a master craftsman, who probably also worked on Charlieu Abbey.

The lintel illustrates the Last Supper: all the heads except two were damaged in 1793. The folds of the tablecloth and of the celestial clothes above are remarkably fluid; a scene depicting the Washing of the feet decorates each extremity.

> **CROSS THIS BRIDGE WHEN YOU COME TO IT**
>
> **Le Pont** – *71110 St-Julien-de-Jonzy -* ☎ *03 85 84 01 95 - closed Feb school holidays - 12.04€ lunch - 13.57/27.59€.* Family restaurant extending a warm, hospitable welcome. The owner, who also runs the nearby bar and butcher's shop, prepares a traditional bill of fare. A few rooms are available for guests' use.

Interior – The former transept crossing surmounted by a dome on squinches forms the narthex of the present church; the four engaged columns have retained their fine capitals; the decoration of the right-hand one, before the nave, is reminiscent of Cistercian art.

Drive east along D 8.

Châteauneuf – The church, standing out against its wooded setting, was one of the last Romanesque buildings erected in Burgundy; the west front is massive, the south doorway has an interesting lintel featuring a naive representation of the 12 apostles. Inside, note the clerestory windows in the nave with their slender columns decorated with capitals and, surmounting the transept, the dome on squinches with its octagonal base and arcaded gallery.

Return to Charlieu along D 987.

Le BUGEY★

Michelin map 328: G-4

The southern Jura region is known by this name. There are two natural divisions: the Haut-Bugey, delimited to the north by a series of transverse valleys, or *cluses*, which run from Nantua to Bellegarde, to the south by the *cluses* of Albarine and Hôpitaux, to the east by the Rhône and to the west by the Ain Valley; and the Bas-Bugey, located in the great meander of the Rhône.

Historical background – The Bugey region was first joined to the kingdom of Burgundy in the 9C; then in 1077 a great part of the territory came under the rule of the Count of Savoy, who gradually managed to appropriate all of it. In 1601, the House of Savoy yielded both the Bugey and Bresse regions as well as the Pays de Gex to Henri IV, King of France, in exchange for the marquisate of Saluces.

A place of transit – It has always been easy to cross the Bugey region, marked as it is by the transverse valleys known as *cluses* linking the smaller mountain chains. Over the centuries the region's geographical location has brought it many sudden changes in fortune. In the 18C Spanish troops rode rough-shod through the region during the Spanish War of Succession; in the 19C, the allied nations rising against Napoleon used the Bugey as their main battleground. It was not until 1855, with the creation of the Lyon-Geneva railway line through the Cluse de l'Albarine, that the region could actually benefit from its position as a place of transit. In 1871 Ambérieu became an important communications node, with the cutting of a passage through Mont Cenis and the construction of the railway line to Italy.

The construction of the A 40 motorway, which required high viaducts (around 100m/328ft high) to be built and long tunnels (more than 3km/1.9mi long) to be dug, helped to open up the Haut-Bugey region.

"Where I die
the country is reborn"

The Ain Resistance movement – In 1943 the Resistance established several camps in the heart of the mountain massif protected by the Rhône and Ain valleys, overlooking the important road and railway routes. The main stronghold in the Valromey was the object of a German assault in 1944. At dawn on 5 February, 5 000 Germans surrounded the mountains and then began the attack of the Hauteville, Retord and Brénod plateaux – in trucks, on foot and on skis. Snow made the going tough. The Resistance forces were forced to scatter after local skirmishes with the enemy. From 6 to 12 February the local villages and population were subjected to enemy violence. Another attack was launched against the Resistance, which had regrouped, in July. This time the fighting affected the entire Bugey region as the Germans sent in 9 000 men reinforced by aircraft and light artillery. The Resistance groups split up and retreated into the highest peaks *(see NANTUA: Musée départemental d'Histoire de la Résistance et de la Déportation de l'Ain et du Haut-Jura)*.

EXCURSIONS

Haut-Bugey *(see NANTUA and BELLEGARDE-SUR-VALSERINE)*

Bas-Bugey *(see BELLEY)*

Grand Colombier *(see GRAND COLOMBIER)*

Château de BUSSY-RABUTIN★

Michelin map 320: H-4

A few miles north of Alise-Ste-Reine, halfway up a hill, stands the château of Bussy-Rabutin; its highly original interior decor is an eloquent testimony of the state of mind of its owner.

The misfortunes of Roger de Bussy-Rabutin – While his cousin, Mme de Sévigné, was very successful with her pen, Roger de Rabutin, Count of Bussy, caused nothing but trouble with his. Turenne, already irritated by his acerbic couplets, described him to the king as "the best officer in his armies – for writing verse". Having compromised himself, in company with other young libertines, in a now famous orgy in which he improvised and sang couplets ridiculing the love affair of young Louis XIV and Marie de Mancini, Bussy-Rabutin was exiled to Burgundy on the orders of the king.

Accompanied in exile by his mistress, the Marquise de Montglat, he passed his time writing his *Histoire amoureuse des Gaules*, a satirical chronicle of the love affairs of the court. This libellous work had its author clapped straight into the Bastille, where he languished for over a year. Then he was sent home to Bussy, where he lived in exile – alone this time, as the beautiful marquise had forgotten all about him.

TOUR ⊙ *45min*

This 15C fortified castle was bought up during the Renaissance by the Comtes de Rochefort, who knocked down the wall which closed in the courtyard and transformed the defensive towers into elegant living quarters. The façade is 17C. Roger de Rabutin's grandfather began works on the ground floor during the reign of Louis XIII; the upper floors, completed in 1649, show the naissant Louis XIV style.

Interior – It was Bussy-Rabutin himself who designed the interior decoration of the apartments, a gilded cage in which he spent his exile, indulging in nostalgia for army and court life and giving vent to his rancour against Louis XIV and his unfaithful mistress.

Cabinet des Devises – Numerous portraits and allegorical paintings along with pithy maxims *(devises)* composed by Roger de Rabutin are framed in the woodwork panels of this room, giving it a most unusual appearance.

The upper panels feature views of châteaux and monuments, some of which no longer exist, and are thus interesting as historical documents. Over the fireplace is a portrait of Bussy-Rabutin by Lefèvre, a student of Lebrun. The furniture is Louis XIII.

Antichambre des Grands Hommes de Guerre – Portraits of 65 great warriors, from Du Guesclin down to the master of the house, Maistre de Camp, Général de la Cavalerie Légère de France, are hung in two rows around the room. Some of the portraits are very good originals, but most of them are only copies from originals of the period (17C) which are nonetheless of historical interest. The woodwork and ceilings are decorated with fleurs-de-lys, trophies, standards and the interlaced ciphers of Bussy and the Marquise de Montglat.

Chambre de Bussy – Bussy's bedchamber is adorned with the portraits of 25 women. That of Louise de Rouville, second wife of Bussy-Rabutin, is included in a triptych with those of Mme de Sévigné and her daughter, Mme de Grignan. Other personalities portrayed include Gabrielle d'Estrées, Henri IV's mistress, Mme de la Sablière, Ninon de Lenclos, the famous courtesan, and Mme de Maintenon.

★ **Tour Dorée** – Bussy-Rabutin surpassed himself in the decoration of the circular room where he worked on the first floor of the west tower. The walls are entirely covered with paintings, on subjects taken from mythology and the gallantry of the age, accompanied by quatrains and couplets. Bussy-Rabutin himself is depicted as a Roman emperor. A series of portraits of the great personalities of the courts of Louis XIII and Louis XIV completes the collection.

Chapelle – The Galerie des Rois de France leads to the south tower, which houses a small, elegantly furnished oratory (16C stone altarpiece depicting the Raising of Lazarus and 18C Visitation in polychrome stone).

Gardens and Park – The park (34ha/84 acres), shaped like an amphitheatre with beautiful stone steps linking the levels, makes a fine backdrop to the gardens with their statues (17C-19C), fountains and pools, apparently designed by Le Nôtre, Louis XIV's own gardener.

Château de Bussy-Rabutin

Ph. Cajic/MICHELIN

CHABLIS

Population 2 594
Michelin map 319: F-5

Tucked away in the valley of the River Serein, between Auxerre and Tonnerre, Chablis is the capital of the prestigious wine-growing region of lower Burgundy. Consider it a big village, or a little town, Chablis itself still has a medieval feel, harking back to its heyday in the 16C. The annual wine fair and the village fairs held in honour of St Vincent, patron of wine-growers, in November and late January *(see Calendar of events)* recall the town's lively commercial past.

White wines of Chablis

As the popularity of light wines has grown along with their export and production around the world, Chablis has virtually become a synonym for dry white wine. Authentic French Chablis has been produced in Burgundy since

the 12C, when the vineyards extended as far as the eye could see, and tending them was the population's sole occupation, the source of an enviable prosperity. Today, the land is used more selectively, and the type of soil is the determining factor in the *appellation* on the bottle, which is a reference to the silica, limestone and clay content of the soil (as in Champagne), rather than to *domaines*, or specific vineyards (as in Bordeaux, for example).

The best vintages are the *Grand Cru*, mostly grown on the steep hillsides of the east bank: Vaudésir, Valmur, Grenouilles, Les Clos, Les Preuses, Bougros and Blanchots; both rich in aroma yet dry and delicately flavoured, distinguished by their golden hue, these generally bloom after three years in the bottle, but are rarely kept more than eight. *Premier Cru* wines are grown on both banks of the river: lighter in colour, less full-bodied; they are best aged three years, never more than six. More than half of the production, bearing the *Appellation Chablis Contrôlée* label, is very dry and pale, to be aged one to three years before reaching its apogee.

Often described as crisp or fresh, a good Chablis made exclusively from Chardonnay grapes is delightful with oysters, fresh-water fish, ham or chicken dishes with creamy sauce. Lesser vintages, including hearty Bourgogne Aligoté or fruity Petit Chablis are best enjoyed young with local country fare (grilled sausage, crayfish) or regional cheese (Chasource, St-Florentin) and fresh bread.

Église St-Martin ⊘ – The church dates from the late 12C. It was founded by monks from St-Martin-des-Tours, who carried their saint's relics with them as they fled the Normans. On the door leaves of the Romanesque south doorway, known as the Porte aux Fers, note the early-13C strap hinges and the horseshoes, offerings made by pilgrims to St Martin. The interior conveys an impression of unity reminiscent of St-Étienne in Sens.

Église St-Pierre – Only three bays remain of the Romanesque church, which is an excellent example of the Burgundian transitional style. It was the parish church until 1789.

Eating out

BUDGET

Le Syracuse – *19 av. du Maréchal-de-Lattre-de-Tassigny - ☎ 03 86 42 19 45 - closed 2 weeks in Oct and 2 weeks in Mar - 12/23€.* This restaurant lying at the heart of the village has many assets: a most appealing rustic setting, lovingly prepared cuisine, thoughtful service and an interesting wine list featuring a fine selection of Chablis.

MODERATE

Le Vieux Moulin – *☎ 03 86 42 47 30 - vxmoulinchablis@aol.com - 16.50/38.50€.* This medieval mill exudes charm and personality. The woodwork and stone walls of the dining hall are decorated with farming tools and the former engine room serves as a backdrop to sumptuous banquets. Enjoy the sight of the clear waters swirling under the foundations. Traditional cooking.

Hostellerie des Clos – ☎ *03 86 42 10 63* - *host.clos@wanadoo.fr* - *closed 23 Dec-17 Jan* - *33/69€*. This hostelry in the old part of town can be approached by the street or by its garden. The handsome dining room giving onto the garden is the setting for delicious meals, washed down with fine Chablis wines. Attractive colour schemes in the bedrooms.

Where to stay

BUDGET

Chambre d'Hôte La Marmotte – *2 r. de l'École - 89700 Collan - 7.5km/4.8mi NE of Chablis by D 150 then D 35* - ☎ *03 86 55 26 44* - ✍ - *3 rooms: 34/42€*. In the heart of a quaint little village, a tastefully restored house built with old stones and beams offers tidy, lovingly kept rooms each decorated with a different colour. Have breakfast in the winter garden graced by a fountain. *Table d'hôte* meals on request during the summer season.

Sit back and relax

Château Long-Depaquit – *45 r. Auxerroise* - ☎ *03 86 42 11 13* - *château-long-depaquit@wanadoo.fr* - *open Mon-Sat 9am-12.30pm, 1.30-6pm* - *closed Christmas, New Year and 1 May*. By appointment only. Visitors are shown round the storehouses and given a tasting of three wines, commented by connoisseurs, and accompanied by *gougère* (choux pastry puff flavoured with cheese, seasoned with pepper and then baked). This is the only estate where the Chablis vintage "La Moutonne" can be found.

Domaine Laroche (wine tastings) – *10 r. Auxerroise* - ☎ *03 86 42 89 28* - *www.michellaroche.com* - *by appointment Apr-Dec, daily 9.30am-12.30pm, 2-6pm; Jan-Mar, Mon-Sat 9am-12.30pm, 2-6pm* - *tour of the Obédiencerie 9.91€*. Visit the Obédiencerie of Chablis, a prestigious 9C and 16C manor house with an authentic 13C press. The cellars house a small crypt which received the remains of the great St Martin between 877 and 887.

EXCURSION

Noyers – *25km/15.5mi SE along D 956*. Upriver from Chablis, this charming medieval town has retained its interesting architectural heritage: timber-framed houses or gabled stone ones with quaint outside stairs, cellar doors opening onto picturesque streets and tiny squares... form a most attractive setting enhanced at night by discreet lighting. Between June and September, the **Rencontres musicales de Noyers** delight music lovers.

Stroll through the town, admiring the 14C and 15C timber-framed houses in **place de l'Hôtel-de-Ville**, the arcaded stone house and Renaissance mansion in **place du Marché-au-Blé**, the Renaissance façade and square tower of the **Église Notre-Dame**, and follow **rue du Poids-du-Roy** to the tiny **place de la Petite-Étape-aux-Vins**. From place du Grenier-à-Sel, a passageway leads to the river bank: here, a **promenade** planted with plane trees offers a pleasant walk and the opportunity to see the seven defensive towers still standing (out of a total of 23), which used to protect the town. Walk through the **Porte Peinte**, a square fortified gate, to return to the town centre.

COUNTRY LIVING

Chambre d'Hôte Château d'Archambault – *Cours - 2km/1.2mi S of Noyers by D 86* - ☎ *03 86 82 67 55* - *chateau-archambault.com* - *5 rooms: 58/69€* - *meals 14/20€*. This imposing 19C mansion once belonged to Napoleon III's private chef. It has been tastefully restored and appointed with contemporary furniture. The rooms look over the park or the vegetable garden. Warm, unpretentious welcome. Self-catering accommodation available.

Le Calounier – *5 r. de la Fontaine, In the village of Arton - 89310 Molay - 8km/5mi N of Noyers by D 86 and then a minor road* - ☎ *03 86 82 67 81* - *info@lecalounier* - ✍ - *5 rooms: 46/51€* - *meals 19€*. Peace and quiet prevail at this superbly restored Burgundy farmhouse, whose name is patois for walnut tree, many of which can be seen on the estate. The rooms are appointed with pieces of antique furniture and decorated with paintings by local artists. Regional cuisine.

Lac de CHALAIN★★

Michelin map 321: E-6 – Local map see Région des LACS DU JURA

This lake, covering 232ha/573 acres, is the most beautiful and impressive of all the lakes in the Jura region. It is particularly well suited for fishing and boating *(see Practical information: Discovering the region)*. The western part of the lake is enclosed by an indentation in the Fontenu plateau and is thus surrounded by steep wooded slopes, whereas the other part, with swampy banks in places, stretches between gently rolling hills. It is fed by resurgent springs from Lake Narlay and in turn spills into the River Ain via the Bief d'Œuf.

Lake dwellings – In June 1904 a severe draught combined with the effect of water catchment for an electricity plant to lower the water level by 7m/23ft, revealed a number of wooden posts on the west bank, which turned out to be the vestiges of a lake community, dating from five millennia ago – the Upper Paleolithic period (polished Stone Age). During successive excavations the remains of dwellings were discovered along about 2km/1.2mi of the west and north shores, beneath the present water level. Among the objects discovered during the excavations and now exhibited at the Lons-le-Saunier municipal archaeology museum, there is a particularly beautiful canoe, 9m/354ft long, hollowed out of the trunk of an oak tree, and also tools and utensils carved from deers' antlers, bone and stone.

Eating out

BUDGET

Ferme-Auberge du Tilleul – *9 r. du Vieux-Lavoir - 39130 Charezier - 13km/8.1mi SW of Lac de Chalain by D 27 -* ☏ *03 84 48 35 07 - closed lunchtime - 10/22€.* Settle in the former stables of this inn and tuck into a delicious *coq au vin* cooked in white Jura wine or a rabbit stew garnished with morels, lovingly prepared by Madame Bailly and her son. The comfortable rooms upstairs give onto the garden and the surrounding countryside.

Sarrazine – *39130 Doucier - 3km/1.9mi S of Lac de Chalain by D 27 -* ☏ *03 84 25 70 60 - closed early Dec to early Jan and Thu out of season - 12.50/20.42€.* A rustic atmosphere pervades this jolly restaurant with farming scenes painted around its walls. Specialities include grilled meat and pig trotters.

Where to stay

BUDGET

Chambre d'Hôte Chez Mme Devenat – *17 r. du Vieux-Lavoir - 39130 Charezier - 13km/8.1mi SW of Lac de Chalain by D 27 -* ☏ *03 84 48 35 79 - ⌦ - 4 rooms: 26/32€ - meals 9.15€.* Quiet, comfortable family house in a pretty village lying half way between Clairvaux-les-Lacs and Chalain Lake. There are more rooms in the cottage near the little wood. *Table d'hôte* meals with new regional specialities every day.

Camping Domaine de Chalain – *39130 Doucier - 3km/1.9mi S of Lac de Chalain by D 27 -* ☏ *03 84 25 78 78 - chalain@chalain.com - open May-18 Sep - booking recommended - 804 sites: 27€ - meals available.* On the edge of Chalain Lake, this camp site is ideal for family holidays. There are a great many organised activities and sporting facilities available during the day and in the evening. Beach for those who love swimming in fresh water. Cabins available.

Camping La Pergola – *39130 Marigny -* ☏ *03 84 25 70 03 - contact@lapergola.fr - open 6 May-15 Sep - booking recommended - 350 sites: 35€ - meals available.* There are several heated swimming pools on the hill above Chalain Lake, and extensive facilities for many water sports. Organised activities for children. You may choose to stay in a fully-equipped camping trailer.

Archaeological site – Listed since 1995 as an archaeological site of national interest, Chalain is a real gold mine for scientists, who are able to perform numerous experiments. It is preferable to see the exhibition before visiting the site.

Exposition A la rencontre des hommes du lac ⊙ – Learn how to make prehistoric tools and discover the settlement and daily life of prehistoric lake dwellers through clear and pleasant explanations.

Maisons néolithiques sur pilotis ⊙ – *Access through La Pergola camp site in Marigny (parking fee).* Two Neolithic houses on pillars have been reconstructed on the shores of the lake, using prehistoric techniques.

Neolithic site

Sports and recreation park – *Restricted parking; parking fee.* One of the largest leisure parks in the region has developed on the shores of the lake, offering swimming facilities, windsurfing and canoeing. This vast expanse of fresh water, abounding in pike and perch, is also the paradise of anglers.

Crêt de CHALAM★★★

Michelin map 328: I-3 – Local map see ST-CLAUDE

This is the highest peak (1 545m/5 069ft) in the range overlooking the Valserine from the west. It is easily accessible to ramblers looking for a challenging change of scenery and a magnificent panorama.

Access – *1hr 30min round trip on foot. We suggest the route leaving from La Pesse.*

Take the road opposite the church. After 4km/2.4mi you come to a crossroads (signposted La Borne au Lion).

🚶 *Park the car and follow the right-hand path (1hr 30min on foot there and back).*

Eating out

BUDGET

Ferme-Auberge La Combe aux Bisons – *39370 La Pesse - 1.5km/0.8mi N of La Pesse by D 25 heading for L'Embossieux - ☎ 03 84 42 71 60 - closed 1-28 Dec, Mon and Tue except school holidays - ✉ - reservations required - 14.48/24.39€.* The decor of this welcoming inn evokes the North American plains with their forests, teepees and charging buffaloes... The chef serves tasty bison meat dishes with local wines and ingredients.

Where to stay

BUDGET

Chambre d'Hôte La Dalue – *39310 Bellecombe - 5km/3.1mi NE of La Pesse by D 25 heading towards Les Moussières - ☎ 03 84 41 69 03 - perrier.ladalue@wanadoo.fr - 4 rooms: 27.44/45.73€ - meals 12.20€.* This old farmhouse lost in the forest is a good stopping-place for hikers and cross-country skiers who have set out to discover the Jura. Simple but pleasant rooms and dormitories have been set up in the former hay loft. Generous, unpretentious cuisine. Preferably for non-smokers.

Hôtel du Commerce – *01410 Chézery-Forens - ☎ 04 50 56 90 67 - closed 1-6 Jan, 17-29 Jun, 16 Sep-12 Oct, Tue evenings and Wed - 9 rooms: 38€ - ☑ 6.10€ - restaurant 12.50/30.50€.* You can look forward to a most enjoyable stay in this family hotel, whose terrace gives onto the Valserine. A smart dining room and simple, carefully kept rooms are available at extremely reasonable prices.

Borne au Lion – A lion (for the Franche-Comté), some fleurs-de-lis (for the kingdom of France) and the date of 1613 can be seen on this milestone, located at the foot of a monument to the Maquis of the Ain and Haut-Jura. It used to mark the border between France, Spain and Savoy. The path soon crosses a plateau planted with spruces, from which the Chalam summit can be seen. The climb becomes very steep towards the end.

A useful marker for ramblers

A. de Valroger/MICHELIN

★★**Panorama** – The entire length of the Valserine Valley can be seen from the summit.

The view to the east stretches as far as the great **Jura range**, the highest and final mountain chain before the land drops down to the Swiss plain. The gullied slopes of Roche Franche can be seen right in front of you; to your left are the Reculet and the Crêt de la Neige (1 717m/5 633ft); to your right is the Grand Crêt d'Eau, beyond the Sac pass. In clear weather, even Mont Blanc can be seen.

There is an extensive view to the west of the mountains and mountain plateaux of the Jura.

CHALON-SUR-SAÔNE★

Population 75 447
Michelin map 320: J-9

Chalon, an inland port situated at the confluence of the River Saône and the Canal du Centre, is an active industrial and business centre; its commercial fairs are well attended. Chalon is also the capital town of an area of arable farming, stock raising and vineyards; the best wines are worthy of their great neighbours from the Côte d'Or.
The vineyards on the banks of the Saône link the Côte de Beaune and the Côte de Nuits to the north and the Mâconnais and the Beaujolais to the south. Famous wines such as Mercurey, Givry, Montagny and Rully (sparkling) come from this region, as do many fine table wines.

From the Roman Empire to the Schneider Empire – Julius Caesar chose Chalon as the main warehouse for his food supplies during his campaigns in Gaul, because of its situation on the banks of the Saône, a magnificent navigable waterway, and at the intersection of a number of major roads.
During the Middle Ages the annual pelt fairs (fox, badger, polecat, stoat, otter, marten, mink etc), known as **Foires aux Sauvagines**, which lasted two months, were among the most popular in Europe.
The building of the Canal du Centre in the late 18C and early 19C, as well as the canals of Burgundy and the Rhône-Rhine link, developed regional commerce on the waterways. At the same time, **Joseph Nicéphore Niepce**, born in Chalon in 1765, devoted himself to scientific research. After perfecting an engine on the same principles as the jet engine (the Pyreolophore), along with his brother Claude, he then devoted his time to lithography and in 1816 succeeded in obtaining a negative image with the aid of a camera obscura, or pinhole camera, and then a positive one in 1822. In 1826 Nicéphore Niepce developed a process of photoengraving: **heliogravure**. The inventor of photography died in Chalon in 1833. A statue in Quai Gambetta and a monument on the edge of the N 6 road at St-Loup-de-Varennes *(7km/4mi S of Chalon)*, where his discovery was perfected, perpetuate the memory of this great inventor.
In 1839, the **Schneider** company from Le Creusot set up a factory in Chalon at the east end of the Canal du Centre; it was initially known as Le Petit Creusot, before becoming Creusot-Loire *(see Le CREUSOT)*. From 1839 the factory produced a series of torpedo boats, submarines and anti-torpedo boats for various countries. Between 1889 and 1906 it produced 81 torpedo boats. The largest ship it produced was the anti-torpedo boat *Mangini*, launched in 1911 for the Bolivian navy. It was 78.10m/256ft long and drew a depth of 3.08m/13ft, making it too big to sail down the Saône. It had to be transported to the Mediterranean on a transport barge. The submarines produced here up until the Second World War were exported to Bolivia and Japan. This factory suffered the full force of the crisis in the steel industry in 1984. Since 1970, however, the economic activity of Chalon has been stimulated by the arrival of other industries such as Kodak, St-Gobain, Framatome, Air Liquide and Water Queen (European leader in the production of fishing gear).

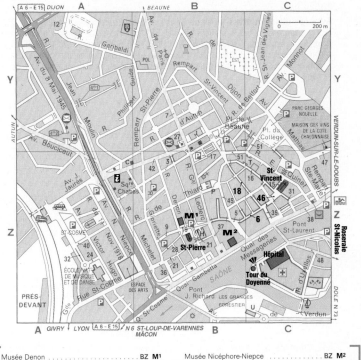

Musée Denon . . . . **BZ M¹**   Musée Nicéphore-Niepce . . . . **BZ M²**

TOWN WALK

Old houses – Some of the many old houses in Chalon have a particular charm. In the streets near the cathedral there are fine half-timbered façades overlooking place St-Vincent (note also at the corner of rue St-Vincent the statue of a saint), rue aux Fèvres and rue de l'Évêché. **Rue St-Vincent** forms a picturesque crossroads at the junction of rue du Pont and rue du Châtelet. No 37 **rue du Châtelet** has a handsome 17C façade with low-relief sculptures, medallions and gargoyles. No 39 **Grande Rue** is a fine 14C house (restored).

Cathédrale St-Vincent – The cathedral of the old bishopric of Chalon (suppressed in 1790) is not uniform in appearance. The oldest parts date from the late 11C; the chancel is 13C. The neo-Gothic façade (1825) conveys a strange appearance to the edifice.

The pillars in the nave are composed of fluted pilasters and engaged columns. A 15C font and a Flamboyant vault adorn the third chapel in the north transept. The north apsidal chapel contains a large contemporary tabernacle in bronze gilt (1986). A finely sculpted canopy adorns the chancel, and a triptych of the Crucifixion (1608) the apse.

The 15C sacristy was divided horizontally in the 16C, and the lower chamber was covered with a vault supported by a central pillar. The ante-chapel is vaulted with five pendant keystones and lit through a beautiful stained-glass window depicting the woman with the 12 stars of the Apocalypse.

The south transept opens into the chapel of Notre-Dame-de-Pitié (15C *Pietà* and Renaissance tapestry) and into the 15C cloisters (restored) which contain four wooden statues. The well in the cloister garth has also been restored.

The south aisle contains many burial stones; some chapels are closed off by stone screens (claustra); the last chapel contains a 16C polychrome *Pietà*.

Hôpital ⊘ – *On the island in the River Saône.*

The Flemish-style building was started in the 16C. The first floor, the nuns' quarters, comprises several panelled rooms, including the infirmary which contains four curtained beds. The buildings were extended in the 17C, and in the 18C certain

Eating out

BUDGET

Bistrot – *31 r. de Strasbourg -* ☎ *03 85 93 22 01 - closed Sat-Sun - 13.26/21.34€.* Wood panelling, old posters, faded postcards and enamelled advertising plaques form the decor of this typical restaurant which well deserves its name! Traditional cuisine with a regional touch.

MODERATE

Auberge des Alouettes – *Rte de Givry - 71880 Châtenoy-le-Royal - 4km/2.5mi W of Chalon by D 69 -* ☎ *03 85 48 32 15 - closed 2-16 Jan and 17 Jul-8 Aug, Sun evenings, Tue evenings and Wed - 16.50€ lunch - 21/46€.* This welcoming restaurant on the road to Givry has two rustic dining rooms and a fine fireplace. Traditional cooking at affordable prices. Meals are served on the terrace in fair weather.

Where to stay

BUDGET

Hôtel St-Jean – *24 quai Gambetta -* ☎ *03 85 48 45 65 - 25 rooms: 33.54/45.73€ -* ☐ *4.57€.* This 19C *hôtel particulier* facing the River Saône has a radiant breakfast room enhanced with painted wrought-iron furniture. Access to the simple yet comfortable rooms is by an imposing stone staircase.

MODERATE

Hôtel St-Régis – *22 bd de la République -* ☎ *03 85 90 95 60 - saint-regis@saint-regis-chalon.fr - 36 rooms: 70/107€ -* ☐ *9€ - restaurant 21/28€.* Country charm permeates this hotel in the town centre. The carefully kept rooms are suffused with light. Relax in the lounge-bar with its wood panelling and leather armchairs. Bright, spacious dining room.

On the town

Place St-Vincent – *Pl. St-Vincent.* Lined by colourful half-timbered houses, this square brings together most of the town's cafés, pubs and wine bars, whose terraces are prettily arranged around a fountain.

Sit back and relax

Aux Colonies des Arômes – *67 Grande-Rue -* ☎ *03 85 93 99 40 - Tue-Sat 8.30am-7pm - closed 2 weeks in Jan.* This tea shop streaming with light enjoys an elegant blue and white decor; the wicker chairs go well with the rush floor covering. Sip scented tea or try one of the many brands of coffee in a refined setting.

Boogie Blues Bar – *35 r. d'Uxelles -* ☎ *03 85 48 84 44 - Mon-Thu 6pm-2am, Fri-Sat 6pm-3am.* Pull up a wicker chair and settle around the fireplace to discuss art and literature in this congenial café, where you can recognise the legendary voice of French singer Georges Brassens. Nice selection of home-made cocktails.

La Maison des Vins de la Côte Chalonnaise – *2 prom. Ste-Marie -* ☎ *03 85 41 64 00 - Mon-Sat 9am-7pm - closed public holidays.* The Maison des Vins organises tastings of around 100 vintages, among the best in the region.

Le Cellier Saint-Vincent – *14 pl. St-Vincent -* ☎ *03 85 48 78 25 - Tue-Sat 9am-noon, 2-7pm; Sun 9am-12.30pm - closed public holidays.* The owner himself designed the barrels made of ash wood where the many wines and liquors have been laid down to mature, as well as the glasses for tasting wine, called Les Impitoyables, which bring out the best of each vintage. Charming welcome.

Paddy Brophy's – *4 bd de la République -* ☎ *03 85 93 15 19 - Mon-Sat 11-1am, Sun 5pm-1am - closed 3 weeks in Aug.* The decor of this pub was almost entirely brought over from Ireland, including the huge fresco representing the Hours and the welcome stone with its inscription in Gaelic.

rooms were decorated with magnificent **woodwork**★. The nuns' refectory and the kitchen passage, which is furnished with dressers lined with pewter and copper vessels, are particularly interesting. The chapel (1873) has a metal structure and displays works of art from the buildings that have been demolished: woodwork decorated with coats of arms, 17C bishop's throne, rare late-15C statue of the Virgin Mary with an inkwell. An 84 piece collection of 18C pots is displayed in the 18C pharmacy.

Tour du Doyenné – The 15C deanery tower originally stood near the cathedral. It was dismantled in 1907 and rebuilt at the point of the island. Near the tower is a magnificent lime tree from the Buffon nursery.

★**Roseraie St-Nicolas** – *4km/2.5mi NE of Chalon-sur-Saône. Take the bridge, Pont-St-Laurent, and continue straight on across the two islands, then turn left onto rue Julien-Leneuveu.*

🚶 *A 5km/3mi trail through the rose garden (1hr 30min) starts from the St-Nicolas recreation ground.*

The **rose garden** is laid out in a loop of the Saône, beyond the municipal golf course. The rose beds (25 000 bushes) are set in vast lawns shaded by conifers or young apple trees. The recommended route runs parallel with a keep-fit trail (2.5km/1.5mi).

Église St-Pierre – The church was built between 1698 and 1713 (19C additions) as the chapel of a Benedictine abbey. It is in the Italian style and has a particularly impressive west front. The huge nave and domed chancel are furnished with statues, some of which date from the 17C: at the entrance to the chancel are St Peter and St Benet, in the transept are St Anne and the Virgin Mary overcoming a dragon. The choir stalls are attractively carved, and the Regency-style organ is surmounted by a figure of Saul playing the harp.

ADDITIONAL SIGHTS

★**Musée Denon** ⊘ – The 18C building, once part of an Ursuline convent, had the Neoclassical façade added to it when it was converted to house the museum which bears the name of one of Chalon's most illustrious citizens, Dominique Vivant **Denon** (1747-1825), a diplomat under the Ancien Régime, who was also a famous engraver and one of the first to introduce lithography to France. During Napoleon's campaign in Egypt he pioneered Egyptology and became artistic adviser to the Emperor, Grand Purveyor and Director of French Museums (including the Louvre), which he endowed with works of art.

The museum displays an important collection of 17C-19C paintings. The Italian School is represented by three large canvases by Giordano, as well as works by Bassano *(Plan of Venice, Adoration of the Shepherds)*, Solimena and Caravaggio. The golden age of Dutch painting (17C) is represented by Hans Bollongier *(Bouquet of Tulips)* and De Heem (still-life paintings). 19C French painting is represented by Géricault *(Portrait of a Black Man)* and the pre-Impressionist landscape painter Raffort, a native of Chalon.

Local history is illustrated by examples of domestic traditions, the life of the Saône boatmen and a collection of local furniture. Also on display is a collection of wood carvings dating from before the Revolution.

The ground floor is devoted to the rich archaeological collections: prehistoric flint implements from Volgu (Digoin-Gueugnon region – the largest and most beautiful Stone Age relics discovered, dating from the Solutré period), many antique and medieval metal artefacts, a magnificent Gallo-Roman group in stone of a lion bringing down a gladiator. There are also Gallo-Roman and medieval lapidary collections.

★**Musée Nicéphore-Niepce** ⊘ –
📷 This museum is housed in the 18C Hôtel des Messageries on the banks of the Saône. The rich collection includes photographs and photographic equipment, and some of the earliest cameras ever made, used by Joseph Nicéphore Niepce, and his first **heliographs**. There are also works by well-known contemporaries of Niepce in the world of photography, including Daguerre, his associate in 1829.

The museum displays photographic equipment from all over the world ranging from luminous projectors and Dagron equipment for microscopic photography (1860) to the camera used on the Apollo space programme.

Note in particular Niepce's first

Chevalier's 19C camera

camera (1816), the machinery for producing **daguerreotypes**, the first colour and relief photographs and the famous 19C cameras: Chevalier's Grand Photographe (c 1850), the Bertsch cameras (1860) and the Damoizeau cyclographs (1890).

▶▶ **Givry and la Voie Verte (the Green Trail)** – 📷 Givry, a peaceful town with a wealth of 18C architecture is the starting point of a 44km/27mi hiking and biking trail laid out along a former railway track.

CHAMPAGNOLE

Population 8 616
Michelin map 321: F-6

This industrial town, which was rebuilt after a fire at the end of the 18C, is a good departure point for excursions into the Ain Valley, La Joux Forest and the lakes region (see *Région des LACS DU JURA*).

The Ain Valley – The Ain springs up at an altitude of 750m/2 467ft, on the Nozeroy plateau. From here (the *Source de l'Ain*), the river flows down a narrow valley with steep, wooded sides. It disappears from view for a short distance, as it vanishes into a deep rift known as the *Perte de l'Ain*, then flows on down to the Champagnole plateau, which is more than 100m/328ft lower than that of Nozeroy. It is this great drop in height which explains the many waterfalls and rapids.

The river flows through a pleasant valley after Bourg-de-Sirod, with pretty meadows rising up to wooded slopes. It cuts through a wooded spur before watering the area around Champagnole. Some 10km/6mi further on, its path is blocked by the steep slopes of the Côte de l'Heute, which force it to make a sharp bend and flow southwards along the edge of the hillside. The valley, 2-4km/1-2.5mi wide, is known as the Combe d'Ain as far as the Cluse de la Pyle.

Musée archéologique ⊙ – *Rue Baronne-Delort.* The archaeological museum contains objects discovered during excavation work in the Gallo-Roman sites of Mont-Rivel and Saint-Germain-en-Montagne; two rooms illustrate the lifestyle of craftsmen and pilgrims who attended services in the Mont-Rivel temples at the beginning of the Christian era. The Merovingian collection consists of objects from the necropolises at Monnet-la-Ville and Crotenay including jewellery, most notably some bronze and iron **buckles**★.

UPPER VALLEY OF THE AIN

84km/52mi – allow 4hr – see local map opposite

Leave Champagnole heading SW on D 471. At Ney, take D 253 to the left; after 2.5km/1.5mi take the unsurfaced road, in poor condition, to the left for about 2.4km/1.4mi, until you reach a car park.

Belvédère de Bénedegand – *15min there and back on foot.*
🚶 A pretty forest path leads to this viewpoint. There is a lovely view of the Ain Valley, Champagnole, Mont Rivel and, in the distance, the forest of Fresse.

Retrace your steps to the main road (D 253), go through Loulle and Vaudioux and turn right on N 5. Take the first road on the left, D 279, and leave the car in the car park at the side of the road, on a level with the Billaude waterfall.

There is a good view of the waterfall and its setting from the platform below.

★**Cascade de la Billaude** – *30min there and back.*
🚶 Take the path marked *Saut Claude Roy* which leads down to the waterfall. Take the steep, sharply twisting footpath down into the ravine, keeping to the right. Then there is quite a stiff climb uphill *(100 steps, many of which are very high)*. At the top, the Lemme can be seen tumbling from a narrow crevice in a wooded setting between towering rock faces, dropping a total of 28m/92ft in two successive cascades. Delicately perfumed cyclamens grow near the waterfall in summer.

Return to N 5 and follow it to the left.

★**River Lemme** – N 5 follows the valley of the River Lemme, a tributary of the Ain, as far as Pont-de-la-Chaux. The sight of this turbulent little river gushing between pines and rocky crags is fresh and exhilarating.

At Pont-de-la-Chaux, take D 16 on the left.

Chaux-des-Croteney – This town, built on a triangular rocky plateau with precipitous rock faces dropping away at the edges, providing a natural defence, is thought by some archaeologists to be the site of ancient Alesia.

Take D 16 and D 127^{E1} to Les Planches-en-Montagne.

★**Gorges de la Langouette** – *30min round trip on foot. Leave the car in the shady car park after the bridge called La Langouette.*

⬛ There is a lovely view from this bridge of the Gorges de la Langouette, only 4m/13ft wide and 47m/154ft deep, cut into the limestone by the River Saine. The three **viewpoints★** over the gorge can be reached by taking the path on the left before the bridge *(access also possible by car: follow the road indicated from the village of Les Planches).* The rather steep footpath is signposted and leads to where the Saine cascades into a narrow crevice, the beginning of the gorge.

Return to Les Planches and turn right at the church; then just before Chaux-des-Crotenay, turn right again onto a forest road.

Vallée de la Saine – The route continues along a pretty road, running through forest along the top of the cliffs which form the sides of the narrow valley of the Saine, a small tributary of the Lemme.

Turn right after coming out of the gorge and cross the bridge.

Syam – Excavations in the Syam plain, near the confluence of the Lemme and the Saine, have enabled a team of archaeologists to say they believe they have located the site of the Battle of Alésia. Having been besieged by Caesar's troops in the oppidum of Alésia for six weeks, the army of the Gauls is thought to have stormed down from the Gyts heights near Syam, where Vercingetorix had an observation post, in an attempt to join up with the Gallic relief forces which were attacking the Roman field camps defending the Crans threshold. In the ensuing battle, involving 400 000 men, the Gauls were unable to break through the Romans' double line of defence fortifications and suffered a crushing defeat.

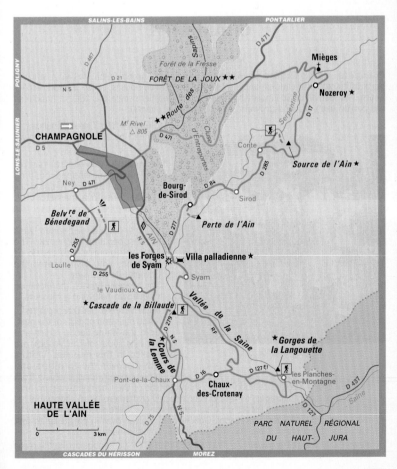

★ **Villa palladienne**  – This amazing Palladian villa was commissioned in 1825 by Emmanuel Jobez, a Forge Master who admired Italian architecture. The square plan underlined by Ionic pilasters, the central rotunda and the Pompeian-style decoration is reminiscent of Italian villas. The interior decoration and period furniture are very attractive. *Concerts are organised regularly. Refreshments are served on the terrace.*

Forges – Built in 1813 on the banks of the Ain, the forge brought prosperity to the village under the First Empire. Today the workshops specialise in rolling processes, perpetuating traditions on machinery nearly 100 years old. The story of the Smithies of Syam is detailed in an exhibit and video presentation.

North of Syam, turn right towards Bourg-de-Sirod.

Bourg-de-Sirod – This village owes its pretty site to the many waterfalls and rapids formed by the Ain as it covers the 100m/328ft drop in altitude between the Nozeroy and Champagnole plateaux.

Leave the car in the car park near the Bourg-de-Sirod town hall (mairie). Follow the path marked Point de vue, Perte de l'Ain.

Perte de l'Ain – There is a superb view of the waterfall formed by the Ain as it disappears into a crevice between fallen rocks.

Carry on through Sirod and Conte.

★ **Source de l'Ain** – *Leave the car at the end of the access road (through forest) which leads off D 283 after Conte.*
▸ Continue on foot *(15min there and back)* to the river's source, which is at the bottom of the thickly wooded, rocky amphitheatre. This is in fact a resurgent spring and has a very variable flow. During the droughts of 1959 and 1964 the mouth was completely dry, and it was possible to climb up a part of the Ain's underground course.

Return to D 283, turn left and continue to Nozeroy.

★ **Nozeroy** – *See NOZEROY.*

Mièges – *See NOZEROY.*

Return to Champagnole by taking D 119, then D 471 to the left, which crosses the pleasantly green Entreportes ravine.

CHAMPLITTE

Population 1 828
Michelin map 314: B-7

Champlitte, an old fortified town, lies in tiers in the green Salon Valley. It still has parts of its old fortifications, and also some Renaissance houses, called *maisons espagnoles*. The festival of St Vincent has been celebrated here since the 18C, in honour of the patron saint of wine-growers *(see Calendar of events)*.

Fête de la Saint Vincent

Church – This Classical building is flanked by an older Gothic tower (1437).

★ **Château** – The central part of this horseshoe-shaped building has a beautiful 16C Renaissance façade beneath a mansard roof. The bas-relief decoration on this superposes Ionic and Corinthian orders, and is enhanced with arabesques and leafwork. The 18C wings are the work of Bertrand, who also created the Château de Moncley.
The château houses the Hôtel de Ville (town hall) and a museum.

★ **Musée des Arts et Traditions populaires**  – Activities and objects of the past, from the Haute-Saône region and the hills south of the Vosges, are evoked in this museum. Visitors will discover the furniture and other typically local artefacts from days gone by – such as the bed-recess characteristic of the Champlitte region, mementoes of itinerant trades, carefully reconstructed craftsmens' workshops, and reconstructions of various places once so central to village life such as the grocer's, the school, the café and the chapel. One section is given over in particular to folk medicine, the chemist's and the realities of the old almshouse.

Musée 1900 – Arts et Techniques  – Two streets lined with workshops evoke the technical progress being made in such a town as this, at the turn of the 20C.

CHAPAIZE ★

Population 153
Michelin map 320: I-10 – 16km/10mi W of Tournus
Local map see MÂCONNAIS

Situated on the River Bisançon, to the west of the magnificent forest of Chapaize, the little village of Chapaize is dominated by the high belfry of its Romanesque church. The church is all that remains of a priory founded in the 11C by Benedictine monks from Chalon.

★ **Église St-Martin** – *30min.* This church was built between the first quarter of the 11C and the early 13C using the fine local limestone. The essentially Romanesque style building shows a strong Lombard influence – Italian stonemasons almost certainly worked on it – and features a strikingly robust, harmonious belfry.

Exterior – The original ground plan was that of a basilica, and the central nave was made higher and had sturdy buttresses added to it in the mid-12C. The west front is fairly plain, with a triangular gable reflected in the pattern of the Lombard arcades.

The mid-11C **belfry** is typical of those found in Lombardy, although this one is set above the transept crossing. It is surprisingly tall (35m/115ft) for a building of such modest proportions. Certain architectural contrivances emphasise its soaring effect: the slightly rectangular shape; the imperceptibly pyramidal first storey as tall as the two storeys above it put together and adorned with Lombard arcades (stresses the vertical); upper storeys decorated with horizontal cornices, windows of different sizes placed at different levels, with width increasing upwards. An external staircase was added in the 18C leading up to the base of the belfry.

The chevet was rebuilt in the 13C, and its elegant simplicity harmonises well with the rest of the building.

In the late 14C, the church roof was recovered with stone slabs, known as *lauzes*. A few weathered sculptures, archaic in style and limited in number, carved with floral decoration or human faces, adorn the capitals of the windows and the belfry. On the north side of the latter a naïve figure carved on a column is a precursor of the statue-column.

St-Martin's

Interior – The stark simplicity of the interior is quite striking. The great cylindrical pillars (4.8m/15ft in circumference) are slightly out of line and are crowned with triangular imposts. Of the total seven bays, two belong to the choir. The nave arcade has very wide transverse arches which support 12C broken-barrel vaulting and also the groined vaulting of the aisles. The transept crossing is covered with an attractive **dome** on squinches and supported by semi-circular transept arches. Both the apse and the apsidal chapels are oven-vaulted. The former is lit through three wide windows and the latter through openings flanked with columns; the one on the left is decorated with sculpted capitals. The side windows are 19C.

La CHARITÉ-SUR-LOIRE★

Population 5 686
Michelin map 319: B-8

La Charité, which is dominated by the belfries of its handsome church, rises in terraces from the majestic sweep of the Loire. The river is spanned by a picturesque 16C
stone bridge which provides a good view of the town. In the days of navigation on
the Loire, La Charité was a busy port.

Ph. Gajic/MICHELIN

The town seen from the far bank of the Loire

The Charity of the Good Fathers – At first the small riverside town was called Seyr
which, according to an etymology which seems to be Phoenician, means Town of the
Sun. The conversion of the inhabitants to Christianity and the founding early in the
8C of a convent and a church marked the beginning of a period of prosperity which
was interrupted by Arab invasions and attendant destruction.
It was in the 11C, when the present church was built, that the reorganised abbey
began to attract travellers, pilgrims and poor people. The hospitality and generosity
of the monks was so widely known that the unfortunate came in droves to ask for
the charity *(la charité)* of the good fathers, and the town acquired a new name.

A check to Joan of Arc – The town, fortified in the 12C, was to be the prize in the
struggle between the Armagnacs and the Burgundians during the Hundred Years War.
La Charité was initially occupied by the Armagnacs, the allies of Charles VII, King of
France. In 1423 the town was taken by the adventurer **Perrinet-Gressard** who was in
the service of both the Duke of Burgundy, who wished to continue the struggle with
Charles VII, and the English, who were anxious to delay for as long as possible a reconciliation between the Armagnacs and the Burgundians. In December 1429 Joan of
Arc arrived from St-Pierre-le-Moutier and besieged La Charité on behalf of Charles VII,
but lack of troops and cold weather obliged her to raise the siege. Perrinet-Gressard
held the town until the Treaty of Arras in 1435, when he returned it to the King of
France against payment of a large ransom and the office of town governor for life.

Les Remparts – From the remains of the ramparts on the esplanade beside the
college in rue du Clos there is another attractive **view**★ of the chevet with its circlet
of apsidal chapels, the Loire, the old town and the ramparts (1164).

★★**Église prieurale Notre-Dame** ☉ – *1hr*. Despite the damage it has incurred over
the centuries (a few bays, the transept and the chancel are all that remain), this
priory church is still one of the most remarkable examples of Romanesque architecture in Burgundy.

Eldest daughter of Cluny – The church and its attendant Benedictine priory, a daughter
house of Cluny, were built during the second half of the 11C. The church was consecrated in 1107 by Pope Paschal II. Its outline and decoration were modified in
the first half of the 12C.
After Cluny the priory church of La Charité was the largest church in France; it
consisted of a nave and four aisles (122m/399ft long, 37m/120ft wide, 27m/89ft
high under the dome). It could hold a congregation of 5 000, carried the hon-
orary title Eldest daughter of Cluny and had at least 50 daughter houses.

Exterior – The façade, which was separated from the rest of the church by a fire in
1559, stands in place des Pêcheurs. Originally two towers framed the central doorway;
only one *(left)*, the 12C **Tour Ste-Croix** has survived. It is square in design with two
storeys of windows surmounted by a slate spire in place of the original one of stone.
It is decorated with blind arcades and sculptured motifs including rosettes.

206

ACCOMMODATION FOR EVERY BUDGET

Camping Municipal La Saulaie – *Quai de la Saulaie* - ☎ *03 86 70 00 83 - silacharite@wanadoo.fr - open 27 Apr-15 Sep -* ✉ *- reservations recommended - 100 sites: 10.98€*. Pitch your tent along the banks of the Loire on the small island of La Saulaie, near the beach. Numerous hiking trails for nature lovers. Swimming-pool on the premises. Facilities for tennis, angling and archery nearby.

Relais de Pouilly – *58150 Pouilly-sur-Loire - 11km/6.8mi N of La Charité-sur-Loire by N 151 then N 7 -* ☎ *03 86 39 03 00 - sarl.relais-de-pouilly@wanadoo.fr -* 🅿 *- 24 rooms: 40/65€ -* ☕ *6.95€ - restaurant 14.50/29€*. Despite its location near the new motorway, this hotel has rooms fitted with double glazing that look out onto a lush setting. Cosy accommodation decorated with bamboo furniture. The dining room gives onto the garden.

Hôtel Le Grand Monarque – *33 quai Clemenceau -* ☎ *03 86 70 21 73 - le.grand.monarque@wanadoo.fr - closed 15 Feb-18 Mar - 15 rooms: 59/104€ -* ☕ *8.40€ - restaurant 21.05/42.50€*. This hotel along the quays was originally built in the 17C. The panoramic dining room opens onto a small garden with a view of the bridge spanning the Loire. A few fine, comfortable rooms. Traditional cooking with special menus for children.

The two doorways are walled up; one of them has preserved its tympanum and shows the Virgin Mary interceding with Christ to obtain protection for the monastery of La Charité, represented by the monk, Gérard, its founder and prior. Scenes from the Life of the Virgin are portrayed on the lintels: the Annunciation, the Visitation, the Nativity, and the bringing of good tidings to the shepherds.

The steps of the Romanesque central doorway, of which very little is left and which was replaced by a Gothic construction in the 16C, lead to place Ste-Croix, on the site of six bays of the nave destroyed in the fire of 1559.

Houses have been built into the former north aisle, which was transformed into a parish church from the 12C to the 18C. The arcades of the false triforium are still visible.

Interior – The present church consists of the first four bays of the original nave, the transept and the chancel. The nave, which was badly restored in 1695, has nothing of interest, but the transept and the chancel constitute a magnificent Romanesque ensemble.

The transept crossing is surmounted by an octagonal dome on squinches. The arms of the transept have three bays and two apsidal chapels dating from the 11C; this is the oldest part of the church. In the south transept, the second Romanesque tympanum of the Tour Ste-Croix is visible, representing the Transfiguration with the Adoration of the Magi and the Presentation in the Temple.

A bestiary of eight motifs accentuates the false triforium; its five-lobed arcades, of Arabic inspiration, are supported by ornamented pilasters. There are good modern stained-glass windows by Max Ingrand.

Leave the church via the south transept.

PRIORY CHURCH OF THE VIRGIN

0   40m

■ Existing buildings
▬ No longer exist

★ **View of the chevet** – The 16C pointed-vaulted passageway (passage de la Madeleine) leads to the east end of the church and from there to the **square des Bénédictins**, which provides a good view of the chevet, the transept and the octagonal tower of the abbey church. In the square, traces of an 11C Cluniac priory have been excavated.

Ancien Prieuré – The vast ensemble formed by the old priory is gradually being restored: note in particular the 14C chapter-house, the 18C cloisters, the refectory, the prior's drawing room and dining room... The prior's lodging (early 16C) with an attractive seven-sided turret overlooks the lower courtyard (now called Cour du Château). Exhibitions relating to the history of the priory or to the restoration work are organised every summer.

Museum ⊙ – Considerable space is devoted to medieval objects found during the excavations behind the church: lapidary fragments and terracotta tiles, implements, pottery, keys, jewellery etc. There are also sculptures by Pina (1885-1966), a pupil of Rodin, and a fine collection of Sèvres ceramics. A separate room traces the development of files and rasps; their production was an important local industry between 1830 and 1960.

▶▶ **Forêt des Bertranges** – This beautiful forest, situated 5km/3mi from the banks of the River Loire, covers an area of some 10 000ha/24 711acres mainly planted with oaks and beeches; it offers a large choice of activities: hikes, riding tours, fishing, mini-golf, themed visits...*(map and information available from the tourist office)*.

CHARLIEU★

Population 3 582
Michelin map 320: F-13

Ancient *Carus locus* was already an active market town in Gallo-Roman times on the road linking the Saône and Loire valleys. The pretty town of Charlieu, standing at the crossroads of several major communications routes, is a centre for the millinery and silk industries, on the scale of both factories and family-run cottage industries.

However, it is Charlieu's archaeological treasures in particular which have won the town its renown.

★ABBAYE BÉNÉDICTINE ⊙ *1hr*

The abbey was founded c 872, attached to Cluny c 930, converted into a priory c 1040 and then fortified on the orders of Philippe Auguste, its protector. The architects and artists from Cluny collaborated here with particularly happy results to rebuild the 11C church and add on the 12C narthex. Excavations thus show that a small 9C church was replaced by a 10C church, which was replaced in turn by an 11C abbey church, on a slightly different axis. This church had a nave with four bays and aisles either side, a transept with transept chapels and an ambulatory with radiating chapels opening off it. The abbey was not to escape the ravages of the Revolution, however; the Benedictine priory, which at the time still housed two monks, was secularised in March 1789. The abbey buildings and the church of St-Fortunat, one of the finest of Cluny's daughters, were largely demolished. All

Tympanum of the great doorway on the north side of the narthex, abbey of Charlieu

Société des Amis des Arts de Charlieu

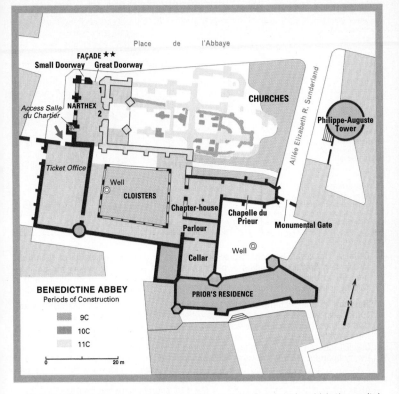

Place de l'Abbaye

FAÇADE ★★
Small Doorway   Great Doorway

Access Salle
du Chartier   NARTHEX

CHURCHES

Philippe-Auguste
Tower

Allée Elizabeth R. Sunderland

Ticket Office

Well

CLOISTERS

Chapter-house

Parlour

Chapelle du
Prieur

Monumental Gate

Cellar

Well

PRIOR'S RESIDENCE

N

BENEDICTINE ABBEY
Periods of Construction

9C
10C
11C

0   20 m

---

that remains of the church are the narthex and the first bay, in which the capitals bear a resemblance to those of the Brionnais. The warm golden glow of the stone of the abbey buildings adds to the charm of the scene.

There is a good view of the two doorways, which are the abbey's best feature, from Place de l'Abbaye.

★★ **Façade** – The north façade of the narthex is entered through a **great doorway**, dating from the 12C, which is decorated with some wonderful sculpture work. Christ in Majesty is depicted on the tympanum in a mandorla, supported by two angels and surrounded by the symbols of the four Evangelists. On the lintel, the Virgin Mary appears with two attendant angels and the 12 disciples. Sadly, the sculptures on the imposts of the engaged door posts are damaged; they depict on the left King David and Boson, King of Burgundy and Provence, and on the right St John the Baptist and Bishop Robert, the abbey's founder.

Above the archivolt note the Paschal lamb with its sharply defined thick curly fleece. The arch mouldings and the columns which frame the doorway are decorated with geometrical and floral motifs. The abbey owed this luxuriant plant-like decoration, of Eastern inspiration, to the Crusades. The inside of the left doorpost bears a representation of Lust, depicted as a woman grappling with frightful reptilian monsters.

The **small doorway**, to the right of the great doorway, also dates from the 12C. The Wedding at Cana is depicted on its tympanum, the Transfiguration of Christ on its archivolt and an Old Testament sacrifice on the lintel.

As you enter, you will see to your left the foundations of the various churches which have stood on this site. They can be seen more clearly from the Salle du Chartrier.

Cloisters – These were built in the 15C to replace the previous ones, which were Romanesque. An old well can still be seen against the west gallery. The east gallery contains six huge arches supported on twin colonnettes, on which the capitals are richly decorated with sculpted acanthus leaves, birds and geometrical motifs.

Chapter-house – This dates from the early 16C and features pointed arches supported on a round stone pillar, into which a lectern has been carved.

Prior's chapel – This dates from the late 15C. The old terracotta floor tiling has been reconstructed based on the original. Above the chapel is a bell turret with a timber roof.

The next two rooms form the Musée Armand-Charnay.

Parlour – This lovely vaulted room dating from the early 16C houses a **lapidary museum** in which, next to old capitals from the priory, note two bas-relief sculptures: a 10C Carolingian one depicting Daniel in the Lions' Den and a 12C one depicting the Annunciation amid interlaced arches.

CHARLIEU

Église St-Philibert . . . . **B**
Maison des Anglais . . . . **E**
Maison des Armagnacs . . . . . **K**
Maison Disson . . . . **N**
Tour Philippe-Auguste . . . . . . **R**

Cellar – The cellar, beneath two semicircular vaults, houses a museum of sacred art (**Musée d'Art Religieux**) including a lovely collection of polychrome wood statues from the 15C to the 18C. Note in particular a Virgin Mary with Bird, from the church in Aiguilly (near Roanne), and a Virgin with Child, both Gothic dating from the 15C.

Narthex – This rectangular building, 17m/56ft long and about 10m/33ft wide, comprises two rooms, one above the other, with ribbed vaulting.
One of these contains a **Gallo-Roman sarcophagus** (**1**) which was found in the crypt of the Carolingian church. The east wall of the narthex is the former west front of the 11C church of St-Fortunat, consecrated in 1094, comprising: a doorway (**2**, on the tympanum framed by three well-defined arch mouldings, Christ is depicted in Majesty in a mandorla held by two angels); two twin windows with arch mouldings, and above, a pair of figures facing each other.
After the narthex, in the first bay of the 11C church, note the interesting decoration on two of the capitals: Daniel in the Lions' Den and mermaids.

Charter room (**Salle du Chartrier**) – A spiral staircase leads up to this room, which is also known as the Salle des Archives. It contains an exhibition on the history of the abbey. The great window to the east has two small blind arcades either side of it, and beautiful arch mouldings above it which are supported on engaged columns with capitals decorated with foliage. From here there is a good view of the site of the previous churches – the outline of each of their foundations shows up in the grass. The view also takes in the Philippe-Auguste tower, the prior's lodging and the rooftops of the town.
Before leaving the abbey, have a quick look down into the courtyard of the prior's lodging.

Prior's lodging (**Hôtel du Prieur**) – *Not open to the public.*
The 16C **monumental doorway** with a basket-handle arch is surmounted by decorative crenellations and the coat of arms of the prior.
The prior's residence runs along an elegant courtyard to the south of the chapel, in the centre of which there is an old well with a wrought-iron cover. The residence dates from 1510 and is a charming half-timbered building with two hexagonal corner towers and steeply sloping tiled roofs.

Tour Philippe-Auguste – This imposing tower, of beautiful ochre-coloured stone, was built c 1180 on the orders of Philippe-Auguste, who considered the fortified town of Charlieu to be of great use to the French crown. The tower was part of the abbey's system of fortifications.

OLD TOWN

Strolling through the streets near place St-Philibert, you will come across numerous picturesque houses dating from the 13C to the 18C.
On the corner of place St-Philibert and rue Grenette stands a 13C stone house which has on its upper floor twin windows with colonnettes as mullions.

Église St-Philibert – This 13C church, which has no transept, has a layout typical of 13C Burgundian architecture: a nave with five bays, side aisles and a rectangular chancel. It houses some beautiful works of art, such as a 15C pulpit hewn from a single block of stone and 15C and 16C stalls with pretty painted panels. One chapel contains a 16C Madonna (Notre-Dame-de-Charlieu). In the chapel of Ste-Anne on the south side of the chancel there is a 15C polychrome stone altarpiece depicting the Visitation and the Nativity. The chapel of St-Crépin on the north side of the chancel contains a 17C *Pietà* and a statuette of St Crispin, patron saint of shoemakers and saddlers, in polychrome wood.

Ancien Hôtel-Dieu – The 18C hospital has a beautiful façade overlooking rue Jean-Morel and consists of two huge rooms for the sick, separated by a chapel in which there is a handsome 17C gilded wood altar. The building now houses two museums.

Musée de la Soierie ⏲ – The silk museum, in the old men's ward, documents the history of the silk industry and silk weaving in Charlieu. The large room on the left houses the statue of Notre-Dame-de-Septembre, patron of the powerful weavers' guild, in whose honour there is an annual procession *(2nd Sunday in September)*. The exhibition includes samples of local silk production (sumptuous clothing, one-off creations commissioned by aristocratic families etc) and impressive old looms, giving a good overview of the technical developments in weaving from the 18C on.

All the equipment on display is still in working order, and from time to time there is a demonstration. Note in particular a large 18C vertical warp beam and some 20C looms which show how the weaving process is becoming increasingly automated.

On the first floor there is a display of materials and designer clothes as well as a video show on traditional and modern silk weaving techniques.

Musée Hospitalier ⏲ – The Hôtel-Dieu, where for three centuries the sisters of the Order of St Martha cared for the sick, closed its doors in 1981 and reopened as a museum. It is a faithful representation of a small provincial hospital from the end of the 19C through the 1950s. The apothecary is fitted with 18C woodwork to accommodate medicinal herbs, flacons with ground-glass stoppers and ceramic urns. Past the operating and treatment rooms, the wooden linen press, the work of regional craftsmen, has room for 850 sheets. The wealth of bedding was due to the infrequency of wash days, which only came around twice a year. One of the two large wards has been recreated with its rows of curtained beds and antique furnishings. Bedridden patients attended mass through the window on the chapel, where the gilded altar bears a frontispiece of Cordova leather.

Continue along rue Jean-Morel and stop outside no 32.

The **Maison des Anglais** dating from the 16C, has mullioned windows on its upper storey with Gothic niches in between them. Two watch-turrets frame the façade.

Turn right onto rue André-Farinet.

No 29: 13C stone house; no 27: 15C half-timbered house, the **Maison Disson**; on the corner opposite, no 22: old 14C salt warehouse.

Turn right again onto rue Charles-de-Gaulle.

At no 9, the 13C-14C **Maison des Armagnacs** has two twin windows surmounted by trefoil arches. That on the left is decorated with a floral motif, and that on the right with a human face. The upper storey is half-timbered and overhangs the street.

Take rue Michon and then rue Chanteloup, a shopping street, to reach rue du Merle.

On the corners of rue du Merle and rue des Moulins (no 11), and of rue des Moulins and place St-Philibert, stand old half-timbered houses.

★**Couvent des Cordeliers** ⏲ – *Leave town via rue Ch.-M.-Rouillier heading W.*
This Franciscan monastery was founded in the 13C in St-Nizier-sous-Charlieu. Its unprotected site outside the town walls meant that it suffered quite a lot of damage both during the Hundred Years War and at the hands of roving bands of mercenaries. The monastery buildings have recently undergone restoration.

The **Gothic cloisters**, of pale gold stone, were sold to the United States and were to be taken down and rebuilt there, but luckily they were rescued at the last minute by the French State, which managed to buy them back in 1910. The arcades (late 14C-15C) are decorated with a fascinating variety of plant motifs. The capitals along the north arcade depict vices and virtues in an amusing series of figures and animals; one capital portrays the expressive face of a monk, another has the dance of death as its theme. The west arcade is adorned with a frieze of oak leaves with snails, rabbits and caterpillars on the capitals.

The single-nave church (late 14C), with no transept, has three side chapels on its south side (late 15C-early 16C) and has been partially restored. Originally, it was entirely decorated with paintings, but only a few mural paintings now remain in the chancel.

RELAX AT A B&B

Chambre d'Hôte La Violetterie – *71740 St-Maurice-lès-Châteauneuf - 10km/6.2mi NE of Charlieu by D 487 then D 987 (heading towards La Clayette) - ☎ 03 85 26 26 60 - closed 11 Nov to Easter - ✍ - 3 rooms: 37/46€.* This 19C mansion is charming with its perron and its gate fronting the courtyard. The bedrooms are light and give out onto the garden. The large dining hall-lounge features wainscoting and a fine fireplace. Charming hospitality.

Chambre d'Hôte Domaine du Château de Marchangy – *42190 St-Pierre-la-Noaille - 5.5km/3.5mi NW of Charlieu by D 227 then a minor road - ☎ 04 77 69 96 76 - marchangy@net-up.com - ✍ - 3 rooms: 68/91€ - meals 25€.* Set in lush parkland, this 18C château features a series of outbuildings, stables, a farmhouse and a courtyard. The calm, cosy and spacious rooms all have canopied beds. Relax on the terrace or by the pool and enjoy the view of the surrounding vineyards.

CHAROLLES

Population 3 027
Michelin map 320: F-11

The little town of Charolles is a pleasant place to stay at and a good starting point for jaunts within a range of 30km/18mi to visit sites as diverse as Cluny, La Clayette, the churches of the Brionnais region and Mont St-Vincent. Bygone capital of the counts of Charollais, the town draws its charm from the rivers (Arconce, Semence) and canals winding through the old streets and the flower-decked squares which invite relaxation.

Charollais cattle – The distinctive white cattle raised on the rich pasture lands in this area are valued for their tasty beef. Regional cattle markets take place several times a year; hundreds of hardy animals are offered for sale by local breeders, valued for their ancestral know-how.

Charollais bull

Ph. Gajic/MICHELIN

TOWN WALK

The town is proud of the 14C vestiges of its castle recalling the counts of Charollais: two towers known as the Tour du Téméraire and Tour des Diamants, the latter now serving as the town hall. There is a nice **view** of the landscape from the terrace gardens. The tourist office can be found at the bottom of rue Baudinot, in a former Poor Clare's convent house, once home to St Marguerite-Marie Alacoque (see PARAY-LE-MONIAL).

ON THE VILLAGE SQUARE

La Poste – *Av. de la Libération, near the church -* ☎ *03 85 24 11 32 - hotel-de-la-liberation-doucet@wanadoo.fr - closed 15 Nov-1 Dec Sun evenings and Mon - 21/55€.* On the village square, next to the post office, this house with its flower-filled façade is typical of the area. The sound-proofed rooms are each decorated in their own style and some of them have a balcony. The tasty meals are served in one of the two attractive dining rooms or on the terrace in summer.

Le Prieuré – Under the authority of the abbot at Cluny, this building welcomed pilgrims on their way to Santiago de Compostela. Note the collection of capitals and the remarkable carved beams of the chapter-house. The priory also houses a **museum** ⓥ, where you can see works by local artists Jean Laronze (1852-1937) and Paul-Louis Nigaud (1895-1937), and a collection of earthenware using the typical, bright motifs of Charolles – flowers, butterflies, dragonflies – and in particular, works by the region's seminal ceramics artist, Hippolyte Prost (1844-92).

Musée René-Davoine ⓥ – *On promenade St-Nicolas.* In the workshop of the sculptor (1888-1962), some major works are on view.

Institut charolais ⓥ – The Institute provides a wealth of information about Charolais beef.

LIFE ON THE FARM

Ferme-Auberge des Collines – *In the hamlet of Amanzé - 9km/5.6mi NW of Clayette by D 989 then D 279 -* ☎ *03 85 70 66 34 - philippe.paperin@wanadoo.fr - closed 1 Nov to Easter -* ✉ *- reservations required - 14.50€.* The pretty square tower of this farmhouse testifies to its long-standing past. The sturdy beams, tiled floors and stone walls make for a strong rustic atmosphere. The quiet rooms look out onto the fields or the blossoming garden. Charolais cows and pigs are reared on the property. Home-grown vegetables.

Ferme-Auberge de Lavaux – *71800 Châtenay - 8.5km/5.3mi E of La Clayette by D 987 then D 300 -* ☎ *03 85 28 08 48 - closed 1 Nov to Easter and Tue – reservations required - 11/20€.* This tastefully restored 19C farmhouse with old-fashioned turrets has a dining room under the eaves and a covered terrace. There is a charming room set up in the square tower, appointed with antique furniture, with a private balcony giving onto the courtyard.

Chambre d'Hôte M. et Mme Desmurs – *La Saigne - 71800 Varennes-sous-Dun - 4km/2.5mi E of La Clayette by D 987 then a minor road -* ☎ *03 85 28 12 79 - michelealaindesmurs@wanadoo.fr -* ✉ *- 3 rooms: 32/40€ - meals 16€.* This converted farmhouse is lost in the countryside. Two rooms are furnished in the old-fashioned style and one suite has been set up under the eaves. You may want to choose the third room, quite charming with its stone walls and tiled floor. Warm, friendly welcome. Charolais cows reared on the property.

EXCURSIONS

★**Mont des Carges** – *12km/8mi E.* From the esplanade, where there are monuments to the underground fighters of Beaubery and the Charollais battalion, an almost circular **view**★ takes in the Loire country to the west, all the Charollais and Brionnais regions to the south and the mountains of Beaujolais to the east.

La Clayette – *19km/11.4mi S.*
The village, host to horse shows and competitions, sits prettily above the Genette Valley and a shady lake. The original 14C château has undergone many transformations. The 17C turrets and orangery are among the most successful. The castle is home to a collection of Rolls-Royces from the roaring twenties.
🎦 Car enthusiasts can visit the nearby **Musée de l'Automobile** ⊘ in **Chaufailles** *(13km/8mi S of La Clayette)* which keeps a stock of some 100 vintage cars. If you visit the gift shop of this museum, you may need a garage to keep your purchase out of the rain!

★**Butte de Suin** – *17km/11mi E half way between Charolles and Cluny, near D 17.* Alt 593m/1 946ft. From the parking area, a footpath leads *(15min there and back)* to a viewing table offering a vast **panorama**★★.

CHÂTEAU-CHINON★

Population 2 307
Michelin map 6319: G-9 – Local map see Le MORVAN

The little town of Château-Chinon, main centre of the Morvan, occupies a picturesque **site**★ on the ridge that separates the Loire and Seine basins on the eastern edge of the Nivernais. Its favourable situation on the top of a hill, a natural fortress site easy to defend and from which one can see both the highlands of the Morvan and the Nivernais plain, made this position successively a Gallic settlement, a Roman camp and a feudal castle, which gave its name to the township. During centuries of battles, sieges and great feats of arms Château-Chinon has earned its motto *Petite ville, grand renom* (small town, great fame).

★**Musée du Septennat** ⊘ – The "seven years" in this museum's name refer to the President's term of office in France (now only 5 years), and the displays include presidential memorabilia and gifts given to **François Mitterrand** (1916-96) during his 14-year tenure beginning in 1981 (he had previously been mayor of the town). The 18C building, on a hilltop above the old town, was a Poor Clare's convent before its current civil, albeit reverential, incarnation.
🎦 Visitors will see photographs of world leaders and international events, medals and honorific decorations. The collection includes a surprising range of art from the five continents: from ancient artefacts to objects designed by famous creators, to handicrafts produced locally in the regions of the world. Jewellery from the Middle East is ornate; oriental furnishings are precisely crafted; African objects are

Eating out

BUDGET

Auberge de la Madonette – *58110 St-Péreuse - 14km/8.7mi W of Château-Chinon by D 978 and then a minor road -* ☎ *03 86 84 45 37 - closed 15 Dec-5 Feb, Tue evenings and Wed except Jul-Aug - 10.52/42.68€.* A thriving garden is the pretty setting for this friendly restaurant full of country charm. The old-fashioned recipes and warm welcome will make your meal here a highly enjoyable experience.

Where to stay

BUDGET

Camping Municipal Les Soulins – *58120 Corancy - 10.5km/6.5mi N of Château-Chinon by D 37, D 12 and D 161 -* ☎ *03 86 78 01 62 - open 15 Jun-15 Sep -* ✍ *- reservations recommended - 42 sites: 10.22€.* This camp site near the lake enjoys a lovely view of the wooded hills nearby. Playground for children.

Chambre d'Hôte Les Chaumottes – *58120 St-Hilaire-en-Morvan - 5.5km/3.5mi W of Château-Chinon by D 978 -* ☎ *03 86 85 22 33 - paul.colas@libertysurf.fr - closed Oct-Apr -* ✍ *- 3 rooms: 30/40€.* A thoroughly restored 14C manor lost in the middle of the countryside. Two of the largish, comfortable rooms look out onto Château-Chinon. Breakfast is served in the colourful dining room decorated in rustic style. Extremely good value. Self-catering accommodation available.

housed in the museum's extension (note the stuffed and mounted lion). Finally, one section has been set aside for gifts from various admirers both famous and anonymous, who thus expressed their affection for their president.

Musée du Costume ⊙ – The costume museum, which is housed in the 18C Hôtel de Buteau-Ravisy, exhibits a large collection of French civilian dress, fashion accessories and folk traditions (replicas).

★★**Panorama from the Calvaire** – *15min on foot there and back from square Aligre.* The calvary (609m/1 998ft) is built on the site of the fortified Gallic settlement and the ruins of the fortress.

There is a very fine circular panorama *(viewing table)* taking in Château-Chinon and its slate roofs, and further off the wooded crests of the Morvan. The two summits of the Haut-Folin (901m/2 956ft) and the Mont Préneley (855m/2 805ft) can be seen to the south-east. At the foot of the hill the valley of the Yonne opens to the east, whereas to the west the view stretches beyond the Bazois as far as the Loire Valley.

★**Promenade du Château** – A road *(starting in faubourg de Paris and returning via rue du Château)* encircles the hill half way up the slope. Through the trees there are glimpses of the Yonne gorge on one side, and the countryside which is visible from the calvary on the other.

Old town – Starting from the Porte Notre-Dame, all that remains of a 15C rampart, you can take a pleasant stroll through the medieval streets of Château-Chinon, particularly lively at weekends.

The **monumental fountain** opposite the town hall, composed of independent articulated sculptures, is the work of Jean Tinguely and Niki de Saint Phalle.

The Gargouillats district around the college features several buildings boasting a futuristic style.

EXCURSION

Lac de Pannesière-Chaumard – *Drive N out of Château-Chinon then bear right onto D 37 and left onto D 12. A scenic road runs right round the lake.*

⊙ The reservoir (7.5km/5mi long), with a capacity of 18 145 million gallons, forms a glorious expanse of water in an attractive **setting**★ amid wooded hills. A road runs all the way round it and along the top of the dam, giving a pretty **view** of the numerous inlets of the lake with the summits of the Haut Morvan outlined against the sky in the background.

Before reaching the dam, make a detour to the NE along D 301 to Ouroux-en-Morvan.

Ouroux-en-Morvan – There is a charming view from this village of the surrounding hills and a stretch of the Pannesière reservoir. Two paths *(15min round trip)* lead up to the **viewpoint**★ from the village square and the church.

Drive back towards the lake on D 12 via Courgermain.

The last mile or so of this downhill run towards the Pannesière reservoir provides superb bird's-eye views of this stretch of water.

Before Chaumard, turn sharp right on D 303, which runs along the bank of the reservoir and across the dam.

Barrage de Pannesière-Chaumard – This 340m/1 115ft-long and 50m/164ft-high dam is supported on numerous slender arches and flanked by massive concrete embankments on either river bank. Twelve supporting buttresses rise from the bottom of the gorge. The dam controls the flow of water in the Seine basin. The hydroelectric power station downstream produces nearly 18 million kWh per year.

Downstream of the main dam (near D 944) is a control dam (220m/722ft long) composed of 33 slender arches. Whereas the turbines consume water at the rate of demand for electricity, the control dam enables the discharged water to be returned to the Yonne at a constant rate and also supplies water to the Nivernais Canal.

Beyond the dam, turn left on D 944 then left again on D 161 and follow the west shore of the lake back to Château-Chinon.

▶▶ **Vallon du Touron** – Drive 9km/5.6mi east to **Arleuf**, where almost all the western gable ends of the houses are slated to protect them against the rain. Head north along the scenic D 500 which crosses the Touron and veers north-west, running along the hillside overlooking the green Touron Valley.

CHÂTILLON-COLIGNY

Population 1 946
Michelin map 318: O-5

The town is situated on the banks of the River Loing and the Canal de Briare which are lined with old wash-houses. It was the birthplace, in 1519, of Admiral **Gaspard de Coligny**, a victim of the St Bartholomew's Day massacre in 1572. In 1937 a monument was erected (over the site of the room where he was born) in the park of the château, by Dutch subscription, to recall the marriage of Louise de Coligny, the admiral's daughter, to William the Silent, Prince of Orange. As the male line of the Coligny family died out in 1657, the Châtillon demesne reverted to the Montmorencys and then to the Montmorency-Luxembourg line.

In 1893 the French writer Colette married Willy (Henri Gauthier-Villars) at Châtillon-Coligny, where she lived with her brother Dr Robineau.

Château – When the Maréchal de Châtillon replaced his medieval castle with a magnificent Renaissance residence in the 16C, he retained the polygonal Romanesque keep (26m/85ft high) built between 1180 and 1190 by the Count of Sancerre. The 12C keep and its underground access passages survived the Revolution, but all that remained of the 16C building were three huge terraces and a well believed to have been carved by Jean Goujon.

Not far from here are an old town gate and the church (16C-17C) with a free-standing bell-tower.

Museum ⓥ – The museum is in the 15C hospital. Besides portraits and literature on the history of the Coligny and Montmorency families, it contains a wonderful Louis-Philippe period pedestal table with Sèvres porcelain plaques which depict the Maréchal de Luxembourg and the Constables of Montmorency. A small room is devoted to local archaeology from the Iron Age to the Merovingian period: Celtic tombs, Gallo-Roman coins, barbarian jewellery. The Becquerel room is devoted to four scientists from the family of the same name. Henri Becquerel was the most famous; he discovered natural radioactivity in 1896 and shared the Nobel Prize with Pierre and Marie Curie in 1903.

▶▶ **Arboretum national des Barres** ⓥ – 8km/5mi NW. ⚑ 3 000 species of trees and bushes, some of them nearly 150 years old.

▶▶ **Rogny-les-Sept-Écluses** – 10km/6.2mi S. ⓒ A series of seven locks dating from the mid-17C built to enable the Briare Canal to negotiate a drop of 34m/112ft. They ceased to operate in 1887. Today, the canal skirts round the hill, flowing through six locks which are more spaced out than the original ones.

J. Damase/MICHELIN

The seven locks at Rogny are dry now

The trim little town of Châtillon is set on the banks of the young Seine, which is joined here by the abundant waters of the River Douix, flowing from a resurgent spring. Sheep breeding has for several centuries been the main source of wealth on the dry plateaux of the Châtillon region (Châtillonnais), and up to the 18C Châtillon was the centre of a very flourishing wool industry.

From one century to the next – A hundred years separate the two major events in the history of Châtillon.

In February 1814, while **Napoleon I** was defending every inch of the approaches to Paris, a peace congress was held in Châtillon between France and the countries allied against her (Austria, Russia, England and Prussia). Napoleon rejected the harsh conditions laid down, the fighting resumed, only to end soon afterwards with the downfall of his Empire.

In September 1914 French troops retreated in the face of a violent attack by the Germans. **Général Joffre**, Commander-in-Chief of the French armies, set up his headquarters at Châtillon-sur-Seine, where he issued his famous order of 6 September: "We are about to engage in a battle on which the fate of our country depends, and it is important to remind all ranks that the moment has passed for looking back...". The German advance was halted and the French counter-attack on the Marne became a great victory.

★**Source de la Douix** – The source of the River Douix is to be found in a spot of astonishing beauty, at the foot of a rocky escarpment (over 30m/98ft high) set in lovely green scenery. This resurgent spring collects the waters of other small springs and infiltrations of the limestone plateau. The normal flow is 132gal a second but this can reach 660gal in flood periods. The promenade, laid out on a rocky platform, affords a view over the town, the valley and the swimming pool.

Église St-Vorles ⊘ – The church, built on a shaded terrace with a view over the lower town and valley, dominates the Bourg district, city of the bishops, which remained independent until the 16C.

The building is over 1 000 years old; it has retained one or two particularities of Carolingian architecture: double bell-tower, double transept, upper chapel. The chancel has an archetypal Romanesque appearance, and in many places there are Lombard arches. The underground chapel of St-Bernard is where the miracle of lactation is supposed to have happened as the saint knelt before the statue of Notre-Dame-de-Toutes-Grâces. The north transept contains a Renaissance sculpture group of the Entombment.

Not far from the church are the ruins of the château and tower of Gissey. In the cemetery, you will find the tomb of Maréchal Marmont, who served under Napoleon and who was born at Châtillon.

★**Musée du Châtillonais** ⊘ – This museum is in the Maison Philandrier, an attractive Renaissance building, but scheduled to move to the old Notre-Dame abbey. There are several interesting Gallo-Roman exhibits – pottery, vases and statuettes – discovered in the 19C and early 20C during local excavations, particularly at Vertault *(20km/12mi W of Châtillon)*. The pride of the museum is however the extraordinary archaeological find made in January 1953 at Mont Lassois near Vix.

★★**The Treasure of Vix** – *A reconstitution of the tomb is displayed behind glass.* The treasures were found in a 6C BC grave containing the remains of a woman: jewellery of inestimable value, the debris of a state chariot, countless gold and bronze items and a huge bronze vase (1.64m/5ft high, 1.45m/4.5ft wide and 208kg/459lb in weight). The rich decoration of the vase – sculpted frieze made of applied panels in high relief portraying a row of helmeted warriors and chariots and Gorgon's heads on

Bronze vase, Treasure of Vix

N. Thibault/HOAQUI

the handles – reveals a highly developed art form influenced by the archaic Greek style. The showcases contain other items found in the tomb of the Gaulish princess: a massive golden diadem, bronze and silver goblets, wine jugs, bracelets and other jewellery.

Other rooms in the museum show items discovered at various sites around the region. Many objects from Vertault illustrate aspects of daily life in Gallo-Roman times. There is a big collection of **ex-votos** in stone which were found in sanctuaries in Tremblois and Essarois, in particular.

▶▶ **Forêt de Châtillon** – This vast forest, extending over 9 000ha/22 240 acres to the south-east of Châtillon-sur-Seine, offers ramblers all the treasures of an unspoilt natural environment. The **Abbaye du Val-des-Choues** ⊘, in the heart of the forest, houses collections relating to forests, hunting and gypsum. *Son et lumière* shows in summer.

Forêt de CHAUX★

Michelin map 321: D-4 to E-4

This 20 000ha/49 420-acre forest, located between the River Doubs and River Loue, is one of the largest forests in France. It originally belonged to the sovereigns, who hunted here; the nearby population also enjoyed extensive rights to the use of the land. These rights disappeared in the 19C, when the areas at the edge of the forest were given to the community *(forêts communales)*, whereas the central part (13 000ha/32 123 acres) became the property of the State *(forêt domaniale)*.

For centuries the forest has been a vital resource for the factories at its edge: salt works at **Salins** and **Arc-et-Senans**, forges at Fraisans, glassworks at La Vieille Loye and so on. The previous layout of the forest in coppices no longer conforms to modern needs, and the forest is now managed with more modern methods. Oak predominates (60%), followed by beech (20%) and various deciduous (15%) and coniferous trees (5%).

A tourist zone has been established to the west of the forest, in order to protect the plants and wildlife elsewhere. Facilities include a bridle path (the *bretelle du Grand-8*), forest footpaths, a Fitness trail, car parks and part of the long-distance footpath GR 59A from Dole to Arc-et-Senans, three game enclosures in which you can see various types of deer and wild boar and a nature reserve (88ha/217 acres) where deer and wild boar roam at liberty. You can observe these from one of two raised observation posts, or by strolling around the forest.

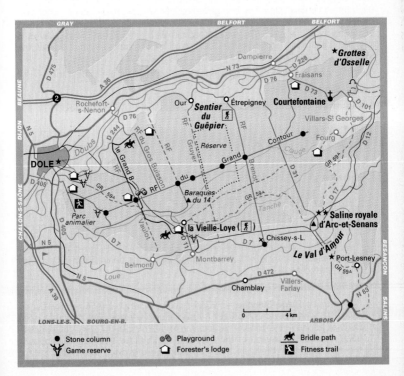

● Stone column	●● Playground	🐎 Bridle path
🦌 Game reserve	⌂ Forester's lodge	🏃 Fitness trail

In the forest

STAND – A group of trees growing on a particular piece of land.

GROVE – A stand of trees grown from seed (unlike copses, where the new shoots grow from old stumps). A grove is said to be regular when the trees are obviously of about the same age.

ROUGH TIMBER – The trunk of a felled tree, stripped of its branches, ready to be turned into timber.

ROND – The French name for a point where forest roads meet. It may be named after a former forest warden or historical event.

There is a 1 400ha/34 594-acre game reserve *(closed to the public)* at the heart of the forest. The Grand Contour forest road between Dole and Fourg is marked with seven stone pillars, 4.5m/177ft tall, which serve as milestones.

La Vieille Loye – This is the only village community in the forest. It used to be inhabited by woodcutters, who lived in huts, or *baraques*, at the centre of each forest area. Some of these woodcutters' huts, the **Baraques du 14** ⓧ, have been restored. A little further on are an old well and a communal village oven (the wood-cutters used to have to pay the landlord a fee – *banalité* – to use the oven, which thus came to be called the *four banal*).

Le sentier du Guêpier – This 4km/2.5mi-long path offers an interesting insight into the history of the forest. In **Etrepigney**, the starting point of the trail, a *bacul* – small woodcutter's cottage – has been reconstructed, and in **Our** a 19C bread oven has been restored.

★**Grottes d'Osselle** ⓧ – ▣ These caves are set in a cliff overlooking a meander in the Doubs. They were discovered in the 13C and have been visited since 1504. During the Revolution, the dry galleries were used as refuges and chapels by local priests; a clay altar can still be seen. A cave bear's skeleton has been assembled from bones found among the debris.

Out of 8km/5mi of long, regularly shaped galleries, leading in the same direction as the mountain ridge, 1.3km/0.8mi have been adapted and opened to visitors. The first galleries, with walls somewhat blackened by the smoke of resin torches, contain concretions which are still being formed by running water. A low passage leads to galleries of stalagmites of almost pure white calcite, some of which have been tinted various colours by iron oxide, copper or manganese. Some niches dec-orated with small, delicate stalactites make pretty tableaux by themselves or reflect in the pools of the cave. The underground river in one of the lower galleries is spanned by a small stone bridge (built in 1751), enabling visitors to see the so-called organ gallery and gallery of the white columns.

Le Val d'Amour – *See Saline royale d'ARC-ET-SENANS.*

★**Dole** – *See DOLE.*

★★**Saline royale d'Arc-et-Senans** – *See Saline royale d'ARC-ET-SENANS.*

DINE IN THE FOREST ...

Auberge de la Lavandière – *R. de la Lavandière - 25440 Lavans-Quingey - 12.5km/7.8mi SE of Courtefontaine by D 101 until you reach Byans-sur-Doubs then D 13 to Quingey and follow directions to Lavans-Quingey -* ☎ *03 81 63 69 28 - la.lavandiere@wanadoo.fr - closed 20 Dec-4 Jan, Sat lunchtime, Sun evenings and Mon - 12/32€.* A vast barn is the setting for this rustic-style restaurant with imposing beams and old-fashioned fireplace. In fine weather, meals can be taken on the large table outside, near the leafy forest and its lively brook. Specialities include veal and salted ham on the bone served with morels and Comté cheese.

... SLEEP UNDER THE STARS

Camping La Plage Blanche – *39380 Ounans - 2km/1.2mi SE of Montbarrey by D 71 -* ☎ *03 84 37 69 63 - reservation@la-plage-blanche.com - open 30 Mar to Sep - reservations recommended - 220 sites: 17.38€ - meals avail-able.* Relax on the shores of the river and watch brave swimmers plunge into the cool waters of the Loue that run alongside this camp site. Riding centre nearby. Recreational facilities for children.

Abbaye de CÎTEAUX

Michelin map 320: K-7 – 14km/9mi E of Nuits-St-Georges.

Cîteaux, like Cluny, is an important centre in western Christendom. It was here, among the *cistels* or reeds, that Robert, Abbot of Molesme, founded the Order of Cistercians in 1098, an off-shoot of Cluny, which under the great driving force of St Bernard (he joined the community of Cîteaux in 1112 and later became abbot of Clairvaux), spread its influence throughout the world.

The abbey of La Trappe, which was attached to Cîteaux in 1147 and reformed in 1664, has given its name to several monasteries which joined the Strict Observance. In 1892, the Order was officially divided into two branches; Cistercian monks who may devote themselves to a pastoral or intellectual life, such as teaching, and the more numerous Trappist monks who follow a strictly contemplative vocation.

During the Revolution, Cîteaux nearly perished in its entirety. The monks were expelled and did not return until 1898 (when the abbey was again proclaimed the mother house of the Order).

Tour of the abbey – The church containing the tombs of the first dukes of Burgundy and of Philippe Pot *(now in the Louvre, Paris)* was completely destroyed. All that remains are relics of the library, faced with 15C enamelled bricks, which incorporates six arches of a Gothic cloister and a vaulted room on the first floor. There is also a handsome 18C building near the chapel and another late-17C building beside the river.

Notre-Dame de Citeaux ⊘ – A new church was built and inaugurated in 1998 to commemorate the 900th anniversary of the foundation of the abbey.

▶**Église de Bagnot** – *9km S of the abbey*. The church has interesting 15C frescoes in a naive style.

From the church in Bagnot

S. Sauvignier/MICHELIN

CLAMECY

Population 4 806
Michelin map 319: E-7

Clamecy is situated in the heart of the pretty country of the Vaux d'Yonne, junction point of the Morvan, the Nivernais and Lower Burgundy. The old town, with its narrow winding streets, is perched on a spur overlooking the confluence of the River Yonne and River Beuvron. There are many pleasant walks along the hillsides.

Clamecy remains "the town of beautiful reflections and graceful hills" described by **Romain Rolland** (1866-1944), the French writer and philosopher, who is buried in the Nivernais not far from his native town.

Bethlehem in Burgundy – It is hard to understand why a bishopric existed at Clamecy, especially when there were already bishops at Auxerre, Nevers and Autun. One has to go back to the Crusades to find the answer.

Guillaume IV of Nevers, who left for Palestine in 1167, contracted the plague there and died at Acre in 1168. In his will he asked to be buried in Bethlehem and bequeathed to its bishops one of his properties in Clamecy, the hospital of Pantenor, on condition that it should be a refuge for the bishops of Bethlehem in the case of Palestine falling into the hands of the infidels.

When the Latin kingdom of Jerusalem fell, the bishop of Bethlehem took refuge at Clamecy in the domain bequeathed to the bishopric by Guillaume IV. From 1225 up to the French Revolution, 50 bishops succeeded each other at Clamecy. This episode is recalled in the dedication of the modern church (1927) of Our Lady of Bethlehem (Notre-Dame de Bethléem).

Log floating – This method of moving timber, which goes back to the 16C, brought wealth to the river port of Clamecy for nearly 300 years. It was organised on the River Cure by a rich timber merchant from Paris, Jean Rouvet.

The logs, cut in the forests of the Upper Morvan, were piled along the banks of the rivers and marked with their owners' signs. On an agreed day, the dams holding back the rivers were opened and the logs were thrown into the flood which carried them in a mass down to Clamecy. This was the floating of *bûches perdues* (free logs). All along the banks an army of workmen regulated the flow of logs as best they could.

At Clamecy, a dam stopped the wood, the timbermen with their long hooks harpooned the logs, dragging them from the water and putting them in piles according to their marks. In mid-March, at the time of the flood-water, immense rafts of wood, called *trains*, were sent down the Yonne and the Seine towards Paris, where the wood was used for heating.

The building of the Nivernais Canal ended this method of transportation by *trains* with the introduction of barges. The last *train* of wood left Clamecy in 1923.

Today all this logging activity has ended on both the Yonne and the Cure but Clamecy continued to operate the largest industrial charcoal factory in France until 1983 using supplies from the local forests.

TOWN WALK

Old houses – From place du 19-Août take rue de la Tour and rue Bourgeoise; turn right on rue Romain-Rolland and rue de la Monnaie (Maison du Tisserand and Maison du saint accroupi). Follow rue du Grand-Marché and place du Général-Sanglé-Ferrière to return to place du 19-Août.

Views of the town – From quai des Moulins-de-la-Ville there is also an attractive view of the houses overlooking the mill-race. From quai du Beuvron the picturesque quai des Îles is visible.

The Bethlehem Bridge, on which stands a tall statue in memory of the loggers, provides a good overall view of the town and its quays.

Upstream on the point overlooking the Nivernais Canal and the river stands a bronze bust of Jean Rouvet.

L'homme du Futur – Bronze statue by the artist César, erected in 1987.

ADDITIONAL SIGHTS

★Église St-Martin – The church was built between the end of the 12C and the beginning of the 16C. Episodes in the life of St Martin are illustrated on the arch stones over the door (damaged during the Revolution).

The interior reveals the rectangular plan and the square ambulatory characteristic of Burgundian churches. The rood screen was constructed by Viollet-le-Duc to counteract the bowing of certain pillars in the chancel. The first chapel in the south aisle, lit by fine stained-glass windows, contains an early-16C triptych of the Crucifixion and two low-relief sculptures from the 16C rood screen (destroyed in 1773) which depict the Last Supper and the Entombment. The organ is by Cavaillé-Coll (1862).

Musée d'Art et d'Histoire Romain-Rolland ⊙ – A bust of the writer stands in front of the museum. The museum is installed in the Duc de Bellegarde's mansion. Paintings include French and Dutch works. There is Nevers and Rouen pottery and an archaeological collection. A display is devoted to the old practice of floating of logs down the river. A room with a fine timberwork ceiling contains works by Charles Loupot (1892-1962), a famous poster designer who lived in Clamecy.

An underground passage leads to the Romain Rolland rooms which exhibit souvenirs of the author and various editions of his works.

EXCURSIONS

Druyes-les-Belles-Fontaines – *18km/11.2mi NW*. The hilltop ruins of the 12C **feudal castle** ⊙ are best seen from the south, along D 148 or D 104. From the road to Courson-les-Carrières, a 14C fortified gate gives access to the rocky outcrop occupied by the old village and the castle ruins.

In the lower part of the village stands the 12C Église St-Romain (fine doorway). The Druyes springs up in a picturesque site near the church.

Carrière souterraine d'Aubigny ⊙ – *6km/3.7mi N of Druyes along D 148.*
◎ This underground stone quarry dates back to the Roman Empire. The limestone was first used for sacred funeral items, later to build castles, and most prominently in the late 19C in Paris, in the construction of monuments

La carrière d'Aubigny

Stonecutters' secrets

such as the Hôtel de Ville and the Opera. In addition to an explanation of the formation and uses of this 150-million-year-old mineral, exhibits display cutting and sculpting tools along with other local minerals and stones.

▶▶ **Vallée de l'Yonne from Clamecy to Corbigny** – *38km/24mi along D 951 and D 985; allow 2hr 30min.* The road runs alongside the river and the Canal du Nivernais overlooked by wooded hills. The itinerary is dotted with pleasant riverside villages such as Armes and hilltop ones such as Metz-le-Comte and Tannay offering wide views of the picturesque Yonne Valley.

CLUNY★★

Population 4 376
Michelin map 320: H-11 – Local map see MÂCONNAIS

The name of Cluny evokes the high point of medieval spirituality. The Order of Cluny exercised an immense influence on the religious, intellectual, political and artistic life of the West. Up to the time of the Revolution, each century left the mark of its style on Cluny. From 1798 to 1823 this centre of civilisation was ransacked but from the magnificence of what remains one can nevertheless get an idea of the majesty of the basilica. For a good overall view of the town, climb the Tour des Fromages.

CLUNY, LIGHT OF THE WORLD

The rise – The influence of the abbey of Cluny developed rapidly from the moment it was founded in the 10C, particularly through the founding of numerous daughter abbeys. "You are the light of the world" said Pope Urban II, himself from Cluny, as were many other popes, to **St Hugh** in 1098. When St Hugh died in 1109, having begun the construction of the magnificent abbey church which **Peter the Venerable**, abbot from 1122 to 1156, was to finish, he left the abbey in a state of great prosperity. In 1155 there were 460 monks resident in the abbey alone, and many young men from all over Europe flocked to this capital of learning.

The decline – Rich and powerful, the monks of Cluny slipped gradually into a worldly, luxurious way of life that was strongly condemned by **St Bernard**. He denounced the bishops who "cannot go four leagues from their house without a retinue of 60 horses and sometimes more... Will the light shine only if it is in a candelabrum of gold or silver?".
The 14C saw the decline of Cluny's influence and power. Its abbots divided their time between the abbey and Paris where, at the end of the 15C, Jacques d'Amboise rebuilt the mansion erected after 1330 by one of his predecessors, Pierre de Châlus. This private lodging (the Hôtel de Cluny) was often used by the kings of France, and gives an idea of the princely luxury with which the abbots of Cluny surrounded themselves. Falling *in commendam* in the 16C, the rich abbey became nothing but a quarry for spoils. It was devastated during the Wars of Religion and the library was sacked.

Destruction – In 1790 the abbey was closed. Its desecration began when the Revolution was at its height. In September 1793, the local authority gave the order for the tombs to be demolished and sold as building material. In 1798 the buildings were sold to a property speculator from Mâcon who demolished the nave and sold off the magnificent abbey church bit by bit until by 1823 all that was left standing was what we see today.

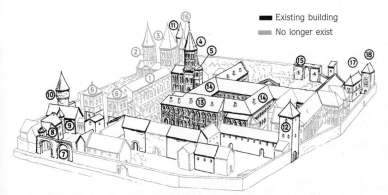

Cluny Abbey at the end of the 18C
1) Abbey Church of St Peter and St Paul – 2) Clocher des Bisans – 3) Clocher du Chœur – 4) Clocher de l'Eau-Bénite – 5) Clocher de l'Horloge – 6) The Barabans – 7) Main Gate – 8) Palais de Jean de Bourbon – 9) Palais de Jacques d'Amboise – 10) Tour Fabry – 11) Tour Ronde – 12) Tour des Fromages – 13) Pope Gelasius Façade – 14) Cloistral Ranges – 15) Garden Gate – 16) Clocher des Lampes – 17) Flour store – 18) Tour du Moulin

Where to stay

MODERATE

Hôtel Bourgogne – Pl. de l'Abbaye - ☎ 03 85 59 00 58 - contact@hotel-cluny.com - closed Dec-Jan Tue and Wed in Feb - 13 rooms: 75/115€ - ⌑ 9.50€ - restaurant 20.50/39€. The poet Lamartine was a regular visitor at this hotel facing Cluny Abbey. The rooms are somewhat sober but they are comfortable and well-kept. Cosy dining room with fireplace. Light meals can be had in the bar at lunchtime. Terrace in the flower-filled patio.

Chambre d'Hôte Le Moulin des Arbillons – 71520 Bourgvilain - 8km/5mi S of Cluny by D 980 then D 22 - ☎ 03 85 50 82 83 - arbillon@club-internet.fr - open Jul-Aug - ⌑ - 5 rooms: 46/72€. This 18C mill stands next to a 19C mansion in the middle of a park, overlooking the village. The rooms have been appointed with family heirlooms. Breakfast is served in the colourful orangery. Wine tastings available and bottles for sale.

EXPENSIVE

Château d'Igé – 71960 Igé - 13km/8.1mi E of Cluny by D 134 - ☎ 03 85 33 33 99 - ige@relaischateaux.com - closed Dec-Feb - ▣ - 8 rooms: 107.50/131€ - ⌑ 13€ - restaurant 33/65€. Feel like a trip back to the Middle Ages? Then this château is the perfect place for you: medieval dining hall with impressive timberwork and a huge fireplace, cosy bedrooms with personalised decor... Thoughtful cuisine made with fresh seasonal produce. Pretty garden.

Shopping

Dentelle Cluny - Aymé de Réa – 15 r. Lamartine - ☎ 03 85 59 31 78 - brunoindiana@aol.com - open Apr-Sep: daily 9am-8pm - closed Oct-Mar. A young craftsman has set up his lacemaking studio in a small medieval building. He designs original pieces inspired by traditional motifs and can demonstrate the legendary Cluny stitch before your very eyes.

Horses galore

Haras National – 2 r. des Prés - ☎ 03 85 59 85 00 - www.haras-nationaux.fr - daily 9am-7pm. Commissioned by Napoleon I, these stables were built with stones taken from the nearby abbey church. They house around 50 stallions which, during the breeding season (Mar to mid-Jul), are sent to the eight stud farms of the area.

Sit back and relax

Au Péché Mignon – 25 r. Lamartine - ☎ 03 85 59 11 21 - open daily 7.30am-8pm - closed 2 weeks in Jan. This patisserie-tea room provides a mouthwatering selection of cakes and delicacies of all kinds: perle d'or (almond paste with griotte cherries), tomato jam...

Le Cellier de l'Abbaye – 13 r. Municipale - ☎ 03 85 59 04 00 - cellier1@club-internet.fr - open Tue-Sat 9.30am-12.30pm, 2.30-7pm; Sun 10am-12.30pm (open Mon 14 Jul-15 Aug) - closed Feb. A total of 250 Burgundy wines, 90 whiskies and a wide choice of local liquors are on offer in this superb store made of 13C stone.

TOWN WALK

Tour Fabry and Tour Ronde – The Fabry Tower (1347) with its pepper-pot roof and the older Ronde Tower are visible from the garden near the town hall.

Hôtel de Ville – The town hall now occupies the building erected for abbots Jacques and Geoffroy d'Amboise at the end of the 15C and beginning of the 16C. The garden front has an original decoration in the Italian Renaissance style.

Romanesque houses – Cluny has preserved fine Romanesque dwellings: note in particular a 12C house at no 25 rue de la République and the 13C mint (restored) at no 6 rue d'Avril; others can be seen along rue Lamartine.

Tour des Fromages ⊘ – From the top (120 steps) of this curiously named 11C tower (cheese tower) there is a good view of Cluny: the abbey, the Clocher d'Eau-Bénite, the flour store and adjoining mill tower, the belfry of St-Marcel and Notre-Dame.

Église Notre-Dame – The square in front of the church has an 18C fountain and old houses. The church, built shortly after 1100, was altered and enlarged in the Gothic period. It was originally preceded by a narthex of which only the flagging remains. The 13C doorway is badly weathered.

The interior is a good example of Cluniac architecture. The lantern tower has carved brackets. The stalls and panelling date from 1644. The stained glass in the choir is modern.

Église St-Marcel ⊘ – This church has a fine octagonal Romanesque **belfry**★ of three storeys, topped by a graceful 15C polygonal brick spire (42m/138ft high). There is an excellent view of the belfry and the apse from the road (D 980).

★★ ANCIENNE ABBAYE ⊘ *1hr*

To visit the abbey, apply to the Musée Ochier.

Most of the abbey church of St Peter and St Paul, called Cluny III, was built between 1088 and 1130 by the abbots St Hugh and Peter the Venerable. The foundations of two previous 10C and 11C buildings have been uncovered, together with those of a Gallo-Roman villa, south of the 12C basilica on the site of the former cloisters in the south-east corner of the present cloisters.

Cluny III, symbol of the primacy of the Cluniac Order, then at its most powerful, was the largest Christian church (177m/581ft long) until the reconstruction of St Peter's in Rome (186m/610ft long). It consisted of a narthex, a nave and four aisles, two transepts, five belfries *(clochers)*, two towers *(tours)*, 301 windows and 225 decorated stalls. The painted apsidal vault rested on a marble colonnade. It is difficult to imagine the full extent of the old building as only the south transepts remain standing.

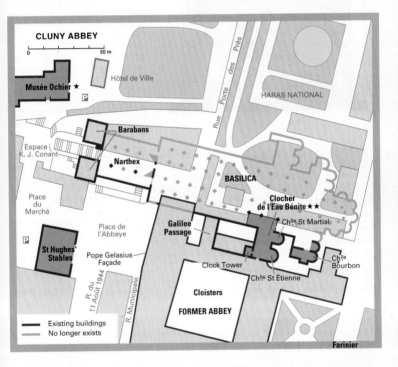

Narthex – The site of the narthex is now bisected by rue Kenneth-J.-Conant. During excavations in 1949 the base of the south end of the façade was uncovered, together with the footings of the doorway which was flanked by the square Barabans towers of which only the foundations survive. Subsequently the south aisle of the narthex uncovered revealing a wall of uniform construction with pilasters attached to semi-columns.

The long Gothic façade (restored) in place de l'Abbaye is named after Pope Gelasius who died at Cluny in 1119 *(abbey entrance)*. By standing well back one can see the belfry and the high clock tower. To the rear are the stables named after St Hugh and the hostel.

Cloisters – The 18C monastic buildings form a harmonious group enclosing the vast cloisters; two great flights of stone steps with wrought-iron railings occupy two corners. There is a handsome sundial in the garth.

Galilee Passage – The 11C passage, which was used by the great Benedictine processions, linked the Galilee (a covered porch) of Cluny II with the south aisle of the great church of Cluny III.

Traces of the church of St Peter and St Paul – From the dimensions of the **south transepts** it is possible to calculate the audacious size of the whole basilica. Its height (30m/98ft under the barrel vaulting, 32m/105ft under the dome) is exceptional in Romanesque architecture. The church consisted of three bays; the central bay, surmounted by an octagonal cupola on squinches, supports the handsome **Clocher de l'Eau-Bénite★★** (Holy Water Belfry). St-Étienne (St Stephen's Chapel) is Romanesque; St Martial's Chapel dates from the 14C. The right arm of the smaller transept contains the Bourbon Chapel with its late-15C Gothic architecture and a Romanesque apse. The contrast between them emphasizes the transition from Romanesque to late-Gothic art.

Monastic buildings – The buildings, which house the School of Arts and Crafts, were nicknamed Little Versailles owing to the elegant Classical east façade.

S. Sauvignier/MICHELIN

Holy Water Belfry

Flour Store – The storehouse (54m/177ft long) was built in the late 13C against the early-13C Mill Tower (Tour du Moulin); in the 18C it was truncated (by about 20m/65ft) to reveal the south end of the façade of the cloister building overlooking the gardens.

The low storeroom with its two ranges of ogive vaulting houses sculptures including a doorway with recessed arches from Pope Gelasius' palace.

The **high chamber**, with its beautiful oak roof, makes an effective setting for various pieces of sculpture from the abbey. The very fine **capitals** *(see photograph)* and column shafts saved from the ruins of the chancel of the abbey church are exhibited by means of a scale model of the chancel: the eight capitals on their columns are set in a semicircle round the old Pyrenean marble altar consecrated by Urban II in 1095. They are the first examples of the Burgundian Romanesque sculpture which was to blossom in Vézelay, Autun and Saulieu. The two models, of the great doorway and of the apse of the basilica, were designed by Professeur Conant, the archaeologist who directed the excavations from 1928 to 1950.

The flour store is the venue of most of the classical concerts on the programme of Les Grandes Heures de Cluny *(late July to late August)*. After the concert, guests are invited to a wine tasting in the cellars. At the end of August, the music scene is taken over by the Orchestre National de Jazz.

ADDITIONAL SIGHT

★**Musée Ochier (Art et Archéologie)** ⓥ – This museum is in the former abbey palace, a gracious building of the 15C, built by Abbot Jean de Bourbon, and is contemporary with the Cluny Mansion in Paris.

Remains of the abbey found during excavations carried out by the American archaeologist KJ Conant are on display together with some outstanding works of lay sculpture. Models in the entrance hall and, upstairs, an audio-visual reconstruction of Cluny III enable visitors to appreciate the greatness of the abbey. Two basement rooms contain stone fragments of the monument: part of the frieze of the narthex and arcading from the choir screen.

Upstairs, sculptures and architectural elements from various façades give an insight into the decoration of medieval houses (harvest frieze, capital decorated with a shoemaker, lintel carved with a tournament scene).

Out of the 4 500 works housed in the library, more than half come from the abbey library (a few incunabula).

Displayed on the ground floor is a collection of 18C objects (sedan chair in painted wood, painted- and gilt-metal tabernacle, chalice, monstrance etc).

On the other side of the entrance hall you can see some ornamental tiling illustrating the techniques used during the Middle Ages.

EXCURSIONS

★**La Voie Verte** – ⓢ Hiking and biking trail. *See CHALON-SUR-SAÔNE.*

Taizé – *10km/6mi N along D 981.* The charming village of Taizé amid the hills of the Grosne region hosts tens of thousands of young people from all over the world every summer, as they meet to pray.

In 1940 Pastor Schutz (now called **Brother Roger**) settled in Taizé and established an ecumenical community which now numbers over 90 brothers, who take life-long vows and are drawn from various Christian churches (Catholic and Protestant) and from about 20 different countries.

Their mission is to be involved worldwide with young people in the search for unity and reconciliation; the brothers organise youth meetings throughout the world. Pope John-Paul II visited Taizé in 1986.

The community is a highly active one with a tented village and group of bunga-lows to accommodate the visitors, and many craft workshops and stands.

Église de la Réconciliation – The low-lying, flat-roofed Church of the Reconciliation was consecrated in 1962 and serves as a place of worship. The five-bell carillon is out in the open air. This concrete building has a large main doorway but small and narrow windows. There are three daily prayer services held here for the community.

The nave is flanked to the right by a passageway leading to the crypt. The stained glass in the seven small windows opening into this passage represent the main feast days.

The first crypt, revolving round a central pillar supporting the choir, is a place of prayer and silence; the second crypt is an orthodox chapel.

Église paroissiale – This Romanesque church is starkly simple and is lit by narrow windows. The church is also used by the community, but is above all a place reserved for personal prayer and meditation.

Cirque de CONSOLATION★★

Michelin map 321: J-4 – 13km/8mi N of Morteau

The natural amphitheatre, from which the Dessoubre and its tributary the Lançot spring, takes the shape of a double semicircle against an awe-inspiring background of partly wooded rocky crags towering majestically to over 300m/984ft.

In one semicircle, the Dessoubre takes its source in a limestone wall (behind the Hôtel Joliot) and immediately forms a waterfall. The source of the Lançot is in the other semicircle. It appears in the park of Notre-Dame-de-Consolation, beneath a cave; when the water level rises, the river spills out of the cave itself.

Eating out

BUDGET

Ferme-Auberge de Frémondans – *25380 Vaucluse - 7km/4.3mi NE of Gigot by D 39 - ☎ 03 81 44 35 66 - closed Oct - open evenings Jul-Aug and Fri evenings to Sun evenings Nov-Sep - ⌷ - reservations required - 10.67/18.29€.* The Moreau family owns this farmhouse overlooking the Dessoubre Valley. Weary travellers will enjoy tucking into their specialities, which include terrine, cheese fondue, kid, stuffed cabbage, goat's cheese and home-made pastries.

MODERATE

La Truite du Moulin – *In Moulin-du-Bas - 25380 Cour-St-Maurice - 0.5km/0.3mi SW of Pont-Neuf by D 39 - ☎ 03 81 44 30 59 - closed Dec, Tue evenings and Wed - 15.38/33.85€.* Take a break and stop at this former mill lying close to a river, converted into a restaurant. Simple but tasty fare served in a welcoming atmosphere. Cosy dining room. Choose your trout from the teeming fish tank. Moderately priced menus.

Where to stay

BUDGET

Chambre d'Hôte Chez Patrick Dorget – *La Joux - 25380 Bretonvillers - 7km/4.3mi N of Gigot by D 125 until you reach Bretonvillers then head for Pierrefontaine and follow directions to La Joux - ☎ 03 81 44 35 78 - ⌷ - 4 rooms: 26/36€.* This old farmhouse typical of the area stands in a vast leafy clearing. The perfect address for nature lovers, this place is a haven of tran-quillity. Pretty rooms adorned with beams. Fine kitchen featuring old-fashioned floor tiling.

MODERATE

Hôtel du Moulin – *25380 Cour-St-Maurice - 1km/0.6mi SW of Pont-Neuf by D 39 - ☎ 03 81 44 35 18 - closed 15 Jan-15 Feb and 1-5 Oct - ▣ - 6 rooms: 40/61€ - ⌷ 6€ - restaurant 16.80/26€.* This handsome 1930s residence embellished with turrets and colonnades has a bright dining room with parquet flooring, large, cosy rooms and a charming garden bursting with flowers bor-dered by a river. Peace and quiet guaranteed.

★VALLÉE DU DESSOUBRE

From St-Hippolyte to the park of Notre-Dame-de-Consolation – 33km/21mi – allow 45min

St-Hippolyte – This town occupies a pretty **site**★ on the confluence of the Doubs and the Dessoubre.

Leave St-Hippolyte on D 39 heading SW.

D 39 follows the course of the Dessoubre quite closely, going through the villages of Pont-Neuf and Rosureux. The peaceful river valley runs between wooded slopes (fir, oak and ash; note several sawmills and furniture factories) crowned by limestone cliffs. Along the bottom of this charming valley, the river flows from pool to pool, sometimes over a bed of white pebbles. On either side of it stretch meadows, dappled by shade in places.

Gigot – The Dessoubre is joined here by a small tributary, the Reverotte, which wiggles its way west upstream of the village along a narrow steep-sided valley which is known as the **Défilé des Épais Rochers** (rocky gorge).

After Gigot, D 39 carries on along the banks of the Dessoubre, making a very pleasant drive indeed amid woods and meadows with the river itself bubbling alongside. In rainy weather, the peaceful little river is transformed into a foaming torrent.

Notre-Dame-de-Consolation – This former Minimist convent was a small seminary until 1981, and now serves as a religious centre. The chapel is in the Baroque style and contains a beautiful marble mausoleum and an 18C carved wooden pulpit.
🚶 The **park** *(allow 1hr)* is a pretty place for a walk through fields, among trees, rocks, waterfalls, springs (Source du Lançot, Source Noire and Source du Tabouret) and the Val Noir (black valley).

★★★LA ROCHE DU PRÊTRE

From La Roche du Prêtre to Loray – 14km/9mi

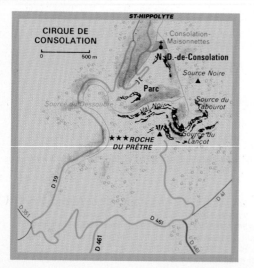

La Roche du Prêtre – This famous viewpoint is located on the edge of a cliff and offers an unforgettable view of the Cirque de Consolation and its surroundings. The summit towers 350m/1148ft above the fresh, green, wooded amphitheatre in which the Dessoubre rises. Here and there craggy rocks break through the greenery. It makes a romantic scene of solitude and rugged grandeur, in sharp contrast to the cosier landscape of the plateau covered with green pastures and dotted with farms.

Grandfontaine-Fournets – This hamlet at the heart of the Haut-Doubs is typical of the Jura region.

It is home to the **Ferme du Montagnon** ⓥ, a farm dating from the 17C and 18C which contains evidence of age-old farming traditions. It still has its **smoking loft**★ *(tuyé)* where meat, hams, bacon and sausages are cured (locally cured products are on sale in the old stables). The way of life on the farm in days gone by is evoked by furniture of the period.

Orchamps-Vennes – This sizeable mountain village occupies a high plateau set back from D 461 from Besançon to Morteau. Its low-roofed houses adorn a charming setting of green meadows and trees.

Église St-Pierre-St-Paul – This 16C church has a 19C belfry porch. There are some interesting tombstones in front of the church. Inside, there is a lovely 17C pulpit in carved oak attributed to Étienne Monnot from Orchamps-Vennes, who also executed the woodwork in the chancel. A Stations of the Cross by Gabriel Saury, a sculptor from Franche-Comté, in 1947, begins at the far end of the north aisle.

Loray – This village contains several houses typical of the region and a neo-Romanesque church with handsome 18C furnishings inside. Not far off stands a 12C **calvary**, the upright of which (over 4m/13ft tall) features a life-size statue of a figure holding a human head in its hand. Higher up are the Virgin Mary, Christ and St Michael overcoming the dragon. At the centre of the village square is a pretty, monumental 19C **fountain wash-house** with fluted columns surmounted by Doric capitals.

Château de CORMATIN★★

Michelin map 320: I-10 – 13km/8mi N of Cluny
Local map see MÂCONNAIS

Cormatin was built in the aftermath of the Wars of Religion between 1605 and 1616 by the Governor of Chalon, Antoine du Blé d'Huxelles.

In August, a theatre and cabaret festival, Les Rendez-vous de Cormatin, takes place in the castle theatre.

At Bois Dernier, situated 1km/0.6mi from the castle, there is an unusual bike museum.

Exterior – The architecture is understated in the style of Henri IV and was probably designed by Jacques II Androuet du Cerceau, architect to the king. Originally the château consisted of three wings round three sides of a courtyard; the south wing collapsed in 1815 during conversion to a cloth weaving factory. The façades are in the French rustic style recommended by Du Cerceau: absence of the Classical orders (except for the two monumental doors in the courtyard), high stone base, matching quoins and window surrounds. The broad moat and the impressive corner pavilions with watchtowers and cannon suggest a defensive concept confirmed by traces of a rampart (demolished in the late 17C) which closed the fourth side of the courtyard.

Interior ⓥ – The north wing contains a magnificent grand **staircase**★★ in an open well (1610); the straight flights of steps, flanked by vigorous balusters, open directly on to the central well. It is the oldest and largest stair of this kind (25m/82ft high), successor to the Renaissance stairs in two flights separated by a wall.

The sumptuous Louis XIII decor in this wing is the work of Marquess Jacques du Blé (son of Antoine) and his wife Claude Phélypeaux, who were close friends of Marie de Medici

M. Simonet-Lenglart/Château de Cormatin

Cabinet de Sainte-Cécile

and the literary salon of the Précieuses. They intended their summer house to reflect the sophistication of Parisian fashion, so they used the artists and craftsmen who had worked for the Queen at the Luxembourg Palace. The gilt, the paintings and sculptures which cover the walls and ceilings are proof of an informed mannerism; each painting has an allegorical meaning reaffirmed in the symbolism of the decorative motifs and the colours used for the panelling.

The **ante-chamber of the Marchioness★** (daughter and sister of government ministers), which was created in the middle of the Protestant revolt (1627-28), is in homage to Louis XIII who is represented above the chimney-piece: the red panelling (colour of authority) celebrates the activities and virtues of the king. The **Marchioness' room★★** has a magnificent French ceiling in gold and blue, symbol of fidelity; the great painting of Venus and Vulcan, a work of the second Fontainebleau School, symbolises love and the baskets of fruit and flowers on the woodwork represent plenty. One of the oldest heavenly ceilings, made fashionable by Marie de Medici, adorns the **Cabinet des Curiosités★★**. The sumptuous Baroque decor in the **Cabinet de Ste-Cécile★★★**, Jacques du Blé's tiny study, is dominated by very blue lapis-lazuli and rich gilding which reflected the glow of the candlelight so necessary in a study; the figure of St Cecilia accompanied by the cardinal virtues represents moral harmony.

Also on view are the kitchens and the Neapolitan bed of Cécile Sorel in a room in the west wing which was refurbished at the turn of the 20C.

Park – The lovely view of the park from the aviary reveals its typical 17C symbolism: the flower beds represent paradise, with the fountain of life in the centre. Within a triangle, the apple tree recalls the forbidden fruit and paradise lost; the labyrinth 🌀 symbolises mankind's errant ways. From the borders inward, the seven walkways culminate in seventh heaven at the highest point. The kitchen gardens and the château's façade may inspire thoughts of more worldly pleasures.

La CÔTE★★

Michelin maps 320: I-6 to J-8

The celebrated vineyards of the Côte d'Or (Golden Hillside) stretch from Dijon to Santenay (60km/37mi) forming a triumphal way for those who love good things to eat and drink. Each place bears a famous name; each village and each hillside has a claim to glory. This is the region of the great wines.

THE GREAT WINES OF BURGUNDY

Natural conditions – The Côte is formed by the eastern edge of the region known as La Montagne, whose rectangular shape is cut by transverse combes in the same way as the blind valleys of the Jura vineyards. Between Dijon and Nuits-St-Georges, the cliffs and rocks of these combes are a favourite spot for the rock-climbers of Dijon. The vineyards cover about 8 000ha/19 768 acres in the Côte-d'Or and 10 000ha/24 711 acres in the Saône-et-Loire and are planted with first-quality vines (Pinot Noir and Chardonnay). They are set in terraces overlooking the plain of the Saône at an altitude varying from 200m to 300m/686ft to 984ft.

Whereas the summits of the hills are covered with box-trees or sometimes crowned with small woods, giving a Mediterranean appearance, the vineyards occupy the limestone slopes, well exposed to the morning sun – the best – and sheltered from cold winds. This position makes the grapes extremely sweet which in turn gives the wine a high alcohol content. Only the southern and eastern-facing sides of the combes are planted with vines; the northern slopes are often covered with woods. In addition, the slopes facilitate drainage; vines like dry soil and the slope is therefore an important factor in the quality of the grape harvest.

The great wines – For the greater part of its run through the vineyards N 74 separates the noble wines from the others. The great wines are generally on terraces half way up the slopes. The high-quality Pinot Noir, king of Burgundian vines, is the only plant for the great red wines. The great white wines are produced from the Chardonnay vines. After the crisis brought about by the phylloxera aphid at the end of the 19C, the vineyards were entirely replanted with American rootstocks, onto which were then grafted the historic Burgundy vines.

South of the Dijon vineyards the Côte d'Or is divided into two parts, the Côte de Nuits and the Côte de Beaune. The wines of both are well known; those of Nuits for robustness; those of Beaune for their delicacy.

Each district has its own hinterland with vineyards higher up in the hills, where the wines are known as Hautes-Côtes, and although they do not pretend to be noble, in a good year they may give pleasure to the most knowledgeable connoisseur. The **Côte de Nuits** extends from the village of Fixin to the southern limit of the Corgoloin region. Its production is almost entirely of great red wines. Its most famous wines, from north to south, are: Chambertin, Musigny, Clos-Vougeot, and Romanée-Conti. Particularly rich and full-bodied, the wines take eight to ten years to acquire their unequalled qualities of body and bouquet.

The **Côte de Beaune** extends from the north of Aloxe-Corton to Santenay and produces great white wines as well as excellent red wines. These wines mature more rapidly than those of the Côte de Nuits and so pass thier prime sooner. Its principal wines are: Corton, Volnay, Pommard and Beaune for the red wines, less full-bodied than those of the Nuits but very smooth, and Meursault and Montrachet for the rich and fruity whites. The great wines, enhanced by delicious cooking, make the Côte a celebrated region in the world of gourmets and connoisseurs.

Eating out

BUDGET

Le Cellier Volnaysien – *Pl. de l'Église - 21190 Volnay -* ☎ *03 80 21 61 04 - closed 28 Jul-8 Aug, 22 Dec-22 Jan Wed and evenings except Sat - 14.94/26.22€.* Walk through the pretty garden planted with rare trees and discover a fine 18C residence fronted by a perron. Vaulted cellars. One of the three dining rooms is located in the former storehouse. Unpretentious local cuisine and Château de Savigny wines at extremely reasonable prices.

MODERATE

La Table d'Olivier Leflaive – *1 pl. du Monument - 21190 Puligny-Montrachet -* ☎ *03 80 21 37 65 - olivier-leflaive@dial.oleane.com - closed Dec-Feb, evenings and Sun - 35€.* Wine buffs will adore this restaurant where meals tend to focus on drink rather than food. Each different wine is commented by a sommelier. An unforgettable experience in a typical village house!

EXPENSIVE

Rôtisserie du Chambertin – *21220 Gevrey-Chambertin -* ☎ *03 80 34 33 20 - closed 7-28 Feb, 1-15 Aug, Sun evenings and Mon - 33/66€.* Grilled meat is the speciality here. You may choose between regional dishes in the vaulted dining hall or light meals in the friendly setting of the Bon Bistrot and its summer terrace. Do not forget to visit the small wax museum re-enacting the daily life of a cooper.

Where to stay

BUDGET

Chambre d'Hôte Les Sarguenotes – *R. de Dijon - 21220 Chambœuf - 6km/3.7mi E of Gevrey-Chambertin by D 31 -* ☎ *03 80 51 84 65 -* ✉ *- 5 rooms: 38/48€.* Take a relaxing break in this modern house dominating the luxuriant countryside. The bedrooms are lacking somewhat in character but they are nonetheless comfortable and each has its own terrace. Reasonable prices.

Chambre d'Hôte Les Brugères – *7 r. Jean-Jaurès - 21160 Couchey - 2km/1.2mi S of Marannay by D 122 -* ☎ *03 80 52 13 05 - closed Dec-Mar - 4 rooms: 45/52€.* This superb 16C residence belonging to a wine-grower has pretty rooms with exposed beams decorated with furniture picked up from antique dealers. The perfect place for wine buffs...

MODERATE

Domaine du Moulin aux Moines – *Auxey-Duresse - 21190 Meursault -* ☎ *03 80 21 60 79 - www.laterrasse.fr - 4 rooms: 55/87€.* This fine manor house lost in the midst of vineyards was once attached to Cluny Abbey. The spacious rooms are tastefully decorated; the ones set up in the mill are particularly nice. Tastings are organised in the wine cellars. Small wine museum.

EXPENSIVE

Hôtel Le Hameau de Barboron – *21420 Savigny-lès-Beaune - 2km/1.2mi N of Savigny by a minor road -* ☎ *03 80 21 58 35 -* ▣ *- 9 rooms: 92/138€ -* ☐ *13€.* Surrounded by 350ha/865 acres of private fields and forest, this old farmhouse has been admirably restored. The luxurious rooms, furnished in the old-fashioned style, enjoy the most refined decoration. Tastings are held in the vaulted cellar that houses the vats of wine, produced and bottled on the estate.

Sit back and relax

Caveau Municipal de Chassagne – *7 r. Charles-Paquelin - 21190 Chassagne-Montrachet -* ☎ *03 80 21 38 13 - jeff.fine.et.rare.wines@wanadoo.fr - open daily 8am-7pm.* The fruity, lively white wines of this region are a delight to drink, whereas the reds are refined and robust. To quote Alexandre Dumas, these wines are to be drunk "kneeling down and bareheaded"...

Château André-Ziltener – *R. Fontaine - 21220 Chambolle-Musigny -* ☎ *03 80 62 81 37 - chateau.ziltener@wanadoo.fr - open daily 9.30am-6.30pm - closed mid-Dec to Feb.* Tourists may visit the cellars, set up as a museum devoted to Cistercian monks. Discover six wines, accompanied by bread and *gougère* (choux pastry puff flavoured with cheese, seasoned with pepper and then baked).

Château de Corton-André – *BP 10 - 21420 Aloxe-Corton - ☎ 03 80 26 44 25 - pandre@axnet.fr - open Apr-Oct: daily 10am-12.30pm, 2.30-6pm; Nov-Mar: Thu-Mon 10am-12.30pm, 2.30-6pm; end of Dec to end of Feb: Thu-Mon.* This magnificent castle with its glazed roof tiling is ideally located in a luxuriant setting. It is the only Côte de Beaune château to boast the Grand Cru *appellation*. Tour of cellars and tastings of wine made on the premises. Bottles for sale.

Clos de Langres - Domaine d'Ardhuy – *Clos des Langres - 21700 Corgolin - ☎ 03 80 62 98 73 - domaine.ardhuy@wanadoo.fr - open Mon-Fri 8am-noon, 2-6pm, Sat 10am-noon, 2-7pm - closed public holidays.* Clos de Langres has an 18C manor house built around an 18C press which is a listed site. Tour of cellars and wine tastings.

★★ THE VINEYARDS

① Côte de Nuits

The road goes along the foot of hillsides covered with vines and passes through villages with world-famous names.

★★★ **Dijon** – *See DIJON.*

Leave Dijon on D 122, known as the Route des Grands Crus (Road of the Great Wines).

Chenôve – The Clos du Roi and Clos du Chapitre recall the former owners of these vineyards, the dukes of Burgundy and the canons of Autun. The great wine cellar of the dukes of Burgundy, **Cuverie des ducs de Bourgogne** ⊙, contains two magnificent 13C presses (some say they are early-15C replicas) which were capable of pressing in one go the contents of 100 wine casks.
Nearby *(on leaving the cellar turn left and first right)* there are picturesque wine-growers' houses, some dating from the 13C, in rue Jules-Blaizet.

Marsannay-la-Côte – Part of the Côte de Nuits, Marsannay produces popular *rosé* wines, obtained from the black Pinot grapes. Wine-growing museum.

Fixin – This is a famous wine-growing village which some believe produces wines among the best of the Côte de Nuits *appellation*. In the **Parc Noisot** ⊙ *(in the centre of town take the rue Noisot for 500m/550yd to a car park and then go on foot via allée des Pins, which is signposted)* there is a commemorative sculpture of Napoleon by **Rude**, *Éveil de Napoléon à l'immortalité*, donated by a loyal officer from the Imperial Guard whose grave is nearby.
A museum houses mementoes of Napoleon's campaigns. From the museum, a path leads to some fountains and to the 100 steps commemorating the 100 days during which Napoleon ruled France once more upon his return from Elba.
The 10C church in the nearby village of **Fixey** is believed to be the oldest in the area.

Gevrey-Chambertin

Brochon – Brochon, which is on the edge of the Côte de Nuits, produces excellent wines. The **château** was built in 1900 by the poet Stephen Liégeard who coined the phrase Côte d'Azur (the Azure Coast) for the Provençal coast and Mediterranean sunshine. The name has stuck long after the poet has faded into obscurity, together with his poem which was honoured by the French Academy.

Gevrey-Chambertin – This village is typical of the wine-growing community immortalised by the Burgundian writer, **Gaston Roupnel** (1872-1946). It is situated at the open end of the gorge, Combe de Lavaux, and surrounded by vineyards. The older part lies grouped around the church and château whereas the Baraques district crossed by N 74 is altogether busier.

The famous Côte de Nuits, renowned for its great red wines, starts slightly to the north.

Chambertin

Among the wines of the Côte de Nuits, full-bodied wines that acquire their body and bouquet as they mature, Chambertin, which comes from the two vineyards of Clos de Bèze and Chambertin, is the most famous and one of the most celebrated wines of all Burgundy. The *Champ de Bertin* (Field of Bertin), which became *Chambertin*, was the favourite wine of Napoleon I and was always to be found in his baggage-train, even on campaigns.

Today there are only 28ha/69 acres producing this celebrated wine, whereas there are 500ha/1236 acres producing Gevrey-Chambertin.

Château ⊘ – In the upper village stands the square-towered fortress, lacking its portcullis; it was built in the 10C by the lords of Vergy. In the 13C it was given to the monks of Cluny who enlarged the windows and installed a fine spiral staircase, wider than the simple ladders used hitherto.

The great chamber on the first floor with its uncovered beams contains a beautiful late-14C credence table. The great tower has retained its watch room and bowmen's room. Beneath the basket-handle vaulting in the cellars, vintage wines are stored.

Church – Dating from the 13C, 14C and 15C, the church still has a Romanesque doorway.

At Morey-St-Denis rejoin N 74.

Vougeot – Its red wines are highly valued. The walled vineyard of Clos-Vougeot (50ha/124 acres), owned by the abbey of Cîteaux from the 12C up to the French Revolution, is one of the most famous of La Côte.

★ **Château du Clos de Vougeot** ⊘ – Stendhal tells how Colonel Bisson, on his return from Italy, paraded his regiment in front of the château and made them present arms in honour of the celebrated vineyard. Since 1944 the château has been owned by the **Confrérie des Chevaliers du Tastevin** (Brotherhood of the Knights of the Tastevin). Ten years earlier in 1934 a small group of Burgundians met in a cellar in Nuits-St-Georges and decided to fight against the slump in wines and to form a society whose aim was to promote the wines of France in general and, in particular, those of Burgundy. The brotherhood was founded and its renown grew fast and spread throughout Europe and America.

Each year several chapter meetings of the order, well known throughout the world, are held in the 12C Great Cellar of the château. Five hundred guests take part in these banquets, at the end of which the Grand Master and the Grand Chancellor, surrounded by high dignitaries of the brotherhood, initiate new knights according to strictly observed rites that are based on the Divertissement in Molière's *Malade Imaginaire*. During these plenary chapter meetings, the knights of the Tastevin celebrate the first of **Les Trois Glorieuses** in the château on the eve of the sale of the wines of the Hospices of Beaune, which is held in the town on the following day. The Monday following is devoted to the *Paulée de Meursault*, a celebration banquet.

The château was built during the Renaissance period and restored in the 19C. The rooms visited include the Grand Cellier (12C cellar) where the *disnées* (banquets) and the ceremonies of the Order are held, the 12C vat cellar containing four huge wine-presses, the 16C kitchen with its huge chimney and ribbed vault supported by a single central pillar, and the monks' dormitory which has a spectacular 14C pitched roof. *Presentation of slides (15min) about the Confrérie des Chevaliers du Tastevin.*

Chambolle-Musigny – The road from Chambolle-Musigny to Curley *(north-west)* passes through a gorge, Combe Ambin, to a charming beauty spot: a small chapel stands at the foot of a rocky promontory overlooking the junction of two wooded ravines.

Reulle-Vergy – *8km/5mi W of Chambolle-Musigny.*

This village has a 12C church and a curious town hall, built on top of a wash-house. Opposite the town hall a barn now houses a **museum** ⊘ describing the arts and traditions associated with the Hautes Côtes wines. Themes covered include the

Clos de Vougeot

day-to-day work in the vineyards, archaeology (items from the Bronze Age, the Gallo-Roman and medieval periods), the flora and fauna, daily life in the 19C (costumes and everyday objects) and the history of the region (evocation of the medieval poem of the Mistress of Vergy).

From l'Etang-Vergy take D 35 and D 25 S and E to Nuits-St-Georges.

Nuits-St-Georges – This friendly and attractive little town is the centre of the vineyards to which it has given its name. It is proud of the famous wines which have a worldwide reputation.

The fame of the wines of Nuits goes back to Louis XIV. When the royal doctor, Fagon, advised the King to take some glasses of Nuits and Romanée with each meal as a tonic, the whole court wanted to taste it.

Among the most famous of the wines, produced from the vineyards since the year 1000, Nuits-St-Georges is the best-known.

Église St-Symphorien ⊘ – This vast church was built at the end of the 13C although it is pure Romanesque in style. The flat chevet is pierced by a large rose window and three windows flanked by small columns and sculptures. A massive belfry surmounts the transept crossing.

The lofty nave, which is covered with groined vaulting, contains an 18C organ loft and a rare late-16C wooden cylinder decorated with open-work carving to enclose a spiral staircase. Traces of frescoes (including the martyrdom of St Christine) and 16C inscriptions are visible in the aisles.

In addition, there are two fine 17C edifices: the **belfry** of the former town hall and the St-Laurent hospital. The present town hall is 18C. The modern church of Notre-Dame has stained glass (1957) by JJ Borghetto.

Museum ⊘ – This museum occupies the premises of an old wine business. In the cellars is an exhibition of archaeological items discovered in the Gallo-Roman settlement excavated at Les Bolards near Nuits-St-Georges (ex-votos, funerary steles and urns, everyday household objects).

A temporary exhibition renewed every year highlights the region's traditional heritage illustrated by the museum collections.

One room is devoted to the Burgundian painter Jean François (1906-80), whose works take wine-growing and wine as their theme.

Vosne-Romanée – *2km/1.25mi N of Nuits-St-Georges.*
These vineyards produce only red wines of the highest quality; they are choice and delicate. Among the various sections *(climats)* of this vineyard, Romanée-Conti and De Richebourg have a worldwide reputation.

Beyond Nuits-St-Georges, the itinerary partly follows N 74 and also some of the picturesque roads of the Burgundian part of La Montagne.

Comblanchien – *4.5km/2.5mi S of Nuits-St-Georges.*
This township is known for the limestone that is quarried from its surrounding cliffs. The stone is very beautiful and is often used for facings, replacing the more costly marble.

S of Comblanchien turn right to Arcenant, 9km/5.5mi NW.

Beyond Arcenant, raspberry and blackcurrant bushes border the road. During a fairly stiff climb, there is a good view over Arcenant, the arable land and the deep gorge of the **Combe Pertuis**.

From Bruant take D 25, D 18 and D 2 S to Bouilland.

During the long run downhill, there is a view of **Bouilland** and its circle of wooded hills.

From Bouilland take D 2 S.

Beyond the hamlet of La Forge the road is dominated on the left by the rocky escarpments crowning the hill and on the right by the rock known as the pierced rock *(roche percée)*. Soon after there is the cirque of the Combe à la Vieille on the left. The road then follows the fresh, green and narrow valley of the Rhoin, between wooded slopes. Shortly before **Savigny-lès-Beaune** *(see BEAUNE)*, the valley opens out.

From Savigny take the minor road E to Aloxe-Corton (3km/2mi).

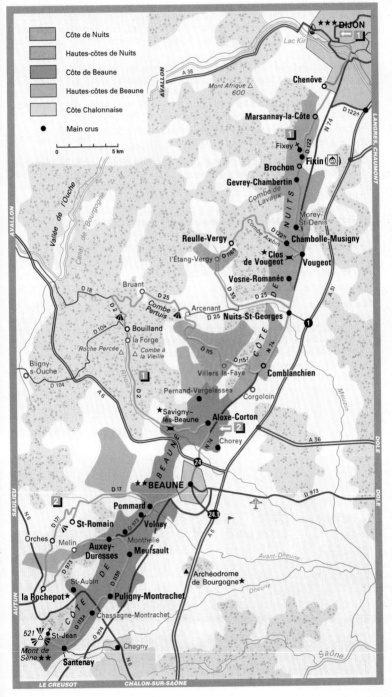

② Côte de Beaune

Aloxe-Corton – This village (pronounced Alosse), the northernmost village of the Côte de Beaune, is of ancient origin. Emperor Charlemagne owned vineyards here and Corton-Charlemagne, "a white wine of great character", recalls this fact. However, red wines are produced almost exclusively at Aloxe-Corton, the firmest and most forward wines of the Côte de Beaune. The bouquet improves with age and the wine remains full-bodied and cordial.

★★ **Beaune** – *See BEAUNE.*

Pommard – *3km2mi SW of Beaune on N 74 and D 973.*
The fairly large village of Pommard takes its name from an ancient temple dedicated to Pomona, the goddess of fruits and gardens. These vineyards of the Côte de Beaune produce red wines that are firm, dark red, full of candour and worth keeping. These wines were greatly appreciated by Ronsard, Henri IV, Louis XV and Victor Hugo.

Volnay – *1km/0.5mi SW of Pommard on D 973.* Its red wines have a delicate bouquet and a silky taste. From the esplanade, below the small 14C church with its squat belfry, there is a good view of the vineyards.
When he acquired the Duchy of Burgundy in 1477, King Louis XI had the entire production of Volnay wine taken to his château of Plessis-les-Tours.

Return to Pommard; take D 17 W to St-Romain (9km/5.5mi).
The road follows the green valley floor between wooded slopes.

St-Romain – This township is made up of two quite distinct parts: St-Romain-le-Haut perched high on a limestone spur, surrounded by a semicircle of cliffs, with the ruins of its 12C-13C castle *(archaeological site: short visitor trail marked out)* on the southern edge. Right at the top stands the terraced 15C church, tastefully restored; it contains 2C fonts and a pulpit dating from 1619. Lower down in St-Romain-le-Bas stands the **town hall** ⊘ *(mairie)*, which contains displays on local archaeology and ethnology.

N of St-Romain turn left on D 17¹ to Orches and La Rochepot.
As the road approaches **Orches**, in its attractive rocky site, there is a fine **view**★ of St-Romain, Auxey, Meursault and the Saône Valley.

Beyond Orches, drive 4km/2.5mi S.

★ **La Rochepot** – The village, now by-passed by the main road, is set at the foot of a rocky promontory on which stands the feudal castle which has been restored. It was the birthplace of Philippe Pot (1428-94), famous statesman and ambassador in London of the dukes of Burgundy. His tomb is a masterpiece of the Burgundian School and is now to be seen in the Louvre Museum.

Château ⊘ – The château is in an impressive **setting**★. The original 12C building was altered in the 15C but the keep was razed during the French Revolution. The complete rebuilding of the castle was undertaken by M Sadi Carnot, son of Président

Château de la Rochepot

Carnot. The outer defences are dominated by huge but graceful towers. The inner courtyard, beyond the drawbridge, contains a well with a wrought-iron well-head; the turrets of the Renaissance wing are roofed with glazed coloured tiles.

The tour includes the guard-room with its vast chimney and handsome ceiling beams, the chamber of the Captain of the Guards, the kitchens, the dining room, which is richly furnished and contains numerous objets d'art, the former chapel, the northern tower with its apartments and the watch-path. From a small terrace at the far end of the courtyard on the right, there is a view over the village and its encircling hills.

Church – This 12C priory church was built by the Benedictine monks from Flavigny. The historiated capitals are similar in style to those at Autun and represent Balaam's ass, the Annunciation and a knight and an eagle in combat. It contains a number of interesting works of art including a 16C triptych by the Dijon painter, Quentin, with a Deposition on the central section.

From La Rochepot take D 973 NE skirting the château.

The road follows a narrow valley and prior to Melin crosses a series of limestone escarpments worn by erosion.

Auxey-Duresses – This village is set in a deep combe leading to La Rochepot and its château. The vineyards of Auxey-Duresses produce fine red and white wines which, before the law on nomenclature, were sold as Volnay and Pommard. The church, with its fine 16C triptych, is worth a visit.

Meursault – *2km/1.25mi SE of Auxey.*
This little town, dominated by the beautiful Gothic stone spire of its church, is proud of producing both red and white wines of high quality. It owes its name to a valley that clearly divides the Côte de Meursault from the Côte de Beaune. This valley, known as the Rat's Leap (*Saut du Rat* – in Latin *Muris Saltus*) is said to have given the present name of Meursault. Its white wines, with those of Puligny and Chassagne-Montrachet, are considered the best white wines in the world. They have a slight taste of hazelnuts and an aroma of ripe grapes which gives a freshness to the subtle qualities of taste and bouquet.

Meursault wines have the rarity of being dry and mellow at the same time. The *Paulée de Meursault*, the final day of a yearly celebration of the grape known as **Les Trois Glorieuses**, is a well-known local fête. At the end of the banquet, to which each guest brings bottles of his own wine, a literary prize is awarded. The happy laureate receives 100 bottles of Meursault.

Puligny-Montrachet – *4km/2.5mi S of Meursault.*
The white wines of Puligny-Montrachet, like those of Meursault, are excellent. Alexandre Dumas, connoisseur of note, declared that this wine "should be imbibed while kneeling with the head uncovered".

The red wines of this old walled vineyard are full-bodied and have subtle qualities of taste and bouquet.

Santenay – *6km/3.5mi SE of Puligny.*
The three localities that go to make up Santenay – Santenay-le-Bas, Santenay-le-Haut and St-Jean – are spread along the banks of the River Dheune as far as the first slopes of Mount Sène or the Montagne des Trois-Croix. Santenay derives its reputation not only from its vast vineyards but also from the local mineral water, which contains lithia and is very salty. The church of **St-Jean** Ⓞ stands at the foot of a semicircle of cliffs; a wooden porch protects the round-headed doorway which opens into the 13C nave; the 15C vaulting in the chancel contains an unusually high number of ribs. Two 15C painted wooden statues of St Martin and St Roch contrast with a 17C Virgin and dragon by the local sculptor J Bésullier.

★★ **Mont de Sène** – *6km/3.7mi W of Santenay via D 113 to Dezize-lès-Maranges, then a minor road to the right; the road is narrow with sharp bends and steep gradients near the top.*
The Mont de Sène is also known as the **Montagne des Trois-Croix** after the three crosses which stand on the summit.

The **panorama**★★ unfolding from the top reveals *(north)* the famous vineyards of the Côte beyond La Rochepot, *(east)* the Saône Valley, the Jura and the Alps, *(south)* the Cluny district dominated by Mont St-Vincent and *(west)* the Morvan.

Conurbation 100 000
Michelin map 320: G-9

Created in 1970, the conurbation of Le Creusot-Montceau has since acquired a strong identity in the field of tourism through the major efforts that have been made to develop the valley's industrial heritage.

Le Creusot basin – The rural setting of Le Creusot-Montceau, on the north-east border of the Massif Central, contrasts with its industrial character. The basin is a natural depression containing the towns of Montceau-les-Mines, Blanzy, Montchanin and Le Creusot, from which it takes its name. It is an important passage, used by the River Dheune and River Bourbince and now by the road, canal and railway, linking the valleys of the River Saône and River Loire.

"Le marteau pilon"
power hammer

Development of industry – Although iron ore was mined in the Middle Ages in the region of Couches, the discovery of vast coal deposits at Épinac, Le Creusot and Blanzy in the 17C marked the real origin of the industrial development of the whole area. Industrial exploitation really began in 1769 and by 1782, The Royal Foundry of Montcenis consisted of a foundry and blast-furnaces.

City of steel – In 1836 **Joseph-Eugène Schneider**, forge-master at Bazeilles, and his brother, **Adolphe Schneider**, set themselves up at Le Creusot, at that time a little township of 3 000 inhabitants. The rapid expansion of the Schneider works was to contribute to the wealth of the town, which from that date increased its population tenfold. The construction of steam and marine engines began the following year. In 1843 the invention of the power hammer by one of the factory's engineers, M Bourdon, resulted in the forging of heavy castings. From that time, besides products for the railways, the factories produced equipment for the great electrical power stations, for ports, factories and mines etc.

Around 1867 steel made its appearance and was mainly used for sheets of armour plating and guns. In 1924 the old power hammer was superseded by the great furnace (forge) equipped with 7 500 to 11 300t hydraulic presses. In 1949 the Schneider works were reconstituted as the Société des Forges et Ateliers du Creusot with factories in the communes of Le Creusot, Le Breuil, Torcy and Montchanin. In 1970 the company amalgamated with the Compagnie des Ateliers et Forges de la Loire to form Creusot-Loire. Following the European steel crisis, Creusot-Loire filed for bankruptcy in 1984. The works were acquired by CLI, a subsidiary of Usinor-Sacilor, by Alsthom Creusot Rail and by Framatome. The blast-furnaces and rows of brick-built workers' houses have been replaced by modern industrial plants.

Today, mining operations continue at the Blanzy pit to supply the thermal power station, Lucy III.

The Creusot factory has also diversified with the establishment of SNECMA, the development of the textile sector and the creation of a nucleus of technological skills directed to high energy and electronics.

The industrial heritage and tourism – In a region rich in reminders of its industrial past (mines, foundries, factories, workshops and workers' settlements) there is now an effort to exploit this industrial heritage for tourism. The towns of Le Creusot and Montceau-les-Mines founded an association in 1983, which organises guided tours under the direction of former employees of Creusot-Loire or the Blanzy mines. There is also a **tourist train service** leaving from Combes station, where waste products from the Schneider factories used to be sent. Its route takes it along the foot of Gros Chaillot hill, giving views of Mont Beuvray, the Mesvrin Valley, and further south Le Creusot.

In the same way, the **Canal du Centre**, which, since its opening for navigation in 1794, had been a vital artery in this hilly region, serving different industrial centres, now provides good possibilities for leisure cruising.

Eating out

BUDGET

Moulin de Galuzot – *In Galuzot - 71230 St-Vallier - 5km/3.1mi SW of Montceau-les-Mines by N 70 and D 974 - ☎ 03 85 57 18 85 - closed 22 Jul-13 Aug, Tue evenings, Sun evenings and Wed - 14.48/34.30€*. A typical country inn situated along the banks of the Bourbince Canal. Meals are served in two dining rooms on a raised platform: one with a colourful setting and old-fashioned chairs, the second with a more rustic touch. Traditional bill of fare.

MODERATE

France – *7 pl. Beaubernard - 71300 Montceau-les-Mines - ☎ 03 85 67 95 30 - hotel.restaurant.lefrance@wanadoo.fr - closed 7-13 Jan and 30 Jul-26 Aug - 18.50/61€*. Tucked away from the bustling town centre, this friendly restaurant is run by a charming young couple. Lovingly prepared dishes are served in an elegant dining room with fireplace. The smallish rooms are light and very quiet.

Where to stay

BUDGET

Hôtel Le Moulin Rouge – *71670 Le Breuil - 3km/1.9mi E of Le Creusot by D 290 - ☎ 03 85 55 14 11 - closed 20 Dec-10 Jan, Fri evenings, Sat lunchtime and Sun evenings -* ▣ *- 30 rooms: 41.16/60.98€ -* ☞ *7.47€ - restaurant 18.30/38.11€*. This hotel located near a farmhouse is a haven of peace. Large, comfortable rooms decorated in the classical tradition. Meals are served in two dining rooms, one of which has a fireplace. Have a nap in the garden or down by the pool.

SIGHTS

Le Creusot

★**Château de la Verrerie** ⓣ – ⓐ The former home of the Schneider family was acquired by the municipality in 1971 and now houses the tourist office, which presents exhibits on the region's industrial heritage.

The crystal manufactory which supplied Marie-Antoinette, transferred from Sèvres to Le Creusot in 1787, was long a prosperous undertaking; in 1833 it was purchased by rivals Saint-Louis and Baccarat, and shut down.

In front of the **château** and in contrast with its dazzling white façade stand two huge conical glass-firing ovens. They were converted in 1905, one into a delightful **miniature theatre** and the other into a chapel which is now used for temporary exhibitions. A collection of 18C and 19C bronze cannon is arrayed in the courtyard.

Écomusée ⓣ – The **museum of man and industry** is devoted to two themes: the history of Le Creusot, its locality and inhabitants (model of the metal works at the end of the 19C); the history of the Schneider dynasty and its achievements. A fine collection of crystal produced here completes the collection.

Salle du Jeu de Paume ⓣ – *Turn left after the entrance*. The building has been set up to display the history of metallurgy in Le Cresusot, through models, panels, instruments and tools: **Metal, Machines and Men** (200 years of local industrial history).

Park – The 28ha/44-acre park offers many recreational opportunities. The terraced gardens were designed by the Duchêne brothers at the beginning of the 20C. The rest of the park is in the less formal English style, with ponds and hothouses, play areas, a swimming pool and a small zoo.

Académie François-Bourdon ⓣ – Founded in 1985 and named after the inventor of the power hammer, the academy is intended to safeguard archives and objects belonging to the industrial heritage of Le Creusot and to exhibit them regularly.

Montceau-les-Mines

Musée des Fossiles ⓣ – Mining operations have led to the discovery of fossils dating back to the formation of the coal deposit some 300 million years ago. Three rooms give an idea of the landscape at the end of the Primary Era by means of these remains of animal (print of an amphibian, fish, shellfish) and plant life (ferns, calamite...). There is also an interesting glass map of the various coal seams in the Blanzy-Montceau basin.

La Maison d'École ⓣ – ⓐ This former school dating from 1881 (annexe of the Écomusée) contains reconstructions of three classrooms from the late 19C to today.

Blanzy *3km/1.7mi NE of Montceau*

Located along the Canal du Centre, the town became prosperous from the 1860s on the strength of its coal mines. Various industries joined the original smelting works: plastics, plumbing, building materials and tyres (Michelin).
Many lakes in the area offer a variety of activities from angling to diving and wind-surfing.

La mine et les hommes ⊙ – A 22m/72ft-high head frame indicates the location of the former St-Claude mine shaft, worked from 1857 to 1881, which has now been refitted with its original equipment: light maintenance, machinery in working order (for operating lifts and pumping water). Former miners show visitors round galleries where extracting and pit-propping techniques are illustrated *(15min audio-visual presentation)*.

Écuisses *10km/6mi SE of Le Creusot*

🖻 The **Musée du Canal** ⊙, an annexe of the Écomusée housed in an 18C lock-keeper's house and in a barge, *L'Armançon*, presents an exhibition on inland water trans-port and bargees. Boat trips are organised in summer.
Beyond Les 7 Écluses, the road runs between the canal and Lake Longpendu.

EXCURSIONS

Promenade des Crêtes (Le Creusot) – *Follow rue Jean-Jaurès, rue de Longwy, D 28 (towards Marmagne) and a sharp right-hand turn to join this scenic moun-tain road.* The switch-back road overlooks the Le Creusot basin. A clearing in the woods *(viewing table)* provides an overall view of the town and its surroundings.

Further on another viewpoint reveals the extent of the old Schneider works and the cen-tral position, in this context, of the Château de la Verrerie.

★ **Mont-St-Vincent** – *12km/7.5mi SE of Montceau-les-Mines.* The Charollais village stands on a bluff, on the watershed between the Loire and the Saône. It is one of the highest peaks (603m/1 987ft) in the Saône-et-Loire *département*, where an old Celtic midsummer cus-tom is perpetuated when a bonfire is lit on or around St John's Day (24 June) to cel-ebrate the return of summer.
At the entrance to the village a sharp right-hand turn leads up to a television and meteo-rological station.

Promenade des Crêtes

From the top of an old mill, converted into a belvedere *(telescope and viewing table)*, there is an almost com-plete **panorama★★**: the Morvan mountains (north-west), the Le Creusot and Autun basins (north), the mountains of the Mâconnais (south-east) and Charollais (south-west).

Church – The church, built at the end of the 11C, was once a priory of Cluny Abbey. A gallery surmounts the square porch. Above the doorway is a carved tympanum, now badly damaged, showing Christ in Majesty between two figures, believed to be St Peter and St Paul. There is transverse barrel vaulting, similar to that in St-Philibert in Tournus, in the nave and groined vaulting in the aisles. The transept crossing is surmounted by a dome on squinches. From the open space beside the graveyard there is an attractive view of the many small valleys to the north.

Musée J.-Régnier ⊙ – The old 15C salt warehouse (restored) now houses a collec-tion of items (from the Neolithic to the medieval period) found in regional archaeological excavations. One room is devoted to Romanesque art.

▶▶ **Signal d'Uchon★** – *18km/11mi W of Le Creusot.* Beacon from the summit of which there is an extensive view of the Morvan.

DIJON★★★

Conurbation 236 953
Michelin map 320: K-6 – Local map see La CÔTE

At the hub of a communications network linking northern Europe to the Mediterranean regions, Dijon has the strategic advantages of a crossroads. Rich in history, the city has also been an influential cultural and architectural centre.

The greater Dijon area is home to almost 240 000 inhabitants; more than two-thirds of the jobs in the area are in the service sector. Industries have settled around the outskirts of the city, mainly mechanical and automotive, but also electric, food and chemical industries. Last but not least, this modern university town, site of the Court of Appeals, administrative and gastronomic centre is the ideal starting point of a tour of great vintage wines (Route des Grands Crus).

View of the city

Origins of the city – The Roman fortress known as Castrum Divionense, located on the military road from Lyon to Mainz, was long a secondary settlement. Sacked, pillaged and burned on numerous occasions, to be built up again, Dijon entered history in 1015, when it was taken by the French king Robert the Pious.

In 1137, a terrible fire razed the city. Duke Hughes II oversaw reconstruction within the broader limits of new fortifications which enclosed the abbey of St-Bénigne as well. Of the 11 gates to the city built at that time, the last (Porte Guillaume) was replaced in 1788 by the triumphal arch on what is today the square Darcy.

The Great Dukes of Burgundy – When Philip the Bold received the duchy of Burgundy from King John the Good, he established the House of Valois as the second ducal dynasty in a fiefdom which was already well organised. Yet Dijon's role was not primordial; Beaune was the seat of the Burgundy Parliament, whereas more northerly cities (in Brabant, Flanders and Picardy) were the region's economic motors, and Philip's marriage to Margaret of Flanders strengthened these ties.

The dukes spent little time in Dijon (Charles the Bold was only there for one week), preoccupied with establishing their authority in recalcitrant corners of their realm, but they did much to develop the city's cultural heritage. The family tombs are in the Chartreuse de Champmol, their sumptuous palace still hosts splendid festivities; the Sainte Chapelle is the headquarters of the Order of the Golden Fleece. Manufacturing grew in the city and as trade prospered wealthy merchants built mansions which still stand today along rue des Forges, rue Vauban, rue Verrerie...

Capital of the Province of Burgundy – Change came when the duchy became an integral part of the kingdom of France. The local population rose up against annexation by Louis XI, and suffered at the hands of the King's troops. But certain concessions were won: The *États de Bourgogne* (regional assembly made up of representatives from the Clergy, the Nobility and the Third Estate) was maintained in the old ducal palace, along with various other privileges and, most importantly, the Burgundy Parliament was transferred from Beaune to Dijon. The King visited Saint-Bénigne in 1479 and solemnly swore to preserve "the freedoms, liberties, protections, rights and privileges" previously enjoyed by the duchy. Nonetheless, he did build a fortress, repair the fortifications and appoint a governor.

A provincial town comes of age – As an administrative centre, seat of the princes of Condé, Dijon underwent significant urban development in the 17C and 18C. Jules Hardouin-Mansart (architect who designed the Versailles Palace) and later his

Eating out

BUDGET

Café du Vieux Marché – *2 r. Claude-Ramey - ☎ 03 80 30 73 61 - closed Sun - 6/15€*. This café located opposite the covered market is fronted by a pretty white and blue terrace. Simplicity and authenticity guaranteed. Light meals and snacks are available.

Le Petit Gascon – *100 r. Berbisey - ☎ 03 80 30 99 66 - closed Sun - 15.24€*. This small restaurant in the modern quarter will give you the opportunity to embark on a gastronomic tour of France as each month it concentrates on a particular region and its specialities. Old-fashioned decor and congenial hospitality.

MODERATE

Le Bistrot des Halles – *10 r. Bannelier - ☎ 03 80 49 94 15 - closed Sun evenings - 15€*. A typical bistrot a stone's throw from the covered market. Choose one of the dishes chalked up on a slate and enjoy the warm and friendly ambience.

La Dame d'Aquitaine – *23 pl. Bossuet - ☎ 03 80 30 45 65 - dame.aquitaine@wanadoo.fr - closed 1-6 Jan, Mon lunchtime and Sun - 21.10€ lunch - 25.70/35.90€*. In the town centre, a porch, a paved courtyard and a long flight of steps will take you down to a superb vaulted dining hall dating back to the 13C. The decor is typically medieval, complete with tapestries, stained glass, sculpted columns and imposing chandeliers. Regional cuisine.

Auberge de la Charme – *21121 Prenois - 13km/8.1mi NW of Dijon by N 71 then D 104 heading towards the Circuit Automobile - ☎ 03 80 35 32 84 - closed Feb school holidays, 1-14 Aug, Sun evenings, Tue lunchtime and Mon - reservations required - 16€ lunch - 22/68€*. Bellows and other old-fashioned tools from the smithy adorn this flower-filled country inn. You will succumb to the rustic charm of the place and will be won over by its hearty and delicious meals.

Where to stay

BUDGET

Hôtel Victor Hugo – *23 r. des Fleurs - ☎ 03 80 43 63 45 - 23 rooms: 28/43€ - ☷ 5€*. You will appreciate the thoughtful service at this traditional hotel. The rooms with their white roughcast walls are simple and quiet, despite their location near the town centre.

MODERATE

Hôtel Wilson – *Pl. Wilson - ☎ 03 80 66 82 50 - hotelwilson@wanadoo.fr - 27 rooms: 64/81€ - ☷ 9€*. This former post house has retained its traditional charm and charisma. The rooms are prettily decorated with light wood furniture. The exposed beams and luminosity make for a cosy atmosphere where one immediately feels at home.

On the town

Hunky Dory – *5 av. du Maréchal-Foch - ☎ 03 80 53 17 24 - open daily 11am-4am*. A popular watering hole among students and young people, with loud music and revolving lights, where karaoke evenings are often held. A separate room is equipped with six billiard tables. Light snacks can be had at any time of day.

L'An-fer – *8 r. Marceau - ☎ 03 80 70 03 69 - Tue-Sun 11pm-5am*. Every evening crowds come from afar to this techno night club, whose reputation is known to all. The famous disc jockey, Laurent Garnier, the ambassador of French techno music, worked here for four years. Gay evening on Sundays.

Sit back and relax

Broc Shop Café – *1 r. du Gén.-Fauconnet - ☎ 03 80 70 93 63 - daily 5pm-2am*. This attic-like building with dilapidated walls is frequented by a lively crowd every evening. Perched up in an alcove beneath a huge chandelier, the disc jockey reigns supreme over the wild nights at this unusual establishment.

Coco Loco – *18 av. Garibaldi - ☎ 03 80 73 29 44 - Tue-Sat 5pm-2am*. The owner of this eccentric café is a colourful character who is well known around town. Dynamic and enterprising, she organises themed evenings and wild nights to which the local youth flock, eager to enjoy the loud and lively atmosphere.

Comptoir des Colonies – *12 pl. François-Rude - ☎ 03 80 30 28 22 - open Mon-Sat 8am-7.30pm*. Around 120 types of tea and 50 brands of coffee roasted by the owner await you in this colonial-style tea shop, which also has a leather and mahogany salon and a large sunny terrace.

Kilkenny Irish Pub – *1 r. Auguste-Perdrix -* ☎ *03 80 30 02 48 - open Mon-Sat 6pm-3am, Sun 7pm-3am.* The typical decoration and furniture of this pub set up in a vaulted cellar were designed by the owners themselves. The cross-Channel touch and the warm welcome combine to convey an extremely cosy atmosphere. Two concerts are organised every month.

La Taverne de Maître Kanter – *Pl. du Marché-les Halles -* ☎ *03 80 30 81 83 - www.tavernes-maitre-kanter.com - open daily 11.30am-midnight.* This inn is set up in a wooden house built in 1889 by the architect Gustave Eiffel, who designed the famous metal tower in Paris. Although the tavern serves mainly meals, it is possible to order drinks in the afternoon.

Le Brighton – *33 r. Auguste-Comte -* ☎ *03 80 73 59 32 - open Mon-Sat 10am-2am, Sun from 5pm.* The room on the ground floor is dominated by a fighter plane, whereas the cellar recreates the interior of a cabin: this pub is patronised by aviators, whose leather jackets can be seen reflected in the blades of a propeller hovering behind the bar.

Mulot et Petitjean – *13 pl. Bossuet -* ☎ *03 80 30 07 10 - mulot.petitjean@wanadoo.fr - open Mon 2-7pm, Tue-Sat 9am-noon, 2-7pm.* This long-standing establishment, which originated in 1796, is specialised in all forms of gingerbread: round biscuits filled with jam, crunchy *gimblettes* with almonds, and sweetmeats shaped as snails, fish, hens, eggs or clogs... The half-timbered house contains a sumptuous decor with marble and wood furniture dating from 1901.

Pâtisserie Liberté – *4 r. François-Rude -* ☎ *03 80 30 27 17 or 03 80 30 47 25 - open daily except Mon 8am-12.30pm, 2-7pm (8.30am on market days).* This sweet shop is known for its *craquelines*, made with praline and *nougatine* (caramel, almond and hazelnut) and for its *délices de Lyon*, macaroons filled with butter cream and *nougatine*.

---

brother-in-law Robert de Cotte rebuilt the ducal palace as the splendid Palais des États de Bourgogne on a monumental esplanade then known as the place Royale. Local officials and parliamentarians built many of the fine houses that give Dijon its character. The University was founded in 1723, the Academy in 1725 and, in 1731, Dijon became the Episcopal See. Under the Revolution, the Chartreuse de Champmol was destroyed; during the periods of the Empire and Restoration, the city remained largely unchanged. From 1851 onwards, the construction of the railway from Paris through Dijon and to the Mediterranean brought new life and new people; the population doubled between 1850 and 1892, as the industrial era took hold.

★★ AROUND THE PALAIS DES DUCS *3hr*

The old district around the palace of the dukes of Burgundy is quite charming. As you stroll along the streets, many of which are for pedestrians only, you will come across beautiful old stone mansions and numerous half-timbered 15C-16C houses. The remains of the ducal palace are now surrounded by buildings in the Classical style.

Place de la Libération – This is the former place Royale. In the 17C, when the town was at the height of its parliamentary power, it felt itself to be a capital and decided to transform the ducal palace, which had stood empty since the death of Charles the Bold, and to re-arrange its approaches. Plans for the fine semicircular design were drawn up by Jules Hardouin-Mansart, the architect of Versailles, and were carried out by one of his pupils from 1686 to 1701; the arcades of place de la Libération, surmounted by a stone balustrade, enhance the main courtyard.

B. Kaufmann/MICHELIN

Place François Rude

Follow rue de la Liberté – formerly rue Condé – to the left of the palace, a pedestrianised shopping street.

Place François-Rude (or place du Bareuzai) – At the heart of the pedestrian zone stands this irregularly shaped, lively square, with one or two half-timbered houses overlooking it. When the statue by the fountain (the *Bareuzai*) was erected in 1904, it provoked some raised eyebrows, but the grape-treading wine-grower, clad only in verdigris, has since been accepted as part of the scenery and is even looked on with some degree of affection by many. The product of his trampling is distributed only during the wine festival *(see Calendar of events)*.

Further on, on the corner of rue des Godrans and rue Bossuet, a department store now occupies the site of the former Maison du Miroir but the locals still agree to meet "on the Miroir corner"!

★ **Rue des Forges** – This is one of the most characteristic old streets of the town.

Hôtel Morel-Sauvegrain – *Nos 52, 54 and 56*. 15C façade.

Ancien Hôtel Aubriot – *No 40*. A Classical doorway contrasts with the elegant 13C arcaded façade of the former Aubriot mansion, built by the first bankers of Dijon. This was the birthplace of Hugues Aubriot, provost of Paris under Charles V. He was responsible for building the Bastille, several of the bridges over the Seine, notably the St-Michel Bridge, and the first vaulted sewers.

Opposite, at no 8 rue Stephen-Liégeard, note the Renaissance façade of the Maison Chisseret.

Maison Milsand – *No 38*. The Renaissance façade is lavishly decorated in the style of Hugues Sambin.

Hôtel Chambellan – *No 34 inner courtyard*. The 15C house, which was built by a rich family of drapers, has a very fine spiral staircase; the central column rises to a flamboyant palm-tree vault supported by the statue of a wine-grower carrying a basket.

★ **Église Notre-Dame** – This church is a good example of 13C Gothic architecture in Burgundy. With only a restricted space in which to work, the master mason showed astonishing technical prowess.

Exterior – The façade is original. Above the great porch with its three bays, closed in laterally as is the porch at Autun, two delicately arcaded galleries are underscored by three tiers of **gargoyles** ⊡. Two graceful bell-turrets top the towers hidden by the façade: that on the right carries the **Jacquemart clock** brought from Courtrai by Philip the Bold in 1382 after his victory over the rebellious Flemish.

Jacquemart and family

The clock has quite a history. The name of Jacquemart, describing the figure of the man who strikes the bell of the clock with a hammer, first appeared in 1500.

The people of Dijon were very fond of him and in 1610 considered that his continued celibacy must be weighing very heavily on the poor man. So he was given a female companion.

In 1714 the poet Aimé Piron took pity on this brave couple, who seemed to have undertaken a vow of chastity. They were given a son, Jacquelinet, whose hammer strikes the little bell for the half-hours; in 1881, a daughter was added, Jacquelinette, who strikes the quarter-hours.

Ph. Cajic/MICHELIN

Interior – The overall effect is harmonious; the triforium of small tapering columns is of great delicacy. Note the height of the transept crossing beneath the lantern tower. The boldly conceived choir, ending with a polygonal chevet, is sober and graceful.

The stained-glass windows of the north transept date from the 13C. The 15C fresco has been restored. The chapel situated to the right of the choir houses the statue of Notre-Dame-de-Bon-Espoir (Our Lady of Good Hope). This 11C Virgin has been the object of particular veneration since the Swiss raised the siege of the town on 11 September 1513; the tapestry given at that time as a votive offering is now to be found in the fine arts museum. After Dijon had been liberated without damage from the German occupation on 11 September 1944, a second tapestry, made by Gobelins, commemorating the town's two liberations, was given as a new votive offering to Notre-Dame-de-Bon-Espoir. It can be seen in the south arm of the transept.

Rue Musette offers an overall view of the west front and leads to the market.

Rue de la Chouette provides a good view of the east end of the church. On one of the buttresses (15C), there is a statue of the owl who gives the street its name. Legend has it that the wise bird will grant the wishes of visitors who stroke it with their left hand.

Map labels:
R. Claude Ramey · R. Quentin · Musette · R. Odebert · R. Rude F. Rue · R. · Rue Chaudronnerie · Rue Verrerie · Hôtel de Vogüé · 8 à 12 · Lamonnoye · Rue de la · Chouette · NOTRE-DAME · Rue du Rabot · Rue Jeannin · 52 à 56 · Place Notre-Dame · 38 · 40 · 34 · Rue des Forges · FORGES · Place des Ducs de Bourgogne · Rue Longepierre · Place F.Rude · RUE · DES · Rue aux Lions · Rue Porte · Cour de Flore · D · V · Salle des États · Cour d'honneur · Cour de Bar · E · S · Pl. de la Sainte Chapelle · T · MUSÉE DES BEAUX ARTS · Rue de Liberté · K · PALAIS DES DUCS · Rameau · Place de la Libération · Rue des Bons Enfants · Place du Théâtre · R. Dauphine · Rue de Bourg · Rue Mercier · R. Neuve Dauphine · R. Jules · Rue du · MUSÉE MAGNIN · Rue Vauban · Hôtel Bouhier · Hôtel Legouz de Gerland · Place Saint-Fiacre · Rue Bouhier · PALAIS DE JUSTICE · Rue Philippe-Pot · Rue du Palais · Rue · 16 · R. Bicot · Place Jean Macé · 29 · Rue Amiral · Rue R. J. B. Liégeard · Roussin · Rue de l'École de Droit · Chabot- · Hôtel Fyot-de-Mimeure · Rue Charrue · Rue Hernoux · 5 · 3 · B · Bibliothèque Municipale · U · Charmy · R. Victor · Dumay · Place des Cordeliers · Rue du · Petit · Potet

0   50 m

Index of street names and sights, see page 244

Hôtel de Vogüé – This early-17C mansion with its colourful tiled roof was one of the early meeting places of the representatives of the province. A portico richly decorated in the Renaissance style opens into an inner courtyard.

The mansion is now occupied by the offices of the city architect and the department of cultural affairs. In July, the main courtyard is the venue of the Estivade, a dance, theatre and singing festival.

Rue Verrerie – Nos 8, 10 and 12 form an attractive group of half-timbered houses. Some of the beams have been richly carved.

If you have time to spare, continue along rue Chaudronnerie.

At no 28, the **Maison des Cariatides**, built in 1603, has 12 caryatids on the street façade. No 66 rue Vannerie is a Renaissance mansion with ornamental windows flanking a watchtower by Hugues Sambin.

Place des Ducs-de-Bourgogne – From this little square, one can imagine what the palace must have looked like at the time of the dukes. The handsome Gothic façade is that of the Salle des Gardes, dominated by Philip the Good's tower.

From place des Ducs, return to the main courtyard of the palace by the vaulted passageway.

DIJON

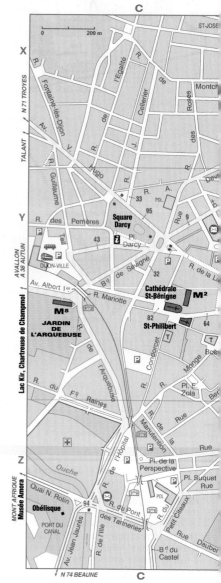

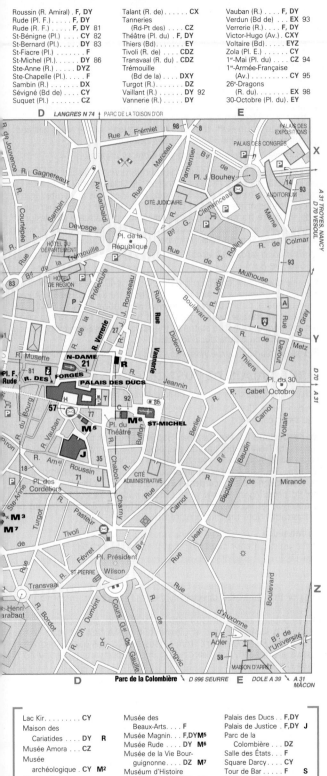

★★ Palais des Ducs et États de Bourgogne

Tour Philippe-le-Bon ⏱ – The tower (46m/151ft high) was built by Philip the Good in the 15C. From the terrace at the top *(316 steps)*, there is a fine **view**★ over the town, the valleys of the Ouche and the Saône and the first foothills of the Jura mountains.

Enter the main courtyard and stand near the railings.

Cour d'honneur – The old Logis du Roi (King's House), a handsome ensemble marked by strong horizontal lines and terminating in two wings at right angles, is dominated by the tall medieval tower of Philippe-le-Bon.
The ducal palace houses, to the left, the various departments of the town hall and, to the right, the famous museum of fine art *(see below)*.

The vaulted passageway to the left leads to the Flore courtyard.

Cour de Flore – The buildings surrounding the courtyard were finished just before the Revolution in 1789. In the north-east corner is the **Chapelle des Élus**; its interior decor and the doors date from the period of Louis XV. Mass was celebrated in the chapel during the sittings of the States of Burgundy. Under the porch which gives access to rue de la Liberté (former rue Condé) a magnificent staircase (**L**), designed in 1735 by Jacques Gabriel, father of the architect who designed the Petit Trianon at Versailles, leads to the **Salle des États** *(not open to the public)*.

Return to the main courtyard, walk across it and through the vaulted passageway leading to the Cour de Bar.

Cour de Bar – The **tower**, built by Philip the Bold in the 14C, preserves the name of an illustrious prisoner who was kept there by Philip the Good: René d'Anjou, Duke of Bar and Lorraine, Count of Provence, who was known as King René. The charming 17C **Bellegarde staircase**, which goes round the tower, leads to the north gallery of the same period. Note the statue of the sculptor **Claus Sluter** by Bouchard and the old **well** backing on to the ducal kitchens.

Leave by the passage leading to rue Rameau.

★ AROUND THE PALAIS DE JUSTICE *1hr*

Leave from place de la Libération by way of rue Vauban heading S.

No 12 rue Vauban has a Classical façade adorned with pilasters and pediments, overlooking the inner courtyard.

Hôtel Legouz de Gerland – Take rue Jean-Baptiste-Liégeard to the left to skirt this mansion with its Renaissance façade pinpointed by four watch-turrets. The Classical inner façade may be seen from no 21 rue Vauban.
At the corner of rue Vauban and rue Amiral-Roussin stands a half-timbered house (no 16) which once belonged to a carpenter. This craftsman embellished his shutters with linenfold panelling and some of the beams with scenes of his craft. The house almost opposite, at no 29, has an elegant courtyard which is screened off by a curved balustrade. Note the fine door of no 27.

Hôtel Fyot-de-Mimeure – *No 23 rue Amiral-Roussin.*
The façade in the pretty interior courtyard is in the style of architect and sculptor Hugues Sambin (16C).

Bibliothèque Municipale ⏱ – *Enter by no 3 rue de l'École-de-Droit.*
The 17C chapel of the former college of Les Godrans, founded in the 16C by the rich Dijon family of this name and directed by Jesuits, has been transformed into a reading room.
This large library contains among its 300 000 or more items precious illuminated manuscripts, including some executed at Cîteaux during the first 30 years of the 12C. The Well of Love *(Puits d'Amour)*, from a house which was demolished when the law courts were extended, has been rebuilt in the courtyard *(enter by no 5 rue de l'École-de-Droit)*.

Follow rue du Palais to reach the Palais de Justice.

Palais de Justice (Law Courts) – This building was formerly the Burgundian Parliament. The gabled façade, in the Renaissance style, has a covered porch supported by columns. The door is a copy of a work by Sambin *(the original is in the Musée des Beaux-Arts)*. The huge Lobby *(Salle des Pas-Perdus)* is covered by a **vaulted ceiling**★ in the shape of an upturned boat. The ceiling of the Chambre Dorée, seat of the Court of Appeal, is adorned with the arms of Fançois I (1522). Opposite the entrance the tiny chapel of the Saint-Esprit contains a screen of carved wood.

Musée Magnin ⏱ – The museum is in an elegant 17C mansion, the home of art lovers Maurice Magnin (a magistrate) and his sister Jeanne, herself a painter and art critic. Their collection covers lesser-known painters, and reveals hidden talents. The more than 1 500 paintings also include works by great masters. On the ground floor, among Flemish and Dutch paintings of the 16C and 17C, hang *The Banquet of the Gods* by Jan Van Bijlert, and *Portrait of a Girl as Diane* by Abraham Van den Tempel. Italian painting has a place of honour with paintings by Cariani, Di Benvenuto, Allori, Cerano, Strozzi and Tiepolo. On the first floor, French paintings from the late 16C through 19C are on display, including works by Claude Vignon *(Expectant Mother Imploring the King)*, Laurent de La Hyre *(Putto Playing the Viola da Gamba* and *Putto Singing)*, Le Sueur, Bourdon, J-B de Champaigne, Girodet, Géricault, Gros and others.

The furnishings from the early 18C through the Second Empire were clearly chosen with as much appreciation and care as the works of art, creating an intimate atmosphere.

Take rue des Bons-Enfants back to place de la Libération.

SACRED ART IN BURGUNDY

Cathédrale St-Bénigne – The ancient abbey church, pure Burgundian-Gothic in style, is the last to occupy this site.

In 1001 Abbot **Guglielmo da Volpiano** built a Romanesque basilica with a large crypt to replace an earlier ruined church; he added a three-storey rotunda to the east which was consecrated in 1018. In 1271 the church collapsed on to the crypt. The present Gothic church was built against the rotunda but during the Revolution the upper parts of the rotunda were destroyed and the crypt filled in. The base of the rotunda and part of the crypt, the only relics of the Romanesque building, were excavated in 1843.

The **west front** of the Gothic church is supported by massive buttresses and projections flanked by two great towers crowned by two octagonal storeys with conical roofs of multicoloured tiles. Within the porch, which is surmounted by a delicately pierced gallery, is the old 12C Romanesque doorway in the centre of the Gothic façade; it is topped by a tympanum, the work of the Bouchardon brothers, which came from the old church of St-Étienne (now the Chamber of Commerce). The transept crossing is marked by a tall spire (93m/305ft) in the Flamboyant style, restored in 1896.

The **interior** is quite austere; its lines are unadorned: plain capitals, simply moulded arcades in the triforium, little columns extending unbroken from the vault to the floor in the crossing and to the tops of massive round pillars in the nave. Since St-Bénigne lost its own works of art during the Revolution, it has provided a home for tombstones and pieces of sculpture from other churches in Dijon. The organ (1743) is by Riepp.

★ **Crypt** ⊘ – The only remaining traces of the Romanesque crypt consist of part of the transept with four apsidal chapels on the east side and a trench in the middle containing the remains of a sarcophagus which was probably used for the burial of St Benignus, the first Burgundian martyr who died in the 3C; there is a pilgrimage to his tomb on 20 November. The sarcophagus faces a broad opening in the lower storey of the **rotunda**★★ which echoes the highly symbolic architecture of the tomb of Christ in Jerusalem built in the 4C; only eight rotundas of this type are known in the world. Three circles of columns radiate from the centre; some have retained their original capitals decorated with palm leaves, interlacing, monstrous animals or praying figures, rare examples of pre-Romanesque sculpture. The eastern end of the rotunda opens into a 6C chapel which may be a *cella* (sanctuary).

★ **Musée Archéologique** ⊘ – The museum is in the eastern wing of what used to be the cloisters of the abbey of St-Bénigne.

Lower level – Two 11C Romanesque rooms hold a collection of Gallo-Roman sculptures. In the first, a pillar representing several divinities gives an interesting perspective on the Gaulish religion in Burgundy. In the second room, the former charter house, the **goddess Sequana**★ reigns, a bronze statue found along with a faun (Roman mythological figure similar to a satyr) during the excavation of the sanctuary at the source of the River Seine.

The fervour brought to the worship of this goddess of the river is expressed in the **collection of ex-voto offerings**★ in stone, bronze, silver and wood, revealing the popular Gallo-Roman beliefs in Burgundy in the early Christian Era.

Level 1 – In 13C Gothic style, this was the monk's dormitory. It is devoted to medieval sculpture from the region of Dijon: alongside architectural fragments, there is a noteworthy head of Christ, made by Claus Sluter for the Chartreuse de Champmol; from St-Bénigne, two Romanesque tympana frame the **Christ on the cross**★★ (1410) attributed to Claus de Werve.

Level 2 – Display of the vestiges of items from different periods, from Paleolithic times to the Merovingian Era. Included in the collection are pottery pieces typical of the Burgundian Neolithic Age, a **gold bracelet** which weighs 1.3kg/3lb found in **La Rochepot** (9C BC), and the **Blanot Treasure**★, a hoard of objects from the late Bronze Age (belt buckle, leggings, necklace and bracelet). In the last room, among some typical stone renderings of Gallo-Roman deities, notice the **frieze**

from Alésia, representing mother-goddesses, and a marble portrait of a woman found in Alise-Ste-Reine. Exhibits on the archaeological digs at Mâlain and the Merovingian Era evoke the way of life of these ancient cultures.

Église St-Philibert – *Closed for restoration.* This church, built in the 12C and altered in the 15C, has been deconsecrated. The west doorway is particularly interesting.

★ **Église St-Michel** – The church, built in Flamboyant Gothic style, was consecrated in December 1529, although its façade was eventually completed in the full Renaissance style; the four-storey towers framing it were finished in the 17C. The façade, on which the three classical orders are superimposed, is the most curious part of the building. The porch, which juts far out, is pierced by three doorways: a long frieze of ornamental foliage and grotesque decorations runs along the upper part of the porch for its whole length. Under it, in medallions, are busts of the prophets Daniel, Baruch, Isaiah and Ezekiel, as well as of David with his harp and Moses with the Tablets of the Law. The right doorway dates from 1537 and is the oldest of the three.

The Last Judgment, presented on the tympanum of the central doorway, is the work of a Flemish artist: Nicolas de la Cour. The 16C statue of St Michael on the pier replaces the original one which was destroyed during the Revolution. It rests on a finely sculpted console. The sculptures on the console were inspired by both pagan traditions and sacred texts; close together one can identify David, Lucretia, Leda and the Swan, Hercules, Apollo, Venus, Judith, the Judgment of Solomon, St John the Baptist and Christ appearing to Mary Magdalene.

The interior is Gothic in style. Note the height of the choir, which like St-Bénigne lacks an ambulatory, the 18C woodwork, and four paintings by Franz Kraus (18C German): *Adoration of the Shepherds* and *The Flight into Egypt* (deteriorated) in the north transept; *Adoration of the Magi* and *Presentation in the Temple* in the chapel of the Saint-Sacrament, which also has a fine Flamboyant altar. The far north chapel contains a fragment of a 15C Entombment.

Musée d'Art sacré ⊘ – The late-17C church of Ste-Anne, with its circular plan and dome, now houses a collection of 13C-19C sacred art: crucifix with delicate decoration in Limoges enamel, chalices, ecclesiastical vestments, wooden statues, including a 12C Virgin Mary in Majesty and an elegant monumental marble altar with stucco work sculpted by the Dijon artist Jean Dubois c 1672. It depicts the Virgin Mary visiting St Elizabeth. The two bronze statues are beneath a Burgundian porphyry baldaquin supported on black marble columns and enlivened by a group of white cherubim in flight.

★ **Chartreuse de Champmol** – *Entrance: 1 boulevard Chanoine-Kir. Follow signs to the Puits de Moïse. Closed for restoration.*

A psychiatric hospital now occupies the site of this monastery, destroyed during the French Revolution in 1793. At the entrance is a 15C doorway which escaped destruction.

The first dukes of Burgundy were buried at Cîteaux but Philip the Bold wanted an almost royal burial place for himself and his heirs and in 1383 he founded the charter house which was consecrated five years later by the Bishop of Troyes. The best artists of the period contributed to the magnificent undertaking but nothing remains except the tombs of the dukes, the retables preserved in the Dijon Musée des Beaux-Arts, and two works by Claus Sluter (late 14C), the sculptor from Haarlem who became the leader of the Burgundian-Flemish School of Art: the chapel doorway and Well of Moses which stands in a courtyard.

Le puits de Moïse

Ph. Gajic/MICHELIN

★★ **Puits de Moïse (Well of Moses)** – *Walk round the buildings to reach the courtyard.*

In fact the well is the base of a polychrome Calvary made between 1395 and 1405 to decorate the font in the great cloisters (the painting is barely visible). It is named after the figure of Moses, probably the most impressive of the six huge and strikingly life-like statues which surround the hexagonal base; the other five figures are the prophets *(going round the monument to the right from Moses)* – David, Jeremiah, Zachariah, Daniel and Isaiah. The angels beneath the cornice are the work of Claus de Werve,

Sluter's nephew; with touching veracity each one through a different pose expresses his suffering before the Calvary (which has disappeared). The generous movement of the draperies brings Baroque sculpture to mind.

★ **Chapel doorway** – The doorway, which is now inside the chapel, consists of five statues sculpted by Claus Sluter between 1389 and 1394. Duke Philip the Bold and Margaret of Flanders, his wife, are depicted kneeling, watched by their patron saints (St John the Baptist and St Catherine), on each side of the Virgin Mary and Child who are portrayed on the central pier.

DOMESTIC ART IN BURGUNDY

Musée de la Vie bourguignonne ⊘ – ⊡ Housed in the Bernardines Monastery, built between 1679 and 1681, the museum covers local history through regional and urban ethnographic collections brought together by Perrin de Puycousin (1856-1949). Furnishings, household items, clothing, and other souvenirs of times past are used to bring to life the daily habits, ceremonies and traditions of Burgundy at the end of the 19C.

On the upper floor, a whole street has been recreated, complete with a beauty salon (some of the tools of the trade look more like instruments of torture) and a corner grocery. A scale model of a 19C manufacture is symbolic of industry in Dijon, whereas a gallery of the busts of significant local figures is an indication of the rich intellectual life here.

There is an electric train in the gallery displaying PLM posters.

Musée Amora ⊘ – *To the west via quai Nicolas-Rolin*. This museum, created by the Amora company, the world's leading mustard manufacturer, recounts the history of this common household condiment, its origins, and every aspect of its production. It is interesting to note that Dijon has become the "Mustard Capital of the World", producing as much as 100t a day, whereas there is not a single mustard field in France! Guided tours of the company museum, led by old-timers from the business, are available on a limited basis.

NATURE AND GREEN SPACES

Square Darcy – The square takes its name from the engineer who brought drinking water to Dijon in 1839. The basins and fountains are complemented by a background of greenery.

At the entrance is Pompon's (1855-1933) imposing statue of a **polar bear**.

★ **Jardin de l'Arquebuse** – This park owes its name to the company of harquebusiers, who occupied the site in the 16C. All the western part is taken up by the botanical gardens (3 500 different species), which were founded in the 18C and joined to the Promenade de l'Arquebuse. In addition there is an arboretum, tropical glasshouses and a vivarium. Magnificent trees surround the colourful flower beds.

★ **Muséum d'Histoire Naturelle** ⊘ – ⊡ The Natural History Museum, founded in 1836 by a nature lover from Dijon, Léonard Nodot, is housed in the old cross-bowmen's barracks (1608). As an introduction to the museum, visit the **ground floor** exhibits on the origins and evolution of the world, including a magnificent **glyptodon★**, a giant armadillo from the Argentinian pampas which first saw the light in the Tertiary Era. Regional geology is also a theme.

The **first floor** is devoted to animal life, and displays include exceptionally good **reconstitutions of the natural habitat★**. Multimedia and hands-on exhibits provide a lively approach to the flora and fauna of the five continents, the Arctic and Antarctic.

On the **second floor**, a surprisingly diverse collection of insects draws the visitor's attention, in particular the superb butterfly display.

The orangery houses temporary exhibitions, a vivarium and beehive.

The Dijon Port

At the entrance to the port, on the city side, stands an obelisk dating from the 1780s, in commemoration of the creation of the **Port de Dijon** and the 1 000km/600mi of canals crisscrossing Burgundy. The Prince de Condé, Governor of the Province, conceived this network as a way of linking Dijon with both Paris and the Mediterranean basin, to the north and south, and with the Loire by the Canal du Centre, thus connecting to the Atlantic Ocean to the west.

The ambitious scheme came under fire during the Revolution and was reduced in scale. The first ship to reach Dijon from the south arrived under Napoleon I, the first arrival from Paris didn't take place until 1820, and the Atlantic connection was dropped entirely.

Today the canals, which intersect at the historic port of the old town, are used for recreational boating only.

Parc de la Colombière – This is reached by way of an avenue of magnificent trees. Clumps of flowering shrubs are intersected by paths and green lawns, all once part of the Condé Princes park. A section of the Roman road *Via Agrippa* which linked Lyon to Trier can be seen in this park.

Lac Kir – This 37ha/91-acre artificial lake, named after its initiator, a famous canon from Dijon, is sought after by the local population for the leisure activities it offers: rambling, angling, swimming and water sports.
The lake also regulates the flow of the River Ouche which the canon used to swim in as a kid.

★★MUSÉE DES BEAUX-ARTS ⊘

The huge fine arts museum created in 1799 is housed in the former ducal palace and in the eastern wing of the palace of the States-General. An engraved plaque, on the wall to the right of the entrance, shows the layout of the Gallo-Roman fortress which covered the central area of Dijon.

Ground floor – On the left, at the far end of the rooms devoted to temporary exhibitions, are the **ducal kitchens**, built in 1435. The six huge chimneys were scarcely sufficient for the preparation of feasts worthy of the Burgundian court; the vaulting converges on the central vent.

Ph. Gajic/MICHELIN

Ducal kitchens

The **chapter-house** of the former 14C ducal chapel (ground floor of the Tour de Bar) illustrates the evolution of religious sculpture – an art form held in high regard in Burgundy – from the 14C to the 17C; precious works of art include: 15C stained-glass windows, reliquaries, 16C silver gilt altarpiece together with St Robert's cross (11C) and a cup belonging to St Bernard.
On the grand staircase stands a statue of the Maréchal de Saxe by **François Rude** (1784-1855).
On the landing is the old door of the Dijon law courts, carved by Hugues Sambin (16C), and some fine medieval and Renaissance pieces of religious gold- and silver-ware and carved ivory.

First floor – This floor houses Italian painting from the 14C to the 16C, with particularly good examples of the Primitive schools of Florence (Taddeo Gaddi) and Siena (Pietro Lorenzetti) and of the Florentine Renaissance (*St Peter Walking on the Water* by Vasari in 1574, the author of the famous artists' biographies). Two galleries contain paintings by 15C and 16C German and Swiss masters; including the Master of the Darmstadt Passion (1425), Conrad Witz *(Emperor Augustus and the Tibur Sibyl)*. Note also the **Annunciation with St Christopher and St Anthony** (German School 15C) and the *Entombment* (16C).

The Prestigious Order of the Golden Fleece

In 1404, Philip the Bold created the Order of the Golden Tree, which John the Fearless and Philip the Good perpetuated and enhanced.
It was this second Philip who, at the time of his marriage to Isabella of Portugal in Bruges, 1429, first wore the insignia of the **Golden Fleece**: a chain encircling his neck, from which hung a sheepskin. The symbolism of the Order relates to Jason of Greek mythology as well as Gideon in the Old Testament. There were two reasons for creating the Order: first, to draw Burgundy closer to the Church by keeping the spirit of the Crusades and chivalry alive, and second, to strengthen the duchy's position in regard to the English crown, the Holy Roman Empire and the Kingdom of France.
The Order was based in the chapel of the ducal palace in Dijon, where the young Count of Charollais, who was later to become Charles the Bold, was knighted in 1433.
The marriage of his only daughter, Marie de Bourgogne, in 1477, to Archduke Maximilian of Austria, brought the Hapsburgs into the Order.
The Order of the Golden Fleece still carries great prestige and implies a commitment to a disciplined life. It is not hereditary, and the official insignia must be returned by the heirs upon a knight's death.

Of the next three galleries *(overlooking the courtyard)*, the first two are devoted to Renaissance art: furniture, medals, enamels and paintings *(Lady dressing, Fontainebleau School)*; the third room is hung with 17C Burgundian paintings (Ph. Quantin).

The wing overlooking rue Rameau is devoted to French painting, starting with 17C works by painters under Louis XIV: Philippe de Champaigne *(Presentation in the Temple)*, Le Sueur, Le Brun and François Perrier. Note also the *Portrait of a Painter* by P Mignard and the *Holy Family Resting* by Sébastien Bourdon. Artists from the late 17C and 18C are represented in two galleries, in particular Burgundian painters such as JF Gilles, known as Colson *(Rest, 1759)* and JB Lallemand (Dijon 1716-Paris 1803), creator of landscapes and genre scenes. A large gallery displays paintings by Nattier *(Portrait of Marie Leszczynska)*, Van Loo *(St George and the Dragon)* and others.

The **Salle des Statues**, in the corner of the west wing, which contains copies of ancient works and 19C pieces including *Hebe and the Eagle of Jupiter* by Rude, has a fine view of place de la Libération; the ceiling depicting the fame of Burgundy and Prince Condé is by Pierre Paul Prud'hon after a Roman piece by Pietro da Cortona. The adjacent **Salon Condé** is decorated with woodwork and stucco of the Louis XVI period; it displays 18C French art: furniture, terracottas and paintings as well as sculptures by Coysevox (bust of Louis XIV) and Caffieri (busts of Rameau and Piron).

The **Prince's Staircase**, which is built against the Gothic façade of the old Dukes' Palace, leads down to the **Salle d'Armes** (Arms Room) on the ground floor: weapons and armour from the 13C to the 18C; cutlery and knives dating from the 16C to the 18C.

The **Salle du Maître du Flémalle**, which contains 14C-15C Flemish and Burgundian painting, including the famous ***Nativity*★★** by the **Master of Flémalle** and several works of art from the Chartreuse de Champmol, provides an excellent introduction to the Salle des Gardes.

◎ The **Salle des Gardes★★★** overlooking place des Ducs is the most famous gallery in the museum. It was built by Philip the Good and used as the setting for the Joyous Entry of Charles the Bold in 1474; it had to be restored in the early 16C after a fire. It houses the art treasures from the Chartreuse de Champmol, the necropolis of the dukes of Valois *(see above)*.

From 1385 to 1410 three men – Jean de Marville, Claus Sluter and his nephew, Claus de Werve – worked successively on the **tomb of Philip the Bold★★★**. The magnificent recumbent figure, watched over by two angels, rests on a black marble slab surrounded by alabaster arches forming a cloister to shelter the procession of mourners composed of 41 very realistic statuettes. The funeral procession consists of clergymen, Carthusians, relatives, friends and officials of the Prince, all hooded or dressed in mourning.

The **tomb of John the Fearless and Margaret of Bavaria★★★**, dating from between 1443 and 1470, is in a similar, although more Flamboyant style.

The two altarpieces in gilt wood commissioned by Philip the Bold for the Chartreuse de Champmol are very richly decorated. They were carved between 1390 and 1399 by Jacques de Baerze and painted and gilded by Melchior Broederlam. Only the **Crucifixion altarpiece★★★** near the tomb of Philip the Bold has retained Broederlam's famous paintings on the reverse side of the wings: the *Annunciation*, the *Visitation*, the *Presentation in the Temple* and the *Flight into Egypt*. At the other end is the **altarpiece of the Saints and Martyrs★★★**. In the centre, note an early-16C **altarpiece of the Passion★★** from an Antwerp workshop.

Above the central altarpiece, between two 16C wall hangings from Tournai, hangs a tapestry dedicated to Notre-Dame-de-Bon-Espoir, protector of the city since the raising of the siege of Dijon by the Swiss on 11 September 1513.

A niche contains a handsome portrait of Philip the Good wearing the collar of the Order of the Golden Fleece, painted by the Rogier Van der Weyden workshop (c 1455). A staircase leads to the tribune, from which there is a good **view★** of the recumbent figures.

Procession of mourners at the tomb of Philip the Bold

The **Galerie de Bellegarde** contains some good examples of 17C and 18C Italian and Flemish painting, in particular *Moses in the Bullrushes* by Veronese and *Adam and Eve* by Guido Reni; there is an unusual panoramic landscape of the *Château de Mariemont* and its grounds by Velvet Brueghel, and a *Virgin and Child with St Francis of Assisi* by Rubens.

Next comes a gallery devoted to 19C French sculpture and displaying works by Rude, Canova, Carpeaux and Mercié.

Second and third floors – These are devoted to modern and contemporary art, including the Granville bequest. Works by the great animal sculptor **François Pompon** (1855-1933) are displayed in an old gallery in the Tour de Bar *(signposted)*.

The other galleries contain paintings, drawings, graphics and sculptures dating from the 16C to the present. Particularly famous names include Georges de la Tour *(Le Souffleur à la lampe)*, Géricault, Delacroix, Victor Hugo (imaginary landscapes in wash), Daumier, Courbet, Gustave Moreau and various painters from the Barbizon School (Daubigny, Rousseau, Diaz de la Peña etc), Rodin, Maillol, Bourdelle and others.

The Impressionists and Post-Impressionists are represented by works by Manet *(Portrait of Méry Laurent* in pastel), Monet, Boudin, Sisley, Cross, Vuillard and Vallotton.

A remarkable collection of African sculpture and masks (Mali, Cameroon, Congo) gives an insight into the art forms which inspired Cubist painters and sculptors: Juan Gris, Marcoussis, Gleizes, Picasso *(Minotaur)*.

Among the rich collection of contemporary painting and sculpture note in particular works by artists in or linked with the Paris School and abstract artists of the 1950s to 1970s: Arpad Szenes and Vieira da Silva, his wife, Lapicque, De Staël *(Footballer)*, Bertholle, Manessier, Messagier, Mathieu and Wols; also several lovely sculptures by Hajdu.

The university's open-air museum contains more contemporary sculpture by Karel Appel, Arman and Gottfried Honegger.

EXCURSIONS

Talant – *On the outskirts of Dijon, heading W. Go up to the church at the top of this former village.* The castle which stood here has completely disappeared apart from an underground cellar. From the viewing table, near the church, there is a fine **view**★ of Dijon and the Ouche Valley.

The restored 13C **church** contains several interesting statues: a 14C Virgin with Child, two 15C *Pietà*, a 16C Christ in Bonds, two 16C Entombments (the finest is in the middle of the south aisle), a medieval Crucifix (in the chancel). Note also the modern **stained-glass window**★ by Gérard Garouste and Pierre-Alain Parot.

Val Suzon

40km/25mi round tour NW of Dijon; add another 21km/13mi for the detour to St-Seine-l'Abbaye.

Messigny-et-Vantoux – *10km/6mi N.* 17C château designed by Jules Hardouin-Mansart.

As you drive out of the village, turn left onto D 7.

The River Suzon, a tributary of the Ouche, flows between wooded banks. The narrow valley widens into the lovely **Ste-Foy** basin. The road then takes a right-angle turn, following the river closely.

In Val-Suzon-Haut, turn left onto N 71 to return to Dijon or turn right onto N 71 to St-Seine-l'Abbaye.

St-Seine-l'Abbaye – This place, about 10km/6mi from the source of the Seine, perpetuates the name of a holy man who founded a Benedictine abbey on his land in the 6C. The abbey church has survived.

Église St-Gilles – This early-13C abbey church marks the transition from the Burgundian-Romanesque style to the Gothic style which came from the Île-de-France. The church was restored in the 14C after a fire; the façade dates from the 15C. The porch is set between two towers, supported by buttresses; the right-hand tower is incomplete. The nave is lit by a clerestory; the flat chevet is pierced by a beautiful rose window, rebuilt in the 19C. The chapels in the flat-ended transept communicate with the side aisles of the choir by means of stone screens pierced by window apertures. There are numerous tombstones in the transept. At the end of the choir stands the former rood screen.

The 18C carved stalls are set against a Renaissance screen, on the reverse side of which are paintings representing the story of St Seine (1504).

On leaving the church, note the fountain of the Samaritan Woman; the basin is surmounted by an 18C bronze.

▶▶ **Sources de la Seine** – *10km/6mi NW.*

◙ It is hard to believe that this tiny stream becomes a world-famous river.

DIVONNE-LES-BAINS‡

Population 6 171
Michelin map 328: J-2
Local map see ST-CLAUDE: Excursion

Divonne is a well-known spa town half way between Lake Geneva and the great Jura mountain range, on the Franco-Swiss border. It is the only town in the Jura region equipped with luxury hotels, a golf course and a racecourse. Many leisure activities can be enjoyed at the 45ha/111-acre reservoir and the sailing base.

To the west, trails lead up Mont Ussy; view over Lake Geneva and the Alps.

Romans enjoyed the waters at Divonne (Divine Source) long ago. An 11km/6.6mi aqueduct carried water to their colonial capital Noviodunum (Nyon). In later centuries, the waters, emerging from five springs at a constant temperature of 6.5°C/43.7°F, ran on forgotten, until 1848, when Dr Paul Vidart founded a spa. It soon became famous, attracting such clients as Prince Jérôme Bonaparte and Guy de Maupassant.

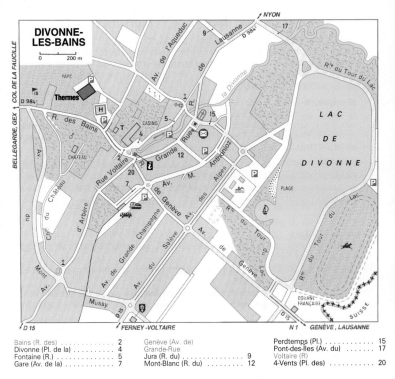

Baths ⊘ – *Avenue des Thermes*. The spa specialises in the treatment of ailments often associated with modern living, such as stress, insomnia, overexertion, tension. Fitness programmes are also available at the spa, set in a pleasant park.

Racecourse – Located near the lake, the racecourse is used in summer for flat racing and also for trotting races.

Lake – This vast artificial lake boasts a popular beach and is sought after by windsurfers and sailing enthusiasts.

EXCURSION

Pays de Gex

Gex – This small village (alt 628m/2 060ft) not far from the mountains and Switzerland is a good departure point for excursions. Mont Blanc can be seen from the terraced village square, place Gambetta. Gex was once a small principality, and until 1601 it belonged to the House of Savoy. It then passed into the hands of the French, who granted it duty-free status for tobacco and salt during the 18C.

Modern residents still benefit from a special tax status exempting them from duty on all products imported from abroad.

Eating out and where to stay

MODERATE

Auberge du Vieux Bois – *1km/0.6mi W of Divonne on the road to Gex - ☏ 04 50 20 01 43 - closed 3-24 Feb, 1-8 Jul, 30 Sep-7 Oct, Sun evenings and Mon - 15/40€.* This unpretentious family inn lying on the edge of a forest extends a warm welcome to guests. Dining room with 1960s decor. During the summer season meals are served on the shaded terrace. Traditional cuisine.

Auberge des Chasseurs – *01170 Échenevex - 11km/6.8mi SW of Divonne by D 984C - ☏ 04 50 41 54 07 - closed 12 Nov-28 Feb, Sun evenings and Mon except Jul-Aug - P - 15 rooms: 84/130€ - ☕ 10€ - restaurant 31/51€.* A peaceful atmosphere characterises this inn offering spruce, tidy bedrooms. The interior boasts a fine wooden staircase and a hallway decorated with photographs and works of art. Relax by the outdoor pool or have a drink on the pretty terrace that looks out onto Mont Blanc.

Playtime, Tea Time, Night-time ...

Joy's Club – *783 av. des Alpes - ☏ 04 50 20 14 12 - open daily 10am-11pm - closed Nov-Mar.* This is the perfect place to come to with the family in a leafy setting near Divonne Lake. There are many organised activities for visitors of all ages (karting, mini-golf) and you can unwind on the shaded terrace while keeping an eye on the children...

Les Quatre-Vents – *Pl. des Quatre-Vents - ☏ 04 50 20 00 08 - Tue-Sat 6.30am-7.30pm, Sun 6.30am-3pm - closed Oct.* If long walks in the countryside have whetted your appetite, then tuck into some delicious home-made pastries in this tea shop. This will give you an opportunity to discover the work of local artists as the room is also used as a painting gallery.

Le 1900 – *49 r. Voltaire - ☏ 04 50 20 42 02 - open daily 9pm-1am.* A warm welcome and a relaxed atmosphere await you in this cocktail bar. The interior decoration is so attractive that it is patronised by tourists as well as by visitors following hydrotherapy treatment.

Creux de l'Envers – *2hr on foot there and back, starting from the bottom of rue du Commerce, then along rue Léone-de-Joinville, and returning via rue de Rogeland on N 5 N of Gex.*

This pleasant walk takes you to a wooded gash in the mountainside through which flows the River Journans.

The narrowest place is known as the **Portes Sarrasines**; the mountain stream rushes through a small gap in the rock flanked on both sides by limestone escarpments looking like a door frame.

★★ **Col de la Faucille** – The viewpoint near the summit affords superb views of Lake Geneva and the Alps.

★ **Monts Jura** – *See MONTS JURA.*

DOLE★

Population 24 949

Michelin map 321: C-4 – Local map see Forêt de CHAUX

The brown-tile roofs of Dole's old houses cluster around the church and its imposing bell-tower. The town is on a hillside overlooking the north bank of the Doubs, which is joined at this point by the Rhône-Rhine Canal. The citizens of Dole are proud of their city; it was the capital of the free province of Burgundy (the Franche-Comté) for many centuries. The present city is adorned with many splendid monuments.

HISTORICAL LANDMARKS

From the free county to the Franche-Comté – Dole was founded in the 11C, largely due to its position at the intersection of major communications routes. Until its annexation by the French, Dole forged links with both the dukes of Burgundy and the emperors of Germany – Friedrich Barbarossa endowed it with a civil charter in 1274. In the 15C, as seat of the Parliament of the Comté and of a university, Dole was already playing the role of a capital city, and it was not long before the flourishing town was noticed – and coveted – by Louis XI and the French.

In 1479 Louis XI laid the town to siege. In spite of the heroic resistance of the inhabitants (which gave rise to a pithy summary of the exchange between the French, demanding surrender *"Comtois, rends-toi"*, and the citizens of Dole, refusing *"Nenni, ma foi!"*), Dole eventually fell and was methodically burned to the ground by its invaders. This is why there is so little architectural evidence left in the town predating the 16C. Furthermore, Louis XI, who was furious that the citizens of Dole had resisted him, forbade the townspeople to rebuild their houses. However, his son Charles VIII returned the Comté to the Habsburgs in 1493, and Dole soon rose to its position as capital again.

The golden age – The 16C and 17C were a period of great prosperity and also a great deal of construction. The collegiate church was built during this period, and a stronger fortified city wall with several bastions. Among the architects and artists responsible for introducing the Renaissance style to the city were Denis and Hugues Le Rupt, Jean Rabicant and the Lulliers.

Dole owed its development and influence up until French annexation primarily to its role as the parliamentary, governmental and university seat.

The **Parliament** was set up by the dukes of Burgundy from the House of Valois when they inherited the Comté in 1384. It exercised supreme justice – even the most noble landowner was not above its jurisdiction – and held major influence in the political, economic, diplomatic and military worlds. Apart from one or two members of the aristocracy, it consisted mainly of lawyers and legal experts from the merchant class. The **university**, founded in 1423, soon won a reputation for the excellent standard of its legal faculty. Lectures were attended by about 800 students, including many young men from abroad. It was customary for these foreign students to have valentines, young local girls who helped them improve their French. Dole's schools produced expert lawyers, providing the count and the emperor with reliable advisers who gradually replaced the members of the aristocracy.

The **States** (États) were formed of three classes: the nobility, the clergy and the citizens. They decided how much tax the province should pay to the count.

Religious life also blossomed, with Dole becoming a leading bastion of the **Counter-Reformation** under Philip II of Spain, an ardent Roman Catholic. Churches and monasteries were built, which still enhance the present city.

The Siege of 1636 and the French Conquest – French attempts to annex the Comté were renewed under **Louis XIII** and his chancellor Richelieu. In 1636 the Prince of Condé, father of the Grand Condé, laid siege to Dole. The French soldiers subjected the town to a steady hail of newly developed, heavy bombs, which crashed through roofs and floors to explode in the basement, demolishing whole buildings. But even after three months of this, French troops were forced to withdraw in the face of the courageous resistance of the townspeople. This unexpected victory for Dole reaffirmed it in its position as independent capital. The episode passed into local legend and even today people recall, for example, the bravery of Ferdinand de Rye, Governor of the Comté and Archbishop of Besançon, who despite being well over 80 years old had himself shut in with the beleaguered townspeople and became the heart and soul of their resistance.

However, in 1668 and 1674 Louis XIV's troops renewed the attack on Dole, which finally succumbed, and in the Treaty of Nijmegen (1678) town and province were officially annexed to France. The Sun King did not forgive Dole for having put up such strong resistance; he made Besançon the capital of the Franche-Comté in its place, stripping Dole of its Parliament, its university and its ramparts.

Dole on the banks of the Doubs

M. Paygnard/MICHELIN

LOCAL HEROES AND ENFANTS TERRIBLES

The Malet conspiracy – Général Malet, cousin of Rouget de Lisle, was born in Dole and embodied most of the characteristics that the French associate with a typical *Comtois*: he was independent-minded and stubborn, loved contention and espoused Republicanism. He was a prime target for Napoleon's suspicion and was eventually imprisoned in Paris on the latter's orders in 1808. Malet escaped during the night of 23-24 October 1812, along with a few supporters, and managed to bring the local barracks, several ministries and the town hall under his control. But a suspicious officer brought the attempted *coup* to an end. Malet was arrested and shot, along with nine of his comrades.

The Pasteur family – The great scientist Louis Pasteur was born in Dole on 27 December 1822. His father Joseph Pasteur had been a sergeant-major in the Imperial Army, but was discharged on the fall of Napoleon and took up his previous trade as tanner. He married Jeanne-Étiennette Roqui in 1816.

When the great scientist, at the peak of his fame, returned to Dole on 14 July 1883 for the unveiling of a commemorative plaque on the house where he was born, he made a vote of thanks, in which he above all expressed his gratitude to his parents. He spoke of his mother's enthusiasm and respect for learning, which she had passed on to him. He said his father had showed him what patience and tenacious application could achieve in even the hardest profession, and described how his father had always admired great people and great achievements, teaching his son to be ever open to learning new things and to strive ceaselessly for self-improvement.

In 1827 the family left Dole to settle in Arbois.

Marcel Aymé's childhood in Dole – The writer and novelist **Marcel Aymé** (1902-67) was sent at the age of seven from the little town of Villers-Robert in the Bresse region to his aunt's at Dole. He was a disruptive, mischievous child at school, but by the age of 17 passed his higher school certificate, specialising in mathematics, and left for Paris to study to be an engineer. Poor health forced him to break off his studies and return to Dole. Here he wrote his first novel *Brûlebois* in 1926. His talent was quickly recognised, and in 1929 he was awarded the Prix Renaudot for his *La Table aux crevés*. He followed this with works such as *La Jument verte* and *La Vouivre*.

Dole is vividly portrayed in Aymé's novels. The fairground, the hospital, the station, rue Pasteur and the market place are just some of the parts of Dole which are evoked in his work. Indeed, the bell-tower of Notre-Dame plays a significant role in the detective thriller *Moulin de la Sourdine*...

★★ OLD TOWN

The old town is clustered around the church of Notre-Dame. Its narrow, winding streets are closely packed with houses, dating from the 15C to the 18C, many of which have interesting details: coats of arms above doorways, turrets, arcaded inner courtyards, various types of stone or timber staircases, wells, statue-niches and wrought-iron window grilles and balustrades.

Leave from place Nationale.

Place Nationale – This charming square in the centre of the old town, surrounded by old houses, has been restored and is once more a busy market square.

In the Sainte-Chapelle

★ **Collégiale Notre-Dame** ⊙ – The collegiate church dates from the 16C and symbolises Dole's rise from the ashes of the fire of 1479. The sturdy belfry-porch (75m/246ft tall) is a reminder also of the religious strife of the period.

The size of the church's interior is striking. Its clear sober lines are a resolute departure from the excessive ornamentation of the Late Gothic style, anticipating the Renaissance. It was furnished and decorated at the expense of local dignitaries and contains some of the first Renaissance works of art to manifest themselves in Dole, such as the beautiful **works in polychrome marble★**. These are characterised by motifs typical of those used by artists in the Dole workshops (foliage, tracery and birds) as, for example, on the façade of the Sainte-Chapelle, the organ case and the pulpit (Denis Le Rupt) and the holy-water stoup. The arch of the Carondelet mausoleum is attributed to a Flemish craftsman. The statues of the Apostles against the

DOLE

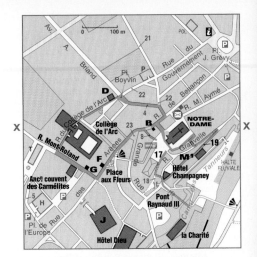

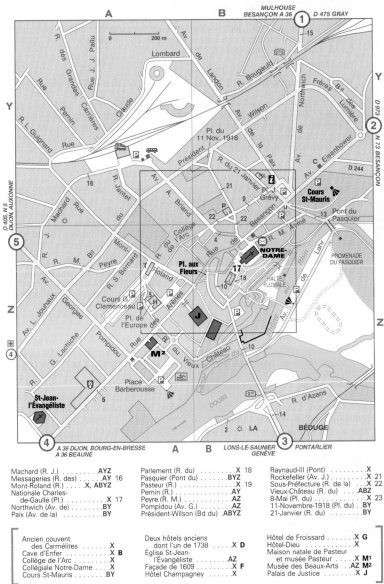

Eating out

BUDGET

La Demi Lune – *39 r. Pasteur - ☎ 03 84 72 82 82 - closed 7-27 Jan and Mon - 13.12/35.40€.* This restaurant with its pretty 16C and 18C vaulted dining room lies close to the Musée Pasteur. Soak up the sun on the terrace running alongside the Canal des Tanneurs. The house specialities include grilled meat, buckwheat pancakes and regional delicacies. Playing area for children.

MODERATE

Les Templiers – *35 Grande-Rue - ☎ 03 84 82 78 78 - closed Sat lunchtime, Sun evenings and Mon - 14.94€ lunch - 24.39/44.21€.* This 13C crypt nestling in a narrow alley in the old quarter enjoys a medieval setting that will appeal to diners: handsome dining hall embellished with ribbed vaulting and chandeliers illuminating the light stone walls. Meals made with good fresh produce.

Where to stay

BUDGET

Chambre d'Hôte La Thuilerie des Fontaines – *2 r. des Fontaines - 39700 Châtenois - 7.5km/4.8mi NE of Dole by N 73 heading for Besançon then D 10 and D 79 until you reach Châtenois - ☎ 03 84 70 51 79 - michel.meunier2@wanadoo.fr - ⊭ - 4 rooms: 34/41€.* The atmosphere is warm and inviting in this 18C guesthouse surrounded by a pretty park. The rooms, reached by a stone staircase, are comfortable and impeccably kept. Take a break down by the pool, near the former stables.

MODERATE

Hôtel La Chaumière – *346 av. du Mar-Juin - ☎ 03 84 70 72 40 - closed 6-15 Apr, 26 Oct-4 Nov, 20 Dec-14 Jan and Sun Sep-Jun - P - 18 rooms: 58.70/74.70€ - ☕ 9.60€ - restaurant 24/64€.* This is the ideal place for lounging around on a deckchair by the pool or showing off on the diving-board. The rooms give onto the peaceful garden. The dining room is bright and comfortable with stone walls and exposed beams. Summer terrace. Family cooking with fresh regional produce.

Sit back and relax

Bar des Sports - Chez Chartier – *12 chemin Thévenot - ☎ 03 84 72 09 48 - open daily 10am-1am (summer); 10am-midnight (the rest of the year) - closed 1 week end of Sep.* The main attraction of this unassuming little café is its remarkable location: facing a beautiful meadow, it offers wonderful views over the Canal Charles-Quint and its procession of ducks paddling in the water. The musical accompaniment covers several decades ranging from the 1970s to the 1990s.

La Navigation – *22 r. Louis-Pasteur - ☎ 03 84 72 11 04 - open daily 9am-1am.* This area was once known for the large number of mills it featured. La Navigation used to be a popular stopping place among boatmen who would come to unload their grain. The terrace is particularly pleasant as the café is set up in a lively pedestrian area.

pillars either side of the chancel were executed by the Burgundian School (early 16C). The marvellous carved wooden **great organ** dating from the 18C is one of the very rare examples of its type in France to have survived virtually intact. The organ builder was Karl Joseph Riepp.

The **Sainte-Chapelle** *(entrance at the far end of the south aisle)* was built in the 17C to house the miraculous Sacred Host of Faverney. In 1608 the church in Faverney burned to the ground, but the ostensory and the Sacred Host survived the fire intact, and have been kept at Dole ever since. The coffered vaulting is adorned with rosettes.

To the right of the old town hall, take rue d'Enfer, which leads to rue de Besançon then place du 8-Mai-1945 and rue des Arènes.

Place aux Fleurs – There is a pretty **view** of old Dole, dominated by the bell-tower of Notre-Dame church.

The fountain in the square, dedicated to childhood, was sculpted by François Rosset. There is also a modern work by Boettchen, *The Gossips*. A 1609 façade graces no 28.

Rue Mont-Roland – Note the polychrome marble and stone doorway of the old Carmelite convent (17C) and the façades of some of the private mansions, for example, the Maison Odon de la Tour (16C) and the **Hôtel de Froissard** (early 17C), where you should pass through the gate to admire the double horseshoe staircase and the loggia in the inner courtyard.

Take rue du Collège-de-l'Arc on the right.

Collège de l'Arc – The Jesuits founded this school in 1582.

Go under the arch which spans the street.

The chapel, deconsecrated today, is distinguished by its beautiful, richly decorated Renaissance **porch**, surmounted by a loggia with arches supported by the figures of angels in flight.

Notice the two mansions on the left, one of which dates from 1738; they still have their small inner courtyards and beautiful balustrades.

Continue to place Boyvin and from there take rue Boyvin, rue de la Sous-Préfecture and rue de Besançon to the right.

Cave d'Enfer – A plaque recalls the heroic resistance of a few Dole citizens during the attack on the town in 1479.

Turn back to reach place Nationale, then take rue Pasteur.

Rue Pasteur – This street used to be called rue des Tanneurs, as it regrouped all the houses of the hemp and leather craftsmen along the banks of the canal. No 43 is the birthplace of Pasteur *(see Additional Sights below)*.

Take the passage on the right of Pasteur's birthplace, follow the canal walk and take the footbridges to get to the Pont Raynaud-III.

Pont Raynaud-III – View of a handsome architectural group: the Charité (18C hospital), the Hôtel-Dieu (17C hospice) and an 18C convent. The Grande Fontaine, an underground spring and wash-house, can be seen under the last arch of the bridge *(to get to it, go down passage Raynaud-III off rue Pasteur).*

Hôtel Champagney – An 17C portal surmounted by a crest leads into a courtyard where two interesting staircases and a beautiful balcony on corbels can be seen.

Take the picturesque rue du Parlement, to the left and then to the right, from which there is a beautiful view of the Notre-Dame bell-tower, which acts as a landmark to get back to place Nationale.

ADDITIONAL SIGHTS

Maison natale de Pasteur and Musée Pasteur ⊙ – The house where Louis Pasteur was born still contains the evidence of his father's trade as a tanner, with old tools and the tannery in the basement. In the living quarters, documents and souvenirs relating to Pasteur are displayed in several rooms. Portraits and personal mementoes recall his family and childhood; note the Légion d'Honneur awarded to the scientist's father by Napoleon I. Among Pasteur's possessions on view are his university cape and cap, his desk, a frame made of grapevines (a gift from local wine-growers), and two pastels executed in his youth.

From the terrace on the first floor there is a view of the tanners' canal and the 16C fortifications.

The **Musée Pasteur** is located in another tanner's workshop next door to Pasteur's birthplace and illustrates the enormous significance of the great scientist's work. A room with old scientific equipment recalls the experiments of the chemist and physicist, who was neither doctor nor biologist, but whose discoveries about bacteria nonetheless made an enormous impact on the worlds of medicine, surgery and the food industry. The famous dried bone marrow from a rabid rabbit still fascinates modern visitors.

Articles and photographs evoke the current 22 Pasteur Institutes throughout the world, which carry out important scientific research particularly in the domain of immunology; a living testimony to this great man.

★ **Musée des Beaux-Arts** ⊙ – *85 rue des Arènes.*

The Museum of Fine Art is located in the 18C Officers' Lodge, hence the military nature of the decoration on the façade.

The lower level is devoted to local and regional archaeology (prehistoric, Gallo-Roman, Merovingian periods and Burgundian sculpture).

The ground-floor rooms are reserved for temporary exhibitions.

On the first floor the museum houses a collection of paintings mainly from France, dating from the 15C to the 20C: Simon Vouet *(Death of Dido)*, Mignard *(Portrait of a Woman and Her Son)*, several landscapes by Courbet and works by Auguste Pointelin (1836-1933) from Arbois, who was creating almost abstract landscapes with large patches of colour as early as 1870. There are also paintings evoking the sieges of various Franche-Comté towns, including that of Dole in the 17C. The top floor exhibits the contemporary art collection.

Hôtel-Dieu – This 17C hospice was the last major construction project before the town fell to the French. The severity of the long façade and high roof of this stately building is softened by a remarkable balcony, supported by sculpted corbels, and the double windows with stone frames. The inner courtyard is laid out like cloisters with two storeys of arcades. The building was splendidly restored and turned into a multimedia library.

Église St-Jean-l'Évangéliste ⓥ – This church was built from 1961 to 1964 by architects Konrady and Cotter. It is strikingly original in style; the sail-like roof is made of two hyperbola-shaped parts. A beautiful wrought-iron **grille★** by Calka, illustrating the Apocalypse, surrounds the glass walls; note particularly the *Lamb* and the *Woman and Dragon*. Extracts from the Revelation of St John are painted on the walls to the right of the altar and over the door. A wrought-iron eagle, the symbol of St John the Evangelist, adorns the base of the lectern. The baptistery and the altar were built from local stone.

FERNEY-VOLTAIRE

Population 7 083
Michelin map 328: J-3

Ferney-Voltaire lies on the Franco-Swiss border and is a literary Mecca for those interested in Voltaire. In 1758 the philosopher, who lived at Les Délices near Geneva, was having trouble with local residents and the strictly conventional Calvinistic city council in particular, who found his plays rather shocking. He therefore decided to buy the estate at Ferney, on French territory but near the border. Depending on whatever situation he found himself in, he would then be able to slip into exile easily from one country to the other.

Portrait of Voltaire

From 1760, Ferney became his favourite home. He extended the château and laid out the park, taking his role as landlord very seriously. He had sanitation installed in the village, part of his estate, and endowed it with a hospital, a school and clockmaking workshops. He had solid homes built for the residents out of stone, around a church in which Voltaire – who would have thought it? – had his own pew.

Life in Ferney – Voltaire as good as held court in Ferney for 18 years, with great lords, merchants, artists and writers all enjoying his hospitality and attending the plays put on in his theatre. The immense fortune which Voltaire had amassed, owing to some fortunate speculation in military supplies, enabled him to entertain 50 guests at all times. The curious came from far and wide to catch a glimpse of him in the park. When he emerged from his château, he would be walking amid a sort of guard of honour of admirers. He wrote his stories here, as well as numerous leaflets and pamphlets, led campaigns against abuse of any kind, particularly against the still-existing serfdom in the Haut-Jura *(see ST-CLAUDE)*. His correspondence was prolific: he wrote or dictated at least 20 letters a day at Ferney, of which over 10 000 were published. Shortly after the 84 year old travelled without his doctor's permission to Paris, where he was rapturously received, he died, exhausted with all the honour (1778).

Château ⓥ – Built by Voltaire to replace a fortress too austere for his tastes, the château, surrounded by a park, is in the Doric style, meant to last a thousand sand years. It contains many mementoes of the philosopher's life, including his portrait at the age of 40, by Quentin de La Tour (library and small cafeteria).

▶▶ **Geneva** – The harbour and the lake shores, the old town, the international district and the Palais des Nations *(see The Green Guide Switzerland)*.

Château de FILAIN★

Population 207
Michelin map 317: F-7

Filain, amid the undulating countryside around Vesoul and the first foothills of the Jura, is one of the finest châteaux in the Franche-Comté region, with a magnificent monumental fireplace.

Tour ⓘ – In the 15C a stronghold flanked by four towers stood on this spur. The right wing of the château dates from this period; the windows were enlarged and mullions were added in the 16C. The central, Renaissance building was linked in the 16C to the earlier buildings. There are large mullioned windows between the two orders of superposed columns (the Roman Doric style can be seen on the ground floor, and the Ionic style on the first floor). The once open gallery on the ground floor was converted to its present state at the beginning of the 19C.
From the garden the 16C south-facing façade is seen at its best, framed by two square towers each topped by a more recent, typically Comtois roof in the Imperial style. Under the First Empire, the old drawbridge was replaced by a staircase with balustrades.
The building is entered through a beautifully sculpted Renaissance doorway, which was carved out of one of the old stronghold corner towers in the 15C.

Salle des Gardes

The tour begins on the ground floor, in the kitchen where a beautiful collection of waffle irons and host moulds are displayed; then come two rooms containing an ornithological collection. On the first floor, the **Salle des Gardes** (guard-room) is embellished by a particularly ornate **Renaissance fireplace★**: the top of the composition features the château's two façades and a superb stag can be seen leaping out of the centre part. The tour now goes through the Grande Galerie and the parlours, before going down to the old kitchens, which have been converted into a library, and the barrel-vaulted passageway which was once the main entrance of the château.

FLAVIGNY-SUR-OZERAIN★

Population 411
Michelin map 320: H-4

Flavigny is built in a picturesque **spot★**, perched on a rock isolated by three streams. Seat of an abbey since the 8C and a fortified township in the Middle Ages, Flavigny no longer has its former importance. Its narrow streets, flanked by old mansions, its fortified gateways and the remains of its ramparts recall its past grandeur.

Aniseed Candy from the Abbaye de Flavigny – This famous local confection, a tiny seed coated in snow-white sugar, has been made in the old abbey since the 9C. The pretty tins and boxes they come in are as attractive as the little sweets inside with their distinctive burst of flavour.

SIGHTS

Park the car on the Esplanade des Fossés. No cars allowed beyond this point.

Old houses – Many houses have been restored; they date from the late Middle Ages and the Renaissance and are decorated with turrets, spiral stairs or delicate sculptures. Note, in particular, the Maison du Donataire (15C-16C) in rue de l'Église.

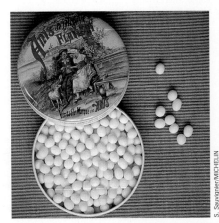

Anis de Flavigny

261

Ancienne abbaye ⊙ – A Benedictine abbey, founded in the 8C, consisted of a great church, the basilica of St-Pierre, and the usual conventual buildings. The latter were rebuilt in the 18C and now house the aniseed sweet factory. There are interesting remains from the Carolingian period of St-Pierre.

Crypte Ste-Reine ⊙ – The upper level of the double-decker Carolingian apse, reached by steps from the nave, contains the high altar. The lower chamber, built c 758, contains the tomb of St Reina. Following her martyrdom at Alise-Ste-Reine her remains were buried here c 866. The finely carved pillar is a good example of Carolingian decorative work.

Chapelle Notre-Dame-des-Piliers – In 1960 excavations revealed the existence of a hexagonal chapel with ambulatory beyond the crypt. The style recalls the pre-Romanesque rotundas of St-Bénigne in Dijon and Saulieu.

Église St-Genest ⊙ – This 13C church, built on the site of an even earlier religious building, was altered in the 15C and 16C. It has a stone central gallery dating from the beginning of the 16C. Other galleries run along the top of the aisles and the first two bays of the nave, something that is very rare in Gothic architecture. They are enclosed by 15C wooden screens. The stalls are early 16C. Among the many interesting statues, note the **Angel of the Annunciation**, a masterpiece of the Burgundian School, in the last chapel on the right in the nave, and a 12C Virgin nursing the Infant Jesus, in the south transept.

Tour of the ramparts – Starting from the 15C gateway, Porte du Bourg, with its impressive machicolations, take chemin des Fossés and chemin des Perrières to reach the Porte du Val flanked by two round towers. Nearby is the Maison Lacordaire, a former Dominican monastery founded by **Father Lacordaire** (1806-61).

EXCURSION

Château de Frolois ⊙ – *17km/10.2mi NW.* The Frolois family established its residence on this site in the 10C; the medieval fortress was often remodelled, leaving only the main building (14C-15C). On the first floor, the family heir, Antoine de Vergy, has a room with a French-style ceiling decorated with the family coat of arms and initials. The ground floor was remodelled in the 17C and 18C, and is hung with attractive late-17C Bergamo tapestries.

Abbaye de FONTENAY★★★

Michelin map 320: G-4

The abbey of Fontenay, nestling in a lonely but verdant valley, is a particularly good example of what a 12C Cistercian monastery was like, self-sufficient within its boundaries.

A Second Daughter of St Bernard – After he had become Abbot of Clairvaux, Bernard founded three religious settlements one after the other: Trois-Fontaines near St-Dizier in 1115, Fontenay in 1118, and Foigny in Thiérache in 1121. Accompanied by 12 monks, he arrived near Châtillon-sur-Seine at the end of 1118 and founded a hermitage there. After he had returned to Clairvaux, Bernard found that the monks he had left under the direction of Godefroy de la Roche had attracted so many others that the hermitage had become much too small. The monks moved into the valley and established themselves where the abbey stands today.

Up to the 16C the abbey was prosperous with more than 300 monks and converts, but the regime of Commendam – abbots nominated by royal favour and interested only in revenues – and the disorders caused by the religious wars brought about a rapid decline. The abbey was sold during the French Revolution and became a paper mill.

In 1906 new owners undertook to restore Fontenay to its original appearance. They tore down the parts which had been added for the paper mill and rebuilt the abbey just as it was in the 12C. The many fountains from which the abbey takes its name are today the most beautiful ornaments of the gardens surrounding the buildings; these were added in 1981 to UNESCO's World Heritage List.

TOUR ⊙

The main doorway of the porter's lodge is surmounted by the coat of arms of the abbey; the upper floor dates from the 15C. Under the archway, note the niche below the staircase: the opening made at the bottom used to permit the watchdog, on guard inside, to keep an eye on the hostel, the long building on the right of the inner courtyard, where pilgrims and travellers were lodged.

After the porch, walk along beside a large 13C building, which used to house the visitors' chapel and the monks' bakehouse, remarkable for its round chimney. Today this houses the reception area and a small lapidary museum. Further on to the right is a magnificent circular dovecot.

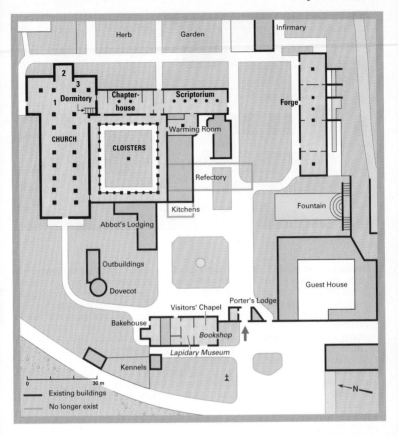

Abbey Church – Built during the lifetime of St Bernard, the church was erected from 1139 to 1147, owing to the generosity of Ebrard, Bishop of Norwich, who took refuge at Fontenay. The church was consecrated by Pope Eugenius III in 1147. It is one of the most ancient Cistercian churches preserved in France.

The expression monastic simplicity is particularly suited to the architectural art of the Cistercians.

The façade, stripped of all ornament, is marked by two buttresses and seven round-headed windows, symbolising the seven Sacraments of the church. The porch has disappeared but the original corbels that supported it are still in place. The leaves and hinges of the doorway are exact reproductions of the original folding doors.

Interior – The Cistercian rules and plans of design have been scrupulously observed and despite the relatively small dimensions of the building (length: 66m/217ft, width of transept: 30m/98ft), the general effect is one of striking grandeur.

The nave, of broken-barrel vaulting, has eight bays; it is supported by aisles of transverse barrel vaulting, forming a series of communicating chapels, lit by small semicircular bays. The blind nave receives its light from openings in the façade and from those set above the chancel arch.

In the huge transept, the arrangement of the barrel vaulting and the chapels in the transept arms is similar to that in the aisles. In the north transept arm, note the statue (**1**) of Notre-Dame de Fontenay (end of the 13C); her smile and ease of pose recall the Champagne School.

The square chancel (**2**) with its flat chevet, is lit by a double row of windows in triplets (symbol of the Trinity). Tombstones and the remains of the 13C paving of small squares of glazed stone, which once covered the floor of the choir and a great part of the church, have been assembled here. On the right, there is the tomb (**3**) of the nobleman Mello d'Époisses and his wife (14C). The stone retable of the former Gothic high altar (late 13C) has been damaged.

The night stair to the monks' dormitory is in the south transept.

Dormitory – The monks slept on straw mattresses on the floor and each sleeping compartment was screened off by a low partition. The magnificent oak timber-work roof is late 15C.

Cloisters

Cloisters – The cloisters, on the south side of the church, are a superb example of Cistercian architecture, both elegant and robust. Each gallery has eight bays marked by fine buttresses; the semicircular archways, except for those of the doorways giving on to the garth, are divided by double arches resting on coupled columns.

The **chapter-house**, with quadripartite vaulting and water-leaf capitals, communicates with the eastern cloister by way of a splendid doorway. The monks' workroom or scriptorium is situated at the end of the east range. From the latter a doorway leads to the warming room. The two fireplaces were the only ones allowed in the abbey apart from those in the kitchen.

The prison is open to view; so too is the forge which was built beside the river to provide water power to activate the hammers and bellows.

The monks cultivated medicinal plants in the gardens next to the infirmary, which is set apart from the other buildings.

The new gardens laid out by an English landscape gardener were designed to moderate the austere appearance of the buildings and to ease the flow of visitors around the abbey.

FOUGEROLLES

Population 3 967
Michelin map 314: G-5

The site of the little town of Fougerolles, in the valley of the Combeauté on the border between the old duchy of Lorraine and the Franche-Comté, meant that in the past, depending on the outcome of the various military skirmishes that took place, Fougerolles was ruled successively by the dukes of Lorraine and the counts and dukes of Burgundy. The town was finally attached to France in the treaty of Besançon signed in 1704 by Louis XIV and Duke Leopold of Lorraine.

The modern town, which has an attractive late-18C church, has earned a reputation for its kirsch, which is produced on both a small and an industrial scale.

Stills

★**Écomusée du Pays de la Cerise et de la Distillation** ⊙ – *2km/1mi N on C 201.*
This interesting local museum, located in the hamlet of Petit-Fahys on the premises of one of the region's earliest industrial distilleries (1831), aims to show visitors an authentic kirsch distillery as it would have been during the 19C and the early 20C. It includes the distiller's house with all its furniture, the

servants' quarters, the maturing loft, the warehouse and the two large workshops with their rows of huge shining stills worked by boilers or steam. Local agricultural activity, and various crafts associated with the distillery (cooperage, basket-making, textiles) are represented by displays of tools and other equipment and reconstructions of workshops.

Adjoining the buildings is a conservatory where orchards bloom, and where local varieties of cherry are cultivated.

EXCURSION

Ermitage St-Valbert – *5km/3mi S*. A hermitage developed in the 17C near the cave where St Valbert lived as a hermit in the 7C. Note the statue of the saint carved in the rock.

🔲 Nearby is a 60ha/148-acre **safari park** ⊘ (roe-deer, deer, chamois...).

Barrage de GÉNISSIAT★

Michelin map 328: H-4
Local map see BELLEGARDE-SUR-VALSERINE

Until January 1948, when the Génissiat dam was flooded, the River Rhône used to disappear in dry seasons into a 60m/197ft-deep fissure, known as the Perte du Rhône, once it got to Bellegarde. The site is now a reservoir 23km/14mi long on which pleasure boats of all shapes and sizes can be seen in summer. The reservoir takes up all of the valley floor and fills the series of gorges the river has cut downstream of Bellegarde, flowing at the narrowest point between cliffs either side only 1.70m/5.5ft apart. The Génissiat dam constitutes the most important power plant in the Jura stretch of the Rhône hydroelectric scheme.

The Rhône in the Jura – The river rises at an altitude of 2 200m/7 218ft in Switzerland, in the glacial cirques of the Oberland between the Furka and Grimsel passes. The Rhône is a torrential mountain river with turbulent muddy waters until it flows into Lake Geneva (alt 309m/1 014ft). From here it emerges into French territory as a remarkably clear, calm river, almost a different river altogether, as the dizzying descent from the high mountains is now over. In crossing the Jura the average drop in altitude is seven times less steep than it was in Switzerland. The river nevertheless flows irregularly; the depth of the water can vary from season to season (0.30-5m/1-16ft).

The fast-flowing, swollen River Arve joins the Rhône shortly after Geneva, bringing with it water from the glaciers of Mont Blanc. Some 30km/19mi further on, the Rhône runs up against the steep ridge of the Jura mountain chain, a natural barrier which it must cross by flowing through a series of *cluses* taking it from one parallel ridge to the next. The first of these is the picturesque Défilé de l'Écluse. The Rhône, which was 350m/1 148ft wide when it left Geneva, is a great deal narrower here as it tries to force its way through – it is now only 20m/65.6ft wide.

The exploitation of the River Rhône – There are nine hydroelectric plants drawing on the resource of the Rhône, between Geneva and Lyon: two in Switzerland, at Verbois and Chancy-Pougny; and seven in France, at Génissiat, Seyssel, Chautagne, Belley, Brégnier, Sault-Brenaz and Cusset-Villeurbanne.

TOUR

The site – The Rhône flows between tall cliffs upstream of the dam, which meant that the level of its waters could be raised by 69m/226ft without risk of serious flooding.

A decisive criterion in the selection of this site for the dam was the density of the limestone, to which 600 000m³/21 189 000cu ft of concrete was to be anchored. There had to be no risk of water seeping under the dam through cracks in the rock beneath it. Once the surrounding limestone was confirmed as being sufficiently solid, work on the dam began in 1937. The reservoir was flooded in early 1948.

The dam – The Génissiat construction is a gravity dam; this means that it resists the push of the water by its sheer weight alone. It measures 104m/341ft high from the foundations to the top, 140m/153yd wide along the crest and 100m/328ft thick at the base.

The reservoir contains 53 million m³/1 872 million cu ft of water and extends over 23km/14mi, as far as the Swiss border. Two evacuation canals were constructed to accommodate the Rhône's violent spates, in which the river's rate of flow can change from 140 to 2 800m³/4 944-98 882cu ft per second; one canal is above ground and makes a *saut de ski* (ski jump) to the west bank, whereas the other runs underground on the east bank.

Barrage de GÉNISSIAT

The **Léon Perrier power station** *(centrale)*, at the foot of the dam of which it is part, was named after the founder of the Compagnie Nationale du Rhône (in charge of the French part of the Rhône hydroelectric scheme). The power station is capable of producing 1 700 million kWh in an average year.

The **salle des machines** ⊙ (machine room) has been open to visitors in the past, but is currently closed for security reasons.

The surrounding area – *30min.*

Leave the car in the car park next to the monument commemorating the construction of the dam.

A **kiosque touristique** (Tourist Information Centre) has been set up at the first viewpoint, with explanatory and descriptive display boards giving information on the construction of the dam, the nature of the installation at Génissiat and the technical details of the other plants in the Upper Rhône hydroelectric power scheme. There is a view from the second viewpoint *(small garden)* which overlooks the west bank evacuation canal with its *saut de ski*. When it is in operation (usually in the early summer), it emits a majestic, foaming jet of water.

Boat trips are available on the reservoir in summer between Bellegarde and the dam.

GOUMOIS

Population 196
Michelin map 321: L-3

Downstream of its spectacular waterfall *(see VILLERS-LE-LAC: Saut du Doubs)*, the River Doubs cuts its way through a deep and narrow gorge before reaching Goumois on the Franco-Swiss border, a pleasant resort sought after by anglers and canoeists.

The municipality was divided into two by the Vienna Treaty in 1815, but the French and the Swiss get together every year on 31 July to celebrate Switzerland's National Day.

G. Magnin/MICHELIN

View over the Doubs from the Corniche de Goumois

ROUND TOUR ⊙

Drive out of Goumois along D 437^B towards Montbéliard. In Trévillers, turn right onto D 201 and continue to the intersection with D 134 leading to Courtefontaine and Soulce, then turn onto D 437^C to St-Hippolyte.

St-Hippolyte – This little town is surrounded by pretty **countryside★**, where the Dessoubre flows into the Doubs.

Leave St-Hippolyte on D 437 towards Maîche.

Les Bréseux – The parish church of this modest village boasts a remarkable set of seven stained-glass windows made in 1948 by the famous glassblower Alfred Manessier.

Maîche – Situated between the Dessoubre and Doubs valleys, Maîche occupies a pleasant site overlooked by the Mont Miroir (alt 986m/3 235ft). The *maîchards* or Comtois horse, a famous breed of draught horses, originate from Maîche. Every summer the village stages a competition to ensure the survival of the breed. A lively carnival takes place in March.

Where to stay and Eating out

BUDGET

Au Bois de la Biche – *Aux Belvédères de la Cendrée - 25140 Charquemont -* ☎ *03 81 44 01 82 - closed 2 Jan-1 Feb and Mon - 14.50/34€*. Listen to the birds twittering and the wind rustling the leaves of the nearby forest... This peaceful establishment serves regional cooking and offers a few sober but pleasant rooms. Choose a table by the picture window to enjoy the view of the Swiss Alps.

Moulin du Plain – *5km/3.1mi N of Goumois by a minor road -* ☎ *03 81 44 41 99 - thomas.choulet@libertysurf.fr - closed 1 Nov-23 Feb -* ▣ *- 22 rooms: 35.10/52.60€ -* ☐ *6.40€ - restaurant 14.50/29.60€*. At the edge of the Doubs, this family inn in the heart of a forest is a favourite haunt among anglers. The simple, well-kept rooms all give onto the river. Regional specialities.

MODERATE

Taillard – *3 rte de la Corniche -* ☎ *03 81 44 20 75 - hotel.taillard@wanadoo.fr - closed early Nov to early Mar -* ▣ *- 18 rooms: 44.20/83.90€ -* ☐ *9.15€ - restaurant 25.90/56.50€*. This hostelry dominating the village and the Doubs Valley has been in the same family since 1874! The guestrooms set up in the annexe are cosier and more attractive. The garden, swimming pool and fitness amenities will ensure that your stay here is a healthy one. Carefully prepared meals.

Note the 18C church and, to the left, the castle of Charles de Montalembert (1810-70), the son of a French émigré exiled in London, who returned to France and became a liberal Catholic advocating freedom in religious practice and education.

Drive S along D 464 to Charquemont and beyond as far as the Swiss border.

★★ Les Échelles de la Mort (The Ladders of Death) – Immediately after the La Cheminée customs *(let the customs official know you do not intend to go into Switzerland)* take the road on the left leading to the Le Refrain hydroelectric plant. This road leads downhill to the bottom of the gorge, where there is an impressive **landscape★** of tall cliffs crowned by firs and spruces.

🚶 *Leave the car left of the plant gates and take the signposted path on the left (45min there and back on foot) to the foot of the Échelles de la Mort (steep climb through undergrowth).*

To reach the **viewpoint** the tourist must climb three steel ladders fixed into a rocky wall, which (despite their name...) have solid reinforced steps and are equipped with hand rails. The climb leads up to a viewpoint about 100m/330ft high, overlooking the Doubs gorges.

Return to Charquemont and take D 10ᴱ to La Cendrée (car park).

Belvédères de la Cendrée – 🚶 Two paths 200m/220yd further on lead to the viewpoints, from which there are very beautiful views of the Doubs gorge and Switzerland. The first path *(30min round trip on foot)* comes to a rocky spur which rises sheer 450m/1 476ft above the Doubs Valley. The viewpoint at the end of the second path *(45min there and back on foot; marked with arrows)* is at the top of the La Cendrée rocks.

Back in Charquemont, take D 201 to the right; drive to Damprichard and turn right onto D 437ᴬ which leads to the Col de la Vierge (altitude of pass: 964m/3 163ft) and the beginning of the famous Corniche de Goumois overlooking the River Doubs.

★★ Corniche de Goumois – This very picturesque road runs along the steep west side of the Doubs Valley, where the river marks the border between France and Switzerland for a while. For 3km/2mi the drive overlooks the depths of the gorge from a height of about 100m/330ft *(best viewpoints have protective railings)*. The steep slopes are wooded or rocky, or carpeted with meadows when they slope less steeply. The landscape exudes a calm grandeur, rather than any particular wild ruggedness. The Swiss Franches Montagnes range can be seen on the other bank of the Doubs *(linked to this itinerary by the Goumois bridge and the no 107 road)*.

GRAND COLOMBIER ★★★

Michelin map 328: H-5
Local map see BELLEGARDE-SUR-VALSERINE

This is the highest peak (1 531km/5 023ft) in the Bugey region, at the tip of the long mountain chain separating the Rhône from the Valromey. The arduous climb affords exceptional panoramic views.

UNDER THE OLD LINDEN TREE

Au Vieux Tilleul – *01260 Belmont-Luthézieu - 10.5km/6.5mi W of Virieu-le-Petit by D 69F then D 54C - ☎ 04 79 87 64 51 - closed Sun evenings and Mon Oct-Apr -* 🅿 *- 15 rooms: 38.10€ -* ☕ *5.34€ - restaurant 16.80/29.80€.* The beautiful interior decoration echoed by yellow and blue fabrics, the comfortable, well-kept rooms and the kind hospitality will ensure that your stay here is a most pleasant one. Pretty vistas of the forest and the Grand Colombier. The meals too are an uplifting experience.

FROM VIRIEU-LE-PETIT TO CULOZ

29km/18mi – allow 2hr

After leaving Virieu, the road climbs the slopes of the Grand Colombier along a series of hairpin bends weaving through a rural landscape. Once it reaches the forest's edge, the road makes its way through stands of magnificent fir trees. The gradient becomes 12% (1:8), then 14% (1:7) and finally even 19% (1:5). After passing the Lochieu road on the left, it comes to a broad shelf of beautiful mountain pastures, at La Grange de Fromentel, from which there is a good view of the Champagne-en-Valromey Valley.

Climbing about 1km/0.5mi further up through the forest, the road branches off to the left towards the Colombier service station and hotel, whereas the final hairpin bend up the mountain leads to the pass.

★★★ **Grand Colombier** – From the car park, there are easy footpaths up to both Grand Colombier peaks. On the rounded northern peak there is a cross and a viewing table *(30min round trip on foot)*; the south peak ends in a steep crest on the west face of the mountain and has a triangulation point *(45min round trip on foot)*.

There are magnificent, extensive panoramas of the Jura, the Dombes, the Rhône Valley, the Massif Central and the Alps; in fine weather three lakes can be seen twinkling in the sun – Geneva, Bourget and Annecy.

On the east face of the mountain the road runs through mountain pastures before entering the forest.

From the hairpin bend 5km/3mi from the Fenestrez summit, take the right turn.

★★ **Observatoire du Fenestrez** – A footpath leads to the edge of the cliff *(benches and hang-gliding take-off strip; no parapet)* from where, at a height of about 900m/2 950ft, there is a view of the Culoz plain.

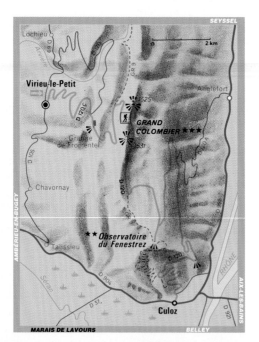

The lakes of Bourget and Chambéry can be seen to the south-east and that of Annecy to the east. Beyond this, the view stretches as far as the Alps in the distance, from La Meije (French Alps) to the Matterhorn.

Return to the main road and turn right (15% – 1:7 gradient downhill). After 4km/2mi keep right towards Culoz when the road forks left to Anglefort.

There are some impressive views of the Bugey region, the Rhône Valley and the Culoz plain on the road downhill *(gradient of 12% – 1:8 in some places: 13 hairpin bends)*, particularly when the road runs along the ridge of the crest, at the edge of the forest.

EXCURSIONS

Réserve naturelle du marais de Lavours – *From Culoz, drive W on D 904 then turn left onto D 37 to Ceyzerieu and left again on a minor road to Aignoz.*
A 2.4km/1.5mi-long didactic trail, raised on piles, enables visitors (free access) to penetrate deep into the marsh.
The **Maison de la Réserve** ⊘, opened in 2001, offers an interactive study of this unique ecosystem *(guided tours of the marsh)*.

Seyssel – Once a major port on the River Rhône, Seyssel is now better known for its excellent white wines. A suspension bridge links the two halves of the town, each having retained its old district.

Barrage de Seyssel – *1.5km/0.9mi upstream of Seyssel.* The dam was built to regulate the flow of the River Rhône downstream of Génissiat. The reservoir lies beneath the spur on which stands **Bassy Church**. The power station has a capacity of 150 million kWh per year.

GRAY

Population 6 773
Michelin map 314: B-8

This handsome town rises up like an amphitheatre from the banks of the Saône, fanning out over the hillside. While it played a significant role in commercial river navigation in the 19C, Gray has now found favour with recreational boaters. There is a pretty view of the town from the 18C stone bridge.
Gray is the birthplace of the mathematician Augustin Cournot and **François Devosge** (1732-1811), founder of the Dijon École des Beaux-Arts (attended by Prud'hon and Rude). It is also home to an **Esperanto museum** ⊘ *(Nacia Espéranto Muzéo)* with comprehensive archives, literature and an exhibition on the history of the international language from its creation in 1887 to the present.

⋆ **Hôtel de ville** – The town hall is an elegant building, with arcades in the Renaissance style (1568), embellished by pink marble columns and a beautiful varnished-tile roof.

⋆ **Musée Baron-Martin** ⊘ – This art museum is in the château of the Count of Provence, brother of Louis XVI, which in the 18C replaced the feudal fortress belonging to the dukes of Burgundy. The Paravis Tower and the cellars date from the original fortress. The first galleries contain works by Primitive artists from various western schools: the Italian (16C-18C), Flemish (17C), Dutch (17C) – including some engravings by Rembrandt – and French (16C-19C). A beautiful collection of **pastels and drawings**⋆ by Prud'hon (1758-1823) can be seen in one gallery,

GRAY

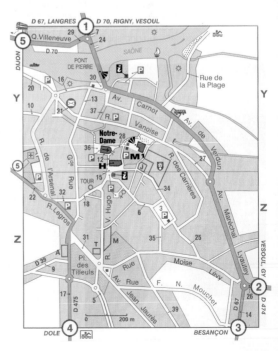

LIFE AT THE MANOR

Château de Rigny – *70100 Rigny - 6km/3.7mi NE of Gray by D 2 - ☎ 03 84 65 25 01 - chateau-de-rigny@wanadoo.fr - ▣ - 29 rooms: 61/185€ - ⌑ 9.50€ - restaurant 29/55€*. Set in the midst of a large shaded park along the banks of the Saône, this handsome 17C and 18C mansion is a haven of peace. The interior decoration features wood panelling, tapestries and period furniture. The bedrooms have each been done up in their own style. Winter garden for enjoying breakfast out of doors.

Château de Nantilly – *70100 Nantilly - 8km/5mi NW of Gray by D 2 - ☎ 03 84 67 78 00 - nantilly@romantik.de - closed 2 Nov-14 Mar - ▣ - 30 rooms: 61/130€ - ⌑ 17€ - restaurant 40/75€*. You will appreciate the peaceful ambience of this 19C manor house standing in a lush park, with a river running by it. The guestrooms have been set up in buildings dating from different periods. Summer pool and facilities for fitness training.

including three portraits which he executed during his stay at the château in 1795 and 1796. The first floor is devoted to contemporary art and to late-19C and early-20C works – extensive sets of prints by Albert Besnard and Aman Jean, Fantin-Latour's lithographic stones, and paintings by Tissot and Steinlen.

The 13C vaulted cellars house, among other things, a collection of coins, fragments of earthenware discovered locally dating mainly from the Gallo-Roman Era and a display case of Hellenic vases.

Basilique Notre-Dame – The church was begun at the end of the 15C. Above the transept crossing is an impressive Baroque dome. The porch was not finished until the 19C. The bays of the nave, three of which are square, have rib vaulting. The sculpted wooden organ case dates from 1746.

▶▶ **Château de Gy★** – *18km/11mi E along D 474*. This imposing 16C-18C castle once belonged to the archbishops of Besançon (Flamboyant-style polygonal **stair-tower★**).

Cascades du HÉRISSON★★★

Michelin map 321: F-7
Local maps below or see Région des LACS DU JURA

The source of the Hérisson is at an altitude of 805m/2 641ft, in the lake of Bonlieu to the south of the waterfalls. The upper course of the river takes it for barely 2km/0.5mi, before it drops down to the Doucier plateau (alt 520m/1 706ft). The Hérisson covers the 280m/920ft difference in altitude in only 3km/2mi, by cutting through narrow gorges, forming spectacular waterfalls. The river owes its picturesque stepped course to the differing textures of the horizontal limestone strata through which it wears its way. Each shelf is formed by strata of more resistant rock. Bear in mind that the flow of small rivers in the Jura, a terrain of mostly porous limestone, is very dependent on the weather.

The Hérisson is a magnificent spectacle during rainy periods. The sight of the water tumbling down in a mighty torrent or in a lengthy series of cascades is well worth the minor inconvenience of having to wear a raincoat and taking care not to slip on the wet ground.

After long periods of fine weather the river, which has no tributaries as it is so near its source, can virtually dry up. Although the falls themselves are not quite so interesting at these times, the river bed, especially between the Gour Bleu and the Grand Saut, features some fascinating evidence of erosion: natural stone steps, giants' cauldrons, multi-storied systems of caves.

B. Kaufmann/MICHELIN

Cascade de l'Éventail

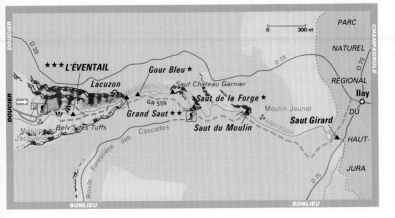

HIKES

🅝 There are several possible departure points, the most logical being **Doucier** *(there is also a charge for parking both here and near the Cascade de l'Éventail).*

From Doucier

Drive 8km/5mi south-east along D 326; leave the car at the end of the road.

Lac de Chambly and Lac du Val – D 326 climbs the Hérisson Valley downstream of the waterfalls, giving the occasional glimpse of these two lovely lakes through the trees. The valley floor is flat and green, the slopes steep and wooded. Once it has passed through the lakes of Chambly and Le Val, the river flows into the Ain.

Continue on D 326 as far as the Jacquand mill (moulin) and leave the car there.

The footpath (Sentier des Cascades) follows the gorges, almost continually through woods. It is sometimes very steep but not dangerous. *Allow 2hr 30min there and back on foot.*

★★★**Cascade de l'Éventail** – After about 400m the path brings you to the foot of this waterfall, where you will get the best view. The water tumbles down a total of 65m/213ft in leaps and bounds, forming a monumental pyramid of foaming water (the name *éventail* derives from its fan shape).
The path then leads very steeply uphill to the top of the Éventail waterfall.
Take the Sarrazine footbridge across the Hérisson, and then follow the path on the right to the Belvédère des Tuffs, from where there is a beautiful view of the Hérisson gorge and the Éventail waterfall.

Return to the footbridge and continue upstream along the river course to the Lacuzon footbridge about 300m further on.

Grotte Lacuzon – *30min there and back on foot from the footbridge.*
Cross the Hérisson and follow the very steep path up to this cave.

Carry on upstream along the south bank, to the Grand Saut.

★★**Cascade du Grand Saut** – The best view of the Grand Saut is from the foot of the waterfall. The water falls from a height of 60m/200ft in a single cascade.

The footpath, now cut into the rock face, is very steep and quite narrow (but with handrails) in places as it leads to the Gour Bleu waterfall.

★**Gour Bleu** – At the foot of the little waterfall known as the Gour Bleu lies a beautiful shallow basin *(gour)* in which the water is a clear blue colour.
The path carries on to the **Saut Château Garnier** and the **Saut de la Forge** waterfalls.

★**Saut de la Forge** – The river, flinging itself from the top of a curving, rocky overhang, makes a very pretty spectacle.

Saut du Moulin and Saut Girard – *1hr 30min there and back on foot from Saut de la Forge.*

🏃 From the path, which runs through woods at some points and meadows at others, the Saut du Moulin can be seen, near the ruins of the Jeunet mill, and, further on, the Saut Girard, falling from about 20m/66ft.

The path crosses the Hérisson at the foot of Saut Girard and leads back to the Ilay crossroads, near the Auberge du Hérisson.

Other possibilites

From Ilay – *Park the car by the Auberge du Hérisson.*

From Bonlieu – *Follow the forest road for 2km/1mi; to the east of Bonlieu church take the signposted road, from which there is a lovely view of the lower reaches of the Hérisson to the left; park the car by the refreshment kiosk at Saut de la Forge and go on foot straight to the Cascade de l'Éventail; from there follow the route described from Doucier.*

Ferme de l'Aurochs ⏱ – *Le Val Dessous; near the Cascades du Hérisson.*
📷 A 2km/1.2mi trail along the Hérisson Valley offers the possibility of meeting some of the ancestors of domestic cattle such as aurochs, bisons and other breeds of wild ox. Feeding time is at 11am and 6pm.

JOIGNY

Population 10 032
Michelin map 319: D-4

Joigny, whose townsfolk have the name of Joviniens, is a busy, picturesque little town set at the gateway to Burgundy on the borders of the forest of Othe. It is built in terraces on the side of a hill, the Côte St-Jacques, overlooking the River Yonne. From the Yonne bridge, which has six 18C arches, there is a pretty view of the river, the quays, the shady promenades and the town built in the shape of an amphitheatre.

The Revolt of the Maillotins – In 1438 the people of Joigny rebelled against their lord of the manor, Count Guy de la Trémoille. They attacked and captured his castle, and put the Count to death with blows from their mauls or mallets, tools used by the wine-growers of those days. Since that event the Joviniens have been known as Maillotins (Maul-bearers) and the maul figures in the town's coat of arms.

Eating out and where to stay

MODERATE

P'tit Claridge – *89410 Thèmes - 8 km/5mi W of Joigny by N 6 then D 182 - ☎ 03 86 63 10 92 - closed 8-15 Jan, 4-15 Mar, 1-15 Oct, Sun evenings and Mon - 22/64€.* A family restaurant at the entrance to the village enjoying a quiet atmosphere and pretty garden bursting with flowers. The dining room streaming with light has French windows opening onto a leafy setting. There are a few simply furnished but well-kept rooms.

EXPENSIVE

Hôtel La Côte St-Jacques – *14 fg de Paris - ☎ 03 86 62 09 70 - lorain@relais-chateaux.fr - closed 6 Jan-5 Feb - 🅿 - 32 rooms: 125/305€ - ⚏ 22€ - restaurant 95/128€.* Treat yourself to a wonderful stay at this sumptuous hotel lying at the water's edge. The spacious rooms and suites giving onto the garden and the River Yonne are a haven of tranquillity. Refined cuisine. Covered pool.

SIGHTS

Porte du Bois – This 12C gateway, flanked by two round towers, was once part of the medieval wall, part of which can be seen in Chemin de la Guimbarde.

St-Thibault – This church, built in both the Gothic and Renaissance styles between 1490 and 1529, is dominated by a 17C square tower crowned by a delicate belfry. Above the door is an equestrian statue of St Theobald (1530) by the sculptor who settled in Spain and took the name Juan de Juni (Jean de Joigny). Inside the church, the chancel slants to the left; this rare asymmetry is emphasised by the chancel vaulting, which has an unusual hanging keystone. There are many works of art *(plan in the north aisle level with the pulpit):* paintings and sculptures including a charming **Smiling Virgin**★, a 14C stone statue *(against the fourth pillar on the right facing the pulpit),* and a series of low-relief Renaissance sculptures from the old rood screen including Christ in hell *(in the lady chapel).*

Old houses – A stroll through the narrow streets in the vicinity of the churches of St-Thibault and St-Jean will reveal several half-timbered houses dating from the 15C and 16C. Most of these were badly damaged, either during the bombardments of 1940 or a gas explosion in 1981, but have been restored. The best-known house is the corner one, called the Arbre de Jessé *(Tree of Jesse)* recalling the genealogical lineae of Jesus, often used in medieval times as a decoration for a wall or window. Others include the Maison du Pilori.

St-Jean – A belfry-porch precedes the west front of this church which lacks transepts but has a pentagonal chevet. The Renaissance-style coffered ceiling has carved medallions framed by decorated ribs.

The south aisle contains a 15C Holy Sepulchre in white marble, ornamented with low reliefs and the 13C recumbent figure of the Comtesse de Joigny. The tomb is lavishly sculptured and includes the figures of the countess' children. The Louis XV woodwork and the furnishings of the sacristy came from Vézelay.

Opposite the Porte St-Jean, there was a passageway between the castle (beautifully restored) and the town.

Rue D.-Grenet leads to the esplanade of the old cemetery.

The **Chapelle des Ferrands**, which forms part of the law courts, is an octagonal funerary chapel (carved panels) erected in 1530 and believed to be the work of a local artist, Jean Chéreau. Nearby, the small doorway of St-André church, dating from the same period, has the discreet elegance of antique monuments.

Fine river **views**, shaded alleyways and an overall view of the city's amphitheatre setting await you if you cross the bridge spanning the Yonne (six 18C arches) and walk along quai de la Butte to the Parc du Chapeau.

EXCURSIONS

★**View from the Côte St-Jacques** – *1.5km/1mi N.* The road climbs in hairpin bends round the Côte St-Jacques. From a right-hand bend there is a fine semicircular **panorama**★ over the town and the valley of the Yonne.

Pressoir de Champvallon ⊘ – *9km/5.4mi SW.*
In the heart of the village of Champvallon, this winepress has a pendular mechanism which is unique in Europe, and still in perfect condition. The design dates from the 12C, and it was built in the early 14C. Once a year, this venerable machine is put to work, and the whole village honours the event with a festive fair *(information in the village)*.

★**Musée Rural des Arts Populaires de Laduz** ⊘ – *15km/10mi S on D 955; take the first left after the motorway bridge.*
⌖ This folk museum at the southeast entrance to the village recalls rural working life before 1914; the tools and products of about 50 craftsmen are on display together with a large collection of old toys and many of the carved figures which were popular in the past.

La Ferté-Loupière – *18km/11mi SW.* This **church** (12C and 15C) in this old fortified market town contains remarkable 15C-16C **mural paintings**★ depicting the parable of the three living and three dead men and a Dance of Death. The latter represents 42 figures from all walks of life and is thus an interesting historical document, as well as a moral lesson (death comes to all). Note also on the larger pillars the archangel St Michael Slaying the Dragon *(left)*, and an Annunciation *(right)*.

Note the **painted panels** on place de la Poste.

Detail from the Dance of Death, La Ferté-Loupière

La Fabuloserie ⊙ – *25km/16mi W by the D 943.*
⌂ At **Dicy** there is a museum of unsophisticated or over the top art which displays unusual and spontaneous works created from a variety of material by untrained people without reference to accepted artistic norms. The world of the irrational extends into the garden where more works are exhibited in the open air.

St-Julien-du-Sault – *10km/6mi N.*
This small village on the banks of the Yonne is home to a 13C-14C **church**, parts of which were restored in the 16C. The side doorways are interesting. Inside, note the high Renaissance chancel and the stained-glass windows dating from the 13C (oval) and the Renaissance (with figures). There is a pretty 16C **half-timbered house** in Rue du Puits-de-la-Caille.

Château de JOUX★

Michelin map 321: I-5 (4km/2.5mi south of Pontarlier)

This château reigns over the extreme end of the Pontarlier *cluse*, used since the Roman Empire as a route linking northern Italy with Flanders and Champagne. This great trade route also served for invading forces: Joux was besieged by the Austrians in 1814, and by the Swiss in 1815; the fortress was used to cover General Bourbaki's army in 1871, on its retreat into Switzerland; and the German invading army used it in 1940.

Château de Joux

The château was built by the lords of Joux in the 11C, and was enlarged under Emperor Charles V. Vauban fortified it, in view of its vulnerable position near the border, after France annexed the Franche-Comté in 1678. The last modernisations were carried out between 1879 and 1881, by the future field marshal, Joffre.
The stronghold has seen many political prisoners, military figures and other famous personalities pass through its gates. Mirabeau was locked inside after his father obtained an order for his arrest from the king. He hoped it would cool down his hot-headed son and protect him from the wrath of his many creditors. In 1802, two insurgents against the Revolution escaped by sawing bars and climbing down curtains. By the time **Toussaint Louverture**, hero of Haitian independence, arrived a few months later, security had been reinforced; the freedom fighter died there on 7 April 1803.
German author Heinrich von Kleist was also held in Joux in 1806.
A renowned theatre festival, **Les Nuits de Joux**, takes place in the castle in summer.

Tour ⊙ – The tour of the five successive curtain walls covering 2ha/5 acres, each separated by deep moats crossed by three drawbridges, unfolds 10 centuries of fortification. There is a beautiful view of the Doubs Valley and the Pontarlier *cluse*, from the terrace of the gun tower.
A **Musée d'Armes Anciennes**, comprising 650 antique weapons, has been installed in five rooms of the old keep. The collection ranges from the first regulation flint-lock rifle (1 717 model) to the repeating firearms from the beginning of the Third Republic (1878). There is also an exhibition of military headgear – including a beautiful collection of shakos – and uniforms.

The Legend of Berthe de Joux

A splendid feast was held to celebrate the marriage of Amaury III de Joux and the young maid Berthe, daughter of a wealthy neighbour. Their joys were immeasurable, until the call of the Crusades came between them. Amaury decided to make the journey to the Holy Land. Months went by with no word from Berthe's noble husband. Several years later, a horseman, exhausted and wounded, rode up to her gate. Wild with hope, Berthe ran to meet him and discovered that he was her childhood companion, Amey de Montfaucon. He was returning from the Crusades, and informed his friend that her husband had disappeared during a battle with the Infidels. Berthe took Amey into her home and cared for him, and he, in turn, comforted her in her loss. When Amaury unexpectedly returned, he discovered them in a very comfortable position indeed! He seized his wife's lover, killed him and had him hung in the neighbouring forest. He had his wife locked up in a miserable cell where the one window looked out on that very same forest.

When Amaury died, his son released Berthe and sent her to expiate her sins at the Montbenoît convent. But the poor woman's prayers haunt the valley still; nights when the wind rises, it seems to carry her melancholy voice through the trees of the forest.

It is possible to visit the cells of Mirabeau, with a beautiful dowelled timber roof frame; that of Toussaint Louverture; and the tiny dark cell of the legendary Berthe de Joux. A 35m/115ft deep vertical gallery *(212 steps)* leads down to the underground section and the great well shaft, 3.70m/12ft in diameter and 120m/394ft deep.

EXCURSION

★★ Cluse de Joux – This is one of the most beautiful examples of a Jura *cluse*. The transverse valley through the Larmont mountain cuts a passage just wide enough for the road and the railway line running from Pontarlier to Neuchâtel and Berne. Two strongholds command the cliffs: that of Le Larmont Inférieur, to the north; and the Château de Joux to the south.

MOUNTAIN RETREAT

Auberge Le Tillau – *Le Mont-des-Verrières - 25300 Les Verrières-de-Joux - 7 km/4.3mi E of La Cluse-et-Mijoux by D 67bis and a minor road - ☎03 81 69 46 72 - Luc.parent@wanadoo.fr - closed 2-10 Apr, 12 Nov-12 Dec - 12 rooms: 32/46€ - ⚏ 6€ - restaurant 16/35€.* City dwellers will love the bracing mountain air at this delightful inn perched at an altitude of 1 200m/3 937ft amid pastures and pine trees. The guestrooms are comfortable and suitable for a short stopover as well as for a longer stay. The traditional cuisine is good and made with fresh seasonal produce.

Le Frambourg – Excellent **view★★** over the Cluse de Joux from the platform of the monument to the fallen of the First World War.

Région des LACS DU JURA★★

Michelin map 321: E-7

The Région des Lacs, or **Jura Lake District**, designates the area between Champagnole, Clairvaux-les-Lacs and St-Laurent-en-Grandvaux, boasting a string of delightful lakes, Chalain, Chambly, Le Val, Ilay, Narlay... They are set in peaceful, restful countryside, in which the light and colours are at their best on a summer afternoon.
The main viewpoint is the Belvédère des Quatre Lacs on N 5.

Wicked as Weimar – In 1635, Richelieu ordered his troops into the Comté, and in the subsequent campaign the lake district was decimated by Swedish troops, allies of the French, under the command of Bernard de Saxe-Weimar. Homes were torched, crops cut down before they could be harvested, and vines and fruit trees uprooted. The resulting famine was so great that people even resorted to cannibalism. Terrible tortures were devised to force people to reveal the whereabouts of their life savings. Entire families, discovered hidden in caves or underground passages, were walled into their refuge, alive. For over a century the expression *Mauvais comme Weimar* (Wicked as Weimar) was still enough to send shivers down anyone's spine.
The entire province was subjected to this nightmare, with the result that large numbers of Comtois fled to seek refuge in Savoy, Switzerland or Italy. Some 10 000 to 12 000 settled in a single district in Rome, where they had a church built, dedicated to St Claude.

Lacuzon, Hero of Independence – One of the caves in the valley of the Hérisson, near the Grand Saut, is named after the popular hero **Lacuzon** (1607-1681), who once sheltered here. His real name was Jean-Claude Prost, and for 40 years he was a leading figure in the battle of the Franche-Comté for independence.

Prost was born in Longchaumois and had an established business in St-Claude when he took up arms at the time of the 1636 invasion. He soon realised that not everyone who wants to be a soldier is born to be one. He would be so terrified before the start of each battle that he would have to bite himself to get a grip on himself. He is said to have cried out as he did so, "Flesh, what have you to fear? You're going to rot one of these days anyway!", echoing the words of another French hero, Turenne, "You tremble, carcass..." Prost's serious, care-ridden expression earned him the nickname of Lacuzon (*cuzon* means worry in the local dialect).

The Bresse plain, in French hands from 1601, was systematically exploited by Lacuzon and his followers, who gave the new French landlords plenty to think about with their numerous successful forays. However, it was the people of the Bresse region who bore the brunt of his attacks; "Deliver us from the plague and from Lacuzon" was a prayer regularly offered up. Many of Lacuzon's ruses went down in local annals. One oft-quoted example is the siege during which he had one of his officers, Pille-Muguet, disguise himself as a Capuchin friar and enter the town. The false monk won the confidence of those defending the town with his constant outspoken criticism of the assailants and their leader and managed to persuade someone to give him the key to one of the gates, which he then opened during the night to his comrades.

The 1648 Treaty of Westphalia brought an end to the Thirty Years War and to Lacuzon's military activities. Despite his age, he took up the fight again, when Louis XIV invaded the Comté. The old soldier found a surprising follower in the priest Marquis of St-Lupicin, who mustered his parishioners and led them himself into battle. He would celebrate mass with a pair of pistols on the altar and during the sermon, he would outline the military exercises which would later take place in the square in front of the church. However, the French army proved too strong in battle for the Franche-Comté partisans, who were killed to a man. In 1674 Lacuzon escaped capture by a hair's breadth, managing to reach Milan, at the time under Spanish rule. He died there seven years later, as uncompromising as ever.

THE LAKES

Boissia – *3.5km/2mi north-west of Clairvaux-les-Lacs (N 78 and D 27).*
A monument has been put up in memory of the 15 young Resistance fighters executed by the Nazis on 17 June 1944.

Bonlieu – The restored church still has a beautiful Renaissance altarpiece, which probably came from the Carthusian monastery in Bonlieu. The village is a departure point for visiting the Hérisson waterfalls, the lake at Bonlieu and the Dame-Blanche viewpoint.

Lac de Bonlieu – *4.5km/3mi south-east of Bonlieu on the picturesque N 78, then D 75^E to the right.*
This pretty lake hidden in the forest is overlooked by a rocky ridge, covered with conifers and beech trees and crisscrossed by numerous footpaths. Boat trips can be taken on the lake.

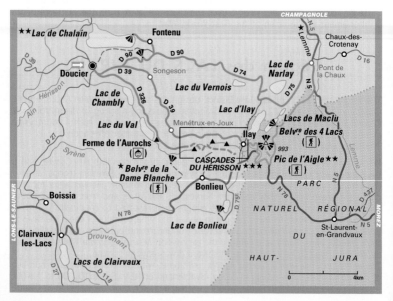

Where to stay and Eating out

BUDGET

Ferme-Auberge Le Coq en Pattes – *Sous-Chalamet - 39150 Les Chalesmes - 10 km/6.2mi E of Chaux-des-Crotenay by D 16 then D 127[E1] to Les-Planches-en-Montagne then D 17 until you reach La Perrena - ☎ 03 84 51 51 62 - closed Sat lunchtime -* ✉ *- reservations required - 9.15/21.34€.* Stuffed boars and weasels adorn the spacious dining room of this farmhouse, which also boasts a monumental fireplace. Sample authentic country cooking (lamb or rabbit) in a warm, friendly atmosphere. Four sober guestrooms.

Camping Le Fayolan – *39130 Clairvaux-les-Lacs - 1.2 km/0.8mi SE of Clairvaux-les-Lacs by D 118 - ☎ 03 84 25 26 19 - relais.soleil.jura@wanadoo.fr - open 8 May-16 Sep – reservations recommended - 516 sites: 19.99€ – Meals available.* This high quality campsite has widely spaced plots of land lying in the vicinity of a lake. Beach, pools, terrace. Snack-bar and shopping mall. There are a great many activities organised for children. Not to mention a fitness trail for adults.

Chambre d'Hôte M. et Mme Grillet – *12 r. de la Maison-Blanche - 39130 Bonlieu - ☎ 03 84 25 59 12 - dominique.grillet@wanadoo.fr -* ✉ *- 4 rooms: 30/42€.* A young couple of farmers have painstakingly restored their old cottage, which they have converted into four comfortable bedrooms. The upstairs terrace looks out onto the garden or onto the lake surrounded by fields. Breakfast is served in the long dining room with its lovely exposed beams and arched windows.

Chambre d'Hôte Les Cinq Lacs – *66 rte des Lacs - 39130 Le Frasnois - 3.5 km/2.3mi N of Ilay by D 75 - ☎ 03 84 25 51 32 - pcolombato@club-internet.fr -* ✉ *- reservations required - 5 rooms: 33.54/42.68€ - meals 13.72€.* This is the perfect base for setting out on long, bracing walks. The comfortable, prettily appointed guestrooms carry the names of local lakes. The half-board formula will give you a chance to enjoy the succulent regional specialities prepared by your hosts. Two chalets have been set up as self-catering gîtes. For non-smokers.

Hôtel La Chaumière du Lac – *21 r. du Sauveur - 39130 Clairvaux-les-Lacs - ☎ 03 84 25 81 52 - Closed 16 Oct-30 Apr -* 🅿 *- 12 rooms: 34/40€ -* ☲ *5.50€ - restaurant 13/35€.* Have a dip in the nearby lake or lounge around on the shore while you wait for your next meal, consisting of Jura specialities. The pleasing bedrooms give onto the lake or the surrounding greenery. Beautiful terrace.

Hôtel L'Alpage – *1 chemin de la Madone - 39130 Bonlieu - ☎ 03 84 25 57 53 - reservation@alpage-hotel.com - closed 15 Nov-15 Dec and Wed except school holidays -* 🅿 *- 9 rooms: 46€ -* ☲ *6.10€ - restaurant 17/30€.* The cosy rooms set up in this chalet perched on the heights command lovely vistas of the lakes and the rolling countryside. Franche-Comté specialities are served in the panoramic dining room or on the sheltered terrace. Two self-catering gîtes.

The Carthusian monastery at the north end of the lake was founded in Bonlieu in 1170; the buildings were demolished in 1944.

A forest road runs up above the east shore, leading to a viewpoint south of the lake, from where there is a beautiful view of the Pic de l'Aigle, the lakes of Ilay, and Maclu, and of Mont Rivel in the distance.

Clairvaux-les-Lacs – The church here contains 15C sculpted stalls from the abbey in Baume-les-Messieurs, and paintings by 18C masters.

Lacs de Clairvaux – *300m south of Clairvaux on D 118 and to the right, along a narrow road.*

These lakes are not quite as pretty as the others in the region. The greater and smaller lakes (Grand Lac et Petit Lac) are linked by a canal, and when the waters are high the two lakes become one. In 1870 the remains of a lakeside community, the first of its type to be found in France, were discovered in the mud of the Grand Lac. Nowadays visitors can swim or explore the Grand Lac de Clairvaux by boat, pedal craft or yacht.

★ **Belvédère de la Dame-Blanche** – *2km/1mi north-west of Bonlieu, then 30min there and back on foot. Drive towards Saugeot from the N 78/D 67 crossroads, and after about 800m take the unsurfaced road to the right on leaving the forest.* 🚶 *At the first crossroads turn left and park the car at the edge of the forest and follow the footpath.*

A rocky bank overlooks the Dessus and Dessous valleys. There is a view of the lakes of Chambly and Le Val to the left and of the Pic de l'Aigle to the right.

Ilay – This is the departure point for visiting the Hérisson waterfalls and the lakes of Ilay and Maclu.

Lac d'Ilay or Lac de la Motte – The lake owes its alternative name to the small rocky island *(motte)* rising near the east shore, a pretty little spot shaded by fir trees and beeches. The priory built there was destroyed during the wars of the 17C. A causeway, now submerged, linked it to the lakeside; the rushes growing on it indicate where it once was. The Lac d'Ilay lies in the centre of a long fault which it shares with the lakes of Narlay and Bonlieu. The waters of the lakes of Maclu flow into it through a canal. The Ilay's waters disappear underground into gullies at its southern end, to flow into the Hérisson, downstream from the Saut Girard.

Lacs de Maclu – These lakes, named after the nearby villages of Grand Maclu and Petit Maclu, lie in a valley overlooked to the east by the wooded cliffs of the Bans, to the west by a rocky outcrop separating them from the Lac d'Ilay, and to the south by the majestic cone of the Pic de l'Aigle.

The Petit Maclu lake empties into the Grand Maclu, which in turns flows into the Lac d'Ilay through a 500m long canal.

Lakes of Maclu and Narlay

★★LAC DE CHALAIN and PIC DE L'AIGLE

Round tour of 46km/29mi – allow 2hr 30min

Leave Doucier east on D 39 towards Songeson and Menétrux-en-Joux; after Ilay turn left on N 78; leave N 78 north of Chaux-du-Dombief, taking the Boissière road, and park the car 250m further on.

★★**Pic de l'Aigle** – 🔏 *45min there and back on foot along a path which is indicated initially but sometimes difficult to make out; it climbs steeply to the right, towards the wooded outcrop of rock called Pic de l'Aigle.*

The **view** from the top of the Pic de l'Aigle (993m/3 258ft), often also called Bec de l'Aigle (eagle's beak), stretches across the entire Jura region, overlooking the Ilay *cluse* and the Chaux-du-Dombief heights. The Jura mountain chains tower on the left, behind which the summit of Mont Blanc can be seen in fine weather; the plateaux extend to the right, as far as their rim above the Saône plain.

Leaving the road to Boissière to the right, take a narrow road uphill.

Belvédère des Quatre-Lacs – 🔏 *15min there and back on foot.* The lakes of Ilay, Narlay, the Grand Maclu and the Petit Maclu can be seen from this viewpoint.

Return to N 5 and take it to the left as far as Pont-de-la-Chaux, then take D 75 to Le Frasnois. Then take D 74 to the right.

Lac de Narlay – The lake is overlooked by wooded slopes. It has a distinctive triangular shape (the other lakes are elongated) and, at a depth of 48m/157ft, it is the deepest lake in the lake district. Its waters drain into several gullies at the west end of the lake and flow underground for 10km/6mi, after which they re-emerge and feed into the Lac de Chalain.

Local hearsay has it that a good fairy cast a spell over the lake so that laundry washed in it came out white without the need of soap (a useful tip for hard-pressed campers).

Lac du Vernois – The lake, surrounded by woods, comes into view suddenly at a bend in the road. There is not a dwelling in sight; the atmosphere is one of absolute peace and seclusion. The waters from this little lake spill into a gully and flow into those from the Lac de Narlay, underground.

Continue along D 74 and take D 90 towards Fontenu.

Fontenu – The church in this village is surrounded by century-old lime trees. About 800m beyond Fontenu is the north shore of the Lac de Chalain, from which there is an excellent **view**★★ *(car park, viewpoint, picnic area).*

★★ **Lac de Chalain** – *See Lac de CHALAIN.*

Turn back and keep right, without going down to the lakeside (one-way), but taking D 90 towards Doucier.

There is a second **view**★★ of the lake 500m/547yd after rejoining the road.

Return to Doucier on D 90 and D 39.

LONS-LE-SAUNIER★

Population 18 483
Michelin map 321: D-6

The capital of the Jura region has an interesting cultural heritage and is an excellent base for tourists wishing to make excursions to the vineyards or the Jura plateaus. It is also a spa town, where mineral-enriched waters are used to treat rheumatism, children's growth problems and psoriasis.

Rouget de Lisle – The author of the French national anthem, the *Marseillaise*, was born in 1760 at no 24 Rue du Commerce, son of a king's counsellor. Rouget enlisted with the army and became a captain of the Engineers, although he was not all that enamoured of warmongering. His tastes ran rather to poetry and music. The products of his fertile mind – the Lons Museum contains four whole volumes of his songs – charmed everyone who frequented the town's salons.

He composed the war song for the Army of the Rhine, later to become known as the *Marseillaise*, in April 1792 at Strasbourg, where he was garrisoned. But the poet-musician was then imprudent enough to write a hymn dedicated to Henri IV, for which he was put into prison as a monarchist.

After his release, Rouget lived on the verge of poverty, scraping a living by copying music and later returning to his family home in Montaigu and becoming a wine-grower (1811 to 1818). He did not meet with much success, so returned to Paris, as poor

Rouget de Lisle Singing the Marseillaise (detail): Painting by Isidor Pils in Strasburg's Historical Museum

as a church mouse. He was imprisoned at Sainte-Pélagie for a debt of 500 francs and was only saved by the generosity of the songwriter Béranger, who paid off his debt to have him freed. In 1830 friends at Choisy-le-Roi took in the now half-paralysed, virtually blind artist. But his luck now finally changed for the better – Louis-Philippe awarded him a pension of 1 500 francs, which at least provided him with some comfort during the last six years of his life.

TOWN WALK

Place de la Liberté – At one end of the square stands a statue by Étex of General Lecourbe (born in Besançon and buried at Ruffey, near Lons). To the east the square is closed off by the imposing Rococo façade of the theatre, with a clock which runs through two bars of the *Marseillaise* before ringing the hour. The clock tower (Tour de l'Horloge) once defended the entrance into the fortified town (the square is located on the site of the old moat).

If you wish, you can first walk along rue St-Désiré to the Église St-Désiré which is not in the town centre but worth seeing.

Église St-Désiré – A beautiful 15C Burgundian School Entombment or Pietà is to the right of the chancel. The 11C **crypt** is one of the oldest in the Franche-Comté. The triple nave has six bays and is roofed with ribbed vaulting. The sarcophagus of St Desiderius is in one of the three apsidal chapels.

Return to the clock tower marking the beginning of rue du Commerce.

★Rue du Commerce – The arcaded houses along this street (146 archways onto the street and under cover) make it very picturesque indeed. The houses were built in the second half of the 17C, after a terrible fire had literally cleared the space. Yet, in spite of the symmetrical balance dictated by the arcades, the people of Lons managed to manifest their taste for beauty as well as the independent spirit common to all Comtois people by varying the dimensions, curve and decoration on the arches. Note the large roofs, with a few dormer windows to let in the light and tall chimneys. The house in which Rouget de Lisle was born (no 24) is now a museum *(see below)*.

Continue to place de l'Hôtel-de-Ville and walk round the buildings.

The town hall (Musée des Beaux-Arts) and the **Hôtel-Dieu** *(see below)*, both 18C, stand close to each other, which highlights their similarities.

Walk across place Perraud and along rue du Puits-Salé to the spring.

Puits-Salé – The town developed around this salt-water spring, used as early as the Roman period.

Turn right onto rue Richebourg then right again onto place de l'Ancien-collège.

Rue de Balerne on the right leads to **place de la Comédie** lined with old wine-growers' houses.

Follow rue du Four to rue des Cordeliers.

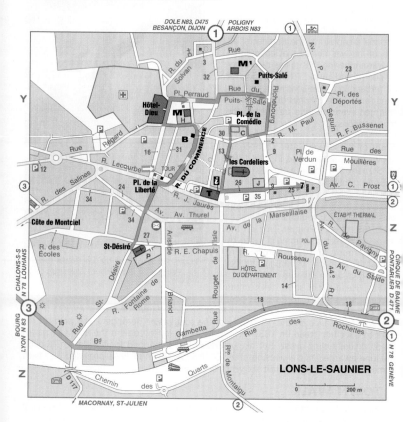

Maison natale
  de Rouget de Lisle . . . .**Y B**
Musée des Beaux-Arts . . . .**Y M**

Musée municipal
  d'Archéologie . . . .**Y M¹**

Théâtre. . . . .**Y T**

Eating out

BUDGET

Ferme-Auberge La Grange Rouge – *39570 Vernantois - 9 km/5.6mi SW of Lons-le-Saunier by D 117 - ☎ 03 84 47 00 44 - closed 25 Aug-17 Sep – reservations recommended - 12€.* Perched on the hills south of Lons-le-Saunier, this inn is a popular address among locals. Phone beforehand to enquire about the day's menu. The large, cosy and quiet rooms exude warm, country-style charm.

MODERATE

Auberge de Chavannes – *39570 Courlans - 6 km/3.7mi SW of Lons-le-Saunier by N 78 - ☎ 03 84 47 05 52 - contact@auberge-de-chavannes.com - closed Jan, 25 Jun-5 Jul, Sun evenings, Tue lunchtime and Mon – reservations required - 29/46€.* You will soon forget that this inn is located near the main road. The meals served here are lovingly prepared and deserve their glowing reputation: the fish come straight from Brittany, the meat from Bresse... In fine weather, eat out on the terrace to soak up the sun.

Where to stay

BUDGET

Nouvel Hôtel – *50 r. Lecourbe - ☎ 03 84 47 20 67 - closed 20 Dec-6 Jan - 🅿 - 26 rooms: 35/49€ - ☕ 7€.* Your host has a passion for warships and the French Navy and the interior of his hotel is decorated with beautiful miniature models of boats. The rooms on the third floor are slightly smaller.

MODERATE

Parenthèse – *39570 Chille - 3 km/1.9mi N of Lons-le-Saunier by D 157 - ☎ 03 84 47 55 44 - parenthese.hotel@wanadoo.fr - 🅿 - 29 rooms: 73/135€ - ☕ 8.50€ - restaurant 15.25/42.70€.* Modern hotel standing close to the Jura vineyards offering comfortable guestrooms, many of which have a balcony giving onto wooded parkland. The restaurant provides generous cuisine with a strong regional touch.

Sit back and relax

Au Prince d'Orange – *1 r. St-Désiré - ☎ 03 84 24 31 39 - store: Mon-Fri 9am-12.30pm, 2-7pm (Sat 7.15pm), Sun 9am-12.30pm; tea room: 2.30-7pm.* Since 1899 the Peten family has been making delicious pastries and sweetmeats such as its *galets de Chalain* (chocolate-coated nougatine with praline) and its "squirrel cake" (praline-hazel nut butter cream on a base of almonds covered with almond paste). The upstairs tea shop is cosy and elegantly appointed.

Grand Café de Strasbourg – *4 r. Jean-Jaurès - ☎ 03 84 24 18 45 - Open daily except Mon Oct-May 8.30-1am - closed 2 weeks in Nov, 25 Dec and 1 Jan.* This popular café is housed in a handsome late-19C edifice which is a listed building. In fair weather, settle on the terrace and sip a drink to the strains of Louis Armstrong, Billie Holiday or Miles Davis.

Grand Café du Théâtre – *2 r. Jean-Jaurès - ☎ 03 84 24 49 30 – open Mon-Sat: 7-1am.* A listed site, this café offers an interesting choice of menus and is conveniently located near the lively shopping district. Nice terrace overlooking the square.

La Maison du Vigneron – *23 r. du Commerce - ☎ 03 84 24 44 60 - Tue-Sat 9am-noon, 2-7pm - closed public holidays.* Discover all about Jura wine at this cellar, where tastings are organised of the main regional *crus*: Côtes du Jura, Vin d'Arbois, Château-Châlon, Crémant, Macvin... Boutique with bottles for sale.

Église des Cordeliers – This Franciscan church is the burial place of the Chalon-Arlays, who were Lons' feudal lords in the Middle Ages. The church was restored in the 18C. Besides the Louis XVI woodwork in the chancel, note the 1728 pulpit executed by the Lamberthoz brothers of Lons.

Continue along the street to place du 11-Novembre.

The square is prolonged by the **Promenade de la Chevalerie**, adorned with the statue of Rouget de Lisle by Bartholdi.

ADDITIONAL SIGHTS

★ **Theatre** ⏰ – Damaged by fire in 1901, the theatre, dating from 1847, had to be partially rebuilt. The architects drew their inspiration from the Opéra Garnier in Paris. The edifice was recently restored with remarkable results.

Musée Rouget-de-Lisle (Donation A Lançon) ⏰ – Rouget de Lisle's birthplace at no 24 rue du Commerce has been turned into a small museum, in which mementoes, documents and a video film relate the story of the French national anthem and its composer.

Hôtel-Dieu ⊘ – 18C. A very beautiful wrought-iron **gate★** closes off the main court-yard. There are porcelain, tin and brass pots in the wood-panelled **pharmacie★** (dispensary).

Musée des Beaux-Arts ⊘ – Housed in a wing of the town hall, this museum exhibits some 30 paintings – by Vouet, Courbet *(Death of a Stag)*, as well as a few Dutch works. – and sculpture – mainly by Perraud but also by Falconet.

Musée Municipal d'Archéologie ⊘ – The archaeology museum's temporary exhibits give an idea of its large regional archaeological collections (prehistory; Neolithic lakeside communities; the metal ages; the Gallo-Roman, Merovingian and medieval periods).
An entire room has been devoted to exhibiting the Bronze Age, dugout canoe found in the Lac de Chalain.
Video films on 40 different themes can be watched on demand.

Colline de Montmorot – *2km/1.2mi west. Leave town on the Cours Colbert (12) and turn right in Montmorot.*
The Montmorot salt works, along with those at Salins, were the biggest in the Franche-Comté. Production stopped in 1966. There is a beautiful view of Lons-le-Saunier from the hilltop crowned with the ruins of a keep.

▶▶ **Montaigu** – *3km/1.7mi south.* Viewpoint overlooking Lons and the sur-rounding area and castle ruins.

▶▶ **La Croix Rochette** – *6km further south and 15min on foot there and back to the Cross. Alt 636m/2 087ft.* Extensive views of the Saône Valley, the Mâconnais hills and the Jura mountains.

THE JURA PLATEAU
19km/12mi – allow 4hr

Leave Lons-le-Saunier along N 78.

Conliège – The 17C **church** has beautiful wrought-iron chancel railings, a richly sculpted 17C pulpit, churchwardens' pews dating from 1525, and a 16C shrine containing the relics of St Fortuné.

★**Creux de Revigny** – This is a beautiful amphitheatre enclosed by limestone cliffs, at the foot of which the source of the Vallière is to be found. This river flows on to Conliège and Lons-le-Saunier. There are many caves in the cliff, hidden amid the dense foliage, which served as a refuge for the nearby inhabitants during the 17C (Ten Years War). These people lived there on a virtually permanent basis; the region was so dangerous during the bloody attacks by the Swedes that even bap-tisms were held here.

The road then heads down into the Ain Valley, which it reaches at Pont-de-Poitte.

Pont-de-Poitte – *See Lac de VOUGLANS.*

LOUHANS★

Population 6 327
Michelin map 320: L-10

Louhans is a picturesque little town and is an important centre for butter, eggs and Bresse poultry, which is known as Louhannaise poultry. The town is also known for its pig and cattle markets.

SIGHTS

★**Grande Rue** – The arches of the old houses with wood or stone pillars, which date from the late Middle Ages, create an impressive decor.

Hôtel-Dieu ⊘ – The 17C-18C hospital contains two large public rooms divided by a wrought-iron screen. Each curtained bed bears a plaque indicating for whom the bed was intended – usually the benefactors offered a bed to the inhabitants of a particular town.
The **pharmacy**, decorated with Louis XIV woodwork, displays a beautiful collection of hand-blown glass vessels and Hispano-Moorish lustreware. There is also a most unusual Burgundian woodcarving of the Virgin of Mercy kneeling before the dead Christ (early-16C).

Church – This building has been greatly restored with stone and brick and is roofed with glazed tiles. On the left is a belfry-porch and large chapel with turreted pavil-ions (14C).

L'Atelier d'un journal ⊘ – ⊡ This annexe of the local museum, the Écomusée de la Bresse Bourguignonne at the Château de Pierre-de-Bresse is housed in the old premises *(no 29 Rue des Dôdanes)* of *l'Indépendant*, a Bresse newspaper aban-doned in 1984 after 100 years of publication. The old machines are still in place; the offices have been reconstructed.

Eating out and where to stay

BUDGET

Cotriade – *4 r. d'Alsace -* ☎ *03 85 75 19 91 - closed 22-28 Jun and Tue evenings except Jul-Aug - 12/32€.* In a lively shopping street in the town centre, this simple restaurant offers regional cooking with special emphasis on fish and sea food. Behind its glass façade, the flowery dining room is furnished in classical style. Menus range from cheap to expensive, with a special formula for children.

BUDGET

Le Moulin de Bourgchâteau – *In Guidon, on the road to Chalon -* ☎ *03 85 75 37 12 - bourgchateau@netcourrier.com - closed 20 Dec-20 Jan and Sun 15 Sep to Easter -* 🅿 *- 18 rooms: 39/85€ -* ⌚ *8€ - restaurant 25/29€.* Delightful 18C mill spanning the waters of the River Seille, whose former machinery now adorns the hotel bar. Comfortable rooms, some of which are nestled under the eaves. Dining room with beams and stone walls.

EXCURSION

Chaisiers et pailleuses de Rancy ⊙ – *12km/8mi south-west by D 971 on the outskirts of Rancy.*
Chair-making, which at the beginning of the 19C was a long-established part-time occupation in Rancy and Bantanges, had become a full-time job by the end of the century. This centre is now the second most important French producer of caned chairs. This annexe of the Écomusée de la Bresse Bourguignonne at the Château de Pierre-de-Bresse illustrates the development of the different stages in this manufacture from the making of the wooden frame to the addition of the straw seat.

LUXEUIL-LES-BAINS ♏

Population 8 814
Michelin map 314: G-6

This well-known spa town is predominantly built in red sandstone and contains many interesting mansions and Gothic or Renaissance houses. After years of decline, the town has made great strides in recent years in the range of leisure facilities it has to offer (concert hall, casino, tennis courts, golf course, swimming pool) to support its activities as a spa.
A 4km/2.5mi walk, known as the **Sentier des Gaulois**, leads from the baths past all the historical monuments of the town.
Luxeuil was the seat of a famous abbey founded by **St Columban**, an Irish monk who came to France in 590 with a dozen companions. He was forced to seek refuge at Bobbio in Italy after he rebuked the king of Burgundy for his loose living.

TOWN WALK

★ **Hôtel du Cardinal Jouffroy** – Cardinal Jouffroy, Abbot of Luxeuil and later Archbishop of Albi, was highly favoured by Louis XI throughout his life. The house in which he lived (15C) is the most beautiful in Luxeuil. In addition to its Flamboyant Gothic windows and arcade, it has some Renaissance features, including, on one of its sides, an unusual corbelled turret (16C) topped by a lantern. Famous figures such as Madame de Sévigné, Augustin Thierry, Lamartine and André Theuriet all lived in this house.
Beneath the balcony, the third keystone from the left depicts three rabbits, sculpted in such a way that each rabbit appears to have two ears, although only three ears in total have been carved.

★ **Maison François-Ier** – This Renaissance mansion *(west of the abbey church)* is named not after the king of France, but an abbot of Luxeuil. Splendid carved faces decorate the Renaissance arcades.

Unique lacework

G. Magnin/MICHELIN

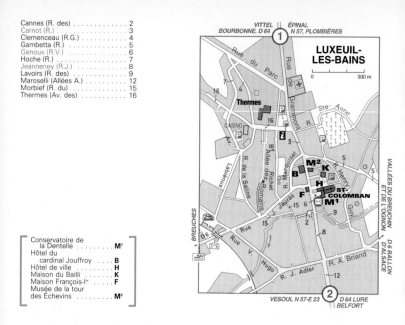

Conservatoire de
    la Dentelle . . . . **M¹**
Hôtel du
    cardinal Jouffroy . . . . **B**
Hôtel de ville . . . . **H**
Maison du Bailli . . . . . . **K**
Maison François-Ier . . . . . **F**
Musée de la tour
    des Échevins . . . . **M²**

★ Ancienne abbaye St-Colomban ◷ – This abbey has survived almost in its entirety, and much of it has been recently restored.

Basilica – The present building, which replaced the original 11C church of which only traces are left, dates from the 13C and 14C. Of the three original towers, only the west bell-tower remains. This was rebuilt in 1527 and the top of it dates from the 18C. The apse was rebuilt by Vauban in 1860. The north façade of the church, with a modern statue of St Columban nearby, can be seen from Place St-Pierre. A Classical doorway with a pediment leads into the interior, which is in the Burgundian Gothic style. The **organ case★** is supported by an atlas and decorated with magnificent sculpted medallions. The pulpit, with sophisticated Empire style ornamentation, stands out from the decor of the rest of the church; it dates from 1806 and came from Notre-Dame, Paris. Lacordaire is among those who preached from it. There are some interesting 16C stalls in the chancel. The south transept houses the shrine of St Columban, and the north transept a 14C statue of St Peter.

Cloisters – Three of the four red sandstone galleries remain. One arcade with three bays surmounted by an oculus dates from the 13C; the others were rebuilt in the 15C and 16C.

Conservatoire de la dentelle – In the Salle des Moines, there is a lace-making workshop and a display of the finest examples of the lace-makers' work.

Conventual buildings – These include, to the south of the church, the 17C-18C *Bâtiment des Moines* (monks' building) and, on Place St-Pierre, the 16C-18C abbot's residence, now the town hall (**H**).

Maison du Bailli – The bailiff's mansion on the square, north of the abbey church, dates from 1473. The courtyard is overlooked by a Flamboyant stone balcony and a crenellated polygonal tower.

★ Musée de la Tour des Échevins ◷ – The Hôtel des Échevins is a large 15C building with crenellated walls. The decoration of the exterior and the splendid Flamboyant Gothic loggia contrast with the building's overall appearance. The museum inside houses on the ground and first floors some remarkable stone funerary monuments from the Gallo-Roman town (Luxovium), votive **steles★**, inscriptions, Gallic ex-votos, a reconstruction of a potter's kiln, sigillate pottery etc. The second and third floors are occupied by the **Musée Adler** containing paintings by Adler, Vuillard and Pointelin. From the top of the tower *(146 steps)* there is a good **view** of the town and, in the distance, the Vosges, the Jura and the Alps.

MÂCON

Population 34 469
Michelin map 320: I-12 – Local map see Le MÂCONNAIS

Mâcon spreads along the west bank of the Saône between the river and the Mâconnais heights with their slopes covered in vineyards. The round roof tiles mark it as a southern town. Its lively atmosphere is due partly to the busy waterfront, the marina and, not least, to the national French wine fair *(see Calendar of events)* held here every year.

Mâcon is the meeting point of the main roads from the Paris basin to the Mediterranean coast and from Lake Geneva to the banks of the Loire. It has always been a busy crossroads; since ancient times waves of invasion have left their mark, such as the prehistoric civilisation excavated at Solutré. At the end of the Roman period, Mâcon, then known as Matisco, was invaded by the Barbarians.

The Prince of French Romanticism – Alphonse de Lamartine *(see MÂCONNAIS 3)* was born in Mâcon in 1790 and took an interest in literature and religious issues from an early age, reading among other things Chateaubriand's *Génie du christianisme*. During his first trip to Italy (1811-12), he fell in love with a certain Antoniella, who inspired his later work *Graziella*. In 1816, he met a great love of his life, Julie Charles, the wife of the physicist Jacques Charles. Julie's premature death drove him to write the melancholy ode *Le Lac*. His *Méditations poétiques*, in which the poet extols Julie under the name of Elvira, were published in 1820, and it was these works which won Lamartine fame. In 1820 he married a young English woman, Mary Ann Birch, and began a very productive period of creativity. In 1829, he was made a member of the Académie Française, and from 1831 to 1833 he fulfilled his childhood dream of making a voyage to the east to visit Nazareth and Jerusalem. However, his daughter Julia died during this voyage, which profoundly shook Lamartine in the religious beliefs which had guided him thus far. The result of this personal crisis was *Jocelyn*, published in 1836, which was enormously well received.

Lamartine's political career – Besides his brilliant literary career, Lamartine enjoyed a no less brilliant career in politics. When King Louis-Philippe came to the throne in 1827, Lamartine gave up his post as embassy secretary to pursue politics. He was elected Deputy of a town in the Nord *département* in 1833, and from 1837 onwards he represented Mâcon, retaining his seat in 1842 and 1846. The news-sheet he founded in 1842, *Le Bien public*, in which he expounded his social theories, had a large readership. His historical work, *Histoire des Girondins*, was also very successful. Following the Revolution of February 1848, he was actively involved in founding the Second Republic and played an important role as Minister of Foreign Affairs. In the election of the French president by universal suffrage in December 1848 he won 18 000 votes, losing to Louis-Napoléon Bonaparte's 5 million.

In 1849 he retired from politics to his homeland, the Mâconnais. The end of his life was beset with financial problems and family grief. He died in Paris in 1869 and is buried in St-Point.

On the banks of the Saône

TOWN WALK

Leave the car in the quai Lamartine car park; the riverside is lined with pavement cafés. Walk along rue St-Vincent, a lively shopping street running parallel (17C house at no 79).

Vieux St-Vincent – All that remains of the old cathedral of St-Vincent, after its destruction by fervent revolutionaries, are the narthex, two octagonal towers and the intervening bay of the main nave. In the **narthex** the 12C tympanum features carvings which were already damaged during the Wars of Religion. Five rows of superimposed sculpture depict scenes from the Last Judgement; the Resurrection of the Dead, and Paradise and Hell are still distinguishable. The cathedral building now houses a **lapidary museum** ⊙.

Maison de Bois – A charming half-timbered Renaissance house with finely sculpted small columns stands at no 22 rue Dombey, on the corner of place aux Herbes. Grotesque carvings and fantastic animals decorate the coping.

Pont St-Laurent – Mâcon was a border town until the treaty of Lyon in 1601, when the Bresse region came under the aegis of the kingdom of France. The existence of the fortified bridge of St-Laurent, part of the border town's fortifications, is first recorded in 1077. The bridge was restored and enlarged in the 18C. From the bridge, there is a good **view** of the banks of the Saône and the town itself, with the twin towers of the old cathedral of St-Vincent rising above the rooftops.

Upstream of the bridge the Saône opens out into the splendid broad reach of water (300m wide) which was used from 1937 to 1939 by seaplanes of the Imperial Airways company on their way from Southampton to Australia via Brindisi and Egypt.

ADDITIONAL SIGHTS

Musée Lamartine ⊘ – The museum dedicated to the famous poet and politician is in the Hôtel Senecé (18C), an elegant, Régence-style mansion and seat of the Académie de Mâcon (founded 1805). It contains paintings, tapestries and furniture of the period. A collection of documents recalls the life and work, both literary and political, of Lamartine.

★**Musée des Ursulines** ⊘ – The museum, which is housed in a 17C Ursuline convent, contains sections on prehistory, Gallo-Roman and medieval archaeology, regional ethnography, painting and ceramics.

Ground floor – After the presentation of the history of Mâcon from antiquity to the present, the prehistory section displays articles from the excavations at Solutré and other regional sites: flint-cutting techniques, tools, weapons and ceramics from the Paleolithic period to the Iron Age. The following rooms are given over to the Gallo-Roman period (statuettes, tools, pottery kiln, collection of funerary urns from the Mâcon necropolis), medieval artefacts (Merovingian weapons and sepulchres, lapidary fragments) and sculpture from the 12C to the 17C. The convent chapel houses temporary exhibits.

First floor – The gallery is devoted to regional ethnography and local traditions and occupations, especially those linked with the river and the land (mason, winegrower, potter).

MÂCON

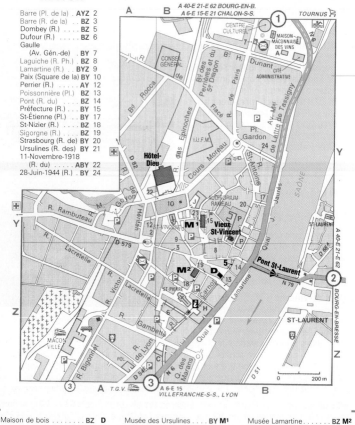

Eating out

BUDGET

Le Poisson d'Or – *Allée du Parc - 1 km/0.6mi N of Mâcon by N 6 and along the banks of the Saône* - ☎ *03 85 38 00 88 - closed Feb school holidays and 20-31 Oct, Tue evenings Oct-Apr and Wed - 17/40€*. Not to be missed, especially if you like frogs' legs and fried fish...Shaded terrace along the banks of the Saône. Neat, tidy dining room with flowered fabrics. Good selection of menus, including one for children.

Where to stay

BUDGET

Hôtel Concorde – *73 r. Lacretelle* - ☎ *03 85 34 21 47 - hotel.concorde.71@wanadoo.fr - Closed 20 Dec-12 Jan and Sun 15 Oct-15 Apr - 13 rooms: 32/44€* - ☲ *6€*. Small, cheap and unpretentious hotel away from the modern quarter. Simple, well-kept rooms. Breakfast is served in the rustic dining room or on the terrace in fine weather.

Chambre d'Hôte Château de Salornay – *71870 Hurigny - 6 km/3.7mi W of Mâcon by D 82 then a minor road* - ☎ *03 85 34 25 73 -* ☲ *- 4 rooms: 40/50€*. A splendid 11C and 15C castle at the entrance to Mâcon, complete with turrets and covered way. The peaceful bedrooms give out onto the fields; the ones in the keep and the tower are more comfortable. The terrace affords a nice view of the city.

Sit back and relax

La Maison de Bois – *13 pl. aux Herbes* - ☎ *03 85 38 03 51 – open Mon 3-9pm, Tue-Sat (summer) 7-2am, (the rest of the year) 9-2am.* The inscription on the façade recounts that this 1480 wooden building once housed an abbey in the 16C. Today it has been converted into a smart and comfortable pub with a large terrace looking out onto the square.

La Traboule – *47 r. Carnot* - ☎ *03 85 38 37 70 – open Mon-Wed noon-2am, Fri-Sat noon-3am, Sun 9pm-2am - closed early Aug.* In Lyon, a *traboule* is a passageway that cuts across a building or a group of houses. This *traboule* has been converted into a cosy pub with a fine wooden door. The comfortable interior is decorated with portraits of famous people who lived in Mâcon. Karaoke evenings.

Le Galion Pub – *46 r. Franche* - ☎ *03 85 38 39 45 - Mon-Sat 3pm-2am.* The mahogany decor of this pub draws its inspiration from boats, as is evidenced by the two bars in the shape of a ship's prow. A stately staircase leads to the mezzanine where the disk-jockey settles for the evening, perched above the entrance. Karaoke evenings.

Maison des Vins – *484 av. Maréchal Lattre-de-Tassigny* - ☎ *03 85 22 91 11 - www.maison-des-vins.com - open daily 11.30am-6.30pm - closed, 1 Janv, 1 May, Christmas.* An exhibition room, a boutique, a bookshop, a playing area for children and, of course, wine tastings commented by connoisseurs who will enlighten you on the art of oenology.

Second floor – This gallery contains 17C and 18C furniture, French and foreign glazed earthenware and painting: 16C Flemish works; Fontainebleau School; 17C and 18C French and Northern schools (Le Brun, de Champaigne, Greuze); 19C Romanticism (Corot), academics and Symbolists (Busière); 20C post-Cubist canvases (Gleizes, Cahn) and contemporary works (Bill, Honneger, Boussard).

Hôtel-Dieu ⊘ – This 18C hospital was designed by Melchior Munet, one of Soufflot's pupils. The Louis XV **dispensary★** has a fine collection of pottery of that period. The Louis XV style panelling is as remarkable as the woodwork of the windows which blends perfectly with the general decor. Frescoes in the chapel.

EXCURSION

Romanèche-Thorins – *15km/9.5mi S Via N 6.* The famous Moulin-à-Vent grows here and in the neighbouring village of Chénas. The **Maison de Benoît Raclet** ⊘ makes an interesting visit. Raclet's empirical discovery of a preventative measure against the pyralis worm, namely pouring boiling water over the vines *(échaudage)*, was used until 1945. The **Musée du Compagnonnage Guillon** ⊘ displays exhibits from days of the traveling craftsman; there are some particularly fine examples of their work. **Le Hameau du vin S.A. Dubœuf★** ⊘ is an interesting modern museum devoted to Beaujolais wine; the wine-growing room contains an impressive winepress dating from

1708, a statue of Bacchus and collections illustrating the daily life of wine-growers. The various stages of wine-making, crafts linked to wine-growing and the different vintages are also illustrated. The visit ends with a convivial wine-tasting session. The **Château du Moulin à Vent** ⏰ produces the most famous of all Beaujolais wines, Moulin-à-Vent: ruby-coloured, round and robust. It is a powerful, full-bodied wine suitable for laying down. Tastings are organised.

Parc zoologique et d'attractions Touroparc ⏰ – *Close to N 6; from the Maison-Blanche crossroads, follow D 466^E towards St-Romain-des-Îles.*

◉ This 10ha/25-acre zoological park and breeding centre set in green surroundings houses animals from all over the world; most of them (except the big cats) roam freely through the park which offers leisure activities, an elevated monorail tourist train, a picnic area with several bars...

Le MÂCONNAIS★★

Michelin map 320: H-10 to I-12

The delightful and varied landscape of the Mâconnais extends from Tournus to Mâcon, between the valley of the Saône and the valley of the Grosne.

The terraced Mâconnais heights on the west bank of the Saône terminate at the northern end in the Chalon plain north of Tournus. On the west side they are separated from the Charollais by the Grosne Valley; in the south they merge imperceptibly into the Beaujolais country.

Southern Burgundy – The Mâconnais does not rise to dramatic heights (Signal de la Mère-Boitier 758m/2 487ft) but the countryside is attractive and varied. The forested peaks and the barren sunless slopes contrast with the lush meadows in the valleys; the terraces bordering the Saône and the hillsides which catch the sun are planted with vineyards.

The Mâconnais contains features more typical of the Mediterranean region to the south: instead of high pointed roofs of slates or flat tiles one sees low-pitched roofs covered with rounded tiles known as Roman or Provençal. The region is a borderland between the north and the south. The climate is less harsh than in northern Burgundy.

The king and the wine-grower

Although he was only a simple wine-grower from Chasselas, **Claude Brosse** decided to try his local wines on the Paris market. He filled two hogsheads with his best wine, loaded them on to a cart drawn by two oxen and after journeying for 33 days arrived in the capital. In Versailles he attended mass in the presence of the King who noticed his great stature. After the service Louis XIV desired to see the unknown man. Unabashed, Claude Brosse explained the purpose of his journey and how he hoped to sell his wine to some noble lord. The King asked to taste the wine on the spot and found it much better than the products of Suresnes and Beaugency then being drunk at court. The wines of Mâcon became very popular with the courtiers and acquired their reputation for excellence; the bold wine producer continued to convey the produce of his vineyards for sale in Paris and Versailles.

Wine – The monks of Cluny planted the first vines in the Mâconnais, of which the Chardonnay, the Pinot and the Gamay are the best known.

The Mâconnais vineyards meet the Beaujolais vineyards on their southern border; they extend from Romanèche-Thorins in the south to Tournus in the north and produce good red wines but, above all, excellent white ones. Annual wine production in the Mâconnais is about 200 000hl/4 400 000gal, two-thirds of which are white wines.

White wines: these come from the Chardonnay stock, the great white grape of Burgundy and Champagne. The most celebrated is Pouilly-Fuissé. This wine has a beautiful green-gold colour, it is dry and crisp; when young it is fruity but with age acquires a bouquet. Pouilly-Loché, Saint-Vérand, Pouilly-Vinzelles, Mâcon-Lugny and Mâcon-Viré, members of the same family as Pouilly-Fuissé, are also well known. The other white wines are sold under the names of White Burgundy, White Mâcon and Mâcon-Villages.

Red wines: without pretending to equal the great wines, these can be considered an excellent value. Fairly full-bodied and fruity, they are generally produced from the Gamay stock, a black grape with white juice.

① LA MONTAGNE
From Tournus to Mâcon *69km/ – 43 miles – 3hr 30min*

This drive passes through a picturesque region of fine views and wide panoramas, dotted with Romanesque churches *(signposted itinerary)* and many other interesting buildings.

★Tournus – *See TOURNUS.*

Leave Tournus along D 14.

The road climbs rapidly, providing views over Tournus, the Saône Valley and the Bresse region. South-west of the Beaufer pass the countryside has many valleys and the crests are covered with boxwood and conifers.

Ozenay – Set in a little valley, Ozenay has an impressive 13C fortified farm (castel) and a rustic 12C church.

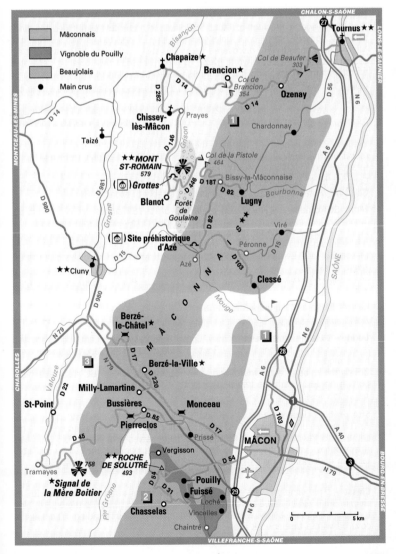

D. Delacroix/mMICHELIN

Fortified farm

Beyond Ozenay outcrops of rocks appear here and there on the slopes.

Most houses have a porch and covered balcony forming a loggia.

From the Brancion pass, take the road to the old market town of Brancion, perched jauntily on a promontory.

★Brancion – *See BRANCION.*

Returning to the pass, go as far as Chapaize, its fine belfry clearly visible from afar.

★Chapaize – *See CHAPAIZE.*

Opposite the church in Chapaize take the road to Lys; turn left.

Chissey-lès-Mâcon – The 12C church with an elegant belfry, typical of Cluny, has curious historiated capitals.

Continue east to Prayes; turn right on D 146.

Blanot – *8km/5mi south of Chissey.*
This old village at the foot of Mont St-Romain is home to the fortified buildings of a 14C **priory★** which once belonged to Cluny. Three tombs dating from the Merovingian period were discovered here. The apse of the late 11C **church** is decorated with a pretty openwork frieze. The Romanesque bell-tower is decorated with Lombard arcades and has a curious widely oversailing roof.

Caves ⊘ – *North of Blanot, take D 446 to Fougnières; 500m/547yd beyond the village, turn left in a bend.*
🔲 The caves are more than 80m/262ft deep. The roof collapsed a long time ago, forming a huge pile of enormous blocks. The visit extends over 1km/0.6mi between the hamlet of Le Vivier and Mont St-Romain *(steep steps and low passages)* and includes 21 chambers. At the end, there is a display of flints and animal bones found on the spot since excavations began in 1988 and dating from the Mousterian period (100000 to 40000 BC).

Carry on north-east. The pretty road *(D 446)* leads through the beautiful forest of Goulaine *(Forêt domaniale)* before climbing steeply to Mont St-Romain.

★Mont St-Romain – *A steep road branching off D 187 climbs up to the summit. Take the path leading to the tower adjacent to the restaurant (parking area).*
From the top of the tower there is a marvellous **panorama★★** of the Saône plain to the east, with the Bresse region and the Jura and Alpine ranges beyond it, the Mâconnais and Beaujolais regions to the south and the Charolais to the west *(viewing table)*.

From Mont St-Romain, continue to the Col de la Pistole, then on to Bissy-la-Mâconnaise.

East of Bissy-la-Mâconnaise lies the Mâconnais vineyard country.

D 82 leads to Lugny.

Lugny – Nestling amid green scenery, Lugny produces an excellent white wine and is situated on the Mâconnais Wine Route *(Route des Vins du Mâconnais)*. The town has a modern wine cooperative.
Beside the ruins of a fortress stands the **church** which has a 16C stone altarpiece portraying Jesus with the twelve Apostles.

Return to Bissy; take D 82 south to Azé.

Site préhistorique d'Azé ⊘ – *8.5km/5.3mi SW of Lugny via Bissy.*
🔲 The **museum** displays over 2 000 artefacts found locally. An arboretum precedes the entrance to the **caves**; the first (208m/682ft long) served as a refuge for cave bears (many bones), prehistoric man, the Aedui, the Gallo-Romans etc; the second cave contains an underground river which can be followed for a stretch (800m/2 625ft).

Take D 15 east then D 103 south-east to Clessé.

Clessé – This wine-growers' village (cooperative) has a late-11C **church** with an elegant small tower and a spire clad with varnished tiles, similar to the one topping the fine octagonal belfry with its twinned openings and arcading. The nave is covered with a timberwork roof.

Continue south on D 103 to Mâcon.

Eating out

Le Moustier – *71960 Berzé-la-Ville -* ☎ *03 85 37 77 41 - dhoquet@aol.com - closed Sun evenings and Tue evenings 1 Oct-30 Apr and Wed - 13/27€.* Handsome 18C house with shaded terrace commanding pretty views of the Mâconnais heights. The stone walls, beams and fireplace convey a warm and cosy atmosphere. Tasty cuisine, homemade specialities. The pasta salad with goat's cheese will restore your appetite after a long, bracing walk.

Where to stay

Chambre d'Hôte Domaine de l'Arfentière – *Rte de Chardonnay - 71700 Uchizy - 10 km/6.2mi S of Tournus by N 6 then D 163 -* ☎ *03 85 40 50 46 -* ⊠ *- 4 rooms: 32/43€.* Take advantage of your stay here to taste or buy some of the wines made on the estate. The bright rooms are decorated in a modern style. Two of them look out onto the vineyards.

Chambre d'Hôte de Rizerolles – *In Rizerolles - 71260 Azé - 8.5 km/5.3mi SW of Lugny by D 82 -* ☎ *03 85 33 33 26 -* ⊠ *- 5 rooms: 34/43€.* An old stone house in a tiny village nestled at the foot of vineyards. You will love the blossoming balcony and shaded courtyard. The decor of the rooms is unusual but the welcome is warm and friendly.

Chambre d'Hôte Mme Noblet – *Les Cochets - 71260 Viré - 4 km/2.5mi N of Clessé by D 403bis then D 15 -* ☎ *03 85 33 92 54 - closed 1 Nov-15 Mar -* ⊠ *- 3 rooms: 38/46€.* This old house in the village offers bright, comfortable rooms sparsely appointed with pine furniture. Note the smith's sign on the lintel above the door. Garden.

Chambre d'Hôte Le Château d'Escolles – *71960 Verzé - 4 km/2.5mi NE of Berzé-la-Ville by D 17 then D 85 -* ☎ *03 85 33 44 52 - 5 rooms: 38/60€.* Pretty outbuilding belonging to a 17C château on the edge of a park. The round windows and Virginia creeper lend it a charming appearance. The rooms set up under the eaves are old-fashioned in style and give onto the vineyards.

② THE VINEYARDS *Round trip 26km/16mi – about 2hr*

This is a pleasant drive in the very heart of the Mâconnais vineyards, through the changing scenery of this lovely countryside.
If you have time, go and visit the **Vignéroscope** ⊘ in Loché (4km/2.5mi south of Mâcon) where the tools used in wine-growing are very tastefully presented.

Leave Mâcon along D 579; turn left on D 54 to Pouilly.

Pouilly – This hamlet gives its name to various wines: Pouilly-Fuissé, Pouilly-Loché and Pouilly-Vinzelles. These wines are highly appreciated and go well with certain Burgundian specialities.

Beyond this village the orderly patterns of the vineyards spread over the gentle curves of the hillsides.

Fuissé – This is one of the communes (Chaintré, Fuissé, Solutré, Pouilly and Vergisson) producing Pouilly-Fuissé, classed as one of the world's great white wines.
Fuissé is a pleasing village, typical of a community of rich and prosperous wine-growers.
Between Fuissé and Solutré, the road affords splendid views over the neat patterns of the vineyards.

Ph. Cajic/MICHELIN

Roche de Solutré

Chasselas – *3.5km/2mi W of Fuissé*. This village is dominated by an outcrop of grey rock which appears amid the heath. The village has developed a vine that produces a well-known dessert grape.

The rock of Solutré stands out against the sky like the prow of a ship.

In the background appear the valley of the Saône, the Bresse countryside and the Jura mountains.

★★ Roche de Solutré – *See Roche de SOLUTRÉ.*

After Solutré the road enters the heart of the vineyard and affords a pretty view of the village of **Vergisson** and its rocky outcrop, a fine limestone escarpment.

Return to Mâcon.

③ LAMARTINE HERITAGE TRAIL *70km/44mi – about 3hr*

All those who are interested in souvenirs of the French romantic poet and statesman Alphonse de Lamartine will be attracted by this tour which passes through the countryside he knew, the scenes and views from which he drew his inspiration.

Mâcon – The memory of Lamartine hangs around the town where you can see his birthplace along rue Bauderon-de-Senecé, opposite the Musée des Ursulines, as well as the Hôtel d'Ozenay at no 15 rue Lamartine, where he lived until his wedding and wrote his first poetid works.

Château de Monceau – *9km/5.6mi W along D 17*. This château (now a convalescence home for the elderly) was one of Lamartine's favourite residences, where he lived as a great vineyard owner but where his creditors pursued him at the end of his life. It was in a little building, known as La Solitude, in the middle of the vineyards, that he wrote his *Histoire des Girondins*.

Milly-Lamartine – *3km/2mi further on*. An ironwork grille stands before the house, the **Maison d'Enfance de Lamartine** ⊘, where the poet spent his holidays as a child, free to enjoy the beautiful countryside nearby. The 12C church has been restored. At the top of the village, in front of the town hall, there is a bronze bust of the poet and a good view over the vineyards. It was at Milly that Lamartine composed his first meditation, *L'Isolement*.

★ Berzé-la-Ville – *2.5km/1.5mi N of Milly*. Towards the end of his life St Hugh of Cluny lived in the Château des Moines, a country house near the priory in Berzé owned by the abbey of Cluny.

Chapelle des Moines ⊘ – This Romanesque chapel belongs to the priory and is well known for its frescoes, a magnificent example of the art of Cluny.

The 12C chapel, built at first floor level in an earlier (11C) building, was decorated with Romanesque **frescoes★★**; only those in the chancel are well preserved.

On the oven-vaulting of the apse, Christ in Majesty is depicted in the centre of an almond-shaped glory. The figure is almost 4m/13ft high and is surrounded by Apostles, bishops and deacons as he hands a parchment of the Law to St Peter; below the windows are groups of saints and martyrs venerated at Cluny. The south wall of the apse shows the legend of St Blaise, and the north wall the martyrdom of St Vincent of Saragossa on a gridiron in the presence of Dacius, the Roman prefect.

The Byzantine influence evident in the murals, which are painted on a blue background, is probably due to the fact that the Cluniac artists who worked at Berzé were directed by Benedictine painters from Monte Cassino in Latium, where the influence of the eastern Roman Empire survived until the 11C.

From the road (D 17) one sees the imposing mass of Berzé-le-Châtel Castle with its impressive fortifications.

★ Château de Berzé-le-Châtel ⊘ – This feudal castle was once the principal seat of the most important barony in the Mâconnais. Henri IV made it a county. The castle protected the southern approaches to Cluny from its highly attractive site on the vineyard covered slopes.

Drive up the Valouze Valley to St-Point (12km/7.5mi SW of Berzé-le-Chatel).

St-Point – The **church**, in the style of Cluny, has a fresco of Christ in Majesty in the apse. It also possesses two pictures painted by Madame de Lamartine, who rests close to her husband and other relatives in the little chapel nearby. To the left of the church, a small door opens on to the park of the **château** ⊘.

This château was bestowed upon Lamartine at the time of his marriage in 1820. It was restored, enlarged, and took on a neo-Gothic colonnade which recalls the British origins of the author's wife, Mary Ann Birch, who supervised the works. She painted portraits of her daughter Julia and her dog Fido, as well as the lovely *Poets' Fireplace* in the bedroom. The study, bedroom and salon have remained much as they were in the days of Lamartine, who particularly favoured this residence and invited many famous guests there (Hugo, Nodier, Lizt).

South of St-Point beside the road (D 22) lies an artificial lake *(see page 293)* which is used as a leisure and water sports centre. East of Tramayes wide views open up from the roadway.

Château de Brézé

★**Signal de la Mère-Boitier** – *A steep road leads up to a car park. 15min round trip on foot.*
From the signal station (758m/2 487ft), the highest point of the Mâconnais region, there is a fine **panorama**★ *(viewing table)* of the Butte de Suin to the north-west, the St-Cyr mountain to the west and the Bresse and Jura to the east.

Château de Pierreclos  – *13km/8mi north-east from the Signal de la Mère-Boitier.* Dating from the 12C (keep) to the 17C, the château has had a troubled existence: devastated several times during the Wars of Religion, it was abandoned in 1950 and saved from imminent destruction in 1986. A wrought-iron gate between two pavilions (17C) closes off the first courtyard. In the inner courtyard, visitors can see the chancel and bell-tower of the old 11C church. The château is associated with Mlle de Milly, depicted as the character Laurence in Lamartine's epic poem *Jocelyn*, and with Nina de Pierrclos, her sister-in-law and the poet's lover. Inside, note the elegant **spiral stairway**, the Renaissance chimney-piece in the guard-room, the kitchen with its 12C fireplace, and the bakery, which used to make bread for the whole village. Under the vaulted ceiling of the cellar, there is an exhibit on wine and barrel-making.

Bussières – **Abbot Dumont**, Lamartine's first master and his great friend, whom he immortalised in *Jocelyn*, was laid to rest by the chevet of the little church.

MALBUISSON★

Population 400
Michelin map 321: H-6

This small holiday resort lies on the east bank of the lake of St-Point in a valley enclosed at both ends by mountains. Legend has it that there is a town at the bottom of the lake (6.3km/4mi long by 800m/0.5mi wide), drowned because its inhabitants refused to give shelter to a young mother and her child.

TOUR OF THE LAKE

Lac de St-Point – Situated in a vale through which the River Doubs flows, this lake and the Remoray Lake formed one single expanse of water. The St-Point Lake is 6.3km/4mi long and 800m/875yd wide. The building of a dam at its north end made it possible to regulate the flow of the Doubs. A path runs right round the lake *(parking areas)*.

Source Bleue – The waters of this spring are so pure and clear that it is possible to see right down into its crystal blue depths. Legend has it that Amaury de Joux returned from the Crusades after five years' absence and discovered that his wife had been unfaithful to him, so locked her up. From her dungeon she could see the gallows where her lover had been hung. The unfortunate woman is said to have wept so much that her tears ran into the spring and dyed its waters blue. Another story goes that the waters took on the colour of the eyes of a young woman who used to use the spring as a mirror.

Chaon – It is from the north end that one can enjoy the best view of the lake.

St-Point-Lac – Climb above the village for another fine view.
Complete your tour of the lake via Granges-Ste-Marie and return to Malbuisson

Lac de St-Point

M. Paygnard/MICHELIN

UPPER VALLEY OF THE DOUBS

Leave Malbuisson heading for Mouthe.

Lac de Remoray-Boujeons – *5km/3mi south along D 437, D 49 to the right then D 46 to the left.* This picturesque lake is separated from St-Point Lake by a strip of marshland.

Découverte de la Réserve Naturelle du Lac de Remoray – Information available at the Maison de la Réserve. Lying at an altitude of almost 1 000m/3 281ft, this nature reserve offers nature lovers a wealth of different ecosystems (lake, marshland, peat bog, meadow, forest...) inhabited by numerous species of birds including a colony of herons. The flora is equally rich with some 400 species.

Maison de la Réserve ⊙ – Located on the way out of Labergement-Ste-Marie towards Mouthe, this new centre offers information about the safeguard of the environment as well as the flora and fauna of the Haut-Doubs region. There are displays of stuffed animals in their natural habitat (reconstituted), aquariums and collections of fossils.

★ **Belvédère des Deux Lacs** – 🖪 *As you reach the end of the Remoray-Boujeons Lake on your way to Mouthe, turn right onto a minor road towards Boujeons. A small parking area situated just beyond the crossroads is the starting point of the path leading to the viewpoint.* There is a beautiful panoramic view of the whole valley and the two lakes.

Val de Mouthe – The area between La Chapelle-des-Bois and Mouthe, which enjoys a microclimate ensuring regular snow coverage throughout the winter, is sought after by cross-country skiers.

Source du Doubs – The road *(signposted – 2km/1.2mi)* which leaves from the war memorial in **Mouthe** leads to the river's source; there is a car park nearby.
The Mouthe Valley, where the Doubs rises, has a mixed landscape of meadows and fir trees. The crystal-clear spring gurgles forth from a cave at the foot of a steep slope in the forest of Noirmont, at an altitude of 937m/3 074ft.

Chaux-Neuve – This ski resort is famous for its ski jumps and is particularly suitable for the practice of Nordic skiing and dog-sledging.

Take D 46 left towards Chapelle-des-Bois.

L'Odyssée Blanche ⊙ – 📷 Here you can see one of the largest packs of huskies in Europe (guided tour, exhibition, film) and you can lead your own team on a 15 to 30km/9 to 22mi off-piste treks across wide snow-covered areas. Possibility of sleeping in tepees.

Continue along D 46 which runs through the Combe des Cives.

Chapelle-des-Bois – This simple mountain village (alt 1 100m/3 609ft) surrounded by meadows at the bottom of a vast coomb at the heart of the Haut-Jura national park, has become a major centre for cross-country skiing. In summer, the surrounding countryside is ideal for long rambles.
📷 Take D 46 along the Combe des Cives to Maison Michaud, now an **écomusée** ⊙ (open-air museum). This sturdy building is one of the oldest farmhouses in the area. It was built in the late 17C and has been completely restored. The immense roof and pretty chimney are covered in the wooden slats known locally as *tavaillons.* The museum gives a good impression of what life in such an isolated dwelling would have been like. Most notably, it would have centred around the chimney, which occupies virtually a room of its own inside, in which the family would have gathered round the fire, cooked their bread, cured their meats and made cheese. *Bread and cakes on sale.*

Eating out

MODERATE

Le Restaurant du Fromage – *Grande-Rue* - ☎ *03 81 69 34 80 - closed 16 Nov-14 Dec - 16.01/18.29€*. Set up in the Hôtel du Lac, this restaurant with its sculpted wooden decor seems to have come straight out of a child's fairy tale. A warm, convivial setting for light meals consisting of cheese platters and other regional specialities. Homemade bread and pastries.

Where to stay

BUDGET

Beau Site (Annexe of the Hôtel du Lac) – ☎ *03 81 69 70 70 - closed 15 Nov-20 Dec except Sat-Sun* - ☑ *- 14 rooms: 26/31€ - ☺ 8€*. This early 19C building fronted by columns offers simple, functional accommodation. The meals, consisting of cheese specialities or traditional cuisine, are served at the Hôtel du Lac.

MODERATE

Hôtel Parnet – *25160 Oye-et-Pallet - 9.5 km/6mi N of Malbuisson by D 437* - ☎ *03 81 89 42 03 - Closed 20 Dec-10 Feb -* ☑ *- 16 rooms: 50/54€ - ☺ 7€*. This house built in the regional style stands in a small village and has a charming park running down to the River Doubs. The bedrooms giving onto the back are quieter. Heated pool and tennis court.

Shopping

Atelier Bernardet – *12 r. Clos-du-château - 25370 Métabief -* ☎ *03 81 49 11 50 – school holidays: open daily 2-7pm; the rest of the year Fri-Sat 2-7pm*. Mr and Madame Bernardet will share with you their passion for beautiful objects and fine craftsmanship by showing you round their workshop, where clocks are made according to the Franche-Comté tradition.

SARL Fonderie de Cloches - Obertino Charles – *15 rte de Mouthe - 25160 Labergement-Ste-Marie -* ☎ *03 81 69 30 72 – exhibition-shop: Mon-Sat 9am-noon, 2-6.30pm; tour of workshop: Jul-Aug Sat 10am-noon; casting of bells: apply for information - closed public holidays*. This foundry set up in 1834 is one of the last of its kind in France. All year round you can watch objects being cast and removed from their mould. The shop offers a wide range of items made on the premises: bronze and steel bells, small spherical bells, chimes, key rings, clocks...

MÉTABIEF-MONT D'OR*

Population 691
Michelin map 321: I-6 – 19km/11mi south of Pontarlier

Just 5km/3mi from the Swiss border, Métabief-Mont d'Or is an international centre of moutain-biking where the World championship wad held in 1993, the European championship in 1994 and where the French national championship takes place every year. Métabief is also a winter sports resort encompassing six villages: Jougne, Les Hôpitaux-Neufs, Les Hôpitaux-Vieux, Métabief, Les Longevilles-Mont d'Or and Rochejean. The quality of local crafts and the many recreational activities available have made Métabief's reputation, summer and winter alike, as an excellent holiday spot.

SIGHTS

Musée de la Meunerie ⊙ – *In Métabief*.
◉ The restored village mill illustrates the miller's ancient craft.

Église Sainte-Catherine – *In the village of Les Hôpitaux-Neufs*. The unassuming church contains a real treasure, one of the finest **Baroque interior*** in the whole region (central altarpiece, side chapels, carved furniture).

Riding high

Y. Vuillaume/DPPI

THE RESORT

Summer activities – The village is popular in the summer for the nearby Saint-Point Lake and for its mountain biking facilities: multi-level permanent tracks for downhill, cross-country and trial practice; access via the Morond cable-car (see below). In addition, there are two 600m/1 968ft toboggan hills, and a climbing wall (70 routes to the top, using 900 possible holds). Karting on grass is another option and guided hikes are organised for those who wish to explore the area.

Ski area

Alpine skiing – Runs for downhill skiing cover some 40km/25mi and include a red run lit for night-time skiing; 40 snowmaking machines make up for the unpredictable weather conditions; 7 chair-lifts and 15 drag-lifts take skiers to the long runs suitable for all levels.
Main access points are: Métabief (X Authier car park), Jougne (Piquemiette-les-Tavins) and Super-Longevilles.
The Métabief drag-lift leads to almost all the runs.

Cross-country skiing – The ski area is especially appreciated by cross-country fans, who can glide over 130km/80mi of tracks, as well as 24km/15mi of cross-Jura trails; double tracks are provided to suit both styles of cross-country skiing.

Other activities – The area also offers **snowshoeing** guided tours along marked trails.

EXCURSIONS

Le Coni'fer ⊙ – 🖼 This tourist trains has brought back to life the old Pontarlier-Vallorbe railway line, disused since 1971. The steam-powered train runs along 7.5km/5mi of track from Les Hôpitaux-Neufs to a natural sight known as *Fontaine ronde*. Various activities are available.

★★ Le Mont d'Or – Alt 1 463m/4 798ft. *About 10km/6mi, then 30min round trip on foot. Leave Métabief on D 45. At Longevilles-Mont d'Or, 200m before D 45 goes over the tunnel covering the railway, turn left at the sign indicating Le Mont d'Or-sommet, which takes you past two chalets, first La Barthelette, then La Grangette-Mont d'Or. At the end of the road, there is a big parking area.*
🗾 From the parking area, climb up to the Belvédère des Chamois, where a wide **panorama** opens up over the Joux Valley, the Swiss lakes and the Alps.

★ Le Morond – Alt 1 419m/4 654ft. *At the church in Métabief, turn left to reach the lower station of the chair-lift; summer: 8min.*

🗾 From Le Morond, there is a spectacular view over the Jura mountains, the Remoray lakes, Lake Geneva and the Alps.

Les Fourgs – This small resort, known as the "roof of the Doubs area" is the highest village in the Doubs *département*, reaching an altitude of 1 246m/4 088ft. The beauty of the surroundings and the quality of the snow cover are particularly sought after by cross-country skiers (60km/37mi of double tracks, including a lit track and two competition tracks). Other possibilities include Alpine skiing (7 drag-lifts) as well as snowshoeing and sledging tours *(apply to the tourist office).*

Plateau des MILLE-ÉTANGS★

Michelin map 314: G-6 to H-6

Bordered by the regions of the Vosges and the Haute-Saône, hemmed in by the Ognon and Breuchin valleys, the Thousand Ponds plateau takes its name from the multitude of small lakes of glacial origin dotted about the area.

The region, isolated and all but forgotten, has the ephemeral charm of places where man lives in total harmony with nature. The woods, paths and cottages have a fairy-tale feel; a place where legends are born and ghosts haunt the wind.

Most of the lakes are privately owned, but some are managed by local authorities: Écromagny, Belonchamp and St-Germain.

Plateau des Mille Étangs

CIRCUIT DES ÉTANGS 28km/16.8mi. About 1hr

This route takes you over part of the Route des Étangs (70km/35mi), departure from Lure. Brochure available from tourist offices.

Lure – An active regional trade centre located on the Paris-Bassel road, Lure had peace and quiet restored in 1976 when the northern by-pass was built. Benedictine monks had even fewer traffic problems when they moved here in the 7C; the 18C vestiges of their building have been incorporated into government offices.

Eating out and where to stay

BUDGET

Auberge Les Noies Parrons – *1 Noies-Parrons - 70270 Mélisey - 2 km/1.2mi NW of Mélisey by D 72 heading for Faucogney - ☎ 03 84 63 23 34 - closed Mon and Tue except public holidays - 14/39€.* A retired butcher from Belfort has settled in this spruce 19C farmhouse standing among trees in a charming lakeside setting. His former profession is easy to guess once you have sampled his succulent specialities: pâté, white pudding, chitterlings sausage, boiled calf's head, knuckle of veal and a special variety of potato, la ratote.

Chambre d'Hôte La Champagne – *70270 Écromagny - 1.5 km/0.9mi E of Écromagny on the road to Melay - ☎ 03 84 20 04 72 - 🖂 - 5 rooms: 28.97/38.11€ - meals 12.19/18.29€.* In a quiet setting in the heart of the forest, this superbly restored farmhouse is a delightful stopping-place for weary travellers. Your German hosts will welcome you with obvious pleasure. The guestrooms are comfortable and the breakfasts generous. The cooking combines French and German traditions. Swimming pool.

Faucogney – This ancient fortified town offered strong resistance to Louis XIV in 1674. As the Franche-Comté was conquered, the château and fortifications were razed. Mont St-Martin rises above the town at the edge of the plateau. The church is one of the oldest in the region.

Leave Faucogney on D 286, towards the chapel and belvedere of St-Martin.

Belvédère de St-Martin – *Follow the signs on a small road which leads upwards to the right.* The road meanders through a magnificent landscape; the dark woods open at times to reveal birch trees bending over lily-covered ponds. *Stop near the chapel.* ◪ A trail goes around it and leads to the belvedere; beneath it the valley spreads open all around.

Go back to D 286 towards La Mer. Notice the many ponds off to the left. At La Mer, take D 266 right towards Melay (or Ternuay). You can take D 315 towards Servance to see the Saut de l'Ognon falls. From Melay, continue on D 239 towards Mélisey.

Stone calvaries line the roadway; the Ice Age left its mark, too, in the form of a lone boulder.

Mélisey – Situated on the north bank of the River Ognon, the village is overlooked by the church with its 12C east end.

Turn right twice to head towards Écromagny on D 73.

Écromagny – This little village is centred around a red-sandstone church, its belfry typical of the region. The Pelvin Pond, one of many surrounding the hamlet, has been improved for recreational visitors.

Turn left towards La Lanterne (D 137), then right on D 72 to return to Faucogney.

Château de MONCLEY★

Michelin map 321: F-3
14km/9mi north-west of Besançon

The concave façade of this rare example of neo-Classical architecture in the Franche-Comté region immediately draws the visitor's attention. However, more pleasant surprises are in store for the château boasts an imposing rotunda and a wealth of interior decoration.

Château de Moncley

Tour ⓥ

The château was built in the 18C by Bertrand, on the site of an ancient feudal fortress, in a pleasant spot overlooking the Ognon Valley. The C-shaped façade is decorated with a group of four Ionic columns supporting a triangular pediment at its centre. The side facing the garden is embellished with a rotunda topped with a dome. Inside, the vestibule is interesting. A dozen Corinthian columns elegantly support a balustraded tribune, which is reached by taking the majestic double staircase. The first floor houses a number of admirable family portraits and Louis XVI furniture, as well as hunting trophies and various stuffed animals.

Eating out and where to stay

MODERATE

La Vieille Auberge – *Pl. de l'Église - 25870 Cussey-sur-l'Ognon - 7 km/4.3mi NE of Moncley by D 14 then D 230 -* ☎ *03 81 48 51 70 - closed 19 Aug-9 Sep, 23 Dec-6 Jan, Mon, Fri evenings out of season and Sun evenings - 14€ lunch - 20/38.50€.* This fine residence covered with Virginia creeper has a dining room with wood panelling and cosy, comfortable guestrooms. The hostess will treat you to regional specialities.

BUDGET

Chambre d'Hôte Les Pétunias – *70150 Hugier - 7 km/4.3mi NW of Marnay by D 67 and D 228 -* ☎ *03 84 31 58 30 - closed Sep -* ⊟ *- 3 rooms: 27.44/38.11€.* Your hosts are an Alsatian couple who have a strong sense of hospitality. Sit out on the pretty verandah amid its greenery, have a dip in the swimming pool or enjoy the barbecue in the flower garden. The interior decoration has been carefully designed and the cosy rooms are appointed with family furniture.

MONTARGIS

Population 15 030
Michelin map 318: N-4

Montargis, capital of the Gâtinais, a region known for shooting and fishing, is dominated by its château which is now occupied by a school. The pleasant town stands on the edge of a forest (4 000ha/9 884 acres) at the junction of three canals – the Briare, the Loing and the Orléans – and at the confluence of three rivers. The main river, the Loing, widens out into **Lac des Closiers** (water sports centre).

Montargis has two claims to fame: the invention of **pralines**, grilled almonds with a sugar coating, which were first produced in the 17C by the Duke of Plessis-Praslin's cook; and the medieval legend of a dog that identified its master's murderer and thus was instrumental in the criminal's execution.

TOWN WALK

The old part of Montargis is crisscrossed by waterways – the Briare canal, smaller canals and branches of the rivers – which are spanned by 127 road and foot bridges. The sight of barges and locks filling and emptying attracts anyone out for a stroll. The canal, which was built in 1642 to link the Loing to the Loire skirts the town to the north and east; the water courses which embellish the old part of the town were used in the past to regulate the Loire which was always liable to burst its banks.

It is possible to park the car in place du 18-Juin-1940. Follow rue du Port, boulevard du Rempart then take boulevard Durzy along the east bank of the canal from the bridge which is level with the Girodet Museum.

Musée Girodet ⊘ – The building, Hôtel Durzy, was designed in the 19C as a museum. It is surrounded by a charming garden with a pond, laid out along the banks of the River Loing.

The museum is devoted to the painter, **Anne-Louis Girodet** (1767-1824), a native of Montargis, who was a pupil of David and a leading light of both Neoclassicism and Romanticism. There is also an important collection of work by the Romantic sculptor, Henry de Triqueti (1804-74), who designed the doors of the church of La Madeleine in Paris. On the first floor the first gallery is hung with 15C to 18C French and Italian paintings, a St Jerome by Zurbaran and 16C and 17C Dutch and Flemish paintings.

★ **Collection Girodet** – The square salon and the second gallery are devoted to Girodet; among his 20 paintings are the extraordinary *Flood* on which the painter spent four years of study, various portraits and the replica, painted by Girodet himself, of his most famous work (now in the Louvre): *The Entombment of Atala*, inspired by Chateaubriand's novel.

The last part of the gallery, in which one of Girodet's pupils has painted the local monuments on the ceiling, is hung with works by 19C French artists.

The furniture of the former library was designed by Triqueti in 1861. This room now houses an important collection of small sculptures from the Romantic period by contemporaries of Girodet, Feuchère, Barre, Gechter and Pradier.

Boulevard Durzy – Shaded by plane trees the boulevard is bordered on one side by the Briare canal and on the other by the Durzy garden. At the southern end is an elegant metal humpback footbridge over the canal offering a fine view of two locks.

Eating out

BUDGET

Les Dominicaines – *R. du Devidet -* ☎ *02 38 98 10 22 - closed Sun and 2nd fortnight in Aug – reservations recommended - 10.10/24.10€.* Miniature clay figurines, mirrors and bursts of lavender against a backdrop of bright yellow walls is the Provençal decor that greets you in this restaurant consisting of three dining rooms, set up in the pedestrian area of the town centre. Traditional cuisine with homemade bread.

MODERATE

Mademoiselle Blanche – *5 r. du Loing -* ☎ *02 38 89 00 87 - closed 2 weeks in Mar, 18-25 Aug, Wed evenings and Sun - 18/27.50€.* You will not be disappointed by this restaurant in the town centre, featuring a pleasant dining room with stone walls, furnished with old-fashioned charm. Smoking area in the lounge for a spot of privacy. Succulent cuisine with fresh regional produce.

Where to stay

MODERATE

Chambre d'Hôte du Domaine de Bel-Ébat – *45200 Paucourt - 6.5 km/4mi NE of Montargis by forest road of Paucourt -* ☎ *02 38 98 38 47 - belebat@wanadoo.fr -* ✉ *- 3 rooms: 70/115€ - meals 35€.* A fine manor house nestled in Montargis Forest, flanked by its stables. The owners will share their passion for horses with you, as well as their love of tradition. Here it is the custom to dress for dinner...

Cross the canal by the footbridge and carry straight on.

Boulevard Belles-Manières – The boulevard runs parallel to a narrow canal with footbridges giving access to the houses, built on the foundations of the rampart towers.

From the east end of boulevard Belles-Manières (retrace your steps) turn left on rue du Moulin-à-Tan; leave place de la République on the left and take rue Raymond-Laforge.

Rue Raymond-Laforge – The bridges over the two canals provide views of the old houses and the wash-houses lining their banks and of the decorative barges, acting as large window boxes, which are tied up to the quays.

Return several yards to take rue de l'Ancien-Palais up the spit of land.

At the end of rue de l'Ancien-Palais turn right into an alleyway which is prolonged by a bridge offering a perspective along the second canal.

Turn right again on rue de la Pêcherie.

The half-timbered houses in this district have been restored. From place Jules-Ferry, rue Raymond-Tellier leads to a bridge providing another **canal landscape** which stretches as far as the Briare canal.

Houses along the Briare Canal

J. Guillard/SCOPE

Take the third turning left, continue along rue du Général-Leclerc which skirts the south side of the Église Ste-Madeleine.

Musée du Gâtinais ⊘ – The archaeological museum is housed in a 15C tannery. The ground floor is devoted to the Gallo-Roman sites at Sceaux-en-Gâtinais and Les Closiers where excavations uncovered a necropolis and a cult complex near a theatre. The other section contains articles from Merovingian burial sites at Grand Bezout. The first floor is devoted to prehistoric regional archaeology; it also contains a small Egyptian section (two sarcophagi, a mummy) from the Campana collection.

In addition, there are paintings illustrating life in Montargis during the 19C.

Musée des Tanneurs ⊘ – Across the street from the Musée du Gâtinais, the old tannery neighbourhood *(Îlot des Tanneurs)* has been restored, and this museum explains the craft, tools and techniques involved in this arduous business over the last century. Upstairs, traditional rural clothing is on display; note the women's headdresses, from the simple *fanchon* (checked kerchief) to the fancier *caline* (worn in town) and the elaborate *coiffe brodée* for special celebrations.

EXCURSIONS

Ferrières – *18km/11mi N along D 315 through Montargis Forest.*
The Benedictine abbey of Ferrières, which was deconsecrated during the French Revolution, was an important monastic centre and fount of learning during the Carolingian period. *Park the car on the shady esplanade marked by the beautiful slim cross of St Apollina.*

Ancienne abbaye St-Pierre-St-Paul – The Gothic church has an unusual **transept crossing★** in the form of a rotunda rising from eight tall columns. It was built in the 12C and is thought to have been inspired by an earlier (9C) Carolingian building. The 13C chancel is illuminated through five Renaissance stained-glass windows. In the north transept there is a collection of 14C-17C statues and a curious baroque liturgical object, a gilt palm tree interlaced with vine tendrils used to display the Holy Sacrament.
The open space below the old cloisters gives a view of the south side of the church and the chapel of Notre-Dame-de-Bethléem, which has been rebuilt many times since the 15C and has long been a highly venerated place of pilgrimage.

Lower town – A stray arm of the Cléry gives this part of town a charming appearance. One of the old wash-houses (Lavoir de la Pêcherie) is still in use. The bridge affords a delightful view of the tanning mill's sluice, the old rooftops and the spire of the abbey church.

▶▶ **Égreville** – *25km/16mi N.* 16C **covered market** with an impressive chestnut timber roof and 13C-15C church with a massive belfry-porch.

▶▶ **Châteaurenard** – *17km/11.5mi SE along D 943.* 11C-12C former castle chapel among ruins; **Bee-keeping Museum** ⊘ along D 37.

MONTBARD

Population 6 300
Michelin map 320: G-4

Montbard rises up the slope of a hill that impedes the course of the River Brenne; it has become an important metallurgical centre specialising in steel tubes and pipes. The memory of Buffon outshines that of the counts of Montbard, who built the fortress that was to become a residence of the dukes of Burgundy.

A GREAT SCHOLAR

Georges-Louis Leclerc de Buffon – Born at Montbard in 1707, Buffon was the son of a counsellor of the Burgundian parliament. At a very tender age he showed his passionate interest in science and went on several journeys in France, Italy, Switzerland and England in order to satisfy his desire to study nature. In 1733, when he was only 26, he entered the Académie des Sciences, where he succeeded the botanist, Jussieu.

His nomination to the post of Administrator of the King's Garden (Jardin du Roi) and museum, now the Jardin des Plantes, in 1739 was to be decisive in his career. Hardly had he taken over his new position than he conceived the vast plan of writing the history of nature. From then on he devoted all his energies to this gigantic task. The first three volumes of his *Histoire naturelle (Natural History)* were published in 1749 and the other 33 volumes followed during the next 40 years.

In 1752 Buffon was elected to the Académie Française. However the honours that were showered on him, just reward for his work and his ability, never went to the great scientist's head.

The crowned heads of all Europe and all the leading figures of his times sought his friendship and were honoured to obtain it.

Helped by the naturalist, Daubenton (1716-99), Buffon reorganised the Jardin du Roi, extending it as far as the Seine, adding avenues of lime trees, a maze, and considerably augmenting the collections of the Natural History Museum.

Buffon at Montbard – Buffon did not really care for Paris as the distractions offered him in the capital did not allow him to work as he wished. So he came back to Montbard, his real home. He set up **forges** on his estate to the northeast of Montbard and took charge of running them himself. As Lord of Montbard, he razed the central keep and the annexes of the château, keeping only the outer walls and two of the 10 towers. Inside he laid out terraced gardens and planted trees of different species as well as flowers and vegetables. It was at Montbard, where he led the life he liked most, that Buffon wrote the greater part of his huge work, which eventually ran to 36 volumes. He died in Paris, in the Jardin du Roi, in 1788.

Eating out

BUDGET

Le Marronnier – *21500 Buffon - 6 km/3.7mi N of Montbard by D 905 -* ☎ *03 80 92 33 65 - closed 20 Dec-20 Jan Fri evenings and Sun - 10/21€.* This house enjoys a fine location opposite the Burgundy Canal. Meals are served in a pretty dining room with stone walls and ornamental fireplace. In summer, relax out on the terrace while admiring the fountain. Traditional cooking.

MODERATE

L'Écu – *7 r. A.-Carré -* ☎ *03 80 92 11 66 - snc.coupat@wanadoo.fr - 16/49€.* Family establishment where you can choose between three dining rooms: one vaulted room, one with huge beams and the latest one, with a modern touch. Traditional cuisine. A few renovated rooms.

Where to stay

BUDGET

Chambre d'Hôte M. et Mme Bacchieri – *La Forge, banks of the Bourgogne Canal - 21500 Rougemont - 10 km/6.2mi NW of Montbard by D 905 -* ☎ *03 80 92 35 99 - closed Christmas -* ⊠ *- 3 rooms: 30.48/41.16€.* This small house facing the Burgundy Canal beckons you to a life of leisure. Cosy, tidy and carefully kept rooms, where nothing will interrupt your peaceful nights. There is a small garden near the lock. Cycling trail along the towing path.

SIGHTS

★ **Parc Buffon** ⊙ – In 1735 Buffon bought the Château de Montbard, which dates from before the 10C and was by then in ruins; he demolished all but two towers and the fortified wall of enclosure. The gardens which he laid out, slightly altered over the years, now form the Parc Buffon. The paths and alleys provide a number of pleasant walks.

Tour de l'Aubespin – Buffon used the height of this tower (40m/131ft) to conduct experiments on the wind. The gargoyles and merlons date from a 19C restoration. From the top there is a fine view of the town and its surroundings. The first of the three rooms contains souvenirs of local history.

Tour St-Louis – The mother of St Bernard was born in this tower in 1070. Buffon lowered the tower by one storey and used it as his library.

Cabinet de travail de Buffon (**D**) – It was in this small pavilion with the walls covered with 18C coloured engravings of various bird species that Buffon wrote most of his *Natural History*.

Chapelle de Buffon – Buffon was buried on 20 April 1788 in the vault of this small chapel adjoining the church of St-Urse (St Ursa) which stands outside the old castle precinct.

Musée Buffon ⊙ – Buffon's stables now house a museum devoted to the great naturalist and to his place in the history of Montbard and of 18C science.

Hôtel de Buffon – Buffon built the large and comfortable mansion from which he had direct access to his gardens and his study.

Musée des Beaux-Arts ⊙ – The fine arts museum is housed in the former chapel (1870) of the Buffon Institute. It contains a magnificent wooden triptych *(Adoration of the Shepherds)* by André Ménassier (1599) and 19C and 20C paintings and sculptures. Three of the artists represented here are natives of Montbard: the sculptor Eugène Guillaume and the painters Chantal Queneville and Ernest Boguet. There are also works by Yves Brayer, Maurice Buffet and three sculptures by Pompon.

EXCURSIONS

Grande Forge de Buffon ⊙ – *7km/5mi north-west.*

Grande Forge

🔲 In 1768 when Buffon, the great French naturalist, was 60 years old he built a forge for the commercial exploitation of his discoveries about iron and steel and to continue his experiments with minerals on a large scale.

His industrial complex was built on two levels: on the lower level were the production shops beside a channel containing water diverted from the River Armançon; on the upper level above the flood line were the houses and other facilities. The **workshops** consist of three buildings separated by two water channels which supplied hydraulic energy to the bellows and trip hammers: the blast-furnace was reached from the upper level by a huge internal staircase which divided into two flights serving platforms where the pig iron was drawn off; next came the refinery, the forge itself, where the pig iron was recast and beaten with the trip hammer into iron bars, and the slitting mill where the bars could be reworked into semi-finished products. Further on is the basin where the raw mineral was washed before being smelted.

Château de Nuits ⊙ – *18km/11mi north-west.* The castle was built in 1560 during the Wars of Religion. The attractive Renaissance façade of pediments and pilasters was formerly screened by a fortified wall. The east façade, facing the Armançon (the old border between Burgundy and Champagne), has retained its austere defensive appearance. The vaulted cellars leading to the east terrace contain a kitchen with an indoor well which enabled the castle to hold out against a siege. A large stone stairway leads to the living quarters above, with its high fireplace in pure Renaissance style and 18C wood panelling. Visitors should also see the buildings occupied by the influential Order of St-Mark (**Commanderie de St-Marc**). Overlooking the River Armançon, the architecture is admirable, especially the late-12C chapel.

MONTBÉLIARD★

Conurbation 113 059
Michelin map 321: K-1

The majestic shape of the castle, framed between two round, fat towers, high above Montbéliard testifies to this city's rich past. The flower-decked old town with its colourful architecture denotes a characteristic Lutheran influence.

HISTORICAL NOTES

The fortified hilltop village of Mons Beligardae began to expand in earnest after the destruction of Mandeure in the 8C. It was ruled as an independent county by a succession of different noble families, including the Montfaucons. As the last Montfaucon died without male issue, the county was inherited by one of his granddaughters, Henriette d'Orbe. In 1397 she married Prince Eberhard IV of Württemberg, thus bringing Montbéliard under the rule of the Germanic Empire.

Mömpelgard, a German principality – For the next four centuries the principality of Montbéliard was a small German enclave, known as **Mömpelgard**, within the borders of France and frequently quite a thorn in the flesh of French rulers. The territory covered an old Gallo-Roman *pagus* (administrative unit), encompassing the seigneurial domains of Héricourt, Châtelot, Clémont, Blamont and Etobon. The princes and dukes of Württemberg, who divided their time between the castle here and their palaces at Stuttgart and later Ludwigsburg, drew many German artists and craftsmen to the town. Although French continued to be the language spoken, German influence was soon evident in economic, cultural and religious fields.

Georges Cuvier

The zoologist Jean Léopold Cuvier (known as Georges) was born in Montbéliard on 23 August 1769. His studies at the local École Française and a period at the Karlsschule in Stuttgart, coupled with his keen early interest in the natural sciences, paved the way for his brilliant scientific career. He began teaching anatomy at the age of only 25 at the botanical gardens in Paris, then from 1799 at the Collège de France, then finally in 1802 at the Natural History Museum. He was elected a member of the Académie Française in 1818 and received the title of baron from Louis XVIII, having established himself as the founder of comparative anatomy and paleontology.

The enclave of Mömpelgard became increasingly problematic for its French neighbours as the ideas of the Reformation began to spread after 1524. The principality officially declared itself Protestant in the mid 16C, and by the end of the century many Huguenots had sought refuge here. Various attempts by the French to seize control, however, met with failure.

The city flourishes – Under the rule of **Friedrich I of Württemberg** (1581-1608), the town blossomed into an elegant city worthy of its princely residents, imbued with the syle of the Renaissance. Much of its transformation was effected by the architect Heinrich Schickhardt *(see below)*. The influx of Huguenot refugees meant that the town had to be extended beyond the medieval fortifications, resulting in the construction of the Neuve Ville.

During the French Revolution, Montbéliard was besieged and finally succumbed to the young French Republic on 10 October 1793.

Heinrich Schickhardt (1558-1634) – During the reign of Friedrich I of Württemberg, the Swabian architect Heinrich Schickhardt played a major role in the construction of modern Montbéliard. Besides being a talented architect and town planner, he was an engineer, a technician, topographer and writer. The carpenter's son, born in Herrenberg in Swabia, learned his trade in the workshops of the architects to the court of the dukes of Württemberg, before being summoned into service of Friedrich I. The Duke took him under his wing and accompanied him on a trip to Italy where the two men were able to perfect their knowledge of the Italian Renaissance. At the age of 42, Schickhardt was put in charge of architecture throughout Württemberg and was finally able to unleash his full creative potential. He introduced the Renaissance style to Montbéliard, as well as endowing cities such as Freudenstadt and Stuttgart with his work. He was promoted architect to the ducal court on the death of Friedrich, but his life ended abruptly and tragically when he was assassinated in December 1635. *There is a 2.8km/2mi signposted tour of what remains of his work in Montbéliard (leaflet available from the tourist office).*

★OLD TOWN

Walk up the steep rue du Château leading to the castle.

Château ⊙ – The **Logis des Gentilhommes** stands on the Esplanade du Château. This town house was built by Schickhardt and has an elegant scrolled gable of Swabian influence.

Château de Montbéliard

All that remains of the castle built in the 15C and 16C are two massive round towers surmounted by lantern turrets, the Tour Henriette (1422-24) and the Tour Frédéric (1575-95). The rest of the castle was demolished in the mid 18C to make way for Classical-style buildings. A beautiful contemporary wrought-iron gate by Jean Messagier closes off the doorway leading to the Tour Henriette.

Museum – *The castle museum is under restoration, following a fire which damaged the towers in 1999.*
Currently, the former vaulted kitchens house a **historical exhibition;** ▣ the **Cuvier natural history gallery** and the archaeology department contain interesting collections (in particular stuffed animals) and extensive contemporary exhibitions are held on the ground floor.

Walk down rue du Château and turn left onto rue A.-Thomas, then left again onto rue Cuvier to rue de l'Hôtel-de-Ville leading to place St-Martin.

Office de Tourisme Montbéliard

Eating out

MODERATE

Le St-Martin – *1 r. du Gén.-Leclerc - ☎ 03 81 91 18 37 - closed 23 Feb-3 Mar, 5-25 Aug, Sat Sun and public holidays - 29/49€.* This time-honoured house with stone walls has a cosy dining room reminiscent of a brasserie. The meals are traditional, made with good fresh produce.

Sur les Rives du Doubs – *25190 Villars-sous-Dampjoux - 2 km/1.2mi W of Noirefontaine by D 36 then D 312 - ☎ 03 81 96 93 82 - closed 2-22 Jan, Mon evenings, Tue evenings and Wed - 31/37€.* This rustic-style inn set up along the banks of the Doubs is the perfect address for a country lunch. The regional specialities are served in one of the two dining rooms or, weather permitting, out on the terrace.

Where to stay

BUDGET

Hôtel Bristol – *2 r. Velotte - ☎ 03 81 94 43 17 - hotel.bristol@wanadoo.fr - closed 26 Dec-3 Jan - 🅿 - 43 rooms: 33/69.50€ - ☕ 6€.* This 1930s hotel is located near the château and the lively pedestrian district. Most of the guestrooms give onto the back and are relatively quiet.

Hôtel Vieille Grange – *25310 Blamont - 18 km/11.2mi S of Montbéliard by D 35 - ☎ 03 81 35 19 00 - closed 4-11 Aug and 22-30 Dec - 10 rooms: 41€ - ☕ 5.32€ - restaurant 20/27€.* As you leave the village, you will come to this 18C farmhouse which has retained all its country charm. The sober bedrooms have been set up in a modern building. Take your meals in the rustic-style dining room with its two fireplaces. Regional cooking.

MODERATE

Hôtel de la Balance – *40 r. de Belfort - ☎ 03 81 96 77 41 - hotelbalance @wanadoo.fr - closed 23-28 Dec - 🅿 - 44 rooms: 58/80€ - ☕ 7.50€ - restaurant 18/25€.* This former residence lying at the foot of the château has been converted into a charming hotel with a pretty pastel façade. The bedrooms are at the top of a splendid staircase carved in wood. The dining room, with its parquet flooring and wood panelling, is warm and inviting.

Sit back and relax

Café de la Paix – *12 r. des Febvres - ☎ 03 81 91 03 62 - open daily 7.30am-11pm.* This small, unpretentious café is the only one in town to offer organised activities on Saturday evenings: philosophical discussions from October to April, jazz concerts from May to September.

Gourmandise – *10 r. Clemenceau - ☎ 03 81 91 09 55 - Tue-Sat 9am-noon, 2-7pm - Closed public holidays.* This confectionery is paradise on earth for those who have a sweet tooth. Among the numerous specialities, try the *montbéliardes* (chocolate-coated almonds), the *cailloux du Doubs* (almond, nougatine and chocolate) and the *clarines* (chocolates with a praline filling).

Le Central – *11 pl. Denfert-Rochereau - ☎ 03 81 91 00 14 - Mon-Sat 7.30am-midnight.* Thanks to its large terrace and attractive decor, the Central is one of the most popular cafés in town, a few steps away from the lively town centre.

Le Pub – *R. des Halles - ☎ 03 81 94 95 98 - Mon-Thu 5pm-1am, Fri-Sat 5pm-2am - Closed 2 weeks in Aug.* This café with an unusual decor extends a warm and friendly welcome that will immediately make you feel at home. The thick wall at the back is believed to be part of the original ramparts.

Place Saint-Martin – This square at the heart of old Montbéliard hosts most of the town's major events, such as the **Lumières de Noël**, a Christmas market in true German tradition (with bretzels, mulled wine and Christmas trees – *see Calendar of events*). Many of the city's most important monuments are to be found on this square.

Musée d'Art et d'Histoire ⓞ – Erected in 1773 by the architect Philippe de la Guépière, the Hôtel Beurnier-Rossel is a typical 18C town mansion.
Beurnier-Rossel's private rooms are especially characteristic. Family portraits and period furnishings give them warmth: note the wood inlays by local craftsman Couleru, the ceramic stove created by Jacob Frey, and the encyclopaedic library, a must in the Age of Enlightenment.
The two upper floors are devoted to the history of the town and the region. The collections are varied: popular illustrations by the Deckherr brothers, religious items from Lutheran churches, a fine collection of traditional headdresses *(bonnets à diari)*. You can also admire a room full of music boxes, bearing the Épée trademark.

Temple St-Martin – *During guided tours of the town, information at the Tourist office*. This is the oldest Protestant church in France (built between 1601 and 1607 by Schickhardt). The architecture of the façade draws its inspiration from the Tuscan Renaissance. The inside would be quite plain, were it not for the original polychrome decoration, rediscovered recently, on the mid-18C **organ** and gallery.

Maison Forstner – This town house (probably from the late 16C) now houses a branch of the Banque de France. The building is named after its former occupant, the Chancellor of Friedrich I of Württemberg. The stately Renaissance façade features four storeys of superposed columns.

Christmas lights

M. Paygnard/MICHELIN

Hôtel de ville – The elegant pink-sandstone town hall was built from 1776 to 1778. There is a commemorative statue of Cuvier by David d'Angers in front of the building.

Hôtel Sponeck – Located near the town hall, this 18C mansion is now the home of the Scène nationale de Montbéliard.

Walk round the mansion along rue du Général-Leclerc, turn left onto rue Georges-Clemenceau and follow the street which turns to the left and joins rue des Febvres. Turn right to reach the covered market.

Halles – The 16C-17C **covered market** has a distinctive roof and long façades with large windows with double mullions. The enormous building was the meeting hall for the town council prior to 1793; it was then used as a store for the town's grain *(éminage)*, as a market and as a customs post.

In Place Denfert-Rochereau, a 15C flagstone can be seen, which is known in Montbéliard as the **pierre à poissons**. The stone was used by fishmongers on market day. In 1524, Swiss reformer Guillaume Farel is said to have used it as a pulpit, to preach the Reformation to the people of Montbéliard.

Walk to place F.-Ferrer and continue along faubourg de Besançon to the Temple St-Georges.

You are now in the suburb, known as the "Neuve ville". Friedrich I commissioned Schickhardt to build this suburb in 1598, to accommodate the waves of Huguenot refugees fleeing France.

Temple Saint-Georges – The church was built between 1674 and 1676 when the Temple Saint-Martin could no longer accommodate all those wishing to attend services; it is now a conference centre.

Église St-Maimbœuf – The lofty mid-19C church with its exaggerated ornamentation offers a striking contrast to the nearby church and is a physical reminder of the Roman Catholic church's reconquest of this bastion of Lutheranism after Montbéliard was reclaimed by France. The interior of St-Maimbœuf is pretty lavishly decorated; monumental tribune with Corinthian columns, extravagant wooden stucco ornamentation, German Baroque style altarpieces and so on.

Instead of returning to the town centre, it is possible to make a pause in the Près-la-Rose gardens.

To reach the gardens, return to place Ferrer, follow rue Ch.-Lalance, walk across the Pont A.-Bermont and follow the Allan to a flight of steps leading down to the park.

Près-la-Rose – This 10ha/25 acre industrial zone near the old town centre has been redeveloped into a science and technology park. A number of large sculptures have been erected on the site, for example *Vaisseau* (Ship) and the eye-catching *Fontaine Galilée* (Galileo Fountain).

Pavillon des Sciences ⊘ – ⊙ This centre offers the young and not so young a good introduction to scientific and technical culture by means of various activities and demonstrations.

A footbridge spans the Allan and leads to rue des Blancheries. Turn left onto avenue du Président-Wilson then right onto rue de la Chapelle.

A short detour via rue de Belfort will enable you to appreciate the tasteful restoration undertaken by the municipality.

MONTBÉLIARD

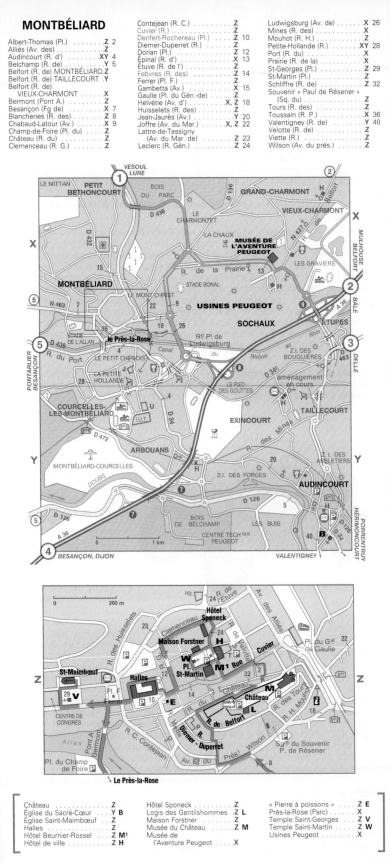

SOCHAUX

This industrial suburb to the east of Montbéliard grew up around the Peugeot factories, after the company had established its largest car manufacturing plant on the Sochaux-Montbéliard plain in 1908. Since the 1930s, it has been the home of a famous football club created by Pierre Peugeot.

The industrial development of the Montbéliard area – By the end of the 18C, Montbéliard had established itself as the economic hub of the Franche-Comté region.

Various factors combined to make the Montbéliard region an obvious location for industrial enterprises; good communication links, new opportunities offered by the region's annexation to France, dynamic neighbours in Switzerland, Baden and Alsace and the receptive attitude of Lutheran management towards Anglo-Saxon economic ideas.

It was not long before major firms such as Peugeot and Japy were attracted to the region.

The first Peugeot car – In the 18C, Jean-Pierre Peugeot was a weaver in Hérimoncourt. When his two oldest sons, Jean-Pierre and Jean-Frédéric, founded a steelworks in the mill at Sous-Cratet in 1810, no one dreamed that this small enterprise would be a huge international industrial concern by the 20C. Soon more factories were founded at Terre-Blanche, in the Gland Valley, Valentigney and Pont-de-Roide, producing laminated steel, saw blades, tools, domestic appliances etc while a factory in the old mill at Beaulieu turned out various types of velocipede and later bicycles. Finally, in 1891, Peugeot produced its first automobile with a combustion engine, called the Vis-à-Vis (face-to-face) because its passengers had to sit facing one another. Since then, the company has manufactured over 600 car models. In the 1970s, Peugeot merged with another French automotive leader, Citroën.

★ **Musée de l'Aventure Peugeot** ⊘ – The Peugeot museum, which opened in 1988 in the premises of an old brewery, houses an extensive collection of automobiles, cycles, tools and other objects (sewing machines, coffee grinders) illustrating the Peugeot firm's output from the early days to the present and introduced by...Colombo himself, whose affection for his old 403 convertible made him the obvious choice.

Phaeton Lion Type V4C3

Musée Peugeot

About 75 models are on show, illustrating the evolution of the car with the lion insignia. Among the *vis-à-vis* quadricycles and traps characteristic from about 1904 on, notice the elegantly decorated model made for the Bey of Tunis (1892). The 1906 Double Phaeton 81B, with four seats facing the way the car was going and inflatable tyres, shows how rapidly cars were evolving. The Bébé, a small car designed in 1911 by Ettore Bugatti, was a huge success. The Phaeton Lion Type V4C3, with a folding back seat, dates from 1913. Beginning with the Peugeot 201 in 1929, all Peugeot models were identified by a three digit number with zero in the middle. The 201 was Peugeot's main defence against the international economic slump; the 1932 comfort model was the first mass-produced car with independent front wheel suspension. Peugeot developed a name for being at the forefront of design; the streamlined bodywork of the Peugeot 402 which appeared at the end of 1935 embodied the latest developments in the field of aerodynamics. A prototype of the 402, the 6 models of which were built by J Andreau, launched in 1936 cut petrol consumption by 35%. The Peugeot 402 Limousine equipped with a gas generator and a coal box (consumption: 15kg/33lb per hour!) bears witness to the extreme shortage of fuel in 1941.

After the war, Peugeot brought out another new model, the Peugeot 203, with an integral all-steel welded body. More recent models and racing cars include: the Darl'mat 302 Roadster, winner of the Le Mans 24 Hour Grand Prix in 1938; the Peugeot 205 Turbo 16, World Rallying Champion in 1989; and the Peugeot 205 Turbo 16 Grand Raid, which came first in the 1990 Paris-Dakar.

Visitors can try their hand at driving a 206 racing model *(paying simulators)*.

Tour of the Peugeot factories ⊘ – Sochaux is the largest Peugeot automobile production centre, above the factories at Mulhouse, Poissy and Valenciennes. The factory is still expanding. Recently, the company gained 12ha/30 acres of land when the River Allan was diverted. The Peugeot 307, 406 and 607 are the main models manufactured at Sochaux.

EXCURSIONS

Église du Sacré-Cœur in Audincourt – *South-east suburb of Montbéliard.* The church, consecrated in 1951, testifies to the aspirations of contemporary artists immediately after the end of the Second World War. A colourful mosaic by Bazaine greets visitors as they enter; inside, the nave is covered with plain oak vaulting and lit by stained-glass windows by Fernand Léger; the interesting **baptistery★**, flooded with yellow and violet light pouring in through the stained-glass windows by Bazaine, contains a font carved out of a block of Volvic stone.

Beaucourt – *7.5km/4.5mi E of Audincourt along D 126.* Since the Franco-Prussian War, Beaucourt has become the third-ranking city of the Territoire de Belfort *département*, having previously been part of the Montbéliard principality, then of the Haut-Rhin *département*. The founding of a Japy clockmaking factory here largely contributed to the town's prosperity in the 19C.

Japy

Jacques Japy was a farmer and a black-smith, who also knew something about locksmithing and the repair of various tools. His son Frédéric Japy founded a clock and watch-making workshop in the area in 1777, a business which was to be at the forefront of the region's industrial development for 180 years. Factories were opened in Feschotte, Isle-sur-le-Doubs, Voujeaucourt, Anzin near Lille and Arcueil in the Paris suburbs. Their activities have diversified over the years; the manufacture of clock parts led to the production of hardware items and electro-mechanical devices, dancing dolls and mirrors for hunting larks. In 1910 Japy was manu-facturing typewriters under a foreign  licence, and by 1955 the firm began production in its own right, taking the name Société Belfortaine de Mécanographie in 1967. SBM is still located in Beaucourt, but no longer manufactures typewriters since production was transferred to Switzerland in 1973.

G. Magnin/MICHELIN

Musée Frédéric-Japy ⊘ – The original clockmaking workshop has been turned into a museum. The industrial genius invented the first machines for manufacturing clocks, at a time when clocks were being made entirely by hand. The display includes examples of the first watches manufactured in Beaucourt, as well as all sorts of clocks: alarm clocks, travelling clocks, mantelpiece clocks etc. The diver-sity of the Japy company's production is illustrated by the many types of screws and bolts, chandeliers, enamel items, typewriters, motors and pumps on display. Explanatory panels describe the evolution of the Japy enterprise.

Pont-de-Roide – *18km/11mi S via D 438 and D 437.* Pont-de-Roide, in a pretty spot on the banks of the Doubs, owes its living in part to the Ugine technical steel factories. There is a 15C bronze holy water stoup in the church, and some beau-tiful stained-glass windows by the firm of J Benoît company in Nancy. In the neighbouring chapel of Notre-Dame-de-Chatey is a 14C Pietà. The woods of Chatey nearby are ideal for pleasant walks.

Mandeure – *9.5km/6mi N of Pont-de-Roide; drive 6km/3.7mi along D 437 then turn right to Mandeure.* This ancient Roman Epomanduodorum still has the ves-tiges of its 2C theatre, a testimony to the past importance of this community, located on the trade route between the Rhine and the Mediterranean.

▶▶ **Mont-Bart Fort** ⊘ – *SW of the city (on N 463).* Altitude 487m/1 598ft. Defensive work built between 1873 and 1877; note in particular the case-mate with its cast-iron armour plating weighing 100t. Fine view of Montbéliard.

MONTBENOÎT★

Population 219
Michelin map 321: I-5

This village is the tiny capital of the Saugeais Valley. It stands on a hillside overlooked by rocky cliffs on the banks of the Doubs, which follows a peaceful pretty course at this point. The old abbey of Montbenoît is among the Jura's most beautiful architectural monuments and draws many visitors.

The rise and fall of the abbey – Montbenoît Abbey was founded by the hermit Benedict (Br *Benoît*) who came to live here, drawing crowds of followers with him. In 1150, the lord of Joux, the region's landlord, was seeking ways of winning divine grace, to compensate for his immoral lifestyle (the Joux were little more than highwaymen). He offered Humbert, Archbishop of Besançon, the sunlit valley, between Arçon and Colombière for the first inhabitants of Montbenoît.
Montbenoît remained under the feudal suzerainty of the lords of Joux. To make his authority clear, every time a new abbot was elected, the landlord would present himself at the monastery gates, surrounded by his vassals and men-at-arms. The abbot, holding a cross and wearing his mitre, would come out and greet him and hand him the keys of the abbey on a silver plate. The landlord would then be in charge of the community for the rest of the day.
The abbey declined in the same way as the abbey of St-Claude. It was held *in commendam* from 1508 onwards; the abbots drew on the abbey's profits without having to either oversee the general administration of the abbey or even take part in the religious life of the abbey. The two most famous abbots were the Cardinal of Granvelle and Ferry Carondelet. Carondelet joined the order after being widowed, and became counsellor to Emperor Charles V. He was a luxury-loving patron who had the church chancel rebuilt and filled it with the most beautiful works of art. He also made generous donations to the cathedral of St-Jean in Besançon, where he was canon and where he is buried. During the Revolution, the abbey of Montbenoît was declared the property of the French state and its lands were sold.

Birth of a republic – In the 12C, Humbert summoned Augustine monks from the Valais region in Switzerland to build a church and buildings, some of which are still standing. They called on some Swiss compatriots, known as Saugets, to help clear and cultivate the land. This name has been given to the valley (the spelling has altered over the years) and to the local residents. Modern Saugets and Saugettes are perceived as having retained the strong individuality of their Swiss forebears. The 12 villages surrounding Montbenoît have their own particular dialect, customs and style of houses. Brass bands and choruses still ring out the Sauget hymn at local festivals. These people are characterised by their lively sense of humour, often caustic.
In 1947 the *préfet* (chief administrative officer of a *département*), who was visiting the Saugeais Valley, was jokingly asked by an innkeeper for his passport to enter the "Saugeais Republic". Amused, he there and then named his host "President of the new republic". When the innkeeper died in 1968, his wife was elected to succeed him!

★OLD ABBEY ⏱ *45min*

Ancienne église abbatiale – The nave of the abbey church dates from the 12C and the chancel from the 16C. The bell-tower was rebuilt in 1903.

Nave – Against the first pillar on the south side is a monument (1522) to a local girl, Parnette Mesnier, who met her death while attempting to resist the unwelcome advances of a young man. Pretty Parnette fled him by clambering up the scaffolding above the chancel, which was under construction at the time. The young man was about to catch up with her at the top, whereupon Parnette threw herself to the ground below. Kind-hearted Ferry Carondelet donated the monument in memory of the young girl's defence of her virtue.
In the Chapelle Ferrée north of the chancel there is a 16C statue of St Jerome and a stone Pièta on the altar.
The beautiful sculpted doors at the entrance to the Chapelle des Trois-Rois south of the chancel were part of the original 16C rood screen.

Chancel – Abbot Ferry Carondelet had travelled all over Italy as ambassador to the court of Rome for the government of the Netherlands and Flanders and sought to recreate at Montbenoît some of the magnificence and refinement of the Italian Renaissance. He personally chose the craftsmen who took just two years to create this harmonious group of sculpture and stained glass, one of the great successes of the early Renaissance in the Franche-Comté. The brilliant colours of the ornamental foliage and arabesques are still visible on the pendentive vaulting, which is decorated with a delicate network of ribs.
The decoration on the magnificent **stalls★★**, dating from 1525 to 1527, is clearly the result of both a lively wit and great artistic talent; unfortunately, very few motifs have survived intact. Note the delicacy and variety of the ornamentation on the upper part between the pinnacles.
One or two cleverly sculpted scenes contribute to the richness of the whole (such as *Women fighting*, symbolising the triumph of Truth over Error) and illustrate ideas taken from the Middle Ages (*Lay of Aristotle*, representing Science being punished by Truth).

There is a beautiful marble **abbatial recess★★** to the right of the altar; a 1526 piscina, also in marble, is next to it.

Above the sacristy door is a low relief commissioned by Ferry Carondelet in memory of the Joux landlords. The sculpted man's head sticking out of the socle is probably a representation of Ferry Carondelet.

Cloisters – The architectural indecisiveness typical of the Franche-Comté is in evidence in the 15C cloisters.

Round arches are still used, whereas the corner doors are surmounted by Flamboyant Gothic ogee arches and sculpted tympanums. The twin colonettes have archaic style capitals, decorated with foliage, fish and animals.

Cloisters

Chapter-house – This chapter-house, which opens onto the cloisters, has diagonal groined arches springing from the door.

Note the 16C painted and gilt wood statuettes, of the Virgin holding Jesus as well as of the Three Kings.

Kitchen – Note a Louis XIV clock with one hand, a beautiful Louis XIII armoire and an enormous mantelpiece.

EXCURSION

Morteau via the Défilé d'Entreroche – *17km/11mi north-east along D 437.*
Downstream of Montbenoît, the charming Saugeais Valley becomes a twisting gorge extending almost all the way to Morteau.

Défilé d'Entreroche – The road cuts between breathtaking craggy limestone cliffs, in which there are two caves:
– The **Grotte du Trésor**, with an incredibly high entrance arch. The cave is located 5min from D 437 on the rock face a little above road level. The beginning of the wooded path leading there is signposted where it branches off from the main road.
– The cave of **Notre-Dame de Remonot**, which has been converted into a chapel and place of pilgrimage, in which the water is said to heal eye afflictions. The opening is at road level; a grille protects the entrance.

The Doubs, the railway and the road twist along beside each other between Remonot and Morteau, squeezing between steep wooded slopes. It is easy to see how the river has gouged its course out of the rocks in many places.

The valley opens up again at the end of the gorge, to form the Morteau basin.

Morteau – This village on the north-west bank of the Doubs grew up around a Benedictine priory during the 12C. There was serious fire in 1865, after which the village was completely rebuilt. Local people earn their living as clockmakers or farmers. A famous gastronomic speciality of the town is the **smoked sausage** which shares its name, and goes down very well with potato salad.

MONTS JURA *

Michelin map 328: I-3

The villages of Mijoux and Lélex, situated in the upper Valserine Valley in southern Jura, joined forces to form, with the Col de la Faucille, the region's most southern winter sports resort, named Monts Jura in 1999. The ski area climbs to 1 680m/5 512ft, affording spectacular views and impressive differences in height.

Where to stay

MODERATE

La Petite Chaumière – *At the pass - 01170 Col de la Faucille - ☎04 50 41 30 22 - info@petitechaumiere.com - closed 2-28 Apr and 14 Oct-20 Dec - P - 34 rooms: 47/57.50€ - ⌑ 8€ - restaurant 17/27€*. A quiet, peaceful stay is guaranteed at this Jura chalet nestled at the foot of the slopes. The rustic-style bedrooms with wainscoting and white walls are simply charming. The dining room is extended by a large terrace that you can enjoy in all seasons.

Chambre d'Hôte Le Boulu – *01410 Mijoux - 4 km/2.5mi SW of Mijoux by D 991 to Lélex - ☎04 50 41 31 47 - open Christmas to Easter and Jul-Sep - ✉ - 5 rooms: 50€ - meals 17.50€*. Stately 18C family farmhouse with sober guestrooms giving onto the garden, where ducks and geese roam freely, or the forest, cut across by the peaceful Valserine River. The owner will extend a warm, inviting welcome and treat you to delicious meals. For non-smokers.

Hôtel La Mainaz – *Rte de Gex - 01170 Col de la Faucille - ☎04 50 41 31 10 - mainaz@club-internet.fr - closed 26 Oct-12 Dec, Sun evenings and Mon except school holidays - P - 22 rooms: 54/95€ - ⌑ 11€ - restaurant 22/46€*. In fine weather this huge wooden chalet overlooking Col de la Faucille commands breathtaking vistas of the Alpine range, Mont Blanc and Lake Geneva. The cosy rooms are adorned with pretty wainscoting. The dining room boasts a lovely wooden ceiling and a fireplace made in red brick.

Lélex – The mountainous features of the upper Valserine Valley are prominent here; the walls of houses are clad with laths on the side exposed to bad weather.

Ascent of Crêt de la Neige ○ – Alt 1 717m/5 633ft.
⬛ In Lélex, take the Catheline gondola *(10min one way)*. On arrival, start walking to the right towards Crêt de la Neige along a safe but slippery path *(allow 3hr there and back; mountain shoes recommended)*.
Beyond le Grand Crêt, to the east, there are views of the Jura mountains, Lake Geneva, and Geneva. The summit reveals a panoramic view of the Alps.
Between Lélex and Mijoux extends the restful Valmijoux countryside with the River Valserine peacefully flowing through green pastures.

Mijoux – This picturesque village is decorated with murals illustrating ancient regional crafts. It is linked to the Col de la Faucille and Mont-Rond by skilifts ○, operating in summer as well as in winter.

In Mijoux, turn right onto D 936 which rises above the Valmijoux, offering views of the Forêt du Massacre, and leads to the Col de la Faucille.

The Vattay ski area is popular with beginners and champions

B. Kaufmann/MICHELIN

★★**Col de la Faucille** – At an altitude of 1 323m/4 341ft, the pass cuts a passage through the great mountainous Jura spine separating the Rhône Valley and Lake Geneva to the east from the Valserine Valley to the west. The pass is well known as one of the main passages through the Jura mountains. It is crossed by N 5, one of the most important roads linking France and Switzerland. The descent to Gex offers unforgettable **views★**.

Ski area

Alpine skiing – The two Alpine ski areas comprise 35 runs (50km/30mi) for all levels of proficiency and a difference in height of 800m/2 625ft; 28 skilifts, including 3 gondolas, are at the disposal of skiers.

Lélex-Crozet (900m to 1 700m/2 953ft to 5 577ft) – The village has a "kindergarden" where youngsters can safely enjoy the pleasures of sliding on the snow. The Lélex gondola leads to Catheline thus giving access to various runs and to the resort's highest point, Monthoisey (1 680m/5 315ft).

Mijoux-La Faucille (1 000m to 1 550m/3 281ft to 5 085ft) – A new chair-lift, inaugurated in 1998, links Mijoux and the Col de la Faucille. From there, a gondola and a chair-lift lead to the summit of Mont-Rond (1 534m/5 033ft), which is not recommended to beginners since most of the runs are red. Very long runs (blue and green) down to Mijoux.

Cross-country skiing – The Vattay and Valserine cross-country ski areas rank among the best in the Jura mountains.

La Vattay (1 300m to 1 500m/4 264ft to 4 920ft) – The area's international renown is fully justified by its extensive facilities (restaurant, bar, equipment hire service, Nordic-skiing school...) and by the quality of its 80km/50mi of pisted down double tracks and competition tracks.

La Valserine (900m to 1 080m/2 953ft to 3 543ft) – Less popular, less challenging but pleasant even so, this area reveals the charm of this yet unspoilt valley. The 60km/37mi of tracks are also pisted down for both styles of cross-country skiing.

Summer activities – The verdant countryside lends itself to rambling while easy access to the summits offers great possibilities for mountain-biking and summer sledging.

EXCURSIONS

★★**Mont-Rond** – 🔃 *500m/547yd from the pass where the access road to the Mont-Rond gondola branches off N 5.*

The Petit and the Grand Mont-Rond peaks constitute one of the Jura's most famous viewpoints. The view from the **Petit Mont-Rond** is the more interesting.

Petit Mont-Rond viewpoint – *The usual way of reaching Petit Mont-Rond is from the Col de la Faucille. Follow the wide road which leads southwards from the pass.*

After about 500m, leave the car in the car park and take the **gondola** Ⓥ (télécabine).

Another possibility is to take the chair-lift (télésiège) from Mijoux up to the lower gondola station at the Col de la Faucille and then, as above, continue to the summit in the gondola.

There is a French radio and television relay near the cable-car station at the top.

Panorama – The sweeping view from the viewing table is breathtaking. Beyond the rift valley in which Lake Geneva lies tower the Alps, extending over an area 250km/155mi wide and 150km/93mi deep, as well as the Jura and Dôle (in Switzerland) chains.

In spring the summit is covered with a glorious carpet of blue gentians, yellow anemones and white crocuses; in summer and autumn alpine asters and mountain thistles lend the peak more subtle tones.

★★★ **Colomby de Gex** – ⬛ *Accessible from the Col de la Faucille; 500m to car park, then about 4hr on foot to the peak. To cut down the length of the walk, take the gondola up to the Petit-Mont-Rond, then follow the GR 9 footpath (signposted) along the ridge.* At 1 689m/5 545ft, the Colomby de Gex is one of the highest points in the Jura range. It offers almost the same view as that from the Petit-Mont-Rond.

Extensive **view**★ of the valley of Lake Geneva, and beyond it a view of the Alps stretching 250km/155mi.

From La Cure to Gex

27km/17mi – allow 30min

N 5 from La Cure leaves the forest of Massacre to the right, beyond the Valmijoux dip where the Valserine flows. The Dôle (1 677m/5 502ft) towers to the left in Swiss territory.

Col de la Faucille – Near the pass, the road runs along for a while between two walls of fir trees. Suddenly Mont Blanc, the giant of the Alps, looms into view directly ahead. At the end of an afternoon of fine weather, the sudden appearance of this immense mound of sparkling snow blushing pink in the rays of the setting sun takes your breath away. There is a beautiful **view**★ down into the Valserine Valley from the end of the pass road from a height of over 300m/984ft.

★★ **Descent to Gex** – Having crossed the La Faucille pass, the road leads through pine forest. It opens up after the La Mainaz hotel, making a great hairpin meander round the green fields and houses of Le Pailly. Leave the car on the roadside where it widens to enjoy the splendid **panorama**★★. Lake Geneva appears in a sort of mist, sometimes even disappearing entirely under a sea of clouds, whereas the peaks of the Alps stand out quite sharply.

The Fontaine Napoléon comes into sight further down, on the side of the road as it makes a tight hairpin bend around a house. The fountain dates from the construction of this road (1805) and recalls its originator. The countryside around Gex appears shortly afterwards, spread out at the bottom of the slopes, a less typically Jura scene with its landscape of cultivated fields laid out like a chessboard.

MOREZ

Population 6 144

Michelin map 321: G-7 – Local map see ST-CLAUDE: Excursion

At the bottom of a gorge in an unusual site, Morez was, until 1860, a centre of the clock and watch industry, and has for two centuries been a leading producer of eyeglasses. The village stretches for about 2km/1mi along the bottom of the Bienne Valley, and the river provided its principal source of energy for centuries. The road up to the nearby passes, Col de la Faucille or Col de St-Cergue, goes through Morez and offers a bird's-eye view of the town. Engineers have designed the route for the railway and the hairpin roads which pass through the town with artistry.

The town of spectacles – Spectacles have been worn to correct poor vision since the 13C. However, the first workshop for their manufacture did not appear on the outskirts of Morez until 1796. The spectacles manufactured there consisted of two heavy wrought-iron side arms welded to two enormous circles. In spite of the primitive nature of this product, it met with resounding success locally. In about 1830, a Morez craftsman took his merchandise to the Beaucaire fair, where he established trade contacts and ended up by making Jura spectacles famous throughout France. Other factories sprang up. In about 1840 Morez introduced the pince-nez, took up the manufacture of optical glass, and gradually became the centre of the French optical industry. As such it can produce up to 12 million pairs of glasses per year. Today, there are 42 manufacturers of eyeglasses in Morez, producing 55% of the eyewear on the French market.

Morbier cheese – Morbier cheese is manufactured throughout Morez and the surrounding area, rather than solely in the little holiday resort of **Morbier**, situated 2km/1.2mi north of Morez

After the milk (about 70-80l/15-18gal for a single cheese) has been left to curdle, it is stirred and heated to about 40ºC/104ºF, then poured into a circular mould. The cheese is lightly pressed and drained and divided into two disks; their flat sides are dusted with ash, which will later appear as a bluish-black line through the middle of the cheese when the two circles are put together. The Morbier is then put into a press and stored in the cellar for two months to complete the maturing process. Every February, the town holds a contest to judge the best Morbier.

The local cheese manufacture, **Fromagerie de Morbier** ⏲, is open to visitors.

MOREZ

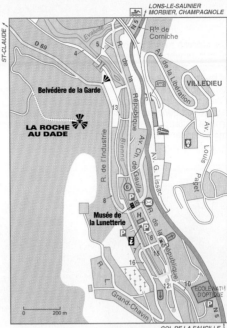

SIGHT

Musée de la Lunetterie ⊙ – This spectacle museum presents the evolution of the most important industrial activity in Morez. Antique machines and tools give the visitor an idea of how the different elements of a pair of spectacles are made. The display cases contain a wide variety of spectacles, both antique (metal frames, frames with side arms, pince-nez) and modern (sunglasses, goggles for sports or industrial use). The visit ends with an audiovisual presentation on the modern spectacle manufacturing industry in Morez. Eyes front! Various workshops can be visited in season *(apply to the tourist office)*.

> **FARM FRESH**
>
> **La Ferme du Grand Vallier** – *N 5 - La Savine - 39150 St-Laurent-en-Grandvaux - ☎ 03 84 60 82 78 - etsrebouillat@wanadoo.fr - open daily 8am-7pm.* Only regional ingredients are used here, whether it be honey, cheese, *charcuterie* or wine. The many house specialities include smoked trout, sausage flavoured with spruce bark and *boulet* (dry sausage with white wine).

EXCURSION

Belvédère de la Garde – This viewpoint is 500m west of Morez, along the St-Claude road *(D 69)*. It gives a good view of the various levels of viaducts running between the hillsides around Morez and, to the right, of the town itself, strung out along the valley.

★ La Roche au Dade – *30min there and back on foot.*
🚶 *Follow the little road leading off from D 69 (north-west on the town plan) a little further west of the Belvédère de la Garde; then take the path indicated with red flashes which goes past the Lamartine family home.*
There is a good **view★** of the Bienne Valley, Morez and its viaducts, and the mountain of Dôle just over the Swiss border.

Le MORVAN★★

Michelin map 319: G-8 to H-10

The Morvan massif is not served by any main roads but it receives a growing number of visitors who are attracted by the vast forests, rocky escarpments, valleys and picturesque sites; canoeists appreciate the mountain streams, fishermen line the banks of the rivers, lakes and reservoirs.

Although the Morvan is a distinct natural region between the Nivernais and Burgundy, it has never been a separate political or administrative entity; it has no historically-established borders. Only its physical characteristics distinguish it from its neighbours. From a distance it is recognisable by its vast and sombre forests; in Celtic etymology morvan means black mountain *(montagne noire)*.

Morvan landscape

Lower and Upper Morvan – The Morvan covers a quadrilateral area (70km/44mi long, 50km/31mi wide) stretching from Avallon to St-Léger-sous-Beuvray and from Corbigny to Saulieu.

Seen from the north the Morvan appears as a vast, slightly undulating plateau, which rises slowly towards the south. The northern section (maximum altitude 600m/2 000ft) descends in terraces sloping gently into the Paris basin; this is Le Bas Morvan (Lower Morvan).

It is the southern section, Le Haut Morvan (Upper Morvan), south of Montsauche, which contains the higher peaks: Mont Beuvray (821m/2 694ft), Mont Preneley (855m/2 805ft), the Massif du-Bois-du Roi or Haut-Folin (901m/2 956ft). Although the peaks do not reach very great altitudes, it is because they end suddenly above the Autun basin that the region is said to be mountainous.

Countryside of water and forest – The Morvan is subject to heavy rain and snow fall because of its geographical location and altitude. Precipitation on the outskirts of the region is on average 1 000mm/39in annually, but can reach over 1 800mm/71in in the Haut-Folin. It rains or snows for 180 days in an average year on the peaks. The heavy rainfall and the melting snow turns the smallest stream into a torrent. As the ground is composed of non-porous rock covered with a layer of granitic gravel (a sort of coarse sand), the Morvan is like a sponge full of water: the rivers – Yonne, Cure, Cousin and their tributaries – become turbulent watercourses. Dams and reservoirs (Pannesière-Chaumard, Les Settons, Crescent, Chaumeçon) have been built to regulate the flow when the rivers are in spate or the water level is low, so as to supplement the output of hydroelectric power when necessary; St Agnan provides a reservoir of drinking water. The characteristic feature of the Morvan massif is the forest which covers a third and often half of the surface area. Gradually the beeches or oaks are being replaced by fir trees. Timber is no longer floated to Paris by water as tree trunks but is now transported by lorry to nearby factories for cabinet-making and particularly charcoal production.

Life in the Morvan – A rough and unfertile country, the Morvan has for a long time been the butt of gibes from its neighbours. In Burgundy they say: "Nothing good comes from the Morvan, neither good people nor a good wind", an unjust statement which expresses the superior attitude of the rich Burgundians towards the Morvan people, whose countryside has neither vineyards nor fertile fields. Since they could extract only small profit from the soil of their native land, the Morvan men often came down to the surrounding plains of Bazois or Auxois, rich lands of cattle-breeding and cultivation, while the women found work as wet-nurses.

In the 19C in particular wet-nursing was a most profitable occupation for the Morvan women.

In the towns at this period it was not considered proper for young mothers to nurse their children and the Morvan women were excellent wet-nurses. Some went to Paris to provide food, some stayed at home to nurse the babies entrusted to their care. Countless Parisian children spent the first months of their lives in the Morvan during this period.

Today the Morvan is still far from being a rich and prosperous region and its population continues to decline. Cattle-rearing on a small scale is no longer a profitable proposition. Forestry, however, is a new resource instituted since the Second World War by the planting of conifers to provide raw material for the developing timber industries.

Another sector of commercial progress is tourism in the Avallonnais and the Morvan. An ⊙ **Écomusée du Morvan** (regional folk museum) is housed in various converted traditional buildings.

In the highest parts of the Massif, south-east of Château-Chinon, a ski area has been established with downhill runs (Haut-Folin) and cross-country routes.

Parc Naturel Régional du Morvan – The majority of the Morvan region was designated a Regional Nature Park in 1970, which contributed a great deal to attracting tourists to the region. The park encompasses 95 *communes* from the *départements* of Côte-d'Or, Nièvre, Saône-et-Loire and Yonne. The image of a galloping horse, taken from an ancient Aedui coin, was adopted as the park's logo. The park lends itself to numerous sports activities, such as hiking, canoeing, cycling, riding or fishing. The long-distance footpath GR 13 crosses the Morvan from north to south *(Vézelay to Autun).*

Shorter rambles are possible on the so-called GR de Pays *(yellow flashes on red background)*, which makes a tour of the Morvan via the big lakes, and a number of smaller footpaths *(marked by yellow flashes)*. There are also plenty of possibilities for accommodation on offer *(on local farms etc)*.

The **Maison du Parc** ⊙ at **St-Brisson** houses the park's administration and an information and exhibition centre. The 40ha/99 acre grounds are home to an arboretum, a herbarium (about 160 local species), a discovery trail at the Taureau lake, an orchard and a conservatory. The **Musée de la Résistance** ⊙ is devoted to the Resistance movement in Morvan during the Second World war.

LE BAS MORVAN

① Round tour from Vézelay

73km/45mi – allow one day

This route enters the Morvan from the north as far as Lormes, returning via the Chaumeçon and Crescent lakes.

★★★**Vézelay** – *See VÉZELAY.*

Leave Vézelay east towards Avallon.

Vézelay and its basilica, set high on their rocky outcrop, are still visible from St-Père.

★**St-Père**– The little village of St-Père, standing at the foot of the hill of Vézelay, on the banks of the River Cure, is home to a beautiful Gothic church.

★**Notre-Dame** – The church, which was begun in about 1200 and completed in 1455, shows all the stages in the development of the Gothic style between the 13C and 15C. In the 16C it became the parish church in place of the church of St-Pierre (from which the name St-Père is derived) which burned down in 1567 during the Wars of Religion and was never rebuilt.

The gable, surmounting a rose window of beautiful design, is hollowed out by arches forming niches. Those in the centre contain statues of Christ being crowned by two angels, and St Stephen, framed on one side by the Virgin and saints Peter, Andrew and James, and on the other by St Mary Magdalene with St John and two evangelists.

The porch added at the end of the 13C and restored by Viollet-le-Duc (1814-79) has three doorways. The centre one, which has a trefoiled archway, depicts the Last Judgment.

Under the porch housing the tomb of the donors (dating from 1258) note the size of the arches and the design of the tracery of the large side windows.

The overall effect is one of great purity of style. Rebuilt in the 15C the choir is encircled by an ambulatory with five radiating chapels. On entering note the two 14C cast-iron fonts shaped like upturned bells.

The vaulting of the nave has painted bosses and corbels carved in the form of expressive faces.

A narrow gallery leads round the building at the height of the clerestory windows. In the north aisle there is a defaced recumbent figure dating from the 13C and in a chapel on the south side of the choir a 10C stone altar which probably belonged to the original church. On leaving the church note the curious painted baptismal font dating from the Carolingian period.

Musée Archéologique Régional ⊘ – The regional archaeological museum is installed in the former presbytery, built in the 17C, and contains objects excavated at Fontaines-Salées, in particular sections of a water conduit made from tree trunks hollowed out by fire to carry mineral water from a spring; it dates from the Hallstatt period (First Iron Age). Also on display are a 4C Gallo-Roman weighing device, enamelled bronze fibulae in the form of sea horses or wild ducks, Merovingian weapons and jewellery found in the tombs at Vaudonjon near Vézelay, and Gratteloup near Pierre-Perthuis. The medieval room contains sculpture from the 12C to the 16C from the Vézelay region including a statue of St James the Great and a 13C statue of Christ conferring His Blessing.

Drive south out of St-Père.

The road follows the upper valley of the River Cure which flows through a wooded gorge.

Fouilles des Fontaines-Salées ⊘– *1.5km/1mi.* These excavations, near D 958, have unearthed Gallo-Roman baths, built on to what was once a Gaulish sanctuary (a 1C BC circular temple with a lustral basin) enclosed within a vast precinct dedicated to the gods of the springs.

These saline springs, which were used in the Iron Age, by the Romans and again in the Middle Ages, were filled in by the salt tax authorities in the 17C. Nineteen wooden casings dating from the first millennium BC have been preserved by the high mineral content of the water. A stone duct from the Roman period gives access to the waters of a spring which is once again being used for treating arthritic complaints.

★**Pierre-Perthuis** – *4km/2.5mi along D 958.* This tiny village in its picturesque **site**★ is named after a rocky spur, **Roche Percée**, which can be seen from the modern bridge spanning the Cure.

Continue south towards Lormes.

★**Bazoches** – *See VÉZELAY: Excursions.*

Drive south for 13.5km/8mi along D 42 to Lormes.

Lormes – This small town on the border between the Morvan and Nivernais regions is an ideal departure point for day trips to the nearby reservoirs. Rue du Panorama, the steep road by the tax office *(Perception)*, leads up to the lookout point by the cemetery, from where there is a broad **panorama**★ of the wooded heights of the Morvan (to the south-east), and the farmland of the Bazois and Nivernais regions dotted with little villages and woods (to the south-west). On the horizon, roughly in the centre of the panorama, stands Montenoison hill.

A popular song festival takes place during the third week in July.

★**Mont de la Justice** – *1.5km/1mi NW; viewing-table.* Alt 470m/1 542ft. The summit affords a fine panorama encompassing Vézelay to the north, the Yonne Valley and Montenoison hill to the west, the Bazois region to the south-west and the Morvan ridge to the south-east.

From Lormes, take D 6 towards Dun-les-Places.

Lac de Chaumeçon – ▣ The twisting road runs across undulating woodland dotted with rocks then across pastoral open country.

Drive over the dyke and turn immediately left; a short section of road (800m/875yd) leads to D 235.

The road overlooks the Chaumeçon reservoir hemmed in by wooded heights, an angler's paradise. Beyond Vaussegrois, the road plunges towards the lake shore and follows it closely before running over the crest of the dam towering 42m/138ft above the gorge of the River Chalaux.

Canoe and kayak competitions are organised regularly between Chaumeçon and Chalaux. *Continue to Plainefas and turn right towards Chalaux.*

Barrage du Crescent – Built between 1930 and 1933 this dam impounds the Cure downstream from its junction with the Chalaux. By its sheer mass the dam retains the accumulated waters flowing from the Cure and the Chalaux. It has a maximum height of 37m/122ft and a total length of 330m/1 083ft.

The reservoir of water (14 million m³/494 million cu ft) is used by the Bois-de-Cure power station to generate electricity and helps to regulate the flow of the Seine.

Take D 944 towards Avallon.

Château de Chastellux-sur-Cure– This château was altered in the 13C and restored in 1825 and has been the seat of the Chastellux family for over 1 000 years. One member of the family, François-Jean de Chastellux (1731-88) took part in the American War of Independence and wrote an account of his journey entitled *Voyage dans l'Amérique septentrionale* (Travels across North America).

The best view of the château is from the viaduct which carries D 944 across the Cure. The building clings to a rocky slope amid much greenery, overlooking the wooded gorge.

Return to Vézelay along D 20 and D 36 (17.5km/11mi).

Eating out

BUDGET

L'Auberge Ensoleillée – *58230 Dun-les-Places* - ☎ *03 86 84 62 76 - closed 24 and 25 Dec - 14/35€.* In summer the façade of this family restaurant is overgrown with Virginia creeper and wisteria. On Wednesdays you can sample famed regional dishes such as *tête de veau* (boiled calf's head), *œufs en meurette* (poached eggs served in red wine sauce with lardoons) and *crapiaux* (thick pancakes cooked with pork fat). Unpretentious accommodation.

La Petite Auberge Chez Millette – *Pl. M.-Basdevant - 58230 Planchez - 10 km/6.2mi S of Montsauche by D 37 and D 520* - ☎ *03 86 78 41 89 - perso.wanadoo.fr/millette* - ✉ - *14/23€.* A truly authentic café which is also the local butcher's shop. Lively ambience around the bar. The upstairs dining room is quieter. Enjoy generous helpings of tasty regional cuisine.

MODERATE

Le Morvan – *89630 Quarré-les-Tombes* - ☎ *03 86 32 29 29 - closed 7-15 Oct, 23 Dec-28 Feb, Mon and Tue except Jul-Aug - 17/40€.* This family restaurant set back from the village offers lovingly prepared regional specialities at reasonable prices. Meals are served in the recently restored traditional dining room. A few modern rooms are available.

Where to stay

BUDGET

Camping Les Genêts – *58230 Ouroux-en-Morvan* - ☎ *03 86 78 22 88 - open 15 Apr-Sep – reservations recommended - 70 sites: 11.61€.* This campsite looking out onto the rolling countryside is extremely pleasant. The sites and their terraces are marked out by hedges and bushes. Tennis court nearby.

Camping La Plage des Settons – *58230 Les Settons – on the edge of Lac des Settons* - ☎ *03 86 84 51 99 - jpbosset@aol.com - open May-15 Sep – reservations recommended - 68 sites: 13.12€.* This quiet, peaceful campsite awaits you in the vicinity of the lake. The lazy can rest on the beach while the more energetic can burn a few calories at the nearby tennis court. Playing area for children.

Chambre d'Hôte L'Eau Vive – *71990 St-Prix - 3.5 km/2.3mi NW of St-Léger by D 179* - ☎ *03 85 82 59 34 - redenis@club-internet.fr - closed Nov-Mar and 15-30 Jun* - ✉ - *4 rooms: 36/42€ - meals 16€.* A stone's throw from Mont Beuvray, this house is the perfect starting-point for long, bracing walks. The drawing room and the bedrooms are pleasantly decorated with holiday mementoes brought back from the islands. *Table d'hôte* meals are served in the dining room embellished with exposed beams, blue pottery and old farming tools on the walls.

Chambre d'Hôte Le Château – *58120 Chaumard* - ☎ *03 86 78 03 33 - closed Dec-Feb, Thu evenings and Sun evenings* - ✉ - *6 rooms: 44€ - meals 15/23€.* Standing in a 2ha/5-acre park in the heart of the Morvan, this large 18C house is a haven of comfort and tranquillity. In summer, have breakfast on the terrace facing Pannessière Lake. Two self-catering gîtes are available. Riding enthusiasts welcome.

Sit back and relax

Les Tombelines – *24 pl. de l'Église - 89630 Quarré-les-Tombes* - ☎ *03 86 32 22 21 – open Jul-Aug daily; the rest of the year Thu-Tue 7am-1pm, 2-7.30pm; the laboratory is open by appointment only.* This confectionery on the church square is unusual in that it has on offer no less than 200 different kinds of jam made with old-fashioned recipes, including one made with dandelions *(cramaillote)* and another with lavender-flavoured apple. The shop also makes chocolates and every year it organises an exhibition on chocolate.

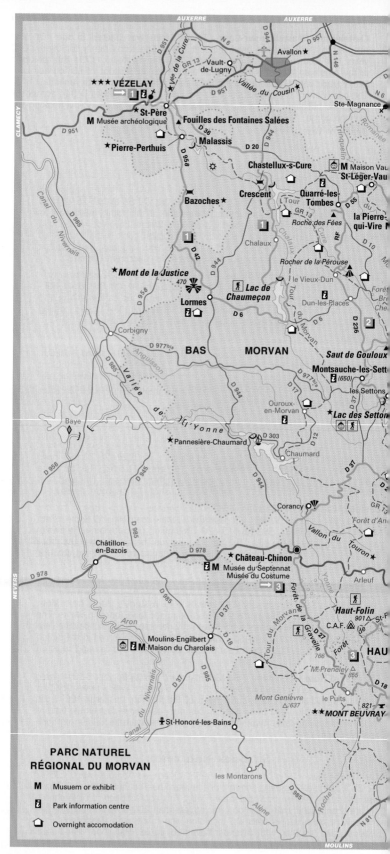

PARC NATUREL
RÉGIONAL DU MORVAN

M Musuem or exhibit

i Park information centre

⌂ Overnight accomodation

Le MORVAN

2 Round tour from Saulieu

80km/50mi – allow one day

The route affords charming views over Les Settons reservoir and the upper valley of the Cure and offers the possibility of visiting a remote abbey and the Musée Vauban.

From Saulieu, head for Dun-les-Places (22km/13.7mi W).

The road runs across a plateau dotted with woods and ponds then through a forested area.

Maison du Parc – *See above: Parc Naturel Régional du Morvan.*

If your children are keen on deer, you can walk to a roe-deer pen near a former forest lodge (information centre), located on D 6, 2km/1.2mi beyond Les Fourches, in Breuil-Chenue Forest. Observation towers located outside the pen enable visitors to watch the animals.

Alternatively, follow D 226 from Les Fourches to St-Agnan.

Lac de St-Agnan– *5km/3mi N. From the village, the road runs across the southern end of the lake, the granite-built dam being at the other end.*

At Les Michaux, follow a minor road on the left towards St-Léger-en-Vauban.

Abbaye de la Pierre-qui-Vire – This monastery, founded in the middle of the last century, is built in a wild and lonely part of the Morvan, on a hilly bank of the Trinquelin, the local name for the River Cousin, a small stream of clear water flowing at the foot of granite rocks in the middle of thick woods. The name of **Father Muard** is closely associated with the foundation of the abbey. He

321

was born in 1809 in the diocese of Sens and showed a desire to enter holy orders at an early age. In 1850 Father Muard laid the foundations of his monastery on land donated by the Chastellux family. It took its name of Pierre-Qui-Vire (the Rocking Stone) from a druidic monument, an enormous block of granite, placed on another rock, which could be made to rock with a push of the hand.

Father Muard's death in 1854, when he was Superior of the abbey, did not stop the development of the community which joined the Benedictine Order in 1859. On the contrary, it grew so fast that the buildings put up between 1850 and 1953 were not big enough to accommodate the 85 monks and many guests who stayed in the abbey. An architectural competition was launched in 1988 and the winning project was by J Cosse. The works, undertaken until 1995, unified the group of buildings which had gone up over time. The church has a narthex, a transitional space which invites meditation; the tympanum was decorated by Brother Marc. On the esplanade, the library can hold 185 000 volumes. Other parts of the abbey, inlcuding the cloisters, have been restored but are closed to tourists.

Tour ⊘ – Although the rules of monastic enclosure forbid tours of the monastery, the **salle d'exposition** is always open to visitors interested in the life of the monks and their work, mainly editing the Zodiaque books on religious art *(audio-visual presentation on the life of the monastery)*. The church is open for **services** ⊘ and one can visit the **druidic stone** *(pierre plate)* which is outside the monastery walls.

St-Léger-Vauban – Sébastien le Prestre, who under the name of the **Marquis de Vauban** became one of the outstanding figures of the Grand Siècle (as the 17C is known in France), was born in 1633 in this little village which was then called St-Léger-de-Foucheret.

Église St-Léger – The church where Vauban was baptised was originally built to a cruciform plan in the Renaissance period; it was transformed in the 19C and boasts some interesting modern additions by the sculptor Marc Hénard: carved wooden panels in the south door; the sculptures and stained-glass window in the chapel of Notre-Dame-du-Bien-Mourir (1625), left of the chancel; the beautiful blue and pink ceramic **tiles★** (1973) which surround the high altar and depict the planets, animals, tools etc revolving round the triangle of the Holy Trinity.

Maison Vauban ⊘ – *In the Maison Communale.*

In a small room information panels and an audio-visual presentation *(20min)* retrace the life and work of this great Frenchman.

Vauban, "the most decent man of his century"

Sébastien le Prestre was left a penniless orphan early in life, and at the age of 17 joined the army of the Prince of Condé, then in revolt against the court, and was taken prisoner by the royal forces.

From that time onwards, he entered the service of Louis XIV. As a military engineer, from the youthful age of 22, he worked on 300 ancient fortified places and built 33 new ones; he successfully directed 53 sieges, thus justifying the saying: "a town defended by Vauban is an impregnable town: a town besieged by Vauban is a captured town". Appointed Brigadier General of the royal armies and then Commissioner General of fortifications, he was made a Field Marshal in 1704. He was extremely inventive in thinking up new tactics for breaking into fortresses and designed a number of weapons and other instruments of war which were revolutionary for his period. He also systematically fortified the north and east borders of France with a belt of fortresses entirely new in conception (Verdun, Metz, Strasbourg, Neuf-Brisach).

Saint-Simon (writer: 1675-1755), who was not renowned for his kind remarks, wrote of Vauban: "A man of medium height, rather squat, who had a very warlike air, but at the same time an appearance that was loutish and coarse, not to say brutal and ferocious. Nothing could be further from the truth; never was there a gentler man, more compassionate, more obliging, more respectful, more courteous, and most sparing in the use of men's lives, a man of great worth capable of giving himself in the service of others..." The last years of this man's life, who never denied his humble origin, were unhappy. Deeply affected by the great misery of the common people, he sent his *Projet d'une dîme royale* (Plan for a Royal Tithe) to the king, in which he proposed ways and means of bettering the living conditions of the lower classes. The work was banned and Vauban, relegated virtually to disgrace by Louis XIV, died of grief on 30 March 1707.

In 1808 Vauban's heart was placed in the Invalides in Paris by Napoleon I; the rest of his body lies in the church in **Bazoches** *(20km/12mi south-west of Avallon)*, near the château which was largely reconstructed by his efforts and from which the view extends to Vézelay.

Quarré-les-Tombes – *About 5.5km/3.2mi via D 55.*
This village owes its name to the numerous limestone sarcophagi dating from the 7C to the 10C discovered near the church. It is thought that there must have been some kind of sanctuary to St George in Quarré, near which knights and other people of rank were buried.

*Follow D 10 towards Saulieu. 3.5km/2.2mi past the path leading to **La Roche des Fées** (rock-climbing site), take the forest track towards Dun.*

*Turn right just before Vieux-Dun onto a forest track and drive 1.6km/1mi to a signposted parking area, situated 200m/218yd from the **Rocher de la Pérouse**.*
A steep footpath climbs to the rocky summit; 30min round trip on foot.
From the top there is an interesting **view** over the isolated Cure Valley and the rounded summits of the massif.

Return to the road leading to Dun-les-Places then continue south on D 236.

Montsauche-les-Settons – This village is the highest resort (650m/2 133ft) in the massif. The village stands at the centre of the Parc Naturel du Morvan. Like Planchez, this township was rebuilt following almost total destruction in 1944.

Saut de Gouloux – *6km/3.7mi north-east then 15min round trip on foot. Access by a path (right) from the first bend in the road after the bridge over the Cure.*
Just upstream from its confluence with the Cure, the Caillot flows over an attractive waterfall.

Base Nautique des Settons ⊘ – In the Parc Naturel Régional du Morvan, the Settons sports centre lies close to a lake at an altitude of 600m/1 969ft. It offers facilities for both water sports (sailing, canoeing, water-skiing, wake-board) and outdoor activities (hiking, cycling) and has a miniature port for children. Many different formulas, including with instructors.

Ph. Gajic/MICHELIN

★ **Lac des Settons** – *South of Montsauche along D 193.* The reservoir was created originally to facilitate logging on the River Cure but is now used to regulate the flow of the River Yonne.
After crossing the River Cure, the road follows the north shore of the reservoir, offering pretty views over the lake and its wooded islands, and leads to the charming resort of Les Settons. The reservoir of Les Settons covering an area of 359ha/887 acres (alt 573m/1 880ft) is a peaceful place, surrounded by fir and larch woods, where wildfowl congregate in the autumn. Footpaths and a lakeside road provide easy access for walking, fishing and water sports.

The road continues through forests and across a plateau, dotted with woods and ponds, before reaching Saulieu via Moux, Alligny and Chamboux Lake.

HAUT MORVAN

③ Round tour from Château-Chinon

84km/52mi – allow one day

This drive crosses several forested massifs and offers far-reaching views.

★ **Château-Chinon** – *See CHÂTEAU-CHINON.*
Leave Château-Chinon by D 27 going south.

A view opens out towards the west of a landscape of meadows, arable fields and woods. The road then rises steeply before entering the ▨ **Forêt de la Gravelle**. It follows the watershed ridge between the basins of the Seine (Yonne to the east) and the Loire (Aron and its tributaries to the west).
At one point quite near to the summit (766m/2 513ft) there is a view to the right of bleak broom-covered moorland. The road then leaves the forest. Another good panorama opens out southwards over a small dam nestling at the bottom of a green hollow dominated by the wooded crests which mark the limit of the Morvan.

The road leads (18km/11mi) to D 18; turn left to Mont Beuvray.

★★ Mont Beuvray – *See Mont BEUVRAY.*

Take D 274 right round and back to D 18 then drive north to Glux-en-Glenne and the Forêt de St-Prix via D 300 and D 500 (very steep). The Bois-du-Roi forest track leads close to Haut-Folin.

Haut-Folin – The Haut-Folin (901m/2 956ft), the highest peak in the Morvan, is crowned by a telecommunications mast. The slopes of this peak have been developed for skiing by the French Alpine Club.

The Bois-du-Roi forest track continues through the **Forêt de St-Prix**, a magnificent stand of spruce and fir trees with immense trunks and joins D 179 at La Croisette.

Gorges de la Canche – *4km/2.5mi north-east.* The road follows the gorge along the side of a hill in a wild landscape of rocks and trees. There is a fine viewpoint in a bend to the right *(partly screened by trees).*

At the bottom of the gorge can be seen the white building of La Canche hydro-electric power station.

Turn left onto D 978 towards Château-Chinon then right 1km/0.6mi further onto D 388 to Anost.

Anost – *8km/5mi north-east.* Set in a pleasant and picturesque spot, Anost offers tourists a choice of numerous walks, especially in the forest *(signposted forest trails)* as well as outdoor swimming. A hurdy-gurdy festival takes place in summer. The village of **Bussy** used to be the main centre of the *galvache* trade (transport by ox-drawn carts) practised in the area until the First World War.

Maison des Galvachers ⊙ – 🖾 The museum is devoted to the men who practised this ancient trade: they would leave home for six months, from May to November, and go as far as the Ardennes in Belgium. The techniques they used for transporting various goods are clearly illustrated.

Notre-Dame-de-l'Aillant – *North-west of Anost: 15min round trip on foot.* From beside the statue there is a semicircular **panorama★** over the Anost basin and beyond the hills of the Autun depression.

Drive through Anost Forest (wild boar in an enclosure) to Planchez then return to Château-Chinon via the twisting D 37 and note the picturesque hilltop village of Corancy on the way.

MOUTHIER-HAUTE-PIERRE★

Population 343
Michelin map 321: H-4

This charming village set in a rocky amphitheatre is, along with Ornans, one of the prettiest spots in the Loue Valley. The village grew up around an old Benedictine priory, first recorded in 870 and deconsecrated during the French Revolution. One or two old houses still stand near the church in the upper part of the village (Mouthier Haut). Mouthier is at its most delightful at the end of April, when the cherry trees are in bloom.

Excellent cherries are harvested downstream of Mouthier in the area known as the Loue orchard; they are also used to make a famous kirsch.

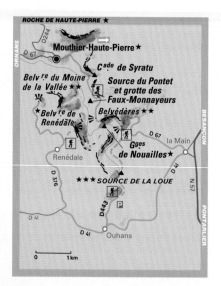

Église – The **village church** was built in the 15C and extended in the 16C; note the carved woodwork (altarpiece, stalls, confessional, pulpit) and the various wooden statues dating from the 13C and 14C.

EXCURSIONS

La Roche de Hautepierre Viewpoint – *5km/3mi N then 15min on foot there and back.* Follow D 244 as far as the entrance to Hautepierre-le-Châtelet and leave the car outside the cemetery.

🔄 *Walk along a steep stony path which levels off as it follows the rocky ridge.*

Alt 882m/2 894ft. Beyond the chapel, the view extends over the gorge and valley of the River Loue; the Jura range and, in fine weather, Mont Blanc can be seen in the distance.

Eating out

BUDGET

Ferme-Auberge du Rondeau – *25580 Lavans-Vuillafans - 15 km/9.3mi N of Mouthier-Haute-Pierre by D 67 heading for Vuillafans then D 27 -* ☎ *03 81 59 25 84 - closed end of Dec to Jan and Mon out of season -* ✉ *- reservations recommended - 15/25€.* This typical Franche-Comté farmhouse lies in a tranquil setting in the middle of fields. You will not be disappointed by the meals, offering homemade bread, vegetarian fare, organic produce, as well as goat and boar reared on the property. The eight comfortable rooms are embellished with wood from floor to ceiling.

Where to stay

BUDGET

Hôtel des Sources de la Loue – *25520 Ouhans - 10 km/6.2mi S of Mouthier-Haute-Pierre by D 67 and D 41 -* ☎ *03 81 69 90 06 - hotel-des-sources-loue@wanadoo.fr - closed 25 Oct-8 Nov, 22 Dec-1 Feb, Fri evenings and Sat lunchtime out of season - 15 rooms: 30.50/43€ -* ☕ *7.60€ - restaurant 13.70/38.15€.* This unpretentious hotel is housed in a building typical of the region. The bar is a popular meeting-place for local residents. Sober guestrooms with wood panelling. Regional specialities.

MODERATE

Hôtel de la Cascade – *2 rte des Gorges de Nouailles -* ☎ *03 81 60 95 30 - closed 12 Nov-2 Mar -* 🅿 *- 19 rooms: 45/59€ -* ☕ *7.20€ - restaurant 17.60/38.50€.* The Loue Valley runs at the foot of this hotel. The rooms are equipped with all modern amenities and some of them have a balcony. Settle in the restaurant (for non-smokers) and enjoy tasty, imaginative dishes.

Lods – This village (pronounced Lo) is on the banks of the Loue, where the river is broken by waterfalls which are particularly beautiful when the water level is high. The old Lods forges are on the opposite bank.

Gorges de la Loue

40km/25mi – about 4hr 30min

The even course of the Loue from Mouthier-Haute-Pierre down to its confluence with the Doubs is easy to follow by canoe. The river's winding course, the few rapids encountered, the crystal clear waters and the picturesque charm of the banks all make for a very pleasant trip.

The valley is at is most interesting between the source of the Loue and Ornans; the river drops 229m/4 507ft in altitude over a distance of 20km/12mi.

The water flows along the bottom of a deep, often wooded gorge in the Jura plateau. The region around Mouthier-Haute-Pierre is positively enchanting in May, when the slopes are white with cherry trees in blossom; in summer, the best light is at the end of the afternoon.

Cascade de Syratu – *Drive out of Mouthier towards Pontarlier.* Visitors climbing back up the valley will see Syratu waterfall, just at the exit to Mouthier-Haute-Pierre, tumbling from a high cliff.

Source du Pontet and Grotte des Faux-Monnayeurs – *45min there and back on foot from D 67.*

🅱 The walk is mostly through woods, climbing up slopes that are sometimes quite steep. Iron ladders lead to these two caves; that of the Faux-Monnayeurs is not recommended to visitors with no head for heights. The source of the Le Pontet is a resurgent spring welling up in a cave at the bottom of a wooded hollow. The Faux-Monnayeurs cave (Counterfeiters' Cave, so named as it is said that counterfeit money was made here in the 17C) is about 30m/98ft higher up; this was the river's original source.

Angling in the River Loue

G. Magnin/MICHELIN

★★ Belvédères – Two viewpoints come one after the other along D 67, from which one of the most beautiful meanders in the river can be seen, from a height of 150m/492ft.

There is another viewpoint, known as the **Belvédère de Mouthier**, 300m further on. The **view★★** is remarkable, taking in Mouthier as well as the upper Loue Valley at the end of the Nouailles gorge. The Mouthier hydro-electric plant is visible in the dip.

★ Gorges de Nouailles – This gorge was the favoured haunt of the Vouivre, the winged serpent of Franche-Comté legend which flew as fast as lightning. Daring country folk eager for riches dreamed of stealing the carbuncle which it wore on its forehead.

🚶 *There is a walk (1hr 30min there and back on foot) from the Café La Creuse to the source of the Loue; take the path along the gorge which branches off from D 67. This wooded path twists along the steep cliff.*

The path gives beautiful **glimpses★** of the gorge, which is over 200m/656ft deep. The walk goes down to the bottom of the cirque in which the Loue rises *(see above)*. A footbridge leads to the cave from which the river springs.

★★★Source de la Loue – *After leaving Ouhans, head for the river's source along D 443, which climbs steeply uphill. Leave the car in the car park next to the little refreshment stall, Chalet de la Loue, and go down the path (30min there and back on foot) to the valley bottom.*

🚶 This spot is one of the most beautiful in the Jura.

A bend in the path suddenly reveals the Loue rising up from a steep-walled basin. It has been proved that the Loue draws its waters from the Doubs. It is also fed by infiltrations from the Drugeon and by rain water draining off the plateau, with the result that the river's flow never falls very low.

The springs swell when it rains and stays muddy and turbulent for a while afterwards, although as a general rule the water is very clear.

The river rises from a vast cave at the bottom of a tall cliff about 100m/328ft high. From the entrance to the cave, there is a good view of the power and size of the Loue's source.

Return to Ouhans and take D 41 on the right towards Levier, then take D 376 on the right shortly afterwards. On leaving Renédale, park the car near the entrance gate of the path leading to the viewpoint.

★ Belvédère de Renédale – *15min there and back on foot.*

🚶 This pleasant path overlooks the Nouailles gorge from a height of 350m/1 148ft. It leads to a platform from which there is virtually a **bird's-eye view** down into the gorge; directly opposite are the cliffs with D 67 winding its way along them.

Take D 376 again to head north; after 2.5km/1.5mi the road ends at the foot of a television broadcasting station, at a viewpoint.

★★ Belvédère du Moine-de-la-Vallée – Touring Club de France bench. There is a superb **panorama** of the Loue Valley north-west to Vuillafans, Roche mountain and the village of Mouthier-Haute-Pierre.

Take the road back to Ouhans and return to Mouthier.

NANS-SOUS-SAINTE-ANNE

Population 125
Michelin map 321: G-5

This charming village grew up close to the source of the Lison, using the river's powerful flow to drive its numerous mills and edge-tool workshop. Nans is also the ideal starting point of splendid excursions through the scenic surrounding area with its cliffs, woods and picturesque river.

Underground, overground... – The River Lison, a tributary of the Loue, actually rises on the slopes of the forest of Scay. Its course on its upper reaches, the Lison-du-Haut, is quite irregular. It will vanish underground for a short distance, only to reappear for a little while, then disappear once more into a gully or crevice. The underground course of the river can be seen at ground level in the largely dry, at times strangely shaped valley which follows it. The valley sides become steeper and steeper, forming a gorge which is spanned by the **Pont du Diable** (devil's bridge) over which D 229 from Crouzet-Migette to Sainte-Anne runs. After heavy rainfall, the river becomes a gushing torrent, filling the valley, before it cascades into the pool known as the Creux Billard.

SIGHTS

★ Taillanderie ⊙ – 📷 Located outside the village *(follow the signposts)* is the 19C edge-tool workshop which turned out agricultural tools until 1969. Working to capacity, it employed 25 workers, most of whom lived on the premises. Hydraulic power was provided by the Arcange, a tributary of the Lison. During the 1hr visit, the process of making a scythe is explained and the large hydraulic wheel (5m/16ft in diameter), dating from 1891, is seen operating; in summer, tools are even made under your eyes.

★★ **Grotte Sarrazine** – *30min there and back on foot.*

🚶 A gigantic natural porch in the steep wooded rockface marks the opening to this enormous cave (90m/295ft high). The sheer size of it can best be appreciated in summer when the resurgent spring is dry and the cave can be visited. During rainy periods the resurgent spring, fed by an underground stretch of the Lison, flows out of the cave as a surprisingly swollen torrent.

Go back to the road on the right and after 200m/220yd take the footpath which climbs up to the source of the Lison.

★★ **Source du Lison** – *1hr there and back trip on foot.*

🚶 The abundant fresh green foliage which surrounds this relatively large pool, going right down to the water's edge, makes a pretty scene. This is the second largest river source in the Jura after the Loue, and even when the water level is low, it flows at 600l/132gal per second.

Slightly downstream, in Nans-sous-Sainte-Anne, the Lison is joined by the Verneau, and they both flow into the Loue shortly afterwards, in a fertile, peaceful landscape.

It is possible to enter the cave through a small tunnel in the rock *(take a torch; slippery underfoot)* which ends at a pulpit-shaped rocky platform *(chaire à prêcher)*.

Retrace your steps along the path and turn right onto a signposted footpath which twists and turns its way up through the woods. The climb down to the Creux Billard can be a bit tricky.

★★ **Creux Billard** – *30min there and back on foot.*

🚶 This deep rocky cirque (over 50m/164ft) is characterised by unusually subtle light. The water in the pool is part of the Lison's underwater course, although the river rises officially further downstream in a nearby cave *(described above)*. The discovery that the Creux Billard is linked with the Lison's source was made after a tragic accident: in 1899 a young girl drowned in the depths of the pool; three months later her body was found downstream of the river's source.

NANTUA★

Population 3 902
Michelin map 328: G-4

Nantua, tucked in a steep-sided, evergreen-forested **cluse**★★ on the shores of a glacial lake, grew up around a Benedictine abbey founded here in the 8C. In the Middle Àges it was a free town surrounded by solid ramparts, which it certainly needed, as it was continually caught up in the turbulent religious and political disputes between the Bugey, the Franche-Comté, Savoy and Geneva, not to mention between France and the Germanic Empire.

Henri IV annexed Nantua to the kingdom of France in 1601.

During the age of stage coaches, Nantua was a busy town as it was the relay post between Bourg-en-Bresse and Geneva. However, in the 19C, when the railway brought an end to handsome teams of horses, Nantua fell into decline and was forgotten.

The development of tourism and the growing popularity of mountain resorts as holiday destinations have injected new life into what is now a charming lakeside resort. Local gastronomic treats include freshwater crayfish *(écrevisses)* and a type of dumpling *(quenelles à la Nantua)*.

★ **Église St-Michel** ⊘ – This church is the last trace of a 12C abbey destroyed during the Revolution. The beautiful Romanesque portal is unfortunately badly damaged, but the Last Supper can nonetheless be discerned on the lintel.

Inside, the height of the great arches of the nave and that of the octagonal lantern tower on pendentives above the transept crossing are striking. The first chapel in the north aisle dates from the Renaissance and is embellished with complex vaulting and a beautiful stone altarpiece.

The chancel contains some beautiful carved woodwork and a pair of kneeling angels on either side of the altar (17C and 18C). Note the **Martyrdom of St Sebastian**★★ (1836) by Delacroix on the north wall *(light switch in the crossing on the opposite side)*. An international music festival takes place in August.

Near the church, on place d'Armes, Nantua has put up a statue in memory of one of its citizens. Deputy **Jean-Baptiste Baudin** served in the National Assembly during the Second Republic (1848-52) and was killed the day after Napoleon III's coup d'état (2 December 1851) at the Faubourg St-Antoine barricades in Paris, probably as he shouted the now famous words, "I'll show you how to die for 25 francs!", thereby attracting the opponents' attention to himself. (Deputies were at that time paid 25 francs a day.)

Musée Départemental d'Histoire de la Résistance et de la Déportation de l'Ain et du Haut-Jura ⊘ – The museum collection (uniforms, weapons, flags, posters, letters and clothes of those deported, parachuting equipment etc) traces the rise

Eating out

BUDGET

Auberge du Lac Genin – *01130 Charix - 16km/9.9mi NE of Nantua by D 74 until you reach Molet then D 95 up to the lake - ☎ 04 74 75 52 50 - denis.godet@wanadoo.fr - closed 13 Oct-28 Nov, Sun evenings and Mon - 11/18€.* You will enjoy the blissfully quiet atmosphere of this mountain inn nestling on the edge of a lake in the heart of woodland. The delightful setting is well worth a visit... The bedrooms are decorated in the rustic style. Grilled meat is the speciality of the house.

MODERATE

Auberge Les Gentianes – *01130 Lalleyriat - 12km/7.5mi E of Nantua by N 84 and D 55^B - ☎ 04 74 75 31 80 - closed 8-31 Jan, Sun evenings, Tue and Wed - 20/36€.* This house is a charming sight indeed with its façade overflowing with flowers. Fine stone fireplace and small terrace for the summer season. Your hosts prepare thoughtful cooking with deliciously fresh produce.

Where to stay

BUDGET

L'Embarcadère – *Av. du Lac - ☎ 04 74 75 22 88 - closed 20 Dec-5 Jan - ▣ - 50 rooms: 45.75/53.50€ - ☲ 7.50€ - restaurant 19/31€.* Relax in a beautiful natural setting in the heart of a forest, a stone's throw from pretty Nantua Lake. Pleasant menus and comfortable guestrooms.

MODERATE

Hôtel des Grandes Roches – *Near motorway exit no 11 - 01100 Oyonnax - ☎ 04 74 77 27 60 - grandesroches-hotel@wanadoo.fr - closed 29 Jul-18 Aug - ▣ - 36 rooms: 53/70€ - ☲ 7.50€.* This hotel perched on the Oyonnax heights commands lovely views of the surrounding mountains and valley. The bedrooms are gradually being renovated one by one for your pleasure. Settle at the restaurant Les Feuillantines, fronted by a pretty terrace.

of Fascism and Nazism and recalls the Vichy administration, the Occupation, the Resistance, the Maquis and deportation. Numerous documents and a film testify to the particularly tough struggle between the Nazis and the Maquis in the Bugey region.

The audio-guided visit includes the voices of former French *maquisards* and of a British soldier.

★**Lac de Nantua** – The 2.5km/1.5mi-long and 650m/0.4mi-wide lake is all that remains of a glacier from the Ice Age which was trapped in the *cluse* by moraine. The lake is fed by several springs, including that of Neyrolles. Its waters flow into the Oignin, a tributary of the Ain, via the so-called Bras du Lac.

NANTUA

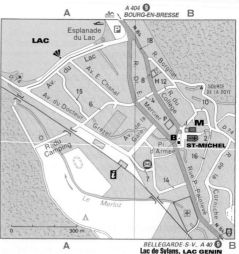

There is a beautiful **view**★ from avenue du Lac and from the lakeside promenade shaded by magnificent plane trees. The lake can be seen framed by the heights of the Haut-Bugey, with the cliffs on the northern side ending abruptly in a wooded scree slope.

Various water sports and leisure activities are available: sailing, pedalos, water skiing, fishing...

EXCURSIONS

Lac de Sylans – *5km/3mi E along N 84*. Water from this natural lake, tucked at the bottom of a deep *cluse*, drains in two opposite directions, towards the Valserine and the Rhône basin to the east, and towards the Lac de Nantua and the Ain basin to the west.

★ **Lac Genin** – *15km/9.3mi NE along N 84 then left past the Lac de Sylans onto D 95*. This small lake, lying in a picturesque setting of pastures and woodland, offers pleasant walks along its shaded shores as well as non-supervised swimming.

Lac de Sylans

1 Haut-Bugey

Allow one day. Leave Nantua to the N on the picturesque N 84, which runs alongside the Lac de Nantua. Turn left at Montréal-la-Cluse; 2km/1.2mi after Ceignes, turn right on a road leading off N 84 and follow it for about 300m/328yd.

Grotte du Cerdon ⊘ – This cave was hollowed out by a subterranean river which has now dried up (it was fed by the Lac de Nantua, which used to be a lot larger than it now is). The tour takes you past beautiful stalactites (the dais), stalagmites (the Cambodian statue) and draperies. It leads into an immense cavern in which a 30m/98ft-high arch is open to the sky. A gallery opened up in 1981 leads to the place where the vanished river emerged from the middle of the rockface as a resurgent spring.

In the past, cheese made locally was left to mature in the cave.

Continue along N 84.

Belvédère de Cerdon – On the way to Cerdon, there is a viewpoint on the right side of the road which offers a superb panoramic view of the Cerdon vineyards and Haut-Bugey region.

Val d'Enfer – On reaching the village of Cerdon, the road enters the Valromey area. By the windswept Pont de l'Enfer a memorial has been set up to the members of the Resistance who fought in the Bugey (bust of a woman against a small wall).

★ **Cerdon** – Nestling inside a deep valley, Cerdon produces renowned sparkling rosé wines. The picturesque narrow streets are decorated with numerous fountains and stone bridges spanning mountain streams. *It is recommended to leave the car in the lower part of the village.*

La Cuivrerie ⊘ – These copper works, set up in 1854 on the site of a former mill, are still operating with mainly obsolete machinery next to a modern enamelling workshop.

Continue along N 84 towards Pont-d'Ain; 6km/3.7mi further on, turn left onto D 36 towards Ambronnay. It is also possible to drive to Jujurieux along D 63 which branches off N 84 as you leave Cerdon; beware as this picturesque minor road is fairly dangerous.

Jujurieux – This village, boasting 13 castles, has retained important evidence of the extraordinary boom it enjoyed during the 19C on account of its weaving industry.

★**Soieries Bonnet** ⊘ – In 1835, CJ Bonnet, a silk manufacturer from Lyon, decided to set up a factory in his native region. This family business, which dealt with all the stages of silk manufacturing, included a training centre, run by nuns, where 400 young girls were taught the various skills connected with silk. Today, the works are specialised in the production of high-quality silk velvet. There is a small museum and the workshops can be visited with the possibility of buying luxury fabrics.

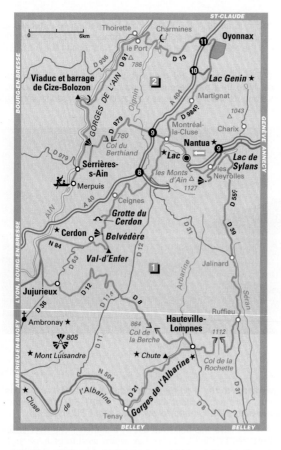

Follow D 12 to Hauteville-Lompnès.

Hauteville-Lompnès – The town, situated on a high plateau (850-1 200m/2 789-3 937ft) is a popular holiday resort, well known for its modern sanatoriums and the superior quality of the air.

Take D 21 on the right.

★**Gorges de l'Albarine** – As the River Albarine flows south-west, it has cut many impressive **gorges**★ along its course. Waterfalls tumble down the towering cliff faces at various points. As the road leaves the gorge, you can see the **Cascade de Charabotte**★, formed as the Albarine cascades down a 150m/492ft drop on the edge of the Hauteville plateau.

Return to Hauteville-Lompnès and take D 9 over the Col de la Rochette, altitude 1 112m/3 648ft, as far as Ruffieu; take D 31 N, D 31ᶠ at the Jalinard junction, D 39 on the left and D 55ᶜ on the right. Then take D 55ᴰ through Granges-du-Poizat to reach Les Neyrolles. From here, take D 39 on the left.

After a few sharp turns in the road there is a remarkable **view**★★ of the steep slopes of the Nantua *cluse* and of the lake; this is a magnificent sight at sunset.

Return to the village of Neyrolles, from where D 39 leads to N 84, which leads off to the left back to Nantua.

② Gorges de l'Ain and Plastics Vallée

Allow one day. Leave Nantua along N 84 to Cluse then drive straight on along D 979 towards Bourg-en-Bresse.

On the way down from the Col du Berthiand, a belvedere offers views of the Ain Valley.

Turn right before the bridge onto D 91ᶜ to Serrières.

Serrières-sur-Ain – Superb scenery round a one-arch bridge spanning the River Ain.

Follow D 91 towards Merpuis and turn right towards the Merpuis site 2km/1.2mi beyond the bridge then take the steep road down to the Allement reservoir.

Boat trips on the River Ain ⊘ – Discover the specificity of this valley where timber-floating once flourished aboard a flat-bottomed boat; hydroelectric installations have considerably modified the valley's landscapes.

Return to Serrières and continue along D 91 which follows the gorge N to Thoirette, affording splendid views of the river.

Viaduc de Cize-Bolozon – This elegant 280m/306yd-long and 53m/174ft-high viaduct, destroyed in 1944 and rebuilt in 1950, carries the railway line running from Bourg to Nantua.

Continue towards Thoirette.

Barrage de Cize-Bolozon – Built between 1928 and 1931, the 156m/170yd-long dam is surmounted by a crane. The valley progressively widens yet remains hemmed in by impressive heights.

At Le Port, do not cross the bridge and follow D 18 towards Oyonnax.

Beyond Matafelon-Granges, the road runs across the narrow end of the reservoir formed by the Charmines dam.

Follow D 13 to Oyonnax.

Oyonnax – Once famous for its wooden combs, Oyonnax has now evolved into a production centre of European importance, turning out a wide variety of plastic objects: household articles, toys, artificial flowers, combs, spectacles, car accessories, and parts for radios and other electrical appliances. The association Plastics Vallée was created in 1986, bringing together 1 200 specialised businesses within a 50km/31mi radius. In addition to the technical college for the science and manufacture of man-made materials (the Lycée technique Arbez-Carme), which has been located here for almost a century, the Pôle Européen de Plasturgie was opened here in 1991 to train plastics engineers from all over the country.

From wooden hair combs to Plastics Vallée

Beautiful wooden combs have been crafted here for centuries by local mountain dwellers during the winter, using Jura boxwood as well as beech and hornbeam. By the end of the 18C other materials were gradually introduced, in particular horn.

The discovery of celluloid in 1869 in the United States opened up new opportunities for comb makers in Oyonnax. In 1878 they began using this material to make not only new kinds of combs, but other accessories and toys. As fast as a new material (galalith, bakelite, cellulose acetate etc) was developed, Oyonnax craftsmen would adapt it to their products, thereby remaining at the forefront of the market. Rhodoid, a thermoplastic derived from cellulose acetate, played a particularly important part in the town's economic prosperity from 1924.

Musée du Peigne et de la Plasturgie ⊘ – *Centre Culturel Aragon, second floor, square G.-Pompidou.*
The museum's collections give a good overview of the evolution and variety of products manufactured in Oyonnax. Exhibits include combs made of boxwood, horn and celluloid, spectacles, buttons, buckles, jewellery, artificial flowers etc. Many objects, such as celluloid mantillas and plastic spectacles, illustrate the manufacturers' skill at their craft and sense for aesthetic design. Machines which once made horn and celluloid combs complete the exhibition.

As you leave the museum car park, turn right towards A 404 then S towards Martignat and Montréal-la-Cluse (D 984D).

NEVERS★

Conurbation 58 915
Michelin map 319: B-10

Situated a few miles from the confluence of the Loire and the Allier, Nevers is the capital of the Nivernais region and the town of fine pottery.
From the great bridge of reddish-brown sandstone that spans the River Loire, there is an overall **view** of the old town, set in terraces on the side of a hill and dominated by the high square tower of the cathedral and the graceful silhouette of the ducal palace.

Julius Caesar checked – In 52 BC, before undertaking the siege of Gergovie, Caesar made the fortified town into an important food and forage depot for his army. Noviodunum Aeduorum, generally considered to have been the Roman name for Nevers, was situated on the borders of the territory of the Aedui tribe. On hearing the news of his check before Gergovie, the Aedui immediately attacked Noviodunum and destroyed it by fire, thus imperilling Caesar's whole position in Gaul.

Pottery and spun glass – Luigi di Gonzaga, the Duke of Mantua's third son who became Duke of Nevers in 1565, brought artists and artisans from Italy.
He introduced artistic earthenware in Nevers between 1575 and 1585. The three Italian brothers Conrade, master potters in white and other colours, taught their art to a group of local artisans. Little by little, the shape, the colours and the decorative motifs, which at first reproduced only the Italian models and methods, evolved into a very distinctive local style.

At the same time, he developed the glass industry as well as the art of enamelling, which became very fashionable. The town's products – spun glass was generally used in the composition of religious scenes – were sent by boat on the Loire to Orléans and Angers.

About 1650 the pottery industry was at its height with 12 workshops and 1 800 workers. The Revolution of 1789 dealt the industry a grave blow. Today, four **workshops** ⊙ maintain the reputation of this traditional craft.

J. Guillot/EDIMEDIA

Nevers faïence plate (late 17-early 18C)

Ver-Vert the parrot – The history of the parrot is told in a piece of light verse written by JB Gresset in 1733.

The famous parrot once lived with the Visitandines in Nevers, coddled and spoiled but impeccably educated. When the Visitandine nuns at Nantes heard of the prodigious reputation of this marvellous parrot, they begged their sisters at Nevers to let them have him for a few days. The nuns at Nevers were reluctant but finally they agreed. Ver-Vert went off for his visit to Nantes but during his voyage in the river boat the Loire rivermen and some Dragoons taught him a vocabulary considerably less virtuous than that he had learned with the nuns:

"For these Dragoons were a godless lot,
Who spoke the tongue of the lowest sot,
... Soon for curses and oaths he did not want
And could out-swear a devil in a holy font."

The nuns in Nantes were horrified at his lurid maledictions; Satan's myrmidon was quickly sent back to Nevers. Brought before the convent's Council of Order, Ver-Vert was condemned to a period of fasting, solitude and, worst of all, to silence. After honourably serving his sentence, Ver-Vert returned to favour once again among the nuns of Nevers but, as in the past, he was spoiled and he died of over-indulgence:

"Stuffed with sugar and mulled with wine,
Ver-Vert, gorging a pile of sweets,
Changed his rosy life for a coffin of pine."

OLD TOWN *Half a day*

A blue line drawn on pavements guides visitors to the main sights.
Start from the Porte du Croux and follow the itinerary shown on the plan.

★**Porte du Croux** – This handsome square tower gateway with machicolations and corbelled turrets, topped by a high roof, is one of the last remnants of the town's fortifications. It was built in 1393, at the time when the fortifications, set up two centuries earlier by Pierre de Courtenay, were being enlarged.

Eating out

BUDGET

La Botte de Nevers – *R. du Petit-Château - ☎ 03 86 61 16 93 - labotte-denevers@wanadoo.fr - closed 5-28 Aug, Sat lunchtime, Sun evenings and Mon - 17.54/34.30€.* This restaurant close to the Palais Ducal has a traditional decor inspired by the legendary boot of the Duke of Nevers. Dining room with tapestries, sturdy beams, stone walls and imposing fireplace. Traditional cooking.

La Gabare – *58000 Challuy - 3km/1.9mi S of Nevers by N 7 - ☎ 03 86 37 54 23 - closed 18-24 Feb, 26 Jul-20 Aug, 27 Oct-4 Nov, Sun Mon and public holidays - 15.24/35.06€.* This farmhouse converted into a restaurant has retained its old-fashioned character with its beams and fireplace. The three en-suite dining rooms are simply furnished with yellow walls. Simple, unpretentious cuisine with fresh ingredients.

MODERATE

Jean-Michel Couron – *21 r. St-Étienne - ☎ 03 86 61 19 28 - closed 2-17 Jan, 15 Jul-5 Aug, Tue, except evenings Mar-Oct Sun evenings Mon - reservations required - 18.30/39.70€.* Discreetly located in an alley of the old town near the Église St-Étienne, this restaurant has three dining rooms, one of which is crowned by the arches of a former chapel. The inventive cuisine is very popular among gourmets.

Where to stay

MODERATE

La Renaissance – *58470 Magny-Cours - 12km/7.5mi S of Nevers by N 7 - ☎ 03 86 58 10 40 - hotel.la.renaissance@wanadoo.fr - closed 9 Feb-4 Mar, 29 Jul-12 Aug, Sun evenings and Mon - 9 rooms: 76.22/152.45€ - ☲ 12.20€ - restaurant 38.11/67.08€.* In a blissfully quiet setting, this hotel at the entrance to the village has a cosy bar-lounge and a bright dining room extended by a terrace. Comfortable rooms appointed with contemporary furniture. Traditional cuisine.

Holiday Inn – *58470 Magny-Cours - 12km/7.5mi S of Nevers by N 7 - ☎ 03 86 21 22 33 - holiday-inn.magny@wanadoo.fr - ▣ - 68 rooms: 81/96€ - ☲ 10€ - restaurant 16/29€.* Situated near the Magny-Cours racing circuit, this modern hotel adjoins an old farm where you will find the reception. Large, bright rooms. The restaurant is built around the terrace with its pool.

Sport

Karting de Nevers / Magny-Cours-Technopole – *Technopôle - 58470 Magny-Cours - ☎ 03 86 21 26 18 - in high season: daily 10am-8pm; out of season: 2-6pm.* This remarkable 1 100m/1 200ft track is covered with special macadam used for Formula 1 races. Discover the excitement of driving a racing car by jumping into a gleaming go-kart; if you are feeling a touch more intrepid, you can try a more sophisticated model. Or why not go for a spin in the company of an experienced racing driver? Thrills guaranteed...

Sit back and relax

Donald's Pub – *3 r. François-Mitterrand - ☎ 03 86 61 20 36 - summer: Tue-Sun 5.30pm-2am; the rest of the year: Tue-Sun 3.30pm-1am (2am Sat).* This pub has kept all its charm since it opened 22 years ago. Warm, friendly welcome in a setting of old wooden benches.

Le Bistro France – *Sq. de la Résistance - ☎ 03 86 61 45 09 - bistro.france@free.fr - summer: Tue-Sat 11.30am-2am; the rest of the year: Tue-Sat 11.30am-1am - closed mid-Aug to Sep and public holidays.* This smart café has a somewhat unusual decor: elegant coffee tables with flowered tablecloths, colourful clowns' portraits on the walls, a long wooden bench snaking its way along the bar... Jazz concerts twice a month. Heated terrace.

Le Négus – *96 r. François-Mitterrand - ☎ 03 86 61 06 85 - Mon 3-7pm, Tue-Sat 9am-noon, 2-7pm.* This confectionery was named after the *négus*, a delicious sweet made with soft caramel coated with crystallised sugar, but it offers a wide choice of many other delicacies. The Moorish decor is a tribute to the emperor of Abyssinia.

Zapping Club – *16 r. de Charleville -* ☎ *03 86 61 59 07 - Wed-Sat 11pm-4am and the day before public holidays.* Installed in a former garage, this huge bar is lit up and decorated like a night club. The space inside is often rearranged to serve as a venue for a variety of events such as concerts, dance performances, roller competitions...

Domaine Hervé-Seguin – *3 r. Joseph-Renaud - 58150 Pouilly-sur-Loire -* ☎ *03 86 39 10 75 - perso-wanadoo.fr/domaineseguinherve - open daily 10am-noon, 2-7pm.* This estate offers three categories of wine: Pouilly-sur-Loire made with the *chasselas* variety, Pouilly-Fumé made with *sauvignon* and Pouilly-Fumé *cuvée prestige.* There is also a special *cuvée,* matured in oak barrels, called La Barboulotte, named after a local species of ladybird.

The tower houses the **Musée Archéologique du Nivernais** Ⓥ which contains ancient sculptures (Greek and Roman marbles) and a large collection of Romanesque sculptures. *Follow the rampart walk.*

Ph. Gajic/MICHELIN

Porte du Croux

Musée Municipal Frédéric-Blandin Ⓥ – The museum, which is housed in the buildings of an old abbey, has a fine collection of **Nevers pottery★** including pieces in the Italian, Persian, Chinese and Nivernais traditions.
Other pieces include delicate enamels and spun glass from Nevers.
Return to the crossroads and turn right onto rue des Jacobins.

★★**Cathédrale St-Cyr-et-Ste-Julitte** Ⓥ – This vast basilica, displaying all the architectural styles from the 10C to the 16C side by side, was consecrated in 1331 before being completed and then altered several times. The plan is characterised by two apses at opposite ends of the nave: Romanesque to the west and Gothic to the east. This arrangement, which was common in the Carolingian period and is to be found in some cathedrals on the banks of the Rhine, notably at Speyer, Worms and Mainz, is rare in France.

Exterior – Walk round the building which bristles with buttresses, pillars, flying buttresses and pinnacles to see the sequence of the different styles and to admire the square tower (52m/171ft high) standing against the south arm of the transept. The tower is flanked by polygonal buttresses; the lower storey is 14C, and the other two, richly decorated with niches, statues and arcades, are 16C.

Interior – The most striking feature is the sheer size of the 13C nave with its triforium and clerestory and the choir encircled by the ambulatory. The 16C clock has a jack o' the clock.
The Romanesque apse, raised by 13 steps and with oven vaulting, is decorated with a 12C fresco representing Christ surrounded by the symbols of the Evangelists.
The stained-glass windows are the work of five contemporary artists. In 1944, allied bombing damaged the Gothic apse and at the same time revealed a 6C baptistery *(open to visitors).*
The nearby Palais de Justice is a former 18C bishops' palace.

★ **Palais Ducal** – The former home of the dukes of Nevers was begun in the second half of the 15C by Jean de Clamecy, Count of Nevers, who was eager to move out of his old fortress which stood on the site of the present town hall. The new ducal residence was completed at the end of the 16C by the Clèves and Gonzagas. The palace is a most beautiful example of early civil Renaissance architecture. The great round towers at the rear give on to a courtyard that overlooks rue des Ouches. The ochre façade is surmounted by a slate roof and flanked by twin turrets; the beautiful canted tower in the centre rising to a small belfry contains the grand staircase; a most graceful effect is created by the placing of the windows which follow the spiralling of the stairs. The modern bas-relief sculptures recall the legends of St Hubert and of the Knight of the Swan *(Chevalier au cygne),* an

NEVERS

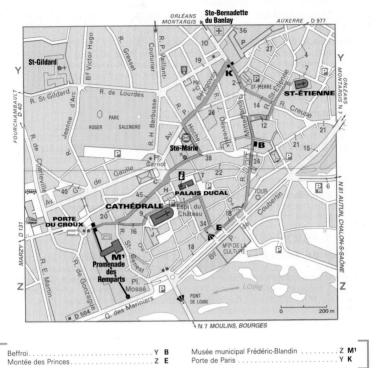

ancestor of the House of Clèves, who inspired the tale of Lohengrin. The dormer windows are flanked by caryatids and the chimneys resemble organ pipes. On the left turret a plaque recalls that several princesses of the Nivernais became queens of Poland.

Montée des Princes – From the terraced garden beyond the esplanade of the Palais Ducal and place de la République, there is a good view of the Loire.

Turn left on quai de Mantoue then rue François-Mitterrand.

Beffroi – The vast 15C belfry, which is dominated by a pointed bell-tower, once housed the covered markets and the council chamber.

Turn right on place Guy-Coquille; turn left on rue St-Étienne.

★**Église St-Étienne** – This beautiful Romanesque church, which once belonged to a priory of Cluny, has remarkable purity and homogeneity of style. It was built from 1063 to 1097, at the instance of Guillaume I, Count of Nevers.
The chevet, best seen from rue du Charnier, has a magnificent tiered arrangement of apse and apsidals. The transept tower, of which only the base remains, was destroyed together with the two towers surmounting the façade, at the time of the French Revolution.
The façade is sober. A line of brackets indicate the former existence of a porch. Apart from the capitals in the ambulatory, the interior is devoid of sculpture but its attraction lies in its fine proportions and the golden colour of the stone. The six bays of the nave are covered by barrel vaulting with transverse arches; there is groined vaulting in the aisles. A Romanesque altar stands in the chancel *(restored)*. The row of windows beneath the vault is of impressive boldness.

Return S; turn right on rue des Francs-Bourgeois and then rue des Ardilliers.

Porte de Paris – This triumphal arch was built in the 18C to commemorate the victory of Fontenoy; verses by Voltaire in praise of Louis XV are engraved on it.

North of the gate turn left on rue Pierre-Bérégovoy, left again on rue Hoche and finally right on rue St-Martin.

Chapelle Ste-Marie – This is the former chapel, now deconsecrated, of the 7th convent of the Visitandines founded in France. At the request of the bishop of Nevers, **Mademoiselle de Bréchard**, a lady of the Nivernais, who had become a nun of the Visitation and Mother Superior of the convent of Moulins, was sent by St Francis of Sales to found this convent.

The façade, of Louis XIII style, is covered with Italian-type ornamentation: niches, entablatures, columns and pilasters.

Rue St-Martin (Maison du Prieur at no 5), rue du 14-Juillet and rue de la Porte-du-Croux lead back to the Porte du Croux.

Promenade des Remparts – A well-conserved section of the town walls, built by Pierre de Courtenay in the 12C, stretches from the Porte du Croux southwards to the Loire. Several of the original towers (Tours du Hâvre, St-Révérien and Gogin) are still standing. From quai des Mariniers, there is a fine view of the Pont de Loire.

ADDITIONAL SIGHTS

St-Gildard ⓥ – *Pilgrimage from April to October.*
It was this convent that Bernadette Soubirous, acclaimed at Lourdes for her many visitations, entered in 1866. She died there in 1879 and was canonised in 1933. Her embalmed body rests in a glass shrine in the chapel of the convent which is the mother house of the Sisters of Charity and Christian Instruction of Nevers.
A small **museum** retraces the saint's life and work and displays some of her personal effects.

Église Ste-Bernadette-du-Banlay ⓥ – *Take avenue Colbert and then rue du Banlay.*
From the outside this church (1966) has all the massive appearance of a blockhouse. Inside however the well-lit nave has a great feeling of spaciousness.

EXCURSION

Circuit de Nevers-Magny-Cours ⓥ – *13km/8mi S.* Between Magny-Cours and St-Parize-le-Châtel, this race track inaugurated in 1960 is the stage for many spectacular automobile and motorcycle races, including the prestigious Grand Prix de France Formula 1 and the Grand Prix de France Moto. The site, which can accommodate 110 000 visitors has been developing over the years and offers a variety of recreational and tourist facilities.

★ **Musée Ligier F1** ⓥ – 🖂 This unique museum devoted to Formula 1 racing displays the cars which made history for the Ligier team. The models on exhibit have all raced and some have won trophies; they bear the initials JS in memory of Jo Schlesser, a friend of Guy Ligier who died in an accident at the Essarts track in Rouen. In the early years, the team, known as the *écurie bleue*, was strongly influenced by the personality and achievements of Jacques Laffite. Before his terrible Brands Hatch accident in 1986, he won several Grands Prix, including the Swedish Grand Prix in 1977 with the JS-7 and the German Grand Prix in 1980 with the JS-11/15. The chronological presentation also offers a look at some recent models, too, such as the JS-39 decorated by illustrator Hugo Pratt and the JS-41 driven by Panis in 1995. In 1996, Panis piloted the JS-43 to victory in Monaco, establishing the team as serious contenders; the following year, Alain Prost bought the team out.
The other section of the building is reserved for **temporary exhibits**. There is a **shop and a movie theatre**, both devoted to car and motorcycle competition.

Musée Ligier F1

NOZEROY ★

Population 422

Michelin map 321: G-6 – Local map see Route des SAPINS

This old market town lies in a picturesque setting, on a solitary hilltop overlooking a vast, pasture-covered plateau. Nozeroy still has a certain old-style flair, along with the more concrete traces of its past such as a 15C gateway (the Porte Nods) and the vestiges of some ramparts north of the town. A medieval festival takes place in July.

Castle seat of the House of Chalon – Nozeroy is tucked up against the ruins of a château, which was built by the most famous member of the Chalon family, Jean l'Antique (the Ancient, 1190-1267). This noble family had several branches – the Chalon-Viennes, Chalon-Auxerres, Chalon-Arlays – and played a very prominent role in the political life of the Franche-Comté. Their history is turbulent; family members fought one another for the leadership of the Comté, joined forces to fight feudal rivals and formed an alliance with the Comté aristocracy to resist the advances of foreign princes. Jean l'Antique put arms, money *(see Salins-les-Bains)*, alliances and diplomacy to his own personal use so skilfully that by the end of his life he had procured over 500 fiefs. His many children, the Chalon-Arlays, inherited the Nozeroy seigneury and expanded its territory still further. Jean de Chalon-Arlay III acquired the title of Prince of Orange through his marriage in 1386.

The château was razed in the 15C and replaced by a magnificent palace, decorated by artists from the court of Burgundy. A century later Philibert, the last of the Chalons, who had attained the rank of commander-in-chief of the Spanish armies and viceroy of Naples, laid on splendid feasts at Nozeroy which drew nobility from all over the province.

Nozeroy and Holland – When Philibert died without issue in 1530, the property of the Chalon family passed to the House of Orange-Nassau, which had links with them. In 1684, a creditor of William of Nassau, *stathouder* of the Netherlands and then king of England, was able to take possession of the prince's domains in the Comté. The Chalon estate is now divided between a number of different families, and the château was completely destroyed during the Revolution.

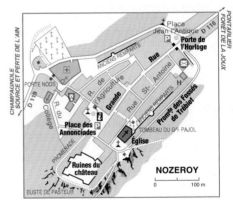

SIGHTS

Porte de l'Horloge – This gateway through a tall square machicolated tower is a remnant of the old fortified curtain wall.

Grande Rue – Several old houses are to be seen along this street.

Place des Annonciades – This square is shaded by a magnificent chestnut tree.

Walk along the tree-lined promenade *(bust of Pasteur)* which leads round the château ruins, providing some beautiful views of the surrounding area.

Église – Most of the church dates from the 15C. Note the 15C stalls and the sculpted wooden pulpit. Lovers of more unusual works of art will appreciate the 17C altar hanging in the right chapel, which was patiently embroidered in woven straw by Nozeroy's Annonciade nuns. Note also the 15C polychrome stone Virgin and Child, against a pillar in the south aisle.

Behind the church is the tomb of Général Pajol (1772-1844).

Promenade des Fossés-de-Trébief – This avenue runs alongside the most interesting section of the old ramparts.

EXCURSION

Mièges – This town grew up around a 16C priory. The inhabitants earn their living mainly from stock raising and cheesemaking. The **church** contains the Late Gothic funerary chapel of the dukes of Chalon; note the ornate pendant keystones on the ceiling.

Close to the church is a small hermitage dedicated to Our Lady, where a pilgrimage takes place twice a year on Whit Monday and on 8 September or on the nearest Sunday to that date.

★ **Source de l'Ain** – *See CHAMPAGNOLE.*

Ornans' history, number of inhabitants and industrial activity justifiably make it the small capital of the Loue Valley which inspired the town's most famous native, the painter Gustave Courbet. The stretch of river flowing between the double row of old houses on piles is one of the prettiest scenes in the Jura.

Riverside living

The Magistrat – Ornans, of which there is no record until the early Middle Ages, received its charter from the lord of Comté in 1244. The town was governed by a municipal council, called the Magistrat, composed of the mayor, four aldermen (now deputies) and 12 members under oath (councillors). These individuals were elected annually by all family heads over the age of 25. The Magistrat designated 12 leading citizens from among the biggest taxpayers to oversee administration of the community. None of these posts were paid. The town had the right to grant sanctuary and made sure that this right was upheld, even by Parliament. In one case, where Parliament had seized a fugitive to imprison him in Dole, the Magistrat brought the affair before Emperor Charles V and had the prisoner returned to sanctuary. Pettifoggery was rife in Ornans, as it was throughout the Comté; the 1 500 inhabitants provided more than enough business for eight barristers, eight solicitors, seven bailiffs and six notaries.

The militia – The men of Ornans were all armed and formed a local militia to defend and keep watch over the château and, if need be, make up a garrison in case of attack. They were less than keen on occupying the feudal towers, which were so well ventilated that they were nicknamed wind-gobblers, or more crudely, bum-coolers. The militia assiduously practised use of the crossbow and the harquebus. There was an annual competition, the victor of which was exempted from the year's taxes. If the same man won three times in a row, he was exempted from paying taxes for the rest of his life.

Processions – Processions were major local events. The priest and 20 chaplains would be at the head, singing loudly, followed by members of the professional guilds in traditional costume with banners, various brotherhoods, penitents in black accompanied by a giant crucifix, young girls in white with flowers in their hair, and women in black with headdresses. Next would come the town sergeants, then the members of the Magistrat, very dignified in their purple robes and caps. The militia would bring up the rear of the procession, with their motley clothes and weapons; despite the beating drums and their purposeful marching and frowning faces, the soldiers nonetheless had a good-natured air.

Gustave Courbet – The great painter Gustave Courbet, master of French Realism, was born in Ornans in 1819. His parents were wine-growers and wanted their son to become a notary, but he eventually abandoned his law books for the painter's easel, teaching himself by studying the paintings in the Louvre. His work provoked a storm of both praise and criticism. He was strongly attached to Ornans and found most of his subjects in and around his birthplace. Landscapes such as *Château d'Ornans* and *Source de la Loue* capture the essence of nature in the Jura. The subjects of his portraits were friends or members of his family; *L'Après-Dînée à Ornans* and *Un* *enterrement à Ornans* are particularly interesting as historical documents. He excelled at psychological portraits, especially of women, such as *L'Exilée polonaise*. In 1868 he made the acquaintance of the painter Wilhelm Leibl, who had been honoured with a gold medal at the Paris Salon, and they became friends.

Courbet was as revolutionary in his politics as he was in his painting. In 1871 he took part in the Paris Commune. He was held responsible for the toppling of the Vendôme column and condemned to six months imprisonment and to a 500 francs fine. In 1873, he was fined a further 323 000 francs for the cost of replacing the column. Financially ruined, revolted by the horrors he had witnessed, no longer able to exhibit his work – the Paris Salon, which was vitally influential in painters' careers at the time, returned his paintings without even looking at them – and all too conscious of the public censure surrounding him, he went into exile in Switzerland in 1873. He died there in 1877, at La Tour-de-Peilz near Vevey, a broken man. His body was brought back to the Ornans cemetery in 1919.

Special **festivities** are put on in Ornans each summer in memory of this painter.

The Route Courbet leads visitors on a tour of the wild Loue Valley which captivated the artist; reproductions of his paintings are exhibited in seven different places along the way.

ORNANS

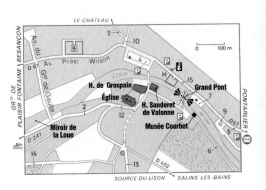

SIGHTS

Grand Pont – This great bridge is the most famous spot in Ornans, with its picturesque **view**★ of the town's old houses reflected in the Loue.

On your way to the church, note two fine mansions: the 17C **Hôtel Sanderet de Valonne** (façade and gate) and the 15C **Hôtel de Grospain** used for a long time as the town hall.

Church ⊘ – The church was rebuilt in the 16C, retaining only the lower part of the 12C bell-tower from the original Romanesque building. The dome and the lantern turret date from the 17C. The church was funded by the Chancellor and the Cardinal of Granvelle, who furthermore ensured that it received a regular contribution for 30 years from the sovereign, in the form of revenue from the sale of 10 loads of salt shipped from Salins every week.

Miroir de la Loue – *Beyond the church, take rue du Champliman along the river bank.*
The pretty stretch of water seen from the bridge downstream of the old town is known as the Loue Mirror. Church, town and cliffs are reflected in the water's silvery surface.

Musée Courbet ⊘ – The museum is in the house where Courbet was born, a beautiful 18C building which used to be the Hôtel Hébert. Works by the artist are exhibited (Jura landscapes, drawings, sculptures), as well as by his students and friends. There are also many objects evoking 19C artistic life in Paris and in the Franche-Comté. Note in particular the *Autoportrait à Ste-Pélagie*, his famous self-portrait painted in prison, and the landscapes *Château Chillon* and *La Papeterie d'Ornans sur le ruisseau de Bonneille*. The rooms downstairs are used for temporary exhibitions.

AROUND ORNANS

Point de vue du Château – *2km/1.2mi N up a steep narrow road.* Fine view of Ornans and the Loue Valley.

Montgesoye – *4km/2.5mi SE.* **Musée du Costume comtois** ⊘ (regional costume museum).

Vuillafans – *7km/4.3mi SE.* Old houses, once the homes of merchants or aristocrats, are still standing here. A charming 16C bridge spans the Loue.

Eating out and where to stay

MODERATE

Château d'Amondans – *25330 Amondans - 12km/7.5mi SW of Ornans by D 101 then D 103 -* ☎ *03 81 86 53 14 - chef@chateau-amondans.com - closed 2 Jan-19 Mar, 11-19 Aug, Wed end of Sep to early Jun and Sun evenings - reservations required - 31/59€.* This stately mansion in a small village lost in the Doubs countryside has undeniable charm. The self-contained guestrooms have been set up in a separate building. The dining room is adorned with old paintings and the meals are lovingly prepared. Swimming pool and park.

Hôtel de France – *R. P.-Vernier -* ☎ *03 81 62 24 44 - hoteldefrance@euro-post.org - closed 15 Dec-13 Feb Sun evenings and Mon except school holidays -* 🅿 *- 26 rooms: 54/80€ -* ☕ *8€ - restaurant 29/37€.* Handsome country residence standing on the slope of a hill, opposite the bridge spanning the River Loue. The rooms giving onto the garden are more peaceful. The dining room is rustic in style, with its exposed beams, fireplace and wood panelling.

▶▶ **Trépot** – *12.5km/8mi N.* **Musée de la Fromagerie** 🕐 (cheese museum).

▶▶ **Gouffre de Poudrey** 🕐 – *14km/9mi NE.* 🖼 Swallow-hole *(150 steps)* with *son et lumière* show.

▶▶ **Dino-Zoo★** 🕐 – *At Charbonnières-les-Sapins, 5km/3mi SW of the Gouffre de Poudrey.* 🖼 Life-size plastic dinosaurs.

FROM ORNANS TO QUINGEY

35km/22mi – allow 3hr

This route follows some charming little roads along the banks of the Loue for the most part, but which wander away from the river in some places. The trip is at its most picturesque between Cléron and the confluence of the Loue and the Lison.

Leave Ornans on D 67 W; after 2.5km/1.5mi take D 101 to the left.

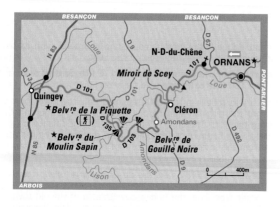

Chapelle de Notre-Dame-du-Chêne – The chapel can be seen from D 101. It was built to celebrate a miraculous revelation in 1803, when a young girl from the area claimed that there was a statue of the Virgin Mary in the trunk of a certain oak tree. The tree was opened up, and an old terracotta Madonna was indeed found inside, the tree bark having grown over it. The statuette, kept in the chapel, has drawn pilgrims ever since – on Whit Monday, the Sunday of Corpus Christi, 15 August (Assumption) and the following Wednesday and the first Sunday in September. A bronze Virgin now stands on the spot where the oak once grew.

Miroir de Scey – *Follow the signs from the road.*
This is the name given to a beautiful meander in the Loue, where the trees and plants on the river banks, and the ruins of a fortress, Châtel-St-Denis, are reflected in the river's waters (*miroir* means mirror).

Cléron – From the bridge over the Loue a well-preserved 14C-16C **château★** 🕐 comes into sight downstream. With its reflection in the river and surrounded by its grounds, it makes a beautiful picture. There is a pretty view of the valley upstream.
The local cheese manufacture, **Le Hameau du Fromage** 🕐, offers guided tours ending with a cheese-tasting session and the possibility of buying what you taste.

There are three viewpoints *(car parks)* between Amondans and the confluence of the Loue and the Lison, all at the edge of cliffs overlooking the river valley which is narrow and deserted at this point.

Belvédère de Gouille-Noire – View of the Amondans stream directly below. This small tributary of the Loue flows between two rocky spurs.

★ **Belvédère de la Piquette** – *15min round trip on foot from D 135.*
🚶 *Follow a wide path for about 100m/110yd, then take the path on the right; turn right at the edge of the cliff.*
There is a **view** of a meander in the Loue, as it swirls around a wooded spur between steep banks.

★ **Belvédère du Moulin-Sapin** – *Beside D 135.* There is a beautiful **view** of the peaceful Lison Valley.
The bridge crosses the Lison

Château de Cléron

just after it flows into the Loue, in a lovely calm **setting**★. The source of the Lison near Nans-sous-Sainte-Anne is one of the most famous sights in the Jura. Soon, the old Châtillon forge comes into sight from the road. Upstream of the dam, there is a pretty view of some little wooded islands.

Quingey – A path, bordered with plane trees, runs along the south bank of the Loue; the view of the little market town on the opposite bank reflected in the water is especially enchanting in the early morning.

PARAY-LE-MONIAL★★

Population 9 191
Michelin map 320: E-11

Paray-le-Monial, cradle of the worship of the Sacred Heart of Jesus, is situated on the boundary between the Charollais and Brionnais regions, on the banks of the River Bourbince beside which flows the Canal du Centre.
The town's Romanesque basilica, where a music festival is held in summer, is a magnificent example of the architecture of Cluny. The building materials industry, which is concentrated in the valley of the Bourbince, is represented at Paray by factories producing tiles and sandstone pavings as well as fire bricks.

Marguerite-Marie Alacoque– Although her desire to become a nun was obvious at a very early age, Marguerite-Marie Alacoque, the daughter of a royal notary in Verosvres-en-Charollais, could not carry out her intention until she was 24.
On 20 June 1671 she entered the convent of the Visitation at Paray-le-Monial as a novice and two months later took the veil.
From 1673 onwards, Sister Marguerite-Marie received a succession of visitations that continued up to her death. Helped by her confessor, Father Claude de la Colombière, she revealed the messages she had received – writing out the revelations that were made to her: "Here is this heart, which so loved mankind" – thus initiating the worship of the Sacred Heart in France. She died on 17 October 1690.

Devotion to the Sacred Heart – It was not until the beginning of the 19C, when the turmoil of the French Revolution had died down, that devotion to the Sacred Heart made any significant progress. In 1817 hearings began before the Vatican Tribunals which ended in 1864 with the beatification of Sister Marguerite-Marie. In 1873, when the first great pilgrimage in Paray-le-Monial took place in the presence of 30 000 people, the decision was made to dedicate France to the Sacred Heart of Jesus. This event was linked to the vow made in 1870 to build a church dedicated to the Sacred Heart with money raised by national subscription; this was the basilica of Sacré-Cœur which now stands on the hill of Montmartre. Pilgrimages have been repeated each year since 1873. Sister Marguerite-Marie was canonised in 1920.
Many religious orders have communities at Paray-le-Monial which has become one of the great centres of Christianity.
Pope John-Paul II visited Paray in October 1986.

PILGRIMAGE AND SACRED ART

★★ **Basilique du Sacré-Cœur** – On the right bank of the Bourbince, approached by a promenade flanked by flowers and weeping willows, stands the church; it was originally dedicated to the Virgin Mary but in 1875 it was raised to the level of a basilica and consecrated to the Sacred Heart.

The church was built without interruption between 1092 and 1109 under the direction of St Hugues, Abbot of Cluny, and restored in the 19C and 20C; it constitutes a contemporary model on a smaller scale of the famous Benedictine abbey at Cluny. Only the architectural style is similar; the builders eschewed decorative splendour and large-scale design to the glory of God, in favour of abstract beauty,

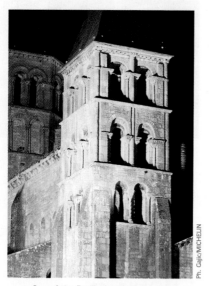

Ph. Gajic/MICHELIN

One of the Basilica's square towers

composed of the rhythmic combination of light and shadow, space and simplicity, which is conducive to contemplation. The rare sculptures make generous use of the geometric motifs found in Islamic art; its enchanting perfection was probably discovered by St Hugues during two visits to Spain.

From the bridge spanning the Bourbince there is a fine view of the basilica; its golden stone is used in many of the churches in the neighbouring Brionnais.

Exterior – Two butressed square towers surmount the narthex, with four storeys of windows; the first tier lights the narthex.

The right-hand tower, built in the early 11C, has sober decoration; the tower on the left, which is of a later date, is more richly decorated – the upper storeys are separated by a moulded cornice and the third storey is pierced by two twinned openings, divided by columns ornamented with capitals; on the top storey, the arch of the opening is formed by two recessed orders instead of three, whereas the capitals of the small columns are joined by a cordon of ovoli (quarter-section mouldings) and lozenges. The octagonal tower which stands over the transept crossing was restored in 1856.

A good vantage point from which to admire the decorative harmony of the chevet is the top of the steps of the old Maison des Pages which now houses the Chambre des Reliques.

Enter the basilica by the north arm of the transept; the beautiful Romanesque doorway is decorated with floral and geometric designs.

Interior – One is struck by the height of the building (22m/72ft in the main nave) and the simplicity of its decoration, characteristic of the art of Cluny. Huysmans (French novelist, 1848-1907) saw the symbol of the Trinity in the three naves, three bays supporting above the great arches three arcades surmounted by three windows. The choir and its ambulatory with three small apses – the Gallery of the Angels – make an elegant ensemble. The historiated capitals of the delicate columns are a typical example of 12C Burgundian art. The oven-vaulted apse is decorated with a 14C fresco, representing a benedictory Christ in Majesty, which was brought to light only in 1935. The transept crossing is covered by a dome on squinches.

Musée du Hiéron ⊘ – The theme of this museum of sacred art is the Eucharist reflected in the life of Christ, the Virgin Mary and the saints. The collection of 13C to 18C Italian art includes primitive paintings; works from the schools of Florence (Donatello, Bramante), Venice, Rome and Bologna; sculptures including a 13C Tuscan Christ and a 13C and 16C ivory eucharistic tabernacle; and gold- and silver-ware. There are also a few works from Flanders and Germany (engravings by Lucas of Leyden and Dürer) as well as from France; a very beautiful 12C **tympanum**★ from the Brionnais priory at Anzy-le-Duc. In the revolutionary turmoil of 1791 the doorway was transported to the park of Château d'Arcy and then given to the Hiéron Museum. The tympanum shows Christ in Majesty enthroned in a mandorla supported by two angels. On the lintel the Virgin Mary bares her breast to the Infant Jesus in her lap; to the left are four virgins bearing a crown and to the right are four Apostles and disciples. The technical achievement of the sculpture is as remarkable as its iconographic richness.

Liturgical items: gold- and silver-ware, ivory, enamels.

Chambre des Reliques – In the former house of the pages of Cardinal de Bouillon, many souvenirs of St Marguerite-Marie have been assembled in a relics chamber. The saint's cell has been faithfully reconstructed.

Parc des Chapelains ⊘ – It is in this large park, containing Stations of the Cross, that the great pilgrimage services take place. A **diorama** in the park depicts the life of St Marguerite-Marie.

Chapelle de la Visitation ⊘ – It was in this little chapel, also called the Sanctuary of the Apparitions, that St Marguerite-Marie received her principal revelations. The silver-gilt reliquary in the chapel on the right contains the relics of the saint.

ADDITIONAL SIGHTS

★ **Hôtel de ville** – The façade of this fine Renaissance mansion, built in 1525 by a rich draper, is decorated with shells and medallion portraits of French kings.

Tour St-Nicolas – This 16C square tower was originally the belfry of the church of St-Nicolas, now deconsecrated. The façade which overlooks place Lamartine is adorned with a beautiful wrought-iron staircase and a corbelled turret at the apex of the gable.

Eating out

MODERATE

Restaurant La Poste et Hôtel La Reconce – *71600 Poisson - 8km/5mi S of Paray-le-Monial by D 34 - ☎ 03 85 81 10 72 - closed Feb, 30 Sep-17 Oct, Mon and Tue except evenings in Jul-Aug - 19.90/72€.* The restaurant set up in a stone cottage consists of a dining room extended by a verandah and a summer terrace. Interesting menus. The comfortable rooms with waxed flooring and cherry wood furniture are housed in a restored 1900 building nearby.

Where to stay

BUDGET

Chambre d'Hôte M. et Mme Mathieu – *Sermaize - 71600 Poisson - 12.5km/7.8mi SE of Paray-le-Monial by D 34 then D 458 (heading for St-Julien-de-Civry) - ☎ 03 85 81 06 10 - closed 11 Nov-15 Mar - ⊠ - 5 rooms: 42/54€ - meals 16€.* This 14C hunting lodge stands proudly in its garden, adorned by a round turret and a square courtyard bursting with flowers. An old-fashioned spiral staircase will take you to the personalised rooms featuring parquet flooring, period furniture and a fireplace. The garden looks out over the surrounding countryside.

EXCURSION

Digoin– *11km/6.8mi W.* This peaceful town, lying on the east bank of the Loire at the junction of two canals, is sought after by anglers, ramblers and those who enjoy river-cruising. The early-19C **canal-bridge** was built 50 years before the Briare Bridge. The **Musée de la Céramique** ⊘, housed in a former 18C inn, illustrates the history of ceramics from the Gallo-Roman period to the present (25 000 items) and the different manufacturing techniques from casting to firing. There is also a fine collection of rocks and fossils.

COUNTRY INN IN TOWN

La Gare – *79 av. du Gén.-de-Gaulle, Digoin - ☎ 03 85 53 03 04 - jean-pierre.mathieu@worldonline.fr - closed Jan, Wed except Jul-Aug and Sun evenings in winter - 17/58€.* A typical country inn extending a warm and friendly welcome. The cooking is thoughtful with a strong regional touch. As for the rooms, they are gradually being renovated to make your stay here even more agreeable.

Digoine: Château and park ⊘ – The main entrance to the château, built in the 18C on the site of a defensive castle, is fronted by a courtyard with a wrought-iron gate. On each side, two pavilions form the wings of the main building. The side facing the park offers a view of two corner towers that were part of the original fortress. The large park has a lake and there are three marked footpaths to guide you around it.

POLIGNY

Population 5 081
Michelin map 321: E-5

This small town, lying at the entrance to a blind valley, the Culée de Vaux, and overlooked by the Croix du Dan has justly earned itself a reputation as the capital of Comté cheese with a dairy industry school and research centre.

Good wines, produced from the rich surrounding farmland for centuries, have greatly contributed to Poligny's prosperity.

The early wine-growers built their homes inside a fortified curtain wall and were under the additional protection of the nearby fortress at Grimont, the ruins of which can still be seen. This fortress belonged to the Comté lords, who kept their records here along with a dungeon for rebellious vassals.

The Grimont dungeons certainly did not lie idle during the reign of the great dukes of Burgundy, since the independent lords of the Comté would keep taking up arms to resolve issues, without first obtaining the permission of their sovereign duke. To uphold their authority, the dukes of Burgundy had declared the Comtois nobility subject to the jurisdiction of the Dole Parliament, which was quite capable of sentencing an insubordinate lord to a 20-year spell in jail, or even to death.

The power struggle came to a head on one occasion in 1455, when Philip the Good imposed a tax of two francs on each household on each seigneury. This was greeted with universal outrage. In particular Jean de Grandson, seigneur of Pesmes, made no secret of his anger; he was forthwith seized and imprisoned in the Grimont fortress where, on being condemned to death by the Dole Parliament, he was suffocated between two mattresses.

Richelieu ordered the invasion of the Franche-Comté in 1635, unleashing the Ten Years War. The town of Poligny was captured and burned by French troops three years later.

Jacques Coitier, Louis XI's crafty doctor, was born in Poligny. Once he fell out of favour, he had reason to fear for his life, until he persuaded his royal patient that he would die three days after his doctor.

Eating out

BUDGET

Le Chalet – *7 rte de Genève - ☎ 03 84 37 13 28 - closed 10-20 Oct, Wed evenings and Thu except Jul-Aug - 10.52€ lunch - 14.49/32€.* Local specialities such as cheese fritters or chicken with morels cooked in white wine are served in this unpretentious restaurant, which extends a warm and inviting welcome. The best Jura wines can be drunk by the bottle, the glass or the pitcher.

La Maison du Haut – *Les Bordes - 39230 St-Lothain - 6km/3.7mi SW of Poligny by D 259 then a minor road - ☎ 03 84 37 35 19 - michel.nicod@libertysurf.fr - reservations required - 12/15€.* This delightful 18C farm in a quiet, secluded spot serves carefully prepared local delicacies in a friendly, family atmosphere. Dormitory for short breaks and simple but pleasantly appointed rooms for those who want to stay longer. Stables and park for horses.

Where to stay

MODERATE

Chambre d'Hôte La Ferme du Château – *R. de la Poste - 39800 Bersaillin - 9km/5.6mi W of Poligny by N 83 then D 22 - ☎ 03 84 25 91 31 - closed Jan - 9 rooms: 52€ - ☕ 5€ - meals 9.15€.* A delightful stay is guaranteed in this 18C farmhouse which has been elegantly restored. The rooms are comfortable and tastefully furnished; they give out onto the leafy countryside, facing both east and west. Painting exhibitions and concerts in summer.

SIGHTS

★ **Collégiale St-Hippolyte** ⌚ – The main doorway beneath the porch features a 15C polychrome stone Virgin on the central pillar. Above this, a low relief depicts St Hippolytus being quartered. On the doorway to the right of the main entrance, a 15C *Pietà* stands on an emblazoned corbel. Inside, note the remarkable wooden calvary on the rood beam above the chancel entrance, and the beautiful collection of 15C Burgundian School **statues★**.

Couvent des Clarisses – *Behind the church.* The entrance is through a great brown door. The convent was founded in 1415 by St Colette. Her relics are in a shrine in the **chapel** which was rebuilt after the Revolution.

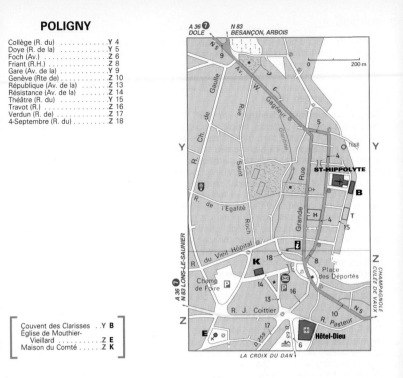

Église de Mouthier-Vieillard ⊙ – All that remains of this 11C Romanesque church are the chancel, part of the transept and the bell-tower surmounted by a 13C stone spire. Of interest inside: a 1534 alabaster altarpiece, a 14C polychrome wooden calvary and some 13C and 15C statues, including one of St Anthony.

Hôtel-Dieu ⊙ – This 17C hospice still has its original cloisters, pharmacy (Nevers and Poligny faience) and vaulted refectory.

Maison du Comté ⊙ – This centre houses a cooperative committee for the promotion of Comté cheese and well as an exhibition outlining the various processes in the making of Comté, from the delivery of the milk to the final ripening of the cheese. Technical progress in the production of this cheese can be followed in the display of machines and other equipment (copper tubs, presses, curd-cutters, churns). An audio-visual presentation shows the landscapes and daily activities of the cheese-producing region.

▶▶ **Croix du Dan** – *3km/1.7mi S along D 68 then left onto D 256*. Alt 511m/1 677ft. ◪ Viewpoint next to the cross *(15min on foot there and back)*; panorama of Poligny at the entrance of its blind valley.

PONTARLIER

Population 18 360
Michelin map 321: I-5

Pontarlier lies near the Swiss border at the foot of the Jura mountains. The town, once famous for the manufacture of absinthe, an aperitif with a very high alcohol content banned in 1915, is today a popular resort both for summer holidays and winter sports.

From the Middle Ages to the 17C – From the 11C, the history of Pontarlier was closely linked to the turbulent relationships between the lords of Salins and of Joux, and between the abbeys of Montbenoît and Mont-Sainte-Marie.
In the mid-13C, Pontarlier and the 18 nearby villages formed a small administrative and ecclesiastical community, the **Baroichage**. Pontarlier's merchant class were the driving force behind this move, which resulted in only minimal independence. The town's economy expanded until the 17C, largely due to the international trade route provided by the nearby pass over the Jura into Switzerland (the Col de Jougne) and four annual fairs.

The anni horribiles: 1639 and 1736 – During the Ten Years War, mercenary troops on the French payroll spread terror and destruction throughout the Franche-Comté. On 26 January 1639, Pontarlier surrendered after a four-day siege led by Bernard de Saxe-Weimar's Swedish forces. The town was pillaged, burned, and over 400 people died.

345

During the 18C, Pontarlier was damaged several times by fire, which caught hold quickly as the town's buildings were largely made of wood. The worst of the fires occurred on 31 August 1736, destroying half the town. As a result of this, Pontarlier was reconstructed following plans by engineer Querret.

Pontarlier became part of France in 1678, when Franche-Comté was officially annexed under the Nijmegen Treaty.

Mirabeau's romantic adventure – In 1776 the Marquis de Monnier, the former president of the Cour des Comptes, retired to spend the summer with his young bride Sophie de Ruffey at his country seat, the Château de Nans near the source of the Lison. The ex-president at the age of 75 had married this 20-year-old woman, who, with only a small dowry, had presumably preferred marriage to a man old enough to be her grandfather to life in a convent. It is hardly surprising, therefore, that a regular guest at the couple's home, namely Mirabeau, supposedly imprisoned at the Château de Joux but nonetheless permitted considerable freedom, all too keenly struck up a friendship with Sophie. The liaison was discovered, and the lovers had to flee the wrath of the Marquis.

The pair had made contingency plans for just such an event. Sophie made a particularly daring escape; at dead of night she slipped through the grounds of the château disguised as a man, climbed over the wall by means of an opportunely placed ladder and leaped onto a conveniently tethered horse which carried her to meet Mirabeau waiting for her on the Swiss border. However, despite the 10 000 livres which were waiting safely for them in Switzerland, having been stolen from the Marquis de Monnier bit by bit and sent on ahead, the couple found they were not able to start an idyllic new life together as they had planned. The Pontarlier tribunal, unmoved by this tale of true love, sentenced, in their absence, the seducer to death and the unfaithful spouse to a lifetime's exile in a convent.

The fugitives were arrested on their way to Amsterdam and brought back to France. Sophie was packed off to the convent in Gien, while Mirabeau managed to save his skin by paying 40 000 livres compensation to the Marquis de Monnier and spending four years imprisoned in the castle at Vincennes. He got himself transferred to the prison at Pontarlier in 1782, and appeared before the tribunal pleading his own defence. After a long and difficult struggle, he got the original sentence annulled.

The flame of romance had died, however, and even Mirabeau's *Lettres à Sophie*, penned while he was incarcerated at Vincennes, could not persuade her to leave her convent for him.

Eating out

MODERATE

La Gourmandine – *1 av. de l'Armée-de-l'Est -* ☎ *03 81 46 65 89 - closed 30 Jan-6 Feb, 1-9 May, 1-18 Jul Tue evenings and Wed - 19.50/37€*. This restaurant located on a main road opposite the Nestlé factories serves copious traditional cuisine. There are several menus, including a special one for children.

Where to stay

BUDGET

Hôtel du Parc – *1 r. du Moulin-Parnet -* ☎ *03 81 46 85 92 - closed 31 Dec-15 Jan and Sun evenings Oct-Mar - 19 rooms: 37/54€ -* ☑ *5.50€*. This hotel a few steps from the busy town centre is a convenient stopping place if you need to spend the night in Pontarlier. The prices are quite reasonable. Choose the renovated rooms as the others are a little bit outdated.

Regional specialities

Distillerie Pierre-Guy – *49 r. des Lavaux -* ☎ *03 81 39 04 70 - www.pontarlier-anis.com - Tue-Sat 9-11.30am, 2.30-5pm - closed 1 week mi-Oct and 1 week beginning of Jan*. This is one of the last two non-industrial distilleries remaining in Pontarlier. Come and see how apéritifs, liquors and brandies are concocted, especially those made with aniseed or gentian. A fascinating experience.

Les Fils d'Émile Pernot – *44 r. de Besançon -* ☎ *03 81 39 04 28 - Mon-Fri 8.30am-noon, 2-6pm - closed public holidays*. Learn everything about the manufacture of liquors and brandies, from the picking of plants right up to the finished product. Local specialities include *Vieux Pontarlier* (aniseed apéritif) and *Sapin* (liquor made with pine flowers).

Fromagerie de Doubs – *1 r. de la Fruitière - 25300 Doubs -* ☎ *03 81 39 05 21 - Mon-Sat 8am-noon, 2-7pm, Sun 10-11am, 6-7pm*. This cheese-making factory will show you how local cheeses like Comté, Morbier and Mont d'Or are prepared and matured in the traditional manner. Tastings are organised on the premises. And don't forget to stop by the shop on your way out.

PONTARLIER

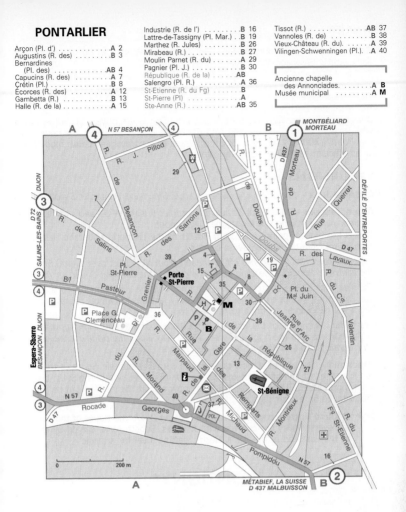

SIGHTS

Ancienne chapelle des Annonciades – This chapel, all that remains of the Annunciade convent, was built in 1612. The **doorway★** dates from the beginning of the 18C. The chapel, now deconsecrated, has been turned into an exhibition centre.

Porte St-Pierre – This triumphal arch was erected in 1771, based on plans by Arçon, to celebrate the reconstruction of the city; the upper section, topped with a small bell-tower, was added in the 19C.
It resembles the Porte St-Martin in Paris, which commemorates the French conquest of Franche-Comté in 1678.

Église St-Bénigne – The church was rebuilt in the 17C and then restored, but it still has an original 15C Flamboyant side doorway.
This curious building has a blind façade on its right side, built after the 1736 fire to make the church blend in with the new houses round the square. The belfry-porch is in the style of mountain churches designed to withstand heavy snowfall.
Inside are two particularly interesting paintings either side of the chancel: that to the left, which depicts Christ surrounded by angels bearing the instruments of the Passion; and that to the right, known as *The Miracle of Lactation* (the Virgin Mary is seen pressing her breast, from which a stream of milk flows to wet the lips of St Bernard). Note also the 1754 pulpit, skilfully carved by the Guyon brothers of Pontarlier; a 17C recumbent Christ; the 18C Black Madonna of Einsiedeln, which was worshipped throughout the Haut-Doubs region; and the 1758 organ case, also the work of the Guyon brothers.
Manessier's 1975 stained-glass **windows★**, with the Paschal Symphony as their theme, harmonise well with the architecture of the church.

Musée Municipal ⊘ – The museum, housed in what was a bourgeois home, built in the 16C and later modified several times (French-style ceilings with painted beams, Art Nouveau windows), is devoted to local history, 19C and 20C Comtois paintings (including *Autoportrait au chien* by Courbet), 18C faience, and objects related to the history of absinthe (posters, engravings, miscellaneous exhibits).

Espera-Sbarro ⊙ – *Take the ring road (Rocade G.-Pompidou) outside of Pontarlier towards Besançon-Montbéliard (N 57).*

⊙ This 4 000m²/4 784sq ft showroom has some very special automobiles on view. They are the work of Franco Sbarro, who transforms every day cars into hot rods and brings legendary models back to life in replica, such as the Ford GT 40, or the Mercedes 540 K. But his imagination really goes for broke in the futuristic prototypes like the *Monster*, a super-powerful four-wheel-drive, 350 horsepower, with its own spare... motorcycle! And the magic is at work under the hood, too: the *Robur* (200 hp), *Chrono* (500 hp), *Isatis* and extravagant *Oxalis* models are all as efficient as they are brightly colourful.

EXCURSIONS

★★ **Cluse de Joux** – *See Château de Joux. 4km/2.5mi; leave Pontarlier S along N 57.*

★★ **Grand Taureau** – *11km/7mi E. Leave Pontarlier S along N 57 and turn left onto a minor road climbing the Montagne du Larmont.*

This is the highest point (1 323m/4 340ft) of the Larmont mountains, less than 1km/0.5mi from the Franco-Swiss border.

Take the road which branches off to the left from N 57, just over 1km/0.5mi S of the centre of Pontarlier, leading up to the ruins of the Larmont-Supérieur fortress.

The **view**★ from here stretches over Pontarlier and the Jura plateaux to the west. The Larmont is equipped with all the necessary facilities for winter sports holidays. For a full panorama, continue to the very top.

Leave the car in front of the little chalet at the end of the road. Climb up the slope which borders it to the right and walk a little way along the ridge overlooking the Morte Valley, continuation of the Val de Travers.

★★ **Panorama** – The all round view takes in the parallel mountain ridges of the Jura, as far as the last line of mountains looming on the other side of the Swiss border, from the Chasseral to Mont Tendre. The snow-capped Berne Alps can be seen in the distance on a clear day.

▶▶ **Défilé d'Entreportes** – *4km/2.5mi E along D 47.* The slopes of this verdant transverse valley are covered with fir trees. Superb rocks carved by erosion at the east end of the *cluse*. Restful setting ideal for a picnic.

PONTIGNY★

Population 748
Michelin map 319: F-4

This little village on the edge of the River Serein is celebrated for its former abbey, the second daughter house of Cîteaux, founded in 1114. Whereas Cîteaux is now in ruins, the abbey of Pontigny (a retraining centre since 1968) has preserved its church intact. Concerts of ancient music take place in summer.

HISTORICAL NOTES

The foundation – At the beginning of the year 1114 twelve monks with the Abbot Hugues de Mâcon at their head were sent from Cîteaux by St Stephen to found a monastery on the banks of the Serein, in a large clearing at a place known as Pontigny. The abbey was situated on the boundaries of three bishoprics (Auxerre, Sens and Langres) and three provinces (counties of Auxerre, Tonnerre and Champagne) and thus from its beginning benefited from the protection and the generosity of six different masters. An old saying recalls that three bishops, three counts and an abbot could dine on the bridge of Pontigny, each one remaining on his own territory. Thibault the Great, Count of Champagne, was the abbey's most generous benefactor: in 1150 he gave the abbot the means to build a larger church than that existing at the time (the chapel of St Thomas), which had become too small for the monks. He enclosed the abbey buildings with a wall (4m/13ft high) sections of which still remain.

A refuge for archbishops – During the Middle Ages Pontigny served as a refuge for ecclesiastics fleeing from persecution in England; three archbishops of Canterbury found asylum there. **Thomas à Becket**, Primate of England, came to Pontigny in 1164 having incurred the anger of his sovereign, Henry II. He returned to his country in 1170 but was murdered in his cathedral two years later.

Stephen Langton took refuge at Pontigny from 1208 to 1213 because of a disagreement with King John.

Edmund Rich, St Edmund of Abingdon, lived in Pontigny in saintly exile for several years until his death in 1240, when he was buried in the abbey church. He was canonised in 1246 and is venerated throughout the region (known locally as St Edme).

Ph. Gajic/MICHELIN

The southern façade

The decades of Pontigny – Abandoned during the French Revolution, the abbey served as a quarry for the nearby villages up to 1840. The ruins were then bought back by the Archbishop of Sens and put at the disposition of the Congregation of Missionary Fathers founded by Father Muard *(see Le MORVAN: Excursion* ②*, Abbaye de la Pierre-qui-Vire)* who restored the church and other buildings.

At the start of the 20C, the fathers were expelled and the property was bought by the philosopher, Paul Desjardins (1859-1940), who organised the famous *Décades* which brought together the most eminent personalities of the period including Thomas Mann, André Gide, TS Eliot and François Mauriac, who had lengthy literary conversations in the celebrated avenue of arbours.

★THE ABBEY *30min*

Opposite the War Memorial in the village, an 18C entrance flanked by small pavilions, opens into a shady avenue which leads past the conventual buildings to the abbey church.

★ **Church** ⊘ – Built in the second half of the 12C in the transitional Gothic style by Thibault, Count of Champagne, this church is austere, in conformity with the Cistercian rule. Of impressive size (108m/354ft long inside, 117m/384ft with the porch, and 52m/171ft wide at the transept), it is almost as large as Notre-Dame in Paris.

Exterior – A lean-to porch, festooned with arcades standing on consoles and small columns, takes up the whole width of the façade. Closed at the sides, it is pierced by twin, double-semicircular bays and a central doorway with a low arch.

The façade, decorated with a tall lancet window and two blind arcades, ends in a pointed gable with a small oculus. The sides of the church are typically bare; no belfry breaks the long line of the roof. The transept and the aisles are of a great simplicity; flat-sided buttresses and flying buttresses support the chevet and the north side.

Interior – The long, two-storey nave has seven bays; it is the earliest Cistercian nave with pointed vaulting to have survived to the present day. The perspective of the nave is interrupted by the wooden screen of the monks' choir.

The squat side aisles of groined vaulting contrast with the more unrestricted nave. The transept, lit at either end by a rose window, is very characteristic with its six rectangular chapels opening on to each arm of the transept.

The choir, rebuilt at the end of the 12C, is very graceful with its ambulatory and its 11 apsidal chapels. The crocketed capitals of the monolithic columns are more elaborate than those of the nave where water-lily leaves, of somewhat rudimentary design, constitute the main decorative element.

At the end of the choir under a heavy baldaquin is the 18C shrine of St Edmund; the earlier wooden shrine, made during the Renaissance, is kept in one of the apsidal chapels.

The beautiful **stalls★**, the transept grille and the organ case date from the end of the 17C. The organ loft, which is heavily ornamented, the choir parclose and the altar date from the end of the 18C.

Monastery buildings – All that is left of the 12C Cistercian buildings is the wing of the lay brothers' building; the rubblestone and delicate Tonnerre stone harmonise well in the façade, which is supported by buttresses.

Of the other buildings, only the southern gallery of the cloisters, rebuilt in the 17C, remains today *(access via the church)*.

POUILLY-EN-AUXOIS

Population 1 502
Michelin map 320: H-6

This small town lies at the foot of Mont de Pouilly, at the exit of the tunnel through which the Canal de Bourgogne flows from the Rhône basin to the Seine basin. It is the ideal starting point of excursions through the surrounding area.

Warping – Barges are towed through the tunnel (3 333m/3 645yd long) by means of an underwater chain. The first steam-powered warping tug was inaugurated in 1867. Information is available from the new **Centre d'interprétation du canal**.

Watershed line – All the water streaming down the southern slopes of Mont Pouilly runs to the Mediterranean sea; all the water streaming down the northern slopes head for the River Seine and the North sea, whereas all the water flowing on the western slopes are directed to the River Loire. Thus the relatively low Mont Pouilly (alt 559m/1 834ft) marks the watershed line between three main river basins: the Rhône, the Seine and the Loire.

Eating out

BUDGET

L'Auberge du Marronnier – *Pl. du Marché - 21320 Châteauneuf-en-Auxois - ☎ 03 80 49 21 91 - closed Dec-Jan - 15€*. This house overgrown with ivy has a dining room decorated with an extensive collection of farming implements. Traditional fare, including dishes such as *coq au vin* and *bœuf bourguignon* (beef stew), is served with an interesting selection of house wines *(vins au pichet)*.

Where to stay

BUDGET

Chambre d'Hôte Mme Bagatelle – *R. des Moutons - 21320 Châteauneuf-en-Auxois - ☎ 03 80 49 21 00 - jean-michel.bagatelle@wanadoo.fr - closed Feb school holidays - ✉ - 4 rooms: 40/58€*. Attractively restored sheepfold in the heart of a small village. The comfortable rooms exude great charm with their stone walls, beams and wooden furnishings. The two rooms featuring a mezzanine are particularly suitable for families. Not to be missed.

Chambre d'Hôte Péniche Lady A – *Canal de Bourgogne - 21320 Vandenesse-en-Auxois - 7km/4.3mi SE of Pouilly-en-Auxois by D 970 and D 18 - ☎ 03 80 49 26 96 - Closed Dec-Jan - ✉ - 3 rooms: 40/50€ - meals 20€*. Feel like staying on a barge? Walk up the gangway of Lady A and your dream will come true. Three small bright cabins await you on this boat anchored along the quays of the Canal de Bourgogne. The deck commands pretty views of Châteauneuf, its castle and the rolling countryside.

MODERATE

Hostellerie du Château Ste-Sabine – *21320 Ste-Sabine - 8km/5mi SE of Pouilly by N 81, D 977bis then D 970 - ☎ 03 80 49 22 01 - chateau-ste-sabine@wanadoo.fr - closed 3 Jan-25 Feb - 🅿 - 30 rooms: 60.99/179.90€ - ☕ 9.16€ - restaurant 22.87/53.37€*. This superb 17C château of Renaissance inspiration is approached by a huge park and a large inner courtyard. Inside the rooms, simplicity and sobriety are the key words. Fine vista of the lake. Summer pool. Animals roam freely on the property.

Église Notre-Dame-Trouvée ⊙ – This small 14C and 15C chapel, a place of pilgrimage, was built to house a very old statue of the Virgin (stolen in 1981), known as Notre-Dame-Trouvée ever since it was discovered miraculously.

The chapel boasts a fine 16C Sepulchre featuring nine main figures and many secondary ones including sleeping soldiers and angels carrying the instruments of the Passion. Various artistic influences (from Burgundy, Champagne and Italy) are recognisable.

EXCURSION

Châteauneuf – This old fortified market town, set in a picturesque **spot**★, is famous for its fortress, which commanded the road from Dijon to Autun and the whole of the surrounding plain.

★ **Château** ⊙ – The southern approach (D18A) provides a spectacular view immediately after crossing the Canal de Bourgogne.

Châteauneuf and the Burgundy CanaL

In the 12C, the lord of Chaudenay, whose ruined castle stands on an attractive site in Chaudenay-le-Château *(6km/3.5mi S)*, built this fortress for his son. It was enlarged and refurbished at the end of the 15C in the Flamboyant Gothic style by Philippe Pot, Seneschal of Burgundy. In 1936 it was presented to the French State by its owner at the time, Comte G de Vogüé.

The impressive structure, enclosed by thick walls flanked by massive towers, is separated from the village by a moat. There used to be two fortified gates; now a single drawbridge, flanked by huge round towers, gives access to the courtyard and the two main buildings.

Although partially ruined, the **guest pavilion**, or *logis de Philippe Pot*, has retained its handsome ogee-mullioned windows. The **grand logis** in the other wing with its high dormer windows has been restored: the guard-room is impressive for its size as well as its huge chimney with a coat of arms. The chapel (1481) has been carefully restored to the advantage of the frescoes executed in the Pot family colours (red and black) and the replica of Philippe Pot's tomb (the original is in the Louvre). The rooms upstairs were decorated in the 17C and 18C. Next to the Charles I of Vienna (1597-1659) room, in the keep, is a room which has kept its original brick partition (15C). From the round room, there is a view over the Morvan foothills and the Burgundy Canal.

The vast guard-room, the chapel (1481) and several rooms decorated in the 17C and 18C are open to visitors. From the circular chamber there is a panoramic view of the Morvan plain.

★ **Village** – This forms a picturesque ensemble with its well-preserved old houses, built from the 14C to the 17C by rich Burgundian merchants, its narrow streets and the remains of its ramparts. Note in particular an interesting old pewter workshop in the main street and carved or ogee door lintels.

▶▶ **Château de Commarin**★ – *8km/5mi N of Châteauneuf along D 977bis.* 14C **castle**★ ⊙ remodelled in the 17C and 18C, containing fine 16C **tapestries**★.

La PUISAYE

Michelin map 319: B-5

The Puisaye region has a reputation for being monotonous and even austere. The uniformity is however only superficial and the visitor will find a variety of scenery.

The forest that once covered the area has now mostly disappeared but the damp climate and the marl and sand soil still favour the existence of numerous pools hidden among the greenery.

The meadows and fields, hedgerows, wooded hills and the silhouettes of the many châteaux – Ratilly, St-Fargeau, St-Sauveur and St-Amand – all add to the interest of a drive in the Puisaye.

This excerpt is from *Tendrils of the Vine*, one of a series of sketches where Colette reveals her deep attachment to her native Burgundy:

"And if you come, on a lovely summer day, to visit my countryside, deep in a garden I know well, a garden so green it is black, flowerless; if you were to watch the colour blue tinge of a far-off hilltop, where stones, butterflies and thistle soak up the same azure hue, purple and dusty, you would forget me, and you would sit there until the end of your days."

Vrilles de la vigne.

La PUISAYE

Pottery in the Puisaye – The soil of the Puisaye contains uncrushed flint coated with white or red clays which were used in the Middle Ages by the potters of St-Amand, Treigny, St-Vérain and Myennes.

It was in the 17C that the pottery trade really began to develop; the fine pieces of pottery, known as the *Bleu de St-Verain* (Blue of St Verain), were followed in the next century by utility products. In the late 19C craftsmen-potters built up a new reputation.

Pottery making is now concentrated in **St-Amand-en-Puisaye**, where there is a training centre, and where, on the outskirts of the town, several potters' shops produce first-rate stoneware. Moutiers, near St-Sauveur, is known for the earthenware and stoneware produced at La Batisse. At the Château de Ratilly *(see below)* those interested in ceramic art can observe the different stages of the potter's craft: casting, moulding and throwing on the wheel.

Eating out

BUDGET

Café Restaurant du Bal – *7 r. du Prof.-Lian - 89520 Treigny -* ☎ *03 86 74 66 18 - closed Wed - 11€ lunch - 14/21€.* With its stone walls and exposed beams, Café Restaurant du Bal is a popular address among the inhabitants of this tiny village. Traditional dishes with a speciality: *tête de veau* (boiled calf's head). Takeaway service available. Warm welcome.

Le Lion d'Or – *37 r. Lucile-Cormier - 89130 Toucy -* ☎ *03 86 44 00 76 - closed 1-20 Dec, Sun evenings and Mon - 16/26€.* The dining room has been set up in the stables of this former post house; access is through the bar. Simple, unpretentious cooking with a traditional touch. Family atmosphere.

MODERATE

La Mare aux Fées – *Le Vieux Pont - 89130 Mézilles - 11km/6.8mi NE of St-Fargeau by D 965 -* ☎ *03 86 45 40 43 - closed Feb, Tue evenings and Wed - 16.50/21€.* Behind the attractive façade overgrown with ivy are two rustic-style dining rooms with beams, stone walls and tiled floors, one of which has a fireplace. Enjoy the warm welcome and generous helpings of traditional food.

Where to stay

BUDGET

Chambre d'Hôte La Bruère – *La Bruère - 89130 Fontaines - 9km/5.6mi SW of Toucy by D 955, rte de St-Sauveur -* ☎ *03 86 74 30 83 -* ✉ *- 3 rooms: 38€ - meals 14€.* This farmhouse is the perfect place to come to for a relaxing break in the country. The spacious rooms have been set up in the former granary. The chef uses fresh organic ingredients grown on the property.

PUISAYE COUNTRY

★★ **Château de St-Fargeau** – *See SAINT-FARGEAU.*
From the castle, drive 3km/1.7mi SE along D 185.

Lac de Bourdon– This 220ha/544-acre reservoir feeds the Briare Canal and offers leisure activities (boat trips, sailing, boating, fishing and swimming).

Parc Naturel de Boutissaint ⊘ – 📷 🗓 Created in 1968, this park was the first of its kind in which wild animals were left to live and roam in total freedom; 400ha/988 acres of pastures, ponds and woods are home to over 400 large animals (deer, bison, wild boars, moufflons) and a multitude of smaller ones (squirrels, rabbits, weasels, stoats) as well as birds, both sedentary and migratory. Visitors can walk, ride or cycle along 100km/62mi of waymarked trails. Picnics are allowed.

A little further on, turn left onto D 955 towards St-Sauveur-en-Puisaye.

Chantier Médiéval de Guédelon ⊘ – 📷 A disused quarry in a forested area was the site chosen for this unique enterprise intended to improve modern man's knowledge of the medieval way of life. The owner of St-Fargeau and the association of master builders of the Puisaye region undertook in 1998 the construction of a medieval castle using only the technical means available in the 13C; the project is due to last 25 years. Pottery made on the premises and regional products are on sale in the barn at the entrance to the site. There is also a workshop which introduces visitors to the delicate art of illuminating manuscripts.

Continue along D 955 towards St-Amand-en-Puisaye then turn left onto D 185.

Château de Ratilly ⊘ – The first sight of this large 13C castle, placed well away from the main roads in a setting of magnificent trees in the heart of the Puisaye region, will charm visitors. Massive towers and high walls of an austere appearance overlook the dry moat surrounding the castle, which is built in fine ochre-coloured stone that time has mellowed.

In the 1730s, Ratilly served as a refuge for the Jansenists, who published a clandestine paper there, safe from the pursuit of the royal police, with the blessing of the bishop of Auxerre.

The left wing now houses a stoneware workshop *(courses available)*. Both the workshop and the showroom, with its small exhibition on the original Puisaye stoneware, are open to the public. Other premises have been refurbished to house temporary art exhibitions.

Drive back down towards the village.

Treigny – This village boasts an unusually vast Flamboyant-Gothic church dating from the 15C. Note the massive buttresses supporting the edifice and the two crucifix inside; the one in the aisle is the work of a 16C leper.

Follow D 66 to Moutiers.

A. de Valroger/MICHELIN

Guédelon work site

Moutiers-en-Puisaye – The parish church once belonged to a priory dependent on the Abbaye d'Auxerre. Note the 13C carvings decorating the narthex and, in the nave, the medieval frescoes dating from two successive periods: 12C frescoes on the north wall (Annunciation, Nativity, Christ surrounded by angels…), on the west wall (large figures) and on part of the south wall; Gothic frescoes (c 1300) on the remainder of the south wall depicting a procession (top), scenes from Genesis (centre) and the story of John the Baptist and Noah's Ark (bottom).

Saint-Sauveur-en-Puisaye – On Colette's namesake street, a red-marble medallion on the façade of her former home simply states, *Ici Colette est née* (Colette was born here).

Housed in one of the pavilions of the Château de St-Sauveur, close to the unusual 12C ironstone-built Tour Sarrasine, the **Musée Colette★** ☉ contains a collection of photographs, objects, furniture, manuscripts and books illustrating Colette's life and career. There is also a recording of some of her writings. Her drawing room and bedroom in Paris, where she spent the last years of her life, have been reconstructed with her own furniture. The visit ends in the library, a reading room filled with 1 500 dummy books containing some of the author's quotes.

Return to St-Fargeau via D 85 (11km/7mi).

Colette

Sidonie Gabrielle, daughter of Jules Colette, her mother's second husband, was born in **St-Sauveur-en-Puysaye** on 28 January 1873. The author spent her first 19 years there. Married to an editor's son, Henry Gauthier-Villars, she wrote the four novels in the *Claudine* series, which her husband, under his pen name of Willy, took credit (and cash) for. Blazing the trail of independent womanhood, she obtained a divorce and took to the stage (inspiration for *La Vagabonde*). Later she married newspaper editor Henri de Jouvenel and bore a daughter. Although this second marriage also ended in divorce, she finally found happiness with author Maurice Goudeket, whom she married in 1935. They set up house, with Colette's legendary cats, in an apartment overlooking the elegant Palais Royal gardens in Paris, where she died, much admired and honoured, in 1954.

Collection André de Jouvenel

Colette's novels, concerned with the pleasures and pain of love, are rich in sensory evocation of the natural environment in her native Burgundy.

She brought a great sensitivity to her descriptions of the animal world *(The Cat, Creatures Comfort)* and childhood *(My Mother's House, Sido)*. Her masterpieces also include post-First World War works steeped in the troubling ambivalence of those times *(Chéri* and *The Last of Chéri)*; *Gigi* (1944) was adapted for stage and screen, a popular musical comedy.

RONCHAMP

Population 2 965
Michelin map 314: H-6

Since the 1950s the name of Ronchamp has evoked the chapel of **Notre-Dame-du-Haut**, designed by Swiss architect Le Corbusier in 1955 to replace a chapel destroyed during the Second World War. Until 1958 when the last colliery was closed down, Ronchamp was a mining town. A museum and archive testify to this industrial past.

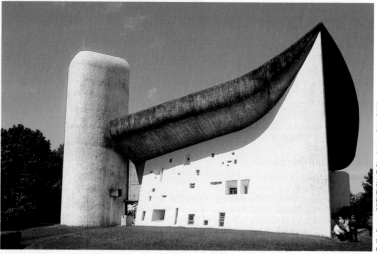

Notre-Dame-du-Haut

B. Kaufmann/MICHELIN/c FLC/ c Adagp, Paris 2003

★★ Notre-Dame-du-Haut ⓥ – *The chapel is 1.5km/1mi N of the town; access via a steep uphill road.*

Le Corbusier's comment on this chapel, which is one of the most important works of contemporary religious architecture, was that he had intended his design to create a place of silence, prayer, peace and inner joy. The chapel was constructed on a hill (alt 472m/1 546ft) overlooking the industrial town of Ronchamp, which had been dedicated to the worship of the Virgin Mary since the Middle Ages. It is built entirely of concrete; the brightness of its whitewashed walls looks dazzling juxtaposed with the dark grey untreated concrete of the roof. The rigid geometric lines of the walls contrast strikingly with the softer curves of the roof, which sweeps upwards in a graceful motion, and the rounded towers. In his conception of this chapel, Le Corbusier broke with the rationalist movement and its inflexible designs, creating a work which has been described as architectural sculpture.

Inside, despite sloping walls and its relatively small size, the chapel seems spacious. The nave widens out towards the altar of white Burgundy stone, and the floor of the chapel follows the slope of the hill it is built on. The image of the Virgin Mary stands bathed in light in a niche in the wall. Light in the church filters through numerous different tiny windows randomly cut in the walls, allowing for a subtle interplay of light and shadow in the half darkness which softens the effect of the bare concrete walls. The three small chapels inside the three towers seen outside contribute to this subdued lighting effect.

Musée de la Mine ⓥ – This museum retraces two centuries of mining in the region. The first gallery contains a display on coal mining – equipment, mining lamps, collections of fossils – and reproductions of common underground catastrophes in the mines.

The second gallery is given over to the life of the miners themselves, both pleasant aspects such as festivals, sports and musical activities, and the ever-present threat of illnesses such as miners' silicosis.

Specialists in the field have access to a large archive on mining which includes information not only about the local mining industry, but also those in other countries in which mining is an important part of the national economy.

Les ROUSSES**

Population 2 927
Michelin map 321: G-8

This resort, situated on a plateau, a stone's throw from Switzerland, is renowned for its extensive ski area (alt 1 100-1 680m/3 609-5 512ft), for the quality of its leisure activities and entertainment and for its convivial atmosphere. As a summer resort, Les Rousses offers ramblers and mountain bikers its wild open spaces whereas the nearby lake attracts water sports enthusiasts.

The resort includes four villages: Les Rousses, Prémanon, Lamoura and Bois-d'Amont

Eating out

MODERATE

Arbez Franco-Suisse – *2.5km/1.6mi S of Les Rousses by N 5 -* ☎ *03 84 60 02 20 - closed Nov, Mon evenings and Tue out of season. - 22/30€.* This bilingual hotel is located on the border between France and Switzerland. As regards meals, you can choose between the informal Brasserie and the dining room with its wooden decor.

Where to stay

MODERATE

Hôtel La Redoute – ☎ *03 84 60 00 40 - hotel.de.la.redoute@wanadoo.fr - closed 5 Nov-15 Dec -* ▯ *- 25 rooms: 60€ -* ☲ *6.10€ - restaurant 14/29€.* This sober family house stands at the entrance to the skiing resort. The accommodation consists of simple but carefully kept bedrooms. Meals are served in a large rustic-style dining room. Good selection of affordable menus, including one for children.

Shopping

Boissellerie du Hérisson – *101 r. Pasteur -* ☎ *03 84 60 30 84 - open daily 9.30am-noon, 2-7pm, Sun 2-7pm.* This shop offers an incredible range of fine, beautifully crafted wooden objects (old-fashioned toys, board games, chests) made for the most part by local artisans.

Sit back and relax

Le Chalet du Lac – *1580 rte du Vivier -* ☎ *03 84 60 30 18 - open daily 10am-1am.* This establishment enjoys an outstanding location: the view from its terrace sweeps over pretty Lac des Rousses, encompassing Noirmont Massif in the far distance. Perfect for a quiet, relaxing break.

SKI AREA

Alpine skiing – There are four linked ski areas, including one in Switzerland offering 40km/25mi of runs of various levels of difficulty: 16 green runs, 7 blue ones, 16 red ones and 4 black ones; these are accessible via 40 ski lifts. There is a choice of ski passes combining several ski areas and free shuttles linking Lamoura, La Serra, Les Jouvencelles, Le Noirmont...

Les Jouvencelles – This ski area, ideal for beginners and families, comprises many runs for children, very long green runs and two red runs. Half way down (or up!) skiers can take a pause in the restaurant-bar Le Beauregard. Maximum altitude: 1 420m/4 659ft. Snowboarding can be practised here or at Le Noirmont.

La Serra – The level here is higher: one beautiful green run but mostly blue and red runs. Maximum altitude: 1 495m/4 905ft.

Le Noirmont – Beginners should avoid this area; even the long green run accessible by chair-lift requires a minimum of self-confidence. The red and black runs are the favourite haunt of snowboarders who speed down the often icy slopes. Maximum altitude: 1 560m/5 118ft.

La Dôle – The highest point of the massif (1 680m/5 512ft) located in Switzerland is crowned with a radar station which controls Geneva airport's traffic. In fair weather, the view of Lake Geneva and of the Alps is unforgettable. Competent skiers will appreciate the blue, red and black runs; there are also a few very short green runs.

Cross-country skiing – 250km/155mi of double tracks suitable for both styles of cross-country skiing; 35 trails varying in difficulty (from green to black). The 76km/47mi Transjurassienne race has been starting from Lamoura ever since 1979.

Snowshoeing – Accessible to all, this activity nevertheless requires a minimum of physical fitness. Practice on the few waymarked trails around the resort is recommended before embarking on long excursions which can prove exhausting. There are guided tours with a member of the École du Ski Français (ESF).

THE RESORT

Les Rousses – The village developed round its church during the 18C. The former wooden houses were replaced by housing estates and hotels. From the terrace in from of the church, there is a fine view of the Lac des Rousses and the Risoux mountain range in the background.

Lac des Rousses – *2km/1.2mi N.* Covering almost 100ha/247 acres, this lake is very lively in summer, its swimming and water sports facilities attracting many holidaymakers.

Prémanon – Overlooked by Mont Fier (1 282m/4 206ft), this village and the nearby hamlets rise in terraces from the banks of the Bienne to the small Dappes Valley which marks the border with Switzerland.

Belvédère des Maquisards – *3km/1.7mi N of Prémanon along D 25.* This spectacular belvedere towers above the gorge of the upper Bienne and its tributary, the Bief de la Chaille.

A break from the slopes

G. Guittot/PHOTONONSTOP

SIGHTS

Fort des Rousses – This fort, built in the 19C, is one of the largest in France; there is a vast network of underground galleries which could house up to 3 000 men.

Fort des Rousses Aventure ⊘ – This adventure park offers three courses graded according to their level of difficulty (children, red and black) and including suspended footbridges, via ferrata etc. The courses are supervised by qualified instructors.

Caves Juraflore ⊘ – The fort contains extensive **maturing cellars** for Comté cheese; the longest measures 214m/235yd. Manufacturing techniques are explained during the visit.

Centre polaire Paul-Émile-Victor ⊘ – *In Prémanon.* 🖾 Housed in an unusual building, this museum initiated by the famous explorer, a native of the region, illustrates the lifestyle of the Eskimo and Same people (traditional objects) as well as Nordic fauna: magnificent 3.10m/10ft-high stuffed white bear.

Musée de la Boissellerie ⊙ – *In Bois d'Amont*. The village has a long-standing woodworking tradition. This activity is presented in a former sawmill turned into a museum. Demonstrations and audio-visual presentations illustrate the various crafts connected with wood, in particular the art of box-making.

L'Atelier – *39220 Bois-d'Amont - 8km/5mi N des Rousses by D 29ᴱ and D 415 - ☎ 03 84 60 94 15 - brocart.patrick@ wanadoo.fr - closed spring holidays, Mon, Tue and Wed except school holidays and Sun evenings - 20/38€*. This former carpenter's workshop has been converted into a restaurant offering a traditional bill of fare. The interior decoration of the wooden house is simple and rustic in style. Upstairs dining room. On Thursday evenings, forget about menus, it's pizza all around.

Musée du lapidaire ⊙ – *In Lamoura town hall*. Gem cutting for the watch-making industry is a traditional craft once widely practised in this region. The museum, which contains a collection of gems and tools, illustrate this precision activity by means of a video film and a demonstration.

FORÊT DU MASSACRE

The forest was given this forbidding name in 1535 when the Duke of Savoie's troops, who were besieging Geneva, trapped and massacred a group of mercenaries sent in reinforcement by King François I.
Consisting mainly of spruce, the forest rises to 1 495m/4 905ft (Crêt Pela) offering views of the Valmijoux, Mont-Rond and the Alps. Several species of fauna and flora date back to the glacial period. Guided tours of the massif are organised in summer.

Round tour – *34km/21mi and 15min on foot there and back.*
Leave Lamoura heading NE along D 25. In Jouvencelles, turn right towards the ski lift parking area then, 100m/110yd further on, take the Chemin des Tuffes. Turn left past the last houses and follow a road branching off the forest track; leave the car 750m/820yd further on.

Belvédère des Dappes – 🔲 *15min there and back. Alt 1 310m/4 298ft*. View *(viewing table)* of Les Rousses, and La Cure, the Lac des Rousses, Le Noirmont, La Dôle and, when the weather is fine, the Swiss Alps. (Les Diablerets).
Continue along the track running right through the forest. You will get a glimpse of Mont Blanc in the vicinity of Crêt Pela, about halfway to Lajoux.
Continue to Lajoux and follow D 436 and D 25 back to Lamoura.

ST-CLAUDE★

Population 12 303
Michelin map 321: F-8

The town of St-Claude, tucked amid delightful countryside between the River Bienne and River Tacon, is the most important tourist centre in the Haut-Jura. It has always been famed for its charming setting (of which there is an excellent overall view from the large bridge spanning the Tacon) and for the abbey which was once here. Since the town has been destroyed several times by fire, most notably in 1799, after which not much consideration was given to aesthetic appeal in its reconstruction, it has no buildings of any note apart from its cathedral. The town thrives on various crafts including pipe making as well as on tourism.

THE RISE AND FALL OF ST-CLAUDE

Pioneers of the Jura – In c 430 the future St Romanus, a young man wishing to lead a reclusive life, left his native village of Izernore (45km/28mi SW of St-Claude) and went to live in the dense forest of the Haut-Jura. He chose a great fir tree, standing next to a spring, as his shelter (this would one day become the site of the cathedral of St-Claude). He lived off wild berries until he was able to harvest something from an area of ground which he broke up and cultivated.
He was joined by his brother Lupicinus (later also made a saint), and then by an ever growing number of followers, attracted by the hermits' saintliness and the miracles they accomplished. St Lupicinus led a particularly austere life. He ate one vegetarian meal every two days, and never drank anything. When his thirst became unbearable he would plunge his hands into cold water and let the fluid seep through his pores into his dried-out body. He wore animal skins and slept seated in one of the stalls in the chapel (if he fell ill, he would allow himself the luxury of lying on the rolled up bark of a fir tree).
By the time St Lupicinus died 50 years later, the monastery of **Condat** had grown up near St Romanus' original fir tree. Linked with it, numerous priories and more basic monastic communities known as *granges*, in which only two or three monks lived,

were founded throughout the Haut-Jura and Switzerland. About 1 500 monks lived in the forest region and cultivated it. They used the boxwood from the forest to carve religious objects for pilgrims: statuettes, crucifixes, rosaries etc. This was the origin of the turned-wood articles that were later to be so important economically to the region.

Saintly monks – Abbey life was a model of piety and morality until the 12C. St Eugendus (Br Oyend), in the 6C, and St Claudius, in the 7C, made major contributions to the illustrious reputation of the abbey; the latter was a great lord and archbishop of Besançon, who gave up his wealth and rank to become a monk and who governed the abbey for over 55 years. During the reign of these saints the abbey gained its reputation for being a place of miracles. By the 12C the monastery and the town depending on it had taken the name of St-Claude, and pilgrims hurried along the roads of Burgundy to visit the relics of the holy monks. Louis XI himself came as well in 1482 to fulfil a vow.

Laxness – Religious discipline began to crumble during the 13C and 14C. The abbey had grown steadily in wealth, thanks to the generous donations from grateful pilgrims, and it simply became too rich. Absolute poverty became increasingly difficult for the monks to practise and many of the new recruits to the abbey were motivated by worldly greed. To increase their individual share of the abbey's wealth, the monks in the know reduced the number of their community – that of the mother abbey at St-Claude fell from 500 to 36 and finally to only 20.

Aristocratic monks – The Comté aristocracy was envious of the rich inhabitants of the abbey, and began taking up places there as they became vacant. Once the nobility held the majority in the chapter, they decreed that admission to the abbey of St-Claude would henceforth be conditional on the applicant's having at least four generations of aristocracy on both maternal and paternal sides of his family. This recruitment policy had disastrous consequences for the abbey, as the monks from established noble families continued leading the life of luxury they were used to, and did not take their spiritual responsibilities at all seriously – religious offices were reduced to a minimum or cut out altogether; on days of abstinence or fasting the monks simply left the abbey to dine in town; monks were seen out hunting in lay clothes, wearing wigs on their heads and swords at their sides; friends and family of both sexes were welcomed into the abbey as visitors.

The Holy See and the episcopal authorities attempted on several occasions to reform the abbey, but were powerless in the face of the political influence of the monks. In 1737, the desperate Pope decided to create an episcopal seat in the town, for which the monks became canons, thus freeing them of the duty to follow the Benedictine observance which was so foreign to them.

A lawyer's paradise – From the 15C to the 18C, armies of lawyers made a living from settling the numerous, incredibly petty disputes between the abbey and the town of St-Claude. The question whether the bell in the monastery or that in the parish church should ring more loudly is just one example of the kind of issue which would provoke a lengthy legal wrangle – in this case 40 years, until the problem was solved by the personal intervention of Emperor Charles V.

The Revolution – The lordly canons, distinctly lacking the moral cachet of their saintly predecessors, were regarded by the 14 000 inhabitants of the abbey lands as nothing more than a handful of utterly shameless over-privileged layabouts. In 1770, shortly before the outbreak of the French Revolution, six Haut-Jura villages, with the help of their lawyer Christin, took out a lawsuit against the chapter to win their freedom. Their case made a tremendous impact; even Voltaire, living at Ferney at the time, came to the aid of the villagers by writing pamphlets. After a court case lasting five years, the canons, who refused point-blank to give any ground, emerged victorious. The bishop suggested that, as their rights had been officially recognised, they might like to make the generous gesture of liberating their serfs on their own initiative, but the monks refused. The bishop appealed to the king, Louis XVI, but even he did not dare intervene in the face of the chapter's stubborn opposition. Finally, the problem was settled by the outbreak of the Revolution: the religious principality of St-Claude was abolished, its goods and lands were confiscated and sold, and the serfs were freed. All that now remains of the once-glorious monastic community is the cathedral surrounded by the ruins of one or two buildings.

THE CAPITAL OF PIPE MAKING

The Romans smoked hemp in terracotta or iron pipes. Pipes were not used in France, however, until 1560, when Nicot, the French ambassador to Portugal, first introduced them and tobacco to the court. The pipe itself consisted of a long tube ending in a little silver bowl. It was not terribly popular initially, but by the end of the 18C pipe smoking had become quite the fashion, and craftsmen in St-Claude, who were already well reputed for their woodturning, began to devote their professional interest to the problems of making pipes.

First of all, they fixed wooden or horn stems made locally to porcelain bowls imported from Germany, then they tried making pipes entirely of wood. Boxwood, wild cherry, walnut and pear wood all produced disappointing results, as they burned along with the tobacco, giving an appallingly bitter aftertaste. In 1854 a Corsican offered to supply a local pipe maker, Daniel David from the village of Chaumont near St-Claude, with briar root, which is far superior to boxwood for making pipes. David tried out this new material and came to settle in St-Claude, where he met with tremendous success. The pipe makers got their briar root from Corsica or countries on the shores of the Mediterranean in the form of lengths of root, weigh-

G. Magnin/MICHELIN

Carved pipe

ing as much as 50kg/110lb. These they dried themselves and then sawed into manageable chunks. Only after a process of about 20 different stages was the polished, varnished pipe ready for the smoker's delight and delectation. The town held a virtual monopoly on this manufacture until 1885, but the two World Wars favoured the development of foreign competitors. However, St-Claude is still an important pipe manufacturing centre.

The town is home to related industries, such as the manufacture of cigarette holders, pipe-cleaners, wooden snuffboxes, pipe accessories in horn etc.

ST-CLAUDE

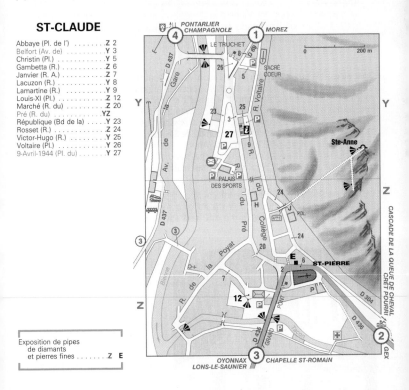

Exposition de pipes
de diamants
et pierres fines . . . . . . .Z E

SIGHTS

★★ **The setting** – In order to fully appreciate the originality of St-Claude's setting on a narrow terrace in between the mountain torrents of the Bienne and the Tacon, stand on the bridge (Grand Pont) spanning the Tacon, from where there is an overall view of the town and the Cirque des Foules.

Then head to place Louis-XI, from where there is a beautiful **view**★ above the old ramparts.

Eating out

MODERATE

Le Carnot – *14 bis r. Carnot -* ☎ *03 84 41 08 10 - closed 5-20 Aug, Sat lunchtime and Sun - 10.67€ lunch - 15.24/22.87€.* A former pipe-making factory provides an unusual backdrop to this restaurant offering regional specialities, salads and pizzas. The dining room is charming with its stone walls, wooden ceiling, spiral staircase and old-fashioned tools. Playing area for children.

Where to stay

BUDGET

Jura Hôtel – *40 av. de la Gare -* ☎ *03 84 45 24 04 - 35 rooms: 33.60/53.35€ -* ☐ *6.10€ - restaurant 13.72/25.15€.* This hotel is located directly opposite the train station. You may prefer one of the 12 larger bedrooms; the other ones are smaller and rustic in style but all are impeccably kept. The dining room looks out over the town.

On the town

L'Américain – *45 r. du Pré -* ☎ *03 84 45 03 85 - Mon-Sat 8am-10pm, Sun 10am-12.30pm, 1-9pm.* Gleaming copper and mahogany wainscoting add a warm touch to this brasserie situated in the centre of town. Mingle with the locals and sip a drink to the lively strains of a jazz band (the owner is a former saxophone player).

Shopping

Roger-Vincent – *2 chemin Combe-du-Marais -* ☎ *03 84 45 27 72 - Mon-Sat 10am-noon, 3-6pm.* Mr Vincent is the only craftsman in France who still cultivates the art of handmade pipes. You can watch him ply his trade in his workshop and admire his collector's pieces.

Other views – There is a view of the Tacon Valley from the bottom of the steep, picturesque rue de la Poyat. This street was once an important link between the upper district (around the abbey) and the suburb inhabited by workers and craftsmen. Before the modern bridges were built, it was also one of the routes taken by pilgrims on their way to revere the relics of St Claudius.

There is a beautiful view from the **Grotte de Ste-Anne**, a cave which overlooks the town from a height of 200m/656ft. Another good viewpoint is to be found on place du 9-Avril-1944. Finally, from the middle of the viaduct the view shows clearly how the lack of level ground has made it necessary to expand the town upwards instead of outwards.

★ **Cathédrale St-Pierre** – This cathedral church, originally dedicated to saints Peter, Paul and Andrew, was once the heart of the abbey community. The present building, originally built in the Gothic style in the 14C and 15C, was finished in the 18C with the addition of a Classical façade. The 15C tower was extended higher in the 18C. The most interesting part of the exterior is the east end, with its watch-turrets topped with spires.

The beautiful rectangular interior is plain, even austere, and is supported by 14 massive octagonal pillars. Left of the entrance, an **altarpiece★** stands against the wall of the nave. It was donated in 1533 by Pierre de la Baume, the last bishop of the Franche-Comté, who lived in Geneva, in gratitude to St Peter for protecting him through all the political and religious disturbances.

The chancel is lit by **stained-glass windows★** restored in 1999 and contains magnificent sculpted

St-Pierre's

A. de Valroger/MICHELIN

wooden stalls★★ which were begun before 1449 and finished in 1465 by the Geneva craftsman Jehan de Vitry. The Apostles and the Prophets are depicted alternately on the backrests, then the former abbots of the monastery; scenes from the abbey's history with the founders St Romanus and St Lupicinus, are represented on the large and small cheekpieces; the 19C restorers added scenes of everyday life to the elbow rests and misericords. Unfortunately the southern section of the stalls was destroyed by fire during the night of 26 September 1983. After years of research, the damaged sculptures were restored under the direction of the regional authority for historic monuments. Meeting this challenge has provided an opportunity to further advance the study of Gothic religious arts.

St Claudius' tomb drew crowds of pilgrims until 1794. Emperors, kings and great lords all came to venerate him. Anne of Brittany had been unable to conceive until her pilgrimage to the Jura, after which she bore a daughter to Louis XII and named her Claude (later to become the wife of François I and Queen of France). The shrine was burned during the Revolution, and the few remaining relics of the saint are kept in a reliquary in the chapel south of the chancel.

Exposition de pipes, de diamants et de pierres fines ⊘ – This collection of 18C and 19C pipes is very varied, containing many examples of different materials (meerschaum, baked clay, brass, enamel, briar root, horn etc), different sizes and different origins (from all over the world). Some pipes are very artistically decorated. The Chancellerie displays a collection of pipes marked with the names of those admitted into the famous pipe makers' guild of St-Claude. Note the sculpting machine, which works on the same principle as the pantograph.

The exhibition also includes displays on diamond cutters themselves; precious stones, both natural and synthetic, cut and uncut; the diamond cutter's and the lapidary's tools; and the various steps involved in cutting a precious stone. There are also one or two crowns and other ceremonial pieces from among the world's famous jewels and treasures.

EXCURSIONS

Chapelle Saint-Romain – *23km/14.3mi via D 436. At the confluence of the Lizon and the Brienne, turn right onto D 470 to Pratz then turn left onto D 300 to Saint-Romain. Leave the car at the entrance to the hamlet and follow (30min on foot there and back) the path leading down to the chapel.* This chapel, built in typical Burgundian Romanesque style, stands in charming surroundings, overlooking the meandering River Bienne (270m/886ft lower) flowing between wooded slopes. A popular pilgrimage takes place on Whit Monday.

Retrace your steps back to Lavans and turn left onto D 118 to make a detour to St-Lupicin before returning to Saint-Claude.

Saint-Lupicin – The village is named after an abbot of St-Claude who founded a priory here in 445. Apart from its 17C vaulting, the church is one of the best-preserved Romanesque buildings in the region. The saint's reliquary is located below the north altar whereas a low-relief sculpture by Maurice Denis can be seen below the south altar.

Parc Naturel Régional du Haut-Jura

The Haut-Jura Regional Nature Park was inaugurated in 1986 and extended in 1998 to preserve the beautiful local forests and cultural heritage and create a new source of income for the region's inhabitants. The park's administration (**Maison du Parc du Haut-Jura**) is located in **Lajoux**, a small town east of St-Claude. It also serves as an information centre for those wishing to go on walking tours or enjoy other activities in the park.

The park covers 145 000ha/358 310 acres and encompasses 96 communities *(communes)*, including St-Claude and Morez. The Crêt Pela (alt 1 495m/4 905ft), the highest summit in the Jura, offers plenty of opportunities for ski enthusiasts in winter, and for nature ramblers and mountain bikers in summer.

There are several museums which give an insight into the development of crafts and industry in the region, which range from independent artisans and cottage-industries to factories. Besides the pipe-making and diamond-cutting workshops of St-Claude, activities include spectacle making in Morez, the manufacture of earthenware in Bois-d'Amont and toys in Moirans-en-Montagne, and traditional cheesemaking at Les Moussières.

The tourist offices in St-Claude and Les Rousses and the Maison du Haut-Jura in Lajoux give information on the park itself and the accommodation and leisure facilities it has to offer visitors.

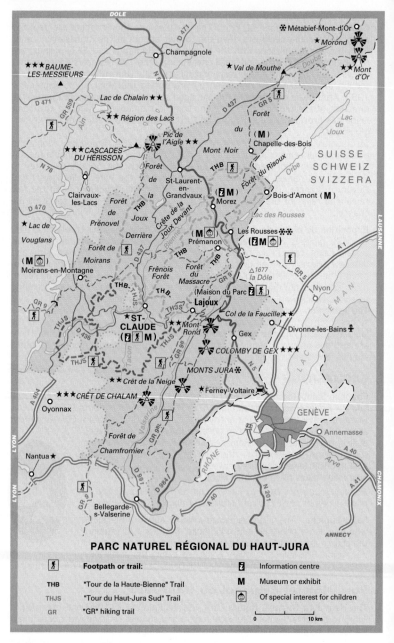

PARC NATUREL RÉGIONAL DU HAUT-JURA

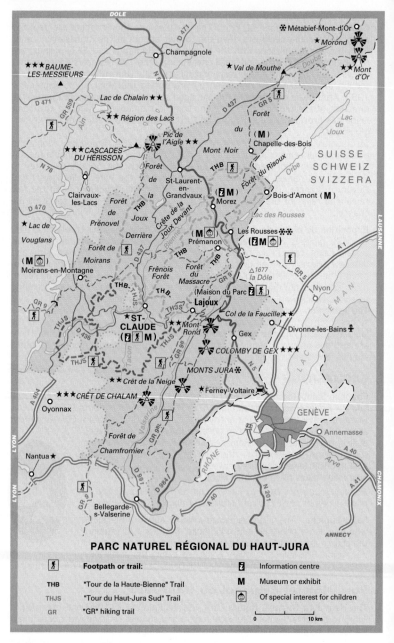	Footpath or trail:			Information centre
THB	"Tour de la Haute-Bienne" Trail		**M**	Museum or exhibit
THJS	"Tour du Haut-Jura Sud" Trail			Of special interest for children
GR	"GR" hiking trail			

0 _____ 10 km

Round tour from Saint-Claude

Drive E out of Saint-Claude towards D 304.

★**Cascade de la Queue de Cheval** – *5km/3mi and 1hr on foot there and back.*
🚶 *On your way out of Chaumont, leave the car in the parking area and take the footpath to the right. It leads to the foot of the 50m/164ft-high waterfall.*

Continue along D 304. Leave the car beyond a bridge in the hamlet of La Main-Morte and follow the path (waymarked in red) leading to Crêt Pourri.

★**Crêt Pourri** – 🚶 *30min on foot there and back.* Alt 1 025m/3 362ft. Fine **panorama**★ from the viewing table.

Follow D 304 to Lamoura, go through the village and continue to Lajoux.

Lajoux – The **Maison du Parc** is located here, in the heart of the nature park, where a few craftsmen try to keep ancient crafts alive; note the strong barn, a free-standing construction where farmers used to keep precious goods and valuables.

Drive along D 292 to Les Molunes then on to Moussières.

Chapeau de Gendarme

At the **Coopérative fromagère de Moussières** ⊙, it is possible to watch the manufacturing process of several local cheeses (Comté, Morbier and Bleu de Gex).

Drive N towards Saint-Claude along D 25. Take the first road left to the belvedere.

Belvédère de la Roche Blanche – *Parking area.* Alt 1 139m/3 737ft. Extensive view of the Flumen Valley, of Saint-Claude and Septmoncel.

There is another belvedere 700m/765yd further on.

★**Belvédère de la Cernaise** – This overhanging promontory offers a bird's-eye **view** of the Flumen Valley, of Saint-Claude and the Septmoncel plateau.

★**Gorges du Flumen** – This mountain stream, a tributary of the Tacon, can be seen cascading through a wild **gorge**★ from the cliff road (D 436) which follows the river between Septmoncel and Saint-Claude. The road offers an impressive view of the main cascade of the Flumen before going through a tunnel to get past a rocky spur.

★**Chapeau de Gendarme** – This natural site is interesting from a geological point of view: it consists of originally horizontal layers of rock which were compressed and lifted during the Tertiary Era and became twisted without breaking.

Belvédère du Saut du Chien – *Parking area.* Fine view of the gorge.

▶▶ **Vallée de la Bienne** – *82km/51mi round tour.* Drive up the east side of the Bienne Valley to Morez and Les Rousses then back again, down the west side of the valley.

ST-FARGEAU

Population 1 814
Michelin map 319: B-6

The clearing of the forests made possible the establishment of smelting works at St-Fargeau, chief town of the Puisaye, to process the minerals extracted from the ferruginous soil. St-Fargeau has a fine château filled with memories of Anne-Marie-Louise d'Orléans, cousin of Louis XIV, better known under the name of Mademoiselle de Montpensier or *La Grande Mademoiselle*. She was an incorrigible supporter of the Fronde (a rising of the aristocracy and Parliament, 1648-53).

A romantic castle – The present château is built on the site of a fortress erected at the end of the 10C; the system of fortifications was completed two centuries later. The present building was begun in the Renaissance period and was built in several stages. The largest tower was built by Jacques Cœur, treasurer to the royal household of Charles VII (reign 1422-61), who owned St-Fargeau for some time.

Antoine de Chabannes, who acquired the château when Jacques Cœur fell into disgrace, carried out many improvements but it is **La Grande Mademoiselle** who can claim the honour of completely changing the appearance of the buildings. Mademoiselle de Montpensier was exiled to St-Fargeau for several years on the orders of Louis XIV as punishment for her attitude during the uprising of the Fronde. When she arrived in 1652 she had "to wade through knee-high grass in the courtyard" and found a dilapidated building. To make her place of exile more comfortable, she called in Le Vau, the king's architect, who laid out the inner courtyard and completely refurbished the interior of the château.

In 1681, Mademoiselle de Montpensier made a gift of St-Fargeau to the Duc de Lauzun, a man of questionable background, whom she later married in a secret ceremony.

Château de St-Fargeau

In 1715 the property was bought by Le Pelletier des Forts. His great-grandson, **Louis-Michel Le Pelletier de St-Fargeau**, became deputy to the National Convention in 1793 and voted for the death of Louis XVI. He was assassinated on the eve of the king's execution and considered by the revolutionaries as the first martyr of their cause; he is buried in the chapel.

Eating out

BUDGET

Ferme-Auberge Les Perriaux – *89350 Champignelles - 3km/1.9mi NW of Champignelles by D 7 (heading towards Château-Coligny) then a minor road - ☎ 03 86 45 13 22 - open Sat-Sun in low season and daily Jul-Aug - reservations recommended - 11/27€.* Today cereals are grown and poultry is reared on this 16C farm, where you can sample fresh home-grown produce: *terrine*, foie gras and cider made on the premises. Rustic setting with fireplace for the long winter evenings. Pleasantly arranged upstairs room.

BUDGET

Auberge la Demoiselle – *1 pl. de la République - ☎ 03 86 74 10 58 - f-dupuy@wanadoo.fr - closed 23 Dec-31 Jan, Wed evenings, Sun evenings and Mon except 14 Jul-31 Aug - 12.96€ lunch - 16.01/32.01€.* Mademoiselle de Montpensier once resided in the château and her portrait hangs above the fireplace in the dining room. Warm, lively decor in yellow hues, complemented by a rustic touch with exposed beams and tiled floors. Nice cooking.

Where to stay

BUDGET

Chambre d'Hôte Le Moulin de la Forge – *89350 Tannerre-en-Puisaye - 11km/6.8mi NE of St-Fargeau by D 18 then D 160 - ☎ 03 86 45 40 25 - ⧖ - 5 rooms: 50€.* You will love this 14C mill surrounded by a park with a landscaped garden, a pool and a pond teeming with fish. Comfortable rooms with beams furnished in the 1930s style.

SIGHTS

Tour de l'Horloge – Brick and stone clock tower (late-15C fortified gateway).

Église Saint-Ferréol – The 13C Gothic west front has a radiant rose window set in a square.
In the nave, note on the right a 16C polychrome *Pietà* in stone and, in the choir, stalls of the same period. At the far end of the choir the wooden statue of Christ dates from the 14C. The chapel in the south aisle contains three sculptures in wood, a 15C triptych representing the Passion, a 16C painted statue of the Virgin Mary and a remarkable 16C carving of St Martin sharing his cloak.

Château ⊘ – The warm rose-coloured brick does much to dispel the grim aspect that the massive towers of the main gateway and the corner towers give to this impressive building, surrounded by a moat. With the exception of the largest tower, known as that of Jacques Cœur, these squat towers are surmounted by slender, pierced lanterns.

Within the feudal enclosure is a huge courtyard of rare elegance bordered by five ranges of buildings (the most recent on the right of the entrance dates from 1735). A semicircular stair in the corner between the two main wings leads to the entrance rotunda. The chapel is housed in one of the towers: on the left is the portrait gallery which led into the apartments of the *Grande Mademoiselle* until they were burned in 1752; on the right is the 17C guard-room. A grand stair leads to the rooms on the first floor. Below the portrait gallery, an exhibition illustrates the planned construction of a feudal castle near St-Fargeau, using medieval techniques and materials *(see La PUISAYE: Chantier médiéval de Guédelon)*. The tour of the attic allows visitors to admire the enormous roof area and the handsome timber-work.

In the English-style park (118ha/292 acres) with its charming groves there is a large lake, fed by the small River Bourdon.

Ferme du Château ⊘ – The buildings have been restored and furnished to house an exhibit on rural life and trades 100 years ago.

★ **Musée de la reproduction du son** ⊘ – The former town hall is now a small museum devoted to the history of ways of reproducing music and to their inventors: Cros, Edison, Bell, Lioret, Pathé, Berliner... Early music boxes, a German calliope from 1910 with a vertical disc, an automatic orchestra dating from 1925, a Limonaire carrousel organ and more make up this charming collection. The set of phonographs, some portable, shows models in fanciful shapes. Demonstrations are provided.

SAINT-HONORÉ-LES-BAINS⌖

Population 763
Michelin map 319: G-10

St-Honoré became popular during the Second Empire and today it is a modern spa and a sought-after holiday resort. Situated on the border of the Morvan, it is the ideal starting point of excursions into this beautiful region.

The spa – The sulphurous, radioactive hot springs of this small spa town were first used by the Romans and are now part of cures for asthma, bronchitis and diseases of the respiratory tracts.

The thermal establishment was built in 1854 on the site of the old Roman baths. A pleasant shaded park and sports facilities are at the disposal of those who come to take the waters.

The **Musée Georges-Per-raudin** ⊘ presents an account of the Resistance movement in the Morvan region.

FAMILY HOTEL

Hôtel Lanoiselée – *4 av. Jean-Mermoz -* ☏ *03 86 30 75 44 - aboizot@club-inter-net.fr - closed 7 Oct-30 Mar -* ▣ *- 18 rooms: 42/92€ -* ⌷ *6€ - restaurant 14/25.50€.* This small family hotel set up in a white house in the heart of St-Honoré-les-Bains exudes charm and discretion. Simple rooms, unpretentious cuisine.

EXCURSION

Vieille Montagne – *Take D 985 S; in Les Montarons turn left on D 502. Car park. 30min round trip on foot.*

From the clearing a path leads to the **belvedere** in its pleasant setting near the ruins of a castle; there is an extensive view, partly through trees, of Mont Beuvray and the Forêt de la Gravelle.

It is possible to return to St-Honoré via Le Niret at the foot of Mont Genièvre (637m/2 090ft) and the picturesque village of Préporché.

Église de ST-HYMETIÈRE★

Michelin map 321: D-8

The beautiful 11C Romanesque church west of St-Hymetière, a rural village in the Revermont, depended originally on a priory in Mâcon.

Church – It has several striking external features: old tombstones as flagstones on the floor of the porch; massive buttresses and narrow archaic windows on the south side

of the church; tall pilaster strips; a protruding apse and a tall octagonal tower. Inside, the oven-vaulted chancel enclosed by plain arcading and the south aisle recall the original Romanesque building, whereas the main vault and north aisle bear signs of the reworking of the masonry carried out in the 17C.

▶▶ **Arinthod** – *4km/2.5mi N.* Square lined with arcaded houses; central fountain dating from 1750; church with large belfry-porch.

▶▶ **Montfleur** – *16km/10mi SE.* **Écomusée vivant du moulin de Pont des Vents** ⊘: 19C watermill in working order.

One of the rare Romanesque churches still standing in the region

ST-THIBAULT

Population 138
Michelin map 320: G-5

This Auxois village is named after St Theobald whose relics were presented to the local priory in the 13C. The priory church has a choir of great elegance and a main doorway which is considered among the most beautiful examples of 13C Burgundian architecture.

★CHURCH ⊘ 30min

The church is approached from the north side. The original church was built to house the relics of St Theobald at the expense of Robert II, Duke of Burgundy, and his wife, Agnes of France, daughter of St Louis; all that remains are the choir, an

apsidal chapel and the carved doorway from the old transept which collapsed together with the nave in the 17C.

The **doorway**★ is a picture book in itself. The sculptures of the tympanum, executed during the second half of the 13C, are devoted to the Virgin. Those in the recessed arches, dating from the same period, represent, on the inner arch, the Wise Virgins to the left and the Foolish Virgins to the right.

About the year 1310, five great statues were added: St Theobald stands with his back to the pier; the other four have been identified as true likenesses of Duke Robert II and his son, Hugh V, benefactors of the church, the Duchess Agnes, and the Bishop of Autun, Hugues

The altar screen depicts the life of St Theobald

d'Arcy. The expressions on the faces and the modelling of the features show great skill; the door itself has beautifully carved 15C panels.

Interior – The nave, which was rebuilt in the 18C, is decorated with period woodwork from Semur-en-Auxois. The chief interest lies in the choir and apse, masterpieces of bold and skilful design, which date from the end of the 13C.

The five-sided **choir**★ is the most graceful Burgundian construction of that period. From the ground to the vault each slender column rises in an unbroken upward movement linking the blind arcades at the lowest level, the lower windows with their delicate tracery, the triforium and the clerestory. In the choir *(left)* stands a late-14C painted wooden statue of young St Theobald, resting a finger on the page of a book.

To the right, in a recess, is the 13C tomb of the founder of the church, Hugues de Thil. The bas-relief sculptures on the back wall of the recess were restored in 1839. Nearby is the piscina for the high altar, with two 13C basins.

The **furnishings**★ are interesting; the altar is decorated with two carved wooden retables representing episodes from the life of St Theobald.

At the far end of the choir is a large 14C Crucifixion and above the high altar a beautiful crosier, decorated with a 16C eucharistic dove.

On the right of the nave, standing against the wall of the choir, is an attractive 14C statue of the Virgin watching Jesus playing with a bird.

In the chapel of St Giles, which is the oldest part of the church, stands the 14C wooden shrine of St Theobald and statues of characters from the Old and New Testaments.

▶▶ **Vitteaux** – *7km/4.3mi NE*. Église St-Germain: 13C doorway; beautiful 15C carved-wood organ loft and stalls.

▶▶ **Château de Posanges** – *10km/6mi NE*. Imposing 15C castle with four round towers and fortified postern.

SALINS-LES-BAINS ✟

Population 3 333
Michelin map 321: F-5

The spa town of Salins lies in a remarkable **setting**★, strung along the pretty, narrow valley of the Furieuse, beneath the fortresses of Belin and St-André.

Like Dole, Salins still has some traces of its medieval fortifications and one or two towers. Lacuzon, hero of the Franche-Comté's fight for liberty, fired his last few cannon balls at the French from one of these towers in 1674.

White gold – In the past, salt was indispensable for preserving foodstuff. However, primitive mining methods made it so scarce and so costly that anyone caught stealing it was sentenced to be hung forthwith (gallows stood in the central courtyard of the salt mine, which itself resembled a fortress). A salt mine was thus a real gold mine. Jean l'Antique, the most famous member of the Chalon family, seized the salt mine at Salins early in the 13C, procuring for himself a source of enormous wealth. The sale of the salt brought him huge sums of cash, which was an exceptionally privileged situation to be in at the time. While most landlords paid for their purchases with goods (mainly grown on their lands), borrowing if necessary small cash sums from Jewish moneylenders and larger

The former saltworks

M. Paygnard/MICHELIN

ones from the bankers of Lombardy, Jean l'Antique was able to put his ducats to astute use, buying fiefs, vassals and the goodwill of bishops, monks, soldiers and wealthy merchants. Delighted with his increased power, he bestowed a charter on the home town of the salt mine, source of his wealth, in 1249, according it a fair degree of autonomy.

The year of the Black Death – Bubonic plague wreaked havoc in Salins, and throughout the Franche-Comté, for six months of 1349. The victims were covered with black, red or bluish patches and died within two or three days. Stringent quarantine regulations were imposed by the town authorities in an attempt to contain the plague, but despite these about 80% of the town's inhabitants died.

The town's recovery from this disaster was slow. In 1374 a public lending house was founded, called the Mont-de-Salins. This is the precursor of the modern French lending houses called Mont-de-Pitié.

The timber trade – Huge quantities of wood, taken from the nearby forests, were needed to heat the cauldrons used to evaporate water in the salt extraction process, as well as for the increasing number of sawmills and industrial needs in general, with the result that the timber trade became almost as important for Salins as its salt mine.

Eating out and where to stay

MODERATE

La Rôtisserie – *39330 Mouchard - 9km/5.6mi NW of Salins-les-Bains by D 472 - ☎ 03 84 37 80 34 - closed 19-26 Jun, 20 Nov-18 Dec, Sun evenings, Mon lunchtime and Wed - 21.61/60.98€.* In a warm, cosy setting, listen to the crackling of the meat grilled on an open fire before your very eyes.

Grand Hôtel des Bains – *Pl. des Alliés - ☎ 03 84 37 90 50 - hotel.bains@wanadoo.fr - closed 6-20 Jan and Sun out of season - ☐ - 30 rooms: 50/68€ - ☐ 6.60€ - restaurant 15.90/26.90€.* This hotel in the town centre provides direct access to the thermal baths, the swimming pool and the fitness centre. Functional bedrooms with white walls; the ones giving onto the back are quieter. Traditional bill of fare and brasserie formula.

As many as 60 000 horse-drawn carts loaded with wood came into the town each year. The waters of the Furieuse were harnessed to drive 12 great sawmills. Salins soon developed a reputation for producing the best ship masts on the market, and became supplier to the French Navy.
By the 17C Salins, with 5 700 inhabitants, was the second largest community in the Franche-Comté after Besançon, which had 11 500.

SIGHTS

Hôtel de Ville – The town hall dates from the 18C. The 17C **chapel of Notre-Dame-de-la-Libératrice**, crowned by a dome, is in the town hall complex.

★ **Salines** ⓥ – ⬚ Salins is the only **salt mine** where visitors can see how salt water was once pumped out of the Jura soil.

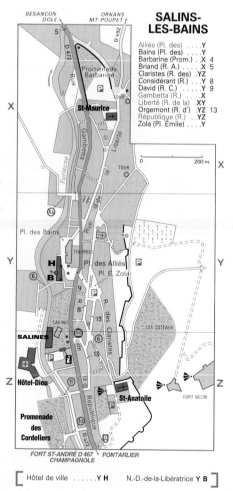

SALINS-LES-BAINS

Alliés (Pl. des)	. . . .Y
Bains (Pl. des)	. . . .Y
Barbarine (Prom.)	. .X 4
Briand (R. A.)	. . . . .X 5
Claristes (R. des)	.YZ
Considérant (R.)	. . .Y 8
David (R. C.)	. . . . .Y 9
Gambetta (R.)	X
Liberté (R. de la)	.XY
Orgemont (R. d')	.YZ 13
République (R.)	. .YZ
Zola (Pl. Émile)	. . . .Y

| Hôtel de ville | . . . . . .Y H | N.-D.-de-la-Libératrice | Y B |

Salt was already being mined in Salins under the Romans, who considered Sequanian salted meats to be a great delicacy. The salt mines then passed into the hands of the Chalon family, followed by the Spanish crown, then the French crown before finally becoming, in 1843, a private business.

The salt waters of Salins-les-Bains are now used exclusively for salt water cures in the local spas.

It is interesting to visit the underground galleries, up to 200m/656ft long, where good lighting shows off the magnificent 13C vaults. The salt water was pumped up from the salt seams, 250m/820ft underground, through boreholes 30cm/15in in diameter. A system using a long beam and a hydraulic wheel activated the pump which drew up the water, which had a high salt content of 33kg/71lb of salt per 100l/22gal. Enormous cauldrons (one of which is on display) were heated over coal fires to evaporate the water and obtain the salt.

Église St-Anatoile – This is the most interesting church in Salins, and one of the best examples of 13C Cistercian architecture in the Franche-Comté, in which there is nonetheless evidence of the local architects' predilection for round arches.

Two protruding Flamboyant Gothic style chapels frame the beautiful Romanesque doorway. Inside, pretty round-arched arcades run along above the pointed Gothic arches separating the nave from the side aisles. Note the 17C pulpit to the right, the 16C choir stalls decorated with striking medallions and woodwork and the carved wooden organ case dating from 1737.

Église St-Maurice – Inside this church there is a wooden statue of St Maurice on horseback in medieval costume at the back of the chapel on the south side. A niche in the south aisle contains a 16C alabaster *Pietà*.

Hôtel-Dieu ⊙ – This hospice dates from the 17C. The pharmacy has some beautiful woodwork as well as a collection of pots in Moustiers faience.

EXCURSIONS

Fort St-André ⊙ – *4km/2.5mi S along D 472 then right on D 94, right again on D 271 and right once more.* Fine example of 17C military architecture (designed by Vauban in 1674). On the right, beneath the ramparts, there is a fine **view**★ of Salins.

★ **Mont Poupet** – *10km/6mi N on D 492 then left on D 273 and left again (parking area near the cross). 15min on foot there and back.*
🚶 A **view**★ from an altitude of 803m/2 635ft of Mont Blanc, the Jura plateau and the Bresse plain. The favourite haunt of hang-gliders and paragliders.

Route des SAPINS★★

Michelin map 321: F to G-6

The beautiful 50km/31mi stretch of road known as the Route des Sapins (Evergreen Forest Drive) runs between Champagnole and Levier, through the forests of La Fresse, Chapois, La Loux and Levier. The itinerary below follows the most interesting stretch with the best facilities *(car parks, rest and picnic areas, signposted footpaths, nature rambles)*.

FROM CHAMPAGNOLE TO LEVIER
55km/34mi – allow 3hr

Champagnole – *See CHAMPAGNOLE.*
Take D 471 NE. At a crossroads on the outskirts of Equevillon, leave D 471 and drive straight on, along the Route des Sapins.

The road climbs through the **Forêt de la Fresse**, offering glimpses of Champagnole to the left.

Turn right on D 21, leaving the Route des Sapins to the left, and go as far as the junction with D 288, where you turn left.

The road follows the line of the hillside, about halfway up, along the coomb through which the Angillon has cut its river bed. To the east of the road lie the magnificent stands of the forest of La Joux, and to the west the 1 153ha/2 849 acres of conifers which make up the forest of La Fresse. Just before the village of Les Nans, turn left onto the forest road known as Larderet aux Nans, which gives a good view of Les Nans and the Angillon coomb. The road rejoins the Route des Sapins at the crossroads, Carrefour des Baumes, then runs through the northern part of the forest of La Fresse, through the village of Chapois and into the forest of La Joux, climbing as it goes.

★★ **Forêt de la Joux** – This is one of the most beautiful pine forests of France.
This wooded area covering 2 652ha/6 550 acres is separated from the Fresse Forest by the Angillon rapids to the south; it borders Levier Forest to the north. Whereas most of the trees are conifers, a few deciduous species can be found. Some of the firs are of exceptional size: up to 45m/148ft tall, with a diameter of 1.20m/3.93ft at 1.30m/4.26ft from the ground. These trees are second in size only to those found in certain tropical regions or California.

Forêt de la Joux

Atelier M. Bevalot

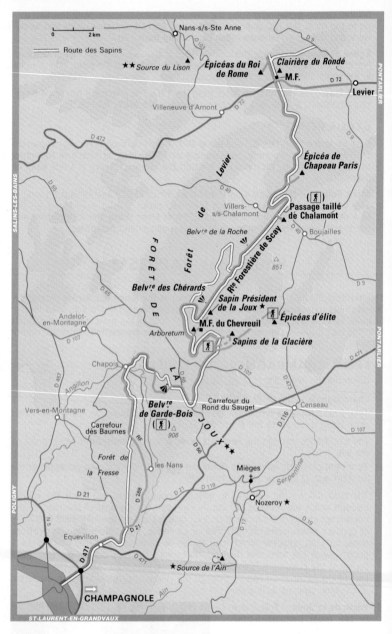

The Administration has divided the forest into five cantons, known as series. The most striking trees are in the cantons of La Glacière and Aux Sources.

Leave the Route des Sapins to take the road to the Belvédère de Garde-Bois, which is near a chapel.

Belvédère de Garde-Bois – 🏃 There is a pretty view of the deep Angillon Valley as well as the forest of La Fresse in the distance.

Carry on east along the road that led to the viewpoint to rejoin the Route des Sapins. The stretch of road from the Rond-du-Sauget crossroads onwards is particularly pretty.

Sapins de la Glacière – 🏃 *30min round trip on foot. Take the path which leads off to the right from the Route des Sapins as you come from Champagnole.*

This canton earned its name from being the coldest part of the forest and the area where the snow lasts longest. Magnificent conifers, as straight as ramrods, grow around a deep hollow in the canton's centre. There is a particularly tall, splendid tree next to the footpath. The peace and quiet in the forest combine with the subdued quality of the light filtered by the trees to create a soothing, meditative atmosphere.

Épicéas d'élite – 🚶 *The Route de la Marine leads to this stand of spruces. Alternatively, there is a signposted footpath leading off from D 473; the beginning of it is indicated about 1km/0.5mi S of the level crossing at Boujailles station (30min there and back on foot).*

These are the most beautiful trees in the Esserval-Tartre spruce forest, hence their name.

Maison Forestière du Chevreuil – The clearing by this forester's lodge is a major tourist attraction in the region. Those interested in forestry will be able to visit the **Arboretum**, a test planting area for trees not native to the region.

Where the Route des Sapins divides into two, take the right fork, signposted Route des Sapins par les Crêtes.

Belvédère des Chérards – There is a glimpse from here of wooded plateaux.

★ **Sapin Président de la Joux** – This fir tree, the most famous tree in the Chérards canton, is over two centuries old. It has a diameter of 3.85m/13ft at a height of 1.30m/4ft from the ground, is 45m/148ft tall and represents the equivalent of 600 planks of wood or 22m³/777cu ft of timber.

> **CHARMS OF THE FOREST**
>
> **Maison Forestière du Chevreuil** – *39300 Supt - 3.5km/2.3mi N of Chapois by D 251 -* ☎ *03 84 51 40 85 - closed 16 Sep-14 Jun -* 🍽 *- 12.81/21.04€.* Standing in a pretty clearing surrounded by pine trees, this unusual house offers simple but delicious meals. Fondue and grilled beef on request. Playing area for children. In bad weather, the restaurant may be closed; it is best to enquire beforehand.
>
> **Chambre d'Hôte Bourgeois-Bousson** – *Grande-Rue - 39110 Andelot-en-Montagne - 2.5km/1.6mi NW of Chapois by D 250 -* ☎ *03 84 51 43 77 - closed Nov to Easter -* 🍽 *- 6 rooms: 28.97/39.64€ - meals 9.91€.* This family establishment close to the forest exudes a quaint, slightly old-fashioned atmosphere. Your hosts are two sisters who will extend a cordial welcome. The guestrooms are simple but comfortable. Traditional cuisine.

The Route des Sapins carries on through the forest, offering a pretty view of the Chalamont dip to the left.

Forêt de Levier – This forest was once the possession of the Chalon family until it was confiscated in 1562 by Philippe II, King of Spain. It became the property of the King of France after Louis XIV's conquest of Franche-Comté in 1674. At that time the forest was used to provide timber for naval construction and for the Salins salt works. Local people also came here to obtain their firewood, so large areas were planted entirely with deciduous trees, in keeping with the forest's role as a useful resource. The modern forest, at an altitude of between 670m/2 198ft and 900m/2 953ft, covers an area of 2 725ha/6 733 acres and consists almost exclusively of coniferous trees (60% fir, 12% spruce). The forest area is managed in three blocks (the *séries* of Jura, Arc and Scay).

Route forestière de Scay – This slightly bumpy road, which crosses the forest of Levier through the so-called quiet zone *(zone de silence)* of Scay, offers some beautiful views of the surrounding area. At the **Belvédère de la Roche** there is a view over the forest of Levier and the clearing in which the village of Villers-sous-Chalamont lies.

Passage taillé de Chalamont – 🚶 Shortly before D 49, a footpath leads off to the right *(30min there and back on foot)*, along what was once a Celtic, then a Roman path. Note the steps cut into the sloping or slippery sections and the grooves which guided chariot wheels. At the point where the path leaves the forest, by the ruins of the medieval tower of Chalamont, it passes through a kind of trench, a technique which was imitated in the building of the nearby modern road linking Boujailles and Villers-sous-Chalamont.

Épicéa de Chapeau-Paris – This tree is to the forest of Levier what the Sapin Président is to the forest of La Joux. It is 45m/148ft tall with a diameter of 4m/13ft and represents an equivalent volume of timber of about 20m³/706cu ft.

Take the Route forestière de Ravonnet and then the Route du Pont de la Marine to the right.

Clairière du Rondé – This clearing contains an enclosure containing Sika deer and a forester's lodge *(maison forestière – exhibitions in summer).*

Épicéas du Roi de Rome – These spruces are over 180 years old and can reach heights of more than 50m/164ft.

Turn back to take D 72 on the left towards Levier.

SAULIEU★

Population 2 837
Michelin map 320: F-6 – Local map see Le MORVAN

Saulieu, pleasantly situated on the boundaries of the Morvan and the Auxois, has a long-standing gastronomic renown upheld by a string of fine restaurants lined alongside the N 6 road. The art lover will find interest in the basilica of St-Andoche and also in the works of François Pompon, a sculptor known for his representations of animals, who was born at Saulieu in 1855.

A gastronomic centre – The gastronomic reputation of Saulieu is linked to the history of road travel and goes back to the 17C. In 1651 the Burgundian states decided to restore the old Paris-Lyon road, which passed along the eastern edge of the Morvan, to the importance that it had before the Middle Ages. Saulieu set about increasing its prosperity by developing local industry and fairs. The town became a post house on the route and obliged itself to treat travellers well. Rabelais had already praised Saulieu and its excellent meals. **Madame de Sévigné** stopped in the town on her way to Vichy on 26 August 1677, and she avowed later that for the first time in her life she had become a little tipsy.

The timber of the Morvan – Although Saulieu's economic activity has always been to a great extent based on forestry there has been a considerable transformation in this sector. There is an ever-growing trade in Christmas trees; each year more than a million of these trees (spruces in particular) are sent to Paris and other large towns in France, Europe and Africa. Despite this shift to conifers there are still large areas of oak and beech. Large tree nurseries now produce several hundreds of thousands of saplings for the French and foreign markets.

The state forest of Saulieu (768ha/1 898 acres) now has many recreational facilities: picnic sites, adventure playgrounds, walks and trails, riding tracks and small lakes providing trout fishing.

SIGHTS

★**Basilique St-Andoche** – *30min.* The basilica stands in place du Docteur-Roclore where there is a pretty 18C fountain. The church, which dates from the beginning of the 12C, is slightly later than the one in Vézelay; it was built to replace an abbey church founded in the 8C on the site of the martyrdom of St Andoche, St Thyrse and St Felix, and was influenced by St-Lazare in Autun of which it was a sister house.

This fine Romanesque building has been sadly maltreated; the choir was burnt by the English in 1359 and rebuilt in 1704 without any attempt at coherence of style; the main doorway was mutilated during the French Revolution and rebuilt in the 19C. Inside, the bases of the pillars are buried nearly three feet deep.

Interior – The main point of interest is the series of historiated or decorated **capitals★★**, inspired by those in Autun. Here one can see the Flight into Egypt, the Temptation of Christ in the Desert, the Hanging of Judas, and Christ appearing to Mary Magdalene.

The choir stalls date from the 14C and the organ loft from the 15C. After its restoration, the tomb of St Andoche was placed in the last chapel in the right aisle. To the right of the choir, note a Renaissance Virgin in stone and a 14C statue of St Roch.

Eating out

BUDGET

La Vieille Auberge – *15 r. Grillot - ☎ 03 80 64 13 74 - closed 6 Jan-6 Feb, Tue evenings and Wed except Jul-Aug - 12/29€.* This country inn at the entrance to Saulieu has a pleasant dining room with pretty tables. Interesting choice of reasonably priced menus combining traditional cuisine with a strong regional touch. Functional rooms.

La Guinguette – *Moulin de la Serrée - 58230 Alligny-en-Morvan - 7km/4.3mi S of Saulieu by D 26 - ☎ 03 86 76 15 79 - open Sat and Sun Easter to 1 Nov and daily Jul-Aug - 15/19€.* This welcoming cabin surrounded by reeds lying at the water's edge is the delight of Sunday afternoon strollers. Fish farm on the property. Trout and salmon can be eaten on the premises or bought to be taken away. Fishing rods available for keen anglers.

EXPENSIVE

La Côte d'Or – *2 r. d'Argentine - ☎ 03 80 90 53 53 - loiseau@relais-chateaux.com - 122/185€.* The illustrious chef Bernard Loiseau, who has earned himself a glowing reputation across the country, reigns supreme over this restaurant. This temple of gastronomy offers a prestigious bill of fare to its gourmet diners, who come from afar to sample the food. Refined atmosphere and smart setting in a former coaching inn.

In the north aisle, there is a handsome tombstone and painted *Pietà*, presented, so it is said, by Madame de Sévigné as a penance for over-indulgence.

Musée municipal François-Pompon ⊙ – Established in a 17C mansion alongside the basilica, this new museum has two curiously different themes: stone (Gallo-Roman tombstones, religious statuary, milestones); and conviviality (exhibits on the art of fine food).

On the **ground floor**, medieval charts and old road markers recall Saulieu's position as an age-old way station. The granite funerary monuments are from the ancient necropolis, and the religious statues from the 12C to the 18C.

The **first floor** is devoted to the sculptor **François Pompon**, born in Saulieu in 1855. A student of Rodin, he is better known for his representations of animals. Pompon's style is distinctive for it smooth, round shapes; **le Taureau★**

Ph. Gajic/MICHELIN

Le Taureau, François Pompon

(Bull), one of his greatest works, was erected on a square at the town's northern entrance in 1948.

As for gastronomy, this subject so close to the Gallic heart is given ample space, inspired by Bernard Loiseau, a local award-winning chef.

EXCURSION

★ **Butte de Thil** – *18km/11mi N along D 980 via Précy-sous-Thil.* Alt 492m/1 614ft. The hill, visible from afar, is crowned with the interesting ruins of a former 14C **collegiate church** and a **medieval castle** (9C-14C) dismantled by Richelieu. The 25m/82ft-tall square tower, from which the view extends 50km/31mi in all directions, was known as the sentry of the Auxois region.

SEMUR-EN-AUXOIS★

Population 4 543

Michelin map 320: G-5 – Local map see Le MORVAN

The **setting★** and the town of Semur, main centre of the Auxois agricultural and stock-raising region, form a picturesque scene. A tightly packed mass of small light-coloured houses stands on the top of a rose-tinted granite cliff, overlooking a deep ravine at the bottom of which flows the River Armançon. Above the houses and cascade of gardens rise the great red-slated towers of the castle keep and the slender spire of the church of Notre-Dame.

From the Paris road, there is a good view of the ramparts and the town during the downhill run to the Joly Bridge.

A stronghold – Semur became the strong point of the duchy in the 14C when the citadel was reinforced by ramparts and 18 towers. The town was divided into three parts each with a perimeter wall. Occupying the whole width of the rock spur and towering above all else was the keep, a citadel in itself and reputedly impregnable. It had a sheer drop both to the north and the south to the Armançon Valley and was flanked by four enormous round towers: the Tour de l'Orle-d'Or, the Tour de la Gehenne, the Tour de la Prison and the Tour Margot. The château stood to the west, on the upper part of the peninsula, encircled by a bend in the river – the ramparts can still be seen. To the east was the town, still the most densely populated district although the town has spread on to the west bank.

TOWN WALK

Porte Sauvigny – This 15C gateway, preceded by a postern, marked the main entrance to the district known as the Bourg Notre-Dame.

Follow rue Buffon lined with shops and 16C houses.

Église Notre-Dame – *30min.* The church stands in place Notre-Dame, flanked by old houses. It was founded in the 11C, rebuilt in the 13C and 14C, altered in the 15C and 16C, extended by the addition of chapels to the north aisle and restored by Viollet-le-Duc (1814-79).

Eating out

BUDGET

Le Calibressan – *16 r. Févret -* ☎ *03 80 97 32 40 - le.calibressan@wanadoo.fr - closed 1-27 Jan, Sat lunchtime, Sun evenings and Mon - 13€ lunch - 16/27.50€.* The name of this restaurant symbolises the Franco-American couple who run the place: she comes from California whereas he is a native of Bresse. The same combination is echoed in the decoration (Indian portraits and dried maize on the walls) and in the cooking (Bresse chicken and hot chili).

Where to stay

BUDGET

Chambre d'Hôte La Maison du Canal – *At Pont-Royal - 21390 Clamerey - 16km/10mi SE of Semur-en-Auxois by D 970 then D 70 (heading for Vitteaux) -* ☎ *03 80 64 62 65 - closed Nov-Apr - 6 rooms: 38/44€.* This early 19C building, set up along the quays of the Burgundy Canal opposite a marina, used to house the post office. The carefully kept rooms look out onto the peaceful Auxois countryside. Information on boating available.

Chambre d'Hôte Les Langrons – *21140 Villars-Villenotte - 5.5km/3.5mi NW of Semur-en-Auxois by D 954 then D 9ᴬ -* ☎ *03 80 96 65 11 - closed Dec - ✍ - 3 rooms: 40/50€.* This beautifully restored farmhouse is located near the village of Villars. The large, comfortable rooms feature exposed beams. The curtains and bedspreads have an unmistakable British touch, which is understandable because the owners come from England. Scrumptious breakfasts. Pretty self-catering *gîte* at the entrance to the farm.

Exterior – The 14C façade, dominated by two square towers, is preceded by a vast porch. In rue Notre-Dame, the 13C door in the north transept (Porte des Bleds) has a beautiful tympanum depicting Doubting Thomas and the bringing of the Gospel to the West Indies. On one of the slender engaged piers which flank the doorway are two sculpted snails, symbolising Burgundian cooking.

The 15C porch shelters three doorways. Although the sculptures of the recessed arches and the niches disappeared during the Revolution, various bas-relief figures line the base of the engaged piers.

From the garden behind the church there is a view of the chevet which, with the narrow and steeply roofed apse and conically roofed chapels, show great purity of line.

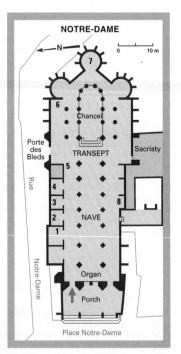

The octagonal tower above the transept crossing is surmounted by a beautiful stone spire (56m/184ft).

Interior – The narrowness of the central nave, dating from the 13C and 14C, emphasizes the soaring height of the vaulting supported by slender columns.

There are several interesting chapels opening off the north aisle. In the second chapel (**1**) is a polychrome Entombment dating from the late 15C with monumental figures typical of Claus Sluter. The third chapel (**2**) with its stellar vaulting has 16C stained glass illustrating the legend of St Barbara. The last two chapels contain panels of stained glass given in the 15C by local guilds – the butchers (**3**) and eight panels from the drapers (**4**).

Behind the pulpit is a 15C stone canopy (**5**), remarkably carved with a 5m/16ft-high pinnacle.

A blind triforium decorates the 13C choir and the transept; its elegant and slender columns are surmounted by capitals in the form of sculpted human heads. The hanging keystone of the choir is brightly painted and represents the crowning of the Virgin amid foliage and angels' heads.

The choir is flanked by double aisles; the three chapels radiating from the ambulatory are separated by triple lancets. The Grantin-Riepp-Callinet organ dates from the 17C to the 19C.

In the last chapel of the outer north aisle is a painted retable (**6**) dating from 1554, representing the Tree of Jesse. The retable is surmounted by a Gothic canopy of carved wood. The Lady Chapel (**7**) is lit by very beautiful stained-glass windows of the 13C restored by Viollet-le-Duc. In the south aisle there is a late-15C polychrome statue (**8**) of Christ bearing the Five Wounds; with a theatrical gesture He indicates the spear thrust in His side; two angels carry His mantle.

Continue along rue Fevret.

Tour de l'Orle-d'Or and Musée – This tower, which is now cracked on the north side, was once part of the keep which was razed in 1602. The tower owes its name to its battlements (demolished), which used to be covered with coppered lead (*ourlée d'or* – trimmed with gold). Its dimensions are impressive (44m/144ft high, walls 5m/16ft thick at the base tapering to about 2.2m/7ft at the top). Prior to the construction of the Joly Bridge (1787), this tower was one of the main entrances to the town. It now houses the headquarters of the local history and natural science society.

Pont Joly – From the Joly Bridge there is an overall **view**★ of the little medieval city. It is particularly charming in the light of the setting sun. The bridge crosses the Armançon at the foot of the castle keep, which once guarded the narrow isthmus joining the rose-coloured cliff, where the city first started, to the granite plateau on which the town has now spread. In the foreground the view sweeps up the valley with gardens, rocks, parks and small cascades on either side.

Promenade des Remparts – The former ramparts along the edge of the granite spur have been converted into a promenade shaded by lime trees which overlooks the valley of the Armançon. To reach the promenade, go past the hospital, a pleasant 18C building, which was once the mansion of the Marquis du Châtelet, Governor of Semur, whose priggish wife was Voltaire's sweetheart.

Rue Basse-du-Rempart skirts the foot of the ramparts. Their grandeur is emphasised by the enormous blocks of red granite, sparkling with mica and quartz, which serve as the foundations of the keep.

Walk back along rue Collenot.

B. Kaufmann/MICHELIN

Le Armançon runs through town

Museum ⊘ – An old Jacobin convent houses the museum and library. The ground floor displays a collection of 13C to 19C sculpture, including many original plaster figures, mostly by Augustin Dumont, who created monumental sculptures and commemorative statues (*Spirit of Liberty* in place de la Bastille in Paris). The first floor houses a rich collection on natural science, particularly zoology and geology (fossils – rare fish fossils – and mineral samples). The second floor contains articles found during the archaeological excavation of prehistoric, Gallo-Roman (votive offerings from the source of the Seine) and Merovingian sites.

A gallery contains 17C to 19C paintings (*Portrait of a Prophet* by Vignon and three works by Corot) and a few 19C sculptures; a small room is devoted to the Middle Ages and the Renaissance (*Angels* by Le Moiturier).

EXCURSIONS

Lac de Pont – *3km/1.7mi S.* ▣ This 6km/3.7mi-long artificial lake was created in the 19C to supply the Canal de Bourgogne. It lies in an attractive green setting dotted with rocks and offers a beach and water sports facilities.

Époisses – *12km/7.5mi W.* This pleasant village, on the plateau of Auxois, a livestock-rearing district, is known for its castle and its soft, strong-flavoured cheese.

★ **Château** ⊘ – The château is set slightly apart from the village and is enclosed by two fortified precincts ringed by dry moats. The buildings in the outer courtyard form a small village clustered round the church, once part of a 12C abbey, and a robust 16C dovecot.

Château d'Épossies

To see the four towers which link the living quarters walk round the outside of the inner precinct before crossing the second moat.

A balustraded terrace precedes the court of honour, which is marked by the presence of a well with an attractive wrought-iron well-head. The château was remodelled in the 16C and 17C and the southern range was demolished during the Revolution. The Guitaut family, owners of the château since the 17C, have preserved many mementoes of famous people who have stayed here.

In the entrance hall, Renaissance portraits are set into the panelled walls. The small room beyond has a richly painted ceiling. The salon's Louis XIV furniture includes chairs covered with Gobelins tapestries.

On the first floor the portrait gallery is hung with paintings of 17C and 18C personalities (Henri IV, Chateaubriand, the Prince de Condé...). When in Burgundy, Madame de Sévigné often stayed at Époisses, with the Guitaut family, as her own château, Bourbilly, was by then in a state of dilapidation.

SENS★★

Pop 26 904
Michelin map 319: C-2

Now a simple sub-prefecture in the *département* of Yonne, Sens is the seat of an archbishopric, proof of its past grandeur. The old town is girdled by boulevards and promenades that have replaced the ancient ramparts. In the city centre stands the cathedral of St-Étienne. The approach from the west *(D 81)* provides a fine view of the town as the road descends from the heights on the left bank of the Yonne.

HISTORICAL NOTES

The Country of the Senones – The tribe of the Senones, who gave their name to the town, was for a long time one of the most powerful in Gaul. In 390 BC, under the command of Brennus, they invaded Italy and seized Rome. When the Romans were masters of all Gaul, they made Sens the capital of a province of the Lyonnaise, known as Lyonnaise IV or Senonia.

An Important Diocese – Up to 1622, the year in which Paris was elevated to the rank of an archbishopric, Sens had pre-eminence over the bishoprics of Chartres, Auxerre, Meaux, Paris, Orléans, Nevers and Troyes, giving the initials forming the device of the metropolitan church, Campont. During the residence in Sens of Pope Alexander III in 1163-64 the city became the temporary capital of Christianity. The church council that condemned Abélard was also held at Sens and the marriage of St Louis and Marguerite of Provence was celebrated in the cathedral in 1234. With the elevation of Paris, the diocese of Sens lost the bishoprics of Meaux, Chartres and Orléans.

TOWN WALK

Marché couvert – The metal framework filled with pink brick of the covered market standing opposite the cathedral is typical of the architectural style in fashion during the latter half of the 19C. The conspicuous pitched roof is ornamented with pinnacle turrets.

South of the museums, rue Abélard is lined with 17C and 18C mansions.

Eating out

MODERATE

Au Crieur de Vin – *1 r. d'Alsace-Lorraine - ☎ 03 86 65 92 80 - closed 3 weeks in Aug, 22 Dec-4 Jan, Sun and Mon - 17€.* Traditional dishes like *tête de veau* (boiled calf's head) and roasted meat (poultry, lamb, pork) are the specialities of this restaurant, served with wines from the Yonne area. As the place is extremely popular among locals, it is recommended to reserve in advance. Wine for sale.

Where to stay

BUDGET

Hôtel Virginia – *3km/1.9mi E of Sens by N 60 heading for Troyes - ☎ 03 86 64 66 66 - 🅿 - 100 rooms: 37/43€ - ⊡ 5.50€ - restaurant 16/22€.* This motel is comprised of several buildings, so you can park the car directly in front of the door leading to your room. Grill-restaurant with special menu for children. Lounge with billiard table.

On the town

Place de la République – *Pl. de la République.* Most cafés in Sens are located around this square facing the cathedral. Relax on one of the many terraces and soak up the sun in a lively atmosphere.

Le Kilt Pub – *16 bd Garibaldi - Sun-Wed. 5pm-1am, Fri-Sat 5pm-2am.* This vaulted cellar, a popular venue for blues, jazz and rock concerts, extends a warm welcome that will make you feel very much at home. Sit down at the piano or sip a drink in a relaxed, friendly atmosphere.

Shopping

There are many nice shops along the pedestrian Grande-Rue.

À la Renommée des Bons Fromages. G. Parret – *37 Grande-Rue - ☎ 03 86 65 11 54 - open Mon, Wed-Sat 7.30am-12.30pm, 3-7.30pm, Sun 7.30am-12.30pm, mornings of public holidays.* A small dairy offering a great many local cheeses: Époisses, Chaource, Soumaintrain, and there is an interesting choice of wines stored in the cellar.

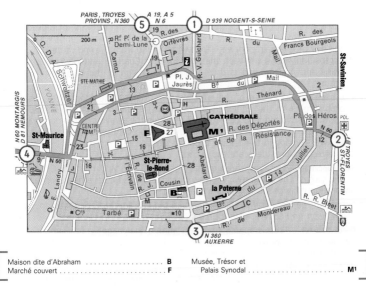

Maison dite d'Abraham	**B**	Musée, Trésor et	
Marché couvert	**F**	Palais Synodal	**M¹**

Around St-Pierre-le-Rond – Beside the **church** ⊘ stands the bell-tower (1728) and a building which in 1927 was faced with the 13C façade of the Sens charity hospital (Hôtel-Dieu). The high lancet windows in the gables of the two façades create a point of harmonious homogeneity of style.

At the corner of rue de la République and rue Jean-Cousin, stands a 16C house, the **Maison dite d'Abraham**. The carved corner post is decorated with a Tree of Jesse. The house next door, at no 50 rue Jean-Cousin, known as the House of the Pillar (Maison du Pilier) (16C), has a curious porch. Further along, at no 8, the Maison Jean-Cousin with a garden façade overlooking rue Jossey also dates from the 16C. The pedestrian shopping street, Grande Rue, has numerous half-timbered houses along it, some of which have plaques indicating their former function.

Église St-Maurice – This church was built in the latter half of the 12C on an island in the Yonne. The square east end is half-timbered; the slate spire rising from the asymmetrical roof is seen to advantage from the right bank of the river.

La Poterne – Traces of the Gallo-Roman walls are visible along boulevard du 14-Juillet, south of the town centre.

Église St-Savinien – *137bis rue d'Alsace-Lorraine, 750m/820yd from boulevard du Mail on the left. Apply to the tourist office.*
The church was built in the 11C on the site of an earlier church. It is basilical in plan with a steep-pitched roof over the nave and three apsidal chapels but no transept. A flight of steps in front of the central apsidal chapel leads to a small crypt. The plain exterior of the building contrasts with the graceful belfry which has two storeys; the lower one in the Romanesque style is pierced by twin bays with round-headed arches; the upper one has tall bays with pointed arches.

★★ CATHÉDRALE ST-ÉTIENNE ⊘ *30min*

The cathedral, started c 1130 by Archbishop Henri Sanglier, was the first of the great Gothic cathedrals in France. Many other buildings have borrowed largely from the design (the layout, the alternating pillars, the triforium); William of Sens, architect, used it as his model when reconstructing the chancel of Canterbury Cathedral (1175-92).

Exterior – The west front, despite the loss of a tower, has nevertheless preserved its imposing majesty and harmony of balance. The north tower (*tour de plomb* or Lead Tower), built at the end of the 12C, used to be surmounted by a timbered belfry covered in lead, which was destroyed during the 19C.

The south tower (*tour de pierre* or Stone Tower), which collapsed at the end of the 13C, was gradually rebuilt in the following century and was completed in the 16C. It is topped by a graceful campanile and is 78m/256ft high. The tower houses two bells, weighing 14t and 16t.

The statues on the upper gallery, which were added in the 19C, represent the leading archbishops of Sens. An immense radiant window, a rose window of smaller size, and a Christ conferring His blessing, framed by two angels (modern statues), rise in tiers above the central doorway.

North doorway – The tympanum of this 12C doorway recalls the history of St John the Baptist. Generosity and avarice are portrayed at the bottom of the low-relief sculptures.

Central doorway – A beautiful statue of St Stephen, in the costume of a deacon and carrying the Gospel, fortunately spared during the Revolution, stands with its back to the pier of the main doorway. This work, dating from the end of the 12C, marks the transition period between the sculptures of Chartres and Bourges and those of Paris and Amiens, and is thus an interesting sign of the beginning of Gothic sculpture.

The bas-relief sculptures of the engaged piers framing the doorway represent the Foolish Virgins on the right and the Wise Virgins on the left. The statues of the Apostles, which used to occupy the 12 niches in the splaying of the doorway, have disappeared. The original tympanum, which supposedly portrayed the Last Judgement, was remade in the 13C: it is devoted to scenes from the Life of St Stephen. Statuettes of saints decorate the arches.

South doorway – The tympanum of the right-hand doorway (early 14C) is devoted to the Virgin. The statuettes, representing the prophets, have been decapitated. A decoration of angels ornaments the arching.

Go round the cathedral to the N and take the passage (14C St-Denis doorway) to the Maison de l'Œuvre, the 16C chapter library. Carry on to impasse Abraham.

North transept – From impasse Abraham admire the magnificent Flamboyant-style façade built by Martin Chambiges and his son between 1500 and 1513. The sculpted decoration is very graceful. The statue of Abraham, surmounting the gable, is modern.

Go back to the west front of the cathedral and enter by the south doorway.

Interior – The nave is impressive for its size and unity; it is divided from the aisles by magnificent arches surmounted by a triforium and roofed with sexpartite vaulting. The alternating stout and slender pillars are characteristic of the Early Gothic style. The original appearance of the church has been somewhat lost in successive alterations: the clerestories in the choir were extended upwards in the 13C and in the nave in the 14C; in the 15C Archbishop Tristan de Salazar added the transept marking the division between the nave and the choir.

The **stained-glass windows★★**, dating from the 12C to the 17C, are magnificent.

In the third bay of the south aisle is a window (**1**) by Jean Cousin, dating from 1530. On the north side of the nave is a Renaissance retable and a monument (**2**) given by Archbishop de Salazar in memory of his parents. The stained-glass windows of the south transept (1500-02) were made in Troyes – those portraying the Tree

The Good Samaritan

of Jesse and Legend of St Nicholas are outstanding; the rose window represents the Last Judgement. Those in the north transept were made between 1516 and 1517 by Jean Hympe and his son, glaziers from Sens; the rose window represents Paradise.

The choir is enclosed by handsome bronze screens (1762) bearing the arms of the Cardinal de Luynes. The large high altar is 18C by Servandoni and the stained glass of the clerestory dates from the 13C.

Both St John's Chapel, which contains a fine 13C calvary (**3**), and the blind arcade round the ambulatory are part of the original building. The oldest stained glass, dating from the late 12C, is in the four windows overlooking the ambulatory: the story of Thomas à Becket (**4**), the story of St Eustache (**5**) and the parables of the Prodigal Son (**6**) and the Good Samaritan (**7**). The tomb (**8**) of the dauphin, father of Louis XVI, by Guillaume Coustou is placed in the next chapel. The 13C apsidal chapel has stained-glass windows (**9**) of the same period. In the chapel of the Sacré-Cœur (**10**) one of the windows is attributed to Jean Cousin. In summer, a 13C staircase leads up to the cathedral treasury *(in winter, go via the museum, as the staircase is closed)*.

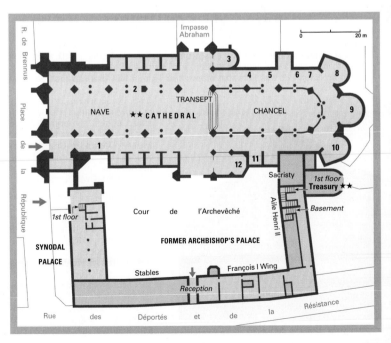

In the chapel beyond the sacristy is a Renaissance retable (**11**). The Lady Chapel contains a 14C seated statue of the Virgin (**12**) above the altar.

Leave by the south transept.

South transept – This was built by Martin Chambiges, master mason who had worked at both Beauvais and Troyes. It is a fine example of the Flamboyant style (1490-1500). The decoration of the Moses doorway is quite remarkable.

★MUSEUM, TREASURY AND PALAIS SYNODAL ⊙

The Musées de Sens are housed in the **ancien archevêché** (16C-18C) and the Palais Synodal which stand on the south side of the cathedral.

François I and Henri II wings – These 16C galleries are devoted to the history of Sens and the Sens district. The first rooms display prehistoric and protohistoric articles: Paleolithic stone tools, Neolithic house and burials (7 500 to 2 500 BC), Bronze Age objects (2 500 to 750 BC) including the treasure of Villethierry (jeweller's stock), many Iron Age weapons and ornaments.

The basement contains pieces of **Gallo-Roman stonework★** reused in the construction of the town walls of Sens: architectural pieces, sculptures, tombstones. Excavations under the courtyard have revealed the foundations of a 4C bathhouse including a collection of bone combs.

Sculpture from the 18C is displayed on the first floor: reliefs from the Porte Dauphine which was erected in memory of the dauphin, Louis XV's son, and of the dauphin's wife, and parts of a rood screen removed from the cathedral in the 19C. The second floor is hung with 17C to 19C paintings.

★★Cathedral treasury (Trésor) – *Access via the museum.*

This treasure house is one of the richest in France. It contains a magnificent collection of materials and liturgical vestments: the shroud of St Victor, a 13C white silk mitre embroidered with gold thread, St Thomas à Becket's alb; handsome 15C high warp tapestries *(Adoration of the Magi* and *Coronation of the Virgin)*; ivories (5C and 6C pyx, the 7C liturgical comb of St Lupus, an 11C Byzantine coffret and a 12C Islamic one) as well as gold plate (late-12C ciborium).

Palais Synodal – This beautiful 13C palace was restored by Viollet-le-Duc. The great vaulted chamber on the ground floor was the seat of the ecclesiastical tribunal *(officialité)*. In the 13C two bays were converted into a prison and there are still traces of graffiti on the walls.

The magnificent hall on the first floor was where the bishops deliberated. The archaeological collection on the ground floor and the collections of the adjoining treasury (Lemoine paintings, tapestries...) will be rearranged once the rooms of the new museum are ready.

▶▶ **Moulin à tan** – *On leaving town S towards Auxerre.* ⊙ This 7ha/17-acre park hosts a rose-garden, an arboretum, an animal pen, a playground...

Roche de SOLUTRÉ★★

Michelin map 320: I-12 – Local map see Le MÂCONNAIS

The **rock of Solutré**, a superb limestone escarpment with a distinctive profile which can be seen from miles away between Mâcon and Bourg-en-Bresse in the east, figures largely in prehistory. It was here that a particular type of flint tool was first identified and given the name Solutrean (18 000 to 15 000 BC). The tools were created by knapping, i.e. knocking off flat flakes to obtain bifaced stones with sharp edges, sometimes called laurel leaves (fine examples in the Musée Denon in Chalon-sur-Saône). The end of this period is marked by the appearance of stone needles with eyes.

Excavations – The first excavations at the foot of the rock in 1866 brought to light a pile of horse bones which, together with a few bison, auroch, deer and mammoth bones, formed a layer 0.5-2m/18in-6.5ft thick covering an area of 4 000m²/4 784sq yd. This hunting ground was used for 25 000 years by the different generations of the Upper Paleolithic Age (Aurignacian, Gravettian, Solutrean and Magdalenian).

Ph. Gajic/MICHELIN

Roche de Solutré

At the end of the last century it was supposed that the horses were rounded up on the top of the rock and forced by noise or fire to jump to their death; this theory is no longer maintained. Excavations carried out between 1968 and 1976 suggest that the wild horses were hunted during their spring migrations to the foot of the rock where they were slaughtered and dismembered.

Panorama – *From Mâcon take D 54 SW through Solutré; beyond the cemetery take the second road on the right to a car park; 45min there and back on foot.* A path leads through Crot du Charnier (where the museum is situated) to the top of the rock of Solutré (495m/1 624ft). Although the range is limited the view embraces the valley of the Saône, the Bresse, the Jura and on a clear day the Alps.

Musée départemental de Préhistoire – The museum, which is buried at the foot of the rock, is devoted to the prehistoric archaeology of the south Mâconnais, the horses and hunting at Solutré in the Upper Paleolithic Age and Solutrean man in the European context (numerous models).

In between the three sections are two viewpoints overlooking the surrounding countryside: the valley of the Saône and the rock of Solutré.

Château de TANLAY★★

Michelin map 319: H-4

The château of Tanlay, built about 1550, is a magnificent architectural composition, and an unexpected surprise in this small village on the banks of the Canal de Bourgogne, which draws fleets of houseboats every summer. The château was built shortly after Ancy-le-Franc, the first example of the Classical Renaissance style, and is a fine monument to French Renaissance architecture at a time when it had broken away from the Italian influence.

Approaching Tanlay from the east by D 965, there is a good general view of this handsome residence and its park; it is particularly attractive in the evening light.

TOUR ⊙ *1hr*

Exterior – The small château (the Portal), an elegant building of Louis XIII style, leads into the Cour Verte (Green Courtyard), which is surrounded by arches except on the left where a bridge crosses the moat and leads to the great doorway opening onto the main courtyard of the large château.

Château de Tanlay

The architect Pierre Le Muet, who oversaw work on the château between 1642 and 1648, designed the pyramidal obelisks which stand at the entrance to the bridge.

The main living quarters are joined by two staircase towers to two lower wings at right angles to the main building. Each wing ends in a round domed tower with a lantern. The Tour des Archives is on the left, the Tour de la Chapelle on the right.

Interior – On the ground floor, the hallway (Vestibule des Césars), is closed off by a handsome 16C wrought-iron doorway leading to the gardens. Go through the great hall and the antechamber (note the lovely Louis XVI desk).

Dining room – The dining room features an eye-catching monumental white-stone Renaissance chimney-piece. Interesting items of furniture include a French Renaissance cabinet and a Burgundian chest.

Drawing room – The 17C woodwork bears the mark of sculptor Michel Porticelli d'Hémery. The pair of sphinxes with women's faces on the chimney-piece are supposed to depict Catherine de' Medici. In the centre, the face of the Amiral de Coligny can be seen.

Bedchamber of the Marquis de Tanlay – *First floor*. Note the late-16C German School painting on copper.

★ **Great Gallery** – The old ballroom on the first floor is decorated with *trompe-l'œil* frescoes.

Tour de la Ligue – The circular room on the top floor of this turret was used for Huguenot meetings during the Wars of Religion. Like his brother Gaspard de Châtillon (assassinated in 1572), François d'Andelot had embraced the Reformation, after which Tanlay, along with Noyers – the fief of the Prince de Condé – became one of the two main centres of Protestantism in the country.

The domed ceiling of the room is decorated with a painting (Fontainebleau School) depicting major 16C Roman Catholic and Protestant protagonists in the somewhat frivolous guise of gods and goddesses.

Gardens – *Only partly open to visitors*. These lie either side of the long canal (526m/1726ft) built by Particelli, which is lined with ancient trees.

Outbuildings – Now a **centre of contemporary art** *(exhibitions in season)*.

TONNERRE

Population 5 979
Michelin map 319: G-4

Tonnerre is a pleasant little town, terraced on one of the hills that form the west bank of the Armançon and surrounded by vineyards and green scenery. Both the old town and the newer quarters are dominated by the church of St-Pierre and the tower of Notre-Dame. From the terrace behind St-Pierre there is a good view of the town and its surroundings.

Few monuments have survived the fire that ravaged the town in the 16C but the old hospital and the beautiful sepulchre it contains are among the treasures of Burgundy.

The Knight of Éon – It was at Tonnerre that Charles-Geneviève-Louise-Auguste-Andrée-Timothée Éon de Beaumont, known as the knight or the lady-knight of Éon, was born in 1728. After a brilliant military and diplomatic career, during which he sometimes had to wear women's clothes, he met with reversals of fortune and was forced to flee to London. He was refused permission to return to France except dressed as a woman. Returning to England, he died there in 1810. To the end of his life, there was widespread speculation as to his sex. The announcement of his death gave rise to a wave of great curiosity ended only by an autopsy. Charles d'Éon was unquestionably a man.

Eating out

BUDGET

Le Saint Père – *2 av. G.-Pompidou* - ☎ *03 86 55 12 84* - *closed 9-18 Mar, 7-30 Sep, Tue evenings and Wed evenings Nov-Mar, Sun evenings and Mon - 11.80/35.50€*. This modest restaurant near the town centre is set up in an old country building. Traditional cooking served in a simple but well-kept dining room. Interesting choice of menus at affordable prices. Note the fine collection of coffee grinders.

Where to stay

BUDGET

Gîte d'Étape La Gravière du Moulin – *7 rte de Frangey - 89160 Lézinnes - 11km/6.8mi SE of Tonnerre by D 905 -* ☎ *03 86 75 60 50 - mairie.lezinnes@wanadoo.fr - 32 guests per night/per guest: 9.80€*. This 19C mill spanning the Armançon offers accommodation for families and groups of friends. There are rooms with two, six or 12 beds: space is obviously not an issue! The rooms are appointed with pine furniture. Library and lab for developing photographs.

Chambre d'Hôte M. et Mme Piedallu – *5 av. de la Gare - 89160 Lézinnes - 11km/6.8mi SE of Tonnerre by D 905 -* ☎ *03 86 75 68 23 -* ✉ *- 3 rooms: 35/40€*. This charming modern house with a round tower has been built in accordance with local tradition. The rooms set up under the eaves are spacious and comfortable and appointed with period furniture. Breakfast is served on the verandah.

TOWN WALK

Start from place de la Gare.

Promenade du Pâtis – Pleasant shady walk.

Walk across place de la République to rue de la Fosse-Dionne.

★**Fosse Dionne** – This circular basin, filled with blue-green water, was used as a wash-house.

It is fed by an underground river that flows through a steeply inclined rock gallery (45m/148yd long) to emerge in the centre of the pool; its flow varies considerably according to season and rainfall. The pool overflows into the Armançon by way of a small stream.

Follow chemin des Roches.

La Fosse Dionne

Église St-Pierre ⊙ – This church stands on a rocky terrace affording a good view of the town and its surroundings. With the exception of the 14C chancel and the 15C square tower, the church was rebuilt in 1556 following the fire that ravaged the town. There is a handsome doorway on the south side with a statue of St Peter on the pier.

Inside, note the interesting 16C paintings on wood, representing scenes from the Passion, and the 17C pulpit, churchwarden's pew and organ loft.

Wallk along rue St-Pierre to see the unusual west front of Notre-Dame then follow rue de l'Hôpital leading to the former hospital; however, before you reach it, turn right onto rue des Fontenilles.

Hôtel d'Uzès – A savings bank occupies this Renaissance dwelling, birthplace of the Knight of Éon; note the design on the doors.

ANCIEN HÔPITAL ⊙ *30min*

This beautiful old hospital, erected between 1293 and 1295 by Margaret of Burgundy, widow of Charles d'Anjou, King of Naples and Sicily and brother of St Louis, has survived intact, apart from minor modifications.

From the outside, the walls of the hall, despite their buttresses, seem to be crushed by the tall roof which covers an area of 4 500m²/5 382 sq yd. The west front was changed in the 18C.

Interior – Although shortened in the 18C, the great hall is of an impressive size (90m/295ft long and 18.2m/60ft wide). The broken-barrel vaulting and the **oak timbering**★ are remarkable. The 40 beds for the sick were set in wooden alcoves built in lines along the walls as at Beaune, which was built 150 years later. The walls themselves were pierced by high semicircular bays, divided by pointed arches. From 1650, the hall was put to many different uses and often served as the parish church. Many citizens of Tonnerre were buried there, which explains the presence of the numerous tombstones.

Note the gnomon (sundial) on the paving, designed in the 18C by a Benedictine monk and the astronomer Lalande (1732-1807).

TONNERRE

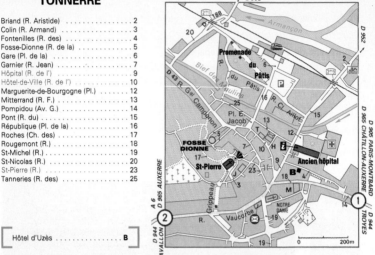

The chapel opens off the end of the hall. The tomb of Margaret of Burgundy, rebuilt in 1826, is in the centre of the choir. Above the altar is a 14C stone statue of the Virgin Mary. To the right of the high altar, a little door leads to the sacristy which contains a carved **Entombment**★, presented to the church in the 15C by a rich merchant of the town. The figures of this Holy Sepulchre make up a scene of dramatic intensity reminiscent of Claus Sluter's style. In the north side chapel is the monumental tomb of the French statesman Louvois, who acquired the county of Tonnerre in 1684 and served as Minister of War under Louis XIV. The bronze statues represent Vigilance by Desjardins and Wisdom by Girardon (1628-1715). The wooden statues in the niches at the end of the hall, above the gallery, representing Margaret of Burgundy and Margaret of Beaumont, Countess of Tripoli, who withdrew here with the foundress, are late 13C.

Among the objects on view in the Salle du Conseil (consultation room) of the hospital is a great golden cross in which is mounted a piece of wood reputed to be part of the True Cross.

Musée Marguerite de Bourgogne ⊙ – In the 18C hospital buildings, the collection includes several objects and manuscripts linked to its history: an 18C silver reliquary; the hospital's founding Charter (1293); the Last Will and Testament of Marguerite de Bourgogne, dated 1305. From the more recent past, a ward (1850) and operating theatre (1908) have been recreated for visitors.

TOURNUS ★

Population 6 231

Michelin map 320: J-10 – Local map see Le MÂCONNAIS

The town stands on the right bank of the Saône between Chalon and Mâcon, near the agricultural land of the Mâconnais hills; the region, which is blessed with a gentle climate, is rich in old buildings and famous wines.

The original Gaulish city of the Aedui tribe became a *castrum* under Roman rule. The few surviving traces of the old fortifications are dominated by the tall towers of the abbey church.

Tournus is one of the oldest and most important of the monastic centres in France owing to the architectural beauty and the harmonious proportions of the church and the conventual buildings, which date from the 10C. The town currently houses the International Centre of Romanesque Studies.

The famous 18C portrait painter, **Jean-Baptiste Greuze**, was born in Tournus in 1725. There are pleasant **boat trips** ⊙ along the River Saône and River Seille.

Monastic centre – When St Valerian, a Christian from Asia Minor, escaped from persecution in Lyon in 177, he travelled to Tournus to convert the people but was martyred on a hillside above the Saône; a sanctuary was built beside his tomb. In the Merovingian period it was converted into an abbey and dedicated to St Valerian.

In 875 the monastery embarked on a period of development following the arrival of monks from Noirmoutier. They had led a wandering life fleeing from the Norsemen since the beginning of the 9C until they were invited by Charles the Bald to settle at St Valerian's abbey. They brought with them the relics of St Philibert, founder of the abbey of Jumièges in Normandy, who died at Noirmoutier in 685; the dedication of the abbey was eventually changed from St Valerian to St Philibert.

A Hungarian invasion in 937 checked the prosperity of the abbey which was destroyed by fire and rebuilt. In about 945 the monastery was abandoned by the monks who retreated to St Pourçain in the Auvergne. In 949 following a decision in council, Abbot Stephen, formerly prior of St Philibert, was ordered to return to Tournus with a group of monks.

The reconstruction which he set in motion was completed in the 12C; it produced one of the most beautiful parts of the church.

Over the centuries the building underwent damage, repair and modification; in 1562 it was sacked by the Huguenots.

The abbey became a collegiate church in 1627 and in 1790 a parish church, so that it avoided irrevocable damage during the Revolution.

Eating out

MODERATE

Le Terminus – *21 av. Gambetta - ☎ 03 85 51 05 54 - closed 12 Nov-6 Dec, Tue evenings and Wed except Jul-Aug - 18/39€.* Before the era of the motorway, Tournus was a popular stopping place for road and train travellers. This house with its comfortable dining room is a tribute to those early days. Note the old barrel organ. The rooms are gradually being renovated one by one.

Aux Terrasses – *18 av. du 23-Janvier - ☎ 03 85 51 01 74 - closed 6 Jan-3 Feb, 17-24 Jun, 11-18 Nov, Sun evenings except Jul-Aug, Tue lunchtime and Mon - 16€ lunch - 22.50/45.50€.* Make a stop at this well-known restaurant away from the town centre and you will certainly not regret it. Carefully prepared dishes of a tasty cuisine will be served to you, some at extremely reasonable prices. A few rooms with white-leaden furniture.

EXPENSIVE

Restaurant Greuze – *1 r. A.-Thibaudet - ☎ 03 85 51 13 52 - greuze@wanadoo.fr - closed 18 Nov-11 Dec - 47/92€.* Housed in a handsome stone building, this restaurant near Tournus Abbey is a temple of French gastronomy. The vast dining hall is sparsely furnished and enhanced by light walls, dark panelling and white tablecloths. First-rate cuisine served in grand style.

Where to stay

BUDGET

Camping Château de l'Épervière – *In Épervière - 71240 Gigny-sur-Saône - 12 km/7.5mi N of Tournus by D 271 - ☎ 03 85 94 16 90 - open Apr-15 Oct - reservations recommended in summer - 100 sites: 25€ - meals available.* This camp site is clustered around a 14C and 18C château amid wooded parkland on the edge of a lake. Shaded sites. Swimming pool with shallow basin for children. Tennis court nearby. Self-catering accommodation available.

Chambre d'Hôte Manoir de Champvent – *In Champvent - 71700 Chardonnay - 11km/6.8mi SW of Tournus by D 56 then D 463 - ☎ 03 85 40 50 23 - closed Nov-Feb - 5 rooms: 34/46€.* Walk through the porch and into this manor house made of yellow stone. The rooms set up in the outbuildings have been appointed with old-fashioned furniture; some of them are under the eaves. Theatrical performances are held on the premises. Large meadow and courtyard bursting with flowers.

TOWN WALK

Parking available near quai de la Saône and rue St-Laurent.

Musée bourguignon – The folk museum is housed in this 17C family mansion, bequeathed to the town by Albert Thibaudet (1874-1936), the celebrated literary critic, who was born in Tournus *(see below)*.

Abbaye – The **Église St-Philipert** is reached from the main road via rue Albert-Thibaudet; the street passes between two round towers, all that is left of the Porte des Champs, the main entrance to the old abbey precinct *(see below)*.

View from the bridge and the quays – From the bridge over the Saône at the end of rue Jean-Jaurès there is a good view of the church of St-Philibert and the town. Many old houses and mansions are to be found in rue du Dr-Privey, rue de la République and rue Désiré-Mathivet. Note the elegant place d' l'Hôtel-de-Ville with a statue of Greuze in its centre.

Continue your stroll to the marina.

★★ANCIENNE ABBAYE (ABBEY) *1hr*

Église St-Philibert ○ – The **façade**, dating from the 10C and 11C and built of beautifully cut stone, has almost the appearance of a castle keep with the dark loophole slits emphasising the warm colour of the stone. The bareness of the strong walls

St-Philibert's nave

is broken by slightly projecting Lombard bands. The crenellated parapet with machicolations linking the two towers accentuates the military appearance of the building. Both this gallery and the porch are the work of Questel in the 19C.

The right tower is topped by a saddle-back roof; the other was heightened at the end of the 11C by the addition of a two-storey belfry surmounted by a tall spire.

Enter the church by the doorway to the right of the main façade.

Chapelle St-Michel (a) – The chapel occupies the upper room in the narthex which was built before the nave *(access via a spiral staircase)*. In plan, it is identical with the ground floor but the astonishing height of the central section and the amount of light give it an entirely different feel. The great arched bay opening into the organ loft was once the entrance to a small oven-vaulted apsidal chapel which was suppressed when the organ loft was built in 1629. The ancient sculpture on the capitals and the blocks which they support have survived from the Carolingian period: the Gerlannus inscription half way up the archivolt may refer to the year 1000 and confirm that the room was built earlier than the nave.

Narthex – This is the place of transition from the outer world to the house of God, where reflection and preparation for prayer are encouraged by the half-light. Its rugged and simple architecture achieves a singular grandeur. Four enormous circular abacus pillars divide it into a nave and two aisles, each of three bays. The nave has groined vaulting whereas the two aisles are covered with transversal barrel vaulting.

One bay of the vault is painted in a black and white chequered pattern, the arms of Digoine, an old and powerful Mâcon family. On the wall above the entrance to the nave is a 14C fresco of Christ in Majesty (**1**); the end wall of the north aisle carries another 14C fresco portraying the Crucifixion (**2**).

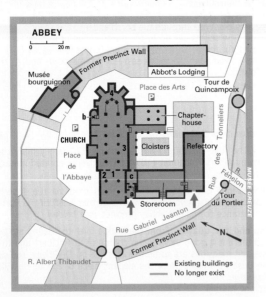

```
ABBEY
0        20 m
```

Former Precinct Wall
Musée bourguignon
Abbot's Lodging
Place des Arts
Tour de Quincampoix
Chapter-house
CHURCH
Place de l'Abbaye
Cloisters
Refectory
Rue des Tonneliers
R. Fénelon
MUSÉE GREUZE
Storeroom
Tour du Portier
Rue Gabriel Jeanton
Former Precinct Wall
N
R. Albert Thibaudet

Existing buildings
No longer exist

The round tombstones are peculiar to this region.

The nave – The luminous and rose-coloured nave, which dates from the beginning of the 11C, is now devoid of decoration.

Magnificently tall cylindrical pillars made from the rose-coloured stone of Préty (a small place near Tournus) are surmounted by ordinary flat capitals, like those in the narthex; they divide the five bays of the nave from the aisles.

A most unusual feature is the central vault which consists of five transverse barrel vaults resting on transverse arches with alternating white and pink arch stones; great columns surmounted by slim columns support the arches, which obscure the clerestory, through which light enters the nave.

Pronounced transverse ribs sub-divide the vaulting in the aisles.

The side chapels in the north aisle date from the 14C and 15C.

A 15C niche in the south aisle contains a 12C statue-reliquary of the Virgin (**3**), Notre-Dame-de-la-Brune, which shows the artistic influence of the Auvergne. The statue, which is made of painted cedar wood (regilded in the 19C) retains an aura of calm and majestic beauty.

Transept and choir – Built at the start of the 12C, the transept and choir contrast strongly with the rest of the building in the whiteness of the stonework; they show the rapid evolution of Romanesque art.

In the transept the contrast can be seen between the spaciousness of the nave and the narrowness of the choir which the architect restricted to the dimensions of the existing crypt.

The oven-vaulted apse is supported by six columns with capitals, surmounted by semicircular windows framed by delicately sculpted decoration. The barrel-vaulted ambulatory built at the beginning of the 11C has three radiating chapels and two oriented chapels; the axial chapel contains the shrine of St Philibert (**4**). The modern stained-glass windows blend well with the rest.

★ **Crypt** (b) – *Access by steps in the north transept.* The crypt with its thick walls was built by Abbot Stephen at the end of the 10C and restored by Questel in the 19C. Inside, note the deep well.

The height of the crypt (3.5m/12ft) is quite exceptional. The central part, flanked by two rows of slender columns (some have a typical archaic bulge) with delightful foliated capitals, is surrounded by an ambulatory with radiating chapels. The 12C fresco, decorating the chapel on the right and representing a Virgin and Child and a Christ in Majesty, is the best preserved in the whole church.

Conventual Buildings – To reach the cloisters one passes through the old alms room (**c**) or warming room (13C) adjoining the south wall of the narthex. It contains a lapidary collection including the column-statues and capitals from the north tower as well as a few sculptures from the cloisters.

Cloisters – Only the north gallery remains; at the end, a 13C doorway leads into the aisle of the church. The buildings on the south side, which hide the refectory, now house both the public and abbey libraries (many illuminated medieval manuscripts). They are dominated by the square Prieuré Tower.

Chapter-house – This was rebuilt by Abbot Bérard following a fire in 1239 and now houses temporary exhibitions. The pointed vaulting is visible through the Romanesque apertures overlooking the cloisters.

Leave by place des Arts.

Admire the east end with its five chapels and the 12C belfry over the transept crossing. This fine tower was inspired by Cluny.

Abbot's Lodging – This is a charming late-15C building.

In rue des Tonneliers stands the Quincampoix Tower which was built after the Hungarian invasion in 937; it was part of the wall of enclosure of the old abbey as was the neighbouring tower, called the Tour du Portier.

Refectory – This magnificent 12C chamber (33m/108ft long and 12m/39ft high) has no transverse arches but is vaulted with slightly broken barrel vaulting. When the abbey was secularised in 1627 the hall was used for tennis matches and was called the Ballon (ball). It is now used for temporary exhibitions.

Storeroom – The storeroom, also 12C, has broken barrel vaulting resting on transverse arches. It is lit by two small windows set high up. The vast cellars below are now occupied by various craftsmen.

ADDITIONAL SIGHTS

Musée Bourguignon ⓥ – This folklore collection was donated to the town by Perrin de Puycousin in 1929.

Wax models in Burgundian costume recreate scenes from daily life of past centuries (about 40 figures in eight rooms).

The scenes include the interior of a Bresse farm, a local Tournus interior with nine variations of the regional costume, the large room of the Burgundian spinners, collections of headdresses, costumes, and, in the basement, the reconstruction of a Burgundian cellar.

Musée Greuze – The museum moved to a new location at the Hôtel-Dieu, rue de l'Hôpital, in 2001. It houses drawings, portraits and red-chalk drawings by Jean-Baptiste Greuze (1725-1805), local archaeological finds, and sculptures by local artists.

Hôtel-Dieu ⓥ – After three centuries of providing health care to the poor, this historic hospital stopped operating in 1982. Yet the old wards through which so many unfortunate people passed remain as a witness to the conditions of life in a hospital from the 17C onwards. The traditional curtained beds in oak wood are still lined up in three vast rooms set around the chapel: one for men, one for women and one for soldiers. The **apothecary★** displays typical 17C Nevers ceramic jars used to store powders and herbs.

Église de la Madeleine – This church stands at the heart of the Roman town and, despite the deterioration of the exterior, remains quite attractive. The east end, adjoined by a cluster of houses, should be admired from the banks of the Saône.
The 12C doorway is interesting for the decorative details. The columns supporting the round-headed recessed arches are adorned with beaded braids and overlapping vertical or slanting garlands; the capitals portray foliage or pairs of birds face to face.
The interior, uniformly white since the restoration, has 15C pointed vaulting. Opening off the north aisle is a Renaissance chapel; its vault is adorned with decorative coffers and ribs. The gilded wood statue represents Mary Magdalene and the tabernacle is in the Empire style. The baptismal chapel also dates from the 15C.

VESOUL

Population 17 168
Michelin map 314: E-7

Vesoul, lying in the delightful valley of the Durgeon, a tributary of the Saône, not far from the border of the Jura region with the southern part of Lorraine, boasts an interesting old town and a pleasant lake offering a choice of outdoor activities.
Vesoul is the home town of Beauchamps (1752-1801), the astronomer who accompanied Bonaparte to Egypt, and the painter-sculptor Gérome (1824-1904).

Birth of a capital – Prehistoric man first settled on the La Motte outcrop overlooking the town to the north. This settlement was replaced by a Roman military camp intended to guard the road between Luxeuil and Besançon. A small market town grew up in the 13C under the sheltering walls of the fort on the plateau. Then the inhabitants moved down into the plain, and Vesoul became an active commercial, religious and military centre. The fort was attacked several times and was finally razed in 1595. The town was the capital of the bailliage of Amont from 1333 to the French Revolution. In 1678 the Franche-Comté, of which Vesoul was a part, was annexed to France. The coming of the railway in the second half of the 19C transformed the town into a major junction for transport routes and spurred the growth of an industrial zone south of the Durgeon.

VESOUL

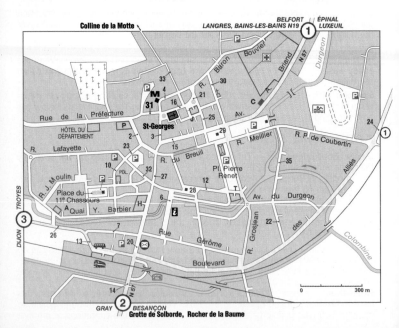

SIGHTS

Musée Georges-Garret ⊘ – This two-storey museum is in the old Ursuline convent (late 17C). The lower floor houses temporary exhibitions and an archaeological department with an interesting collection of Gallo-Roman **funerary steles**. The upper floor is devoted to painting and sculpture, including a large collection of work by local artist Gérome. The 15C representation of Christ Bound near the entrance is particularly eye-catching.

Église St-Georges – This church is a beautiful 18C Classical building. The nave and aisles are the same height, suggesting Rhenish Gothic influence. Note the splendid 18C allegorical marble sculpture of **Faith★** by the Italian Canova and the chapel of St-Sépulcre, which houses a 16C Entombment.

In the Musée Georges-Garret

Old town – The 15C-16C buildings are remarkable for their façades, which show strong Gothic influence. Of particular interest are the Hôtel Thomassin (rue Salengro) and the Maison Baressois, facing the northern side of the church. But the most prolific period was the 18C, as represented by the many buildings with harmonious and symmetrical lines: Hôtel Lyautey de Colombe, Hôtel Raillard de Granvelle (place du Grand-Puits) and Palais de Justice (place du Palais).

Colline de la Motte – *30min round trip on foot.*
The hill of La Motte (alt 378m/1240ft) overlooks the valley from a height of about 160m/525ft. A road twists and turns its way up the hill to some open level ground and a little chapel which houses a number of ex-votos. Further on the road comes to a terrace with a statue of the Virgin Mary, from which there is a beautiful **panorama★** *(bronze viewing table in the shape of the valley)* of the Langres plateau to the west and the Jura mountains, and sometimes even the Alps, to the south.

EXCURSIONS

Grotte de Solborde; Rocher de la Baume – *5km/3mi S. Leave Vesoul along N 57 and turn right beyond La Providence.*
These caves are located close to each other, in very pleasant surroundings ideal for rambling. Fine view of the Vesoul basin.

Lac de Vesoul – *3km/1.7mi W of town on D 13.* This lake has been developed as a recreational park.

▶▶ **The Saône Valley from Vesoul to Gray** – A relaxing drive along the meandering River Saône: medieval **castle** ⊘ in Rupt-sur-Saône, fine Romanesque **church** with 11C crypt and 13C frescoes in Crandecourt.

Eating out

Caveau du Grand Puits – *R. Mailly -* ☎ *03 84 76 66 12 - closed 15 Aug-1 Sep, 24 Dec-3 Jan, Wed lunchtime, Sat lunchtime, Sun and public holidays - 14.95/21.35€.* Walk down a few steps and enter a lovely vaulted cellar with stone walls that serves as a setting to this family restaurant. Traditional bill of fare. Terrace giving onto the courtyard. A highly popular address among local residents.

Where to stay

Camping International du Lac – *2.5km/1.5mi W of Vesoul -* ☎ *03 84 76 22 86 - open Mar-Oct -* ✉ *- reservations recommended - 160 sites: 13.20€.* If you are keen on sporting activities, this is the place for you. Spread out over a huge recreational area on the edge of a lake, it offers facilities for swimming, sailing, fishing, archery, tennis, ping-pong and basket-ball. Hiking trails and cycling paths.

VÉZELAY★★

Population 492
Michelin map 319: F-7 – Local map see Le MORVAN

The beautiful setting of Vézelay, built on a hill overlooking the Cure Valley, the basilica of Ste-Madeleine towering over the town with its old houses and ramparts, constitute one of the treasures of Burgundy and France.

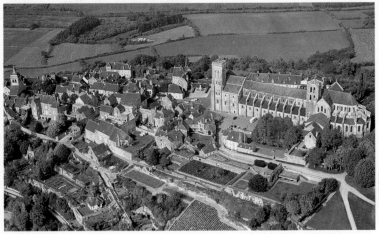

Vézelay

HISTORICAL NOTES

Girart de Roussillon, the founder – It was this Count of Burgundy, a legendary hero whose exploits were sung in the ballad-chronicles of the Middle Ages, who was the founder of the abbey of Vézelay.

In the middle of the 9C he established a group of monks where St-Père stands today. After the destruction of the monastery during the Viking invasions, a new monastery was established on a nearby hill, a natural position more easily defended.

Pope John VIII consecrated the foundation of the abbey of Vézelay in 878.

The call of St Bernard – The abbey was at the height of its glory when St Bernard preached the Second Crusade at Vézelay on 31 March 1146. For a century the church had sheltered the relics of Mary Magdalene, the beloved and pardoned sinner. Vézelay was then one of the great places of pilgrimage and the start of one of four routes that led pilgrims and merchants across France into Spain and Santiago de Compostela.

It was from the side of this hill of inspiration that St Bernard launched his vibrant call for the Crusade, in the presence of King Louis VII of France and his family as well as a crowd of powerful barons. Such was the authority of the Abbot of Clairvaux that he was considered as the real leader of Christianity. His call was received with great enthusiasm by all present who undertook to leave for the Holy Land without delay.

Although the Third Crusade, undertaken in 1190, was not preached at Vézelay, it was there that King Philippe-Auguste of France and King Richard the Lionheart of England met before their departure.

It was also the place chosen by St Francis of Assisi for the first of his monasteries of Minorities in France. In about 1217 two of his friars, whom he had entrusted with the task, chose to settle near the small church of Ste-Croix, which had been built on the spot where St Bernard had addressed the crowd massed in the Asquins Valley; the church was later given into the care of the Franciscans. From 1248, the year of the Seventh Crusade, St Louis, who was a Franciscan tertiary, made several pilgrimages to Vézelay.

Reformation, decline and revival – Vézelay was the birthplace of Theodore Beza (De Bèze in French) (1519-1605) who preached the Reformation with Calvin. In 1557 a Protestant community settled in Vézelay. Plundered by the Huguenots in 1569, the abbey was partly destroyed during the Revolution.

Restored in the 19C after centuries of neglect, the church of Ste-Madeleine is once more the scene of great pilgrimages. The Franciscans have charge of both the church and the chapel of Ste-Croix, which retains some of the original Romanesque arches.

Where to stay and Eating out

BUDGET

Chambre d'Hôte Cabalus – *R. St-Pierre* - ☎ *03 86 33 20 66* - contact@cabalus.com - *closed Mon in low season and Tue* - *6 rooms: 28/50€* - ☐ *8€* - *meals 15€*. This former 12C hostelry attached to Vézelay Abbey has been converted into a tea shop. The fine vaulted room is adorned with sculptures, paintings and pottery pieces. Soup and different spreads for open sandwiches are on offer. Six imaginative rooms are available for guests' use.

MODERATE

Chambre d'Hôte La Palombière – *Pl. du Champ-de-Foire* - ☎ *03 86 33 28 50* - *closed Jan* - *9 rooms: 54/77€* - ☐ *6€*. This 18C mansion overgrown with Virginia creeper has tremendous character. The rooms are both cosy and charming: they have satin bedspreads, old-fashioned bathrooms and are decorated with Louis XIII, Louis XV and Empire furniture. Enjoy the home-made jams for breakfast on the verandah.

Hôtel Crispol – *Rte d'Avallon* - *89450 Fontette* - *5km/3.1mi E of Vézelay by D 957* - ☎ *03 86 33 26 25* - *closed 10 Jan to end of Feb, Tue lunchtime and Mon* - ▣ - *12 rooms: 67/74€* - ☐ *9€* - *restaurant 20/46€*. The elegant, carefully kept rooms of this hotel are furnished in contemporary style and boast lovely bathrooms. The big, bright dining room affords pretty views of Vézelay hill. Delicious meals with fresh market produce.

TOWN WALK

Promenade des Fossés – *From place du Champ-de-Foire at the lower end of the town follow promenade des Fossés.*

The road is laid out on the line of the ramparts which encircled the town in the Middle Ages and which were punctuated by seven round towers.

The 14C-16C **Porte Neuve**, which bears the coat of arms of the town of Vézelay, is flanked by two rusticated towers with machicolations and opens on to a charming promenade shaded by walnut trees. From **Porte Ste-Croix** (or the Porte des Cordeliers), which provides a good view of the Cure Valley, a path leads down to the La Cordelle where St Bernard preached the Second Crusade in 1146; a cross commemorates the great event.

The promenade ends at the château terrace behind the basilica.

Old houses – From place du Champ-de-Foire (lower end of the town) it is possible to drive up to the basilica via the Porte du Barle and a steep one-way street to a parking area near the church. Alternatively, walk up from place du Champ-de-Foire via promenade des Fossés and return by Grande Rue.

The narrow winding streets still contain many old houses in the picturesque setting of the old town: carved doorways, mullioned windows, corbelled staircase turrets and old wells surmounted by wrought-iron well-heads.

Romain Rolland (1866-1944), who loved the "breath of heroes" and wished to awaken the conscience of Europe, spent the last years of his life at no 20 Grande Rue.

★★★ BASILIQUE STE-MADELEINE *1hr*

The monastery founded in the 9C by Girart de Roussillon was dedicated to Mary Magdalene. The miracles that happened at her tomb soon drew so great a number of penitents and pilgrims that it became necessary to enlarge the Carolingian church (1096-1104); in 1120 a fierce fire broke out on the eve of 22 July, day of the great pilgrimage, destroying the whole nave and engulfing more than 1 000 pilgrims.

The work of rebuilding was immediately begun, the nave was soon finished and, about 1150, the pre-nave or narthex was added. In 1215 the Romanesque-Gothic choir and transept were completed.

The discovery at the end of the 13C of other relics of Mary Magdalene at St-Maximin in Provence created misgivings. Pilgrimages became fewer and the fairs and market lost much of their importance. The religious struggles caused the decline of the abbey, which was transformed into a collegiate church in 1538, was pillaged from cellar to roof by Huguenots in 1569 and finally partially razed during the French Revolution.

The abbey church became a parish church in 1791 but was elevated to a basilica in 1920.

In the 19C **Prosper Mérimée** (novelist: 1803-70), in his capacity as Inspector of Historical Monuments, drew the attention of the public works' authorities to the building, which was on the point of collapsing. In 1840 Viollet-le-Duc, who was then less than 30 years old, undertook the work, which he finally finished in 1859.

Exterior

The façade – This was reconstructed by Viollet-le-Duc according to plans contained in the ancient documents. Rebuilt about 1150 in pure Romanesque style it was given a vast Gothic gable in the 13C, with five narrow bays decorated with statues. The upper part forms a tympanum decorated with arcades framing the statues of Christ Crowned, accompanied by the Virgin Mary, Mary Magdalene and two angels.

The tower on the right – Tour Saint-Michel – was surmounted by a storey of tall twin bays in the 13C; the octagonal wooden spire (15m/49ft high) was destroyed by lightning in 1819. The other tower remained unfinished.

Three Romanesque doorways open into the narthex; the tympanum of the central doorway on the outside was remade in 1856 by Viollet-le-Duc, who took the mutilated original tympanum as his inspiration: the archivolt, decorated with plant designs, is authentic, but the rest of the arches and the capitals are modern.

Ph. Gajic/MICHELIN

Central doorway

Tour of the exterior – Walk round the building anticlockwise to appreciate its length and the flying buttresses which support it. This side of the church is dominated by the 13C tower of St-Antoine (30m/98ft high) which rises above the junction of the nave and the transept; the two storeys of round-headed bays were originally intended to be surmounted by a stone spire.

The chapter-house, built at the end of the 12C, abuts the south transept. The gallery of the cloisters was entirely rebuilt by Viollet-le-Duc. Beautiful gardens *(private property)* now cover the site of the former abbey buildings. Remains of the 12C refectory still stand.

Château Terrace – *Access by rue du Château.* From this terrace, shaded by handsome trees, situated behind the church on the site of the old Abbot's Palace, there is a fine **panorama**★ *(viewing table)* of the valley of the River Cure and the northern part of the Morvan.

Continue round the basilica past the attractive houses built by the canons of the chapter in the 18C.

Interior

Enter the basilica by the door on the south side of the narthex.

Narthex – This pre-nave, consecrated in 1132 by Pope Innocent II, is later than the nave and the interior façade. Unlike the rib-vaulted church, the Romanesque narthex is roofed with pointed arches and ogival vaulting.

The narthex is so large it seems like a church in its own right. The nave is divided into three bays flanked by aisles surmounted by galleries. The four cruciform pillars of engaged columns decorated with historiated capitals are extremely graceful. The capitals portray scenes from both the Old Testament (Joseph with Potiphar's wife, Jacob, Isaac and Esau, the death of Cain and Samson slaying the lion) and the New Testament (the life of St John the Baptist and St Benedict resurrecting a dead man).

Three doorways in the narthex open into the nave and the aisles of the church. When the central door is open, there is a marvellous perspective, radiant with light, along the full length of the nave and choir.

A detailed examination should be made of the sculptures of these doorways, executed in the second quarter of the 12C, and particularly of the tympanum of the central doorway. This is indisputably a masterpiece of Burgundian-Romanesque art, ranking with that of St-Lazare at Autun.

★★★**Tympanum of the central doorway** – At the centre of the composition a mandorla surrounds an immense figure of Christ Enthroned (**1**) extending his hands to his Apostles (**2**) assembled round him; the Holy Ghost is shown radiating from the stigmata to touch the head of each of the Twelve. All around, on the arch stones and the lintel, are crowded the converts to be received at the feet of Christ by St Peter and St Paul (**3**), symbols of the universal Church. People of every sort are called: on the lintel are *(left)* archers (**4**), fishermen (**5**), farmers (**6**), and *(right)* distant and legendary people – giants (**7**), pygmies (climbing a ladder to mount a horse **8**), men with huge ears (one with a feather-covered body **9**). The arch stones show Armenians (wearing clogs **10**), Byzantines perhaps (**11**), Phrygians (**12**) and Ethiopians (**13**); immediately next to Christ are men with dogs' heads (the cynocephalics converted by St Thomas in India **14**). The next two panels show the miracles that accompanied the divine word preached by the Apostles: two lepers show their regenerated limbs (**15**) and two paralytics their healthy arms (**16**). Lastly two Evangelists record all that they have seen (**17**).

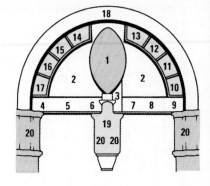

The large-scale composition seeks to demonstrate that the word of God is intended for the whole world. The signs of the zodiac which alternate with the labours of the months on the outer arch stone (**18**) introduce the notion of time: the Apostles' mission must also be transmitted from generation to generation.

On the central pier John the Baptist (**19**) carrying the paschal lamb (unfortunately missing) is shown at the feet of Christ as if supporting Him and introducing Him to His rightful place in the centre. Below Him and on the flanking piers are more Apostles (**20**).

The power of the Holy Ghost which fills the 12 Apostles is symbolised by a strong wind creating turbulence which ruffles the garments and drapes, and sways the bodies. The linear skill, which is the dominant feature of this masterly work, suggests that in the principal scene the sculptor was following the work of a calligrapher, whereas in the medallions, showing the signs of the zodiac and the months of the year, he felt free to carve humorous interpretations of his contemporaries at work.

Tympana of the side doors – Two recessed arches with ornamental foliage and rosettes frame the historiated tympana on the side doors.

The one on the right represents the Childhood of Christ: on the lintel are the Annunciation, the Visitation and the Nativity; on the tympanum is the Adoration of the Magi. The one on the left represents the apparitions of Christ after His Resurrection; on the tympanum is the apparition to the Apostles; on the lintel is the apparition to the disciples at Emmaus.

Nave – Rebuilt between 1120 and 1135 after a terrible fire, this Romanesque nave is noteworthy for its huge size (62m/203ft long), the use of different coloured limestone, the lighting, and above all, the fine series of capitals.

The nave is much higher than the side aisles and is divided into 10 bays of groined vaulting separated by transverse arches with alternating light and dark stones. These do much to mitigate the severity of the lines.

The great semicircular arches, surmounted by windows, rest on cruciform pillars ornamented with four engaged columns decorated with capitals. A graceful decoration of convex quarter-section mouldings, rosettes and pleated ribbons goes round the arches, the main arches and the string course that runs between the windows and the arches.

★★★**The capitals** – As they are more beautiful than those in the narthex they deserve to be examined in detail *(details and plan below)*.

The sculptors – five different hands have been detected in the work – must have had an astonishing knowledge of composition and movement; their genius is expressed with spirit and malice although their realism does not exclude lyricism, a sense of the dramatic and even of psychology.

Transept and chancel – Built in 1096, when the original Carolingian church was enlarged, the Romanesque transept and chancel were demolished at the end of the 12C and were replaced by this beautiful Gothic ensemble completed in 1215. The arcades of the triforium continue into the transept.

The relics of Mary Magdalene (**a**), preserved in the base of a column surmounted by a modern statue, are to be found in the south transept.

A vast ambulatory, with radiating chapels, surrounds the choir.

Right side
1) A duel.
2) Lust and Despair.
3) Legend of St Hubert.
4) Sign of the Zodiac: Libra.
5) The mystical mill.

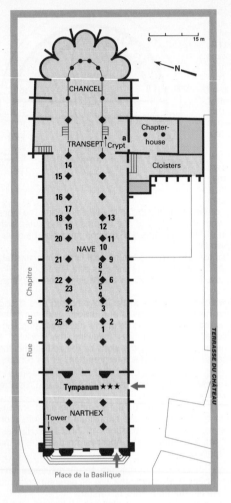

CHANCEL

Chapter-house

TRANSEPT | Crypt   a

Cloisters

14
15

16
17
18   13
19   12
20   11
NAVE   10
21   9
           8
           7
22   6
23   5
           4
24   3
25   2
           1

Rue du Chapitre

TERRASSE DU CHÂTEAU

Tympanum ★★★

NARRHEX
Tower

Place de la Basilique

6) The death of Dives and Lazarus.

7) Lamach kills Cain.

8) The four winds of the year.

9) David astride a lion.

10) St Martin avoids a tree about to fall on him.

11) Daniel subdues the lions.

12) An angel wrestling with Jacob.

13) Isaac blessing Jacob.

Left side

14) St Peter delivered from prison.

15) Adam and Eve.

16) Legend of St Anthony.

17) The execution of Agag.

18) Legend of St Eugenia.

19) Death of St Paul the hermit.

20) Moses and the Golden Calf.

21) Death of Absalom.

22) David and Goliath.

23) Killing of the Egyptian by Moses.

24) Judith and Holophernes.

25) Calumny and Greed.

Crypt – The Carolingian crypt was completely altered during the second half of the 12C. It used to contain the tomb of Mary Magdalene at the time of the great medieval pilgrimages and still houses part of her relics. The painting on the vaulting is 13C.

Chapter-house and cloisters – Built at the end of the 12C, shortly before the choir of the basilica, the chapter-house has pointed vaulting. It was completely restored by Viollet-le-Duc. The cloisters, which were razed during the French Revolution, used to have a huge cistern in the centre of the close, the only water reserve for the town. Viollet-le-Duc rebuilt one gallery in Romanesque style.

EXCURSIONS

★**Château de Bazoches** ⏱ – *10km/6mi S.* 🅿 This 12C château was once the favoured dwelling of the famous military engineer and marshal of France, **Vauban** (1633-1707). Visitors are reminded that he was an author as well, and mementoes recall his family life and work habits. From the reception rooms, decorated with a large Aubusson tapestry (17C), there is a good view of the Vézelay hill. The Grand Gallery built by Vauban was used as a design and drafting office; parts of it have been set up to look as they must have when the engineer was at work there. Note the models, armour, Vauban family genealogical tables (coats of arms in Limoges porcelain) and the family trees of the château's different owners. Vauban would have easily recognised his own **room**, with its well-crafted bed and six arm chairs (17C); the portrait of Louis XIV above the mantle is by Van der Meulen. The small study

FARM INN

Ferme-Auberge de Bazoches – *Domaine de Rousseau* - ☎ *03 86 22 16 30 - closed 15 Dec-1 Feb Sun evenings and Wed -* ✉ *reservations recommended - 14€.* Sows and Charollais cows are reared at this imposing 18C farmhouse located opposite the château. The attic rooms with exposed beams and sloping roofs are appointed with old-fashioned furniture. Tuck into the succulent home-made pies, chicken and guinea fowl dishes and pork roasted with honey.

has a charming decor of birds on the ceiling and a collection of small portraits, three of which are by Clouet. On the ground floor, more memorabilia is exhibited in his wife's room; she lived here until her death in 1705.

Vauban's tomb is in the church in Bazoches (12C-16C), whereas his heart has been laid to rest in the cenotaph erected in his memory in the Invalides, in Paris.

Chamoux – *7km/4.3mi W on the road to Clamecy*. Situated just before the village on the right side of the road, **Cardo-land** ◷ 🖼 is a prehistoric park created by a Spanish artist; a succession of reconstructed scenes beginning in a science museum (less ambitious than Jurassic Park's) and ending in a decorated cave. At the entrance, an exhibition of Cardo's work illustrates the extent of his talents.

VILLERS-LE-LAC★

Population 4 196
Michelin map 321: K-4

This small town lying in the picturesque Doubs Valley, where the river spreads to form the Chaillexon Lake, is the starting point of excursions to the magnificent waterfall known as the **Saut du Doubs**.

★**Musée de la Montre** ◷ – This fine museum illustrates the history of watch-making, a long-standing tradition of the Jura region on both sides of the Franco-Swiss border. Watches of all shapes (even that of a skull!), depicting a variety of themes from the religious to the daringly suggestive, are on display next to the latest models (computer-watches, television-watches...), not forgetting precision tools and reconstructed workshops of bygone days.

EXCURSION

★**Lac de Chaillexon** – The two slopes on either side of the River Doubs crumbled in here and blocked a part of the valley, creating a natural dam which in turn formed the lake. There are two principal parts to it: in the first, the water is a single open stretch between the gentle slopes of the valley; in the second, it lies between abrupt limestone cliffs which divide this part of the lake into a number of basins. The serpentine lake is 3.5km/2.1mi long, and on average about 200m/220yd wide.

★★**Saut du Doubs** – From the raised level of the lake, the Doubs tumbles to its natural level in a magnificent cascade.

This excursion is less interesting during long periods of drought, when the Saut du Doubs has a tendency to dry up.

Le Saut du Doubs

G. Magnin/MICHELIN

By boat – There is a **boat service** ⊘ from Villers-le-Lac to the Saut du Doubs. The boats follow the river's meanders as they gradually open up to form the Chaillexon Lake; then they take their passengers through a gorge, the most picturesque part of the trip. From the landing-stage, take the path *(30min round trip on foot)* which leads to the two viewpoints overlooking the Saut du Doubs (height: 27m/88.5ft).

On foot – ▣ *Take rue Foch (D 215) behind the Hôtel de France, towards Maîche; 5km/3.1mi after Villers, take the road on the right towards Pissoux; then take a downhill road, which leads to a car park. From there it is possible to walk to the downstream end of Chaillexon Lake (1hr 30min round trip) then the Saut du Doubs.*

Take the path by keeping left after the souvenir shops; it leads to the main lookout point over the waterfall, directly opposite the waterfall.

There is a very beautiful view indeed of the impressive Saut du Doubs and the cascade a little further downstream, 27m/88.5ft high, at the beginning of the lake contained by the Chatelot dam.

Another viewpoint, towering right above the fall, offers a very impressive sight of the water thundering into the narrow basin.

Return to the landing-stage or car park along the path skirting the river bank.

Take the car to the road linking Villers-le-Lac and Pissoux and drive on to Pissoux. At the entrance to the village, take the road on the right which leads to a viewpoint 70m/230ft above the Chatelot dam and its reservoir.

Barrage du Chatelot – The dam, built in a horseshoe on the Franco-Swiss border, was a joint project realised by the two countries. It is an arch dam supported by the rocks on the two shores, standing 148m/162yd wide, 73m/240ft high, 14m/46ft thick at the base and 2m/6.5ft thick at the top. The crest serves as an overflow.

Lac de VOUGLANS★

Michelin map 321: D-8

A flooded village! This was the terrible yet inevitable price for the local population to pay when the Vouglans dam was built, creating a huge reservoir... Years have passed and today Vouglans Lake delights tourists and water sports enthusiasts.

This very long lake follows part of the Ain gorge; the finest viewpoints are situated on the east shore, but the best way to enjoy the scenery is to take a boat trip.

The Ain is a beautiful, powerful river. Only 15km/9mi separate its source from that of the Doubs, which flows into the Rhône making an immense detour of 430km/267mi via the Saône, whereas the Ain joins the Rhône more directly, after covering only 190km/118mi.

The river flows through the Jura region almost entirely at the bottom of a deep gorge, tumbling down waterfalls, churning along as rapids or threading its way among rocky crags.

The Ain and its tributaries supply energy to a number of hydroelectric plants, the largest of these being the Vouglans plant.

From gorges to lakes – The Ain once flowed through striking gorges after the Cluse de la Pyle, until it left the Jura region; the walls of the gorges now rise up on either side of several broad lakes created along the river's course by a series of dams. The confluence of the Bienne, a tributary from the east, and the Ain divides the valley into two sections, reflecting the different types of relief that the river is flowing through. To the north of the confluence lies the plateau through which the Ain has carved a course. To the south lies the Bugey mountain range. The river cuts through the folds of the southern Jura in a series of stunningly beautiful transverse valleys or *cluses*. At Neuville-sur-Ain, the Ain breaks through the edge of the Jura mountain massif, known as the Revermont, and then flows on through the plain in sinuous loops parallel to the Rhône for a while, before finally joining the great river itself.

The events of 1944 – On 11 July 1944, the southern section of the Ain Valley was the backdrop for military conflict, as 3 000 German troops coming from Bourg attempted to cross the river at Neuville, heading towards the Bugey mountains. They were held off until the evening by 200 men from the secret armies of Neuville-sur-Ain and Poncin, who formed the front guard of the *maquis*.

Eating out

BUDGET

Ferme-Auberge La Bergerie – *39260 Crenans - 3km/1.9mi N of Moirans-en-Montagne by D 296 - ☎ 03 84 42 00 50 - closed Nov - 12.20/27.44€.* This farmhouse is a lovely sight indeed, perched in its tiny village. The rooms are smart and carefully kept. Savour young goat, rabbit, organic lamb and cheese in the old living room, the stables or out on the terrace. Interesting choice of good Jura wines. Pretty, cosy rooms and stables for horses.

Le Regardoir – *At the Moirans-en-Montagne Belvedere - 39260 Moirans-en-Montagne - ☎ 03 84 42 01 15 - closed 30 Sep-20 Apr, Mon evenings, Tue evenings and Wed evenings except 15 Jun-30 Aug - reservations recommended - 12.50/15€.* Book a table under the oak trees or on the sheltered terrace for a traditional lunch or a pizza cooked in an open oven. Superb views over the turquoise waters of the lake and the lush rolling countryside.

Where to stay

BUDGET

Camping Trelachaume – *39260 Maisod - 2km/1.2mi S of Maisod by D 301 - ☎ 03 84 42 03 26 - trelachaume@ifrance.com - open 27 Apr-14 Sep - booking recommended - 180 sites: 14€.* Pleasant camp site with outstanding views over Vouglans Lake, the mountains and the leafy forests. Many sporting facilities including sailing, volley ball, bathing and hiking.

Camping Surchauffant – *At Pont de la Pyle - 39270 La Tour-du-Meix - ☎ 03 84 25 41 08 - surchauffant@chalain.com - open May-15 Sep - booking recommended - 180 sites: 15.60€.* Those keen on bathing, water-skiing and fishing will be able to indulge in their favourite sport in Vouglans Lake, a few steps away from the camp site. Children too will be delighted as they have a special playing area.

Chambre d'Hôte La Baratte – *39270 Présilly - 5km/3.1mi N of Orgelet by D 52 then D 175 - ☎ 03 84 35 55 18 - ⬜ - 4 rooms: 46/52€ - meals 17€.* The former barn and stables of this old farmhouse have been converted into a series of impeccably kept rooms enjoying all modern conveniences. The dining room has old-fashioned charm with its typical floor tiling. The menu focuses on regional dishes from the Franche-Comté area. Accommodation is provided for horses.

★TOUR OF THE LAKE

The Vouglans dam flooded 35km/22mi of the Ain gorge with water, forming the Lac de Vouglans. No road skirts the lake all the way round but the itinerary below *(try and do this excursion during the late afternoon)* often gets close to the shores and offers superb views of the lake.

Pont-de-Poitte – There is a view of the River Ain from the bridge. When the water is low the giants' cauldrons are very much visible. When it is high, the rocky bed disappears under the foaming torrent, making an impressive scene.
Canoe trips ⊘ are organised by Cap Loisirs.

Leave Pont-de-Poitte on D 49. 6km/4mi further on, take D 60 to the left, then turn left again towards St-Christophe.

St-Christophe – This little village is set against a high cliff, overlooked by the remaining walls of a château as well as the **pilgrimage church of St-Christophe**. This was built in the 12C and 15C and contains interesting works of art and wooden statues. In the single side chapel there is a fragment of a 16C naïve wooden altarpiece, and a 15C Virgin and Child of the Burgundian School.
Go down to the village of Tour-du-Meix and take D 470 to the left.

Pont de la Pyle – The bridge is in prestressed concrete and is 351m/384yd long and 9m/10yd wide. The waters of the reservoir partially hide the three piles, each 74m/243ft high. The view upstream is of the beautiful stretch of water which now occupies the old Pyle ravine.

From the Pyle Bridge, follow D 301 to the right (200m/220yd after crossing the bridge).

As you turn, there is a lovely **view★** of the whole stretch of water contained by the dam. More **glimpses★** of the reservoir appear in between the oaks and evergreens which line the twisting road as you continue.

Maisod – *1hr there and back on foot.*

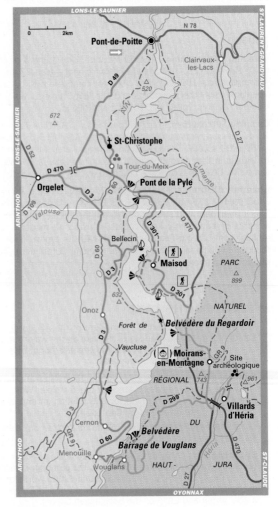

There is a signposted footpath in Maisod by the entrance to the château. A pleasant, shady walk leads to the cliff overlooking the reservoir, and then continues along its edge.

Carry on along D 301. A road leading to the edge of the lake leads off 1.5km/1mi beyond Maisod.

Turn right on D 470 towards Moirans.

★ **Belvédère du Regardoir** – *15min round trip on foot.*
There is a superb **view** from the platform overlooking the crescent-shaped section of reservoir, against a background of greenery.

Moirans-en-Montagne – This small industrial town tucked in a wooded combe has an interesting 16C church, which was partially rebuilt in the 19C. It houses a 17C wooden *Pietà*. Moirans itself is a centre for crafts and toy manufacture.

★ **Musée du jouet** ⊙ –
5 rue Murgin.
The contemporary architecture of this toy museum is inviting, fluid and colourful. The first section presents the region's close ties to the toy industry; several films trace the history of methods of manufacture, from woodworking to plastic moulding. There is a performance by automated figures; the collections fill two storeys with more than 5 000 toys, organised by themes. There is a play area for children.

Take D 470 S.

Villards d'Héria–
On the left, a small, steep road leads to the excavations.

Archaeological site ⊙ –
Recently protected by huge, high-tech structures (translucent Teflon), the Gallo-Roman site was used for worship; two temples and the baths were certainly a place for pilgrimage for the Sequani resident here in the 1C.

Belvédère du barrage de Vouglans – *2km/1.2mi from D 299. Platform and shelter.*
There is an interesting view here of the Vouglans dam and the electricity (EDF) plant which was built at its base.

At Menouille take D 60 right, which leads to the level of the top of the dam.

Barrage de Vouglans – The 103m/338ft-high and 420m/1 378ft-long arch dam, which was first put in service in 1968, is only 6m/20ft thick at the top. Containing 600 million m³/2 119 million cu ft, it is the third largest reservoir in France after the dams at Serre-Ponçon and Ste-Croix (*see The Green Guide French Alps*).

Drive N along D 60.

One of the most beautiful meanders of the flooded valley can be seen after Cernon, shortly before the intersection with D 3. There is a **view★★** of a wild landscape, including the wooded peninsula which extends to the middle of the lake *(car park right of the road).*

Vaucluse Forest (named after the Carthusian monastery flooded when the dam was built) stretches a little further to the right. On the way to Orgelet, the road runs past the Bellecin water sports centre which includes an artificial beach.

Turn left to Orgelet at the intersection with D 3.

The road climbs and the view extends towards the wooded heights of Haut-Jura.

Orgelet – To the west of the church lies a large, grassy square with beautiful plane trees. The interior of the **church** is surprisingly spacious, with a tall Gothic vault and wide galleries across the west end of the nave (the organ loft) and above the first arches of the aisles on either side of the nave. The balustrade is extended by an arch which seems to close off the bay of the transept.

Moirans-en-Montagne – Play time!

G.B. à la Guillaume/Musée du Jouet, Moirans

Return to Point-de-Poitte along D 470 and D 49.

Admission times and charges

As times and charges for admission are liable to alteration, the information below is given for guidance only. Every sight for which there are times and charges is indicated by the symbol ⊙ in the main part of the guide.

Order: The information is listed in the same order as the entries in the alphabetical section of the guide.

Dates: Dates given are inclusive.

Last admission: Ticket offices usually shut 30min before closing time; exceptions only are mentioned below.

Charge: The charge is for an individual adult; where appropriate the charge for a child is given.

Tourists with special needs: Sights which are accessible to tourists of reduced mobility are indicated by the symbol ৬ below.

Guided tours: The departure time of the last tour of the morning or afternoon will be up to 1hr before the actual closing time. Most tours are conducted by French speaking guides but in some cases the term "guided tours" may cover group visiting with recorded commentaries; some of the larger and more popular sights may offer guided tours in other languages. Enquire at the ticket office or bookstall. Other aids commonly available for the foreign tourist are notes, pamphlets or audio-guides.

Lecture tours: These are regularly organised during the tourist season in towns of special interest. In towns labelled "Villes d'Art et d'Histoire", ◤, tours are conducted by specially certified lecturers/guides.

Churches: Admission times are indicated if the interior is of special interest. Churches are usually closed from noon to 2pm. Visitors should refrain from walking about during services. Visitors to chapels are accompanied by the person who keeps the keys. A donation is welcome.

Tourist offices: The addresses and telephone numbers are given for the local tourist offices ◨, which provide information on local market days, early closing days etc.

A

ALISE-STE-REINE

Les Fouilles (Mont Auxois) – Jul and Aug: 9am-7pm (last admission 30min before closing); Apr-Jun and early Sep to mid-Nov: 10am-6pm. 5€ museum and archeological digs (children: 4€). ☎ 03 80 96 10 95.

Musée Alésia – As for the archeological digs.

AMBRONAY

Ancienne abbaye – Apr-Sep: 9am-noon, 2-6pm, Sun 2-6pm; Oct-Mar: 9am-noon, 2-4pm, Sun 2-4pm; No charge. ☎ 04 74 34 52 72.

ANCY-LE-FRANC

Château – Mid-Apr to end Oct: guided tours (1hr) daily except Mon at 10.30am, 11.30am, 2pm, 3pm and 4pm (Jun-Aug: additional tour 5pm). 6€ (under 11s: 3€). ☎ 03 86 75 14 63.

ARBOIS   ◨ 10 r. de l'Hôtel de Ville, 39600 Arbois, ☎ 03 84 66 55 50. www.arbois.com

Guided tours of the town – Contact the tourist office.

Maison de Louis Pasteur – Jun-Sep: guided tours (30min) 9.45am, 10.45am and 2.15-6.15pm; Apr, May and early to mid-Oct: 2.15pm, 3.15pm, 4.15pm and 5.15pm. 5.34€. ☎ 03 84 66 11 72.

Musée Sarret-de-Grozon – Jun-Aug: Contact the tourist office. ☎ 03 84 66 55 50. www.arbois.com

Château Pécauld: Musée de la Vigne et du Vin – Jul and Aug: possibility of guided tours 10am-12.30pm, 2-6pm; May, Jun, Sep and Oct: daily except Tue 10am-noon, 2-6pm; Nov-Feb: daily except Tue 2-6pm. Closed 1 Jan, 1 May, 25 Dec. 3.30€. ☎ 03 84 66 40 45.

Pupillin: Grottes des Moidons – Jul and Aug: guided tours (45min) 9.30am-5.30pm; mid to end Jun and early to mid-Sep: 10am-noon, 2-5pm; early to mid-Jun and mid to end Sep: daily except Wed 2-5pm; Apr and May: daily except Wed 2-5pm. 5.50€ (children: 2.80€). ☎ 03 84 51 74 94.

Grotte des Planches – Mid-Jul to end Aug: guided tours (1hr) 10am-6pm; early Apr to mid-Jul and Sep: 10am-noon, 2-5pm; Oct: daily except Fri (apart from school holidays) 10am-noon, 2-5pm; 1st week in Nov: 10am-noon, 2.30-4.30pm. 5.40€ (children: 2.70€). ☎ 03 84 66 13 74.

Plasne: Fruitière – Ideal for tasting the region's wines, Comté cheese is also one of the region's major assets. La Fruitière de Plasne offers guided tours of the production workshop and cellars. Tours by appointment. Information ☎ 03 84 37 14 03.

Château du Pin – Jul-Sep: 1-7pm. 4€. ☎ 03 84 25 32 95.

Château d'Arlay – Mid-Jun to mid-Sep: guided tours (30min) of the château, unaccompanied tours of the park and Jurafaune 2-6pm. 5.90€. ☎ 03 84 44 41 94. www.arlay.com

ARC-ET-SENANS

Saline Royale – Jul and Aug: 9am-7pm; Jun and Sep: 9am-6pm; Apr, May and Oct: 9am-noon, 2-6pm; Nov-Mar: 10am-noon, 2-5pm. Closed 1 Jan and 25 Dec. 6.50€. ☎ 03 81 54 45 45.

AUTUN
🛈 2 av. Charles-de-Gaulle, 71400 Autun, ☎ 03 85 86 80 38. www.autun.com

Hôtel de ville: library – In summer, the library organises exhibitions of its rare book collection. ☎ 03 85 86 80 35.

Musée Rolin – Apr-Sep: daily except Tue 9.30am-noon, 1.30-6pm; Oct-Mar: daily except Tue 10am-noon, 2-5pm, Sun 10am-12pm, 2.30-5pm. Closed 1 Jan, 1 May, 14 Jul, 1 and 11 Nov, 25 Dec. 3.05€. ☎ 03 85 52 09 76.

Muséum d'Histoire Naturelle – Jun-Aug: daily except Mon and Tue 2-5.30pm; mid-Apr to end May and early Sep to mid-Nov: daily except Mon and Tue 2-5pm; mid-Nov to mid-Apr: Sat-Sun 2-5pm. Closed public holidays. 3.05€. ☎ 03 85 52 09 15.

Musée Lapidaire – Tours by appointment at the Musée Rolin.

Château de Sully – Aug: guided tours (45min) 10am-7pm; Apr-Jul and Sep-Nov: 10am-6pm. 2.50€. ☎ 03 85 82 09 86. www.chateaudesully.com

Couches: château – Jul and Aug: guided tours (45min) 10am-noon, 2-6pm; Jun and Sep: 2-6pm; Apr, May and Oct: Sun and public holidays 2-6pm. 5.50€ (children: 4€). ☎ 03 85 45 57 99.

AUXERRE
🛈 1 quai de la République, 89000 Auxerre, ☎ 03 86 52 06 19. www.ot-auxerre.fr

Guided tours of the town – 🄽 discovery tours (1hr30min to 2hr) 4.60€. Information available at the tourist office or on www.vpah.culture.fr

Cathédrale St-Étienne – Tour of the treasury and crypt by appointment with the Amis de la Cathédrale Association. ☎ 03 86 52 23 29.

Ancienne abbaye St-Germain – Jun-Sep: guided tours of the crypt (45min) daily except Tue 10am-6.30pm; Oct-May: daily except Tue 10am-noon, 2-6pm. Closed public holidays. 4€ (combined ticket including entrance to the musée Leblanc-Duvernoy), no charge 1st Sunday in the month. ☎ 03 86 18 05 50.

Musée Leblanc-Duvernoy – Daily except Tue 2-6pm. Closed 1 Jan, 1 and 8 May, 1 and 11 Nov, 25 Dec. 2€, no charge 1st Sunday in the month. ☎ 03 86 18 05 50.

Musée d'Histoire Naturelle – 10am-noon, 2-6pm, Sat-Sun and public holidays 2-6pm. Closed 1 Jan, 1 May and 25 Dec. 1.50€, No charge Sunday. ☎ 03 86 72 96 40.

AUXONNE
🛈 R. Berbis, 21130 Auxonne, ☎ 03 80 37 34 46.

Musée Bonaparte – May-Sep: 10am-noon, 3-6pm. No charge. ☎ 03 80 31 15 33.

Château de Talmay – Jul and Aug: guided tours (45min, last admission 15min before closing time) daily except Mon 3-6pm. 5.50€. ☎ 03 80 36 13 64.

AVALLON
🛈 6 r. Bocquillot, 89200 Avallon, ☎ 03 86 34 14 19. www.avallonais-tourisme.com

Avallon: Musée de l'Avallonnais – May-Oct: daily except Tue 2-6pm. 3€. ☎ 03 86 34 03 19.

Avallon: Musée du Costume – Mid-Apr to end Sep: guided tours (45min) 10.30am-12.30pm, 1.30-5.30pm. 4€. ☎ 03 86 34 19 95.

Château Montjalin – ♿ 9am-7pm. 5€ (children: 2.50€). ☎ 03 86 34 46 42.

B

Massif du BALLON D'ALSACE

Giromagny: Musée de la Mine – Apr-Oct: Thu, Fri and Sat-Sun 2.30-5.30pm. 2€. ☏ 03 84 29 03 90.

Ski area – In winter, Le Ballon offers a perfectly adequate range of snow sports. Proud of its 19 ski slopes, it is most of all a site dedicated to cross-country skiing: 8 slopes, 40 km. Ask for information at the ski school, ESF chalet in la Gentiane, ☏ 03 84 29 06 65.

Château-Lambert: Musée de la Montagne – Apr-Sep: 9am-noon, 2-6pm (last admission 30min before closing); Oct-Mar: daily except Tue and Sun mornings 9am-noon, 2-5pm. Closed 1 Jan, 1 Nov, 25 Dec. 4€. ☏ 03 84 20 43 09.

BAUME-LES-DAMES   🚹 6 r. de Provence, 25110 Baume-Les-Dames, ☏ 03 81 84 27 98.

Église abbatiale – Closed for renovation.

Usine de pipes Ropp – ♿ Jul and Aug: guided tours (1hr30min) daily except Tue 2.30-4.30pm. 3€. ☏ 03 81 84 27 98.

Clerval: church – Guided tours Sun 10.30-11.30am. Contact the parish priest, 24 r. de la Porte-de-Chaux, Clerval.

Grotte de la Glacière – Jun-Aug: guided tours (1hr) 9am-7pm; Mar to May: 10am-noon, 2-6pm; Sep: 10am-noon, 2-5pm; Oct: 2-4pm, Sat-Sun 10am-noon, 2-5pm. 4.50€. ☏ 03 81 60 44 26.

BAUME-LES-MESSIEURS

Abbaye – Mid-Jun to mid-Sep: 10am-noon, 2-6pm. 3€. ☏ 03 84 44 61 41.

Grottes de Baume – Jul and Aug: guided tour (45min) 10am-6pm; Apr-Jun and Sep: 10am-noon, 2-5pm. 4.50€ (children: 2.20€). ☏/fax 03 84 48 23 02.

BEAUNE   🚹 R. de l'Hôtel-Dieu, 21200 Beaune, ☏ 03 80 26 21 30. www.ot-beaune.fr

Guided tours of the town – 🄰 discovery tours (1hr30min) early Jul to mid-Sep: at 3pm. Information available at the tourist office or on www.vpah.culture.fr

Hôtel-Dieu – ♿ Early Apr to mid-Nov: 9am-6.30pm; mid-Nov to end Mar: 9-11.30am, 2-5.30pm. 5.10€. ☏ 03 80 24 45 00.

Musée du Vin de Bourgogne – Apr to Dec: daily except Tue 9.30am-6pm; Jan-Mar: daily except Tue 9.30am-5pm. Closed 1 Jan and 25 Dec. 5.10€. ☏ 03 80 22 08 19.

Musée des Beaux-Arts – Apr-Sep: 2-6pm; Mar: daily except Tue 2-5pm; mid-Nov to end Dec: 10am-5.30pm. Closed early Oct to mid-Nov. 5.10€. ☏ 03 80 24 56 92 or 03 80 24 98 70 (Sat-Sun).

Musée Étienne-Jules-Marey – Apr-Oct and 3rd Sat-Sun in Nov: 2-6pm. 5.10€. ☏ 03 80 22 56 92.

Château de Savigny-lès-Beaune – Apr-Oct: 9am-6.30pm; Nov-Mar: 9am-noon, 2-5.30pm. Closed first 2 weeks in Jan. 6.50€ (children: 3€). ☏ 03 80 21 55 03. chateau-savigny.com

Archéodrome de Bourgogne – ♿ Jul and Aug: 10am-7pm; Apr-Jun and Sep: 10am-6pm; Feb, Mar, Oct and Nov: Daily except Mon and Tue 10am-5pm. 6.10€ (children: 4.40€). ☏ 03 80 26 87 00. www.archeodrome-bourgogne.com

BELFORT   🚹 2 bis r. Clemenceau, 90000 Belfort, ☏ 03 84 55 90 90. www.mairie-belfort.fr

Guided tours of the town – Contact the tourist office.

Hôtel de Ville – Contact the reception desk at the town hall. ☏ 03 84 54 24 24.

Belfort Lion: viewing platform – Apr-Sep: 10am-noon, 2-6pm; Oct-Mar: 10am-noon, 2-5pm. Closed 1 Jan, 1 Nov, 25 Dec. 0.90€. ☏ 03 84 54 25 51.

Fortifications – Jul to Sep: guided tours (1hr30min) 10am-5pm. ☏ 03 84 54 25 51.

Musée d'Art et d'Histoire – Apr-Sep: daily except Tue 10am-6pm; Oct-Mar: daily except Tue 10am-noon, 2-5pm. Closed 1 Jan, 1 Nov, 25 Dec. 2.79€, no charge 2nd Sunday in the month. ☏ 03 84 54 25 51.

Donation Maurice Jardot - Cabinet d'un amateur – ♿ Apr-Sep: daily except Tue 10am-6pm; Oct-Mar: daily except Tue 10am-noon, 2-5pm. Closed 1 Jan, 1 Nov, 25 Dec. 3.88€. ☏ 03 84 90 40 70.

Étueffont: Forge-Musée – Palm Sunday to 1 Nov: guided tours (1hr30min to 2hr, last tour leaves 1hr30min before closing time) daily except Tue 2-6pm. Closed 1 Nov. 3€. ☎ 03 84 54 60 41.

BELLGARDE-SUR-VALSERINE
🛈 24 pl. Victor Bérard, BP 253, 01202 Bellegarde-Sur-Valserine, ☎ 04 50 48 48 68.

Fort de l'Écluse – Jul and Aug: daily except Mon 2-7pm, Sun 1-7pm; Sep-Jun: call for information. 4€. ☎ 04 50 59 68 45.

Lochieu: Musée Rural du Valromey – Jul and Aug: daily except Tue and Wed 2-7pm, Sun and public holidays 10am-7pm; Apr-Jun, Sep and Oct: daily except Tue and Wed 2-6pm, Sun and public holidays 10am-6pm. 4€. ☎ 04 74 32 10 60.

BELLEY
🛈 34 Grande-Rue, 01300 Belley, ☎ 04 79 81 29 06.

Guided tours of the town – Contact the tourist office.

Izieu: Musée-Mémorial – Mid-Jun to mid-Sep: 10am-6.30pm; mid-Sep to mid-Jun: 9am-5pm, Sat-Sun and public holidays 10am-6.30pm. Closed mid-Dec to mid-Jan. 4.57€. ☎ 04 79 87 20 08 or 04 79 87 21 05.

Château des Allymes – Jun-Sep: daily except Tue 10am-noon, 2-7pm (last admission 30min before closing); May: daily except Tue 10am-noon, 2-6pm; Mar, Apr, Oct and Nov: daily except Tue 2-6pm; Dec-Feb: Sat-Sun 2-5pm. 3.50€. ☎ 04 74 38 06 07.

St-Rambert-en-Bugey: Maison de Pays – Daily except Sun, Mon and public holidays 9am-noon, 2-5.pm. 2€ (children under 8: no charge). ☎ 04 74 36 32 86.

Château de BELVOIR

Tour of the castle – Jul and Aug: 10am-11.30pm, 2-5.30pm; Apr-Jun, Sep and Oct: Sun and public holidays 10-11.30am, 2-5.30pm. 5€.

Musée de la Radio et du Phonographe – Jul and Aug: guided tours by request daily except Mon 10am-noon, 2-6pm; Apr-Jun, Sep and Oct: Sat-Sun and public holidays 10am-noon, 2-6pm. 3.05€ (children: no charge). ☎ 03 81 86 80 18.

BESANÇON
🛈 2 pl. de la 1re-Armée-Française, 25000 Besançon, ☎ 03 81 80 92 55. www.besancon.com

Guided tours of the town – 🅰 discovery tours: Information available at the tourist office or on www.vpah.culture.fr.

Cathédrale St-Jean – Daily except Tue 9am-6pm.

Horloge astronomique – Apr-Sep: guided tours (15min) daily except Tue at 9.50am, 10.50am, 11.50am, 2.50pm, 3.50pm, 4.50pm and 5.50pm; Oct-Mar: daily except Tue and Wed at 9.50am, 10.50am, 11.50am, 2.50pm, 3.50pm, 4.50pm and 5.50pm. Closed Jan, 1 May, 1 and 11 Nov, 25 Dec. 2.44€. ☎ 03 81 81 12 76. www.monuments.fr

Hôpital St-Jacques – Contact the tourist office.

Citadelle and museums – Jul and Aug: 9am-7pm; Apr-Jun, Sep and Oct: 9am-6pm; Oct: 10am-5.30pm; Jan-Mar, Nov and Dec: daily except Tue 10am-5pm. Closed 1 Jan and 25 Dec. Same opening times for all the citadel's museums. 6.10€ (children: 3.10€; combined ticket for all the citadel's museums). ☎ 03 81 87 83 33. www.citadelle.com

Musée des Beaux-Arts et d'Archéologie – & Daily except Tue 9.30am-noon, 2-6pm. Closed 1 Jan, 1 May, 1 Nov, 25 Dec. 3€ (under 18s: no charge), no charge Sat afternoon. ☎ 03 81 87 80 49. www.besancon.com

Musée du Temps – & May-Sep: daily except Mon and Tue 1-7pm; Oct-Apr: daily except Mon and Tue. 1-6pm. Closed 1 Jan, 1 May, 1 Nov, 25 Dec. 3€, no charge Sat afternoon. ☎ 03 81 87 81 50.

Bibliothèque Municipale – During temporary exhibitions: ☎ 03 81 87 80 91.

Nancray: Musée de Plein Air des Maisons Comtoises – Jul and Aug: 10am-8pm (last admission 1hr before closing); May-Jun: 10am-6pm; Apr, Sep and Oct: 2-6pm; February school holidays: 1.30-5.30pm. Closed rest of the year, 1 Jan and 25 Dec. 5.30€. ☎ 03 01 55 29 77. www.maisons-comtoises.org

Mont BEUVRAY

Musée de la civilisation celtique – & Jul and Aug: 10am-7pm; mid-Mar to end of Jun and early Sep to mid-Nov: 10am-6pm. 5.50€ (children under 12: no charge). ☎ 03 85 86 52 39.

Oppidum de Bibracte – Unaccompanied tours in the afternoon. Jul and Aug: guided tours (1hr) 2pm and 4pm (if weather permits); between 8 and 11€ site and museum (children: no charge). ☎ 03 85 86 52 39.

BOURBON-LANCY

Musée de l'Uniforme Militaire – Jun-Aug: daily except Mon 10am-noon, 3-7pm; Mid-Apr to end May, Sep and Oct: daily except Mon 2.30-6.30pm. 4€. ☎ 03 85 89 14 55.

Bourbon-Expo – ᕫ Jul and Aug: Sat 9am-noon, 3.30-7pm, Tue 9am-noon, Wed, Thu and Fri 3.30-7pm. No charge. ☎ 03 85 89 23 23.

Église St-Nazaire and museum – ᕫ Jul and Aug: 3.30-6.30pm. No charge. ☎ 03 85 89 23 23.

BOURG-EN-BRESSE

Brou: Church – Mid-Jun to mid-Sep: possibility of guided tours 9am-6.pm; early Apr to mid-Jun and mid-to end Sep: 9am-12.30pm, 2-6pm; Oct-Mar: 9am-noon, 2-5pm. Closed 1 Jan, 1 May, 1 and 11 Nov, 25 Dec. 5.50€ (ticket combined with the museum and the cloister). ☎ 04 74 22 83 83.

Museum – Mid-Jun to mid-Sep: 9am-6.30pm; early Apr to mid-Jun and mid-to end Sep: 9am-12.30pm, 2-6.30pm; Oct-Mar: 9am-noon, 2-5pm. Closed 1 Jan, 1 May, 1 and 11 Nov, 25 Dec. 5.50P ☎ 04 74 22 83 83.

BRANCION

Château – Mid-Mar to mid-Nov: 9.30am-7pm; mid-Nov to mid-Mar: Sun and public holidays 10.30am-5pm. 3€. ☎ 03 85 51 03 83.

La BRESSE

Cuiseaux: Maison de la Vigne et du Vigneron – Mid-May to end Sep: daily except Tue 3-7pm. 3€. ☎ 03 85 76 27 16.

St-Germain-du-Bois: Agriculture Bressane – ᕫ Mid-May to end Sep: daily except Tue 3-7pm. 3€. ☎ 03 85 76 27 16.

Pierre-de-Bresse: Écomusée de la Bresse bourguignonne – Mid-May to end Sep: 10am-7pm; early Oct to mid-May: 2-6pm. Closed 25 Dec-1 Jan. 6€ (children: 2€). ☎ 03 85 76 27 16.

Perrigny: Maison de la Forêt et du Bois – Mid-May to end Sep: daily except Tue 3-7pm. 3€. ☎ 03 85 76 27 16.

Buellas: church – Contact the town hall, ☎ 04 74 24 20 38 or M. Perrin (opposite the church).

Vonnas: Harness and coach museum – 9am-noon, 2-6pm. Closed 1 Jan and 25 Dec. 4.60€. ☎ 04 74 50 09 74.

St-Cyr-sur-Menthon: Musée de la Bresse – Jul and Aug: 2-7pm, Sun and public holidays 10am-7pm; Apr-Jun and early Sep to mid-Nov: daily except Tue and Wed 2-6pm, Sun and public holidays 10am-6pm. 4.50€ (children: 2€). ☎ 04 85 36 31 22.

Pont-de-Vaux: Musée Chintreuil – ᕫ Apr-Oct: daily except Tue 2-6pm. 3€. ☎ 03 85 51 45 65.

St-Trivier-de-Courtes: Ferme-Musée de la Forêt – Jul-Sep: 10am-noon, 2-7pm; Apr-Jun and Oct: Sat-Sun and public holidays 10am-noon, 2-7pm. 2.50€ (under 12s: no charge). ☎ 04 74 30 71 89.

BRIARE

Musée de la Mosaïque et des Émaux – ᕫ Jun-Sep: 2-6.30pm; Feb-May and Oct-Dec: 2-6pm. Closed 25 Dec. 4€. ☎ 02 38 31 20 51.

La Bussière: Château de Pêcheurs – Jul and Aug: guided tour (45min) 10am-6pm; Apr-Jun and early Sep to mid-Nov: daily except Tue 10am-noon, 2-6pm. 6€. ☎ 02 38 35 93 35.

Le BRIONNAIS

La Bénisson-Dieu: church – Jul and Aug: 10am-7pm; Easter to Jun: daily except Mon 10am-6pm; early Jun to early Aug open Fri evening at 10pm, from mid-Aug to end Sep Fri at 9pm. ☎ 04 77 66 64 65.

Marcigny: Tour du Moulin – Mid-Jun to mid-Sep: 10.30am-12.30pm, 2-7pm; mid-Mar to mid-Jun and mid-Sep to mid-Oct: 2-6pm. 3.50€. ☎ 03 85 25 37 05.

Semure-en-Brionnais: Église St-Hilaire – Guided tours available by request to the Vieilles Pierres association, Château St-Hugues, 71110 Semur-en-Brionnais. ☎ 03 85 25 13 57.

Semur-en-Brionnais: Château St-Hugues – Mid-May to mid-Sep: 10am-noon, 2-7pm, Sun and public holidays 1.30-7pm; early Mar to mid-May: 10am-noon, 2-6.30pm, Sun and public holidays 1.30-7pm; mid-Sep to mid-Nov: 10am-noon, 2-6pm, Sun and public holidays 1.30-6.30pm. 2.50€. ☎ 03 85 25 13 57.

Château de BUSSY-RABUTIN

Jun-Aug: guided tours (45min) 9.30am-12.30pm, 2-7pm; Apr, May and Sep: 9.30am-12.30pm, 2-6pm; Oct-Mar: daily except Tue and Wed 10am-noon, 2-6pm. Closed 1 Jan, 1 May, 1 and 11 Nov, 25 Dec. 5.50€ (children: 3.50€). ☎ 03 80 96 00 03.

C

CHABLIS
🛈 BP 38. 89800 Chablis, ☎ 03 86 42 80 80.

Église St-Martin – Jul and Aug: 11am-1pm, 3-6pm, Fri and Sat 11am-1.30pm, 2.30-6pm, Sun 2-6pm. ☎ 03 86 42 80 80.

Lac de CHALAIN
🛈 36 Grande-Rue, 39130 Clairvaux-Les-Lacs, ☎ 03 84 25 27 47.

Exposition "À la rencontre des hommes du lac" – Jul and Aug: daily except Sat 10.30am-5.30pm. 2.50€.

Maisons néolithiques sur pilotis – Jul and Aug: unaccompanied tours daily except Sat 4-7pm, guided tours 5-6.30pm. For information, contact the musée archéologique in Lons-le-Saunier. ☎ 03 84 47 12 13.

CHALON-SUR-SAÔNE
🛈 Bd de la République, 71100 Chalon-Sur-Saône, ☎ 03 85 48 37 97. www.chalon-sur-saone.net

Guided tours of the town – 🅰 discovery tours (1hr30min) 4.60€. Information available at the tourist office or on www.vpah.culture.fr.

Hôpital – May-Sep: guided tours (1hr15min) Wed, Thu and Sun 2.30; Oct-Apr: Wed and Sun 2.30pm. 3€. ☎ 03 85 44 65 87.

Musée Denon – Daily except Tue 9.30am-noon, 2-5.30pm (Closed 1 Apr, 1, 8, 9 and 20 May, 14 Jul, 15 Aug, 1 and 11 Nov, 25 and 31 Dec. 3.10€, no charge Wed. ☎ 03 85 94 74 41.

Musée Nicéphore-Niepce – Jul and Aug: daily except Tue 10am-6pm; Sep-Jun: daily except Tue 9.30-11.30am, 2.30-5.30pm. Closed public holidays. 3.10€, no charge 1st Sunday in the month. ☎ 03 85 48 41 98.

CHAMPAGNOLE
🛈 av. de la République, 39304 Champagnole, ☎ 03 84 52 43 67. www.tourisme.champagnole.com

Musée Archéologique – Jul and Aug: daily except Tue 2-6pm. 2€. ☎ 03 84 52 48 23.

Syam: Villa paladienne – Mid-Apr to mid-Oct: daily except Tue 11am-6pm. 5.50€ (children: 4€). ☎ 03 84 51 64 14.

Syam: Forge – ♿ Jul and Aug: daily except Tue 10am-7pm; May, Jun and Sep: Sat-Sun and public holidays 10am-6pm. 3€. ☎ 03 84 51 61 00.

CHAMPLITTE

Musée des Arts et Traditions Populaires – Apr-Sep: guided tours (2hr, last admission 30min before closing) daily except Tue 9am-noon, 2-7pm, Sun and public holidays 2-6pm; Oct-Mar: daily except Tue 10am-noon, 2-5pm, Sun and public holidays 2-5pm. 6€. ☎ 03 84 67 82 00.

Musée 1900: Arts et Techniques – ♿ Apr-Sep: guided tours (1hr30min, last admission 30min before closing) daily except Tue 9am-noon, 2-6pm, Sun and public holidays 2-6pm; Oct-Mar: 9am-noon, 2-5pm, Sun and public holidays 2-5pm. 6€ (under 16s: no charge). ☎ 03 84 67 62 90.

La CHARITÉ-SUR-LOIRE
🛈 Pl. Ste-Croix, 58400 La Charité-Sur-Loire, ☎ 03 86 70 15 06. www.ville-la-charite-sur-loire.fr

Guided tours of the town – Contact the tourist office.

Église Prieurale Notre-Dame – Contact the tourist office.

Museum – Jul and Aug: daily except Tue 10am-noon, 2-6pm; Apr-Jun and Sep-Nov: Daily except Mon and Tue 2-5pm. No charge. ☎ 03 86 70 34 83.

CHARLIEU

🏛 Pl. Saint-Philibert, 42190 Charlieu, ☎ 04 77 60 12 42.

Guided tours of the town – Contact the tourist office.

Abbaye Bénédictine – Mid-Jun to mid-Sep: 9.30am-7pm; early Mar to mid-Jun and mid-Sep to end Oct: daily except Mon 9.30am-12.30pm, 2-630pm; Nov-Feb: daily except Mon 10am-12.30pm, 2-5.30pm. Closed Jan and 25 Dec. 4€. ☎ 04 77 60 09 97.

Musée de la Soierie – Mid-Jun to mid-Sep: 10am-7pm; mid-Sep to mid-Jun: daily except Mon 2-6pm. Closed Jan and 25 Dec. 3.25€. ☎ 04 77 60 28 84.

Musée Hospitalier – ♿ As for the Musée de la Soierie.

Couvent des Cordeliers – Mid-Jun to mid-Sep: 10am-7pm; early Mar to mid-Jun and mid-Sep to end Oct: daily except Mon 10am-12.30pm, 2.30-6pm; Feb and Nov: daily except Mon 10am-12.30pm, 2.30-5pm. 3.25€. ☎ 04 77 60 12 42.

CHAROLLES

🏛 Couvent des Clarisses, 71120 Charolles, ☎ 03 85 24 05 95.

Le Prieuré: museum – Jun-Sep: daily except Tue 2.30-6.30pm; Oct-May: contact the tourist office in Charolles. 2.50€. ☎ 03 85 24 24 74 or 03 85 24 05 95 (tourist office).

Musée René-Davoine – Jun-Sep: daily except Tue 2.30-6.30pm. 2€. ☎ 03 85 24 05 95.

Institut charollais – ♿ 10am-6pm. 4.50€. ☎ 03 85 88 04 00.

Chaufailles: Musée de l'Automobile – Jun-Sep: 9am-noon, 2-6.30pm; Oct-May: 9am-noon, 2-6pm; Sat-Sun and public holidays 10am-noon, 2-6.30pm. 6€ (5-12 years: 3€). ☎ 03 85 84 60 30.

CHÂTEAU-CHINON

🏛 Pl. Notre Dame, 58120 Château-Chinon, ☎ 03 86 85 06 58.

Musée du Septennat – Jul and Aug: 10am-1pm, 2-7pm; May, Jun and Sep: daily except Tue 10am-1pm, 2-6pm; from beginning of Feb school holidays to end Apr and Oct-Dec: daily except Tue 10am-noon, 2-6pm. Closed 25 Dec. 4€. ☎ 03 86 85 19 23. www.cg58.fr

Muséée du Costume – ♿ Jul and Aug: 10am-1pm, 2-7pm (last admission 30min before closing); Apr-Jun and Sep: daily except Tue 10am-1pm, 2-6pm. 4€ (children: 2€). ☎ 03 88 85 18 55.

CHÂTILLON-COLIGNY

🏛 2 pl. Coligny, 45230 Châtillon-Coligny, ☎ 02 38 96 02 33.

Guided tours of the town – Contact the tourist office.

Museum – Apr-Oct: daily except Mon 2-5.30pm, Sat-Sun and public holidays 10am-noon, 2-5.30pm. Jan-Mar, Nov and Dec: Sat-Sun and public holidays 2-5pm. Closed 1 Jan and 25 Dec. 2€. ☎ 02 38 92 64 06.

Arboretum national des Barres – Mid-Mar to mid-Nov: 10am-6pm. 5€ (children: 2.50€). ☎ 02 38 97 62 21. www.engref.fr/arboretum.des.barres

CHÂTILLON-SUR-SEINE

🏛 4 pl. Marmont, 21400 Châtillon-Sur-Seine, ☎ 03 80 91 13 19.

Église St-Vorles – Mid-Jun to mid-Sep: 10am-noon, 2.30-5.30pm; early Apr to mid-Jun: Wed, Sat-Sun and public holidays 10.30am-noon, 2.30-5.30pm; mid-Sep to mid-Nov: Sat-Sun and public holidays 2.30-4.30pm. ☎ 03 80 91 24 67.

Musée du Châtillonnais – Jul and Aug: 10am-6pm; Sep-Jun: daily except Tue 9.30am-noon, 2-5pm. Closed 1 Jan, 1 May and 25 Dec. 4.30€. ☎ 03 80 91 24 67.

Abbaye du Val-des-Choues – Jul and Aug: 10am-6pm; early Apr to mid-May: Sat-Sun and public holidays 10am-5pm; mid-May to end Jun: daily except Tue 10am-5pm. 4€ (children: 2€). ☎ 03 80 81 01 09.

Forêt de CHAUX

Vieille Loye: Baraques du 14 – ♿ Jul and Aug: daily except Fri 2-6.30pm. 2€. ☎ 03 84 71 72 07.

Grottes d'Osselle – Jul and Aug: guided tours (1hr15min) 9am-7pm; Jun: 9am-6pm; Apr and May: 9am-noon, 2-6pm; Sep: 9am-noon, 2-5pm; Oct: 2.30-5pm, Sun and public holidays 9am-noon, 2-5pm. 5.40€ (children: 3€). ☎ 03 81 63 62 09.

Abbaye de CÎTEAUX

Notre-Dame de Cîteau – Mid-Jun to mid-Sep: guided tours daily except Mon 9.45am-6.30pm, Sun noon-6.30pm; early May to mid-Jun and mid-Sep to mid-Oct: daily except Mon and Fri 9.45am-12.45pm, 2.15-6pm. 6.50€ (children: 3.25€). ☎ 03 80 61 32 58.

CLAMECY

Musée d'Art et d'Histoire Romain-Rolland – ⟨ゟ⟩ Jun-Sep daily except Mon-Tue, 10am-noon, 2-6pm, Sun 2-6pm. Closed Jan. ☎ 03 86 27 17 99.

Druyes-les-Belles-Fontaines: Feudal castle – ⟨ゟ⟩ Jul and Aug: 3-6pm, Sun guided tours at 4pm; mid-Apr to end Jun and Sep: Sat-Sun and public holidays 3-6pm. 3.50€. ☎ 03 86 41 51 71. www.chateau-de-druyes.fr.fm

Carrière souterraine d'Aubigny – ⟨ゟ⟩ Jul and Aug: guided tours (1hr30min) 10am-6.30pm, Sun and public holidays 2.30-6.30pm; Apr-Jun and early Sep to mid-Nov: daily except Mon 10am-noon, 2.30-6.30pm. 5€. ☎ 03 86 52 38 79. www.carriereaubigny.org

CLUNY

Guided tours of the town – 🅰 The Centre des Monuments nationaux (National Monuments Centre) offers a range of discovery visits. Information at the tourist office and at the National Monuments Centre. ☎ 03 85 59 82 04.

Tour des Fromages – Jul and Aug: 10am-7pm; Sep: 10am-12.45pm, 2-7pm; Apr-Jun: 10am-12.30pm, 2.30-7pm; Oct: daily except Sun 10am-12.30pm, 2.30-6pm; Nov-Mar: daily except Sun 10am-12.30pm, 2.30-5pm. Closed 1 Jan, 1 May, 1 and 11 Nov, 25 Dec. 1.25€. ☎ 03 85 59 05 34.

Église St-Marcel – By request. ☎ 03 85 59 07 18.

Ancienne Abbaye et musée Ochier d'Art et d'Archéologie – Jul and Aug: 9am-7pm; Sep: 9am-6pm; Apr-Jun: 9.30am-noon, 2-6pm; Oct: 9.30am-noon, 2-5pm; early Nov to mid-Feb: 10am-noon, 2-4pm; mid-Feb to end Mar: 10am-noon, 2-5pm. Closed 1 Jan, 1 May, 1 and 11 Nov, 25 Dec. 5.50€ combined ticket with the Musée d'Art et d'Archéologie (18-25s: 3.50€). ☎ 03 85 59 12 79 or 03 85 59 89 97.

CIRQUE DE LA CONSOLATION

Grandfontaine-Fournets: Ferme du Montagnon – ⟨ゟ⟩ Apr: 2-6pm; May-Oct: 9am-noon, 2-6.30pm. No charge. ☎ 03 81 43 57 86. www.montagnon.fr

Château de CORMATIN

Mid-Jul to mid-Aug: guided tours (45min) 10am-6.30pm; early Jun to mid-Jul and mid-Aug to end Sep: 10am-noon, 2-6.30pm; Apr and May: 10am-noon, 2-5.30pm. Grounds open to visitors. 6.50€. ☎ 03 85 50 16 55.

LA CÔTE

The vineyards

Chenôve: Cuverie des Ducs de Bourgogne – ⟨ゟ⟩ Mid-Jun to mid-Sep: 2-7pm; early Oct to mid-Jun: by appointment (3 weeks in advance) No charge. ☎ 03 80 51 55 00.

Fixin: Parc Noisot – Mid-Apr to mid-Oct: Wed, Sat-Sun 2-6pm. 1.5€. ☎ 03 80 52 45 52.

Gevrey-Chambertin: Château – Apr-Oct: guided tours (1hr) daily except Thu 10.30am-noon, 2-6pm, Sun and public holidays 11am-noon, 2-6pm; Nov-Mar: daily except Thu 10am-noon, 2-5pm, Sun and public holidays 11am-noon, 2-5pm. Closed Easter, 1 Nov and 25 Dec. 4.57€. By appointment with Mme Masson (3 days in advance). ☎ 03 80 34 36 13.

Château du Clos de Vougeot – ⟨ゟ⟩ Apr-Sep: guided tours (1hr) 9am-6.30pm, Sat 9am-5pm; Oct-Mar: 9-11.30am, 2-5.30pm, Sat 9-11.30am, 2-5pm. Closed 1 Jan and 24, 25, 31 Dec. 3.2€. ☎ 03 80 62 86 09.

Reulle-Vergy: Museum – Jun-Sep: 2-7pm, by appointment with Mme Griuot. 1.52€. ☎ 03 80 61 40 95.

Nuits-St-Georges: Église St-Symphorien – Closed for renovation work.

Museum – May-Oct: daily except Tue 10am-noon, 2-6pm. 2€. ☎ 03 80 62 01 37 or 03 80 62 01 35.

Côte de Beaune

St-Romain: town hall – Mid to end of Jul: 4-8pm, Sat-Sun and public holidays by request; Aug: 4-8pm; early Sep to mid-Jul: by request. No charge. ☎ 03 80 21 28 50.

La Rochepot: Château – Jul and Aug: daily except Tue 10am-6pm; Apr-Jun and Sep: daily except Tue 10-11.30am, 2-5.30pm; Oct: daily except Tue 10am-11.30am, 2-4.30pm. 5.5€ (children: 2.75€). ☎ 03 80 21 71 37. www.larochepot.com

Santenay: Église St-Jean – Closed for renovation work.

Le CREUSOT
🖪 Château de la Verrerie, 71200 Le Creusot, ☎ 03 85 55 02 46. www.lecreusot.net

Château de la Verrerie – Early Jun to mid-Sep: 10am-7pm, Sat-Sun and public holidays 2-7pm; mid-Sep to end May; 9am-noon, 2-6pm, Sat-Sun and public holidays 2-6pm. Closed 1 Jan and 25 Dec. 5.95€ (children: 3.81€). ☎ 03 85 55 02 46.

Écomusée – Early Jun to mid-Sep: 10am-7pm, Sat-Sun and public holidays 2-7pm; mid-Sep to end May; 10am-12.30pm, 2-6pm, Sat-Sun and public holidays 2-6pm. Closed 1 Jan and 25 Dec. 5.95€ (ticket combined with the F. Bourdon academy exhibition). ☎ 03 85 73 92 00.

Salle du Jeu de Paume – Jun-Sep: 10am-7pm, Sat-Sun and public holidays 2-7pm; Oct-May: 10am-12.30pm, 2-6pm, Sat-Sun and public holidays 2-6pm. Closed 1 Jan and 25 Dec. 5.95€. Contact the tourist office (☎ 03 85 55 02 46).

Académie François-Bourdon – Jun-Sep: 10am-7pm, Sat-Sun and public holidays 2-7pm; Oct-May: 10am-12.30pm, 2-6pm, Sat-Sun and public holidays 2-6pm. Closed 1 Jan and 25 Dec. 5.95€. Contact the tourist office (☎ 03 85 55 02 46).

Montceau-les-Mines:

Musée des Fossiles – Early Jun to mid-Sep: daily except Mon 2-6pm; mid-Sep to end May; Wed and Sat 2-6pm, 1st Sun in the month 3-6pm. Closed public holidays. 2.3€. ☎ 03 85 69 00 00 or 03 85 57 64 88.

La Maison d'École – Mid-Jun to end Aug: daily except Mon 2-6pm and the last Sun in each month 2-6pm; rest of the year: by request 3€ (children: 1.5€) ☎ 03 85 57 29 36.

Blanzy: La mine et les hommes – ♿ Mid-Mar to mid-Nov: guided tours (1hr30min) 2-5.30pm. 5€ (children under 10: no charge). ☎ 03 85 68 22 85.

Écuisses: Musée du Canal – Early Jul to mid-Sep: 3-6pm, Sun and public holidays 2-7pm; mid-Apr to end Jun and mid-Sep to end Oct: 3-6pm. 2.8€ ☎ 03 85 78 97 04.

Mont-Saint-Vincent: Musée J.-Régnier – Early Apr to mid-Sep: Sun and public holidays 3-7pm. No charge. ☎ 03 85 69 00 00.

D

DIJON
🖪 34 r. des Forges, 21022 Dijon, ☎ 03 80 44 11 44. www.ot-dijon.fr

Guided tours of the town – ◪ discovery tours (1hr30min to 2hr). Information available at the tourist office or on www.vpah.culture.fr.

Tour Philippe-le-Bon – Mid-Apr to mid-Nov: 9am-5.30pm; mid-Nov to mid-Apr: Wed 1.30-3.30pm, Sat-Sun 9-11am, 1.30-3.30pm. Closed public holidays. 2.30€. ☎ 03 80 74 52 71.

Bibliothèque Municipale – Daily except Mon, Sun and public holidays 9.30am-12.30pm, 1.30-6.30pm, Wed and Sat 9.30am-6.30pm. Closed public holidays. No charge. ☎ 03 80 44 94 14.

Musée Magnin – Jun-Sep: 10am-12.30pm, 2-6pm; Oct-May: daily except Mon 10am-noon, 2-6pm. 3€, no charge 1st Sunday in the month. Closed 1 Jan and 25 Dec. ☎ 03 80 67 07 15.

Cathédrale St-Bénigne: Crypt – 9am-6.30pm. 1€.

Musée Archéologique – Mid-May to end Sep: daily except Tue 8.55am-6pm; early Oct to mid-May: daily except Mon and Tue. 9am-12.30pm, 1.35-6pm. Closed 1 Jan, 1 and 8 May, 14 Jul, 1 and 11 Nov, 25 Dec. 2.20€, no charge Sun. ☎ 03 80 30 88 54.

Musée d'Art Sacré – Daily except Tue 9am-noon, 2-6pm. Closed 1 Jan, 1 and 8 May, 14 Jul, 1 and 11 Nov, 25 Dec. 2.80€, no charge Sun (combined ticket with the Musée de la Vie bourguignonne). ☎ 03 80 44 12 69.

Musée de la Vie Bourguignonne – ♿ Daily except Tue 9am-noon, 2-6pm. Closed 1 Jan, 1 and 8 May, 14 Jul, 1 and 11 Nov, 25 Dec. 2.80€, no charge Sun (combined ticket with the Musée d'Art Sacré). ☎ 03 80 44 12 69.

Musée Amora – Daily except public holidays. Contact the tourist office. ☎ 03 80 44 11 41.

Muséum d'Histoire Naturelle – Daily except Tue mornings 9am-noon, 2-6pm, Sat-Sun 2-6pm. Closed 1 Jan, 8 May, 14 Jul, 15 Aug, 1 and 11 Nov, 25 Dec. 2.20€, no charge Sun and public holidays. ☎ 03 80 76 82 76.

Musée des Beaux-Arts – ♿ Daily except Tue and public holidays 10am-6pm. The Granville donation, Ducal kitchens, Egyptian and Weapons rooms are closed between noon-2pm. 3.40€, no charge Sun. ☎ 03 80 74 52 70.

DIVONNE-LES-BAINS

🛈 r. des Bains, BP 90. 01220 Divonne-Les-Bains, ☎ 04 50 20 01 22. www.divonnelesbains.com

Thermes de Divonne (baths) – Av. des Thermes, 01220 Divonne-les-Bains, ☎ 04 50 20 27 70.

DOLE

🛈 Pl. Grévy, 39100 Dole, ☎ 03 84 72 11 22. www.dole.org

Guided tours of the town – ◪ discovery tours. For information, contact the tourist office or the heritage dept., ☎ 03 84 69 01 54 and on www.dole.org and www.vpah.culture.fr

Collégiale Notre-Dame – For access to the top of the bell-tower, contact the town hall.

Maison natale de Pasteur et Musée Pasteur – Jul and Aug: 10am-6pm, Sun and public holidays 2-6pm; Apr-Jun, Sep and Oct: 10am-noon, 2-6pm, Sun and public holidays 2-6pm; Nov-Mar: Sat-Sun and public holidays 2-6pm. 4.50€. ☎ 03 84 72 20 61.

Musée des Beaux-Arts – ♿ Jul and Aug: daily except Mon and Tue 10am-noon, 2-6pm; Sep-Jun: daily except Mon 10am-noon, 2-6pm. Closed 1 May and 24 Dec-2 Jan. No charge. ☎ 03 84 79 25 85.

Église St-Jean-l'Évangéliste – 9am-noon, 2.30-5.30pm. Contact the presbytery. ☎ 03 84 72 05 14.

F

FERNEY-VOLTAIRE

Château – May-Sep: guided tours (1hr) daily except Mon 10am-6pm, Sat-Sun and public holidays 10am-6.30pm. 4€ (children: no charge), no charge 1st Sunday in the month (Oct-May). ☎ 04 50 40 05 40. www.auberge-europe.org

FILAIN

Château – Mid-Apr to end Oct: guided tour (1hr) 10am-noon, 2pm-6pm. 6€ (children: 2.50€). ☎ 03 84 78 30 66. www.filain.com

FLAVIGNY-SUR-OZERAIN

Ancienne Abbaye – Guided tours (15min) by appointment daily except Sat-Sun 8.30-10.30am. Closed in Aug, 25 Dec-1 Jan and public holidays. No charge. ☎ 03 80 96 20 88.

Crypte Ste-Reine – Audio-tours (15min) daily except Sat-Sun 8.30-11.30am, 2-5pm. 1€. ☎ 03 80 96 20 88.

Église St-Genest – 9am-6pm, by appointment. ☎ 03 80 96 00 29.

Château de Frôlois – Jul and Aug: guided tours (30min) 2.30-6.30pm. 4€. ☎ 03 80 96 22 92.

Abbaye de FONTENAY

♿ Early Apr to mid -Nov: 10am-noon, 2-5.30pm; mid-Nov to end of Mar: 10am-noon, 2-5pm. 7.50€ (children: 3.75€). ☎ 03 80 92 15 00.

FOUGEROLLES

🛈 1 r. de la Gare, 70220 Fougerolles, ☎ 03 84 49 12 91. www.otsi-fougerolles.net

Écomusée du Pays de la Cerise et de la Distillation – Jul and Aug: guided tours (1hr30min) 10am-7pm, 2-7pm; Apr-Jun, Sep and Oct: daily except Tue 2-6pm. 3.81€. ☎ 03 84 49 52 50.

Ermitage Saint-Valbert: Safari park – Guided tours (2hr, leaving from the Blanzey car park) in the company of a forest guide Sat-Sun at 3pm. No charge. ☎ 03 84 49 54 97.

G

Barrage de GÉNISSIAT

Centrale Léon-Perrier: Salle des machines – Visits cancelled due to the government Vigipirate security plan. ☎ 04 78 24 16 16.

GRAND COLOMBIER

Aignoz: Maison de la Réserve naturelle du marais de Lavours – ⊙ Free access all year round. Jun-Aug: 10am-6.30pm; end Mar to early Jun and Sep: daily except Mon 10.30am-6pm; rest of the year: Sat-Sun and public holidays 1.30-6pm. 5€ (children: 3.5€). ☎ 04 79 87 90 39.

GRAY
🅱 Île Sauzay, 70100 Gray, ☎ 03 84 65 14 24. www.ville-gray.fr

Guided tours of the town – Jul and Aug: Thu 10am; Sep-Jun: by request at the tourist office. 3€.

Esperanto museum – For information or visits, contact the museum, 19 r. Victor Hugo, ☎ 03 84 67 06 80.

Musée Baron-Martin – May-Oct: daily except Tue 10am-noon, 2-6pm; Nov-Apr: daily except Tue 2-5pm. Closed 1 Jan, 1 May, 11 Nov, 25 Dec. 3.35€. ☎ 03 84 64 83 46.

H

Cascades du HÉRISSON

Ferme de l'Aurochs – Early Jun to mid-Sep: 9.30am-7.30pm; May and mid-Sep to mid-Oct: Sun and public holidays 9.30am-7.30pm. 4.70€. ☎ 03 84 25 72 95.

J

JOIGNY
🅱 Quai H.-Ragobert, 89300 Joigny, ☎ 03 86 62 11 05. www.joigny.com

Guided tours of the town – ▲ discovery tours (1hr30min). Jul and Aug. 4.60€. Information available at the tourist office or on www.vpah.culture.fr

Pressoir de Champvallon – ⚹ Easter to All Saints: guided tours (45min). 2.30€. By appointment on ☎ 03 86 91 07 69 or at the Nucra, ☎ 03 86 63 41 27.

Musée rural des Arts populaires de Laduz – Jul and Aug: 10am-7pm; Apr-Jun, Sep and Oct: Wed, Sat-Sun and public holidays 2-6pm; Nov-Mar: Wed 2-5pm. 6€ (under 14s: 3€). ☎ 03 86 73 70 08.

Dicy: La Fabuloserie – Jul and Aug: guided tours (2hr) 2-6pm; Mid-Apr to end Jun, Sep and Oct: Sat-Sun and public holidays 2-6pm. 5.50€ ☎ 03 86 63 64 21.

Château de JOUX

Château – Jul and Aug: 9am-6pm; Apr-Jun and Sep: 10-11.30am, 2-4.30pm; Oct-May: 10am, 11.30am, 2pm, 3.15pm and 4.15pm. Closed 25 Dec. 5€. ☎ 03 81 69 47 95.

L

LONS-LE-SAUNIER
🅱 Pl. du 11-Novembre, 39000 Lons-Le-Saunier, ☎ 03 84 24 65 01. www.ville-lons-le-saunier.fr

Guided tours of the town – Contact the tourist office.

Théâtre – Jul and Aug: "Visages de Pierre" guided tours alternating with "Visages de Fer" guided tours (1h) Tue 3pm. 3€ (children under 12: no charge). ☎ 03 84 24 65 01.

Musée Rouget de Lisle (Donation A. Lançon) – Mid-Jun to mid-Sep: 10am-noon, 2-6pm, Sat-Sun and public holidays 2-5pm. No charge. ☎ 03 84 47 29 16.

Hôtel-Dieu – Jul and Aug: guided tours (1hr) Sat 3pm. 3€. ☎ 03 84 24 65 01.

Musée des Beaux-Arts – Daily except Tue 10am-noon, 2-6pm, Sat-Sun and public holidays 2-5pm. Closed 1 Jan, 1 May, 25 Dec. 2€, no charge Wed and 1st Sunday in the month. ☎ 03 84 47 64 30.

Musée Municipal d'Archéologie – Daily except Tue 10am-noon, 2-6pm, Sat-Sun and public holidays 2-5pm. Closed 1 Jan, 1 May, 25 Dec. 2€, no charge Wed and 1st Sunday in the month. ☎ 03 84 47 12 13.

Conliège: church – By request to M. Broutet, 34 r. Neuve, 39570 Conliège.

LOUHANS

1 Arcade St.-Jean, 71500 Louhans, ☎ 03 85 75 05 02.

Hôtel-Dieu – Mar-Oct: guided tours (1hr15min) daily except Tue 10.30am, 2.30pm, 4pm and 5.30pm; Nov-Feb: daily except Tue 2.30pm and 4pm, Mon 10.30am, 2.30pm and 4pm. Closed 1 Jan, 1 May and 25 Dec. 3.70€. ☎ 03 85 75 54 32.

L'Atelier d'un journal – & Mid-May to end Sep: 3-7pm; early Oct to mid-May: daily except Sat-Sun 2pm-6pm. Closed 25 Dec-1 Jan. 3€ (children: 1.50€). ☎ 03 85 76 27 16.

Chaisiers et pailleuses de Rancy – & Mid-May to end Sep: daily except Tue 3-7pm. 3€. ☎ 03 85 76 27 16.

LUXEUIL-LES-BAINS

1 av. des Thermes, 70303 Luxeuil-Les-Bains, ☎ 03 84 40 06 41.

Ancienne abbaye St-Colomban – For guided tours, ask at the tourist office. ☎ 03 84 40 06 41.

Musée de la tour des Échevins – May-Sep: daily except Mon and Tue. 2-6pm; Oct-Apr: Wed, Fri and Sat-Sun 2-6pm. Closed in Nov and 25 Dec. 2€. ☎ 03 84 40 00 07.

M

MÂCON

1 pl. St-Pierre, 71000 Mâcon, ☎ 03 85 21 07 07. www.macon-bourgogne.com

Guided tours of the town – Contact the tourist office.

Vieux St-Vincent: Lapidary Museum – Jun-Sep: daily except Mon 10am-noon, 2-6pm, Sun and public holidays 2-6pm. Closed 14 Jul. 1.50€. ☎ 03 85 39 90 38.

Musée Lamartine – Daily except Mon 10am-noon, 2-6pm, Sun and public holidays 2-6pm. Closed 1 Jan, 1 May, 14 Jul, 1 Nov, 25 Dec. 2.30€. ☎ 03 85 39 90 38.

Musée des Ursulines – Daily except Mon 10am-noon, 2-6pm, Sun and public holidays 2-6pm. Closed 1 Jan, 1 May, 14 Jul, 1 Nov, 25 Dec. 2.30€. ☎ 03 85 39 90 38.

Hôtel-Dieu – & Jun-Sep: daily except Mon and Tue. 2-6pm; Oct-May: contact the Musée des Ursulines. Closed 14 Jul. 1.50€. ☎ 03 85 39 90 38.

Romanèche-Thorins: Maison de Benoît Raclet – Guided tours by appointment (2 weeks in advance). Closed Dec-Apr. No charge. ☎ 03 85 35 51 37.

Musée du Compagnonnage Guillon – Jul and Aug: 10am-6pm; Apr-Jun, Sep and Oct: daily except Tue 2-6pm. Closed 1 May 3.50€, no charge 1st Sunday in the month. ☎ 03 85 35 22 02.

Le Hameau du vin S.A. Dubœuf – Apr-Oct: 9am-6pm; Jan-Mar, Nov and Dec: 10am-5pm. Closed 25 Dec. 11.50€ (children: 6.10€). ☎ 03 85 35 22 22. www.hameauenbeaujolais.com.

Château du Moulin à Vent – Mon-Sat 8am-noon, 2-6pm, Sun and public holidays by appointment - Closed early Aug to mid-Aug ☎ 03 85 35 50 68.

Parc zoologique et d'attractions Touroparc – & Mar-Oct 10am-7pm, Nov-Feb 10am-noon, 1.30-5.30pm. 14€. ☎ 03 85 35 51 53. www.touroparc.com

MÂCONNAIS

La montagne

Blanot: Caves – Apr-Sep: guided tours (1hr) 9.30am-noon, 1.30-6pm. 5€ (children: 3€). ☎ 03 85 50 03 59.

Site préhistorique d'Azé – & Jul and Aug: guided tours (1hr30min) 10am-7pm; Apr-Jun and Sep: 10am-noon, 2-7pm; Oct: Sun 10am-noon, 2-6pm 5.34€ (children: 3.81€). ☎ 03 85 33 32 23.

The Vineyards

Loché: Vignéroscope – & Domaine St-Philibert. Jun-Aug daily except Tue 3-6.30pm. 6.50€ ☎ 03 85 35 61 76.

Route Lamartine

Milly-Lamartine: Maison d'Enfance de Lamartine – May-Sep: guided tours (1hr) daily except Mon and Tue at 10am, 11am, 3pm, 4pm and 5pm. Closed 1 Jan and 25 Dec. 6€ (children under 12: no charge). ☎ 03 85 37 70 33.

Berzé-la-ville: Chapelle des Moines – Closed Nov-Apr. 2.50€. ☎ 03 85 38 81 18.

Berzé-le-Châtel: **Château** – Jul and Aug: guided tour (45min) 10am-6pm; Jun and Sep: daily except Tue 2-6pm. 5€. ☎ 03 85 36 60 83.

St-Point: **Château** – May-Sep: guided tours (30min) 10am-noon, 3-7pm; mid-Mar to end Apr and early Oct to mid-Nov: daily except Wed and Sun morning 10am-noon, 3-6pm. Closed public holidays (morning). 4.60€ (6-11 years: 2.50€). ☎ 03 85 50 50 30.

Pierreclos: **Château** – Apr to Nov: 9am-6pm; Dec-Mar: 9am-noon, 2-6pm. 6€ (children: no charge). ☎ 03 85 35 73 73.

MALBUISSON
🆔 33 Grande Rue, 25160 Malbuisson, ☎ 03 81 69 31 21.
☎ 03 81 69 31 21. www.malbuisson.com

Maison de la Réserve Naturelle du Lac de Remoray – Jul and Aug: 10am-7pm; short school holidays: 10am-noon, 2-6pm; outside school holidays: daily except Tue 2-6pm. Closed 1 Jan and 25 Dec. 5€ (5-14 years: 2.50€). 03 81 69 35 99. www.maison delareserve.com

Le Cernois-Veuillet: **L'Odysée Blanche** – ♿ Jul and Aug: 10am-7pm; Christmas school holidays and Jan: 10am-5pm; February school holidays: 10am-6pm; Mar to Jun: 10am-noon, 2-6pm; Sep to Oct: 10am-noon, 2-5pm. Closed rest of the year and certain public holidays. 5.80€. ☎ 03 81 69 20 20.

Chapelle-des-Bois: **Écomusée** – Early Jul to mid-Sep: 2-6pm, Tue, Thu and Fri 10am-6pm (last admission 1hr before closing); mid-Sep to end Dec and Apr-Jun: Fri 10am-noon, 2-6pm, Sat-Sun and public holidays 2-6pm; Jan-Mar: daily except Sat-Sun 2-6pm, Tue, Thu, Fri 10am-noon, 2-6pm. Closed mid-Oct to mid-Dec, early to mid-Apr, 1 Jan, 1 May and 25 Dec. 3.65€. ☎ 03 81 69 27 42.

MÉTABIEF-MONT D'OR

Musée de la Meunerie – School holidays: 10am-7pm; outside school holidays: daily except Mon 10am-noon, 3-6pm. 3.81€. ☎ 03 81 49 49 89.

Le Coni'fer – Early to mid-Jul. Wed and Sat 5pm, Sun and public holidays 2.30 and 5pm; mid-Jul to end Aug: Thu, Fri and Sat 5pm, Wed, Sun and public holidays 2.30 and 5pm; Jun and Sep: Sun and public holidays 3pm. 6.70€. ☎ 03 81 49 10 10.

MONCLEY

Château – Apr-Oct: guided tours (1hr30min) 1 Sun each month at 3pm, by request at the tourist office. 6€. ☎ 03 81 80 92 55.

MONTARGIS
🆔 Bd Paul-Baudin, 45205 Montargis, ☎ 02 38 98 00 87.

Musée Girodet – Daily except Mon and Tue 9am-noon, 1.30-5.30pm, Fri 9am-noon, 1.30-5pm. Closed 25 Dec-1Jan, 4th Sun in Jul (local feast day) and public holidays. 3.05€. ☎ 02 38 98 07 81.

Musée du Gâtinais – Wed and Sat-Sun 9am-noon, 1.30-5.30pm. Closed 25 Dec-1Jan, 4th Sun in Jul (local feast day) and public holidays. 2.74€. ☎ 02 38 93 45 63.

Musée des Tanneurs – Sat 2.30-5.30pm. Closed 1 Jan and 25 Dec. 2€. ☎ 02 38 98 00 87.

Châteaurenard: **Bee-keeping Museum** – ♿ Feb to 11 Nov: Wed and Sat-Sun 10am-6pm (Jul and Aug: daily). 4.25€ (children: 3€). ☎ 02 38 95 35 56.

MONTBARD
🆔 R. Carnot, 21500 Montbard, ☎ 03 80 92 03 75.

Parc Buffon – Jun-Sep: guided tours (1hr30min) daily except Tue 10am-noon, 2-7pm; Apr, May and Oct: daily except Tue 10am-noon, 2-6pm; Nov-Mar: daily except Tue and Sat 2-5pm, Sun and public holidays 10am-noon, 2-5pm. Closed 1 Jan, 1 May, 25 Dec. 2.50€, no charge 1st Sunday in the month. ☎ 03 80 92 50 42.

Musée Buffon – Apr-Oct: daily except Tue 10am-noon, 2-6pm; Nov-Mar: daily except Tue 2-5pm, Sat-Sun and public holidays 10am-noon, 2-5pm. Closed 1 Jan, 1 May, 25 Dec. 2.50€, no charge 1st Sunday in the month. ☎ 03 80 92 50 42.

Musée des Beaux-Arts – Jun-Sep: daily except Tue 2-6pm. 2.50€, no charge 1st Saturday in the month. ☎ 03 80 92 50 42.

Grande Forge de Buffon – ♿ Apr-Sep: daily except Tue 10am-noon, 2.30-6pm (last admission 30min before closing). 5€. ☎ 03 80 92 10 35.

Château de Nuits – Apr-Oct: guided tours (1hr) 9.30am-11.30am, 2.30-5.30pm. 5€. ☎ 03 86 55 71 80.

MONTBÉLIARD

🅩 1 r. Henri-Mouhot, 25200 Montbéliard, ☎ 03 81 94 45 60. www.agglo-montbeliard.fr

Guided tours of the town – 🄰 discovery tours, information at the tourist office or on www.vpah.culture.fr ☎ 03 81 94 45 60 or on www.agglo-montbeliard.fr/tourisme. Jun-Sep: 2-6pm; May and Oct: Sun and public holidays 2-7pm. 2.50€. ☎ 03 81 97 51 71.

Château – Daily except Tue 10am-noon, 2-6pm. Closed 1 Jan, 1 May, 1 Nov, 25 Dec. 1.50€, no charge 1st Sunday in the month. ☎ 03 81 99 22 61.

Musée d'Art et d'Histoire (Hôtel Beurnier-Rossel) – As for the château. 1.50€. ☎ 03 81 99 23 90.

Pavillon des sciences – ♿ Jul and Aug: 10am-7pm, Sat-Sun 2-7pm; Sep-Jun: 9am-noon, 2-5pm, Wed 9am-noon, 2-6pm, Sat-Sun and public holidays 2-6pm. 3.10€ espace Galilée and 2.30€ espace Chenevière. ☎ 03 81 91 46 83 or 03 81 97 19 79.

Sochaux:

Musée de l'Aventure Peugeot – ♿ 10am-6pm. Closed 1 Jan and 25 Dec. 7€. ☎ 03 81 99 42 03.

Tour of the Peugeot factories – Guided tours (2hr30min) daily except Sat-Sun 8.30 by appointment (at least 1 week in advance and 2 weeks in advance during school holidays). Minimum age: 14 years. Closed 3 weeks in Aug, 25 Dec-1Jan, Easter, Ascension and Whitsun. No charge. ☎ 03 81 33 28 25.

Beaucourt: Musée Frédéric-Japy – ♿ Daily except Mon and Tue 2-5pm, Sun 2.30-5.30pm. Closed 1 Jan, 1 May, 1 Nov, 25 Dec. 2€. ☎ 03 84 56 57 52.

Mont-Bart: Fort – Jun-Sep: possibility of guided tours 2-6pm (last admission 1hr before closing); May and Oct: Sun and public holidays 2-7pm. 2.50€. ☎ 03 81 97 51 71.

MONTBENOÎT

🅩 , 25650 Montbenoît, ☎ 03 81 38 10 32.

Old Abbey – Jul and Aug: guided tours (1hr) 10am-noon, 2-6pm, 2€ unaccompanied tours with written commentary sheet (by request at the tourist office). ☎ 03 81 38 10 32.

MONTS JURA

Ascent of the Crêt de la Neige – Jul and Aug: 9am-1pm, 2.15-5.30pm, Sat-Sun 9am-1pm, 2.15-5.30pm (continuous). Shuttle 9am, 10am, 11am and 4pm. 7€. Answering machine for info on the station: ☎ 08 36 68 39 01.

Mijoux: Skilitfs (télésiège du Val Mijoux) – Val Mijoux chair-lift; Jul and Aug: 9am-6pm; Sep-Jun: 9am-4pm. Gondola from Mont-Rond to col de la Faucille: 9am-6pm (continuous). 4.42€ return (children: 3.51€); gondola and chair-lift 6.40€ (children: 5.18€). Times liable to modification depending on weather conditions. ☎ 04 50 41 35 37.

Petit Mont-Rond viewpoint (by gondola) – Jul, Aug and mid-Dec to mid-Apr: leaves from col de la Faucille (15min). 4.50€ return, 4€ single.

MOREZ

🅩 pl. Jean Jaurès, 39402 Morez, ☎ 03 84 33 08 73. www.haut-jura.com

Fromagerie de Morbier – Feb, Jul and Aug, 9-11am, reservations required ☎ 03 84 33 59 39.

Musée de la Lunetterie – Opening planned for Jan 2003. Call for information on ☎ 03 84 33 39 30.

MORVAN

St-Brisson: Maison du Parc – ♿ Morvan Ecomuseum Centre, temporary exhibition and tours early Apr to mid-Dec: 10.30am-6pm. Mid-Nov to end Mar: tours daily except Sat-Sun 8.45am-noon, 1.30-5.30pm. Tours of the site (botanical garden, arboretum, étang du Taureau discovery path, interactive terminal). No charge. ☎ 03 86 78 79 00.

Musée de la Résistance – Early Apr to mid-Nov: 10.15am-6pm. 4€. ☎ 03 86 78 79 06 or 03 86 78 72 99.

St-Père: Musée archéologique régional – ♿ Easter to All Saints: 10am-12.30pm, 1.30-6.30pm (last admission 20min before closing). 4€. ☎ 03 86 33 26 62.

Fouilles des Fontaines Salées – Same opening times as the Archeological Museum. ☎ 03 86 33 26 62.

Abbaye de la Pierre-qui-Vire: Tour– ♿ 10.15am-12.15pm, 3pm-5.30pm, Sun and public holidays 11.15am-12.15pm, 3-5.30pm. Closed Jan. 2.30€. ☏ 03 86 32 19 20.

Services – ♿ Service at 9.15am, Sun and public holidays 10am; vespers at 6pm. The monastery is not open to visitors. ☏ 03 86 33 19 20.

St-Léger-Vauban: Maison Vauban – ♿ Jul and Aug: 10.30am-1pm, 2.30-6.30pm; May, Jun and Sep: daily except Tue 10.30am-1pm, 2.30-6pm; Apr and Oct: Sat-Sun and public holidays 10.30am-1pm, 2.30-6pm. 4.50€ (children: 1.50€). ☏ 03 86 32 26 30.

Base Nautique des Settons – ♿ Lac de Settons - 58230 Montsauche-les-Settons - ☏ 03 86 84 51 98 - www.activital.net - Open May-Sep: daily 9am-12.30pm, 1.30-7pm; Oct-Apr: Mon-Fri 8.30am-noon, 1.45-5.30pm - Closed public holidays Oct-Apr.

Anost: Maison des Galvachers – Jul and Aug: daily except Tue 2-6pm; Jun and Sep: Sat-Sun 2pm-6pm. 1.50€. ☏ 03 85 82 78 16 or 03 85 82 73 26.

N

NANS-SOUS-SAINTE-ANNE

Taillanderie – Jul and Aug: 10am-7pm; May, Jun and Sep: 10am-12.30pm, 2-6.30pm; Mar, Apr, Oct and Nov: school holidays, Sun and public holidays, 2-6pm. 4.40€. ☏ 03 81 86 64 18.

NANTUA   🏢 Pl. de la Déportation,, 01130 Nantua, ☏ 04 74 75 00 05. www.ville-nantua.com

Église St-Michel – For guided tours, ask at the tourist office. ☏ 04 74 75 00 05.

Musée Départemental de la Résistance et de la Déportation de l'Ain et du Haut-Jura – May-Sep: daily except Mon 10am-1pm, 2-6pm. 4€. ☏ 04 74 75 07 50.

Grotte du Cerdon – Jul and Aug: guided tours (1hr15min) 10am-6pm; Jun and Sep: Sat-Sun 1-6pm; Oct-May: call for information. 5.50€ (children: 4€). ☏ 04 74 37 36 79. www.les-grottes-du-cerdon.com

Cerdon: La Cuivrerie – ♿ May-Sep: guided tours (45min) at 10am, 11am, 2pm, 3pm, 4pm and 5pm; Oct-Apr: Sat-Sun and public holidays 10am, 11am, 2pm, 3pm, 4pm and 5pm. Shop: 9am-noon, 1.30-6.30pm, Sat-Sun and public holidays 9.30am-noon, 2-6.30pm. Closed 1 Jan and 25 Dec. 3.90€. ☏ 04 74 39 96 44.

Jujurieux: Soieries Bonnet – ♿ Early May to mid-Nov: guided tours (1hr) daily except Tue 2-6pm. 4€ (children: 2.50€). ☏ 04 74 37 12 26.

Boat trips on the River Ain – ♿ Early Jul to mid-Sep: trips (1hr15min) at 2.30. 4pm and 5.30pm. 6.10€ (under 16s: 3.80€). ☏ 04 74 50 81 61.

Oyonnax: Musée du Peigne et des Matières Plastiques – ♿ Jul and Aug: daily except Sun 2.30-6.30pm; Sep-Jun: daily except Sun and Mon 2-6pm. Closed public holidays. 3.50€. ☏ 04 74 81 96 82.

NEVERS   🏢 Palais Ducal, 58000 Nevers, ☏ 03 86 68 46 00. www.ville-nevers.fr

Guided tours of the town – 🗺 discovery tours (2hr) Jul and Aug. 5€. Information available at the tourist office or on www.vpah.culture.fr.

Workshops – Exhibition hall: daily except Sun 9am-noon, 2-7pm; Workshops: early Jul to mid-Sep by request. 2€. ☏ 03 86 71 96 90. www.faience-montagnon.fr

Musée Archéologique du Nivernais – By request only.

Musée Municipal Frédéric-Blandin – May-Sep: daily except Tue 10am-6.30pm; Oct-Apr: daily except Tue 1-5.30pm, Sun and public holidays 10am-noon, 2-5.30pm. Closed 25 Dec-1 Jan and 1 May. 2.40€. ☏ 03 86 71 67 90.

Cathédrale St-Cyr-et-Ste-Julitte – Jul and Aug: daily except Sat-Sun 3pm. ☏ 03 99 77 09 46 or 03 86 59 06 74.

Église St-Gildard and museum – Apr-Oct: 7am-12.30pm, 1.30-7.30pm; Nov-Mar: 7.30am-noon, 2-6pm, Sun and public holidays 8am-noon, 2-6pm. No charge. ☏ 03 86 71 99 50.

Église Ste-Bernadette-du-Banlay – During religious services.

Circuit de Nevers-Magny-Cours – Daily except Sun 9am-6pm, Sat and public holidays 9am-5pm (except during race meetings). 11€ (children: 7€). ☏ 03 86 21 80 00. www.magnyF1.fr

Musée Ligier F1 – ♿ May-Oct: 2-6pm. Times liable to modification: call for information. 7€ (children: 4€). ☏ 03 86 21 82 01.

NOZEROY

Guided tours of the town – Contact "Les Amis du Vieux Pays de Nozeroy". ☎ 03 84 51 17 43.

O

🏛 7 r. P.-Vernier, 25290 Ornans, ☎ 03 81 62 21 50. www.pays-ornans.com

ORNANS

Church – Closed for restoration.

Musée Courbet – Apr-Oct: 10am-noon, 2-6pm; Nov-Mar: daily except Tue 10am-noon, 2-6pm. Closed 1 Jan, 1 May, 1 Nov, 25 Dec. 3€ (during summer exhibitions: 6€). ☎ 03 81 62 23 30. www.museecourbet.org

Montgesoye: Musée du costume comtois – ♿ Jul and Aug: daily except Tue 2-6pm (last admission 15min before closing); Jun and Sep: Sun 2-6pm. 2€. ☎ 03 81 62 18 48.

Trépot: Musée de la fromagerie – ♿ Jul and Aug: guided tours (45min) 10.30am-noon, 2-6pm, Sun and public holidays 2-6pm; Jun: Sun and public holidays 2-6pm. 3.05€. ☎ 03 81 86 71 06.

Gouffre de Poudrey – Jul and Aug: guided tours (45min) 9.30am-7pm; May-Jun: 9.30am-noon, 1.30-6pm; Sep: daily except Wed (except 1st Wed in the month) 9.30am-noon, 1.30-6pm; Apr: daily except Wed (except during Easter school holidays) 11am, 2pm, 3pm and 4pm; Mar and Oct: Tue, Thu and Sat-Sun 2pm, 3pm and 4pm; Feb and Easter school holidays: 2pm, 3pm and 4pm. Closed rest of the year. 5.30€. ☎ 03 81 59 22 57. www.gouffredepoudrey.com

Dino-Zoo – Jul and Aug: 10am-7pm; May, Jun and Sep: 10am-6pm; February school holidays: 11am-5pm; Mar: daily except Mon and Fri 11am-5pm; Apr: 11am-6pm; Oct: 11am-5.30pm; Nov school holidays: 11am-4.30pm. Closed rest of the year. 6€ (children: 4.30€). ☎ 03 81 59 27 05.

Cléron: château – Mid-Jul to mid-Aug: Tour of the outside 2.30-6pm. 2.50€.

Hameau du Fromage – In its new industrial complex, and for a charge of 5.50€, you can observe the cheese dairy's production process from inside glazed galleries, then by means of a film and exhibition halls. Cheese tasting and shop at the exit. Daily 9am-7pm (last visit at 6.15pm), ☎ 03 81 62 41 51.

P

PARAY-LE-MONIAL

🏛 25 av. Jean-Paul-II, 71600 Paray-Le-Monial, ☎ 03 85 81 10 92.

Guided tours of the town – 🅰 discovery tours (1hr30min to 2hr) Jul and Aug: daily except Sun morning 10am and 3pm; mid-Apr to end Jun: Sun and public holidays 3pm. 4.50€. Information available at the tourist office or on www.vpah.culture.fr.

Musée du Hiéron – Closed for renovation work.

Parc des Chapelains – ♿ 9.30am-noon, 2-6pm. Closed in Jan. No charge. ☎ 03 85 81 62 22.

Chapelle de la Visitation – Possibility of guided tours by request at the Pilgrimage office. ☎ 03 85 81 62 22.

Digoin: Musée de la Céramique – Jun-Oct, guided tours (90 min) Mon-Sat 10.30am, 2.30-5pm; Apr-May 10.30am, 3pm, 4.30pm; Nov-Mar, Tue-Sat 3pm, 4.30pm. Closed 24 Dec to mid-Jan and holidays. 3.35€. ☎ 03 85 53 00 81

Château de Digoine – Mid-Jul to mid-Aug: 1-7pm; early May to mid-Jul and mid-Aug to end Oct: Sat-Sun and public holidays 1-7pm. 5.50€ (park and gardens: 3€). ☎ 03 85 47 96 44.

POLIGNY

🏛 Cours des Ursulines, 39800 Poligny, ☎ 03 84 37 24 21.

Visite guidée de la ville – Jul and Aug: several tours per week. Contact the tourist office.

Collégiale St-Hippolyte – Jul and Aug: possibility of guided tours Tue and Thu 10.30am-noon, 3-5.30pm. ☎ 03 84 37 24 21.

Église de Mouthier-Vieillard – Jul and Aug: guided tours by request. ☎ 03 84 37 24 21.

Hôtel-Dieu – Guided tours available, ask at the tourist office. ☎ 03 84 37 24 21.

Maison du Comté – Daily except Mon 9.30am-noon, 2.30-5pm in summer; 9.30am-noon in winter. ☎ (022) 346 47 09.

PONTARLIER

🏠 14 bis r. de la Gare - BP 187. 25300 Pontarlier, ☎ 03 81 46 48 33. www.ville-pontarlier.fr

Musée Municipal – ♿ Daily except Tue 10am-noon, 2-6pm, Sat 2-6pm, Sun and public holidays 3-7pm. Closed 1 and 2 Jan, 1 May, 1 Nov, 25 Dec, 24 and 31 Dec afternoon. 3€. ☎ 03 81 38 82 14.

Espera-Sbarro – ♿ Jul and Aug: 10am-7pm; school holidays: 10am-noon, 2-6pm; rest of the year: daily except Tue 2-6pm. 5€. ☎ 03 81 46 23 67. www.espera-sbarro.com.fr

PONTIGNY

🏠 22 r. Paul-Desjardin, 89230 Pontigny, ☎ 03 86 47 47 03. 0

Abbey church – Guided tours available by request, ask at the Association des Amis de Pontigny. ☎ 03 86 47 54 99.

POUILLY-EN-AUXOIS

🏠 Le Colombier, 21320 Pouilly-En-Auxois, ☎ 03 80 90 74 24.

Église N.-D.-Trouvée – During religious services.

Châteauneuf: Château – Jun-Aug: guided tours (45min) 9.30am-12.30pm, 2-7pm; Apr, May and Sep: 9.30am-12.30pm, 2-6pm; Oct-Mar: daily except Tue and Wed 10am-noon, 2-6pm. Closed 1 Jan, 1 May, 1 and 11 Nov, 25 Dec. 4€ (children: 2.50€). ☎ 03 80 49 21 89.

Commarin: Château – Apr-Oct: guided tours (45min) daily except Tue 10am-noon, 2-6pm. 6.10€ (children: 3€). ☎ 03 80 49 23 67. www.commarin.com

La PUISAYE

Parc Naturel de Boutissaint – 8am-7pm. 8€ (children: 5€). ☎ 03 86 74 07 08. www.boutissaint.com

Chantier Médiéval de Guédelon – Jul and Aug: 10am-7pm (last admission 1hr before closing); Apr-Jun: daily except Wed, 10am-6pm, Sat-Sun and public holidays 10am-7pm; Sep: daily except Wed 10am-5.30pm, Sat-Sun and public holidays 10am-6pm; Oct: 10am-5.30pm. 8€. ☎ 03 86 74 19 45.

Château de Ratilly – Mid-Jun to mid-Sep: 10am-6pm; mid-Sep to mid-Jun: call for information. 3.50€. ☎ 03 86 74 79 54.

Musée Colette – ♿ Apr-Oct: daily except Tue 10am-6pm; Nov-Mar: Sat-Sun and public holidays 2-6pm; school holidays: daily except Tue 2-6pm. Closed 1 Jan and 25 Dec. 4.30€. ☎ 03 86 45 61 95.

R

RONCHAMP

Chapelle Notre-Dame-du-Haut – Apr-Sep: daily except Tue 9.30am-6.30pm; Oct-Mar: daily except Tue 10am-4pm. Closed 1 Jan. ☎ 03 84 20 65 13.

Musée de la Mine – Jun-Aug: daily except Tue 10am-noon, 2-7pm; Sep-May: daily except Tue 2-6pm. Closed 1 Jan, 1 and 8 May, 14 Jul, 25 Dec. 3.05€. ☎ 03 84 20 70 50.

Les ROUSSES

🏠 r. Pasteur, 39220 Les Rousses, ☎ 03 84 60 02 55. www.lesrousses.com

Fort des Rousses Aventure – Jul and Aug: tree-climbing and hiking over the ramparts of the fort 9am-noon, 2-6pm. Bookings can be made with the Les Rousses sports club. 20€. ☎ 03 84 60 35 14.

Les caves Juraflore – Guided tours (1hr30min) with projection of a film. Bookings can be made at the sports club (☎ 03 84 60 35 14) or at the tourist office (☎ 03 84 60 02 55). 5€ (under 12s: 3.50€). Wear warm clothes.

Prémanon: Centre polaire Paul-Émile-Victor – School holidays: 10am-noon, 2-6pm; outside school holidays: daily except Tue 10am-noon, 2-6pm. Closed from mid-Nov to mid-Dec, 1 Jan and 1 May. 4€. ☎ 03 84 60 77 71. www.centrepev.com

Bois-d'Amont: Musée de la Boissellerie – Mid-Jul to end Aug: 10am-noon, 2-6pm (last visit 1hr before closing); mid-Jun to mid-Jul, early to mid-Sep and school holidays: 2-6pm; mid-Sep to mid-Jun: Wed-Sun 2.30-6pm. Closed early Nov to mid-Dec. 4€. ☎ 03 84 60 90 54.

Mairie de Lamoura: Musée du Lapidaire – ♿ Christmas to Easter, Jul and Aug: guided tours (45min) daily except Sat-Sun 2.30pm-6pm; Jun and Sep: Sun 2.30-6pm. Closed rest of the year. 3€ (children: 2€). ☎ 03 84 41 22 17.

S

ST-CLAUDE
🛈 19 r. du Marché -BP 94. 39200 St-Claude, ☎ 03 84 45 34 24.

Guided tours of the town – Contact the Atelier de l'Environnement (Environmental work group) CPIE du Haut-Jura), 39170 Saint-Lupicin. ☎ 03 84 42 85 96.

Exposition de pipes, de diamants et pierres fines – ♿ Jul and Aug: 9.30am-6.30pm; May, Jun and Sep: 9.30am-noon, 2-6.30pm; Oct, Jan-Apr and Christmas school holidays: daily except Sun and public holidays 2-6pm. Closed rest of the year. 4€. ☎ 03 84 45 17 00.

Moussières: Coopérative Fromagère – In the cheese dairies where Bleu de Gex Haut Jura cheese is produced, the Coopérative fromagère de Moussières has installed a glazed gallery from which the production process of its various AOC cheeses (Comté, Morbier and Bleu de Gex) can be observed, starting at 8.15am, ☎ 03 84 41 60 96.

ST-FARGEAU
🛈 3 pl. de la République, 89170 St-Fargeau, ☎ 03 86 74 10 07.

Château – ♿ Early Apr to mid -Nov: 10am-noon, 2-6pm. 7€ (children: 4€). ☎ 03 86 74 05 67.

Ferme du Château – Jul and Aug: 10am-7pm; Apr-Jun and Sep: daily except Mon (except school holidays) 10am-6pm. 5€ (children: 3€). ☎ 03 86 74 03 76.

Musée de la reproduction du son – Jul and Aug: 10am-noon, 2-7pm; Apr-Jun and early Sep to mid-Nov: 10am-noon, 2-6pm. 3.80€. ☎ 03 86 74 13 06.

ST-HONORÉ-LES BAINS
🛈 13 r. Henri-Renaud, 58360 St-Honoré-Les-Bains, ☎ 03 86 30 71 70. www.st-honore-les-bains.com

Musée Georges-Perraudin – Jun-Sep: daily except Mon and Tue. 2.30-6.30pm. 3.50€. ☎ 03 86 30 72 12.

Église de St-HYMETIERE

Montfleur: Écomusée vivant du moulin de Pont des Vents – Jul and Aug: guided tours 3pm, Sun 3pm and 5pm; Mar-Jun and Sep-Dec: Wed, Fri and Sat-Sun 3pm. Unaccompanied tours and shop: 4-7pm. 3€. ☎ 03 84 44 33 51.

ST-THIBAULT

Church – Mid-Mar to mid-Nov: 9am-6pm. Visit of the chapel of St Gilles by request. ☎ 03 80 64 66 07 or 03 80 64 62 63.

SALINS-LES-BAINS
🛈 Pl. des Salines, 39110 Salins-Les-Bains, ☎ 03 84 73 01 34. www.salins-les-bains.com

Guided tours of the town – Contact the tourist office.

Les Salines – Early Apr to mid-Sep: guided tours (1hr) at 9am, 10am, 11am, 2.30pm, 3.30pm, 4.30pm and 5.30pm; mid-Sep to end Mar: 10.30am, 2.30pm and 4pm. Closed Dec and Jan. 4€. ☎ 03 84 73 01 34.

Hôtel-Dieu – ♿ By request at the tourist office. No charge. www.salins-les-bains.com

Fort St-André – Jul and Aug: 11am-5.30pm; Apr-Jun and Sep: Sat-Sun and public holidays 10am-7pm. 1.52€. ☎ 03 84 37 90 29 or 06 84 42 81 84 or 06 28 78 24 84.

SAULIEU
🛈 24 r. d'Argentine, 21210 Saulieu, ☎ 03 80 64 00 21.

Musée municipal François-Pompon – Mar to Dec: daily except Tue 10am-noon, 2-6pm, Sun and public holidays 10.30am-noon, 2-5.30pm. Closed 1 May and 25 Dec. 4€. ☎ 03 80 64 19 51.

SEMUR-EN-AUXOIS
🛈 2 pl. Gaveau, 21140 Semur-En-Auxois, ☎ 03 80 97 05 96. www.ville-semue-en-auxois.fr

Guided tours of the town – Contact the tourist office.

Museum – Mid-Jun to mid-Sep: 10am-noon, 2-6pm, Sat-Sun and public holidays 2-6pm; early May to mid-Jun and mid to end Sep: daily except Tue 2-6pm; Oct-Apr: daily except Sat-Sun 2-5pm. Closed 1 Jan, Easter, 1 and 8 May, 14 Jul, 1 and 11 Nov, 25 Dec. 3.04€, no charge 1st Sunday in the month. ☎ 03 80 97 24 25.

Époisses: Château – Park 9am-7pm. Jul and Aug: guided tours of the château (45min) daily except Tue 10am-noon, 3-6pm. 5€ (park: 3€). ☎ 03 80 96 40 56.

SENS

🛈 Pl. Jean-Jaurès, 89100 Sens, ☎ 03 86 65 19 49. www.office-de-tourisme-sens.com

Guided tours of the town – Contact the tourist office.

Église St-Pierre-le-Rond – Closed for renovation work.

Cathédrale St-Étienne – Possibility of guided tours. Contact the Museum-Treasury. ☎ 03 86 64 46 22.

Museum, Treasury and Palais Synodal – Jul and Aug: 10am-6pm; Jun and Sep: 10am-noon, 2-6pm; Oct-May: daily except Tue (not incl. school holidays). 2-6pm, Wed, Sat, Sun and public holidays 10am-noon, 2-6pm. Closed 1 Jan and 25 Dec. 3.20€, no charge 1st Sunday in the month. ☎ 03 86 83 88 90.

Roche de SOLUTRÉ

🛈 Rte des Vins, 71960 Roche De Solutré, ☎ 03 85 35 81 00.

Musée Départemental de la Préhistoire – & Jun-Sep: 10am-7pm; May: daily except Tue 10am-noon, 2-6pm; Oct-Apr: daily except Tue 10am-noon, 2-5pm. Closed Dec, Jan and 1 May. 3.50€, no charge 1st Sunday in the month. ☎ 03 85 35 85 24.

T

Château de TANLAY

Apr to mid-Nov: guided tours (1hr) daily except Tue at 9.30am, 10.30am, 11.30am, 2.15pm, 3pm, 3.45pm, 4.30pm and 5.15pm. 7€ (children: 3€). ☎ 03 86 75 70 61.

TONNERRE

🛈 42 r. de l'Hôpital, 89700 Tonnerre, ☎ 03 86 55 14 48. www.tonnerre89.com

Église St-Pierre – For guided tours, ask at the tourist office or at the town hall.

Ancien Hôpital – Jun-Sep: guided tours (1hr) daily except Tue 10.30am-12.30pm, 1.30-6.30pm; Apr, May and Oct: daily except Wed 10am, 11am, 2.30pm and 3.30pm, Sat-Sun and public holidays 1.30-6.30pm. Contact the tourist office. ☎ 03 86 55 14 48.

Musée Marguerite-de-Bourgogne – Jun-Sep: daily except Tue 10.30am-12.30pm, 1.30-6.30pm; Apr, May and Oct: Sat-Sun and public holidays 1-6pm. 3.80€. ☎ 03 86 54 33 00.

TOURNUS

🛈 2 pl. Carnot, 71700 Tournus, ☎ 03 8527 00 20.

Boat trips – Go for an unforgettable cruise on the River Saone, which runs past the town, or on the wilder River Seille aboard a comfortable river cruiser. Information available from Pavillon Saône, ☎ 03 85 40 55 50. www.house-boat.net

Église St-Philibert – Jul and Aug: guided tours available daily except Sat and Sun morning at 10.30am, 3.30pm and 5pm, ☎ 03 85 27 00 20.

Musée Bourguignon – Apr-Oct: daily except Mon 11am-6pm. Closed 1 May. 2.80€. ☎ 03 85 51 29 68.

Hôtel-Dieu – & Apr-Oct: daily except Tue 11am-6pm. 4.60€. ☎ 03 85 51 23 50.

V

VESOUL

🛈 R. des Bains, 70002 Vesoul, ☎ 03 84 97 10 85.

Guided tours of the town – Mid-Jun to mid-Sep: 4pm (Pl. de l'Église). Contact the tourist office. 3€.

Musée Georges-Garret – Daily except Tue 2-6pm. Closed 1 Jan, 1 May, 14 Jul, 1 Nov, 25 Dec. No charge. ☎ 03 84 76 51 54.

Rupt-sur-Saône: Castle – Jul: 10am-noon, 2-6pm; Apr-Jun and Aug-Oct: Sat-Sun and public holidays 10am-noon, 2-6pm. No charge. ☎ 03 84 92 70 41.

VÉZELAY

🛈 R. St-Pierre, 89450 Vézelay, ☎ 03 86 33 23 69.

Bazoches: Château – Apr-Oct: 9.30am-noon, 2.15-6pm; Nov-Mar: 9.30am-noon, 2.15-5pm. 5.64€. ☎ 03 86 22 10 22.

Chamoux: Cardo-land – & Jun-Aug: 10am-6.30pm; Apr, May and early Sep to mid-Nov: Sun and public holidays 10am-6pm, Sat and school holidays 1.30-6pm. 7€ (children: 4€). ☎ 03 86 33 28 33.

VILLERS-LE-LAC

Musée de la Montre – ♿ Mid-Jun to mid-Sep: daily except Tue 10am-noon, 2-6pm; other school holidays and early to mid-May: daily except Tue 2-6pm. 5.50€. ☎ 03 81 68 08 00 or 06 07 15 74 91.

Boat service: Vedettes du Saut du Doubs (Droz-Bartholet) – Les Terres Rouges - ☎ 03 81 68 13 25. Easter to All Saints: cruises to Besançon and the Saut du Doubs.

Lac de VOUGLANS

Boat trips – Apr to end Oct: departure daily. Contact Bateau Croisières - pont de la Pyle - 39270 La Tour-du-Meix - ☎ 03 84 25 89 54 (high season) and 03 84 25 46 78 (low season) or ☎ 06 08 45 48 76.

Moirans-en-Montagne: Musée du Jouet – ♿ Jul and Aug: 10am-6.30pm; Sep-Jun: 10am-noon, 2-6pm, Sat-Sun 2-6pm. Closed 1 Jan and 25 Dec. 5€ (children: 2.50€). ☎ 03 84 42 38 64.

Villards d'Héria: Archeological sit – Jul and Aug: guided tours (1hr) 10.30am, 2pm, 3.15pm and 4.30pm. 2€. ☎ 03 84 47 12 13.

Index

Notes